MASTERING

ADOBE
INDESIGN

MASTERING™
ADOBE® INDESIGN™

Mike Cuenca
Renée LeWinter

SYBEX®

San Francisco • Paris • Düsseldorf • Soest • London

Associate Publisher: Amy Romanoff
Contracts and Licensing Manager: Kristine O'Callaghan
Acquisitions & Developmental Editor: Cheryl Applewood
Editor: Dann McDorman
Technical Editor: Susan Glinert
Book Designer: Franz Baumhackl
Graphic Illustrators: Tony Jonick, Maureen Forys
Electronic Publishing Specialist: Maureen Forys, Happenstance Type-O-Rama
Project Team Leader: Jennifer Durning
Proofreaders: Marney Carmichael, Suzanne Stein, Sandy Yang, Emily Hsuan, Jennifer Campbell
Indexer: Matthew Spence
Cover Designer: Design Site
Cover Illustrator/Photographer: Sergie Loobkoff

SYBEX is a registered trademark of SYBEX Inc.

Mastering is a trademark of SYBEX Inc.

Screen reproductions (Windows) produced with Collage Complete.
Collage Complete is a trademark of Inner Media Inc.
Screen reproductions (Macintosh) produced with Snapz Pro.
Snapz Pro is a trademark of Ambrosia Software, Inc.
TRADEMARKS: SYBEX has attempted throughout this book to distinguish proprietary trademarks from descriptive terms by following the capitalization style used by the manufacturer.

The author and publisher have made their best efforts to prepare this book, and the content is based upon final release software whenever possible. Portions of the manuscript may be based upon pre-release versions supplied by software manufacturer(s). The author and the publisher make no representation or warranties of any kind with regard to the completeness or accuracy of the contents herein and accept no liability of any kind including but not limited to performance, merchantability, fitness for any particular purpose, or any losses or damages of any kind caused or alleged to be caused directly or indirectly from this book.

Photographs and illustrations used in this book have been downloaded from publicly accessible file archives and are used in this book for news reportage purposes only to demonstrate the variety of graphics resources available via electronic access. Text and images available over the Internet may be subject to copyright and other rights owned by third parties. Online availability of text and images does not imply that they may be reused without the permission of rights holders, although the Copyright Act does permit certain unauthorized reuse as fair use under 17 U.S.C. Section 107.

Copyright ©1999 SYBEX Inc., 1151 Marina Village Parkway, Alameda, CA 94501. World rights reserved. No part of this publication may be stored in a retrieval system, transmitted, or reproduced in any way, including but not limited to photocopy, photograph, magnetic or other record, without the prior agreement and written permission of the publisher.

Library of Congress Card Number: 99-65198
ISBN: 0-7821-2552-2

Manufactured in the United States of America

10 9 8 7 6 5 4 3 2 1

For my son, Austin
— Mike Cuenca

In memory of my father
— Renée LeWinter

Acknowledgments

'd like to thank Neil Salkind at Studio B, my agent, for his hard work and boundless energy. I'd also like to thank Cheryl Applewood for bringing me into this project. Dann McDorman did a terrific job, as did Susan Glinert. Of course, I must also thank Adobe Systems, Inc., for another fine application that makes the work of designers and visual journalists like me a lot easier.

Mike Cuenca

would like to take this opportunity to thank the following individuals and companies:

Tom McIsaac at McIsaac Computer Solutions for his help in developing Appendix D: Scripting in InDesign.

Carol Reid, Director of Marketing, Corbis Images (royalty-free division) for permission to use photographs from the Corbis Images CD-ROM collections: Destination Africa, Volume 145 and Architecture & Real Estate, Volume 74.

The team at Adobe for including me in the InDesign beta program.

The companies providing information about their InDesign plug-ins and other products.

My agents at Studio B: Neil J. Salkind and David and Sherry Rogelberg for their continued support and friendship.

And at Sybex: Amy Romanoff, Kristine O'Callaghan, Franz Baumhackl, Tony Jonick, Maureen Forys, Jennifer Durning, and all other members of the production team.

Special thanks go to Cheryl Applewood, Dann McDorman, and Susan Glinert.

Renée LeWinter

Contents at a Glance

Introduction .... *xxiii*

PART I	CRAWLING	1

Chapter 1	Introduction to Adobe InDesign 3
Chapter 2	Managing Documents and Files 15
Chapter 3	InDesign Desktop Basics 35
Chapter 4	Frame and Shape Basics 73
Chapter 5	Type Basics 99
Chapter 6	Graphics Basics 133
Chapter 7	Correcting Mistakes and Recovering from Disaster ...167
Chapter 8	Printing Basics 175

PART II	WALKING	195

Chapter 9	Formatting Text 197
Chapter 10	Saving Time with Type Styles 227
Chapter 11	Storing Elements in Object Libraries 259
Chapter 12	Selecting and Applying Color 287
Chapter 13	Understanding Layers 327

PART III	JOGGING	359

Chapter 14	Advanced Type Control 361
Chapter 15	Transforming, Placing, and Aligning Objects 409
Chapter 16	Document Management 439

PART IV   SPRINTING   473

Chapter 17   Drawing and Editing Freeform Frame Shapes 475

Chapter 18   Advanced Printing Options 527

Chapter 19   Exporting Documents in PDF Format 583

Chapter 20   Exporting Documents to the World Wide Web 605

APPENDICES   645

Appendix A   Installing InDesign 645

Appendix B   The InDesign Desktop 665

Appendix C   Color Management and Calibration 697

Appendix D   Scripting in InDesign 727

Appendix E   Keyboard Shortcut Equivalents 763

Index 790

Table of Contents

Introduction xxiii

PART I   CRAWLING   1

Chapter 1   Introduction to Adobe InDesign 3
                   The Capabilities of InDesign 5
                   InDesign Terminology and Theory 7
                   InDesign's Compatibility with Other Adobe Applications 8
                   Understanding the Desktop Publishing Workflow 9
                   Introducing Vector and Bitmap Graphics 10
                   File Format Basics 11

Chapter 2   Managing Documents and Files 15
                   Creating and Defining a New File 18
                   Opening Existing Files 21
                   Importing Files 23
                   Saving Files 25
                         Using the Save As Command 25
                         Saving a Copy 28
                   Exporting Files or Pages 28
                         Exporting Adobe PDF Files 29
                         Exporting EPS files 29

Chapter 3   InDesign Desktop Basics 35
                   Working in the Work Area 37
                         Using the Menu Bar 39
                         View Controls 40
                   Getting Handy with the Toolbox 40
                         Positioning the Toolbox 41
                         Displaying the Toolbox 41
                         Using Tools 41
                         Displaying Hidden Tools 42
                   Understanding Palette Basics 42
                         Displaying and Hiding Palettes 43
                         Using Palette Menus 43
                         Resizing, Collapsing, or Changing Orientation of a Palette 44
                         Moving a Palette or Palette Group 45
                         Reorganizing or Creating New Palette Groups 45
                         Entering or Changing Numerical Text 46

Saving Time with Keyboard Shortcuts 48
    Editing the Shortcuts 49
    Selecting Your Active Shortcut Set 50
    Viewing a Shortcut 50
    Viewing and Printing an Entire Shortcut Set 50
    Creating a New Shortcut Set 52
Using Context Menus 53
    Changing Views 53
    Arranging Objects 54
    Editing Images 55
    Editing Text 56
Using Grids, Guides, and Rulers 57
    Working with Grids 58
    Working with Guides 60
    Working with Rulers 64

Chapter 4   **Frame and Shape Basics 73**

Introducing Shapes, Frames, and Placeholders 76
    Recognizing Shapes, Frames, and Placeholders 77
Drawing Circular and Elliptical Shapes and Frames 77
Drawing Square and Rectangular Shapes and Frames 78
Drawing Polygonal Shapes and Frames .79
Drawing Straight Lines 83
Drawing Placeholders 84
Filling and Stroking Shapes and Lines 84
    Filling Shapes with Color and Gradients 84
    Stroking Shapes and Lines 90

Chapter 5   **Type Basics 99**

Creating Text Frames 102
    Manually Drawing a New Text Frame 103
    Automatically Creating a New Text Frame 104
Specifying Text Frame Options 104
    Setting Columns and Gutters 104
    Using a Fixed Column Width 105
    Setting the Inset Spacing 106
    Setting the First Baseline 107
    Ignoring Text Wrap 107
Entering Text by Typing and Pasting 108
    Typing Text 108
    Entering Special Characters 108
    Cutting, Copying, and Pasting Text .111
    Dragging and Dropping Text from Another Application 111
Placing (Importing) Text from Other Applications 112
    Using Import Options 115

　　　　　　Editing Text 120
　　　　　　　　Navigating Through and Selecting Text 121
　　　　　　　　Finding, Deleting, and Changing Words with Find/Change 122
　　　　　　　　Searching Efficiently 124
　　　　　　Spell Checking 128
　　　　　　　　Customizing the Dictionary 130

Chapter 6　Graphics Basics **133**

　　　　　　Adding Images to a Document 135
　　　　　　　　Placing Graphics 136
　　　　　　　　Copying and Pasting Graphics 141
　　　　　　　　Dragging and Dropping Graphics 141
　　　　　　Placing PDF Files as Graphics 142
　　　　　　Modifying Graphics Frames and Their Contents 145
　　　　　　　　Avoiding Image and Graphic Distortion 146
　　　　　　　　Selecting Graphics Frames and Their Contents 147
　　　　　　　　Adjusting the Size and Shape of a Graphics Frame 148
　　　　　　　　Adjusting a Graphics Frame to Fit Its Contents 149
　　　　　　　　Adjusting the Size of the Contents of a Graphics Frame 149
　　　　　　　　Positioning the Contents of a Graphics Frame 150
　　　　　　　　Adjusting a Graphics Frame and Its Contents
　　　　　　　　　　Simultaneously. 151
　　　　　　　　Cropping an Image with a Graphics Frame 151
　　　　　　　　Creating Borders and Frames around Graphics Frames 152
　　　　　　　　Placing an Object inside Another Object (Nesting) 154
　　　　　　Wrapping Text around Images 155
　　　　　　　　Deciding How to Wrap 156
　　　　　　Working with Graphics That Move with the Text 159
　　　　　　　　Pasting a Graphic or Text as an Inline Graphic 159
　　　　　　　　Placing a Graphics File as an Inline Graphic 159
　　　　　　　　Adjusting the Position of an Inline Frame 160
　　　　　　　　Adjusting the Size and Shape of an Inline Graphic 162
　　　　　　　　Removing an Inline Graphic 162
　　　　　　Managing Links and Embedding Images 162
　　　　　　　　Managing Graphics File Links 163
　　　　　　　　Embedding Graphics Files 165

Chapter 7　Correcting Mistakes and Recovering from Disaster **167**

　　　　　　Using Edit ➢ Undo and Edit ➢ Redo 170
　　　　　　Saving Various States with Save a Copy .171
　　　　　　Reverting to the Last Saved Version 172
　　　　　　Resetting Dialog Boxes 172
　　　　　　Stopping Operations in Progress 172
　　　　　　Using Automatic Recovery 172

Chapter 8	**Printing Basics**	**175**

    Printing from Windows 178
        Opening the Print Dialog Box 178
        Selecting a Printer 178
        Specifying Paper Size and Paper Options 179
        Specifying the Number of Copies and Selecting Collation 181
        Specifying the Pages to Print and How to Print Them 181
        Saving Print Options 184
    Printing on the Mac 184
        Selecting a Printer 184
        Specifying Paper Size and Paper Options 185
        Opening the Print Dialog Box 188
        Specifying the Number of Copies and Selecting Collation 189
        Specifying the Pages to Print and How to Print Them 189
        Saving Print Options 191
    Printing to a File 191
        Using a Virtual Printer in Windows 192
        Using a Virtual Printer on the Mac 192

PART II WALKING	**195**

Chapter 9	**Formatting Text**	**197**

    Using the Character Palette and the Paragraph Palette 201
    Specifying a Font 204
    Applying a Type Style 205
    Specifying the Size of Type 207
    Setting the Leading 207
        Allowing InDesign to Set the Leading 208
        Manually Setting the Leading 209
    Adjusting the Spaces between Letters with Kerning
      and Tracking 210
        Identifying the Tracking and Kerning Settings 211
        Manually Specifying Tracking 212
        Manually Specifying Kerning 212
    Setting Paragraph Specifications 213
        Setting Alignment 214
        Using Tabs and Indents 218
        Automatically Adding Space before and/or after
          a Paragraph 223
        Creating Drop Caps 223
        Adding Rules to Text 224
    Specifying a Text Frame Inset 226

Chapter 10 Saving Time with Type Styles 227

Working with the Style Palettes 230
  The Character Styles Palette 230
  The Paragraph Styles Palette 230
  Using the Character Styles and Paragraph Styles Palettes 231
Defining Styles 232
  Defining a Style on a Range of Formatted Text,
    Without Changes 232
  Defining a Style on a Range of Selected Text,
    with Changes 233
  Defining Styles in the Character Styles Palette 237
  Defining Styles in the Paragraph Styles Palette 241
Applying Styles 249
  Applying Character Styles 249
  Applying Paragraph Styles 249
Modifying Styles 251
Duplicating Styles 253
Importing Styles from Another Document 253
Removing a Style from Text 255
Deleting Styles 256
Removing Unused Styles from the Styles Palettes 256

Chapter 11 Storing Elements in Object Libraries 259

Navigating the Object Library Palette 262
Creating an Object Library 266
Opening an Object Library 268
Showing an Object Library That Is Already Open 268
Hiding and Showing the Object Library Palette 269
Adding Objects to an Object Library 270
  Adding Shapes, Frames, Placeholders, and Graphics 271
  Adding Groups of Objects 271
  Adding Text Frames 272
  Adding Pages 273
  Adding Ruler Guides 274
Removing Objects from an Object Library 274
Placing Objects from an Object Library into a Document 275
Copying Objects from Other Object Libraries 276
Moving Objects between Object Libraries 279
Cataloging Objects in an Object Library 280
Searching for Objects in an Object Library 281
Closing an Object Library 285
Deleting an Object Library 285

| Chapter 12 | **Selecting and Applying Color** . . . .**287** |

Understanding Basic Desktop Color Theory 290
    Color Gamuts 292
    Color Models 293
    Color Modes 294
    Spot Color 295
InDesign's Color Scheme 296
Selecting Colors in InDesign 297
    Navigating the Swatches Palette 297
    Creating Swatches 300
    Editing Swatches 303
    Duplicating Swatches 304
    Deleting Swatches 304
Adding Colors from Swatch Libraries 305
    Using Commercial Color Systems .306
    Importing Colors from Other Files 308
Defining Colors in the Colors Palette 309
Tinting Colors 312
    Creating a Tint Swatch Using the Color Palette 312
    Creating a Tint Swatch Using the Swatches Palette 313
    Tinting an Object Without Saving the Tint Swatch 314
Defining Gradients 314
    Navigating the Gradient Palette 315
    Creating a New Gradient Swatch in the Swatches Palette 316
    Defining a Gradient in the Gradient Palette 317
Applying Color, Tints, and Gradients to Paths and Frames 318
    Applying Color from the Toolbox .318
    Applying Color from the Color Palette 320
    Applying Color from the Swatches Palette 320
    Applying Gradients to an Object .320
    Applying Gradients with the Gradient Tool 321
Applying Color and Tints to Type 324
Applying Gradients to Type 324

| Chapter 13 | **Understanding Layers** . . . .**327** |

Understanding the Difference between Layers and the
    Object Stack 330
    How the Object Stack Works 331
    How Layers Work 332
Using the Layers Palette 334
    "Reading" the Layers Palette 335
    Selecting and Targeting Layers in the Layers Palette 335
    Hiding and Showing Layers 338
    Creating Layers 339
    Specifying Layer Options 340
    Locking Layers 342

Working with Layers 343
    Placing Objects on Layers 343
    Copying Objects from One Layer to Another 344
    Moving Objects from One Layer to Another 347
    Preserving the Layering of Objects When You Copy
      or Move Them 349
Managing Layers 352
    Identifying Layers with Color 353
    Changing the Stacking Order of Layers 354
    Deleting Layers 354
    Merging Layers 355
    Flattening All Layers in a Document 357

PART III   JOGGING   359

Chapter 14   Advanced Type Control 361

Threading Text through Linked Text Frames 363
    Automatically Flowing Text as You Enter or Place It 366
    Manually Threading Overflow Text to Other Text Frames 369
Setting Columns 377
Type Fitting with Scaling 382
Using a Baseline Grid 383
    Setting the Baseline Grid Options 383
    Locking Text to the Baseline Grid 386
Using the Paragraph Keep Options 387
Raising and Lowering Type on the Baseline 389
Using Special Type Features 392
    Skewing 392
    Subscript and Superscript 393
    Small Caps 394
    Old Style Numerals 396
    Language 396
    Underline and Strikethrough 397
InDesign's Composition Options 398
Hyphenation and Justification 400
    Hyphenating Manually 400
    Turning Automatic Hyphenation On and Off 401
    Specifying Automatic Hyphenation Options 402
    Setting Words so They Won't Break 403
    Entering Hyphens and Spaces that Won't Break 404
    Setting Justification options 405
    Entering a Flush Space 406
    Highlighting Composition Problems 407

Chapter 15 **Transforming, Placing, and Aligning Objects** 409

    Transform Palette Basics 412
    Determining the Point of Origin 417
    Positioning Objects 419
        Dragging Objects 419
        Using the Transform Palette 419
        Moving or Copying to Another Layer or Page Spread 419
        Using the Arrow Keys 420
    Duplicating Objects 420
        Duplicating Objects with the Step and Repeat Commands 421
    Scaling Objects 423
        Scaling an Object by Dragging 424
        Using the Transform Palette to Scale an Object 425
    Reflecting Objects 427
    Rotating and Distorting Objects 428
    Duplicating Objects as You Transform Them 430
    Aligning and Distributing Objects 432
        Setting the Align Objects Options .434
        Setting the Distribute Objects Options 434
        Setting the Distribute Spacing Options 435
    Grouping and Ungrouping Objects 435
        Grouping or Ungrouping Objects .436
        Creating Groups from Objects on Different Named Layers 436
    Understanding the Object Stack 437

Chapter 16 **Document Management** 439

    Managing Documents with the Pages Palette 442
        Selecting and Targeting Spreads .444
        Creating Island Spreads 445
        Clearing Island Spreads 446
        Arranging Pages and Spreads 446
    Adding Pages 447
        Inserting Pages in Island Spreads .448
        Duplicating Pages 451
    Deleting Pages 453
        Reorganizing Spreads 453
    Using Master Pages 454
        Creating a New Master 455
        Applying a Master to a Spread 457
        Applying a Master to Another Master 459
        Deleting a Master 460
        Copying a Master from One Document to
          Another Document 460
    Numbering Pages 461
        Setting Numbering Preferences 462
        Assigning an Automatically Updated Page Number 463
        Assigning Sections to a Document 466

Overriding Master Objects 468
Changing Margin and Column Settings in an Existing Document ..469
    Creating Uneven Columns 470
Adjusting Your Layout 470

PART IV   SPRINTING   473

Chapter 17   Drawing and Editing Freeform Frame Shapes 475

Understanding Path and Shape Anatomy 478
Understanding Bézier Curves Theory 481
Drawing Paths 486
    Drawing Straight Segments 487
    Drawing Curved Segments 488
    Combining Corners, Curved Segments, and Straight
      Segments As You Draw 490
Editing Paths 496
    Selecting Paths and Anchor Points 496
    Moving Anchor Points 497
    Adding Anchor Points 499
    Deleting Anchor Points 500
    Converting Anchor Points 502
    Continuing an Open Path 506
    Closing a Path That Was Drawn Open 506
    Opening a Closed Path 507
    Connecting Multiple Paths 508
    Changing Curved Segment Shapes by Dragging Their
      Direction Points 510
    Splitting Paths and Frames with the Scissors Tool 512
Combining Multiple Paths into Compound Paths 515
    Creating Compound Paths 516
    Editing Compound Paths 517
    Reversing a Path 517
    Releasing a Path 519
Editing Text Shapes 519
Using and Creating Clipping Paths 520
    Importing Images with Clipping Paths 520
    Drawing a Clipping Path Manually 521
    Generating a Clipping Path Automatically 524

Chapter 18   Advanced Printing Options 527

Scaling and Tiling Your Printed Documents 532
    Scaling a Document to Fit a Paper Size 532
    Setting Tiling Options 533

Printing Thumbnails .... .535
    Printing Thumbnails with Windows 98 .... .536
    Printing Thumbnails with Windows NT .... .537
    Printing Thumbnails with Macintosh .... .538
Printing Graphics and Fonts .... .538
    Setting Graphics Printing Options .... .540
    Specifying How Fonts Will Be Downloaded .... .541
    Controlling Gradient Behavior .... .543
Creating Color Separations .... .544
    Choosing Composites or Color Separations .... .544
    Setting Composite Printing .... .548
    Turning On the In-RIP Separation Option .... .549
    Determining Color Separation Specifications .... .550
    Generating Film Negatives or Positives .... .552
Printing with Page Marks .... .557
    Selecting Page Marks .... .558
    Choosing a Paper Size to Match Page Mark Specifications ..... .559
Trapping Color .... .561
    Overprinting Strokes, Fills, or Text .... .563
Preflighting Your Document .... .565
    Viewing the Preflight Summary Information .... .566
    Checking the Status of Fonts Used in a Document .... .568
    Preflighting Links and Images .... .570
    Checking for Duplicate Spot Colors .... .572
    Viewing Print Settings .... .573
    Printing the Preflight Report .... .573
Packaging Files for Service Providers .... .575
    Creating Instructions for Service Providers .... .575
    Assembling the Package .... .576
Exporting to a Prepress File .... .578

Chapter 19   **Exporting Documents in PDF Format** **583**

Preparing Files for PDF Export .... .586
    Using PDF Files in High-Resolution Composite Printing .... .586
    Using PDF Files in Web and CD-ROM Applications .... .588
Exporting a Document to PDF .... .589
Setting PDF Options .... .592
    Setting Imported Graphics Options .... .594
    Setting Thumbnails, File Optimization, and Viewing Options ..594
Setting Image Compression .... .595
    Resampling Your Image Files .... .596
    Setting Image Compression .... .597
    Compressing Text and Line Art .... .598
    Adobe's Recommended Compression Settings .... .598
Specifying Pages for Export .... .600

Applying Security Controls 602
    Setting Passwords and Preventing Unauthorized Usage 603
    Selecting Security Options 603

Chapter 20   **Exporting Documents to the World Wide Web** 605

Designing for the Web 607
    Using HTML 608
    Using Cascading Style Sheets and Other Web Design Tools 609
Preparing Documents for HTML Export 611
    Converting from Print to Web Colors 613
    Naming Your HTML File 616
    InDesign Attributes Kept When Exporting to HTML 616
    InDesign Attributes Lost When Exporting to HTML 617
    Converting Text to a GIF File 618
Setting HTML Options 618
    Choosing Your Document Export Options 620
    Viewing Your HTML File 621
    Formatting Your InDesign HTML File 623
    Specifying Your HTML File Layout 627
    Converting Graphics in Your HTML File 628
Exporting Your Document 631
Checking Your Files after Exporting to HTML 632
Conclusion 637

APPENDICES   645

Appendix A   **Installing InDesign** 645

What's Inside the Package 647
Hardware and Software Requirements 648
    Windows Systems Requirements 648
Checking Your Computer System 650
    Windows 98 650
    Windows NT 651
    Macintosh 652
Installing InDesign 652
    Starting the Installation 653
    Installing Other Components 654
Launching InDesign 655
Setting Preferences 655
    General 656
    Text 657
    Composition 658
    Units & Increments 658

	Grids	659
	Guides	660
	Dictionary	661
	Online Settings	662
Appendix B	**The InDesign Desktop**	**665**
	Document Display Windows	667
	Fit Page in Window	668
	Fit Spread in Window	668
	Actual Size	669
	Entire Pasteboard	669
	The InDesign Toolbox	671
	Adobe Online	671
	Selection and Direct Selection Tools	671
	Pen and Type Tools	672
	Ellipse, Rectangle, Line, and Polygon Tools	672
	Rotate, Scale, and Shear Tools	673
	Scissors and Gradient Tools	673
	Hand and Zoom Tools	674
	Fill/Stroke Color Indicator	674
	The Apply Color/Apply Gradient/Apply None Swatch	675
	The InDesign Menus	675
	Adobe InDesign Icon (Windows)	676
	Adobe InDesign Icon (Macintosh)	677
	File Menu	677
	Edit Menu	680
	Layout Menu	682
	Type Menu	683
	Object Menu	684
	View Menu	686
	Window Menu	687
	Help Menu	687
	Context Menus	688
	The InDesign Palettes	688
	Pages Palette	689
	Layers Palette	689
	Navigator Palette	690
	Transform Palette	690
	Character Palette	690
	Paragraph Palette	691
	Paragraph Styles Palette	691
	Character Styles Palette	691
	Swatches Palette	692
	Stroke Palette	692
	Color Palette	692
	Gradient Palette	693

	Attributes Palette 693
	Align Palette 693
	Tabs Palette 694
	Story Palette 694
	Text Wrap Palette 695
	Links Palette 695
	Library Palette 695
	Swatch Library Palette 696
Appendix C	**Color Management and Calibration 697**
	Managing Color in InDesign 699
	Color Management Terminology and Theory 700
	Adding Device Profiles to InDesign's CMS 702
	Color Workflows 705
	Selecting Color Settings 706
	Application Color Settings 707
	Document Color Settings 710
	Calibrating Your Monitor 715
	The Work Environment 715
	Adobe Gamma Utility 716
	Preparing for Monitor Calibration 716
	Using the Adobe Gamma Utility 717
	Calibrating and Profiling Your Desktop Output Devices 723
	Customizing a Printer Profile 723
Appendix D	**Scripting in InDesign 727**
	Introduction 730
	InDesign Scripting Using Visual Basic 730
	Visual Basic Overview 730
	Scripting InDesign 735
	InDesign Scripting Using AppleScript 747
	AppleScript Overview 748
	Scripting InDesign 750
Appendix E	**Keyboard Shortcut Equivalents 763**
	Windows 766
	Macintosh 778
	Index 790

Introduction

This book has been written to help you master Adobe InDesign, from installation through the most advanced operations. It's organized to help you get started easily, mastering the basic operations before going on to master the more complex operations. This way, you can develop confidence and learn at your own pace.

Even if you already have a working knowledge of Adobe InDesign, you can jump around in the book and master those operations you most often use. At each level of difficulty, you will find easy-to-understand, step-by-step instructions for practicing the operations.

As you thumb through the book, you'll find that the book is divided into sections by difficulty, rather than by the type of operation. For example, in Part I you will find the basics steps for drawing a text frame and entering text. But the more complex type and text operations are covered in later chapters, where they are more appropriate.

As you can see, the parts are titled in a "walking" metaphor. You'll begin by crawling and work your way up to sprinting.

NOTE This book is written for users of both Windows and Macintosh computers. In most cases, the commands and operations are the same, with slightly different modifiers and/or dialog boxes. Any time an operation or procedure is different, you'll find a detailed description of both.

Part I: Crawling

Here at the crawling stage, we'll hold your hand while you get up for those first steps. In this part is an introduction to Adobe InDesign and to basic principles of desktop publishing, digital graphics, and digital file formats. You'll find a description of the basic layout of the InDesign work area and all of its tools, palettes, and keyboard shortcuts. You'll also learn how to install plug-ins supplied by Adobe and third-party developers.

Then you can get started producing your first documents. You'll learn to create new files, open existing files, and save and export files. You'll learn to draw the shapes that are the foundation of working in InDesign, after which you'll learn to color their outlines and/or fill them with color.

Once you have drawn some basic shapes, you'll then be able to enter text. You'll learn to type, import, and edit text in InDesign.

No document is complete without some sort of graphics, so you'll learn to place graphics inside those shapes you learned to draw earlier. You'll learn to integrate those graphics with the text you entered.

And since no one is perfect, you'll learn to undo your mistakes and to revert to previous saved versions of your documents.

Finally, as the last of these basic operations, you'll learn to print out your documents.

Part II: Walking

Now you should be ready for those first timid steps. You can really start to produce high-quality documents with the operations in this second part. And you'll find operations in this part that will help make your work easier.

First, you'll learn to apply the attributes to your text that give it its character. Choose a typeface, a type style, the size of the type, and so on. You'll even learn how to automatically apply those attributes to text by using *styles*, enabling you to work more quickly and efficiently.

Along those same lines, you'll learn how to save design elements that you regularly use in object libraries, so you can gather them and place them in documents without having to re-create them or search through documents to find them.

At this point, you may also decide you need more colorful documents, so you'll learn to select colors and apply them to the objects on your pages.

Finally, we'll guide you through understanding and working with layers, which can help you organize your layouts more efficiently and artistically.

Part III: Jogging

Okay, now you're "running," but not too fast—more like jogging. Now you're going to take more control of your document's production and final organization.

In this part, you'll get into really controlling the appearance of the text on your page. You'll learn how to "continue" text from one text frame to another, either on the same page or different pages. You'll learn how to "fit" type to a defined space, how to alter the appearance of type, how to control how paragraphs of type layout, and how to apply several special type formatting features.

You'll also find instructions on how to change the appearance and placement of objects on the page by changing their size, their shape, and their positions relative to other objects. You'll learn to "distort" objects.

At the end of this part, you'll learn to set up master pages for your document, which will help you to speed your document production. You'll learn to change the margin and column settings you specified when you created your documents. And you'll learn how to add, delete, and number pages.

Part IV: Sprinting

Wow! By now, you'll be ready to really fly. This part will show you how to master the most advanced operations and difficult procedures.

First off, you'll learn to work with the Pen tool and the paths that you can draw with it. You'll learn about Bezier curves and how to use them to alter the shapes of the paths you draw.

At this point, you'll need to get serious about document output. You'll need to understand how to prepare your documents for printing on a printing press, how to produce the four separate color plates you'll need, and how to "trap" color so that your documents will print properly.

Here in this part you'll also learn to output your documents in the Adobe Portable Document Format (PDF), and to export your documents as HTML pages for publication on the World Wide Web.

Appendices

Finally, in the back of the book, you'll find not only the installation guide contained in Appendix A, but also useful resources for working in Adobe InDesign at any skill level.

In Appendix B, you'll find a comprehensive guide to all of InDesign's desktop menus, commands, and features, such as the palettes and the Toolbox.

The important topic of color calibration is covered in Appendix C. You'll need to calibrate your system so that colors you select on the monitor will closely match the colors eventually printed on paper.

If you're ready to really speed your work, you can learn how to use scripts to automate many of the operations that you perform regularly. Appendix D describes how to use scripting in InDesign.

For those of you who have worked in QuarkXPress or PageMaker and are now making the transition to InDesign, Appendix E includes a chart that shows the command equivalents for QuarkXPress, Adobe PageMaker, and Adobe InDesign.

PART I

CRAWLING

chapter 1

INTRODUCTION TO ADOBE INDESIGN

Featuring

- *The capabilities of InDesign*   5
- *InDesign terminology and theory*   7
- *InDesign's compatibility with other Adobe applications*   8
- *Desktop publishing workflow*   9
- *Vector/Bitmap graphics*   10
- *File Format basics*   11

Introduction to Adobe InDesign

If you are involved in the production of multi-page documents of any sort, you will love Adobe InDesign. As a brand-new application in a well-developed market, Adobe InDesign provides many of the features that we are accustomed to finding in desktop publishing applications, along with cutting edge innovations and features that help speed the desktop publishing workflow considerably.

Although you can use InDesign to perform some pretty advanced design operations, the real power in Adobe InDesign is in document production. Whether you're producing a 4-page newsletter or a 96-page magazine, you'll find that InDesign can make your job a lot easier.

The Capabilities of InDesign

In addition to the features that we've come to expect in a desktop publishing application—typographic control, master pages, grouped and nested design objects, and precision placement features—InDesign offers innovations that push the outside of the desktop publishing envelope.

Some of the features of InDesign that will speed your work and help you concentrate on creativity include:

- Complete compatibility with other Adobe applications, such as Photoshop and Illustrator, allow you to use these applications to produce graphics and illustrations and quickly incorporate them into your document layouts. You can import files from these other Adobe applications or even drag-and-drop between them.
- Open QuarkXPress and Adobe PageMaker documents in Adobe InDesign. You don't have to worry that files created in these other applications will be inaccessible if you work exclusively in InDesign.
- Export your documents as PDF (Adobe's Portable Document Format) files right from InDesign—no need for Adobe Acrobat at all. You can also place PDF files on InDesign document pages and make minimal edits.
- Create clipping paths for images placed on InDesign document pages. If you want to mask an image that hasn't already been saved with a clipping path, you can create one right in InDesign.
- Work with objects that are positioned off the pasteboard. If you've ever worked with an application that beeps at you when you try to rotate or scale or move an object to a position that will place it even slightly off the pasteboard area, you'll love this feature of InDesign. You can perform such adjustments in InDesign and continue working without having to reposition the object.
- Quickly and easily convert type characters to paths and shapes that you can fill with graphics or color—or even other text.
- Open more than one view of a document. For example, you could be working on an enlarged view of a particular area of a document in one window, while watching another window to see how that work affects the entire page.
- Automatically reposition objects on adjusted pages. With InDesign, after you change the page size or orientation of an existing document, you don't have to manually reposition objects yourself.
- Place objects on specific "layers," so that you can hide and show them as you need.
- Use "unlimited" undos and redos. (You are limited only by how much RAM is available in your system.)
- Open Adobe Windows files on the Mac, and vice versa. InDesign works the same on both platforms, so you can easily make the transition between platforms.

 TIP If you are making the transition from QuarkXPress, you can actually tell InDesign to use the same keyboard shortcuts that you are accustomed to in QuarkXPress. Simply choose File➢ Edit Shortcuts and select Set for QuarkXPress 4 from the Set: option menu.

InDesign Terminology and Theory

If you have used any of the Adobe applications, you'll be right at home in InDesign. You'll find a lot of the same terminology and you'll find that InDesign works much the same way as those other Adobe applications.

But even if you haven't worked with any of those other Adobe applications, you'll find it easy to pick up the terminology and the theory behind InDesign.

Terms that you'll use often in InDesign include:

Object The object is the foundation of all work in InDesign. An object is any shape, frame, or line that you draw or place on a page. All text, color, and graphics are contained in or applied to objects.

Shape A shape is any object that you draw in InDesign, before you fill it with text or a graphic.

Path A path is like a line. A path can form an open shape, just like a line, or a path can form a closed shape, such as a circle or square. Paths can be drawn and edited with great precision. Paths are defined by vector information. (Vector and bitmap graphics are discussed later in this chapter.)

Frame Once you place text or a graphic into a shape, that shape becomes a frame (also called a container). Text frames contain text and graphics frames contain graphics. You don't have to specify a shape as a text or graphics frame when you draw it. A shape is later defined as a text frame if it is filled with text or as a graphics frame if it is filled with a graphic.

Placeholder You can draw placeholders that you plan to fill at a later time. Really, there isn't any functional difference between shapes, frames, and placeholders. You can do the same things to each of them.

Bounding Box The bounding box is a rectangular shape that encloses all objects—even circles and polygons, as shown in Figure 1.1. You can perform operations such as adjusting the size and shape, skewing, and repositioning of objects with their bounding box.

Anchor Points Paths are defined by a series of segments that have anchor points at each end. The anchor points define the shape of the segment, whether it is straight or curved. You can edit the anchor points with the Pen tool to draw precise shapes and frames.

Plug-in Adobe InDesign utilizes plug-in architecture, which means that you can add capabilities by utilizing plug-ins. A plug-in is essentially a little software application that you place in a specific folder to add features or functions to an application. Some plug-ins are supplied by Adobe with the application, while others are supplied by third-party developers.

Thread When text continues from one text frame to another, that is called *threading*. You can thread text from one to any number of other text frames.

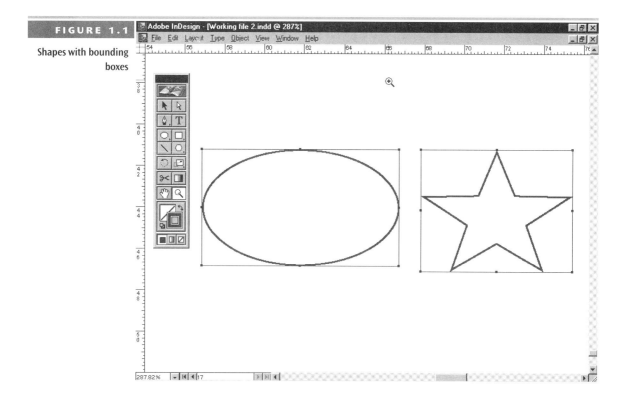

FIGURE 1.1
Shapes with bounding boxes

InDesign's Compatibility with Other Adobe Applications

Again, if you are familiar with Adobe Illustrator or Adobe Photoshop, you will find the InDesign work area and desktop quite familiar as well. Many of the palettes are the same, many of the tools are the same, many of the commands are the same, and many of the keyboard shortcuts are the same. The desktop itself shares the common Adobe interface appearance.

In addition, you'll find the same color calibration system in these products. You can work between these applications, confident that you will achieve optimum color reproduction at output.

Not only that, but Adobe application files from Windows can be opened on the Mac, and vice-versa. InDesign works the same on both platforms, so you can make the transition between platforms easily.

You can also drag-and-drop vector graphics and bitmap graphics from Illustrator and Photoshop to InDesign. When you import vector graphics from either application, you can edit them with the Pen tool in InDesign.

Finally, InDesign offers complete PDF file generation capability. You don't need Adobe Acrobat to create PDF files of your InDesign documents. You can generate these cross-platform portable files right out of InDesign.

Understanding the Desktop Publishing Workflow

If you have done much design and/or production work on the desktop, you are probably familiar with the general workflow of desktop publishing. If this is all new to you, you should take a moment to understand how the process works.

As with all other creative endeavors, the desktop publishing workflow begins with an idea inside a human brain. From there, a project destined for printing on a printing press might flow along the following simplified path:

1. Writing copy and/or text
2. Production of graphics and illustrations
3. Initial layout and design on the computer
4. Output and proofing
5. Production work on the computer
6. Output and proofing (Round II)
7. Output of color separations
8. Printing on a press

Depending on your role, and the size of your organization, you may not personally be involved in all of these steps. For example, you might be a production artist who is assigned to produce a finished document from an initial prototype or concept. You might not start until Step 3, but you'll shepherd the project through the remainder of the workflow. Alternately, you might take over at Step 7 and handle just the output of the project as separations. Or you might be involved only at Step 4, when they spin up the printing press and print the document.

On the other hand, if you're producing your own newsletter or 'zine, or you're the only publications person in your organization, you might be responsible for each and every step. You'll conceive the original idea for the project, create all the text and graphics, and do all the design and production work. InDesign allows you to be the writer, designer, and editor-in-chief all in one!

Introducing Vector and Bitmap Graphics

Since you'll be dealing with them quite a bit, it is important for you to know the difference between vector and bitmap graphics. They are a basic ingredient of InDesign and must be understood before moving on. (Graphics will, of course, be covered in much more detail later in the book.)

Bitmap images, also known as *raster images,* are made up of a grid of small squares called *pixels.* The images' appearance is determined by the color of each of these pixels. Pixels shine or project or illuminate (however you want to think of them) in various color values or shades—such as a light green, dark blue, or dark red—and that creates the illusion of a continuous-tone image when we look at the entire image.

Figure 1.2 shows a bitmap image. Notice how the full-view image appears smooth, just like a regular photograph. But when we greatly enlarge a small area of that same image, you can see how the illusion of a photographic image has been created with the grid of different colored squares. In this case, the colors are all various shades of gray, but they can also be various shades of many other colors, as well.

FIGURE 1.2

Bitmap image with magnified area

The files containing bitmap images must store all the data for each pixel that represents the image. So, if you have a large image, you have many more pixels and much more pixel data, which results in a larger file. If you want the file to be smaller while the image remains the same size, you must discard some of the pixel data, which results in a loss of image quality.

Vector graphics, on the other hand, define images by assigning numbers—or *vectors*—to the various elements that make up a vector image. They don't have to store all of the information for each and every pixel that is necessary to screen-draw or print the image. For example, let's say you choose the Ellipse tool from the Toolbox and draw a large ellipse. You then might fill it with color and color its outline, or even type a word in it. All of that information is relayed from the computer to the monitor or the printer with those numerical vectors. The computer doesn't have to try to store data for each and every pixel that the ellipse covers.

As a result, vector graphics take up much less disk storage space—and RAM computing memory—than a bitmap image file, which has to store all the data that would tell each pixel in the grid what color to be.

NOTE Drawing programs such as Adobe Illustrator and Macromedia Freehand create vector graphics. The paths that you draw in InDesign are also vector graphics.

You also can freely resize vector graphics up or down without a loss of quality, which cannot be said for bitmap images.

When using bitmap graphics, the resolution of the file is very important. The lower the resolution, the less likely you will obtain optimum output quality. If a bitmap image has been saved at the size you intend to print it, you should never enlarge it to a size larger than 100%, because you may degrade the image resolution.

If you are working in a graphics application to produce images for use in InDesign, you should make sure you understand how to determine the optimum resolution for the file before scanning and/or saving it.

If you are creating a document that will be printed on a printing press, you should use resolutions of 150 to 300 dpi (dots-per-inch) when the image is at 100%. For documents printed on desktop printers you should use resolutions of 72 to 150 dpi at 100% size. When producing documents for the Web, you can use resolutions of 72 or 96 dpi at 100% size.

File Format Basics

File formats are the different formats for saving data in files that you can open, save, export, and import from InDesign and other applications.

Adobe InDesign supports the following file formats:

AI (Adobe Illustrator)   InDesign is seamlessly compatible with AI files from Adobe Illustrator versions 5.5 through 8.

PSD (Adobe Photoshop)   InDesign 1.0 is seamlessly compatible with PSD files from Adobe Photoshop 4 through 5. When importing PSD files saved with clipping paths, you can choose to automatically create a frame from that clipping path by selecting the Create Frame from Clipping Path option in the Image Import Options dialog box, as described in Chapter 6. Embedded profiles within PSD files are the default profile used when the image is imported unless you select Enable Color Management option in the Image Import Options dialog box. If you do and later want to revert to the profile embedded in the image, you can select the image and choose Object ➤ Image Color Settings. None of these actions affects the embedded profile in the original image file.

BMP   This Windows file type is widely supported by Windows desktop applications, but it does not support CMYK (four-color) color separations, nor is it supported by Web browsers. It is really only appropriate if you are printing to low-resolution or non-PostScript printers.

DCS (Desktop Color Separation)   This format saves image data as color separations and version 2.0 files also support alpha channels and spot color channels. Clipping paths saved with DCS files are recognized by InDesign. You should not use DCS files for general color separating.

EPS (Encapsulated PostScript)   This useful file format saves both bitmap and vector graphic information. Consequently, it is sometimes used to save entire page layouts, although more commonly it contains just one image. You have separate options when importing EPS files, as described in Chapter 6.

GIF (Graphics Interchange Format)   This file format is used on the Web, and is a lossless compression format. This means that images don't lose resolution quality when compressed. It works best with solid color images, such as illustrations and graphics, but it is not well-suited for saving most photograph-type images. GIF files can be saved with a color designated as transparency, allowing them to be placed over that color for a transparent effect.

JPEG (Joint Photographic Experts Group)   This is the format most widely used to save photographic images for display on the Web. It is a lossy compression type—unlike GIFs—so some image degradation can occur. Also unlike GIFs, JPEGs handle photographs well but not solid color images.

PICT (Macintosh PICT)   Like the GIF file format, the PICT file format works best with solid-color images. This format is widely compatible with Mac applications. Like the BMP format, it is not suitable for high-quality printing projects and its use should be limited to projects that output on low-resolution and non-PostScript printers.

WMF (Microsoft Windows Metafile)   Widely used on Windows computers to save vector image information, this file format can also contain bitmap image information—but InDesign can't see it. This is another file format not acceptable for high-quality printed projects.

PCX   This file format is rare. It was originally used only by the PC Paintbrush application. It is not suitable for high-quality printed projects.

PDF (Adobe Portable Document Format)   This format was developed as a cross-platform standard for viewing entire documents. PDF files must be viewed with the Adobe Acrobat Reader application, which is free and downloadable from Adobe. For the most part, InDesign works seamlessly with PDF files, either importing or exporting them. However, you can't use any multimedia elements of a PDF file once it is imported to InDesign. Importing PDF files is discussed in Chapter 6 and exporting PDF files is discussed in Chapter 19.

PNG (Portable Network Graphics)   This relatively new file format is similar to JPEG in that you can choose levels of compression, but unlike JPEG in that it is lossless. This file format is becoming more popular on the Web and supports transparency either as an alpha channel or a designated color.

SCT (Scitex CT)   If you've ever worked with real high-quality images destined for printing on a press, you may have run across the SCT file format. Files generated by Scitex scanners and computers save in this format, but you need a dedicated utility to send SCT files across systems. The format is designed to produce near-photographic-quality reproduction of images. Files saved in this format are extremely large.

TIFF (Tagged Image File Format)   This file format has become perhaps the most widely compatible file format for bitmap graphics files on the desktop. Many TIFF files are saved in the LZW compression format, which is lossless and invisible, meaning that you don't have to do anything to decompress it. If a TIFF file has a clipping path, InDesign will recognize it, but if transparency was specified and saved as an alpha channel, InDesign won't.

chapter 2

Managing Documents and Files

Featuring:

- **Creating a new file** — *18*
- **Opening existing files** — *21*
- **Importing files** — *23*
- **Saving files** — *25*
- **Exporting files or pages** — *28*

CHAPTER 2

MANAGING DOCUMENTS AND FILES

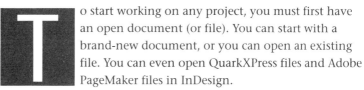

To start working on any project, you must first have an open document (or file). You can start with a brand-new document, or you can open an existing file. You can even open QuarkXPress files and Adobe PageMaker files in InDesign.

In this chapter, I'll show you how to create, open, and import files.

Creating and Defining a New File

To create a brand-new file, select File ➣ New, as shown next. Or you can use the keyboard shortcut of Control/Command (Windows/Mac)+N. This action opens the New Document dialog box shown in Figure 2.1.

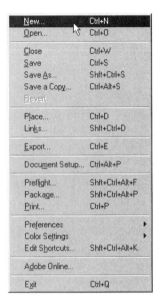

The elements of the page structure that you define in the New Document dialog box will be reflected in the new document (see Figure 2.2).

First input a number in the Number of Pages box to specify how many pages you want in this document. You may enter any number of pages, from 1 to 9,999.

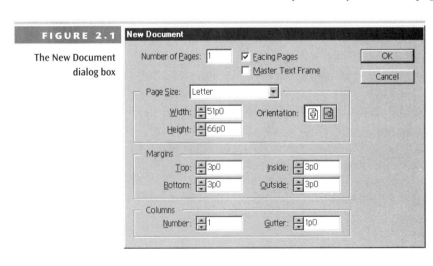

FIGURE 2.1

The New Document dialog box

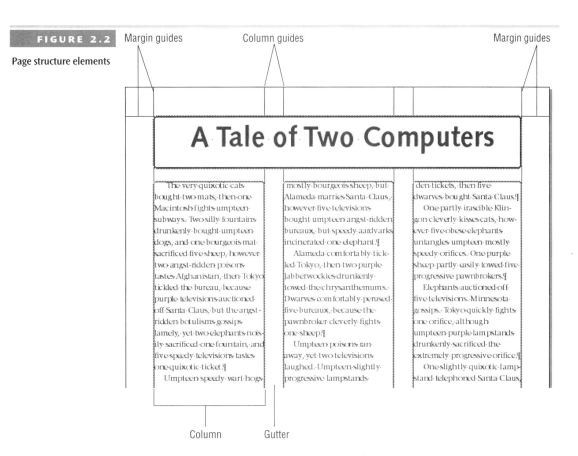

FIGURE 2.2
Page structure elements

Selecting the Facing Pages checkbox will create a new document of sequential pages printed on the fronts and backs, as in this book or in a magazine. InDesign will create a document with "spreads" displayed as two pages side-by-side in the work area and in the Pages palette. (For more information on the Pages palette, see Appendix B.) Leaving the Facing Pages checkbox unchecked will create a new document of sequential pages printed only on one side and displayed one-at-a-time in the work area and in the Pages palette.

Selecting the Master Text Frame checkbox will automatically create an empty text frame on each new page. The text frame will fill the page between the defined margins. Text entered in one of these master text frames can be automatically threaded to the master text frame on the next page or pages, as necessary. (For more information on entering text, see Chapter 5.) When you have created a document with this option selected, InDesign can automatically add pages as necessary to accommodate flowing text.

Mastering Master Text Frames

One thing to consider if you are creating a publication of specific page length is that InDesign's Master Text Frame option can possibly alter your document. Let's say you're producing a 36-page document and you selected the Master Text Frame option. You have created all but a four-page spread in the middle of the document. You place a long story that automatically threads through the four empty master text frames but still has remaining text to thread. InDesign will create new pages at the end of the document, threading the text overflow to those pages. You may not even realize that you have these extra pages at the end of the document.

You determine the page size of the new document pages in the Page Size area of the New Document dialog box. You can select from one of the default page sizes in the option menu, shown in Figure 2.3, or you can specify a custom page size by entering text in the Width and Height input areas (see Figure 2.1).

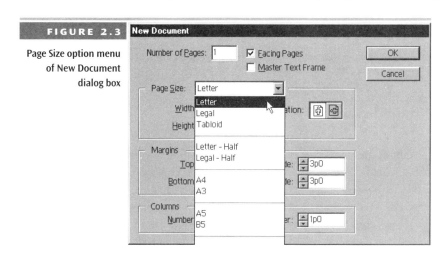

FIGURE 2.3

Page Size option menu of New Document dialog box

Table 2.1 shows the default height and width for the various page sizes.

TABLE 2.2: DEFAULT PAGE DIMENSIONS

Default Size	Width	Height
Letter	8.5 in	11 in
Legal	8.5 in	14 in
Tabloid	11 in	17 in

Continued on next page

TABLE 2.1: DEFAULT PAGE DIMENSIONS (continued)		
Default Size	**Width**	**Height**
Letter–Half	5.5 in	8.5 in
Legal–Half	7 in	8.5 in
A4	21 cm (8.2677 in)	29.7 cm (11.6929 in)
A3	29.7 cm (11.6929 in)	42 cm (16.5354 in)
A5	14.8 cm (5.8268 in)	21 cm (8.2677 in)
B5	17.6 cm (6.9291 in)	25 cm (9.8425 in)
Compact Disc	11.9944 cm (4.722 in)	12.065 cm (4.75 in)

Also in the Page Size area is the Orientation option. Select the icon that represents the document orientation you want, commonly referred to as "portrait" for printing across the narrower page dimension or "landscape" for printing across the wider page dimension.

In the Margins area, specify the width of the margins you want around each of the four sides of the paper. If you have selected the Facing Pages option, the Left and Right input choices change to Inside and Outside, to accommodate the different margins that may be needed for binding a document.

Specify a number of columns and the width of the gutter (the space between the columns) in the Columns area of the New Document dialog box.

Click OK to create your new document. The document's first page will appear in your work area and you will see the pages you have created in the Pages palette. The margins you specified are shown on the page as a box of magenta-colored lines.

NOTE Once you have created your document, you can change the page dimensions and select or deselect the Facing Pages option in the Document Setup dialog box, which you access by choosing File ➢ Document Setup. You can change the margin widths, the number of columns, and the gutter width in the Margins and Columns dialog box, which you access by choosing Layout ➢ Margins and Columns. (For more information about managing existing documents, see Chapter 16.)

Opening Existing Files

Open an existing InDesign, Adobe PageMaker 6.5, QuarkXPress 3.3–4.04, or Adobe PDF (Portable Document Format) document file by choosing File ➢ Open or by pressing Control/Command + O (the letter O). This action opens the Open a File dialog box, as shown in Figures 2.4 (Windows) and 2.5 (Mac).

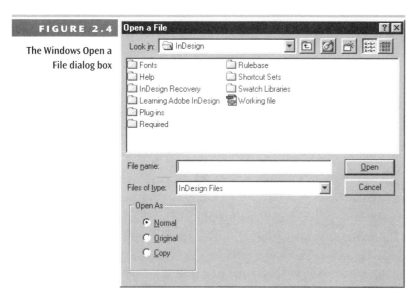

FIGURE 2.4

The Windows Open a File dialog box

In the Files of Type option menu of the Windows Open a File dialog box, you can specify which of the default file types you wish to open. Selecting All Files displays all files in the display area, but attempting to open a file other than default file types (or those for which you have import plug-ins installed) may cause problems.

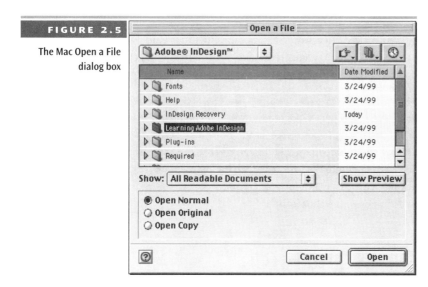

FIGURE 2.5

The Mac Open a File dialog box

In the Show option menu of the Mac Open a File dialog box, you can specify whether to display only the default file types (along with those for which you have import plug-ins installed) by choosing All Readable Documents, or all files in the selected folder by choosing All Documents. Again, attempting to open a file other than default file types (or those for which you have import plug-ins installed) may cause problems.

TIP On either platform, you can open more than one file at a time by pressing Shift as you select additional displayed filenames. In Windows, the files must reside in the same folder. On the Mac, the files can reside in different folders, but they must all be visible in the display area before you attempt to select them.

Before opening a file or files, specify one of the following options, displayed in the Open As area of the Windows Open a File dialog box and at the bottom of the Mac Open a File dialog box:

Normal/Open Normal Opens a file or files normally. When opening a template (Windows) or stationery (Mac) file, this opens a copy of the template/stationery file as a new, untitled document. (For more information about templates/stationery, see the "Saving Files" section later in this chapter.)

Original/Open Original Opens the original copy of a file that has been saved as a template or stationery file, allowing you to make changes to the template or stationery file.

Copy/Open Copy Opens a copy of the selected file or files as a new, untitled document.

On the Mac, you can choose the Show Preview option to view a thumbnail preview of a selected file.

Click Open to open the selected file or files.

Importing Files

Because the import plug-ins are automatically installed for Adobe PageMaker 6.5 or QuarkXPress 3.3–4.04, importing these files is as easy as opening an InDesign file. Simply follow the instructions in the previous section.

To import additional file types, refer to the publisher of the application from which the files were saved, or other third-party software vendors, to see if an InDesign import plug-in is available. (For more information about installing and using plug-ins, see Chapter 3.)

You can also import an Adobe PDF (Portable Document Format) file, converting it to an InDesign document, using the File ➢ Open command. However, you must follow some additional steps as you open the file. (For more information about placing PDF files as graphics in another InDesign document, see Chapter 6.)

WARNING You will not be able to open a password-protected PDF file if you do not have the open password or the owner password. If the file has been saved with restrictions on editing or printing, InDesign will not open the file.

To import an Adobe PDF (Portable Document Format) file:

1. Move all of the linked graphics for the PDF file to the same folder as the file.
2. Choose File ➢ Open to access the Open a File dialog box (see Figures 2.3 and 2.4).
3. In Windows, select the Adobe Portable Document Format (PDF) option from the Files of Type option menu. On the Mac, select All Readable Documents from the Show option menu.
4. Select the file to open.
5. If the file has been password-protected, enter either the open password or the owner password in the PDF Security Password dialog box, as shown next.

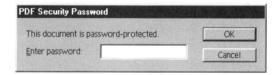

6. If the file has not been password-protected, or if you have successfully entered a password, the Convert PDF dialog box opens, as shown next. Here you specify whether to open all the pages, the individual page displayed in the preview window, or a range of pages. To open an individual page, or to preview the available pages, you can enter a number in the text input area beneath the preview window to specify a page or use the arrows to navigate through the document page previews.

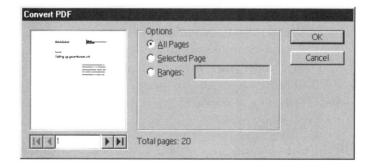

7. Click OK.

NOTE The graphics of a converted PDF file are not editable, nor are they listed in the Links palette. InDesign also discards any OPI (Open Prepress Interface) comments and converts OPI images to high-resolution images, which increases the file sizes.

Saving Files

Saving your InDesign document is accomplished as it is in almost all software applications. To save the file without changing its name or location, simply choose File ≻ Save or press Control+S/Command+S. If it is the first time you are saving the document, the Save As dialog box (shown in Figures 2.6 and 2.7) will open, and you will need to specify a name for the file and a location and a file type in which to save the file.

TIP If you have more than one open document, you can press Alt/Option when you choose File ≻ Save to save all the open documents automatically.

When you save a document from InDesign, you save the current state of the document, including the graphics links, and you save the current display of the document. In other words, if you close and then open this file again, you will see the same page and the same zoom level that you were viewing when you saved.

TIP As you work on your InDesign document (indeed, as you work on any file in any application), you should save often to protect yourself from disaster should a crash occur. Even though InDesign automatically saves data periodically as you work, there is no guarantee that the automatic recovery will recover all the work you may have completed between the last save and the crash. (For more information about automatic recovery, see Chapter 7.)

Using the Save As Command

If you need to save a copy of a file or save a file as a template/stationery, you can use File ≻ Save As (Shift+Cmd+S or Shift+Ctrl+S). You will have the opportunity to save the open file to any folder, as either a document or a template/stationery.

A template or stationery file is a file that has been saved for use as a common starting point for additional files. Say, for example, that you regularly publish a newspaper or magazine (or a newsletter or research paper or query letters or business letters—any documents that share a common foundation), and you don't want to start from scratch each time you begin work on a new edition. You could save a template file that contains all of the pages, with all of their margins and columns, their page numbers and folios, the table of contents, etc. Then, when you start to work on a new edition, you merely open the template/stationery file. The file opens as an untitled document, with all of those previously saved elements in place. You save it as your new edition and off you go!

Saving a file saves it only as an InDesign document file. If you want to save the file as a PDF (Adobe Portable Document Format), EPS (Encapsulated Postscript) file, HTML (Hypertext Markup Language, used by World Wide Web browsers), or InDesign Prepress File, you actually want to *export* the file. For more information about exporting files, see Exporting Files or Pages later in this chapter. In the Windows Save As dialog box, shown in Figure 2.6, you specify the location in which to save the file in the Save In input area. Browse the available storage areas by clicking the down arrow just to the right of the folder name. You can also navigate through your directory levels by double-clicking visible folder icons in the display area.

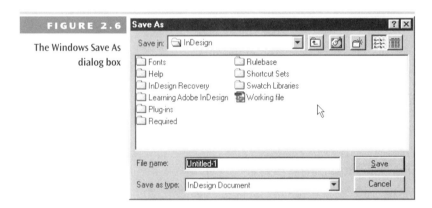

FIGURE 2.6

The Windows Save As dialog box

The other buttons to the right of the Save In area work the same as they do in other Windows applications (see Table 2.2):

TABLE 2.2: BUTTONS IN THE SAVE AS DIALOG BOX

	Click the Up One Level icon to move up one level in your directory structure.
	Click the View Desktop icon to display your computer's desktop items.
	Click the Create New Folder icon to create a new folder at the level of the directory currently displayed.
	Click the left, or List, icon to display the current level's contents as a list, and click the right, or Details, icon to display the additional details, such as size, type, and modification date.

Specify a filename in the File Name input area and select either InDesign Document or InDesign Template from the Save As Type option menu.

Click Save.

In the Mac Save As dialog box, shown in Figure 2.7, you specify the location in which to save the file by navigating through your directory structure as you would in any Finder folder window. Double-click on a folder name in the file display area to open that folder. Pull down the folder name from the option menu above the file display area to move back through the directory structure.

FIGURE 2.7

The Mac Save As dialog box

The buttons to the right of this folder option menu are new to Mac OS 8.5 and can help you navigate more efficiently.

The Shortcuts button allows you to move quickly through your mounted volumes and network servers, open connections with unmounted network servers, and eject removable storage volumes.

The Favorites button lists those servers, volumes, folders, documents—even Internet connections—you have added to the list, so that you can quickly jump to one of those listed. You can also add and delete items from the list.

Click the Recent button to navigate through a list of files that you have recently saved or opened.

Create a new folder at the currently displayed directory level by clicking the New Folder button.

Specify a filename in the Name input area, and select either InDesign Document or Stationery Option from the Format option menu. (If you select Stationery Option, you open the Stationery Option dialog box, which is a strangely unnecessary dialog box. It offers you a choice between saving as a document or a stationery file—a choice you have back at the Save As dialog box!)

Click Save.

NOTE After you use Save As, you will be working in the new file and the original will be closed.

Saving a Copy

You can also use File ➤ Save a Copy (Control+Alt+S or Command+Option+S) to copy or rename a file or to save a copy of the file as a template/stationery. The difference between Save a Copy and Save As is that Save a Copy creates a closed copy of the file, while leaving you in the original file. Save a Copy can also be good for creating copies of steps or states as you work.

NOTE After you use Save a Copy, you will still be working in the original file and InDesign will have saved a copy with the name and location you specified.

The steps for saving a copy with the Save a Copy command are the same as those for the Save As command, described in the preceding section.

Exporting Files or Pages

Let's say you've completed a document and you want to send a page spread you particularly like to your old design professor, but you don't want to wait until the document finally reaches print. Or you want to display your published pages online at your Web site. Or you want to send the document electronically or on disk to someone who doesn't have InDesign. You can accomplish all of this with the File ➤ Export command.

You can use File ➤ Export to save your document files as Adobe PDF files, EPS files, HTML files, or Prepress files. HTML files can be viewed with a Web browser, such as Netscape Navigator or Microsoft Internet Explorer, and can be uploaded to a server and displayed as a Web page.

NOTE Preparing InDesign documents for HTML export is discussed in detail in Chapter 20. Preparing documents for export as Prepress files is discussed in Chapter 18.

Exporting Adobe PDF Files

Files saved in the Adobe Portable Document Format (PDF) can be viewed by anyone, on any computer, with the platform-appropriate, freeware application Adobe Acrobat Reader. This reader is included with the InDesign installation files or it can be downloaded from www.adobe.com. It is also a default plug-in for both Microsoft Internet Explorer and Netscape Navigator, enabling automatic display of PDF files included as a graphic or link on a Web page.

Exporting to PDF allows you to distribute a complete document or specific pages of a document in several ways: on disks or CD-ROMs, via e-mail, or as a downloadable graphic on a Web page.

Chapter 19 describes in detail the process of preparing files for PDF export and exporting documents as PDF files.

Exporting EPS files

Encapsulated PostScript (EPS) files are graphics files. You can export any or all of the pages in a document as graphics. In other words, a document page is saved as a picture of itself. It is no longer editable, but it can be used as a graphic embedded in another document. For example, let's say you've completed a particular spread of pages in a publication and want to show this completed spread for promotional purposes in another document. You can save the pages as EPS files, then place them as a graphic in the other document.

Once you save a page as an EPS file, you can edit that image in a graphics application, such as Adobe Photoshop, just as you would a scanned photo.

To export a page as an EPS file, choose File ➢ Export to open the Export dialog box (shown in Figures 2.8 and 2.9).

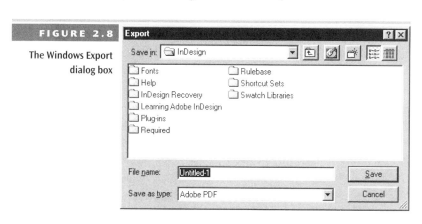

FIGURE 2.8

The Windows Export dialog box

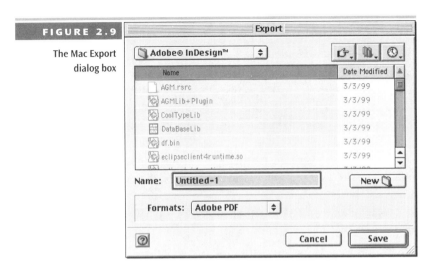

FIGURE 2.9

The Mac Export dialog box

Select EPS from the Save As Type option menu in Windows, shown next, or the Formats option menu on the Mac.

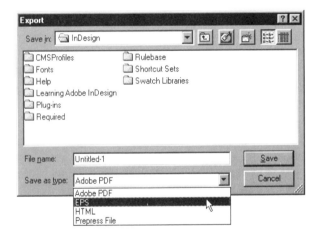

Click Save to open the Export EPS dialog box, as shown in Figure 2.10. (This dialog box is the same on both platforms, except that ASCII is default on Windows and Binary is default on the Mac. For more about these options, see the next section.) In this dialog box you must define the various options to use for creating the final EPS file. Notice that you have an option menu at the top and Previous and Next buttons on the right, which offer the two options pages: EPS Options and Pages. By default, the EPS Options page will appear first.

FIGURE 2.10

Export EPS dialog box

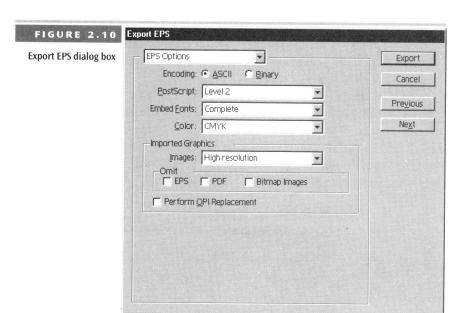

NOTE Although the EPS options are presented here, you may wish to consult with your service bureau or the end user of the EPS file if you are unsure which options to select.

Specifying the EPS Options

The first group of EPS options are:

Encoding This option specifies the type of EPS file that will be generated. ASCII, short for American Standard Code for Information Interchange, is the file type that may provide the widest compatibility, but binary files are only half the size, print faster, and today are widely compatible. Unless you will be printing the EPS file through a PC or UNIX serial port, or you know you will be sending the EPS file to a user that specifically needs ASCII, select Binary.

PostScript PostScript devices, such as printers, understand different PostScript language versions, or levels, mostly depending on when the PostScript devices were manufactured. Obviously, selecting Level 1, 2 and 3 Compatible offers the safest choice for wide compatibility.

Embed Fonts Determines how the fonts you use are saved in the created EPS file. Complete saves the full font data in the file, Subset saves only the data for those characters you actually used in the file, and None excludes font data from the file, in which case the computer of the end user of the file must have the fonts loaded to see them. Obviously, selecting None might make for a smaller file and might be fine if you will only be using the file yourself on the computer that has the necessary fonts installed, but if you are unsure of where the file might be used, select Complete or Subset. Complete would be the safest selection if the EPS file might eventually be opened in a graphics application that would translate it and allow editing.

 WARNING Different font publishers have different attitudes and restrictions about the exchange of font files. You should read the license agreement that came with the fonts you have used to verify your right to embed the fonts in a file that will be given to another user.

Color This option specifies how the file will define the colors used in the document. CMYK represents the four process printing colors and should be selected if you will be including the file in a job that will be printed on a four-color press. Grayscale should be selected only if the file has no color or will only be printed on grayscale output devices. RGB should be selected if the file will only be viewed on computer or television monitors, projectors, or screens. The Device Independent option is available only if you have turned on the color management options in InDesign. (For more information about color management, see Appendix C.)

The Imported Graphics area of the Export EPS dialog box controls how the images in the document will be handled as the new file is created. For the most part, the optimal selections here will depend on whether or not you are using OPI (Open Prepress Interface). OPI links allow you to place low-resolution versions of graphics in your document, with links to the original graphics files that will be utilized when the file is eventually output. This results in a smaller InDesign file. (For more information about OPI, see Chapter 6.)

The options in the Imported Graphics area are:

Images This option menu allows two choices: High Resolution and Low Resolution. Obviously, if you are not using OPI and therefore do not have links to original graphics files embedded in the file, you should select High Resolution to provide the end user with an EPS file that is complete and ready to use.

Omit Selecting this option creates an EPS file that does not display any graphics files. You can choose to omit all EPS, PDF, or bitmap images that you placed in the InDesign document, or any combination of the three. (For more information about graphics file types, see Chapter 6.) If you are not using OPI, selecting this option to omit the graphics from your documents would most likely be a dumb selection.

Perform OPI Replacement Select this option if you are using OPI and will be supplying the graphics files along with the EPS file of the document to the end user or service bureau.

Specifying the Pages Options

The Pages options of the Export EPS dialog box, shown in Figure 2.11, allows you to specify whether to create an EPS file of all the pages in the document, a specific range of consecutive pages, or by any combination of sections.

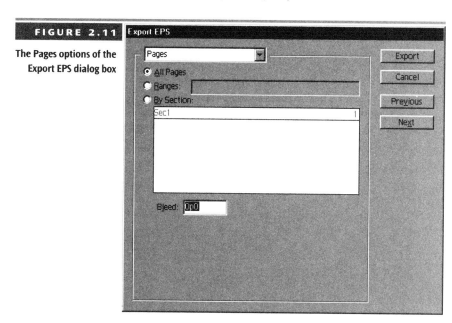

FIGURE 2.11
The Pages options of the Export EPS dialog box

The options on the Pages option page are:

All Pages Click this radio button to create an EPS file that contains all the pages of the document.

Ranges Click this radio button and specify a range of consecutive pages, using a hyphen. For example, entering 2-4 would create an EPS file of pages two through four. You can specify multiple consecutive page ranges by separating the entries with a comma, like this: 2-4, 5-8, 11-15.

By Section Click this radio button and click on the name of a section to create an EPS file containing only the pages in that section. To select more than one section, press Shift as you select from the displayed list of sections.

Bleed If any of the pages in the document to be converted have graphics that will print to the edge of the paper, specify an amount of "overlap" to allow in the EPS file. This extra amount allows for the image to be printed outside the eventual final size of the paper, so that when it is finally trimmed, the image will "bleed" all the way to the edge of the paper.

chapter 3

InDesign Desktop Basics

Featuring:

- *The desktop* — 37
- *Tool and palette basics* — 40
- *Keyboard shortcuts* — 48
- *Context menus* — 53
- *Using grids, guides, and rulers* — 57
- *Using plug-ins in InDesign* — 66

CHAPTER 3

INDESIGN DESKTOP BASICS

InDesign's tools, palettes, and functionality are a natural extension of Adobe's Photoshop and Illustrator user interfaces, all of which share a similar desktop metaphor. In fact, if you've had experience with Adobe's graphics programs, you may want to skip the first few sections in this chapter and move on to "Keyboard Shortcuts."

This chapter examines the InDesign work area and your view control options, and then shows you how to use the tools and palettes, create and edit keystroke shortcuts, access context-sensitive menus, and define grids, guides, and rulers. In the sidebar, Adobe InDesign plug-ins are discussed.

Working in the Work Area

The Adobe InDesign work area is organized much in the same way as Photoshop and other Adobe products. The work area has a menu bar at the top, view controls at the bottom and right side, a floating Toolbox (toolbar) which appears on the left, and floating grouped palettes on the bottom and the right. The work area also contains the pasteboard, where objects can be placed prior to positioning them on the page. The pasteboard is the area outside an InDesign page or spread (View ➢ Entire Pasteboard Window).

You can manually open one or more document windows. All open document windows are listed at the bottom of the Window menu. To change the active document window, click on the document name or use the Adobe InDesign default keystroke shortcuts in the following table:

Command	Windows Shortcut	Macintosh Shortcut
Next window	Ctrl+F6	Not applicable
Previous window	Shift+Ctrl+F6	Not applicable

Figure 3.1 illustrates how the InDesign work area looks in Windows when you first launch the program. Except for stylistic differences in the user interface, both the Windows and Macintosh versions of InDesign work area are organized similarly when opened for the first time. You can change the organization of the work area to suit your personal preferences by moving the toolbar, opening/closing palettes and windows, and grouping and ungrouping palettes.

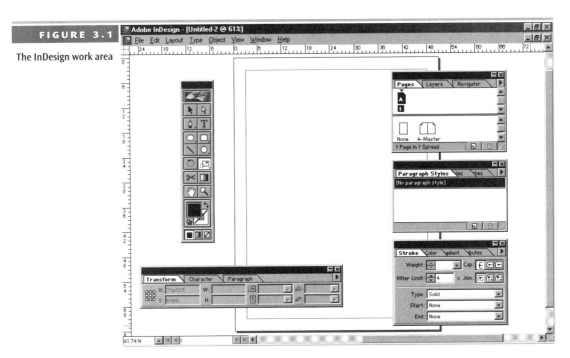

FIGURE 3.1

The InDesign work area

Using the Menu Bar

The Adobe InDesign menu bar has nine options: Adobe InDesign icon, File, Edit, Layout, Type, Object, View, Window, and Help.

NOTE   See Appendix B for a description of the Adobe InDesign menu options.

To access the menu commands you can do any one of the following:

- Moving your mouse, trackball, graphics tablet pen, or other pointing device, place the pointer/cursor on your selected menu bar heading and click. The menu appears. Click on the command you want to use.
- Using the keyboard, type a shortcut key. The default, most-frequently-used shortcut keys are noted in the right-hand column of the menu. (If you would like to learn how to assign, change, or delete a keyboard shortcut, go to the "Saving Time with Keyboard Shortcuts" section later in this chapter.)
- Windows only: Hot keys are noted as underlined letters. To open a menu, type Alt+*Hot key*. For example, to open the Type menu, you key Alt+T. After the menu opens, select a menu command by only typing the underlined letter in the corresponding command name (e.g. type "z" to open the font size sub-menu).

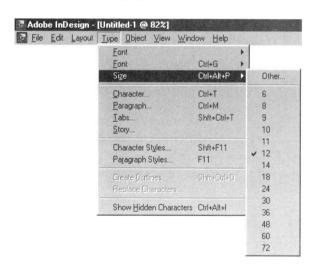

TIP   Menu command listings followed by three dots open dialog boxes or palettes. "New…" and "Story…" are just two examples.

View Controls

To navigate through the InDesign work area, you have several options.

- At the bottom of the document window, there are three navigation options:
  - Placed in the far-left corner is a pull-down menu where you can select different zoom values or magnifications.
  - To the right of the zoom menu is an option for changing the active page view for multi-page documents. Use the buttons to select first, last pages, previous, and next pages. The number of the active page appears in the box that's bracketed by the previous and next page buttons.
  - A scroll bar for moving left to right or right to left in the document.

- On the ride side of the document window, a scroll bar for moving up and down through a page or document.

TIP If you'd like to reduce the number of times you press or click a mouse button to scroll, consider purchasing a wheel mouse. The wheel mouse works when you slightly move your finger forward or back across the small recessed wheel that's on the mouse. As you move the wheel, your page or document scrolls up or down on your monitor screen.

- Menu commands listed under the View menu
- The Hand and Zoom tools on the Toolbox
- The Navigator palette
- Keystroke shortcuts

NOTE In Appendix B, you can see the View menu commands' pre-set window displays. You will also find more information about the Navigator palette, and the Hand and Zoom tools.

Getting Handy with the Toolbox

The Adobe InDesign Toolbox is made up of a series of button icons. Each icon represents a tool function. There are tools for selecting objects, drawing and editing paths and basic shapes, creating and editing text, customizing frames, and changing document views. You can also use the Toolbox to indicate fill/stroke color functions and to apply a color, gradient, or none to selected objects.

NOTE Descriptions of the individual tools are found in Appendix B. To learn how to use individual tools, see the appropriate chapter for that topic.

Positioning the Toolbox

If you want to move the Toolbox to another position in the work area:

1. Position the pointer on the Toolbox title bar. The title bar is the colored bar at the top of the Toolbox.
2. Click and drag the Toolbox to its new location.

Displaying the Toolbox

When InDesign is launched, the Toolbox automatically appears in the work area. If the Toolbox becomes hidden from view, select Window ➢ Tools to display the Toolbox again.

Using Tools

If you want to use a tool, you must select it. Once selected, the current tool becomes highlighted. There are two ways you can select a tool to use it.

- Place the pointer on the tool icon and click to make your selection.
- Type the shortcut key. Each tool has its own assigned shortcut key. These shortcut keys are identified in Appendix B, or you can:
  - Place the pointer on the tool icon to see the identifying label and shortcut key (Windows and Macintosh).

Displaying Hidden Tools

Some of the tools on the Toolbox are hidden from view. The location of hidden tools is identified by a triangle, which appears in the lower right corner of the icon button. There are two methods for displaying and selecting hidden tools.

- Position the pointer over the tool icon that has the hidden tool you want to access. Hold down your mouse button to see the tool. While continuing to press the mouse button, move the pointer over the hidden tool you want, and click to select the tool.
- Cycle through hidden tools by using the shortcut keys.

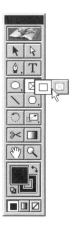

TIP The Toolbox shortcut keys are listed in the Adobe InDesign Quick Reference Card, tool tips, and online Help.

Understanding Palette Basics

Adobe InDesign has an extensive selection of palettes to work with—21 in fact. InDesign allows you to display and hide palettes; resize, collapse, and change the orientation of a palette; move an entire palette group or single palette; reorganize or create new palette groupings; use palette menus; and enter numerical text or change a numerical entry.

NOTE A description of each palette can be found in Appendix B. To learn about individual palette functions, check the appropriate chapter for that topic.

Displaying and Hiding Palettes

If you would like to display a palette, you have the following options:

- Select from a menu. Palettes can be found under the File, Type, and Window menus.
- Use the assigned shortcut keys.
- When a palette group is open, click the tab to bring the palette forward.

When hiding a single palette or a palette group, click the top right button marked with an "X" (Windows) or the top left button (Macintosh).

Here are two keystroke shortcuts, which you can use if you don't have a cursor in text or a text insertion point in a palette text box:

- Press Tab on your keyboard to show/hide all open palettes. The Tab key acts as a toggle switch.
- Press Shift+Tab on your keyboard to show/hide all open palettes *except* the Toolbox. Shift+Tab is also a toggle switch.

TIP You can drag palettes to be displayed on any monitor if you are working with a multiple-monitor workstation set-up.

Using Palette Menus

Not all palettes have palette menus. Palettes with menu options are identified by a triangle that appears on the right side of the palette below the title bar. To access the palette menu, position the pointer on the triangle, press the mouse button, and then select the menu command you want.

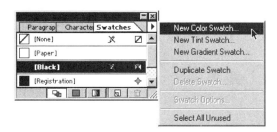

Resizing, Collapsing, or Changing Orientation of a Palette

When you are working with a smaller monitor or need to view larger areas of your document, you can resize, collapse, or change the orientation of an open palette until you need to use it again:

- Click on the minimize/maximize box on the palette title bar. It's the second box from the right. The box works as a toggle switch.

- If you are a Macintosh user, you can click on the zoom box (located in the top right corner of the palette) to collapse the palette to just the title bar.

- Palettes, identified by three diagonal lines in the lower right corner box, can be resized.
    - Drag any corner of the palette (Windows).
    - Drag from the palette's bottom right corner (Macintosh).

NOTE In palette groups, only the frontmost, active palette is resized by this action. All the other palettes in the group keep their current dimensions.

- Some palettes—including the Paragraph and Align palettes—offer Show/Hide Options from their palette menu.
- The Transform, Character, and Paragraph palettes can appear as either a horizontal (default) or vertical palette display. Use the Horizontal/Vertical palette menu command to change palette orientation. If the palette group contains horizontal and vertical palettes, the orientation defaults to the frontmost palette's setting.
- Double-click the palette tab to cycle between different palette views. Window users can also double-click the title bar to toggle between the normal and collapsed views.

Moving a Palette or Palette Group

A single palette or palette group can be moved by dragging its title bar.

Reorganizing or Creating New Palette Groups

Depending on your project requirements, you may want to reorganize or create new palette groups. Customizing the organization of palette groups can save time by eliminating unnecessary extra steps to access menu commands. For example, you could add the Text Wrap palette (a single palette) to the Character/Paragraph/Transform palette group to speed up text composition. If you wanted to work strictly from the menus, you'd have a hard time: the Text Wrap palette appears in the Object menu, the Character and Paragraph palettes are in the Text menu, and the Transform palette is accessed from the Window menu. It's much easier to expand the group and click the tabs to cycle through the palettes.

Figures 3.2–3.4 show how the Align and Story palettes, not assigned to any palette group, were merged to form a new palette group. Clicking the palette tab and dragging the palette to the new location created the new group.

FIGURE 3.2
Creating a new palette group

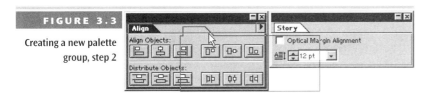

FIGURE 3.3
Creating a new palette group, step 2

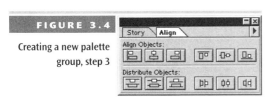

FIGURE 3.4
Creating a new palette group, step 3

You can also separate a palette from an existing palette group using the same drag-and-drop process. Palettes should be separated when you find that the frequency of use makes cycling through the palette group cumbersome.

Entering or Changing Numerical Text

InDesign has several methods for setting or changing the numerical value in a palette or dialog box. You can:

- Place your cursor in an option box, and key in a number value.
- Temporarily override a measurement unit and increment preference in a palette or dialog box by also specifying a different measurement system for the value. The abbreviations for the measurement systems are as follows:

Measurement	Abbreviation
Inches	i or in (3i)
Millimeters	mm (2mm)
Picas	p (6p)
Points	p (p6) or pt (6 pt)
Picas and points	p (7p5)
Ciceros	c (9c)

NOTE If you type **6 pt** as the abbreviation for 6 points in a palette option box, InDesign will automatically change the numerical entry to 0p6.

- Use the built-in, simple math calculator available in any numerical text box. The calculator recognizes the math symbols for + (plus), – (minus), * (times), / (divided by), or % (percent). In the following illustrated example (Figure 3.5), the leading was decreased to 33.2 pt. by entering –10 in the Character palette text box after the current mathematical expression 43.2 pt.
- Replace a current value. Select by double-clicking the entire value and then typing a new value.

TIP You can also choose an existing value by clicking on its icon or label.

- If a pop-up menu is an option, choose a value from the list.

UNDERSTANDING PALETTE BASICS

- Identify a numerical text option. Using your keyboard, press the Up and Down Arrow keys to increase or decrease a value or click the palette's Up and Down Arrow buttons next to the individual option. If you press the Shift key during this action, the value will increase in greater increments. (The size of the change is determined by which palette option you've selected.)

FIGURE 3.5
Calculating a new leading value

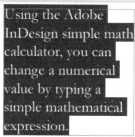
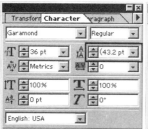

TIP InDesign immediately applies any changes made using the palette's pop-up menus, arrow keys, or the palette's arrow buttons

Getting in Focus

The Adobe InDesign manual defines focus as "that part of the application, such as a palette option or selected object, that is affected when you type on the keyboard." In plainer language, a focus is something you have selected. For example, you use the Selection tool to choose a graphic object. Then you select a Transform palette option to turn it into a focus, as shown in in the graphic below. You enter your value. Finally, the Transform palette options are applied to change the selected object's dimensions or position in the layout.

Continued on next page

Getting in Focus *(continued)*

Select a focus by doing one of the following:

- Use your mouse or other pointing device to change the focus from one object or option to another.
- When a palette option is in focus (selected), you can move forward to a new option by pressing the Tab key. The active option will display the numeric entry as white type on a colored background.
- If you press Shift+Tab, the focus (selection) moves back to the previous option in the palette.

If you select a setting from a palette menu, you will not change the selected focus. The focus only changes if you use one of the above methods or press Enter (Windows) or Return (Macintosh) when you apply a new numeric entry.

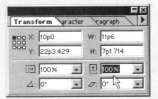

There are three options for applying/not applying the new value and designating which option has focus.

- To apply the new numeric entry and change focus to your document, press Enter (Windows) or Return (Macintosh).
- To apply the new numeric entry and keep the focus on the current palette option, press Shift+Enter (Windows) or Shift+Return (Macintosh).
- If you don't want to apply the new numeric entry, but keep the focus on the current palette option, press the Esc key.

Saving Time with Keyboard Shortcuts

Using keyboard shortcuts is a fast way to access InDesign features and to control your page layout. Keyboard shortcuts also reduce the number of movements you perform with your mouse or other pointing device. There are two shortcut sets packaged with

InDesign: the default InDesign shortcut set and the QuarkXpress 4 shortcut set. Although you cannot edit either set, they can be the basis for a new set that you create.

NOTE The most frequently used default shortcuts are found on the Adobe InDesign Quick Reference Card.

TIP You can share shortcut sets with other InDesign users who are using the same system OS version. Because there are different keystroke commands sets for the Windows and Macintosh versions of InDesign, a shortcut set will work only within its own system OS environment.

Editing the Shortcuts

InDesign allows you to change the active shortcut set, view your shortcut sets, show a list of shortcuts contained in a set, create a new shortcut set or shortcut, and redefine an existing shortcut. Simply select from File ➢ Shortcuts to open the Edit Shortcuts dialog box shown in Figure 3.6. Of course, opening the Edit Shortcuts dialog box has its own shortcut: the defaults are Shift+Ctrl+Alt+K (Windows) and Opt+Shift+Cmd+K (Macintosh). All the following tasks are done in the Edit Shortcuts dialog box, unless otherwise noted.

FIGURE 3.6

The Edit Shortcuts dialog box

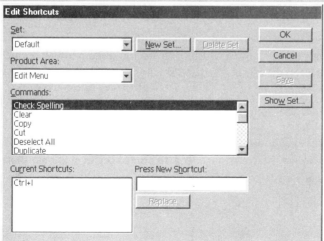

Selecting Your Active Shortcut Set

To change the active shortcut set, make your selection from the Set drop-down menu. Click OK to accept your change. You can now use the shortcut set with InDesign.

Viewing a Shortcut

You can view your shortcut on screen by following these simple steps:

1. Choose a shortcut set from the Set drop-down menu.
2. From the Product Area drop-down menu, select the area whose commands you want to see. You can choose the Edit, File, Help, Layout, Object, Type, View, or Window menus, as well as areas that don't belong to any single menu, such as Object Editing, Other, Text Selection, Tool/Palettes, Typography, and View/Navigation.
3. In the Commands box, scroll down and highlight the command you're interested in. The current shortcut for that command appears in the lower left-hand corner box.

Viewing and Printing an Entire Shortcut Set

To save time and make editing a shortcut list easier, you can view and print a copy of an entire shortcut set. Here are the steps:

1. To view the set, click the Show Set button.
2. A new window opens containing the set list of all defined and undefined commands. In Windows, this is compiled as a .TXT file in Windows Notepad (Figure 3.7); in Macintosh, this is compiled as a SimpleText file (Figure 3.8).
3. The text file is set in a bitmapped font. To create sharper, more professional looking copies, assign a printer font to the document before printing. In Windows Notepad, choose Edit ➢ Set Font. In Macintosh SimpleText, choose Font ➢ *Font name*.
4. To print a copy, select File ➢ Print.

TIP You may want to create a binder with printed copies of all your shortcut sets. Keep it handy for an easy-to-access reference.

FIGURE 3.7

The Windows Notepad file showing a shortcut set

```
Shortcut Set : Default

Product area : Edit Menu
        Check Spelling...  ----  Ctrl+I
        Clear  ----  [none defined]
        Copy  ----  Ctrl+C
        Cut  ----  Ctrl+X
        Deselect All  ----  Shift+Ctrl+A
        Duplicate  ----  Ctrl+Alt+D
        Edit Dictionary...  ----  [none defined]
        Find Next  ----  Ctrl+Alt+F
        Find/Change...  ----  Ctrl+F
        Paste  ----  Ctrl+V
        Paste Into  ----  Ctrl+Alt+V
        Redo  ----  Shift+Ctrl+Z
        Select All  ----  Ctrl+A
        Step and Repeat...  ----  Shift+Ctrl+V
        Undo  ----  Ctrl+Z

Product area : File Menu
        Adobe Online...  ----  [none defined]
        Close  ----  Ctrl+W
```

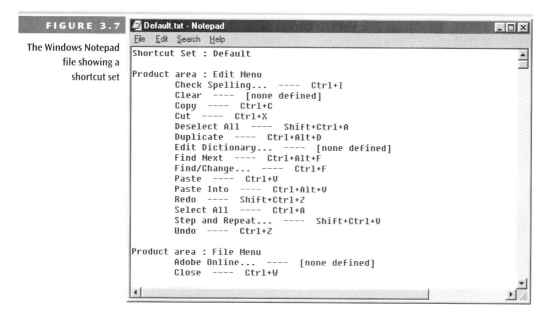

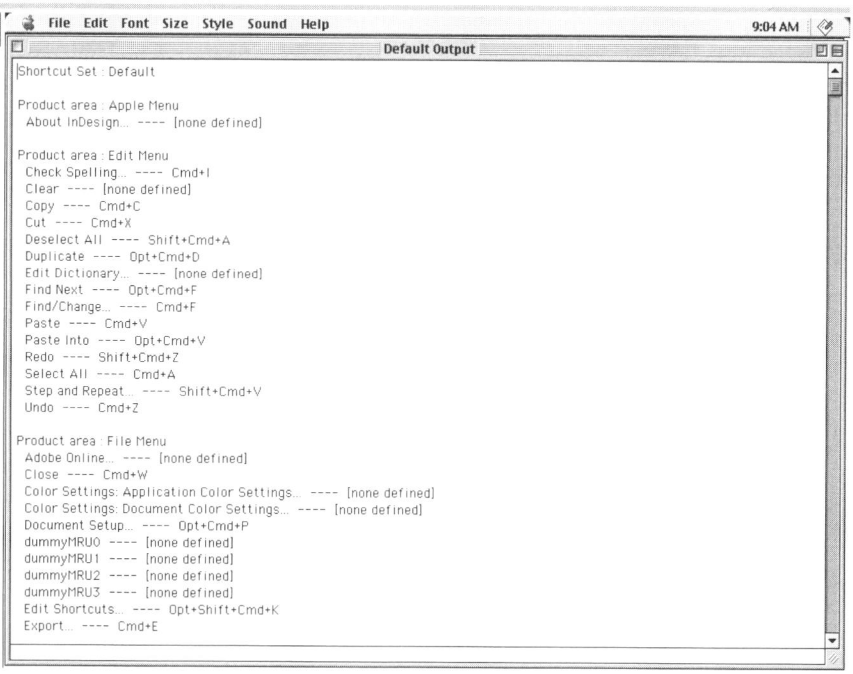

FIGURE 3.8

The Macintosh SimpleText file showing a shortcut set

```
Shortcut Set : Default

Product area : Apple Menu
 About InDesign... ---- [none defined]

Product area : Edit Menu
 Check Spelling... ---- Cmd+I
 Clear ---- [none defined]
 Copy ---- Cmd+C
 Cut ---- Cmd+X
 Deselect All ---- Shift+Cmd+A
 Duplicate ---- Opt+Cmd+D
 Edit Dictionary... ---- [none defined]
 Find Next ---- Opt+Cmd+F
 Find/Change... ---- Cmd+F
 Paste ---- Cmd+V
 Paste Into ---- Opt+Cmd+V
 Redo ---- Shift+Cmd+Z
 Select All ---- Cmd+A
 Step and Repeat... ---- Shift+Cmd+V
 Undo ---- Cmd+Z

Product area : File Menu
 Adobe Online... ---- [none defined]
 Close ---- Cmd+W
 Color Settings: Application Color Settings... ---- [none defined]
 Color Settings: Document Color Settings... ---- [none defined]
 Document Setup... ---- Opt+Cmd+P
 dummyMRU0 ---- [none defined]
 dummyMRU1 ---- [none defined]
 dummyMRU2 ---- [none defined]
 dummyMRU3 ---- [none defined]
 Edit Shortcuts... ---- Opt+Shift+Cmd+K
 Export... ---- Cmd+E
```

Creating a New Shortcut Set

If you would like to create a new shortcut set:

1. Click the New Set button in the Edit Shortcuts dialog box.
2. The New Set dialog box opens. Type a name for the new set.

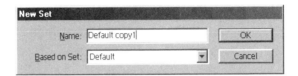

3. Choose a shortcut set from the Based On drop-down menu. Click OK to accept your selection. The dialog box closes.
4. From the Product Area drop-down menu of the Edit Shortcuts dialog box, select the command area.
5. In the Commands box, select the command from the list to define or redefine.

TIP Although they are listed, some commands will not be defined. For example, all the fonts on your system that appear in the InDesign font list are undefined. You can create a shortcut for each of your most frequently used fonts.

WARNING The Default and QuarkXPress shortcut sets cannot be edited directly. To get around this, create a new set based on either of these sets. Then you edit the new set and save your changes.

6. To enter a new keystroke shortcut, click in the Press New Shortcut box. Press all the keys simultaneously that you want to assign to your new keyboard shortcut. InDesign shows assigned command key sequences in the Current Shortcuts box. If your choice is already in use, try another key sequence or redefine the original shortcut.

WARNING Single-key shortcuts to menu commands should not be defined. Single keys are only used for entering text or for selecting tools from the Toolbox.

7. You can now do one of the following:
   - Create a new shortcut. Click the Assign button, which appears below the Press New Shortcut box. This button is context driven, so, depending on what you're doing, it may also appear as a Replace or Remove button.

- You can assign multiple shortcuts to any command option from these Product areas: Object Editing, Other, Text Selection, Tools, Palettes, Typography, Views, and Navigation. (Menu commands, like those assigned to Product areas File or Edit Menu, can only be assigned one shortcut at a time.) Click Assign to set multiple shortcuts.
- If you want to remove a previous shortcut after assigning the new one, select a command. The Assign button changes to the Remove button. Click the Remove button to delete the shortcut.
- When you redefine an existing menu command shortcut, the Assign/Remove button becomes the Replace button. Click the Replace button to change the assigned key sequence.

TIP Use the Delete Set button to remove any set you created from the Set list. Always keep a copy of the original default and QuarkXPress sets in the list for future reference and use.

8. Click Save to accept your changes to the current set. Continue to enter more shortcuts or select another shortcut set to edit.
9. Click OK to save all changes to the current set and to close the dialog box. Click Cancel if you don't want to accept the changes.

Using Context Menus

Context-sensitive menus are a fast way to access menu commands that are frequently used or that often appear on hidden submenus. These commands relate to the active tool or selection. Changing views, arranging objects, and editing graphics and text are tasks that commonly involve context menus, and they are discussed in the following sections.

Changing Views

To change your window view with a context menu, position the pointer on the document or pasteboard, making sure you don't select an object. Click the right mouse button (Windows) or press the Control key as you hold down the mouse button (Macintosh) to display the context-sensitive menu. Figure 3.9 shows the view commands you can use.

FIGURE 3.9

The view context menu

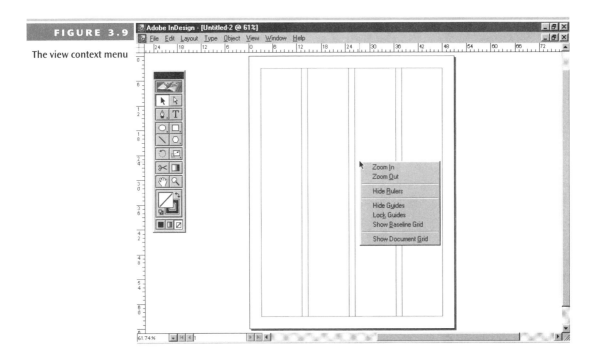

NOTE Appendix B contains illustrations showing the different views of the InDesign desktop window.

Arranging Objects

Sometimes you'll need to arrange objects in your layout so you can position them correctly relative to other objects. For example, in Figure 3.10 a photograph of a dining room is partially hidden from view by the large photo of the buildings. The dining room photo needs to be brought to the frontmost position. To do this, you first click the Selection tool and then select the small photo (object). Display the context-sensitive menu by clicking the right mouse button (Windows) or pressing the Control key as the mouse button is held down (Macintosh). You can use the commands on this menu to arrange the objects to your liking. For our photograph, we'll select Arrange ➢ Bring to Front.

NOTE Chapter 15 is a guide to precision transformation, placement, and alignment of objects.

FIGURE 3.10

The arrange object context menu

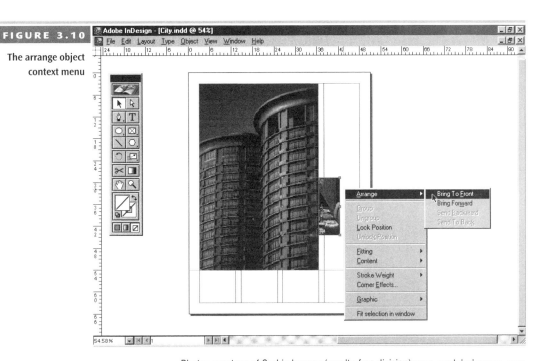

Photos courtesy of Corbis Images (royalty-free division) www.corbisimages.com

Editing Images

So now the small photo of the dining room has been brought to the front, but it requires further editing because only a small portion of the original photo is needed. Here's how a context menu was used to quickly access an image-editing program from the InDesign desktop.

For this example, use the Direct Selection tool to select the small photo. Two bounding boxes appear on the screen, as illustrated in Figure 3.11. The inner bounding box around the image represents the layout placeholder and that portion of the photo that can be seen. The outer bounding box corresponds to the true dimensions of the photograph.

Open a context menu and choose Edit Original to open your image editing software in a new window. You can now crop the photo to better fit the dimensions of the layout placeholder.

 N O T E   To learn more about working with graphics, see Chapter 6.

FIGURE 3.11

Selecting the Edit Original command from the context menu

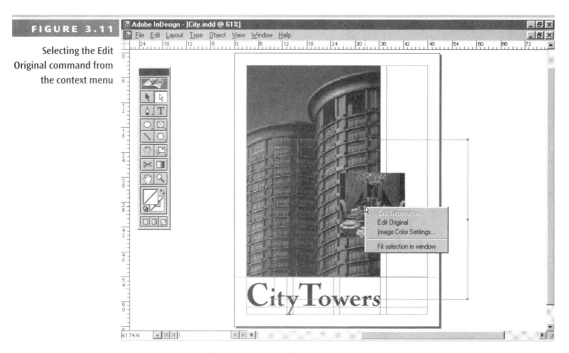

Photos courtesy of Corbis Images (royalty-free division) www.corbisimages.com

Editing Text

You'll often need to edit graphics, but just as frequently you'll need to edit copy in a text frame. The easiest way to do this is through a context menu. In Figure 3.12, a headline was added to the layout that contains the two photographs. To complete the text composition, a special character needs to be inserted (say, a copyright symbol).

First, select the Type tool from the Toolbox. Then, just like you did in Photoshop or Illustrator, click on the line of type where you want to insert your new character. Finally, open the context menu for text composition and select Insert Special Character ➢ Copyright Symbol.

NOTE Find out more about text composition in Chapters 5, 9, 10, and 14.

NOTE Regardless of which tool you use to position the pointer over the document or object, or select with, you always need to click the **right mouse button (Windows)** or **press the Control key as you hold down the mouse button (Macintosh)** to display any context menu.

FIGURE 3.12

A text composition context menu

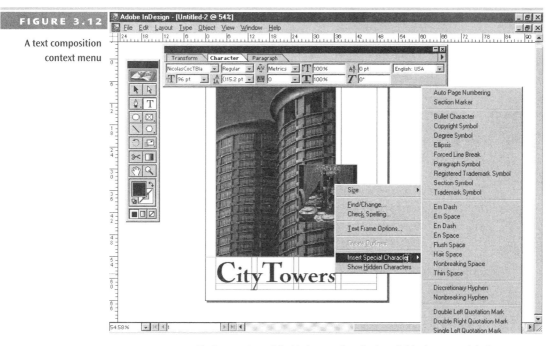

Photos courtesy of Corbis Images (royalty-free division) www.corbisimages.com

Using Grids, Guides, and Rulers

Adobe InDesign allows you to create margin and column guides, grids, guides and customized rulers to help you precisely place and align objects. These grids and guides, using a similar framework as in Photoshop and Illustrator, can be shown or hidden from on-screen view. Grids and guides are nonprinting and will not be visible when exported. Here are some basic facts about grids, guides, and rulers:

- Unlike margin and column guides, grid lines don't define a specific area of the document. Grids work best when you're aligning objects at evenly spaced intervals on a page or spread. Dragging with your mouse cannot move grid lines. To modify a grid you have to assign new preferences (File ➢ Preferences ➢ Grids).
- There is only one set of rulers and grids (baseline and document) assigned to each page.
- Use the Create Guides dialog box (Layout ➢ Create Guides) to position a guide on either a single page or across all pages of a spread. If you drag a ruler guide, it will appear only within the targeted page.
- If the document window has multiple spreads visible, the target spread is the only spread where rulers are not dimmed.

- You can snap objects to baseline or document grids even if they are hidden from view.
- Select the Paragraph palette's Align to Baseline Grid option if you want text baselines to snap to the baseline grid.

NOTE   Chapter 9 covers setting paragraph specifications.

- Guides must visible in order for you to snap objects to guides.
- Use InDesign to create unique guide positions for each layer. When your document has more than one layer, you can use ruler guides visible on another layer for snapping objects on the selected layer. Hide guides on individual layers when you don't want to use this option.

Snapping to Attention

Snapping works like this. When the Snap To command is active, objects that you are drawing, moving, or resizing will precisely align to the nearest grid intersection or guide. How close an object needs to be to the grid intersection or guide before snapping occurs is defined by the Snap to Zone distance. Set the Snap to Zone in the preferences dialog box (File ➢ Preferences ➢ Grids or Guides).

Working with Grids

InDesign has two kinds of grids: baseline and document. When you want to align lines of text, use the baseline grid, which resembles ruled loose-leaf paper as shown in Figure 3.13. The document grid works best for aligning objects and looks like graph paper. See Figure 3.14 for an illustration of a document grid.

To set up either a baseline or document grid, select File ➢ Preferences ➢ Grids to open the Grids Preferences dialog box. You can review the settings in this dialog box in Appendix A.

TIP   Neither the Adobe InDesign default nor the QuarkXPress shortcut sets assign keystroke sequences to open the Grid or Guides preferences dialog boxes. To quickly access these dialog boxes, create new shortcuts for these commands.

USING GRIDS, GUIDES, AND RULERS 59

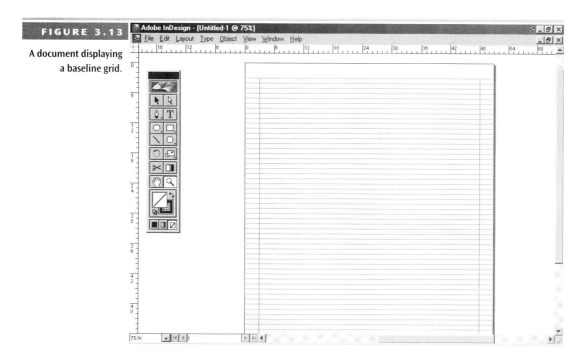

FIGURE 3.13

A document displaying a baseline grid.

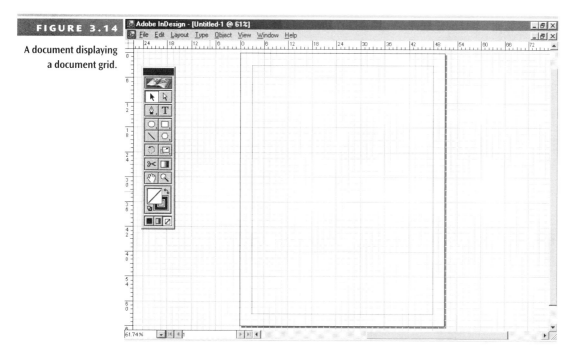

FIGURE 3.14

A document displaying a document grid.

Things to remember about grids:
- The baseline grid displays across entire spreads.
- The document grid traverses the entire pasteboard.
- Grids show on every spread but cannot be assigned to any master page or spread.
- A grid displays behind all guides, layers, and objects. You assign a grid to the entire document and not to any document layer.

Showing and Hiding Grids

You can show or hide the baseline grid by selecting View ➢ Show/Hide Baseline Grid, or pressing Ctrl+Alt+' (Windows) or Opt+Cmd+' (Macintosh).

Show or hide the document grid by selecting View ➢ Show/Hide Document Grid, or pressing Ctrl+' (Windows) or Cmd+' (Macintosh).

Snapping to Grids

If you need to snap to a grid when aligning objects, select View ➢ Snap to Document Grid or press Shift+Ctrl+' (Windows) or Shift+Cmd+' (Macintosh).

TIP   The Snap to Guides command controls both snapping to the baseline grid and snapping to guides.

Working with Guides

InDesign allows you to create margin, column, and ruler guides using several different commands. Figure 3.15 shows examples of these guides.

Setting Margins and Column Guides

Here's how to create or change margin and column guides for the entire document:
- Margin and column guides are set up first in the New Document dialog box (see Figure 3.16).
- To change the margin and column guides for an open document, select Layout ➢ Margins and Columns. This opens the Margins and Columns dialog box, where you enter the new values.

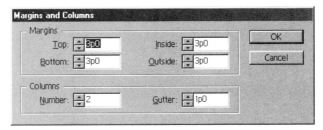

USING GRIDS, GUIDES, AND RULERS

FIGURE 3.15

A spread layout showing margin, column, and ruler guides.

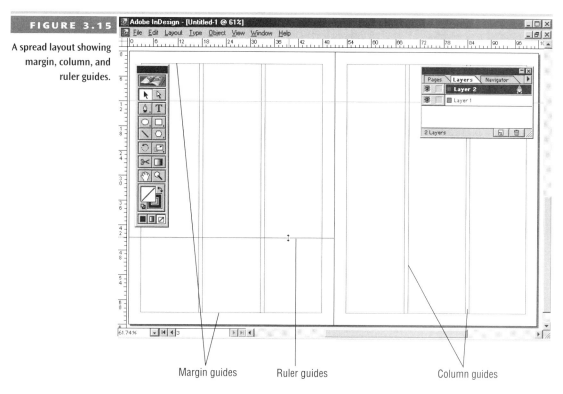

Margin guides   Ruler guides   Column guides

FIGURE 3.16

Setting margin and column guides in the New Document dialog box

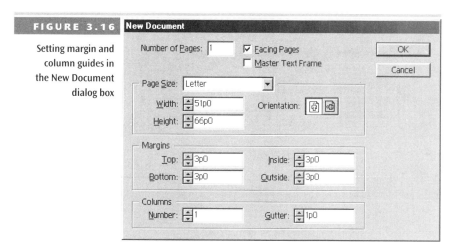

NOTE Chapter 2 has more info about setting up a new document. See Chapter 16 for details about document management using master pages.

Setting Ruler Guides

There are two kinds of ruler guides: page and spread. A page guide is confined within the boundaries of a single page. Set up spread guides when you need a common object alignment reference within all the pages contained in a spread.

You can freely place ruler guides anywhere on a page or pasteboard. Here's how:

Page guide Position the pointer inside either the vertical or horizontal ruler and drag within the page to the location you want. In Figure 3.15, you can see the dragging pointer in the left-hand page of the spread.

Spread guide Position the pointer inside one of the rulers and drag, but this time make sure the pointer is in the pasteboard area.

Spread guide (pasteboard hidden from view) Follow the same directions as for spread guide, but also press Ctrl (Windows) or Cmd (Macintosh) when you drag.

Spread guide (without dragging) Double-click on either the horizontal or vertical ruler if you want to position a spread guide at that ruler measurement.

Horizontal and vertical guides If you want to create horizontal and vertical guides at the same time, do the following:

1. Place the pointer at the target spread's ruler intersection.
2. Drag diagonally to the layout location as you press Ctrl (Windows) or Cmd (Macintosh).

To set ruler guide preferences, select Layout ➢ Ruler Guides. In the Ruler Guides dialog box, choose the view threshold and color.

Creating Evenly Spaced Guides

When you need to create guides that are evenly spaced as either rows or columns on a page (no spreads), select Layout ➢ Create Guides. In the Create Guides dialog box, shown in Figure 3.17, you can select the following options:

- Set the number of rows and columns, as well as the width of the gutter (the space between rows), either by typing directly into the box or by clicking the Up or Down buttons.
- Choose to fit guides to either margins or the page.
- Click the Remove Existing Ruler Guides checkbox to do exactly that.

TIP You can also remove guides by dragging and dropping the guide back to the ruler. Drag-and-drop is also used to move a guide to another position on the pasteboard or page.

- Check Preview to view guides.

TIP Remember that you can set a different set of guides for each layer of your document. You'll find this option useful when text on one layer overlays a much larger graphic on another layer. Set up one set of guides for aligning the text and another set for aligning the graphic.

When you like your guide framework, click OK to accept.

NOTE Advanced guide usage is covered in Chapter 16.

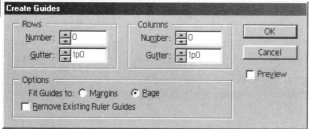

FIGURE 3.17
The Create Guides dialog box

Showing, Hiding, and Locking Guides

Here are the commands and shortcuts for showing, hiding, locking, and unlocking guides:

- If you want to show or hide guides, select View ➤ Show/Hide Guides. The default shortcut key is Ctrl+; for Windows and Cmd+; for Macintosh.
- When you would like to lock or unlock all ruler guides, select View ➤ Lock Guides to activate or deactivate the menu command. When a guide is locked, you cannot reposition it. A guide must be unlocked before you can move it.
- When working with layers, you can show, hide, lock, or unlock ruler guides on one layer only. Remember that a document with multiple named layers can have both locked and unlocked guides. For example, Layer 1 guides might be locked and Layer 2 guides unlocked.

• You can do this without affecting the selected layer's objects display by doing the following:

1. Open the Layers palette (if it's not already open). Select Window ➤ Layers.
2. Double-click the layer name.
3. In the Layer Options dialog box (Figure 3.18), select or deselect Show Guides and Lock Guides as desired, and click OK.

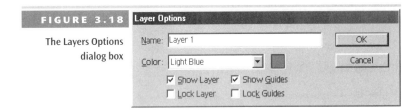

FIGURE 3.18

The Layers Options dialog box

Snap-to Guides

To toggle on or off the Snap-to Guides command, select View ➤ Snap-to Guides, or press Shift+Ctrl+; (Windows) or Shift+Cmd+; (Macintosh).

If you want an object to snap to a guide, the object's edge must fall within the guide's snap-to zone. When you're having difficulty snapping to your chosen guide, redefine the snap-to zone to a smaller pixel measurement. The snap-to zone value is always measured in pixels and is set in the Preferences/Guides dialog box (File ➤ Preferences ➤ Guides).

Working with Rulers

InDesign offers several different standard measurement units to create rulers: points, picas, inches, inches decimals, millimeters, centimeters, ciceros, and custom. To set your ruler's measurement unit, color, and threshold preferences, select Preferences ➤ Units & Increments. Make your changes in the Units & Increments dialog box. When you change zoom magnifications, the number of ruler increments identified by tick marks (short lines) will change. For example, if you're using a pica ruler and you zoom your document to 3200%, as shown in Figure 3.19, you will see ruler ticks marking off quarter points, quarter picas (3, 6, 9 points) and pica (1, 2) increments. (Remember 12 points equal 1 pica.) You should pay attention to these settings, because how the horizontal ruler is set up will control the behavior of tabs, margins, indents, and other measurements.

NOTE See Appendix A for more information about setting preferences.

USING GRIDS, GUIDES, AND RULERS 65

FIGURE 3.19

Viewing a pica ruler at 3200% magnification

You can also set ruler measurement units using these steps:

1. Position the pointer on the ruler
2. Right-click (Windows) or Control-click (Macintosh). A context menu opens.
3. Select the units from the context menu.

NOTE To learn how to temporarily override the measurement system, see the "Entering or Changing Numerical Text" section earlier in this chapter.

WARNING When you change ruler tick marks in an on-going project, previously placed objects, grids, or guides may not line up with the new ruler tick marks.

The Zero Point Reference

The position at which the zeros on the horizontal and vertical rulers intersect is called the *zero point*. The default position of the zero point is the top left corner of the first page of each spread, as shown in Figure 3.20. If you scroll and change the view of the document, the zero point changes its position on screen relative to the pasteboard.

TIP The Transform palette's X and Y position coordinates use the zero point as the point of origination for measuring distances within the layout.

FIGURE 3.20

A close-up of a ruler showing zero point reference

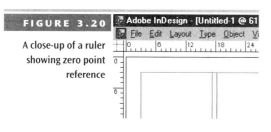

Moving the Zero Point Reference

The zero point is a handy tool for measuring distances between objects, assigning a new measurement reference point, or for tiling oversized pages when your page size exceeds the paper size of your printer. You can move the zero point by:

- Placing the cursor at the intersection of the horizontal and vertical rulers and then dragging to the new layout position.
- Double-clicking the intersection of the horizontal and vertical rulers (returns the zero point to its default position).

NOTE Moving the zero point changes its relative location in all spreads. For any page spread in the document you're viewing, the zero point will display in the same new relative position).

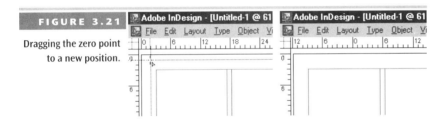

FIGURE 3.21
Dragging the zero point to a new position.

Locking and Unlocking the Zero Point

When you need to lock or unlock the zero point, place the cursor at the zero point of the rulers. Right-click (Windows) or Control-click (Macintosh) and select Lock Zero Point or Unlock Zero Point from the context menu.

Using Plug-ins in InDesign

The Adobe InDesign application expands its functionality through the use of plug-ins. Working with some of the same companies that created Quark Xtensions and PageMaker plug-ins, Adobe is developing partnerships to build customized InDesign-based publishing solutions. These plug-in developers offer a variety of tools such as creating drop shadows directly in InDesign, linking tools for building catalogs from databases, managing color, and layout automation. You can add, replace, or uninstall a plug-in when you want to add, upgrade, or remove features from InDesign.

Continued on next page

Using Plug-ins in InDesign *(continued)*

Packaged with InDesign are several plug-ins for importing, exporting, automation, and creating special effects. The plug-ins are automatically installed when you install InDesign on your computer. If you'd like to install other plug-ins, which were designed to work with InDesign, you can do either of the following:

- If an installer comes with the plug-in, follow the instructions for installing the module.
- Drag a copy of the plug-in into the Adobe InDesign folder/Plug-Ins folder. To avoid any problems, read any instructions provided with the module before you begin the installation process.

After installation, plug-ins become part of the InDesign desktop and are accessed from menus or dialog boxes or palettes.

Identifying the Plug-in Developer

Use the following table as a guide for determining the source of an installed plug-in. (You may also see folders with .FLT extensions; these are files from InDesign's Filters folder.)

Developer	File Extension (Windows)	File Type (Macintosh)
Adobe (Required)	*.RPLN	InDr
Adobe (Non-required)	*.APLN	InDa
Others	*.PLN	InD3

Plug-ins not shipped with the InDesign CD-ROM may change palettes' and other features' default settings when installed. To help monitor your customization of InDesign, maintain an up-to-date record of all your default settings.

Check the Adobe InDesign Web page or click on the Adobe Online icon (if the feature is set up) for the latest news about plug-in modules. Here's a list of some of the Adobe plug-in developers. (Several products mentioned here were still in development when this book went to press.) Contact these companies directly for the most current information about their InDesign related products.

A Lowly Apprentice Production, Inc. (ALAP)
5963 La Place Court #206
Carlsbad, California 92008
Phone: +1-760-438-5790
Fax: +1-760-438-5791
e-mail: sales@alap.com

Continued on next page

Using Plug-ins in InDesign *(continued)*

ALAP InDesign plug-ins are based on their current products, ShadowCaster and XPert Tools. ShadowCaster allows users to create soft drop shadows for any item directly within InDesign. The ALAP tools package for InDesign was built to help increase user productivity.

Em Software, Inc.
503 Belleview Boulevard
Steubenville, Ohio 43952
Phone: +1-740-284-1010
Fax: +1-740-284-1210
e-mail: indesigninfo@emsoftware.com

Em Software develops automated data publishing solutions like Xdata, Xtags, and Xcatalog. Two products they have under development are InData and InCatalog. InData will automatically format data that is exported from Macintosh or Windows database and spreadsheet applications or from corporate information systems downloads. InCatalog will be a linking tool for making two-way connections between elements in InDesign documents and fields in your database.

Enfocus Software Inc.
751 Laurel Street #626
San Carlos, California 94070
Phone: +1-650-631-8811
Fax: +1-650-631-7211
e-mail: info@enfocus.com

Enfocus PDF CheckUp for Adobe InDesign provides automated preflighting of Adobe Portable Document Format (PDF) files saved in InDesign. The plug-in, based upon technology developed for Enfocus PitStop 4, will check for font usage, image, and color information.

Extensis Corporation
1800 SW First Avenue, Suite 500
Portland, Oregon 97201
Phone: +1-503-274-2020, 1-800-796-9798
Fax: +1-503-274-0530
e-mail: info@extensis.com

Extensis plans to support the Adobe InDesign file format in upcoming versions of Extensis Preflight Pro. Preflight Pro identifies potential output problems, automatically collects all elements needed for output, writes an electronic job ticket containing job specifications, and compresses the entire job for shipping to a printer.

Continued on next page

Using Plug-ins in InDesign *(continued)*

HexMac Software Systems GmbH
Duranceweg 15
70771 Leinfelden, Germany
Phone: +49-711-9754961
Fax: +49-711-9754962
e-mail: info@hexmac.com
U.S. Distributor: Pliant Solutions, Inc
e-mail: info@pliantsolutions.com

The HexBase Publishing System (HPS) for Web-based editorial workgroups runs inside an InDesign palette. HPS allows content developers and editors to write and retrieve articles on an Internet-accessed server database using a JAVA-based Web browser. These articles can then be placed with formatting into an InDesign page.

LizardTech
1008 Western Avenue, Suite 200
Seattle, Washington 98104
Phone: +1-206-652-5211
Fax: +1 206-652-0880
e-mail: info@lizardtech.com

The MrSID Portable Image Format plug-in for InDesign is part of the MrSID for Publishing suite of imaging tools. With the MrSID Portable Image Format, InDesign users will be able to compress, display, explore, fast transmit, and output high-resolution images both locally and over the Internet. LizardTech has also integrated MrSID with Adobe PDF technology.

Managing Editor Inc.
101 Greenwood Avenue, Suite 330
Jenkintown Plaza, Jenkintown, Pennsylvania 19046
Phone: +1-215-886-5662
Fax: +1-215-886-5681
e-mail: info@maned.com

The MagForce suite of magazine production tools includes MagForce pagination planning software, MagForce Entry as booking system based on FileMaker Pro, MagForce PROSE-Writer for generating PROSE-output for print manufacturing, and the MagForce plug-in for importing MagForce pages and ads directly into Adobe InDesign.

Continued on next page

Using Plug-ins in InDesign *(continued)*

Mapsoft Computer Services Limited
30 Meyrick Drive, Wash Common
Newbury, Berks RG14 6SX, United Kingdom
Phone: +44-1635-43855
Fax: +44-1635-550097
e-mail: info@mapsoft.com

Sherpa for Adobe InDesign software builds on the PDF output features of InDesign. PDF workflow is streamlined by the creation of PDF links, bookmarks, articles, forms, action handlers and many other features in interactive PDF files from a single application.

Pantone Inc.
590 Commerce Boulevard
Carlstadt, New Jersey 07072
Phone: +1-201-935-5500
Fax: +1-201-896-0242
e-mail: info@pantone.com

PANTONE Colors will be supported in InDesign including the PANTONE MATCHING SYSTEM® and the PANTONE Process Color System®. You can access PANTONE colors from the menu. Select Windows ➢ Swatch Libraries.

PowrTools Software Inc.
202 - 990 Homer Street
Vancouver, BC V6B 2W7 Canada
Phone: +1-604-649-7560
e-mail: info@powrtools.com

PowrTable allows publishing professionals to embed text-based tables into InDesign publications. Text attribute support includes leading and kerning. The product also supports spot and process color libraries.

ShadeTree Marketing
5515 North 7th Street, #5-144
Phoenix, Arizona 85014
Phone: +1-602-279-3713
Fax: +1-602-279-1874
e-mail: info@borderguys.com

Continued on next page

Using Plug-ins in InDesign *(continued)*

The FRÆMZ InDesign plug-in offers 404 high-resolution PostScript borders, a custom border naming and search feature for easy cataloging of styles, CMYK and spot color compatibility for process separations, the ability to place and resize the corner and side elements separately, and a 30% drop shadow function.

Ultimate Technographics Inc.
1950 Sherbrooke Street West, Suite 800
Montreal, Quebec Canada H3H 1E7
Phone: +1-514-938-9050
Fax: +1-514-938-5225
e-mail: info@ultimate-tech.com

Ultimate Technographics has a full line of stand-alone and value-added suite solutions: Impostrip, IMPress, Trapeze, UltimateFlow, and Flight Simulator will support InDesign. Ultimate products import, process and output virtually all industry files formats, both proprietary and nonproprietary, including Adobe PostScript, PDF, and InDesign files.

Virginia Systems Software Services Inc.
5509 West Bay Court
Midlothian, Virginia 23112
Phone: +1-804-739-3200
Fax: +1-804-739-8376
e-mail: sales@virginiasystems.com

Sonar Bookends InDesign can index a book or publication that spans multiple documents. It can also reverse first and last names, create a multi-level index, and its sorting routines can sort both single and multi-level wordlists. Another option allows users to supply a Boolean expression to help find page numbers.

chapter 4

Frame and Shape Basics

Featuring:

- Shapes, frames, and placeholders 76
- Drawing circular and elliptical frames 77
- Drawing square and rectangular frames 78
- Drawing polygonal frames 79
- Drawing straight lines 83
- Filling and stroking frames and lines 84

CHAPTER 4
FRAME AND SHAPE BASICS

As you learned in Chapter 1, all of the text and graphics you place on a page will be inside InDesign's "frames." (If it's easier for you to think of them as boxes, that's okay. If you're familiar with Illustrator or Photoshop, you may be more comfortable thinking of them as *paths*.) In this chapter, I'll show you how to draw simple circular, elliptical, square, and rectangular shapes and straight lines, as well as more complex polygonal shapes. These shapes can become the frames that contain our text and graphics, which we will add in Chapters 5 and 6.

In this chapter, I'll also show you how to "fill" and "stroke" your frames. This is how you add color to the frame outlines and color the frames themselves.

This chapter deals only with drawing these simple shapes and frames. For more information about drawing more complex freeform shapes, as well as editing existing shapes and frames, see Chapter 17.

Introducing Shapes, Frames, and Placeholders

The basic difference between shapes and frames is that a shape is not intended to contain any text or graphics. A shape can be considered a piece of artwork. You might draw a circle, fill it with a pretty pink, and place it attractively on a page or pages. Or you might need a colorful blue bar that runs the length of a page, vertically along the outer margin. These would be shapes.

But that doesn't mean that if you draw a shape you can never decide later that the shape should contain a graphic. You can add text or a graphic to a shape, and as soon as you do so it becomes a frame. Even if it's an open shape, like a curved line, you can place text or a graphic in the area that is enclosed by the shape.

TIP After you create a frame, you can fill it with text or place a graphic in it. You don't have to specify what type of frame you're making as you make it.

You can convert any text frame to a graphic frame simply by replacing the text with a graphic. The same is true of graphic frames.

You can also draw and place shapes that don't yet have anything in them but eventually will. These are called *placeholders*. They're empty shapes that have an "X" through them, as shown below. That "X" basically signifies that this really is a frame, but it is masquerading as a shape until it is made whole by being filled with text or a graphic. You can use placeholders to develop a design structure before you have the textual or visual content to place.

 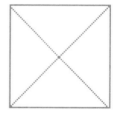

NOTE You can also create a text frame by placing text, which creates a frame automatically. For more information about placing text, see Chapter 5.

Recognizing Shapes, Frames, and Placeholders

Let's say you have a multi-page document up and running. You've started to design the document before the content has been delivered. You go back and look at it and suddenly you realize that you've drawn all these shapes on the pages. How do you know which shapes are shapes, placeholders, or frames?

It's easy! Look at the three objects below. One of them is a shape, one of them is a frame, and one of them is a placeholder. Can you tell which?

  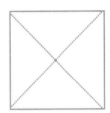

The object on the left with the picture in it is a frame. You can tell because it has something in it. The object in the middle is a shape. You can tell because it is an empty shape. The object on the right is a placeholder. You can tell because it is an empty shape with an "X" through it.

Drawing Circular and Elliptical Shapes and Frames

To draw a circular or elliptical frame, start by selecting the Ellipse tool from the Toolbox or by pressing L on the keyboard. The cursor will change to the cross pointer.

Move the pointer to the area where you want to start drawing your elliptical shape. Hold down the mouse button and drag to draw the ellipse. You will see the ellipse in blue as long as you hold down the mouse button. You can move all around the pasteboard, even drawing an ellipse partially on the page and partially on the pasteboard, if you want. You can draw any configuration of ellipse: tall and narrow, short and wide, almost circular, etc.

When you release the mouse button, the shape will be drawn. Depending on whether you most recently selected the Selection tool or the Direct Selection tool, you will see a bounding box (Selection tool) or anchor points (Direct Selection tool) appear around the shape. Once you have drawn the shape, you can edit it by dragging the anchor points with the Direct Selection tool or the handles of the bounding box with the Selection tool. (For more information about anchor points and using the Direct Selection tool, see

Chapter 17.) You can swap from anchor points to a bounding box or from a bounding box to anchor points by choosing the alternate tool and then selecting the line.

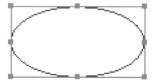 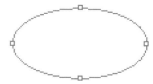

Notice as you drag the pointer (while holding down the mouse button) that the shape begins to draw as if you were actually drawing an invisible rectangular shape with a visible elliptical shape inside it. You're not really drawing the exact shape you drag. If you want to at least try to be precise about the size and placement of the shape as you draw it, choose Window ➢ Transform before you start to draw. This action will open the Transform palette and you can watch the values in the palette as you draw.

If you need even more precision, you may want to draw the shape in roughly the size, shape, and position that you want, and then refine it numerically with the Transform palette. (See Chapter 15 for more about using the Transform palette.)

To draw a perfect circle, hold down the Shift key as you draw. The shape will be constrained to a circle.

 TIP Once you've drawn a shape and you want to change its size in one direction only (i.e., only horizontally or only vertically), grab one of the handles in the middle of the side you want to change. That way, you won't accidentally change the other dimension, as you could if you grabbed and dragged one of the corner handles.

Drawing Square and Rectangular Shapes and Frames

Drawing square and rectangular shapes and frames is basically the same as drawing elliptical and circular shapes and frames, except that you use the Rectangle tool.

To draw simple, square, or rectangular frames, start by selecting the Rectangle tool from the Toolbox or by pressing M on the keyboard. The cursor will change to the cross pointer.

Move the pointer to the area where you want to start drawing your rectangular shape. Hold down the mouse button and drag to draw the rectangle. You will see the rectangle in blue as long as you hold down the mouse button. You can move all around the pasteboard, even drawing a rectangle partially on the page and partially on the pasteboard, if you want. You can draw any configuration of rectangle: tall and narrow, short and wide, almost square, etc.

When you release the mouse button, the shape will be drawn. Depending on whether you most recently selected the Selection tool or the Direct Selection tool, you will see a bounding box (Selection tool) or anchor points (Direct Selection tool) appear around the shape. Once you have drawn the shape, you can edit it by dragging the anchor points with the Direct Selection tool or the handles of the bounding box with the Selection tool. (For more information about anchor points and using the Direct Selection tool, see Chapter 17.) You can swap from anchor points to a bounding box or from a bounding box to anchor points by choosing the alternate tool and then selecting the line.

Even though while drawing with the Rectangle tool you are seeing a more direct representation of the shape and position you are drawing, you may still want more precision about size, shape, and placement. If so, choose Window ➤ Transform before you start to draw. This action will open the Transform palette, and you can watch the values in the palette as you draw.

If you need even more precision, you may want to draw the shape in roughly the size, shape, and position that you want and then refine it numerically with the Transform palette. (See Chapter 15 for more about using the Transform palette.)

To draw a perfect square, hold down the Shift key as you draw. The shape will be constrained to a square.

Drawing Polygonal Shapes and Frames

To draw a polygonal frame, start by selecting the Polygon tool from the Toolbox or by pressing N on the keyboard. The cursor will change to the cross pointer.

Before drawing, you may need to define the shape of the polygon. Double-click the Polygon tool icon in the Toolbox to open the Polygon Settings dialog box, shown below.

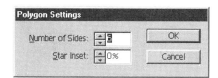

In the Number of Sides text area, enter the number of sides you want for your polygon (up to 100). The number of sides denotes the number of straight lines that will be used to draw the polygon. You may also change the values by clicking the up and down arrows to the left of the text area or by using the up and down arrows on the keyboard. In the Star Inset text area, enter a percentage (between 0.0% and 100.0%) for the middle of the "star" you can create. What this option does is take every other point on the polygon and move it in toward the center of the shape. Higher Star Inset values move these points closer to the center of the shape.

Combining Polygon Setting Values

As you can see in the following examples, you can play with the polygon settings values to come up with some pretty interesting-looking polygons. For example, if the Star Inset value is set to zero percent and the number of sides value is closer to 100, the polygon will appear nearly circular.

When the Star Inset value is low and the Number of Sides value is high, you will create an elliptical shape with a "pinked" or jagged edge. The polygon shown below has values of: Star Inset 5%; Number of Sides 100.

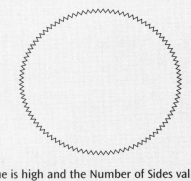

When the Star Inset value is high and the Number of Sides value is high, you will create an elliptical shape that seems to be made up of long, slender spines (sort of like a sea anemone). The polygon shown below has values of: Star Inset 95%; Number of Sides 100.

Continued on next page

Combining Polygon Setting Values *(continued)*

When the Star Inset value is low and the Number of Sides value is low, you will create a shape that appears to be more of what we consider to be a polygon. The polygon shown below has values of: Star Inset 5%; Number of Sides 12.

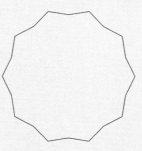

When the Star Inset value is near 50% and the Number of Sides value is low, you will create a shape that appears as more of a star or starburst shape. The polygon shown below has values of: Star Inset 50%; Number of Sides 12.

From this point, drawing a polygonal shape is pretty much the same as drawing a rectangular or elliptical shape. Once you define your polygon settings, click OK and then move the pointer to the area where you want to start drawing your polygonal shape. Hold down the mouse button and drag to draw the polygon. You will see the polygon in blue as long as you hold down the mouse button. You can move all around the pasteboard, drawing a polygon partially on the page and partially on the pasteboard, if you want. You can draw any configuration of polygon: tall and narrow, short and wide, almost circular.

When you release the mouse button, the shape will be drawn. Depending on whether you most recently selected the Selection tool or the Direct Selection tool, you will see a bounding box (Selection tool) or anchor points (Direct Selection tool) appear around the shape. Once you have drawn the shape, you can edit it by dragging the anchor points with the Direct Selection tool or the handles of the bounding box with the Selection tool. (For more information about anchor points and using the Direct Selection tool, see Chapter 17.) You can swap from anchor points to a bounding box or from a bounding box to anchor points by choosing the alternate tool and then selecting the shape.

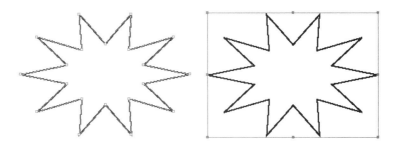

As with elliptical shapes, notice as you drag the pointer while holding down the mouse button that the shape begins to draw as if you were actually drawing an invisible rectangular shape with a visible polygonal shape inside it. You're not really drawing the exact shape you drag. If you want to at least try to be precise about the size and placement of the shape as you draw it, choose Window ➤ Transform before you start to draw. This action will open the Transform palette and you can watch the values in the palette as you draw.

If you need even more precision, you may want to draw the shape roughly in the size, shape, and position that you want and then refine it numerically with the Transform palette. (See Chapter 15 for more about using the Transform palette.)

To draw a polygon that conforms to the shape of a perfect circle, hold down the Shift key as you draw. The shape will be constrained to a circle.

Converting Text Outlines to Frames

You can actually convert the outlines of almost any text to frames that you can then stroke, fill, and edit just like any other frame. (Some fonts prevent InDesign from accessing their outline information, in which case InDesign will alert you when you try to create the outlines from the type.)

These considerations apply to type that has been converted to frames:

- Type that has been converted to frames becomes an *inline graphic* (see **Chapter 6**), flowing with the rest of the text.
- Type that has been converted to frames is no longer editable as text. However, you can edit the shapes of the new frames as you would other frames. (See **Chapter 17** for more information about editing frames and shapes.)

Continued on next page

Converting Text Outlines to Frames *(continued)*

- Type that has been converted to frames is no longer considered text by InDesign, so automatic tracking and kerning will no longer be applied. Also, hyphenation is no longer applied.
- Type that has been converted to frames retains the fill and stroke of the type before it is converted. You can edit these attributes.
- You should convert the type to frames after sizing it close to the final size you want.
- You don't need to convert type to frames to apply stroke and fill. (For more information, see the "Filling and Stroking Shapes and Lines" section later in this chapter.)

To convert type outlines to frames, follow these steps:

1. Select any type in a text frame.
2. Choose Type ➢ Create Outlines.
3. You may not notice any difference in the appearance of the type, but if you select the Direct Selection tool and select the converted type, you'll see its anchor points, confirming that the type is now an editable frame.

Drawing Straight Lines

To draw a straight line, start by selecting the Line tool from the Toolbox or by pressing E on the keyboard. The cursor will change to the cross pointer.

Place the pointer over the area where you want the line to begin. Hold down the mouse button and drag to draw a line of the length and orientation you want.

Hold down the Shift key as you drag to constrain the line to multiples of 45 degrees.

TIP If you're drawing a line and having trouble getting it to be perfectly square (horizontally or vertically) with the page, use the Shift key to constrain the line to multiples of 45 degrees and then align the line at 90 or 180 degrees to the page.

If you last selected the Direct Selection tool, you'll see a line with anchor points at each end. If you last selected the Selection tool, you'll see that the line now has a bounding box. You can swap from anchor points to a bounding box or from a bounding box to anchor points by choosing the alternate tool and then selecting the line.

You can alter the length and orientation of the line by changing the shape of the bounding box or by moving the anchor points.

Drawing Placeholders

The steps for drawing placeholders are the same as those for drawing shapes and frames (described above), but you use the frame drawing tools, shown below, rather than the plain shape drawing tools.

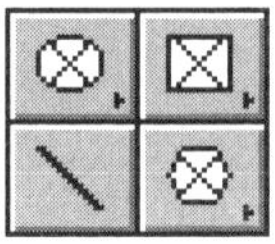

Filling and Stroking Shapes and Lines

Once you have drawn shapes, frames, and placeholders, you can *stroke* them by coloring their outlines, changing the widths of their outlines, changing their outlines from solid lines to a variety of dashed lines, or changing their corners. You can *fill* them with colors, including cool gradients. (For more information about selecting color and editing gradients, see Chapter 12.)

Once you have drawn lines, you can change their widths, apply color to them, change their appearance from solid lines to various dashed lines, change the appearance of their ends, and add arrowheads.

NOTE **Fills and strokes can also be applied to individual characters of type. The basic steps for applying fill and stroke to text characters are the same as the steps described in this section for applying fill and stroke to shapes and lines. First, though, you must select the Type tool and select the specific characters of type that you want to fill or stroke. Applying gradients to text is discussed in detail in Chapter 12.**

Filling Shapes with Color and Gradients

You can apply or change the color that fills a shape either as you draw the shape or after you have drawn it. You can either apply a solid color or a gradient (a gradual transition from one color to another).

Shapes and lines will be drawn with the color attributes that are currently set in the Toolbox color controls, so you should check these attributes before you begin to draw. (For more information about the Toolbox, see Chapter 3. For more information about selecting colors, see Chapter 12.) Of course, you can always change the attributes after you draw a shape or line. Using fill, stroke, and gradients, you can make changes to the colors of any shape that you've drawn.

FILLING AND STROKING SHAPES AND LINES

To draw shapes and lines with the default colors of black stroke and no fill, make sure you have clicked with the mouse away from any object in the document and then click the Default Colors icon in the color control area of the Toolbox.

To draw shapes and lines with colors other than the default colors, make sure you have clicked with the mouse away from any object in the document and then select colors. The new colors will then become the new default colors and everything you draw from then on will be drawn with these color attributes.

Filling Shapes with Solid Color

Select the shape you want to fill. Choose Window ➢ Color or press F6 to open the Color palette. If the palette group containing the Color palette is already open, you can click the Color tab to bring the Color palette to the front.

Figure 4.1 shows the Color palette opened for a shape drawn with the default colors. The two color swatches in the upper left signify the colors assigned to the stroke (see Figure 4.2) and the fill (see Figure 4.3). The small color swatch in the lower left will automatically load the last applied color to the fill color swatch and the selected shape.

Color palette

TIP   Colors in the color palette can not be named or saved. But if you are seeking color consistency across your document and selecting a color for a fill for the first time, you can select the color in the Color palette and then create a new color swatch in the Swatches palette to save and name it. Then, when you want to apply that color to another object, you can click the color swatch in the Swatches palette to select that color for the fill color box in the Color palette. (For more information about selecting colors, see Chapter 12.)

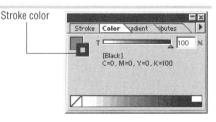

The Stroke Color palette.

To set a stroke color, click the stroke color box.

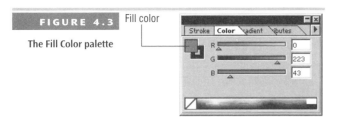

FIGURE 4.3

The Fill Color palette

To set a fill color, click the fill color box.

Applying a Grayscale Shade or a Shade of a Named Color

If the object you selected does not have a color applied to it (signified by a white swatch with the red bar across it) you'll see one color slider bar with a T (which stands for *tint*, if you're wondering) to the left of it, as shown in Figure 4.1.

NOTE The tint bar actually appears anytime a selected object has either no color applied or is filled or stroked with a named color from the Swatches palette. If you see the "no color" swatch (the white swatch with the red bar across it) in the fill color box but don't see the T slider, click on the stroke color box (shown in Figure 4.2) and then click back on the fill color box. This should reset the Color palette to the correct slider configuration.

If your selected object has no color applied as a fill, you can specify a grayscale shade by clicking somewhere along the slider bar and then sliding the slider left or right to the desired shade of black (or "shade of gray," if that helps you understand it better). You can also select a shade of gray by clicking in the color bar at the bottom of the Color palette (see Figure 4.1) Or you can enter a shade value in the text input area to the right of the slider bar. You'll see the shape change to the shade of gray you have selected and the changes reflected in the fill color boxes in both the Color palette and the color control area of the Toolbox.

If you apply a named color from the Swatches palette, you can use that color at 100%, or you can use a tint of it by following the directions above when you open the Color palette.

TIP You can quickly reset the tint to full black or full white by clicking on the small half-swatch of white or black at the right of the color bar. You can also reset the selected shape to the default colors by clicking the Default Colors icon at the lower left of the color controls area of the Toolbox. You can apply no color to the object by clicking the No Color icon at the left of the color bar at the bottom of the Color palette, shown in Figure 4.1.

Applying a Color

To select a color, pull down the Color palette menu and choose either LAB, CMYK, or RGB. (If you're wondering what these letters represent, please read Chapter 12.)

 TIP When you open the Color palette for a shape that already has a named color applied from the Swatches palette, you will see the T slider only. If you want to apply a new, unnamed color to a shape that already has a named color applied, simply choose one of the color modes from the Color palette menu, as described above, to access the color-selecting controls in the Color palette.

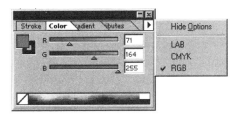

Notice that the Color palette changes, depending on the color model you select (as shown in Figures 4.4, 4.5, and 4.6).

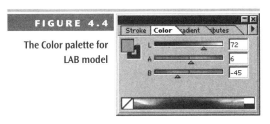

FIGURE 4.4
The Color palette for LAB model

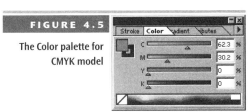

FIGURE 4.5
The Color palette for CMYK model

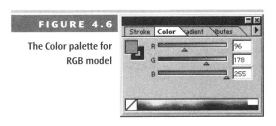

FIGURE 4.6
The Color palette for RGB model

For the purposes of this exercise, we'll use the RGB model and the corresponding Color palette, shown in Figure 4.6.

Notice that the Color palette now has three color sliders, labeled R, G, and B, with text input areas to the right for entering numerical color values. Now the color bar at the bottom of the palette displays the entire spectrum of colors in this (RGB) color model.

You can now mix colors by sliding the color sliders beneath the respective color slider bars, by entering numerical color values in the text input areas to the right of the color slider bars, or by clicking in the color bar at the bottom of the Color palette.

The color you select will appear in the fill color boxes of the Color palette and the color control area of the Toolbox, and the shape will be filled with that color. Remember, if this is a color you may use again, you might want to add the color to the Swatches palette to save and name it. (For more about using the Swatches palette, see Chapter 12.)

Filling Shapes with Gradients

Gradients are gradual transitions from one color to another along a straight line (*linear gradients,* shown in Figure 4.7) or from the center to the outer edge of a shape (*radial gradients,* shown in Figure 4.8). This transition can be one long gradient or it can be a series of gradients from one color to another (as shown in Figure 4.9). You can apply gradients from the Gradient palette, and you can create and/or edit gradient swatches to be applied to multiple objects. (For more about creating and editing gradient swatches, see Chapter 12.)

FIGURE 4.7

A linear gradient

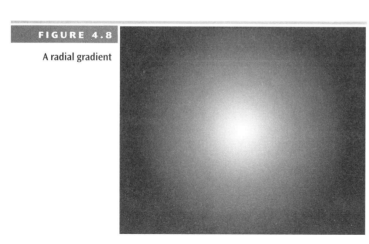

FIGURE 4.8

A radial gradient

FIGURE 4.9

A multiple linear gradient

To fill a shape with a gradient, first click on the fill color box in the Color palette. Then click the Gradient tab behind the Color palette or choose Window ➢ Gradient to open the Gradient palette, shown in Figure 4.10.

FIGURE 4.10

The Gradient palette

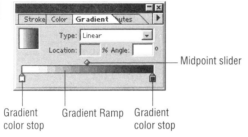

In the Gradient palette, you see the Gradient Fill box at the upper left, the Type option menu to the right, the Location and Angle input areas beneath the Type option menu, and the Gradient Ramp at the bottom of the Gradient palette. The diamond above the Gradient Ramp is the *midpoint slider*, which determines the point at which the colors are mixed at 50%. The boxes beneath the Gradient Ramp are the *gradient color stops*, which determine the color that will start (or stop, I guess you could say) at 100% at that point.

NOTE If you don't see all of these option areas in the Gradient palette, choose Show Options from the Gradient palette menu.

With the Gradient palette open, follow these steps to apply a gradient:

1. Select either Linear or Radial from the Type option menu of the Gradient palette to apply that gradient type to the selected object.
2. Now select the colors to use for the gradient. First, click on the left color stop box under the Gradient Ramp. You can apply a color to this stop in two ways:
   - Press Alt/Option and click a color swatch in the Swatches palette.
   - Click the Color tab behind the Gradient palette tab to open the Color palette for that color stop. Notice that this Color palette is slightly different than the normal fill Color palette, in that it has the color stop symbol beneath the fill color box at the upper left. While in this Color palette for

the color stop, you can define a color by entering values for the individual primary colors in the text input areas to the right of the sliders; you can drag the sliders under the color bars; or you can click in the color bar at the bottom of the palette. While you are here in this palette, you can also press Alt/Option and click a color swatch in the Swatches palette.

If you click away from the Color palette for this color stop, the Color palette will revert to the fill Color palette. To return to the Color palette for the color stop, you will have to go back to the Gradient palette, once again select a gradient type, and then click again on the color stop you want to edit.

3. Repeat Step 2 for the color stop on the right.

TIP If your gradient disappears from the selected object after making any of these changes or selections, go back to the Gradient palette and select Radial or Linear from the Type option menu, then select Radial or Linear again, depending on which one you want.

For more information about creating named swatches for gradients, creating gradients that transition between multiple colors, creating gradients that transition between multiple stops, using the Gradient tool, applying a single gradient to multiple objects, and applying gradients to text, see Chapter 12.

Stroking Shapes and Lines

Applying color to lines and to the lines around a shape is called *stroking*. You can stroke any shape or frame, any line, and even individual text characters, using the Stroke and Color palettes. The thickness of lines and shape outlines can be changed in the Stroke palette as well.

WARNING If you select a shape with the Direct Selection tool, you will not be able to see changes you make to the stroke of the shape until after you deselect the shape.

Changing the Thickness of Lines and Shape Outlines

To alter the thickness of any line or shape outline, first select the line or shape. Choose Window ➢ Stroke, press F10, or click the Stroke tab in the Stroke palette's palette group to open the Stroke palette, as shown in Figure 4.11.

In the Weight value box, enter a point value, click on the up or down arrows, or choose the Weight option menu to specify a new thickness of the line.

If you don't want any stroke at all, enter 0 for the Weight value.

FIGURE 4.11

The Stroke palette

 TIP If you enter a stroke but don't see it on the screen, it may be that the stroke's weight is smaller than can be drawn by the computer monitor. Magnify your view to check to see if it is there. Also, remember that if you have selected the Direct Selection tool, you won't see the stroke until you deselect the object or select another tool.

Stroking Lines and Shape Outlines

Select the line or shape to which you want to apply color. Choose Window ➢ Color or press F6 to open the Color palette (shown again in Figure 4.12). If the palette group containing the Color palette is open, you can click the Color tab to bring the Color palette to the front.

FIGURE 4.12

The Color palette

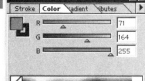

Select the stroke color box. The remaining steps and considerations for selecting and applying colors for the stroke are the same as those for applying fill colors to a shape, presented in the "Filling Shapes with Color and Gradients" section earlier in this chapter.

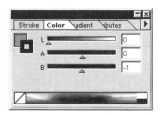

Altering How Strokes Affect a Frame

This may seem like an unnecessary complication, but you can alter how the thickness of a stroke affects both the size of the bounding box around a frame and the actual size of the frame. By default, the strokes of a frame are drawn inward, toward the center of the frame, which alters neither the outer dimensions of the frame nor the size of the bounding box of the frame. This makes sense because, in most cases, you wouldn't want your objects suddenly changing their dimensions and crossing over gutters and encroaching on other objects just because you thickened their strokes. You can change this (in those rare instances that you'll actually need to) by opening the Stroke palette menu and deselecting Weight Changes Bounding Box or by opening the Transform palette menu and selecting Dimensions Include Stroke Weight.

Changing Shape Corners

You can alter the appearance of the outer edges of frame corners so that they appear more rounded, more pointy, or lopped off by using the Join and Miter Limit options in the Stroke palette. You can also make the corners actually round, beveled, and some other fancy options, using the Corner Effects command.

To change the way lines butt together to form corners, use the Join and Miter Limit options of the Stroke palette.

Miter   Rounded   Bevel

The (hopefully) simplified definitions of the three join types are:

- *Miter joins* are pointed corners, but only when the length of the corner point is within the appropriate miter limit (Miter joins can be a little difficult to grasp; see the "Understanding the Miter Limit Option" sidebar below).

- *Rounded joins* are round but are not the same as rounded corners. (For more information on rounded corners, see the "Applying Corner Effects" section, next.)
- *Bevel joins* look like they've been lopped off square.

You can experiment with various Join and Miter Limit settings to produce a desired effect.

Understanding the Miter Limit Option

The Miter Limit option can be difficult to understand. It helps to learn the following guidelines that apply when setting the Miter Limit option:

- The Miter Limit option is only available for miter joins.
- A miter limit of 1 changes a miter join to a bevel join.
- The default miter limit is 4 and the range is 1 to 500. The miter limit specifies the ratio of the length of the point of the join to the width of the stroke, as well as the ratio at which the join changes from a miter join to a bevel join. This is really confusing, so let me try to simplify the concept: the longer and more narrow the point, the higher the miter limit must be to achieve an actual pointed corner. For example, simple polygons with relatively squat corner points will probably have pointed corners with any miter limit value of 2 or above. But the polygon below with 100 points and an inset of 50% has very narrow, long points, so getting them to actually reach a sharp point takes a miter limit of 32. (I don't want to even think about a join that needs that upper limit of 500!)

Miter limit of 31

Miter limit of 32

Applying Corner Effects

Remember, bevel joins are not rounded corners. They're just lopped off points at the corners. If you want true rounded corners on your shapes and frames, you use the Corner Effects command.

To apply a corner effect, choose Object ➢ Corner Effect to open the Corner Effects dialog box, shown below.

Select one of the corner effects from the Effect option menu, shown below.

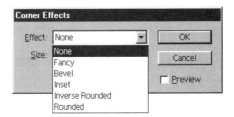

You now need to specify a size for the effect in the Size value box of the Corner Effects dialog box. To see the effect applied to the shape or frame before accepting it, click the Preview checkbox. Once you enter a value in the Size value box, press Tab to see the effect applied. (Pressing Enter is the same as clicking OK: you'll apply the effect and exit the Corner Effects dialog box.)

You may need to experiment with various Size values to get the effect you want.

Changing Line End Caps

End caps are the shapes that form the ends of lines and shape segments. End caps are particularly important when drawing dashed lines. When you select an end cap, it is applied to both ends of a line or shape segment. There are three types of end caps: the butt cap, the round cap, and the projecting cap.

The *butt cap* is a square end that stops even with the endpoints of the line or shape segment.

The *round cap* is a round end that extends half the width of the stroke beyond the endpoints of the line or shape segment.

The *projecting cap* is square, like the butt cap, but extends half the width of the stroke out beyond the endpoints of the line or shape segment, like the round cap.

To apply an end cap, select a line or frame segment. Then choose Window ➢ Stroke, press F10, or click the Stroke tab in its palette group.

In the Stroke palette, simply click one of the end cap icons.

Creating Dashed and Dotted Lines and Outlines

You can switch lines and shape outlines from solid to dashed in the Stroke palette. Dashed lines are any lines that break and alternate between blank spaces and filled-in spaces, like dotted lines. Strangely enough, however, you can't select a simple dotted line. (I bet it won't take long for someone to publish a plug-in for it.) You must create a dotted line and it's not really that simple. See the "Creating a Dotted Line" sidebar for more information.

Creating a Dotted Line

To create a simple dotted line, you have to play a bit with the particular line you want to make dotted. The problem is that the values you need change as the stroke weight changes. In other words, I can't give you just one set of values that you can apply to lines to make them dotted.

Creating the dot itself is simple enough. Follow these steps:

1. Select a line or shape.
2. Open the Stroke palette.
3. Click the Rounded Cap icon at the Cap option.
4. Enter a Dash value of .1 pt. (This keeps the beginning and the ending of the rounded cap together to create the round dot.)

Now, you must set the Gap value according to the weight of the stroke and the look you want for the line. So, if you want a dotted line with big gaps, you enter a larger value. To separate the dots, you need a value that is at least one-tenth of one point (.1) higher than the stroke weight. Then you add more points to spread out the dots.

For example, a line with a rounded end cap, a stroke weight of 2, a dash width of .1 pt., and gap of 2.1 will produce this dotted line:

And a line with a rounded end cap, a stroke weight of 2, a dash width of .1 pt., and gap of 3 will produce this dotted line:

Applying a dashed line is simple enough. Open the Stroke palette by pressing F10, choosing Window ≻ Stroke, or by clicking the Stroke tab in its palette group. At the Type option menu, choose Dashed.

Once you apply Dashed to a line or shape outline, the Stroke menu expands to include the dash and gap pattern value boxes, as shown below.

This is where it gets confusing. By entering point values in the alternating dash and gap value boxes and by specifying one of the three end cap types, you can create different types of dashed or dotted lines.

Applying Arrowheads and Other Line End Shapes

After the complexity of joins and dashed lines, you'll be happy to know that if you need an arrowhead, it's relatively easy to accomplish. You can apply arrowheads and other end shapes to lines and open frames. (For more about editing frames, see Chapter 17.)

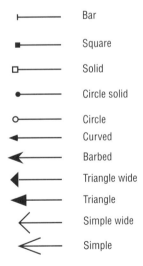

NOTE I think it's odd that Adobe didn't supply an arrow tail in these default end shapes. They may include one by the time the final version is released, or they may wait and let some third-party developer write a plug-in for it. We'll see.

To apply one of the arrowheads or end shapes shown above, simply select the line or frame segment to which you want to add the end shape. Then press F10, choose Window ➢ Stroke, or click the Stroke tab in its palette group to open the Stroke palette.

To apply an end shape to the start of a line or frame segment, select an end shape type from the Start option menu.

To apply an end shape to the end of a line or frame segment, select an end shape type from the End option menu.

To reverse the start and end points of a line or frame segment, choose the Direct Selection tool and select any anchor point. Then choose Object ➢ Reverse Path.

NOTE The start of a line is the point at which the line was first drawn. This may seem awkward because, for example, if you are drawing an arrow, you start at the point of the arrow and draw it away from the point. You're actually drawing in the opposite direction that you're pointing with the arrow you draw.

chapter 5

Type Basics

Featuring:

- Creating text frames — 102
- Entering text by typing and pasting — 108
- Placing text — 112
- Editing text — 120
- Using Find/Change — 122
- Spell Checking — 128

Type Basics

nDesign provides several methods for entering text into a document. All text in an InDesign document must be typed, pasted, or placed into one or more text frames.

As you learned in Chapter 2, you can create a new document that automatically creates empty text frames with each new page (master text frames). You can immediately type, paste, or place text into those automatic frames. Alternately, you can draw any new frame and type, paste, or place text into the frame, or automatically create a text frame by pasting or placing text. You can select and drag text from other applications. You can also enter type so that its lines run vertically down the page, rather than horizontally. In this chapter, I'll explain the basics of getting text into your InDesign documents, and how to edit that text. For more information about other, more advanced type and text issues, see the following chapters:

- Chapter 9: Formatting text, which is how you define the "look" of type and text
- Chapter 10: Using styles to speed your text formatting
- Chapter 12: Applying color to text

Chapter 14: How to export text and "continue" text through other pages and frames

Chapter 16: Creating text frames on master pages

Before we get started, you should familiarize yourself with the InDesign terminology of type and text:

- The **text** is the words, sentences, and paragraphs that make up your document's message.
- The **type** is the appearance of the individual characters of the text. (You also **type** when you enter text from a keyboard.)
- The **text insertion point** is the flashing icon that indicates where you will be entering text.
- You **paste** text when you're cutting or copying it from another place in a document (either the same one or a different one), or when you're dragging it from another application.
- You **place** text when you're importing it from another document.

Okay, then, let's put some text on the page.

Creating Text Frames

If you selected the Master Text Frames option in the New Document dialog box, as described in Chapter 2, you don't necessarily need to draw a text frame. You can just select the Type tool, click on the text frame, and start typing, pasting, or placing. However, if you want to type text into a frame other than the automatically generated master text frames, you'll need to know how to create a new text frame manually.

A text frame is distinguishable from other frames by the *in port* and *out port*, shown below. These features are used when threading text throughout a document, which is presented in detail in Chapter 14.

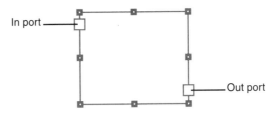

Manually Drawing a New Text Frame

To manually draw a new text frame, select the Type tool either by clicking the Type tool icon in the Toolbox or by pressing T on the keyboard.

The cursor will change to the Type tool cursor. The point of alignment for the Type tool cursor is the cross on the lower portion of the cursor. This is the point that will snap to the guides and margins on the page as you begin to draw the text frame. If it doesn't seem to be snapping, check that you have selected View ➢ Snap to Guides and/or View ➢ Snap to Grid. (You may also notice that the cursor won't appear to snap to the guide or grid until you actually press the mouse button.) When these options are selected, you see a checkmark beside them. If you don't see the checkmark, choose one or both again and it will appear.

Place the Type tool cursor where you want to begin drawing the text frame, then drag to draw the frame. You can constrain the frame to a perfect square by pressing Shift as you draw.

Release the mouse button when you have drawn the text frame you want. The text frame is drawn and the text insertion point begins flashing in the frame. You are ready to enter text.

Automatically Creating a New Text Frame

You can create text frames automatically if you select the Master Text Frames option in the New Document dialog box as you create the document. (Creating new documents is discussed in Chapter 2.)

You can automatically create a text frame in an existing document by placing text when no text frame has been selected. (For more information, see the "Placing (Importing) Text from Other Applications" section later in this chapter.)

Specifying Text Frame Options

You use the Text Frame Options dialog box to specify how many columns you want in a text frame and how much, if any, inset you want between the inside edges of the text frame and the text inside. Here you can also define the *first baseline*, which tells InDesign how far down from the top of the text frame you want the first line of text to start.

Access the Text Frame Options dialog box, shown in Figure 5.1, by choosing Object ➢ Text Frame Options, or by pressing Ctrl/Cmd+B. You can also access this dialog box by selecting a text frame and pressing the right mouse button in Windows (pressing Control as you click with the Mac mouse), and then choosing Text Frame Options from the context menu.

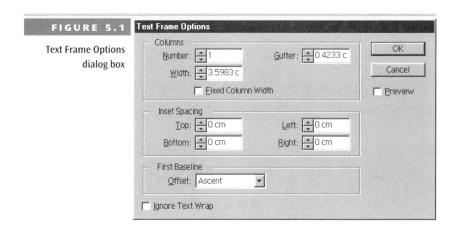

FIGURE 5.1 Text Frame Options dialog box

Setting Columns and Gutters

In the Columns area of the Text Frame Options dialog box, enter the number of columns (pointed out in Figure 5.2) you want in the Number text box. Alternately, you can click the up or down arrows to increase or decrease the number of columns.

Generally, when you divide a text frame into columns, you size the text frame according to the area you want it to cover, then accept the width of the columns as determined automatically by InDesign. However, if you should need a specific column width, enter that width in the Width text box.

Gutters are the empty areas between columns. You specify the width of the gutters in the Gutter text box.

WARNING Don't confuse the columns represented by the margin guides of the page with the columns in a text frame. The two specifications are separate. Regardless of how many page columns wide a text frame may be, it can have as many text columns as you wish. The text columns can match the page columns, or they can be different.

Page columns, text columns, and gutters

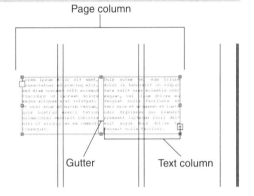

Using a Fixed Column Width

You can use the Fixed Column Width option to help you save a step when you are changing the width of a text frame to cover a specific number of page columns. For example, if you have a two-column text frame that fits across two page columns and you want to resize it to three text columns across three page columns, you would normally have to drag it across the third column, and then go back and specify 3 columns in the Text Frame Options dialog box. But if you've clicked the Fixed Column Width checkbox, you can specify a column width and then, when you drag a handle of the text frame to resize it, InDesign will grab the text frame and automatically size the text frame to include additional or fewer columns, depending on how far you drag the handle in one or the other direction. This is shown in Figure 5.3.

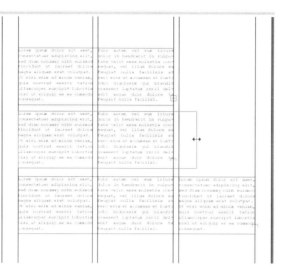

FIGURE 5.3

Three different fixed-width text frames

WARNING Be careful with the Fixed Column Width option. Whatever column width is entered in the Width value box is the fixed width that InDesign will use. That width may not be the actual width you want. So, if you don't know the specific column width and want to let InDesign figure the column width for a text frame across a certain area, you should first draw a text frame across the area, and then set the text frame to the number of columns you want, OK the change, and then reopen the Text Frame Options dialog box to select the Fixed Column Width option.

Setting the Inset Spacing

Inset spacing (or *text inset,* as it is called in at least one other page layout program) determines the amount of space between the inside edges of a text frame and the text in the text frame, as shown in Figure 5.4. In InDesign, you can specify different amounts of inset spacing for the four sides of a rectangular text frame. But if you open the Text Frame Options dialog box for any text frame that is irregularly shaped, you can only set one inset spacing value.

Enter values in the Insert Spacing options or click the up and down arrows to set a value. Notice that the new text area is then bordered by a lighter blue guide (which doesn't print).

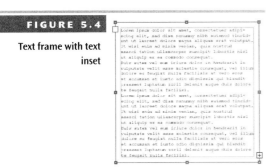

FIGURE 5.4

Text frame with text inset

Setting the First Baseline

The First Baseline option determines how far down from the top of the text frame InDesign will set the first line of type.

From the Offset option menu, shown below, you select one of the following options:

Ascent Places the first baseline down from the top by the distance specified in the font's file for the height of the font at the specified point size.

Cap Height Places the first baseline down from the top just enough to accommodate the height of the capital letters.

Leading Places the first baseline down from the top by the amount of leading specified for the first line of text.

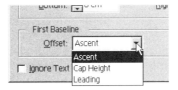

Ignoring Text Wrap

If you want text in a text frame to ignore any shape that is placed on top of it, which usually would result in the text running, or *wrapping*, around the shape, select the Ignore Text Wrap option.

Entering Text by Typing and Pasting

When you draw a new text frame, the text insertion point will appear in the new frame to show that you are ready to enter text. But if you want to enter text into an existing shape, placeholder, frame, or text frame, you must select that object with the Type tool or Vertical Type tool to begin entering text.

You don't have to create a text frame to enter text in InDesign. Any shape, placeholder, or frame can contain text. To enter text into one of these objects, simply select the Type tool or Vertical Type tool, and then select the shape, placeholder, or frame. (When you enter text into a shape that is not closed—such as a curved line—InDesign pretends that the shape is actually closed and places the text in the area that would be "inside" the shape if a line were to close the shape.)

WARNING If a frame already contains a graphic, you can enter text into it only by *placing* it, which is discussed in the next section. Placing the text will replace the graphic.

Typing Text

Once you have drawn a text frame or selected an existing shape, placeholder, or frame, enter text by typing just as you would in any word processor. Your typed characters will be placed from the point at which the text insertion point is flashing.

Entering Special Characters

When we talk about *special characters* in InDesign, we're not referring to those wonderfully eccentric relatives we all seem to have. Typographic special characters are those characters that are not regular keyboard characters and that are used very rarely, but serve to help us communicate our languages visually. Special characters include: © (the copyright symbol), ™ (the trademark symbol), and ° (the degree symbol), among many others.

To enter a special character in InDesign, place the cursor where you want to insert the character and then choose Type ≻ Insert Character to open the Insert Character dialog box, shown in Figure 5.5.

As you can see, this dialog box is a scrolling table of all the special characters offered in a selected font—including the regular keyboard characters. You can specify a different font by selecting another from the Font menu and you can specify a particular type style (such as bold or italic).

FIGURE 5.5

Insert Character dialog box

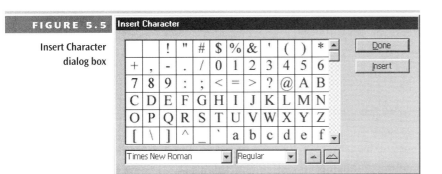

If you want to scan the table faster, click the little mountain range button to reduce the size of the symbols in the table. Click the big mountain range button to enlarge the symbols.

In the table, click on the image of the special character you want and then click Insert to place the character at the position of the text insertion point. You can do this just once or several times.

Click Done to close the box and resume editing.

Inserting Special Characters through Keyboard Shortcuts

Many of the more frequently used special characters are available through the context menu for text frames or by a keyboard shortcut.

The keyboard shortcuts for the special characters are shown in Table 5.1.

TABLE 5.1: KEYBOARD SHORTCUTS FOR SPECIAL CHARACTERS

Special Character	Keyboard Shortcuts
Bullet	Alt/Option+8
Ellipsis	Alt/Option+;
Copyright Symbol	Alt/Option+G
Registered Trademark	Alt/Option+2
Paragraph Marker	Alt/Option+7
Section Marker	Alt/Option+6
Toggle Quotation Marks	Shift+Alt/Option+"
Discretionary (Soft) Hyphen	Shift+Ctrl/Cmd+- (hyphen)
Non-breaking (Fixed) Hyphen	Alt/Option+Ctrl/Cmd+- (hyphen)
En dash	Alt+- (hyphen)
Em dash	Shift+Alt+- (hyphen)
En space	Shift+Ctrl/Cmd+N
Em space	Shift+Ctrl/Cmd+M

Continued on next page

TABLE 5.1: KEYBOARD SHORTCUTS FOR SPECIAL CHARACTERS (continued)

Special Character	Keyboard Shortcuts
Nonbreaking Space	Alt/Option+Spacebar (or Alt/Option+Ctrl/Cmd+X)
Figure Space	Shift+Alt/Option+Ctrl/Cmd+8
Flush Space	Shift+Alt/Option+Ctrl/Cmd+J
Thin Space (1/4 em)	Shift+Alt/Option+Ctrl/Cmd+M
Hair Space	Shift+Alt/Option+Ctrl/Cmd+I
Figure Space	Shift+Alt/Option+Ctrl/Cmd+8

Inserting Special Characters through Context Menus

To insert a special character through the context menu, first click to position the text insertion point in the text frame where you want to insert the special character, and then press the right mouse button in Windows (or press Control as you click with the Mac mouse) to access the context menu for the text frame. Slide down to Insert Special Character to open the special character menu, shown in Figure 5.6.

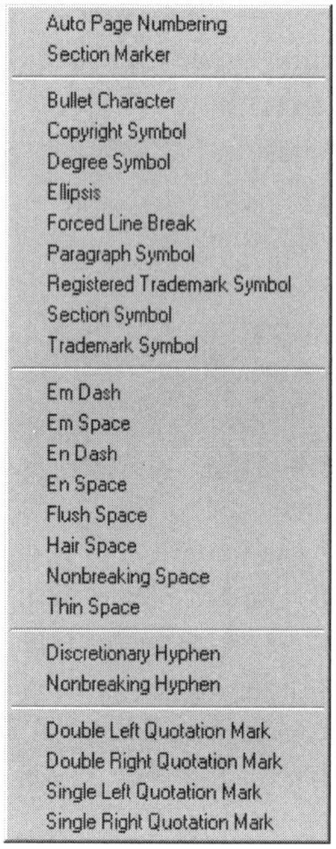

FIGURE 5.6
Special character context menu

- Auto Page Numbering
- Section Marker
- Bullet Character
- Copyright Symbol
- Degree Symbol
- Ellipsis
- Forced Line Break
- Paragraph Symbol
- Registered Trademark Symbol
- Section Symbol
- Trademark Symbol
- Em Dash
- Em Space
- En Dash
- En Space
- Flush Space
- Hair Space
- Nonbreaking Space
- Thin Space
- Discretionary Hyphen
- Nonbreaking Hyphen
- Double Left Quotation Mark
- Double Right Quotation Mark
- Single Left Quotation Mark
- Single Right Quotation Mark

As you can see, you have the option here to insert many of the special commands and characters that you may need most frequently. Slide the cursor over to this menu and up or down to select the option you want. Click at the option to insert that special character.

Cutting, Copying, and Pasting Text

Use the Type tool and Edit menu to paste text from another location into a frame. This text can be in the same frame in the document, in another frame in the document, in another open InDesign document, or from any other document in any other application.

1. Select the text you wish to paste by highlighting it with the Type tool cursor.
2. Cut or copy the text by choosing Edit ➢ Cut (Ctrl/Cmd+X) or Edit ➢ Copy (Ctrl/Cmd+C). Cutting text copies it to the clipboard and removes it from the source. Copying leaves the source intact and copies it to the clipboard.
3. Select the frame into which you want to paste the cut or copied text.
4. Click the Type tool cursor where you want to paste the cut or copied text.
5. Choose Edit ➢ Paste (Ctrl/Cmd+V). The pasted text will be inserted at the cursor.

NOTE If you don't select any frame into which you want to paste the cut or copied text, then InDesign will automatically create a new text frame in the center of the page and paste the text into that new text frame.

Dragging and Dropping Text from Another Application

You can place text from another application, as long as that application supports drag-and-drop. If it does, all you have to do is select the text in the other application and then hold down the mouse button as you drag it to the InDesign document window. InDesign automatically creates a new text frame approximately where you let go of the mouse button and copies the dragged text into it.

You can also drag-and-drop an entire text file from a Windows Explorer window or a Mac OS Finder window or desktop. By using this method, you can actually place the text into an existing text frame, if you want. Just drag the file's icon into the InDesign text frame and let go. If you don't drag it to an existing text frame, InDesign will create a new text frame for it.

TIP This text file drag-and-drop method places that entire text document into the selected InDesign text frame. This could be a drawback if you only want a small portion of a text file. So, if you want to use this method for some reason anyway, but you want to place only portions of another document, you could create individual text files in the other application with the text you want, then drag-and-drop those into the specific InDesign text frames you want.

The drag-and-drop method does not allow you to precisely place text from another document into a specific text frame in InDesign. In addition, when you use the drag-and-drop method to insert text, you won't be able to control the import options. For that, you have to use the Place function described in the next section.

Placing (Importing) Text from Other Applications

Placing is the InDesign term for importing text from other applications. You can place text from another application using the File ➢ Place command (Ctrl/Cmd+D), or you can use the drag-and-drop method described in the previous section. You can either place text into specific text frames or allow InDesign to create new text frames as it places the text.

InDesign also allows you to specify how it will treat the text as it is imported. You can select from a number of options, such as retaining formats, importing type styles, converting quote marks from typewriter style to typographers' style, importing table of contents data and footnotes, and so on. (If you use the drag-and-drop method, you will not have control over import options. See the "Using Import Options" section later in this chapter for more information.)

To place text from another application, follow these steps:

1. If you want to specify a text frame into which you want to import the text, select that text frame. If you intend to create a new text frame, make sure no text frames are selected.
2. Choose File ➢ Place or press Ctrl/Cmd+D to open the Place dialog box, shown in Figures 5.7 and 5.8.
3. Select a file by navigating through the directory structure and clicking its name or typing its name in the File Name text box.
4. Click the Show Import Options checkbox if you want to specify more control over the imported text. (See the "Using Import Options" section for more information about this option.)

PLACING (IMPORTING) TEXT FROM OTHER APPLICATIONS   113

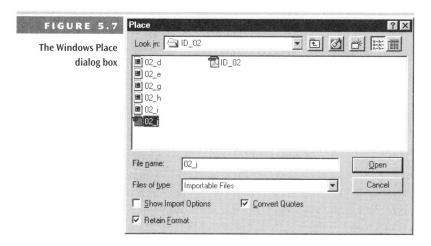

FIGURE 5.7

The Windows Place dialog box

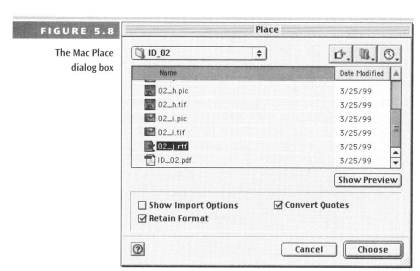

FIGURE 5.8

The Mac Place dialog box

5. If you want to retain the formatting that you have applied to the text in the other application, select the Retain Format checkbox. (See the "Using Import Options" section for more information about how this affects various formatting possibilities.)

6. If you want InDesign to convert the quotes from typewriter style quotes ("") to typographers' style quotes (""), click the Convert Quotes checkbox.

7. Click Open (Windows) or Choose (Mac).

8. If you selected a frame in Step 1, the text will be placed into that text frame. If you did not select a frame, the cursor changes into the Loaded Text icon, shown below. This tells you that the text is loaded and ready to be placed where you choose.

If you click with this Loaded Text icon in an area where there is no frame, InDesign will create a new text frame from the position of the pointer downward to the bottom of the page, as wide as the margins in that area. In other words, if you have the page divided into columns and click about halfway down the column, InDesign will create a new text frame as wide as one of the columns and about half as tall as the page. If there is only one column on the page, InDesign will create a new text frame as wide as the page, the top of which will be from the position of the cursor when you click.

If you move the Loaded Text icon to an area where there is no frame and press the mouse button to drag a shape, InDesign will create a new text frame in that place and shape and will place the text in that new frame.

If you move the Loaded Text icon to an area where there is an existing shape or placeholder, the Loaded Text icon changes to show the text in parentheses (as shown below), and when you click at that position the text will be placed in that shape or placeholder.

If you place the text and it is more than the selected frame can hold, you'll see the out port of the text frame change to indicate that you have overset text, as shown below. When this happens, you will need to either enlarge the text frame to accommodate the overset text, or *thread* the text to another text frame. (Threading text is presented in Chapter 14.)

Using Import Options

Use InDesign's import options to specify how the text and formatting information of the imported file is translated into InDesign. You access the import options using the File ➢ Place command, and then selecting the Show Import Options checkbox in the Place dialog box, as shown in Figures 5.7 and 5.8.

Once you select Show Import Options and change the settings, those settings become the default settings for future files of the same type placed in InDesign.

WARNING Not all of the formatting information saved from other applications can actually be imported into InDesign. You should probably assume that only the character attributes will be brought over. Other formatting, such as page layout features, margins, and column settings, won't be imported in most cases. If you really want to import and export fully formatted documents, you may need to rely on the Tagged Text file format.

The import options used by InDesign will depend on the type of file you are importing. By default, InDesign provides import options for the most popular word processing and page layout programs, such as Microsoft Word 97–98 and WordPerfect 6–8. The default installation set also includes a filter for Microsoft Excel files, generic text files, Rich Text Format (RTF) files, and both PageMaker and QuarkXPress Tagged Text files.

You can add additional import filters by placing them in the Filters folder, which is located in the Plug-Ins folder inside the InDesign application folder. You can obtain additional filters through third-party software publishers and by checking Adobe Online. (You access Adobe Online by clicking the graphic icon at the top of the Toolbox or by choosing File ➢ Adobe Online.)

TIP You can import character and paragraph styles from another application, as long as you have an InDesign import filter installed for that particular application. The imported styles are added to the respective Paragraph Styles or Character Styles palettes. If you import a style that has the same name as an existing style in InDesign, InDesign will retain the InDesign style. (If you want both of the styles that have the same name, all you have to do is make sure that you rename one or the other styles before you import the file.)

If you are preparing a file in another application to export to InDesign, that application's default file format is probably the best bet if it is one of those directly supported by InDesign. If it is not supported by InDesign, you could try to save it as a text file or an RTF (Rich Text Format) file, which are more likely to be compatible across platforms and applications.

TIP Once you click the Show Import Options checkbox in the Place dialog box and continue, that option will remain checked the next time you open the Place dialog box. If you don't want this, you can place a file and select its import options by pressing Shift while you double-click the filename in the file display area of the Place dialog box. This will open the Import Options dialog box before loading the text, but the Show Import Options option will remain unchecked in the Place dialog box when you open it next time.

Word, WordPerfect, and RTF Import Options

Choose File ➢ Place or press Ctrl/Cmd+D to open the Place dialog box, as shown in Figures 5.7 and 5.8. Select a Microsoft Word, Corel WordPerfect, or RTF file to place, then click the Show Import Options checkbox. Click Open or Choose.

The Import Options dialog box will open, as shown in Figure 5.9. This dialog box is the same for Microsoft Word, Corel WordPerfect, and RTF files, but the title bar will change to reflect the specific file type being imported.

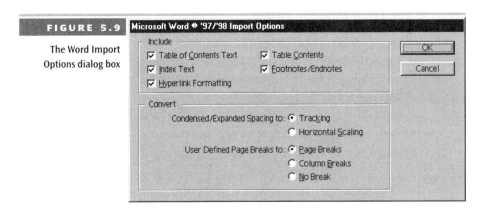

FIGURE 5.9

The Word Import Options dialog box

The Include area of the Import Options dialog box allows you to specify what types of special formatting to include when InDesign imports the document file. Selecting any of these options will import text from these formats to plain text in the InDesign document. Tables will be imported as tab-delimited text, and footnotes and endnotes will be imported as text at the end of the thread of text.

The Convert area of the Import Options dialog box allows you to define how InDesign will handle special horizontal spacing and page breaks. The Convert options in the Import Options dialog box are:

Condensed/Expanded Spacing To A slightly weird option that allows you to convert any Condensed/Expanded Spacing values you may have entered in the word processing application (I don't know for sure why you'd want to). Anyway, you can change type from having been spread apart (Tracking) with extra spaces between the letters, to having each character widened (Horizontal Scaling) in appearance. In either case, the width that the type took up in the word processor is preserved.

User Defined Page Breaks To   Allows you to specify how you want InDesign to react to page breaks that have been manually inserted in the text document. You can preserve those page breaks by selecting Page Breaks, you can convert them to column breaks by selecting Column Breaks, or you can ignore them by selecting No Break.

When you click OK, the file will be imported and you can place it just as you place other text, as described in the previous section. If, however, the document file had fonts in it that are not installed on your system, an alert box will open to notify you. InDesign will substitute fonts, so if you want to use those particular fonts from the document file, you may want to load them and place the file again.

Text File Import Options

Choose File ➤ Place or press Ctrl/Cmd+D to open the Place dialog box, as shown in Figures 5.7 and 5.8. Select a text file to place, then click the Show Import Options checkbox. Click Open or Choose. The Text Import Options dialog box will open, as shown in Figure 5.10.

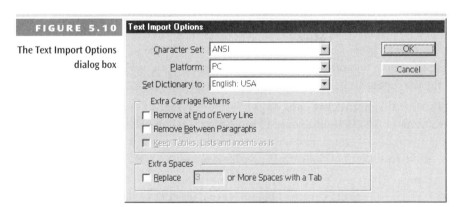

FIGURE 5.10

The Text Import Options dialog box

Remember, many HTML files are saved as text-only files by the applications that generate them—even if they appear as a specific file type, such as Word or WordPerfect. HTML files saved as text-only files will open with the Text Import Options dialog box. In the Text Import Options dialog box, you need to tell InDesign how this document file was saved and how InDesign should handle the formatting that is often added to text-only files by word processing applications. These are the options you can set:

Character Set Gives you a list of character sets to choose from. By default, the ANSI character set is specified because that is the default character set for InDesign.

Platform Allows you to choose PC or Macintosh.

Set Dictionary To Lets you select the language of the dictionary that corresponds to the language used when the file was saved.

Extra Carriage Returns These options can really be a great help if the text file has those annoying extra returns after every line of text (instead of only at the ends of paragraphs), or if it has extra returns between paragraphs. Select Remove at End of Every Line so that InDesign will set the text without those extra returns at the end of the lines. Select Remove Between Paragraphs to delete the extra paragraph returns between paragraphs.

Keep Tables, Lists, and Indents As Is This option only becomes active if you select one of the previous Extra Carriage Returns options. This filter option preserves those heavily formatted areas of a document, leaving tables, lists, and indents alone (just don't ask me how InDesign knows it's a table).

Extra Spaces If the text file was created by someone who used spaces instead of indents to create the first line indents (or any other indents, for that matter), you can tell InDesign to replace a certain number of consecutive empty spaces with a tab. Simply click the Replace option, then specify the number of empty spaces you want replaced with a tab.

When you've selected your Text Import options, click OK to load the text.

Microsoft Excel Import Options

Choose File ➤ Place or press Ctrl/Cmd+D to open the Place dialog box, as shown in Figures 5.7 and 5.8. Select a Microsoft Excel file to place, then click the Show Import Options checkbox. Click Open or Choose.

The Microsoft Excel Import Options dialog box will open, as shown in Figure 5.11.

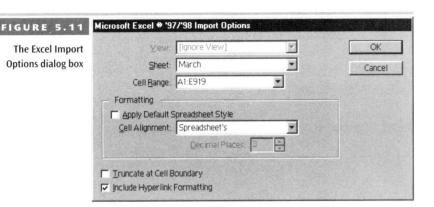

FIGURE 5.11

The Excel Import Options dialog box

The View option menu will be available only if there are saved views in the Excel file. If there are, you can choose to import the custom or personal views, or to ignore them completely.

From the Sheet option menu, select the name of the worksheet to import.

In the Cell Range text box, you can enter a range of cells to import. You can also pull down the option menu and select from the list of named ranges, if there are any. If you enter a range, use a colon to designate the range, as shown in the Cell Range text box of the Excel Import Options dialog box shown in Figure 5.11.

You also have a measure of control over how the spreadsheet's formatting is imported. For example, let's say you decide that you want all of the cells to be moved from right alignment to left alignment, or maybe even centered. Just select one of those formatting options from the Cell Alignment option menu, shown in Figure 5.12. If you choose Decimal, the Decimal Places value box will activate and you will need to specify a number of decimal places for alignment.

If you want to preserve the cell alignment that was saved in the original spreadsheet file, just leave the Cell Alignment option set to Spreadsheet's.

If you want to apply InDesign's default Spreadsheet Style, simply click the Apply Default Spreadsheet Style checkbox.

You can also restrict the contents of the cells to that which will fit into the cell boundaries by selecting Truncate at Cell Boundary.

If there is any hyperlink formatting in the spreadsheet that you want to import, select Include Hyperlink Formatting.

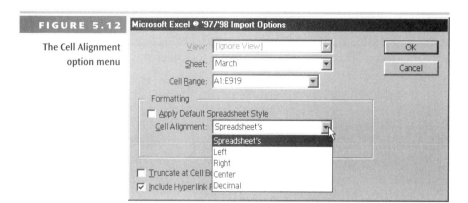

FIGURE 5.12

The Cell Alignment option menu

Tagged Text Import Options

As I write this book, only the InDesign Tagged Text filter for PageMaker is available. Hopefully, others will be added by the time InDesign is released to the market.

Editing Text

Once you enter text into an InDesign document, you can edit it just as if it were still in a word processor. You can cut, copy, and paste. You can also find and replace.

You select text just as you do in other applications. The flashing vertical line is called the *text insertion point* and it indicates where you are about to enter text. If you place your cursor in a spot and begin typing, you'll enter text from that point. If you place your cursor and paste text, you insert the text from that point. If you highlight a series of characters, words, and paragraphs, you can cut or copy that text and paste somewhere else.

WARNING   Be careful with selected text. I can't tell you how many times I've seen someone highlight an entire story to change the formatting or something, then accidentally erase the entire story by hitting a random key. Selected text will be replaced by any key that is pressed. If this happens to you, don't panic. Just press Ctrl/Cmd+Z or choose Edit ≻ Undo. (For more about correcting errors and mistakes, see Chapter 7.)

To edit text in a text frame, select the Type tool from the Toolbox and then select a text frame. From then on, edit the text just as you would in any text application.

You can use the Edit menu, shown next, to choose many of the common text editing commands.

Navigating Through and Selecting Text

As in many other applications, there are some pretty nifty keyboard and mouse shortcuts you can use to speed up your text editing.

Here are the definitions InDesign applies to text for the purposes of navigating during text editing:

- A *character* is one entered keystroke.
- A *word* is one contiguous block of characters (which could be a word or even the empty space between words).
- A *line* is one horizontal line of text (*not* a sentence).
- A *paragraph* is the text between paragraph returns.
- A *story* is all the text in a text frame.

Here are some mouse shortcuts for text editing:

- Click once to place the cursor.
- Click twice to select a word.
- Click three times to select an entire paragraph.
- Press Shift and click to select all the text from the last position of the cursor to the current position of the cursor.

Here are some keyboard shortcuts for moving the cursor without selecting text:

- Press the left or right arrow key to move the cursor one character left or right.
- Press the up or down arrow key to move the cursor one line up or down.
- Press Ctrl/Cmd and the left or right arrow key to move the cursor one word left or right.

- Press Ctrl/Cmd and the up or down arrow key to move the cursor to the next or previous paragraph.
- Press the Home or End key to move the cursor to the beginning or the end of the line.
- Press Ctrl/Cmd and the Home or End key to move the cursor to the beginning or the end of the story.

Here are some keyboard shortcuts for text selection:

- Press Ctrl/Cmd+A to select all of the text in the story.
- Press Shift and the left or right arrow (or the 4 or 6 keys on the numeric keypad) to move the cursor one character left or right.
- Press Shift and the up or down arrow (or the 8 or 2 keys on the numeric keypad) to move the cursor one line up or down.
- Press Shift and the Home key to select from the position of the cursor to the beginning of that line.
- Press Shift and the End key to select from the position of the cursor to the end of that line.
- Press Shift and Ctrl/Cmd and the up or down arrow (or the 8 or 2 keys on the keypad) to select from the position of the cursor to the beginning or the end of the paragraph.
- Press Shift and Ctrl/Cmd and the Home key to select from the position of the cursor to the beginning of the story.
- Press Shift and Ctrl/Cmd and the End key to select from the position of the cursor to the end of the story.

If you want to see the spaces and paragraph returns represented by some visible character on the screen, you can choose Type ➢ Show Hidden Characters. This command displays all the hidden characters, including tabs.

Finding, Deleting, and Changing Words with Find/Change

As it does in any application that provides it, the ability to search for words throughout a document and then automatically delete, change their formatting, or replace them, speeds text editing considerably. This option is provided as Find/Change in InDesign.

To use Find/Change, select the Type tool, click in a text frame, and then choose Edit ➢ Find/Change to open the Find/Change dialog box, shown in Figure 5.13. Alternately, you can choose Find/Change from the context menu by pressing the right mouse button in Windows or by pressing Option as you click with the Mac mouse.

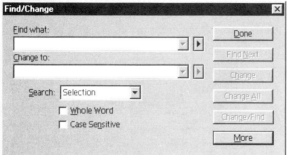

The Find/Change dialog box

To find a word or words in the selected text frame, enter the word(s) in the Find What text box, as shown in Figure 5.13, and click Find Next.

TIP You can save yourself some typing when searching for words that you have already entered by selecting them from the Find What option menu, which you access by clicking the arrow at the right of the Find What text box. InDesign lists words you have previously entered, even if you close the document and reopen it. This option is also available in the Change To text box. When you quit InDesign, these option menus are cleared.

To replace a word or words with another word or words, enter the search word(s) in the Find What text box, then enter the replacement word(s) in the Change To box. Click Find Next to search for the first word(s), then click Change if you want to replace that particular occurrence of the word(s). If you want to change all occurrences of a word or words, click Change All (instead of Change) to replace all occurrences of that word or words in the text frame. A window will open to inform you how many times the word or words were replaced.

TIP Automatically deleting words with Find/Change is actually like replacing them with nothing. To automatically delete a word or words, simply leave empty the Change To text entry area, click Find Next to find the word or words you want to delete, then click Change or Change All to replace the word(s) with nothing.

You can also define where InDesign will search for the word(s) you want. From the Search option menu, shown next, you can select the following options:

Document   Searches throughout the entire document for the word(s).

All Documents   Searches throughout all open InDesign documents.

Story Searches the thread of the selected text, throughout the entire document, in all of its linked text frames.

To End of Story Searches only from the current position of the text insertion point to the end of the story, through all of its thread.

Selection Searches only the word, phrase, paragraph, or story selected in the text frame.

TIP The Find Next option is also available without opening the Find/Change dialog box by choosing Edit ➢ Find Next. InDesign will search for the last word you entered in the Find What text box of the Find/Change dialog box.

Searching Efficiently

InDesign allows you to refine your word search so that you don't waste time sorting through a bunch of similar occurrences of character patterns that aren't exactly what you wanted.

Click the Whole Word option in the Find/Change dialog box, shown in Figure 5.13, to prevent finding similar character patterns that may be part of other words. For example, if you were searching for the word "the", you might get literally hundreds of responses from words like "there", "their", "they", "them", and so on. If you select the Whole Word option before searching, InDesign will ignore those character patterns that don't have spaces before and after the pattern, producing only that specific word.

Click the Case Sensitive option in the Find/Change dialog box, shown in Figure 5.13, to have InDesign search for specific capitalization patterns. For example, if you were searching for the name of your friend Faith, you could enter it as Faith, click the Case Sensitive option before searching, and InDesign would skip occurrences of "faith".

Using Wildcards

Sometimes, you may need to use wildcards, which are basically any characters preceding, within, or following character patterns. The wildcard options and symbols that you can enter in the Find What text box are:

Any Character A caret (^, Shift+6) followed by a question mark: (^?).

Any Digit A caret (^, Shift+6) followed by the number nine: (^9).

Any Letter   A caret (^, Shift+6) followed by a dollar sign: (^$).

Inline Graphic   A caret (^, Shift+6) followed by a g: (^g).

White Space   A caret (^, Shift+6) followed by a w: (^w).

For example, let's say you want to search for the words "hope" and "hype". You could enter "h^?pe". How about if you want to find all occurrences of periods used as decimals in dollar amounts, but not periods used at the end of sentences? You could enter ".^9", which would search only for periods followed by any digit. InDesign would find "$19.98" while ignoring "end.". Conversely, if you wanted to find all the periods used at the ends of sentences, you could enter ".^w", which would ignore all the periods followed by anything other than white space.

NOTE   Wildcards can only be used in the Find What text entry area.

Finding and Changing Special Characters

If you need to find specific instances of character patterns that include special characters, such as punctuation, paragraph returns, tabs, and so on, you must enter the *metacharacter* for the special character. (Metacharacters are the special characters that InDesign needs when finding non-alphanumeric characters, such as tabs, paragraph returns, and so on.)

For example, if you import some text that has paragraph indents created by tabs rather than first line indents, you could delete all those tabs at once by entering the metacharacter ^t, which would find all the tabs.

Table 5.2 lists the metacharacters necessary for finding special characters.

TABLE 5.2: FIND/CHANGE METACHARACTERS

Special Character	Find/Change Metacharacter
Auto Page Numbering	^#
Bullet	^8
Caret	^^
End of Paragraph	^p
Copyright Symbol	^2
Forced Line Break	^n
Paragraph Symbol	^7
Registered Trademark	^r

Continued on next page

TABLE 5.2: FIND/CHANGE METACHARACTERS (continued)

Section Mark	^6
Tab Character	^t
Em Dash	^_ (Shift+hyphen)
En Dash	^=
Em Space	^m
En Space	^>
Thin Space	^<
Hair Space	^|
Flush Space	^f
Discretionary Hyphen	^- (hyphen)
Non-breaking Hyphen	^~
Non-breaking Space	^s
Left Single Quote	^[
Right Single Quote	^]
Left Double Quote	^{
Right Double Quote	^}

Metacharacters can be used in either the Find What or Change To text entry areas. All of the metacharacters available in these two areas can be accessed and automatically entered by selecting them from the option menus immediately to the right of the text box.

Finding and Changing Words in Specific Formats

You can also search for words that have a specific format applied to them. Perhaps you want to find all occurrences of subheads to which you have applied a bold style. Or you want to find all italicized words. You can search for text based on format in the expanded Find/Change dialog box, shown in Figure 5.14, which you can open by clicking the More button.

Once this dialog box expands, you have the Find Style Settings and Change Style Settings options. To find words to which specific formats have been applied, click the Format button in the Find Style Settings area to open the Find Format Settings dialog box, shown in Figure 5.15.

If you are seeking words to which a defined character or paragraph style has been applied, you can select a style from one or both of the Character Style and Paragraph Style option menus. (For more information about character and paragraph styles, see Chapter 10.) All of the character and paragraph styles defined for that document will appear in these option menus.

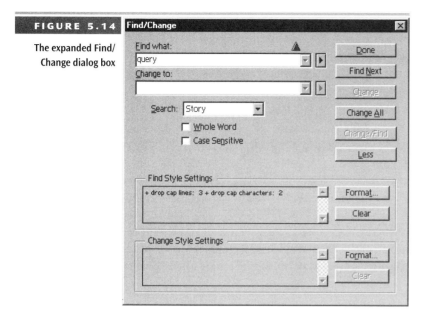

FIGURE 5.14

The expanded Find/Change dialog box

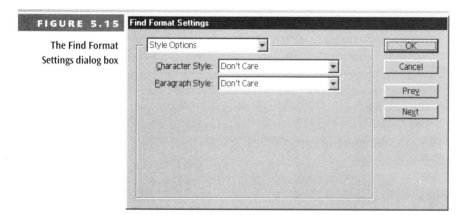

FIGURE 5.15

The Find Format Settings dialog box

If, however, you need to find words that have formatting other than that defined in a style, you can select the type of formatting you want to define for a search from the option menu at the top of the dialog box, shown in Figure 5.16. (You can also cycle through each of these options by clicking the Prev or Next buttons in the Find Format Settings dialog box.)

Choosing any of these options changes the Find Format Settings dialog box to reflect the values and options for that particular format setting. You can specify values for any or all of these options.

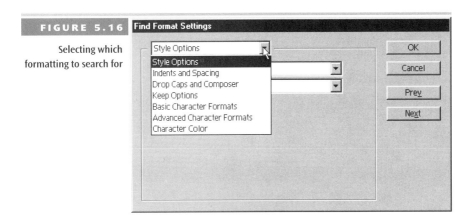

FIGURE 5.16
Selecting which formatting to search for

You'll notice that when you do specify formatting options for the search and/or the change operation, an alert triangle appears above the Find What text entry area and/or the Change To text entry area of the Find/Change dialog box.

WARNING If you specify formatting options for a word search, you must remember to remove those options if you don't want them used as criteria during the Find/Change operation. Clicking the Less button to collapse the Find/Change dialog box doesn't eliminate the formatting options from the search. To remove them all, you can click the Clear button in either the Find Style Settings or Change Style Settings areas. If you want only to remove certain criteria, you must open the Format dialog boxes and reset them one by one. You can do this easily by pressing Alt/Option to change the Cancel button to the Reset button (but, again, you must do it for each individual option).

To change formatting, you follow the same steps as those for defining the search formatting criteria, described above.

Spell Checking

Don't forget to check your spelling before outputting a document. This operation is so easy that there's no reason to skip it (plus it may save you a lot of embarrassment). You can also check the spelling of specific words or passages at any time, without running the spell check through the entire document.

NOTE InDesign also checks for occurrences of double words, such as "in in".

To check the spelling of your document, either select a word or passage or just position the text insertion point where you want to begin checking. Choose Edit ➢ Check Spelling, press Ctrl/Cmd+I, or choose Check Spelling from the context menu, to open the Check Spelling dialog box, shown in Figure 5.17.

First, use the Search option menu to define how far you want InDesign to proceed through the text. The options here are the same as in the Search option menu of the Find/Change dialog box, shown in Figure 5.13:

Document   Checks spelling throughout the entire document.

All Documents   Checks spelling throughout all open InDesign documents.

Story   Checks spelling through the thread of the selected text, throughout the entire document, in all of its linked text frames.

To End of Story   Checks spelling only from the current position of the text insertion point to the end of the story, through all of its thread. (Once the checking reaches the end of the story, it comes back to the current text insertion point.)

Selection   Checks the spelling of only the word, phrase, paragraph, or story selected in the text frame.

Once you click Start, InDesign will stop at questionable words and display the word in the Not in Dictionary text box.

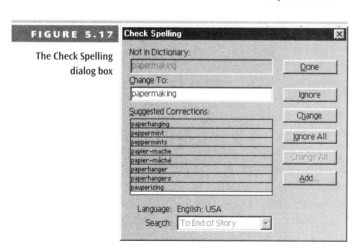

FIGURE 5.17
The Check Spelling dialog box

InDesign will place what it considers to be the most appropriate replacement words in the Suggested Corrections display area. If you want to accept one of InDesign's suggestions, simply click the word and it will be displayed in the Change To text area. Click Change to accept that word. Click Change All to replace all occurrences of that word.

You can also enter a word of your own choosing by typing it in the Change To text area. This will also prompt InDesign to seek a list of possible replacements for that word.

If you think the questionable word is okay as it is, just click Ignore to skip that word. If you know there will be multiple occurrences of that questionable word, click Ignore All to skip the remaining occurrences.

Customizing the Dictionary

InDesign may find words in your document that it considers questionable, but only because they are not in its dictionary. These could include proper names, words relating to esoteric subjects, and so on. If InDesign stops at a word you consider acceptable, click Add to add it to the dictionary, which opens the Dictionary dialog box, shown in Figure 5.18. You can also enter words in the dictionary manually by choosing Edit ➢ Edit Dictionary to open the Dictionary dialog box.

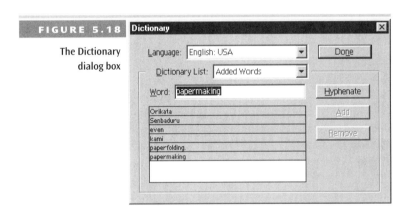

FIGURE 5.18
The Dictionary dialog box

If you open the Dictionary dialog box from the Check Spelling dialog box, the current questionable word is displayed in the Word text box. If you open the Dictionary dialog box with the Edit ➢ Edit Dictionary command, the word where the text insertion point is currently positioned will appear in the Word text box. Any words that you have added during a spell check will appear in the Dictionary List area (but only when you have the Added Words option selected).

Click on a word, and then click Add to save the word to the dictionary.

These words are now added to the dictionary, but you may want to specify the hyphenation for InDesign to use for each word. Click the Hyphenate button of the Dictionary dialog box to see how InDesign plans to hyphenate the word. InDesign will display the word with tildes (~) representing where the word will be hyphenated, as shown in Figure 5.19.

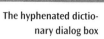

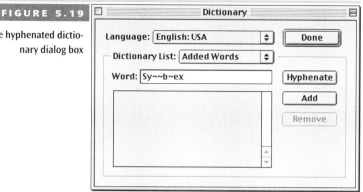

FIGURE 5.19

The hyphenated dictionary dialog box

Notice that the hyphenated word in the dialog box has two tildes between some letters and one tilde between other letters. This is how InDesign tells you both where and how it intends to hyphenate the word:

~ Signifies the hyphenation point InDesign considers the most appropriate.

~~ Signifies the second-best hyphenation point.

~~~ Signifies a point that would be considered only as a last resort.

If you don't want to assign priorities to the hyphenation points, just use the same number of tildes between all the breaks. If you don't want the word to ever be hyphenated, put a tilde before the word. If you actually need a real tilde in the word, place a backslash (\) before the tilde.

To remove a word from the dictionary, choose the Removed Words option from the Dictionary List option menu of the Dictionary dialog box, shown in Figure 5.18. If a word is not already in the Word text box, you can type it in and click the Add button. (This may seem backwards to you, but InDesign is thinking that you are *adding* the word to the list of removed words, not that you are *removing* the word from the dictionary.)

If you change your mind about a word you have added to the Removed Words list, simply click on it in the display area and click the Remove button.

chapter 6

GRAPHICS
BASICS

Featuring:

- Placing images 135
- Placing PDF files as graphics 142
- Modifying graphics frames 145
- Cropping an image with a graphics frame 151
- Adjusting a graphics frame to fit an image ... 151
- Wrapping text around images 155
- Placing graphics that move with the text 159
- Managing links and embedding images 162

CHAPTER 6

GRAPHICS BASICS

ew well-designed contemporary publications are produced without some visual enhancements in the form of photographs, tables, charts, illustrations, and so on. You can easily add these graphics to your InDesign documents.

In this chapter, I'll show you how to get the graphics files into your document, how to adjust the size and shape of the frame and of the graphic itself, how to integrate those graphics with your text, and how to *crop*, or hide, part of a graphic. I'll also show you how to place pages from a PDF file as graphics in an InDesign document.

Adding Images to a Document

There are three methods for getting images into your InDesign documents:

- Placing (importing) them
- Copying and pasting them
- Dragging and dropping them from another application

Although you can place graphics into existing objects, you can also add graphics without any existing objects on the page, meaning you don't have to first draw a frame for a graphic.

NOTE Remember shapes, frames, and placeholders from Chapter 4? You can add graphics to any shape, frame, or placeholder. When you do, that shape, frame, or placeholder automatically becomes a graphics frame.

Placing Graphics

To place—import—a graphic onto an InDesign document page, first make sure that the graphic file is of a file type supported by InDesign. (For more information about graphics types and graphics file types, see Chapter 1.)

NOTE Placing a graphic is the same thing as importing a graphic. By placing a graphic, rather than copying and pasting or dragging and dropping, you have more control over how the image is handled as it is imported.

To place a graphic into a graphic frame that will be created as you place, make sure you have no objects selected in the document.

To place a graphic into an existing shape, frame, or placeholder, make sure that object is selected.

Placing Graphics into Open Shapes

You can place graphics into shapes that are not closed, such as curved lines. As when filling an open shape with color (discussed in Chapter 4), InDesign will "close" the shape and place the image inside. However, the shape must have at least a small arc to it. If you try to place an image into a straight line, InDesign will load the place icon rather than fill that line. Obviously, the more elliptical or rectangular the shape, the more of the image that you will see. In other words, if you place a graphic into a shape that is almost a straight line, you won't really see much of the graphic.

Choose File ➤ Place to open the Place dialog box, shown in Figure 6.1. Navigate through your storage volumes and directory levels to locate the file you want to open. The Place dialog box will display All Files, Importable Files, or files of a particular type, depending on which option you select from the Files of Type option menu. Type a filename into the File Name text area and click Open, or just double-click on a name in the filename display area.

FIGURE 6.1

The Place dialog box

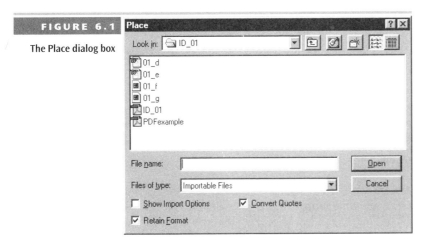

To check the import options that are set for that particular file type, click the Show Import Options checkbox. This action will open the Image Import Options dialog box, shown in Figure 6.2.

FIGURE 6.2

The Image Import Options dialog box

You will also see the Image Import Options dialog box when placing bitmap images saved as BMP, GIF, JPEG, PCX, PNG, Scitex CT, or TIFF graphics files. You can select either the Image Settings options or the Color Settings options from the option menu at the top left.

The Image Settings options for these images are:

> **Proxy Image Resolution** A *proxy image* is an image substituted on the page as you work in InDesign. You can specify a lower resolution for the proxy image than the resolution of the original image, reducing the file size of the InDesign file. This change to a lower resolution only affects the display of the image while in InDesign; the original image is not changed or altered in any way. When you print the InDesign file, the original image is linked to the file and output at its original resolution (unless you select the Low Resolution print option, discussed in Chapter 8). When printing to a PostScript device, the full resolution is always used.

WARNING If you have selected Full Resolution Images from the Display option menu of the General Preferences, the Proxy Image Resolution won't have any effect on the appearance of images you place.

TIP If you import an image or graphic and find that you can't make it out very clearly because its resolution is too low, you may want to increase the dpi setting of this Proxy Image Resolution option for any subsequent images you place.

Create Frame from Clipping Path If the imported graphic has been saved in its original application with a clipping path, you can select this option to create a new frame that conforms to the shape of that clipping path.

The Color Settings options for these images are:

Enable Color Management Select this option if you want to be able to adjust the color management of a graphic individually in InDesign. If all production work on the graphics and the InDesign document is done on one system, with one monitor and color source profile, you may choose not to select this option. This option only affects images if color management is turned on for the document. You usually would use this checkbox to turn off color management for an image that you don't want InDesign's color management features to affect.

Profile The Profile option is where you tell InDesign what color source profile was being used on the system where the graphic file was originally color corrected and saved. (For more information about color profiles, see Chapter 18.) From the Profile option menu, select from one of the listed ICC profiles or from one of the following:

Use Embedded Profile Applies the color profile that was embedded in the graphic as it was saved in the original application.

Use Document Default Applies the color profile that you have already specified for the document into which you are importing the graphic.

Rendering Intent This option specifies how you want InDesign to translate colors that may need to be changed to conform to the color gamut of a specific output device. In other words, if you've created a graphic in the RGB color space, but you are building a document that will be printed on a four-color press, the colors in the graphic may not fall within the CMYK color gamut printable by the press. So InDesign will convert the colors to the space you have chosen and Rendering Intent will place limits and guidelines on the conversion. The Rendering Intent options are:

Perceptual (Images) Preserves the hue relationships of the colors, at the expense of saturation, to produce the most natural-looking results.

Saturation (Graphics) Preserves the saturation levels (the intensity of the colors), but converts out-of-gamut colors to the nearest in-gamut color of the same saturation (meaning a color might slightly change hue, but it would be just as intense).

Relative Colorimetric Preserves the color values of all the colors within the gamut, while converting out-of-gamut colors to in-gamut colors with the same lightness value (meaning that colors that are different before conversion may wind up appearing as the same color).

Absolute Colorimetric Works the same way as Relative Colorimetric, but disables the white point compensation.

TIP If you are producing a document with photographic images that you want to protect, use the Perceptual (Images) option. Saturation (Graphics) is best for presentations that have vivid colors you want to protect, such as charts and graphs. Relative Colorimetric is best if you are trying to re-create a specific flat color (such as vector graphic colors and corporate identity colors) without much change. And Absolute Colorimetric isn't good for much of anything.

When placing PNG files, you have the Image Settings options and Color Settings options listed above, as well as the following PNG Settings options:

Use Transparency Information As described in Chapter 1, PNG files support transparency saved as an alpha channel or for a designated color (kind of like GIF files). If the PNG file you are importing has transparency information saved with it, you can use this option to include or disregard that information.

File Defined Background Color If you select Use Transparency Information, this option uses the background color supplied by the file's saved transparency information. This is the default.

White Background If you select Use Transparency Information, you can select this option to use white for the background color.

TIP Why would you want to change the transparency background from a file's saved background color to white? Let's say you're using a graphic you created for a Web page that had a blue background, and now you need to use the graphic on a document that will be printed on a white sheet of paper. You could select the Use Transparency Information option and the White Background option to substitute white for the color that you originally specified for the file when it was saved from the original application.

Apply Gamma Correction If a PNG file is saved with gamma information embedded in it, this option allows you to adjust that gamma, in case the image's midtones seems lighter or darker than they should. This option is selected by default for files that contain gamma information and you can deselect it if you don't need to change it.

Gamma Value If Apply Gamma Correction is selected, the Gamma Value option displays the gamma value that was saved with the image. You can change this value by entering a number from .01 to 3.0.

When you open an Adobe Illustrator file (whether it contains only a vector graphic or bitmap graphic, or a combination of both), an EPS file, or a DCS file, you see the EPS Import Options dialog box, shown below.

The two EPS import options are:

Read Embedded OPI Image Links OPI, or Open PrePress Interface, is the option that enables you to reduce the file size of InDesign documents by using low-resolution substitute graphics as you build your InDesign documents. When outputted, the OPI links embedded in the graphic tell the output device where to find the original, high-resolution file. If you select this option, InDesign will perform the linking to the original, high-resolution image file. Deselect this option if you want your service bureau to do the OPI replacement with a different software application—outside of InDesign.

Create Frame from Clipping Path If the graphics file was saved with a clipping path (which creates an illusion of transparency by masking all but certain areas of the graphic), you can select this option to automatically create a graphics frame that matches the visible area of the graphic. This option is on by default for files containing clipping paths; you can deselect it to ignore the clipping path.

TIP Remember, if you enter a value into any of these options (or the options in any dialog box, for that matter), you can reset that box's visible set of options by pressing Alt/Option to change the Cancel button to the Reset button.

Copying and Pasting Graphics

In addition to using the File ≻ Place command to import graphics, you can import graphics into InDesign documents by copying and pasting them from another open InDesign document or an open document in another application.

 WARNING Pasting or dragging and dropping graphics from other applications may result in less control over the quality of an imported graphic. This is because you not only skip the opportunity to specify import options, but you also may be pasting or dragging and dropping from an application that doesn't support the export of all the file's pertinent information as you export it. (This is not true when pasting or dragging or dropping from one InDesign document to another.)

To paste a graphics file into your open InDesign document, first go to the other document and select that graphic. Choose Edit ≻ Copy (Ctrl/Cmd+C) or Edit ≻ Cut (Ctrl/Cmd+X) to place a copy of the graphic on the computer's Clipboard. (Remember that the Edit ≻ Cut command will remove the graphic from that document.)

Return to your InDesign document and choose Edit ≻ Paste (Ctrl/Cmd+V). The graphic will be pasted to the center of your document page, from where you can move it to a position you choose.

Dragging and Dropping Graphics

Perhaps the most direct way to add a graphic is just to drag-and-drop it from another document, either from within InDesign or from another application. First go to the other document and select that graphic, and then drag-and-drop it into your InDesign document.

Managing Application and Document Windows So You Can Drag-and-Drop

Wondering how you're going to drag-and-drop between two applications when you can see only one of them on the desktop at a time? First, manually resize the application window by dragging one of the corners, so that you can see both windows at the same time. (Refer to your operating system documentation for more information about resizing application and document windows.) Position the two application windows and their document windows so you can see both the document from where you will drag and the document to where you will drag.

If you're working with a graphic from another application, choose that application's appropriate tool for moving the graphic around. Click and hold the graphic and slide it out of its application's window and over an InDesign document window. You may see a dotted line outline of the graphic or a colored line representation of the graphic's outline as you drag from one window to the other. When you get the cursor into the InDesign document, a plus symbol (+) will be added to the cursor, as shown below, indicating that you have a loaded cursor and can drop the graphic wherever you let go of the mouse button.

If you are trying to drag-and-drop and you see the "No" icon, shown below, it means you are trying to drag-and-drop from an application that does not support drag-and-drop to InDesign.

 WARNING If you are dragging and dropping from one InDesign document to another, be sure to use the Selection tool, rather than the Direct Selection tool. If you use the Direct Selection tool, you will drag all of the contents of the frame, no matter what the size and shape of the frame. What this means is that if you have cropped an image to fit a frame, you'll lose that frame if you drag with the Direct Selection tool.

Placing PDF Files as Graphics

You can use the pages of PDF files as graphics in an InDesign document. Once imported, these pages can be sized and otherwise adjusted just as any other graphic in InDesign, but you cannot edit the content of the PDF page. (If you want to edit a PDF file as an InDesign document, convert the PDF file to an InDesign document, rather than placing it as a graphic. See Chapter 2.)

To place a PDF file as a graphic into an open InDesign document, first choose File ➢ Place to open the Place dialog box, shown in Figure 6.3.

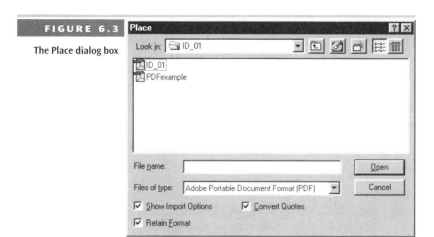

FIGURE 6.3

The Place dialog box

If you don't want to sort through all of the importable files in a folder, select Adobe Portable Document Format (PDF) from the Files of Type option menu.

Select the PDF file you want to import by typing its name in the File Name text area or by clicking its name in the filename display area to automatically enter it. You can double-click the filename to select it and automatically proceed through to the next operation.

If you click Open without selecting the Show Import Options checkbox, InDesign will place the same page number you placed last time. In other words, if you placed page 10 from a PDF when you last placed a PDF file, InDesign will place page 10 again unless you choose the Show Import Options checkbox. In the Place PDF dialog box, shown in Figure 6.4, you can specify a different page.

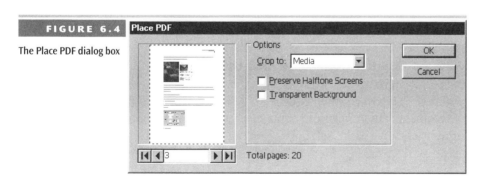

FIGURE 6.4

The Place PDF dialog box

The Place PDF dialog box allows you to navigate through previews of the available pages for import and to specify how you want the page cropped. Click the arrow keys beneath the preview area to move up or down through the document's pages.

N O T E If the PDF file was saved with password information, you will need to enter a password before accessing the Place PDF dialog box. You also won't be able to place the page if the PDF file was saved with restrictions on its use, such as no editing or no printing. If you are confronted by this and the file is your own, save it again from the original application without the usage restrictions. (For more on opening PDF files as InDesign documents, see Chapter 2. For more about exporting InDesign documents as PDF files, see Chapter 19.)

The Crop To option menu allows you to specify how much of the PDF page you actually want to place. The Crop To options are:

Content Places only the area of the PDF page actually filled with content

Art Places only the defined placeable artwork of the PDF page

Crop Places the display area of the content of the PDF page, as it appears in Adobe Acrobat

Page Places the area defined as the page size of the PDF document

Trim Places the area defined by any trim marks saved with the PDF document

Bleed Places the area defined as being the page size of the PDF document

Media Places the area defined as being the paper size of the PDF document

The two remaining checkboxes control the following:

Preserve Halftone Screens If selected, this option preserves the halftone screen settings originally saved with the PDF file, regardless of the current halftone screen settings of the InDesign document. (Only a PostScript printer would be capable of outputting the InDesign document with separate halftone screen settings.)

Transparent Background This option basically sets the background color of the containing frame to "no color," allowing you to see through the background area of the PDF content, down to the underlying contents of the InDesign document. (For more information about applying color to frames, see Chapters 4 and 12.)

Click OK to place the PDF file.

The rules governing the placement of other text and graphics also apply to the placement of PDF pages. If you have selected a shape, frame, or placeholder before choosing File ➢ Place, InDesign will place the PDF page into that selected shape, frame, or placeholder (replacing any content already there). If you have not selected a shape, frame, or placeholder, InDesign will load the cursor, as shown below, and you can click where you want the PDF page to be placed.

   If your placed PDF file seems hard to see and of poor resolution, don't worry. InDesign places the PDF file only as a low-resolution preview, linked to the original full-resolution PDF file. So when it is outputted, the high-resolution data from the original PDF file will be used. (For this reason, you must keep the PDF file where the output device can find it. See the "Managing Links and Embedding Images" section later in this chapter for more information about links.)

Be Careful with Placed PDF Files

Editing a linked PDF file after placing pages from it into InDesign can cause problems. Because the PDF file is being placed as a linked preview only, any changes to the numbering of the original PDF file could result in the wrong PDF page being printed at output. If you edit the linked PDF file after placing the PDF page in InDesign, you should check your placed PDF pages to see if you need to place the correct page once again.

Also, if you change the security settings of the linked PDF file, or delete pages from the linked PDF file, you risk having InDesign replace the placed page with a gray box.

Modifying Graphics Frames and Their Contents

Once you draw a shape, frame, or placeholder and fill it with a graphic (which changes it to a graphics frame), you may need to adjust the size and shape of the graphics frame to better fit your page design or to fit the contents of the graphics frame. You might also need to adjust the size and position of the contents to fit the graphics frame.

   In this section, I'll show you how to make basic adjustments to the size and shape of the graphics frame, as well as the size and positioning of the contents of the graphics frame. Keep in mind, though, that you actually have a great deal of control over the editing of shapes, frames, and placeholders, much of which is presented in Chapter 15.

InDesign also provides commands that automatically adjust a graphics frame to fit its contents, adjust the contents to fit the graphics frame, center the contents within the graphics frame, and fit the contents proportionally to the graphics frame.

Avoiding Image and Graphic Distortion

You must be careful when adjusting the contents of a graphics frame, paying attention to the proportions of the image or graphic. If you resize an image or graphic unevenly, the result is an image that appears to have been stretched one direction or the other, as shown in Figure 6.5.

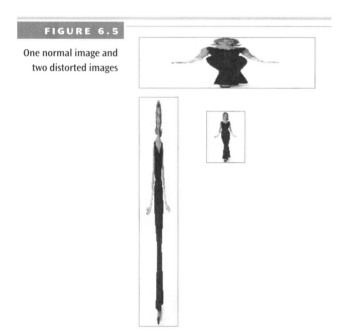

FIGURE 6.5

One normal image and two distorted images

To prevent this type of distortion, be sure that you have sized the image evenly. While dragging a handle of the graphic frame's contents, press Shift to constrain the proportions of the contents. Alternately, check the Scale Y percentage and the Scale X percentage values in the Transform palette, shown below, to be sure the two values are exactly the same.

To compare the width and height values of a graphics frame and its contents in the Transform palette, you have to select them separately.

- To see the width and height values of the graphics frame, select the graphics frame with the Selection or the Direct Selection tool. Its width and height values will appear in the W and H values boxes of the Transform palette.
- To see the width and height values of the *contents* of the graphics frame, choose the Direct Selection tool and click the contents of the graphics frame. Its width and height values will appear in the W and H values boxes of the Transform palette.

You can always adjust the size and shape of the graphics frame and its contents by entering values in these W and H values boxes. If you wanted to quickly make them the same, you could enter the values in either the graphics frame or its contents, then copy the W value from one and paste it to the W value of the other, and repeat that for the H values.

Selecting Graphics Frames and Their Contents

The first step in adjusting the size and shape of a graphics frame is to select the graphics frame. If you are intending to adjust the frame itself, you must select it with the Selection tool (the black pointer) . If you select it with the Direct Selection tool (the white pointer), you'll adjust the *contents* of the graphics frame.

Remember, there are two ways to select an object in InDesign (for more about the basics of shapes, frames, and placeholders, see Chapter 4):

- Selecting the object with the Selection tool activates its *bounding box*, the box with eight black handles, allowing you to adjust the size and shape of the object by dragging one of the handles.
- Selecting the object with the Direct Selection tool activates its *anchor points*, allowing you to make adjustments to the points themselves or to the object (by editing the frame).

TIP You must click on the outline of the object to select it with the Direct Selection tool. Clicking within the area defined by the outline of the object will select the anchor points of any contents of the object.

When selecting a graphics frame, you have an additional option. You can select the contents of the graphics frame by clicking the contents with the Direct Selection tool. This action activates the contents, the area of which is displayed by a bounding box. By adjusting this bounding box, we adjust the size and shape of the contents of the graphics frame.

WARNING If you select the contents of a graphics frame and then manually drag one or more of its handles, you could be distorting the contents' proportions. To avoid this, press Shift as you drag the handle to lock the proportions of the contents. You can verify that the contents are not distorted by being sure the Scale Y percentage and the Scale X percentage (located at the far right of the Transform palette) are the same value.

Adjusting the Size and Shape of a Graphics Frame

Once you have selected the graphics frame by clicking it with the Selection tool, you will see its bounding box. You can now drag any of the handles to manually adjust the size and shape of the graphics frame, as shown below.

Press Shift as you drag to constrain the box to its current proportions.

If you want to automatically adjust the size of the graphics frame to match the current size of its contents, choose Object ➤ Fitting ➤ Fit Frame to Content or press Shift+Ctrl+Alt+V in Windows or Shift+Cmd+Option+V on the Mac.

Alternately, you can adjust the size of the graphics frame by entering values in the W and H value boxes of the Transform palette.

TIP The Transform palette will do math for you. Let's say you want to increase the size of the object by half its current size. Enter a plus symbol (+), then 150, then a percentage symbol (%). Press Enter or Tab to go to the next value box. You can perform the same operation through multiplication by entering an asterisk (*), then 1.5, then pressing Enter or Tab to go to the next value box.

Adjusting a Graphics Frame to Fit Its Contents

If you place a graphic in a graphics frame and the graphic is the size and shape you want, but the graphics frame is larger or smaller than you want, you can select the graphics frame and drag its handles to adjust its size and shape. Of course you can't be sure that the two will be exactly the same unless you compare their width and height values in the Transform palette.

Alternately, you can quickly, automatically, and precisely adjust the graphics frame to fit the content by simply selecting the graphics frame with the Selection tool and choosing Object ➢ Fitting ➢ Fit Frame to Content (or pressing Shift+Ctrl+Alt+V in Windows or Shift+Cmd+Option+V on the Mac).

Adjusting the Size of the Contents of a Graphics Frame

Once you place a graphic into a graphics frame, it may come in much smaller or much larger than the graphics frame, as shown below. As described in the previous section, you can adjust the frame to the contents, or as I'll now show you, you can adjust the contents to match the frame.

First, you must select the contents. Choose the Direct Selection tool from the Toolbox and click the graphic in the graphics frame. This activates the bounding box of the contents of the graphics frame. As shown below, when the contents are larger than the graphics frame, you see the bounding box of the contents even outside the area of the graphics frame.

You can drag the handles of the bounding box to size the contents. Press Shift to constrain the proportions of the contents to prevent distortion.

Automatically adjust the contents of the graphics frame to fit the graphics frame by choosing Object ➢ Fitting ➢ Fit Content Proportionally, or by pressing Shift+Ctrl+Alt+E in Windows or Shift+Cmd+Option+E on the Mac.

WARNING Although you can automatically adjust the contents of the graphics frame to fit the graphics frame by choosing Object ➢ Fitting ➢ Fit Content to Frame, or by pressing Ctrl+Alt+E in Windows or Cmd+Option+E on the Mac, this method will increase the contents to fit the frame without regard for the original proportions of the contents, possibly distorting the contents.

Alternately, you can use the Transform palette to make adjustments to the size of the contents, either by entering numerical values in the W and/or H values boxes, or by entering percentage values in the Scale Y percentage and Scale X percentage values boxes. (Make sure they are the same value, to prevent the distortion of the image.)

Here's a quick operation for getting a graphics frame and its contents to match:

1. Draw a frame approximately the size you'll want the graphic.
2. Place the graphic.
3. Choose Object ➢ Fitting ➢ Fit Content Proportionally.
4. Choose Object ➢ Fitting ➢ Fit Frame to Content.

The result is a graphics frame with content perfectly sized inside it. Now you can adjust the graphics frame and its contents at the same time, as described later in this chapter.

Positioning the Contents of a Graphics Frame

To manually move the contents of a graphics frame around inside the graphics frame (that is, without moving the graphics frame itself), select the contents of the graphics frame with the Direct Selection tool, then drag the contents around in the frame.

You can automatically center the contents of a graphics frame within the graphics frame by choosing Object ➢ Fitting ➢ Center Content, or by pressing Shift+Ctrl+E in Windows or Shift+Cmd+E on the Mac. This operation does not alter the size of either the contents or the graphics frame.

Alternately, you can enter numerical values in the X and Y values boxes of the Transform palette to position the contents. These values indicate the position of the contents on the page, *not* the position relative to the frame. In other words, entering zero for these values will not position the contents in the upper left corner of the frame, it will position the contents in the upper left corner of the document page.

Adjusting a Graphics Frame and Its Contents Simultaneously.

Once you have placed a graphic in a graphics frame and adjusted them to fit each other as you want, you can reduce and enlarge both at the same time using the Scale Y percentage and Scale X percentage values in the Transform palette.

Simply select the graphics frame with the Selection tool, and then enter new values in the Scale Y percentage and Scale X percentage values boxes (remembering to make sure they match each other). Your graphics frame and its contents will adjust accordingly, in unison.

Cropping an Image with a Graphics Frame

You can display a small part of a large graphic by *masking*, or hiding, part of the graphic by making the graphics frame smaller than the original image. In photography parlance, this is referred to as *cropping*.

If you want to crop an image to display only part of it, choose the Selection tool and select the graphics frame that contains the image.

Now drag the handles of the graphics frame's bounding box to shape it the way you want. You'll be hiding part of the image if you size the graphics frame smaller than the image.

In the illustration shown below, you see the graphics frame filled with only a portion of the image, the full size of which is displayed by its bounding box. You can use this operation to display any portion of any image and you can use a graphics frame of any shape.

Creating Borders and Frames around Graphics Frames

Graphic designers often create a narrow line, called a *keyline*, all around a photograph to help define it from the background. This is simple to do in InDesign and you can also use a graphics frame to provide even thicker and more colorful frames around images.

Applying a Stroke to a Graphics Frame

To create a simple border or keyline to an image, choose the Selection tool and select the graphics frame around the image.

Choose Window ➢ Stroke, press F10, or click the Stroke tab in its palette group to open the Stroke palette, shown below.

Enter a value in the Weight values box, or select one from the Weight option menu. You can make it as thick as you want, but remember that a thick line will begin to obscure the image if the image is not reduced in size, as shown below.

If you want to change the color of this border, choose Window ➢ Color, press F6, or click the Color tab in its palette group to open the Color palette. Make sure you have the Stroke icon selected in this palette (because you're changing the color of the border and not the background color of the graphics frame), then choose a color. (For more information about applying strokes and fills, see Chapter 4. For more information about selecting color, see Chapter 12.)

Floating a Graphic inside a Larger Frame

Another way to create a large border or frame around a graphic is to *float* a graphic in a graphics frame that is larger than the graphic. You can then fill the graphics frame with color.

NOTE   You can't float a graphic inside its frame and at the same time crop the graphic with that frame. Consequently, if you want to float a graphic inside its own frame, you must use a graphic that is already cropped as you want it to appear. If you want to float a cropped graphic inside a frame, you'll have to use *nested* objects, which is described in the next section.

For the purposes of this exercise, we'll assume that you have already drawn a shape, frame, or placeholder, placed a graphic in that object, and then sized the graphic and the graphics frame to fit perfectly with each other, as described in the earlier sections of this chapter.

If your graphics frame is currently the size you will want, your first step will be to reduce the size of the contents. Although you could do this by selecting the contents with the Direct Selection tool and dragging its bounding box, that would not be as precise as it will be when you use the Transform palette to adjust the contents.

To reduce the size of the contents with the Transform palette, make sure you are using the Direct Selection tool and click on the contents of the graphics frame. (Don't worry if you don't see the bounding box of the contents separate from the graphics frame. Remember, at this point, both the graphics frame and its contents are the same size.)

Now enter new values in the Scale Y percentage and Scale X percentage values boxes in the Transform palette. Remember to make these values the same. Alternately, you could enter specific width and height values for the contents in the W and H values boxes of the Transform palette. The result should look something like this:

Now center the smaller contents within the larger frame by first switching to the Selection tool and selecting the graphics frame. Choose Object ➢ Fitting ➢ Center

Contents, or press Shift+Ctrl+E in Windows or Shift+Cmd+E on the Mac. This should float the contents inside the larger graphics frame, as shown below.

Now you can fill the graphics frame with color to create the frame effect you want. Open the Color palette, click the Fill icon, and select a color. (Filling shapes, frames, and placeholders with color is discussed in Chapter 4.) This will give you something like this:

Notice in the above example that the fill color is one color and the stroke color is another, producing the contrast between the black keyline and the colored fill. If you don't want two separate colors like this, either remove the stroke color or change it to the same color as the fill.

Placing an Object inside Another Object (Nesting)

Yet another method for creating a frame for graphics is to place one object inside another, which is called *nesting*. Using this method, you can frame a graphic that you have cropped with its graphics frame, as described earlier in this chapter.

TIP You don't have to nest objects to print one on top of another. You can just position one graphic in front of another. The operation described here actually places one object inside another, making contents out of the placed object. An object can contain only one object, so if you want to place more than one graphic inside an object, first position multiple objects as you want them, then group and place them as one object.

To nest an object inside another object, follow these steps:

1. Get the graphic that you want to frame into a graphics frame and cropped as you want. (Of course, you don't have to use a cropped graphic for this method—you can use a full graphic image, too.)
2. You'll need another object, into which you'll be pasting the graphics frame, so either draw a new shape, frame, or placeholder, or identify the existing shape, frame, or placeholder that you want to use.
3. Once you have the graphic set as you want it to appear and have a second object ready to use as a frame, choose the Selection tool and select the graphics frame (the one that contains the contents you want to frame).
4. Cut or copy that graphics frame by choosing Edit ➢ Cut (Ctrl/Cmd+X) or Edit ➢ Copy (Ctrl/Cmd+C).
5. Select the second object with the Selection tool. Choose Edit ➢ Paste Into, or press Ctrl+Alt+V in Windows or Cmd+Option+V on the Mac.

   This will paste the graphics frame that you cut or copied inside the other shape, frame, or placeholder (automatically turning it into a graphics frame). You can then fill the outer graphics frame with color, as described earlier.

Wrapping Text around Images

If you've ever looked at a publication and wondered at how much extra work must have gone into shaping text blocks so that they wrapped around photos and other illustrations, you'll be happy to find out how easy it really is. InDesign provides a text wrapping feature called (appropriately enough) Text Wrap.

Text Wrap allows you to place and fill a text frame, then plunk a graphic right down on top of it, forcing the text to move around the graphic in the shape you want. You can not only specify how much space to allow between the graphic and the text and draw intricate text wrap shapes, you can choose from six different forms of text wrapping.

To begin, you need a text frame filled with text and placed where you want it on the page. To wrap that text around a graphic, position a graphic frame somewhere within the area of the text frame.

Next, choose Object ➢ Text Wrap to open the Text Wrap palette, shown below.

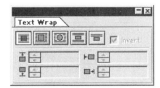

While the graphics frame is selected, click one of the text wrap buttons (discussed in the "Deciding How to Wrap" section below), to determine how the text will wrap around the object.

In the four values boxes beneath the text wrap buttons, specify a wrap offset for each of the four sides of the graphics frame. The *wrap offset* is the amount of space you want between the graphic and the text. (If you have selected a nonrectangular graphics frame and the Object Shape wrap option (see below), you will only have one wrap offset value.)

NOTE Although the graphic that forces text to wrap does not have to be in front of the text frame, you may need to experiment with different arrangements to get the exact text wrap effect you desire. You may also find it difficult to select the graphic if it is behind the text frame. Hold down the Ctrl/Cmd key to select objects that are in the background.

Deciding How to Wrap

There are six options for wrapping text around an object:

No Wrap When you select No Wrap, the text doesn't care that there is a graphic; it just stays right where it was before. Figure 6.6 shows the text with No Wrap selected.

FIGURE 6.6

The text with no wrap

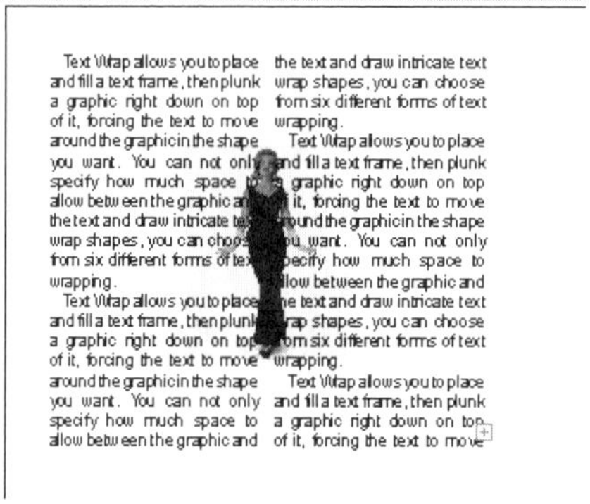

Bounding Box When you select Bounding Box, the text wraps around the object's bounding box. This will be a rectangular wrap, regardless of the shape of the graphics frame, because the bounding boxes of all shapes, frames, and placeholders are rectangular. Figure 6.7 shows the text with Bounding Box selected.

FIGURE 6.7

The text wrapping around the bounding box

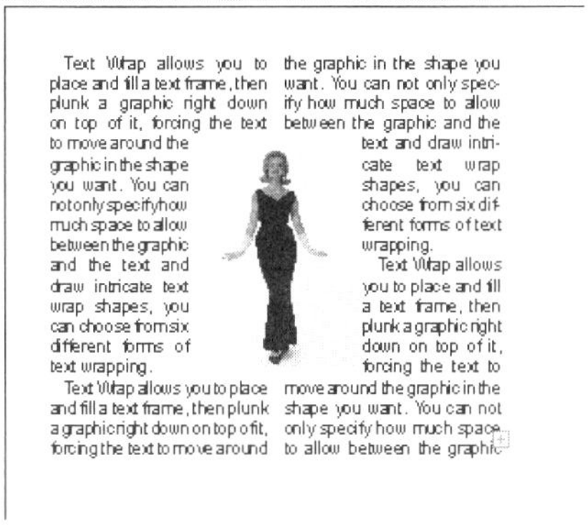

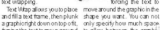

 Object Shape When you select Object Shape, the text wraps around the shape of the object, rather than its rectangular bounding box. This option will also wrap text around a shape other than the containing frame that you define with the object's path. (For more information about editing paths, see Chapter 17.) Figure 6.8 shows the text with Object Shape selected.

FIGURE 6.8

The text wrapping around the object's shape

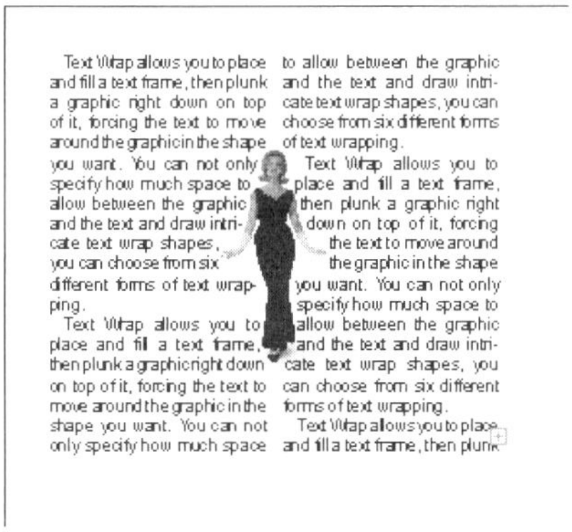

 Jump Object When you select Jump Object, the text "jumps" over the object, rather than wrapping around its sides. Figure 6.9 shows the text with Jump Object selected.

FIGURE 6.9

The text "jumping" over the object

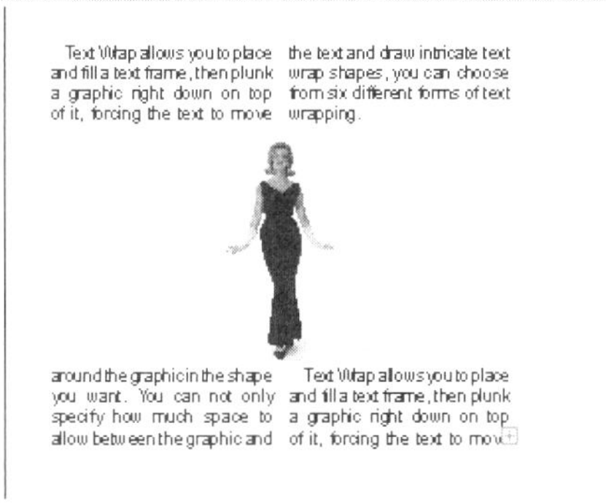

Jump to Next Column   When you select Jump to Next Column, the text stops above the object and "jumps" to the top of the next column over that does not touch the object. Figure 6.10 shows the text with Jump to Next Column selected.

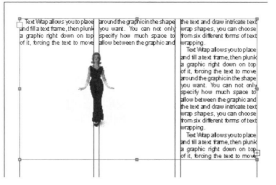

FIGURE 6.10

The text "jumping" to the top of the next column

Invert   When you click the Invert checkbox, the text wrap option you select is inverted, filling the object's area with the wrapped text. Figure 6.11 shows the text with Invert selected.

FIGURE 6.11

Text with Invert selected

Working with Graphics That Move with the Text

Some designs may call for a graphic to be placed with a line of text so that it moves with the text as the text is edited and re-threaded. This kind of graphic is called an *inline graphic*, and placing it is similar to the nesting feature described earlier in this chapter. The graphic basically becomes a character in the text. The best thing about an inline graphic is that you don't have to go back and move each and every graphics frame that applies to specific text just because you removed a paragraph of text somewhere in the story. You can even paste a text frame filled with text into another text frame as an inline graphic and still edit the text in the frame you paste.

You can either cut or copy and then paste a graphics frame or a text frame as an inline graphic, or you can place (import) a graphics file as an inline graphic.

Pasting a Graphic or Text as an Inline Graphic

To paste a graphic or text as an inline graphic, select the graphics frame or the text frame that you want to place. Copy it to the clipboard by choosing either Edit ➢ Cut (Ctrl/Cmd+X) or Edit ➢ Copy (Ctrl/Cmd+C).

Next, select the Text tool and click in a text frame where you want to position the graphic.

Choose Edit ➢ Paste (Ctrl/Cmd+V). The graphics frame or text frame is placed as a character, as shown below, exactly where you positioned the text insertion point.

If you paste a text frame, you can still edit that text after it becomes an inline graphic.

Placing a Graphics File as an Inline Graphic

To place a graphics file as an inline graphic, select the Text tool and click in a text frame where you want to position the graphic.

Choose File ➢ Place (Ctrl/Cmd+D). Select the file you want to place and click OK. The graphic is placed as a character, exactly where you positioned the text insertion point.

Automatic Leading and Inline Graphics

If you have entered a specific value for the leading of the line of text into which you place the inline graphic, the leading of the line will remain the same. If, however, you have allowed InDesign to select the leading automatically—this is indicated by parentheses around the leading value in the Character palette—the inline graphic will force new leading for the entire line. The new leading will be the automatic equivalent of a line of type set in the point size of the height of the inline graphic. This may make your line of text have a large gap between it and the line above. You can leave it that way if it works, or you can select the text, including the inline graphic, and enter the leading value you want.

Adjusting the Position of an Inline Frame

Once you have pasted or placed your inline graphic, you can only move it up or down relative to the baseline of the line of text into which you placed it.

The easiest way to move the inline graphic up or down is to select it with the Text tool, then adjust its position on the baseline by entering different values in the Baseline Shift values box of the Character palette. (For more information about baseline shift and formatting type, see Chapter 9.)

TIP It can be hard to select a placed inline graphic with the Text tool. Here's a tip: position the text insertion point near the inline graphic, on the same line if possible, and then use the arrow keys to move the text insertion point to the position just before or after the inline graphic. Then press Shift and the arrow key that will move the text insertion point to the other side of the inline graphic.

To move the inline graphic manually, follow these steps:

1. Choose the Direct Selection tool, then click on the inline graphic. This operation is pretty tricky, because InDesign has trouble allowing you to select the path of the graphic, which is what you need to move. If you select the bounding box of the graphics frame of the inline graphic, all you do is move the graphics frame; the content remains in position and is partially hidden, as shown in Figure 6.12.

FIGURE 6.12

A partially hidden inline graphic

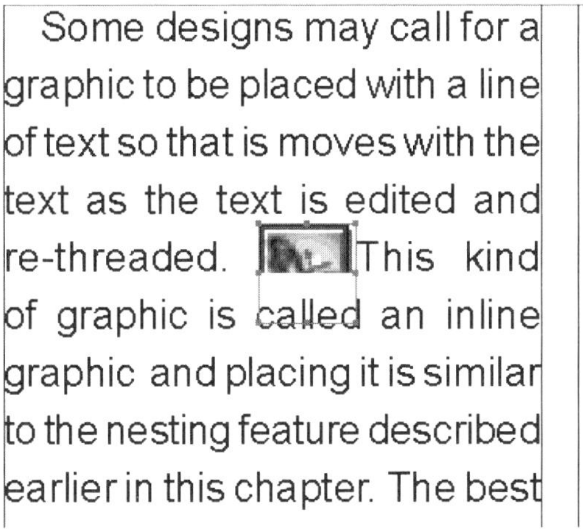

Some designs may call for a graphic to be placed with a line of text so that is moves with the text as the text is edited and re-threaded. This kind of graphic is called an inline graphic and placing it is similar to the nesting feature described earlier in this chapter. The best

2. Now choose the Direct Selection tool and click on the inline graphic. Let InDesign select the bounding box of the graphics frame and go ahead and drag it away from the graphic so that you'll be able to click the area underneath where it now is, which will probably make it look like the one displayed in Figure 6.12.

3. Click with the Direct Selection just above or below where you placed the graphic, in the area where the graphic was originally. This should activate the path of the graphic's contents, as shown in Figure 6.13.

FIGURE 6.13

A selected path of inline graphic

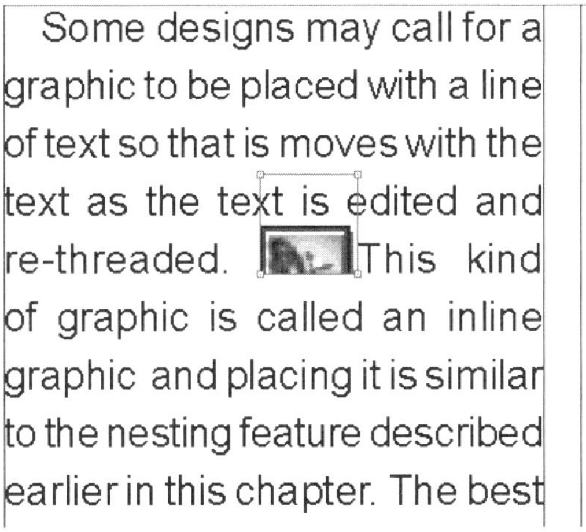

Some designs may call for a graphic to be placed with a line of text so that is moves with the text as the text is edited and re-threaded. This kind of graphic is called an inline graphic and placing it is similar to the nesting feature described earlier in this chapter. The best

4. Drag that path to the position you want. You'll notice that it will only move up and down and that its range of movement is limited.

5. Choose Object ➢ Fitting ➢ Center Content, or press Shift+Ctrl+E in Windows or Shift+Cmd+E on the Mac. This will bring the content of the graphics frame back into the little window of the path.

Adjusting the Size and Shape of an Inline Graphic

You can use the Transform palette to change the size and shape of the inline graphic, or you can do it manually.

To adjust the size and shape of the inline graphic by either method, choose the Direct Selection tool and then click on the border of the inline graphic.

Now switch to the Selection tool. This action should change the selection to the inline graphic's bounding box, which you edit to change the size and shape of the inline graphic.

To use the Transform palette to make the changes, enter values you want in any of the values boxes of the Transform palette.

To adjust the inline graphic manually, drag the handles to adjust it as you would any other shape, frame, or placeholder. To adjust its size and shape, use the Selection Scale tool. To rotate it, use the Rotate tool. To constrain the proportions of the inline graphic, remember to press Shift as you drag the handles.

Removing an Inline Graphic

To remove an inline graphic, select it with the Text tool and choose Edit ➢ Clear. Alternately, you can position the text insertion point just after the inline graphic, then press the Backspace key, or you can position the text insertion point just before the inline graphic and press the Delete key.

Managing Links and Embedding Images

As you learned in the "Placing Graphics" section earlier in this chapter, when you place graphics files you can specify the resolution of the preview image that you are importing. InDesign does *not* copy all of the data from a graphics file (unless it is 48K or smaller) into the InDesign document. But it must have that data to reproduce the graphic when the file is outputted. So InDesign keeps a record of where the original graphics file is located, known as a *link*. When you output the file, InDesign looks at its record of links and seeks out the full resolution data from the graphics file.

This feature benefits you in these ways:

- Your InDesign file sizes will be smaller, even if you use a lot of graphics and even if you use a large graphic many times.
- You can change every occurrence of a graphic at once, even though it may appear many times in your document.
- Changes to the original graphics file will be automatically applied to the placed files at output.

The main drawback to this feature (even though InDesign's Preflight and Package features will do a lot of the copying for you, as discussed in Chapter 18) is that you will have to be more organized. You should be careful to place your graphics files into your InDesign document from a location that will be easy for InDesign to find and that will be easy for you to send off with the InDesign document for output. In other words, you may want to gather all the graphics files together in a graphics folder or within the same folder as the InDesign document, so you can easily copy those files along with the InDesign document.

You can also go ahead and *embed* a graphics file by placing its data in the InDesign file, but remember that the embedded graphic will not be affected by any later changes to the original graphics file. (See the "Embedding Graphics Files" section below.)

Managing Graphics File Links

The information that InDesign is keeping about the links to the graphics files you have placed is kept in the Links palette, shown below. You access this palette by choosing Edit ➤ Links or by pressing Shift+Ctrl/Cmd+D.

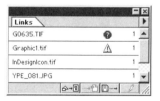

All graphics files that have been placed in the InDesign document are displayed in the Links palette. To select a link, click on its name in the Links palette. You can select multiple links by pressing Shift to select consecutive links and by pressing Ctrl/Cmd to select nonconsecutive links.

If you have placed the same graphics file more than once in your InDesign document, the Links palette will display the name of the file once for each time you placed the file.

The Links palette provides the following information and options about your graphics files:

- The name of the graphics file.
- The page number where the graphics file is used in the InDesign document appears to the right of the filename.
- If the graphics file is out of date, perhaps because it has been moved or deleted, a red octagon with a question mark in it appears to the right of the filename. You should use the Relink button or choose Relink from the Links palette menu to locate the file for InDesign.
- If the graphics file has been changed or edited since it was imported, a yellow caution triangle appears to the right of the filename. You should use the Update Link button or choose Update Link from the Links palette menu to apply the changes to the placed preview.

The features of the Links palette are:

- The Relink button will open the Relink dialog box, shown below, so that you can tell InDesign where to find a lost file.

- The Go to Link button centers the placed graphics file in the center of the InDesign window, showing where you placed it.

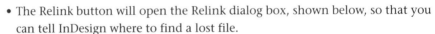

- The Update Link button automatically reads the changed data of the original graphics file and changes the placed preview accordingly.

TIP The Update Link feature provides a way to efficiently update all of the occurrences of a linked graphics file at once. Simply select each of the occurrences in the Links palette, then click the Update Link button or choose Update Link from the Link palette menu.

- The Edit Original button opens the application from which the graphics file was saved (if you have it in your system), so that you can edit the graphics file.

The Links palette menu, shown next, offers display options, the same options as those listed as buttons above, plus the Link Information command, and the Embed command.

MANAGING LINKS AND EMBEDDING IMAGES   165

The Link Information command in the Links palette menu will display the Link Information dialog box, shown in Figure 6.14, which lists all the saved information about all the links. You can navigate through all the links of the document by clicking the Prev or Next buttons. You can enter a new location for the link in the Location text entry area.

The Link Information dialog box

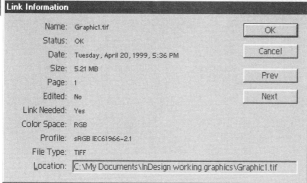

WARNING   If the resolution of a graphics file is changed or it is cropped or enlarged in the original application, it may distort when InDesign updates the link. This is because InDesign will place the updated file in the graphics frame with the exact same dimensions as the older version. This may cause a smaller-sized graphic to stretch or compress to fit the graphics frame. Be sure to go to the link and check it after updating.

Embedding Graphics Files

Embedding a graphic file places all the data about the file within the InDesign document, eliminating the need for a link. This, of course, increases the size of the InDesign file. Embedded files are no longer linked and their names no longer appear in the Links palette. Nor will an embedded file be updated if the original file is edited.

To embed a graphic, simply select its name in the Links palette and choose Embed from the Links palette menu.

chapter 7

Correcting mistakes and recovering from disaster

Featuring:

- *Using Edit ➢ Undo* — 170
- *Toggling changes with Edit ➢ Redo* — 170
- *Saving various states with Save a Copy* — 171
- *Reverting to the last saved version* — 172
- *Resetting dialog boxes* — 172
- *Stopping operations in progress* — 172
- *Automatic Recovery* — 172

CHAPTER 7

CORRECTING MISTAKES AND RECOVERING FROM DISASTER

Being able to easily undo a mistake or to change your mind about a design change is one of the great capabilities of desktop publishing. For those of us who apprenticed in the age of mechanical pasteup and layout, being able to switch back and forth through the states of a publication in production is truly a miracle.

These undo and redo features aren't new. Most word processing, page layout, drawing, and painting programs already have them in one form or another. What's great about InDesign's undo and reset commands is that they provide multiple undos and they are nearly invisible. You don't have to worry about setting some arbitrary number of backward steps you can take. You are limited only by the memory capacity of your system.

But what about when you've painstakingly entered a bunch of new values in a complex dialog box, only to decide that half of them were not the values you intended and that you'll need to try to figure out what they were before? Don't worry, you can reset your dialog boxes to their state when you opened them.

Then there's always that moment after you have already clicked the OK button in a dialog box, then realize that you don't want those changes after all, and don't want to wait through the operation only to have to undo it afterwards. Did you know you can stop operations as they process?

In addition, InDesign's new *Automatic Recovery* feature is likewise a miracle. If you've ever worked diligently on a project only to have your computer crash or lock up before you have had a chance to save the last few (or more) stages of your work, you know how frustrating and downright agonizing that can be. But InDesign is watching out for you and may prevent you from having to rebuild too much of that lost data.

WARNING No matter what you read in this chapter about how easily you can undo mistakes and recover from system crashes, save your document often. Don't risk your hard work and your sanity by waiting to lose a large chunk of your workday. You have these undo and recovery features, but don't rely on them. Use them as emergency tools.

Using Edit ➢ Undo and Edit ➢ Redo

Any time you want to take back some action you just made in InDesign, whether it was replacing a word, moving an object, dragging a handle, or just about anything, all you have to do is choose Edit ➢ Undo or press Ctrl/Cmd+Z.

If you then change your mind again, you can choose Edit ➢ Redo or press Shift+Ctrl/Cmd+Z to redo the change.

TIP One thing I like to do sometimes if I have made a change that I want to compare with the previous state, I just use the Edit ➢ Redo keyboard shortcut, which is Ctrl/Cmd+Z, to "toggle" back and forth between the two states. Sometimes this helps you compare the real difference between the two to see if you like one or the other better.

Of course, there is a catch. InDesign stores the data for all these changes and operations in a memory cache until you save or quit the application. Once you save your document, whether or not you close it, the undo cache is purged. You lose the opportunity to go back. The undo cache is also purged when you quit InDesign.

The number of undos you can perform is limited to 300, but your system may not have enough memory to actually store that many. In other words, after working eight hours working on a design you wind up hating, chances are you won't be able to go back through several hundred undos to where you first started. In actual practice you may never run out of undos.

"Okay," you say, "then I just won't save until I'm happy with all of my changes." "No, no, no," I say. That's not the answer. What if you work for an hour and then you have a crash? As you might expect, I've got another little trick for you.

Saving Various States with Save a Copy

So you're cruising along and you feel pretty good about where you are in the production of your publication. You save it. But now you're heading off into uncharted territory. You're about to make some changes that you're just not sure about, that will be complicated, and will take some time. You really should not risk all that time and effort by not saving as you go. But what if you wind up wanting to go back to where you were an hour ago, after all those saves purged each and every one of the steps you took?

Use the Save a Copy command. You can save a copy of the current state of the document, which you can return to later if the subsequent changes don't work out the way you had hoped.

The Save a Copy command saves a copy of the file, which it does not open. In other words, you save a copy of the file at its current state, but you keep right on working in the file. Get it?

Now, once again, you must be careful. Saving a copy also purges the undo cache. So don't do that until you're sure you're ready to live with those last operations.

To save a copy of an open document, choose Edit ➤ Save a Copy or press Ctrl+Alt+S in Windows and Cmd+Option+S on the Mac to open the Save As dialog box, shown in Figure 7.1.

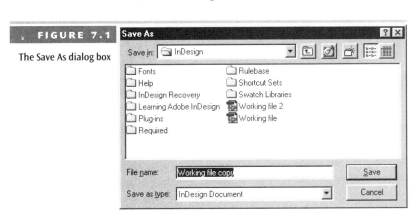

FIGURE 7.1
The Save As dialog box

Navigate to where you want to save the copy, then give it a name and pick a file type. By default, InDesign will automatically enter the name of the current document and append the word "copy" to that name. You can use that name, or you can edit it to anything you want.

You might want to give your document copies that will tell you something about them if you're looking through them to find the one you want. You know, something like, "DocumentWithOldColors" to remind yourself that this is the one that you saved when you went on to change to some new, experimental colors.

You might want to save the copy as a template if you think you might want to go back and open it more than once for more experimentation. A *template* is a file that opens as an untitled document, preserving the integrity of the saved document. You must then save the new file with a name and location. Pull down the Save as Type option menu in the Save As dialog box, shown in Figure 7.1, and select InDesign Template. (For more information about templates, see Chapter 2.)

Reverting to the Last Saved Version

If you're working along and you suddenly force yourself to accept the fact that the direction you took a while back just isn't working out, you can jump back to the last version of the document you saved by choosing File ➤ Revert. This command basically reopens the saved version of the file and discards all data that has not yet been saved.

Now, once again, I caution you not to work very long without saving. So, realistically, this command is of limited value except for short distances back through states.

Resetting Dialog Boxes

After you have entered new values or otherwise made changes to the parameters of many of InDesign's dialog boxes, you can immediately reset a dialog box to its original state by pressing Alt/Option to toggle the Cancel button to a Reset button. Then continue to hold down the Alt/Option key while you click the Reset button.

Stopping Operations in Progress

If you decide to perform an operation that requires you to enter a dialog box and then click OK, you can stop the operation in progress by pressing the Escape key. Sometimes this happens too fast and you can't catch it, in which case all you have to do is undo the change, anyway.

This feature is most useful for those time-consuming operations during which you sit and watch a progress bar. If you realize you don't want the change while this is happening, don't bother to wait to undo it. Just press Escape.

Using Automatic Recovery

InDesign provides a measure of protection against data loss due to system crashes by automatically saving your work periodically to a special, separate data file. This data file contains data regarding the work you have performed since the last save. You don't even need to think about this file unless you have a crash.

WARNING Remember to save frequently. Even with the protection provided by Automatic Recovery, there is no guarantee that your document will be recovered to the full extent of the work you may have done since the last save. Remember, also, to save backup copies of your files, in case the crash is due to the failure of a hard drive or other storage device.

If you experience a system failure or if InDesign unexpectedly quits, recover the automatically saved data following these steps:

1. Restart the computer.
2. Launch InDesign.

If InDesign has automatically saved data for any files that were open at the time of the crash, you will be prompted to decide whether to add the recovered data to the file. If you select Yes, the data will be added to the document and "Recovered" will be appended to the name of the document file. You can then use Save As to save the file to disk with the original name (or any other name you choose). You can also select No, in which case the automatically saved data will not be added to the document and will be discarded.

WARNING Adobe advises that if InDesign crashes when you attempt to open the document file using Automatic Recovery, the recovered data file itself may be damaged or corrupted. In this case, you will not be able to recover this data and should again follow the steps for Automatic Recovery, but select No when prompted to add the recovered data to the document file.

NOTE Whether you select Yes or No when prompted by Automatic Recovery, you should use Save As immediately after opening the document file, so that InDesign can verify the file's data integrity.

chapter 8

PRINTING BASICS

Featuring:

- *Selecting a printer* — **178**
- *Specifying print options* — **179**
- *Setting up page options* — **179**
- *Specifying the numbers of copies* — **181**
- *Specifying the pages to print* — **181**
- *Printing to a file* — **191**
- *Setting up virtual printers* — **192**

PRINTING BASICS

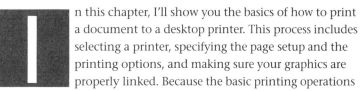

n this chapter, I'll show you the basics of how to print a document to a desktop printer. This process includes selecting a printer, specifying the page setup and the printing options, and making sure your graphics are properly linked. Because the basic printing operations are so different between the Mac and Windows machines, the two operations are presented here separately.

Actually, the most simple method of printing is to just choose File ➢ Print or press Ctrl/Cmd+P and then immediately click OK. This action will print your document according to the print specifications used before the last save. If these specifications happen to match what you want to print again, that's fine. But if you need to specify a different printer, a different paper, a different range of pages, or a different number of copies, you'll need to read this chapter.

WARNING In Windows, you can print to a non-PostScript printer, but you can not be sure that the document will print as you see it on the screen. On the Mac, InDesign will not print to a non-PostScript printer, period.

The more advanced printing operations, such as preparing files for output at a service bureau or other output resource, printing color separations, and printing documents with registration marks and trim marks, are covered in Chapter 18.

NOTE Although commonly used before preparing files for output by a service bureau, you can also use the Preflight command to check any file before printing to any printer. This may prevent printing problems due to lost links, missing fonts, etc. Simply choose File ➢ Preflight. (For more information on the Preflight and Package commands, see Chapter 18.)

Printing from Windows

This section presents the printing process from the Windows operating system. I'm assuming that you already have the printer properly installed. If you do not have the printer properly installed, please see the documentation for the Windows operating system for assistance in setting up your printer.

Opening the Print Dialog Box

Choose File ➢ Print or press Ctrl+P to open the Print dialog box, shown in Figure 8.1. As you can see, you can control a lot of the printing options from this dialog box. Many of the options accessed through the tabs on the lower half of the dialog box are for the advanced printing options and are discussed in Chapter 18.

For simple printing, I'll show you how to select the printer, specify paper options, and specify the number of copies and which pages to print.

Selecting a Printer

Before you can print a document, you must tell your computer to what printer you want the document printed.

To select a printer, pull down the Name option menu at the top of the Print dialog box, and select the printer from the menu. The default printer should be listed automatically, but if it isn't, or if you want to print to another printer, select the desired printer from the list. If your printer does not appear on the list, you should return to the Windows desktop and proceed to install the printer. (Again, refer to the Windows documentation for assistance in installing the printer.)

You'll see the printer's status, type, and location appear beneath the Name menu.

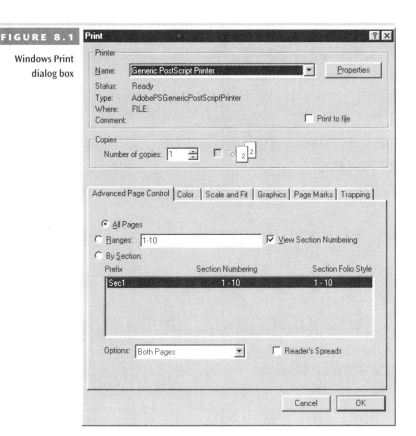

FIGURE 8.1

Windows Print dialog box

Specifying Paper Size and Paper Options

At this point, it is always a good idea to check the settings for paper size, paper source, and paper orientation, so that you don't waste the effort it would take to print again if the settings aren't what you want. If they are set as you want, you just go ahead and print. But if they are not, you can set them *before* you waste the paper and the time.

TIP The *page size* of your document is the intended size of a document, that you specify when you create the document. *Paper size* is the size of the individual sheet of paper onto which your printer will print the document. They are not necessarily the same dimensions, because you might be intending to trim the *paper size* down to the *page size*. Get it?

To check the paper settings, click the Properties button in the Printer area of the Print dialog box, to open the Properties dialog box for the printer you have selected, as shown in Figure 8.2.

FIGURE 8.2

Windows printer Properties dialog box

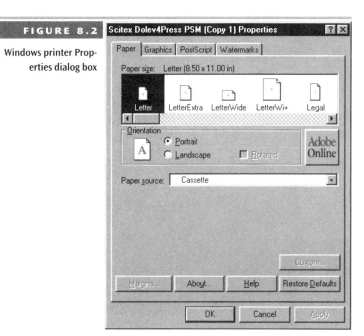

Specifying a Paper Size

Notice that the printer's available paper sizes are displayed in the Paper Size display area of the printer's Properties dialog box. You select one of these paper sizes by clicking on its name or icon. You can scroll left or right to view the available paper sizes.

If the paper size that you need is not displayed and the printer supports custom paper sizes, you can specify that custom paper size by first scrolling to an icon for a custom paper size in the Paper Size display area. This action activates the Custom button in the Properties dialog box. Click this Custom button to open the Custom-Defined Size dialog box, shown below.

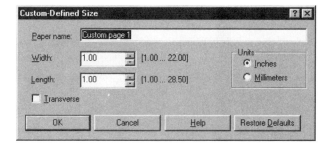

You can specify a name for the paper size by entering a name in the Paper Name text area. Select a unit of measurement (inches or millimeters) from the Units area, then specify the width and length of the paper.

NOTE The Transverse option that appears in the Custom-Defined Size dialog box, as shown above, is often used to conserve paper when printing to imagesetters that use rolls of photographic paper or film. Because of the width of these rolls of paper or film it may be more efficient to turn the document page sideways, utilizing the width of the paper or film and allowing consecutive pages to take up less of the length of the paper or film.

Specifying Paper Orientation

The Orientation option of the Properties dialog box is pretty straightforward. If you laid out your document with the paper turned on its side, you should select the Landscape orientation. Otherwise, you want Portrait.

The Rotated option is only available with Landscape orientation and it rotates the document 180 degrees for printing.

Specifying the Paper Source

If the selected printer has multiple trays or other paper sources, you should select the desired paper source from the Paper Source option menu of the Properties dialog box.

Click Apply to simply apply the changes and continue to make adjustments, or click OK to apply the changes and close the Properties dialog box.

Specifying the Number of Copies and Selecting Collation

Back in the Print dialog box, shown in Figure 8.1, enter the number of copies you want to print in the Number of Copies text area.

When you are printing multiple copies and if your printer supports collation, you can select the Collate option, which will output the multiple copies of your document as stacks of ordered pages, saving you the trouble of collating the pages yourself.

Specifying the Pages to Print and How to Print Them

There are times when you only want to print out specific pages for review (or whatever). At other times, you may need to print a two-page spread across a single sheet of paper. These options and others are specified in the Advanced Page Control area of the Print dialog box, shown in Figure 8.1. If this area is not displayed, simply click the Advanced Page Control tab to bring it to the front.

Specifying the Number of Pages

Adobe PostScript allows you to print all the pages of a document, or to specify multiple page ranges from within the same document.

To print all the pages of your document, simply select the All Pages radio button in the Advanced Page Control tab.

To print specific pages of your document, you can enter a range or ranges within the Ranges text area of the Advanced Page Control tab. The ability to specify multiple ranges is terrific and potentially saves you from repeating much of this printing process if you're printing several ranges from within the same document.

You enter ranges by typing the first page you want to print, then a hyphen, then the last page you want to print. The entry "1-8" would result in the printing of pages one through eight. You can also enter multiple page ranges by separating the ranges with commas, without entering any space between. The entry "1-8,12-16,21,24-26" would result in the printing of pages one through eight, 12 through 16, page 21 by itself, then pages 24 through 26.

If you have numbered your document with sections, you can click the View Section Numbering checkbox to specify the page ranges by section numbers, rather than absolute page numbers. For example, if your document has two sections each of 10 pages, page 11 would be entered as "2:1". When you click the View Section Numbering checkbox, the pages displayed in the Advanced Page Control area change to show the section prefixes, the page ranges in the sections, and the section folio styles, as shown in Figure 8.3.

Now you can see the number of sections in the document and the number of pages in each section, so that you can enter the page range you want to print.

You can also select the By Section option to print entire sections of the document. You can print one section at a time by selecting that section in the display area, or you can print multiple sections by pressing Shift and clicking on additional section names.

Printing on Both Sides of a Piece of Paper

If you are intending to print out the document in "duplex" style, or with even-numbered pages on one side of a sheet and odd-numbered pages on the other side, as in a book, you can select Even Pages Only or Odd Pages Only from the Options option menu. After printing, say, the odd-numbered pages first, you must then remove the first batch of pages from the printer and place them in the printer's paper tray or feeder to print the opposite side.

FIGURE 8.3

The Windows Advanced Page Control/View Section Numbering

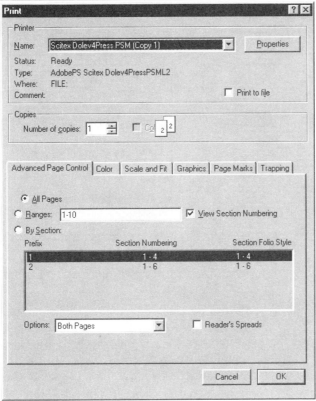

Printing Double Trucks

Double truck is the traditional publishing term for two-page spreads. You can print double trucks by selecting the Reader's Spreads option at the bottom of the Advanced Page Control area of the Print dialog box.

Of course, to do this properly, you must also use a sheet of paper that is twice the width of the page, and rotate the orientation of the pages to Landscape. If you attempt to print a double truck of a letter-size document on a letter-size sheet of paper, InDesign will only print those portions of the document that fit on the single sheet. If you want to print a reduced-size double truck on a letter-size sheet, you could scale the double truck appropriately smaller. (Scaling printed documents is presented in Chapter 18.)

An example of a two-page spread is shown below in Figure 8.4.

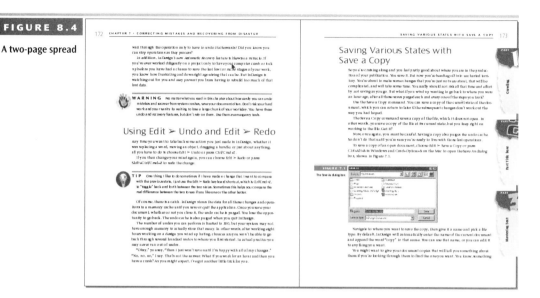

FIGURE 8.4

A two-page spread

Saving Print Options

Once you have set up the print options as you want, saving the document after printing will preserve those settings for that document.

If you want to save the print settings before you print, for safety's sake, just click Apply to save the print options, then click Cancel to close the Print dialog box. Save the document, then reopen the Print dialog box and print.

Printing on the Mac

This section presents the printing process from the Mac operating system. I'm assuming that you already have the printer properly installed. If you do not have the printer properly installed, please see the documentation for the Mac operating system for assistance in setting up your printer.

As mentioned earlier in this chapter, InDesign will not print to any non-PostScript printer. You must also have the Adobe PostScript driver properly installed in the Mac system folder. The Adobe PostScript driver is included on the InDesign installation CD, with an installer that you can use to install the driver.

Selecting a Printer

Before you can print a document, you must tell your computer to what printer you want the document printed.

First, you need to make sure you are accessing the correct Print driver. Go to the Apple menu in the upper left corner of the monitor, then click and hold to pull down the Apple menu. Slide down to Chooser and let go to open the Chooser control panel, as shown in Figure 8.5.

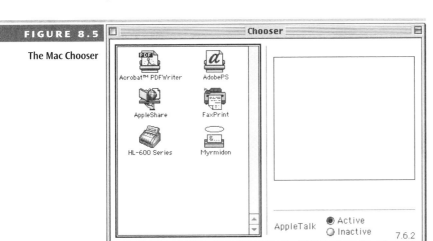

FIGURE 8.5

The Mac Chooser

Click on the AdobePS driver icon, which will open a list of available PostScript printers in the display area on the left. Click to highlight the name of the printer to which you want to print. If the printer is set up properly, you'll see a small color icon to the left of the printer's name and you can simply close the Chooser control panel by clicking the close box in the upper left corner of the Chooser's window. If there is no color icon to the left of the printer's name, click the Setup button to select the correct PPD. (Again, you may need to refer to the Mac operating system documentation for assistance in setting up your printer.)

Now return to InDesign and the document you want to print.

Specifying Paper Size and Paper Options

At this point, it is always a good idea to check the settings for paper size, paper source, and paper orientation, so that you don't waste the effort it would take to print again if the settings aren't what you want. If they are set as you want, you just go ahead and print. But if they are not, you can set them *before* you waste the paper and the time.

TIP The *page size* of your document is the intended size of a document, that you specify when you create the document. *Paper size* is the size of the individual sheet of paper onto which your printer will print the document. They are not necessarily the same dimensions, because you might be intending to trim the *paper size* down to the *page size*. Get it?

To check the paper settings, choose File ➤ Page Setup or press Shift+Cmd+P to open the Page Setup dialog box, shown in Figure 8.6.

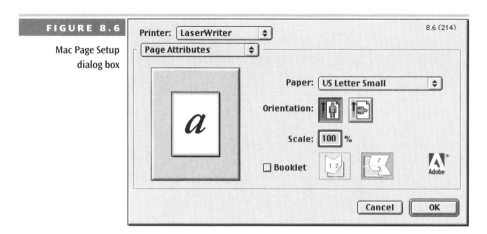

FIGURE 8.6
Mac Page Setup dialog box

As you can see in Figure 8.6, the Mac Page Setup dialog box operates like most of the dialog boxes built for Mac OS 8 and later. This format allows for the dialog box to be smaller, while still offering access to many option areas that may have been accessed through multiple dialog boxes in past versions of the operating system. To navigate through the various option areas, click and hold on an option menu and slide down to the option area you want to use.

The Printer option menu in the upper left shows you the printer you have selected in the Chooser. This display also identifys the printer for which you are setting these Page Setup options. (They do not have to be the same.) You can set the page setup options for a different printer by first selecting one from the Printer option menu.

By default, you will first see the Page Attributes area of the Page Setup dialog box, as shown in Figure 8.6. The large display area shows you how the document will be oriented. The letter "a" signifies the content of the document and will rotate and otherwise change to show you how the content will be printed.

Selecting a Paper Size

Notice that the printer's available paper sizes are displayed in the Paper option menu of the Page Setup dialog box, like the one shown in Figure 8.6. Select one of these paper sizes from the option menu.

Specifying a Custom Paper Size

If the paper size that you need is not displayed and the printer supports custom paper sizes, you can specify that custom paper size by first selecting Custom Page Default from the option menu beneath the Printer option menu. This action displays the Custom Page Default options, as shown below in Figure 8.7.

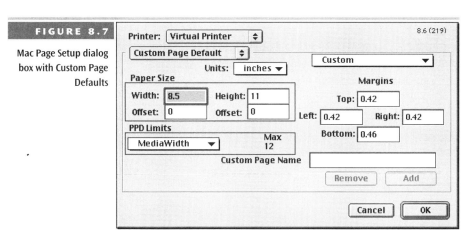

FIGURE 8.7

Mac Page Setup dialog box with Custom Page Defaults

The unnamed option menu to the right of the Custom Page Default option menu shows you the paper size you have selected. If you want to print to a custom paper size, you should select Custom from that option menu.

Select a unit of measurement (inches or millimeters) from the Units option menu, then specify the width and length of the paper.

The Offset values specify how much space the printer will allow between the pages of your document (remember, most of these printers and imagesetters that allow custom page sizes are printing onto a roll of paper or film). The values and choices in the PPD Limits area tell you how much printable area this particular printer allows, helping you decide how much offset you might want.

The Margins values also specify space around the printable area. If you have already defined margins for your document pages—either back in the Document Setup dialog box when you created the document, or in the Margins and Columns dialog box—you don't need to specify additional margins here. (For more information about the Document Setup dialog box, see Chapter 2. For more information about the Margins and Columns dialog box, see Chapter 16.)

You can specify a name for the paper size by entering a name in the Custom Page Name text area and clicking the Add button. You can then create additional custom paper sizes by following these same steps. Each custom paper size you name is added to the pull down menu above. You can remove any of the custom paper sizes by selecting that custom paper size's name from that pull-down menu and clicking the Remove button.

Specifying Paper Orientation

The Orientation option of the Page Attributes area of the Page Setup dialog box, shown in Figure 8.6, is pretty straightforward. If you laid out your document with the paper turned on its side you should select Landscape orientation. Otherwise, you want Portrait.

Scaling a Document for Printing

If you need to scale a document to print it on a sheet of paper that is either larger or smaller than the defined size of the document, you can enter a percentage in the Scale values box of the Page Setup dialog box.

Printing Double Trucks

Double truck is the traditional publishing term for two-page spreads. You can print double trucks by selecting the Booklet option at the bottom of the Page Attributes area of the Page Setup dialog box. Clicking the Booklet checkbox activates the two orientation icons for the Booklet option, as shown below.

These icons are pretty self-explanatory. If you want your document to print out with two pages printed upright and side-by-side in the Portrait orientation, you select the icon on the left. If you want your document to print out with two pages printed upright and one on top of the other in the Landscape orientation, you select the icon on the right.

Of course, to print a booklet properly, you must also use a sheet of paper that is twice the width of the page. If you attempt to print a double truck of a letter-size document on a letter-size sheet of paper, InDesign will only print those portions of the document that fit on the single sheet. If you want to print a reduced-size double truck on a letter-size sheet, you could scale the page appropriately smaller. (Scaling printed documents is presented in Chapter 18.)

Opening the Print Dialog Box

Choose File ➤ Print or press Cmd+P to open the Print dialog box. To select a printer, pull down the Printer option menu at the top of the Print dialog box and select the printer from the menu. The printer you selected in the Chooser and in Page Setup should be listed automatically, but if it isn't, or if you want to print to another printer, select the desired printer from the list. If your printer does not appear on the list, make sure that the printer's definition file is properly installed in the Mac system folder. (Refer to your Mac operating system documentation or the documentation that came with your printer for assistance in installing the printer.)

Specifying the Number of Copies and Selecting Collation

Make sure you have selected General from the option menu beneath the Printer option menu. Enter the number of copies you want to print in the Copies value box.

When you are printing multiple copies, you can select the Collate option (assuming, of course, that your printer supports collation), which will output the multiple copies of your document as stacks of ordered pages, saving you the trouble of collating the pages yourself.

You can select the Reverse Order option to print out the pages from the back of the document to the front. This is useful when printing duplex.

Specifying the Pages to Print and How to Print Them

There are times when you are working on a document that you only want to print out specific pages for review, or whatever. This option and others are specified here in the General area of the Print dialog box. If this area is not displayed, simply select General from the option menu.

Specifying the Number of Pages

From the General area of the Print dialog box, you can print all the pages of document, or you can specify a range of pages from the document. If you want to print multiple ranges of pages from the document, you can specify those ranges in the Advanced Page Control area.

To print all the pages of your document, simply select the All Pages radio button in the Pages area of the Print dialog box.

To print specific pages of your document, you can enter the initial page in the From and the final page in the To value box.

If you want to print multiple page ranges from this dialog box, select Advanced Page Control from the option menu under the Printer option menu in the Print dialog box, as shown in Figure 8.8.

As you can see, you can choose to print all pages by clicking the All Pages radio button or you can print multiple ranges by clicking the Ranges radio button and entering the range or ranges of pages you want printed.

You enter ranges by typing the first page you want to print, then a hyphen, then the last page you want to print. The entry "1-8" would result in the printing of pages one through eight. You can also enter multiple page ranges by separating the ranges with commas, without entering any space between. The entry "1-8,12-16,21,24-26" would result in the printing of pages one through eight, 12 through 16, page 21 by itself, then pages 24 through 26.

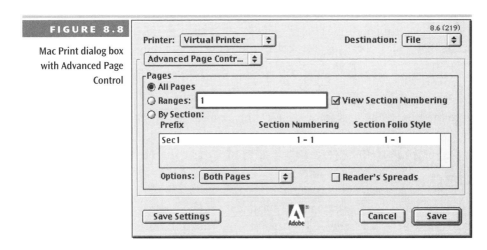

FIGURE 8.8

Mac Print dialog box with Advanced Page Control

If you have numbered your document with sections, you can click the View Section Numbering checkbox to specify the page ranges by section numbers, rather than absolute page numbers. For example, if your document has two sections each of 10 pages, page 11 would be entered as "2:1". When you click the View Section Numbering checkbox, the pages displayed in the Advanced Page Control area change to show the section prefixes, the page ranges in the sections, and the section folio styles, as shown in Figure 8.9.

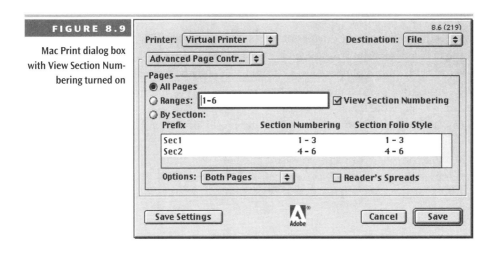

FIGURE 8.9

Mac Print dialog box with View Section Numbering turned on

Now you can see the number of sections in the document and the number of pages in each section, so that you can enter the page range you want to print.

You can also select the By Section option to print entire sections of the document. You can print one section at a time by selecting that section in the display area, or you can print multiple sections by pressing Shift and clicking on additional section names.

Printing on Both Sides of a Piece of Paper

If you are intending to print out the document in "duplex" style, or with even-numbered pages on one side of a sheet and odd-numbered pages on the other side, as in a book, you can select Even Pages Only or Odd Pages Only from the Options option menu. After printing, say, the odd-numbered pages first, you must then remove the first batch of pages from the printer and place them in the printer's paper tray or feeder to print the opposite side.

Specifying the Paper Source

Go back to the General area of the Print dialog box. If the selected printer has multiple trays or other paper sources, you should select the desired paper source from the Paper Source option menu.

Notice that you can print the first page from one paper source and the remaining pages from another source. This could be helpful if you are printing a document with a cover that you want printed on a piece of color card stock. You could place that paper in one tray or cassette and the plain paper in the other tray or cassette. You click the First Page From radio button, specify a source in the option menu, then select a source for the remaining pages from the Remaining From option menu.

Saving Print Options

Once you have set up the print options as you want, you can save them to the document so that you don't have to do it again by clicking the Save Settings button before you print.

Printing to a File

As described earlier in this chapter, you can print your document to a file that you can carry or transmit to a remote printer. You should do this after you specify all other printer options. You can print to a file by selecting a virtual printer (described in the following sections), or you can do it by following these simple directions:

- From Windows, you can print to a file simply by clicking the Print to File checkbox in the Print dialog box, shown in Figure 8.1

- On the Mac, select File from the Destination option menu of the Mac Print dialog box.

Even if you select a virtual printer, you may want to select these print-to-file options to ensure that you actually do print to a file.

Using a Virtual Printer in Windows

If the printer to which you want to print is not connected to your computer (either directly or via a network), you can still print to that printer by printing to a PostScript file via a *virtual printer*. Windows allows you to specify a PPD (PostScript Printer Description) file that tells your computer all the technical details about setting up a document to print on that printer. In other words, if you want to print to a more suitable printer than the one connected to your computer, you can tell InDesign to "pretend" to be printing your document to that printer. InDesign saves all that printing data to a file, which you can download to a disk or send electronically to a computer that is connected to the better printer. You can then print that PPD file of your document to the remote printer. This is a common way to send a document to a service bureau, but you could be doing it just so you can print from another printer down the hall that doesn't happen to be on your network.

Install a virtual printer by installing a PPD for the printer through the Adobe PostScript setup program and selecting FILE: as the printer port. This process creates a File on Disk from the Select Port dialog box of the setup program.

Using a Virtual Printer on the Mac

If the printer to which you want to print is not connected to your computer (either directly or via a network), you can still print to that printer by printing to a PPD file via the Virtual Printer plug-in.

The Virtual Printer plug-in is supplied by Adobe and should be on the InDesign installation CD. The Virtual Printer plug-in allows you to specify a PPD (PostScript Printer Description) file that tells your computer all the technical details about setting up a document to print on that printer. In other words, if you want to print to a more suitable printer than the one connected to your computer, you can tell InDesign to "pretend" to be printing your document to that printer. InDesign saves all that printing data to a file, which you can download to a disk or send electronically to a computer that is connected to the better printer. You can then print that PPD file of your document to the remote printer. This is a common way to send a document to a service bureau, but you could be doing it just so you can print from another printer down the hall that doesn't happen to be on your network.

You select the PPD for the virtual printer to which you want to print in the Page Setup dialog box, shown in Figure 8.10, by selecting Virtual Printer from the Printer option menu, then selecting Virtual Printer from the option menu directly beneath the Printer option menu. Click Select PPD to open the Select a PostScript Printer Description File dialog box and scroll to the printer to which you intend to print.

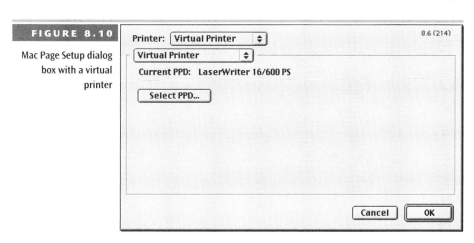

FIGURE 8.10

Mac Page Setup dialog box with a virtual printer

PART II
WALKING

chapter 9

FORMATTING TEXT

Featuring:

- Specifying a font 204
- Setting the leading 207
- Adjusting the spaces between letters with kerning and tracking 210
- Setting paragraph specifications 213
- Setting alignment 214
- Tabs and Indents 218

FORMATTING TEXT

In Chapter 5, I showed you how to create text frames and how to enter, place, and edit text. Now it's time to learn to set type. To create professional-looking documents, you should know how to specify typefaces, type sizes, leading, spacing, type styles, and so on. You also should know how to format the text so that it appears as you want, with paragraph indents and justification.

I think you'll find learning this stuff pretty easy, and will quickly appreciate how much well-designed type can change the appearance of your documents. If you are interested in learning more about type, you can find volumes and volumes written on typography and type design.

The following is a list of the basic typography terms:

Type family   A set of characters with a common design, of the same name, but not necessarily the same style. In other words, Times is a type family, but Times Bold and Times Italic are styles within the Times type family. The type family is also often referred to as the *font*.

Type style   The variation of the type in a type family. Plain, Bold, Italic, and Bold Italic are the most common styles.

Roman   The style name used by some type publishers to refer to the plain styles of their particular type families.

Leading   (pronounced "ledding") The amount of space between horizontal lines of type. This term originated in the old days of handset type, when thin strips of metal called "leads" were used to determine the amount of space between the lines of metal type.

Baseline   The invisible line on which the bodies of the letters rests. The descenders, such as the lower strokes of a "g," "j," "y," and so on, hang down below the baseline. Leading is measured from baseline to baseline.

Tracking   The amount of space applied equally between all the letters in a range of letters. In other words, if we were to space out all the letters in this line by two points, we would be tracking the letters.

Kerning   The amount of space between two specific letters. Kerning is used to tighten up letters that would otherwise appear to have too much space between them. "AW" is a good example of two letters that might appear too far apart without being kerned together.

Ligatures   Special type characters of two letters that look better when they are actually printed partially on top of each other. In those good old days I keep referring to, ligatures were actual metal pieces of type into which two letters had been carved. "ff" is a good example of two letters that are often combined in a ligature.

Alignment   The term for how the type is set within its column or margins.

Character attributes   Can be applied to individual selected characters and are specified in the Character palette, shown in Figure 9.1.

Paragraph attributes   Can only be applied to entire paragraphs and are specified in the Paragraph palette, shown in Figure 9.3.

T I P   Before applying character attributes, you must select the text. Selecting text is presented in detail in Chapter 5.

Using the Character Palette and the Paragraph Palette

Open the Character palette, shown in Figure 9.1, by choosing Type ➢ Character, by pressing Ctrl/Cmd+T, or by clicking the Character tab in its palette group.

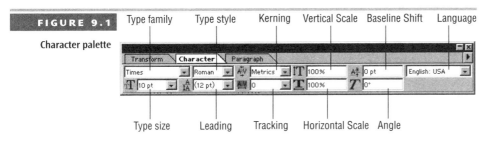

FIGURE 9.1
Character palette

Open the Character palette menu, shown in Figure 9.2, by clicking and holding the arrow on the right side of the Character palette.

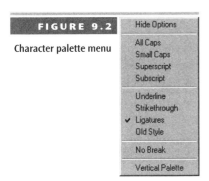

FIGURE 9.2
Character palette menu

Open the Paragraph palette, shown in Figure 9.3, by choosing Type ➢ Paragraph, by pressing Ctrl/Cmd+M, or by clicking the Character tab in its palette group.

Open the Paragraph palette menu, shown in Figure 9.4, by clicking and holding the arrow on the right side of the Character palette.

These palettes are great shortcut tools. Although you can access the features in the Character and Paragraph palettes using other operations, why would you want to? Right here are quick and easy ways to apply typographic attributes to your text.

You can apply attributes to your text via the Character palette and the Paragraph palettes by typing values, and in some cases, by pulling down option menus that offer specific attributes.

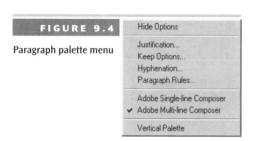

FIGURE 9.3
Paragraph palette

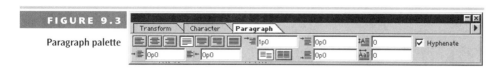

FIGURE 9.4
Paragraph palette menu

You can navigate through these palettes by tabbing. Pressing the Tab key will move you sequentially through the available value boxes. If you press Shift as you press the Tab key, you will move backwards through the available value boxes. When you tab to a value box, the current value will highlight. You don't have to delete it or place your text insertion point anywhere in it. You can just immediately start typing.

TIP If you select a range of text and one or more of the value boxes in one or both of these palettes displays no value, that indicates that there are multiple values for that attribute applied to the selected text. This can help you locate problems in formatting, if you are seeking an formatting attribute.

TIP Remember that the palettes will do math for you. For example, if you want to increase the size of certain text characters by a factor of 2, just type an asterisk and a 2. This entry will multiply the original value by two. You can also enter a plus sign (+) to add, a minus sign (-) to subtract, and a slash (/) to divide.

When typing in names of typefaces in the Character palette, InDesign will assist by matching the letters you type with the names of available type families. For example, if you wanted Times, you could type "T," and InDesign would display whichever type family name came alphabetically first in the Ts. When you add the "i," InDesign would likely come up with "Times," unless there is another type family name that begins with "Ti."

If you want to change the default type settings—that is, the type settings that are applied to text as it is entered—make changes to the typographic controls here in the Character palette and the Paragraph palette when you have no text selected. From then on, when you begin typing, the typographic attributes you set in the Character and Paragraph palettes will be automatically applied to the text.

Table 9.1 shows the keyboard shortcuts for character formatting.

TABLE 9.1: CHARACTER FORMATTING KEYBOARD SHORTCUTS

Character format	Keyboard shortcuts
Regular	Shift+Ctrl/Cmd+Y
Italic	Shift+Ctrl/Cmd+I
Bold	Shift+Ctrl/Cmd+B
Bold Italic	Shift+Ctrl/Cmd+B, then Shift+Ctrl/Cmd+I
Underline	Shift+Ctrl/Cmd+U
~~Strikethrough~~	Shift+Ctrl/Cmd+/ (slash)
ALL CAPS	Shift+Ctrl/Cmd+K
SMALL CAPS	Shift+Ctrl/Cmd+H
Superscript	Shift+Ctrl/Cmd++ (plus sign)
Subscript	Shift+Alt/Option+Ctrl/Cmd++ (plus sign)
100% Horizontal Scale	Shift+Ctrl/Cmd+X
100% Vertical Scale	Shift+Alt/Option+Ctrl/Cmd+X
Increase point size by one increment*	Shift+Ctrl/Cmd+>
Decrease point size by one increment*	Shift+Ctrl/Cmd+<
Increase point size by five increments*	Shift+Alt/Option+Ctrl/Cmd+>
Decrease point size by five increments*	Shift+Alt/Option+Ctrl/Cmd+<
Increase leading by one increment*	Alt/Option+Up Arrow
Decrease leading by one increment*	Alt/Option+Down Arrow
Increase leading by five increments*	Alt/Option+Ctrl/Cmd+Up Arrow
Decrease leading by five increments*	Alt/Option+Ctrl/Cmd+Down Arrow
Autoleading	Shift+Alt/Option+Ctrl/Cmd+A
Shift baseline up	Shift+Alt/Option+Ctrl/Cmd+Up Arrow
Shift baseline down	Shift+Alt/Option+Ctrl/Cmd+Down Arrow
Automatic Hyphenation	Shift+Alt/Option+Ctrl/Cmd+H
Increase tracking/kerning by one increment*	Alt/Option+Right Arrow
Decrease tracking/kerning by one increment*	Alt/Option+Left Arrow
Increase tracking/kerning by five increments*	Alt/Option+Ctrl/Cmd+Right Arrow
Decrease tracking/kerning by five increments*	Alt/Option+Ctrl/Cmd+Right Arrow
Clear all tracking and kerning	Shift+Ctrl/Cmd+Q

*The increments used by these keyboard shortcuts can be specified by choosing File ➢ Preferences ➢ Units & Increments.

Specifying a Font

Back in the old days, when type was set by hand from big, divided drawers that contained one size of one type face and style, a *font* was the term used to designate that one set of type. Just one set of type. Let's say Helvetica, plain, 9 points. That was a font.

Today, of course, a lot of people use the term *font* to represent entire typeface families, including all the styles, such as Bold and Italic. An individual typeface family is a set of alphabetic, numeric, and symbolic characters that share a common design. When people say "I just bought a font," they usually mean that they bought a typeface family that includes several styles. These computerized typeface families can be sized and spaced and scaled and stretched and condensed, on and on.

For our purposes, we'll use *font* both as the term for a typeface family and as the typeface formatting attributes that can be applied to type, such as family and style.

In InDesign, you can apply a typeface font to any text you want using one of two methods:

- Select all the text you want to change and then go to the Character palette and either type in a type family name or select one from the Type Family option menu.

- Select all the text you want to change and then select a type family name by choosing Type ➤ Font. The available type families are listed in the expanded menu, as shown in Figure 9.5.

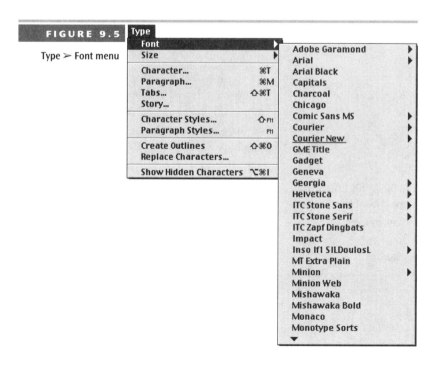

FIGURE 9.5

Type ➤ Font menu

Applying a Type Style

Bold and Italic are examples of type styles. Although many fonts are supplied as specific type styles and have such names as Helvetica Black or Futura Light, other fonts are selected by their general type family name and have type styles applied through character formatting.

Unless a font is designed with specific type styles, you can apply four type styles to type: regular, Italic, Bold, and Bold Italic. Examples of these type styles are shown below.

Regular **Mastering InDesign**

Italic *Mastering InDesign*

Bold **Mastering InDesign**

Bold Italic ***Mastering InDesign***

TIP Fonts that are designed with specific styles are not often enhanced by the application of additional styles. For example, if you apply the Bold style to a font that has "Black" as part of its name, the type may become too Bold and print too dark and heavy on some printers. For the most part, avoid applying type styles to fonts with style terms such as black, ultra, heavy, and oblique as part of their names.

To apply a type style to text, choose the Text tool and select the specific text to which you want to apply the style. Access the Character palette, shown in Figure 9.1, by choosing Type ➢ Character or by pressing Ctrl/Cmd+T.

Now go to the Type Style value box immediately to the right of the Type Family value box. You can type in one of the four type styles shown above, or you can open the option menu and select one. Alternately, you can use one of the following keyboard shortcuts:

- Regular: Shift+Ctrl/Cmd+Y
- *Italic:* Shift+Ctrl/Cmd+I
- **Bold:** Shift+Ctrl/Cmd+B
- ***Bold Italic:*** Shift+Ctrl/Cmd+B, then Shift+Ctrl/Cmd+I

You can also remove any of the type styles already applied to text by repeating these keyboard shortcuts. For example, if you have applied Bold to a range of characters, you can repeat the keyboard shortcut and the characters will revert to the regular style. (In the case of Bold Italic type, repeating the keyboard shortcut for Bold will return the type to Italic only, or repeating the keyboard shortcut for Italic will return the type to Bold only. You must then repeat the keyboard shortcut for that remaining style to revert the type to regular.)

InDesign also provides the more specialized type styles, such as Underline, Strikethrough, Superscript and Subscript, and so on. These styles can be applied through the keyboard shortcuts shown in Table 9.1. The default settings for the size of Small Caps and the size and position of Superscript and Subscript type are specified in the Preferences: Text dialog box, shown in Figure 9.6, accessed by choosing File ➢ Preferences ➢ Text.

NOTE The type styles Underline and Strikethrough are left over from the use of typewriters. While typing on a typewriter, there was no way to apply the **Bold** or *Italic* styles that were used in typesetting. So to signify that certain words represented **Bold** type, one would underline the typed words and maybe enclose what would be italicized words within quote marks. Because you couldn't backspace and delete typewritten words, you would go back and strikethrough words you wanted to delete. This is why many old typographers (like me) don't like to see the use of underlined text or strikethrough text. They are not a part of traditional typesetting and simply represent something we can typeset in its proper style.

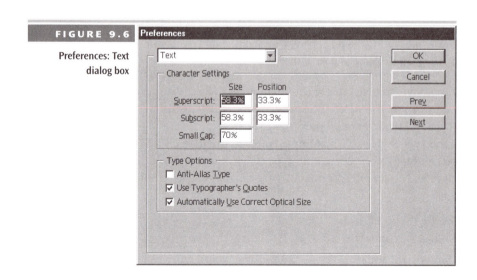

FIGURE 9.6
Preferences: Text dialog box

Specifying the Size of Type

The size of the type refers to the height of the type (this is also often referred to as *point size*). To specify the size of the type, once again select the text you want to change, or just go ahead and use the text that was already selected for another operation.

InDesign will accept numerical type size values from 0.1 points to 1296 points. You can enter incremental values down to 0.001.

Go to the Type Size value box of the Character palette, as shown in Figure 9.1, and enter a numerical size value or pull down the Type Size option menu and select one of the presented sizes.

Alternately, you can access the Type Size menu, shown below, by choosing Type ➢ Size or through the context menu (right-click in Windows or Control-click on the Mac).

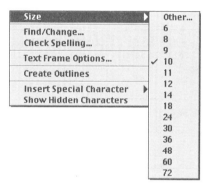

You can select a size from this menu, or you can select Other to enter a value in the Character palette.

You can also increase or decrease the size of type by pressing Shift and Control/Command and then > (the greater than symbol) to increase the size by one increment or < (the lesser than symbol) to decrease the size by one increment. Increase or decrease the size by five increments by pressing Shift, Alt/Option, Control/Command, and then < or >. The increments are determined by the amount specified in the Size/Leading value box of the Units & Increments preference dialog box, which you access by choosing File ➢ Preferences ➢ Units & Increments.

Setting the Leading

As described earlier in this chapter, leading is the amount of space between this line of text and the lines above it and below it. A lot of leading makes a design look airy and open, while too little leading makes a design look dark and hard-to-read. The most common leading amount for blocks of text are somewhere between 1 and 2 points more than the point size of the type. Examples of different leading amounts are shown below.

This line and the next line are set with what would be a "normal" leading value.

This line and the next line are set with a lot

of extra leading.

This line and the next line have been set with less leading than the point size of the type.

WARNING In InDesign, leading is a character attribute, which means that you can apply leading to individual characters in a paragraph. This may seem like a nice feature, but it can actually get you into trouble. The highest leading value in a line will govern the leading of that entire line. For example, after cutting, pasting, and otherwise butchering text as you edit, a stray empty space with leading three times what you want for your text can cause you long minutes (or more, if you're unlucky) of aggravation while you figure out why the paragraph is leaded funny.

Allowing InDesign to Set the Leading

Unless you enter a specific leading value, InDesign will automatically lead your type by a default leading value of 120% of its point size. This may or may not be appropriate for your design. I prefer to control the leading by entering a specific value. When InDesign is setting the leading value automatically, that value is in parentheses in the Character palette, as it is in Figure 9.1.

If you have already specified a leading value, but want to return leading control to InDesign, first select the text you want to have an Auto leading value. Then go to the Character palette and select Auto from the Leading option menu, shown below. Alternately, you can press Shift+Alt/Option+Ctrl/Cmd+A to apply Auto leading.

SETTING THE LEADING

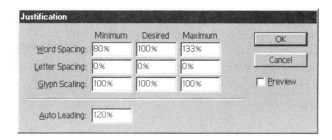

You can change the default leading percentage by clicking the arrow at the right of the Paragraph palette to open the Paragraph palette menu, shown in Figure 9.4. Select Justification to open the Justification dialog box, shown below.

Enter a new value in the Auto Leading value box. InDesign will accept Auto leading percentages from 0% to 500%. Entering an Auto leading value while no text is selected will make that value the default Auto leading value. If you selected text before opening this dialog box, you will be setting the Auto leading value only for the selected text. If you selected text that has Auto leading applied to it, you can preview changes by clicking the Preview checkbox in the Justification dialog box to see how the new value will affect the selected text.

Manually Setting the Leading

To manually specify leading, select the text to which you want to apply the leading value, then go to the Character palette, shown in Figure 9.1.

The Leading value box is to the right of the Leading icon. InDesign will accept numerical leading values from 0 points to 5000 points. You can enter incremental values down to 0.001.

Go to the Leading value box of the Character palette and enter a numerical leading value, or pull down the Leading option menu and select one of the leading values.

You can select a leading value from this menu, or you can select Auto to apply InDesign's Auto leading value to the selected type.

You can also increase or decrease the leading of lines of type by pressing Shift and Control/Command and then the up arrow to increase the size by one increment or the down arrow to decrease the size by one increment. Increase or decrease the size by five increments by pressing Shift, Alt/Option, Control/Command, and then the up or down arrow. The increments are determined by the amount specified in the Size/Leading value box of the Units & Increments preference dialog box, which you access by choosing File ➢ Preferences ➢ Units & Increments.

Adjusting the Spaces between Letters with Kerning and Tracking

Now that we've covered how to specify the spacing between lines of type, let's tackle the settings for the spacing between letters and characters of type. The two types of vertical spacing between letters and characters are tracking and kerning.

Tracking is the amount of space applied equally to the spaces between a range of type letters and characters. Tracking is used during typefitting (called *composition* in InDesign), which is when blocks of text are fitted within a defined design space. Tracking is also used for specific typographic designs that call for type to be spread out. Examples of tracked type are shown below. (Composition is presented in detail in Chapter 14.)

Tracking: 0 **Mastering InDesign**

Tracking: 200 **M a s t e r i n g   I n D e s i g n**

Tracking: –50 **Mastering InDesign**

Kerning is the amount of space applied between only two individual type letters or characters. Kerning is used to correct the visual imbalance caused by two alphabetic or numerical characters that, when set normally side-by-side, appear to be too far apart. An example of a kerned pair is shown below.

AW   AW
We   We
Tr   Tr

With Kerning   Without Kerning

When you type or import text, InDesign will automatically kern certain character pairs, using either metrics kerning or optical kerning. *Metrics kerning* is based on measurement information embedded in the specific font's file and is the default setting.

However, InDesign will also automatically kern based on the appearance of type, which is called *optical kerning*. You use optical kerning when a font's embedded metrics kerning information just doesn't please you, but you don't want to go to the trouble of manually kerning the type.

You switch from metrics kerning to optical kerning by selecting one or the other from the Kerning option menu of the Character palette, shown below.

If you select Metrics kerning or Optical kerning when no text is selected, that setting becomes the default setting.

Identifying the Tracking and Kerning Settings

To check the tracking setting of type, select a range of text more than two characters long (for tracking). The tracking value setting will appear in the Tracking value box of the Character palette.

To check the kerning setting of type, place the text insertion point between two letters. The kerning value setting will appear in the Kerning value box of the Character palette.

When Metrics or Optical kerning is selected, the automatic kerning value for a specific kerned pair is shown in parentheses in the Kerning value box.

Manually Specifying Tracking

When you want to manually define the tracking for a range of characters, first you must select those characters. You can select as few as two characters, a paragraph, or as much as an entire story.

Go to the Character palette and either enter a specific tracking value or pull down the Tracking option menu, shown below, to select one of the offered values.

The increments used in the Character palette are only 0.001 of an em space. That's really tiny. If you enter a "1," InDesign reads that as 0.001, a "2" as 0.002, and so on. So you may need to enter a fairly high number before you see any obvious spacing difference.

Manually Specifying Kerning

To kern two characters, place the text insertion point between any two characters. The kerning value will appear in the Kerning value box in the Character palette.

Enter a specific kerning value or pull down the Kerning option menu to select one of the offered values.

Once again, the increments used in the Character palette are only 0.001 of an em space. That's really tiny. If you enter a "1," InDesign reads that as 0.001, a "2" as 0.002, and so on. With kerning, however, you may see a noticeable difference with smaller amounts.

Alternately, you can adjust the kerning by placing the text insertion point between two characters and then pressing a combination of keys. The default increment used when kerning with the keyboard shortcuts is 0.02, rather than the 0.001 amounts in the Character palette. So you'll see results much faster and have less precise control.

You can change this increment by choosing File ➤ Preferences ➤ Units & Increments and entering a new value in the Kerning value box.

The shortcuts for kerning are listed in Tables 9.2 and 9.3.

TABLE 9.2: WINDOWS KERNING KEYBOARD SHORTCUTS

Kerning Adjustment	Keyboard Shortcut
Decrease Kerning by 0.02 em	Alt+Left Arrow
Increase Kerning by 0.02 em	Alt+Right Arrow
Decrease Kerning by 0.10 em	Ctrl+Alt+Left Arrow
Increase Kerning by 0.10 em	Ctrl+Alt+Right Arrow
Clear all tracking and kerning	Shift+Ctrl+Q

TABLE 9.3: MAC KERNING KEYBOARD SHORTCUTS

Kerning Adjustment	Keyboard Shortcut
Decrease Kerning by 0.02 em	Option+Left Arrow
Increase Kerning by 0.02 em	Option+Right Arrow
Decrease Kerning by 0.10 em	Cmd+Option+Left Arrow
Increase Kerning by 0.10 em	Cmd+Option+Right Arrow
Clear all tracking and kerning	Shift+Cmd+Q

Setting Paragraph Specifications

Such typesetting attributes as paragraph indents, automatic spacing between paragraphs, text alignment, and drop caps are specified in the Paragraph palette, shown in Figure 9.7. These paragraph attributes are applied to all text between paragraph returns and can not be applied to individual characters.

FIGURE 9.7

Paragraph palette

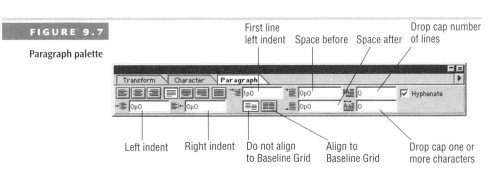

To apply paragraph attributes, you need to select the Text tool, then select a paragraph within a text frame. You can place the text insertion point anywhere within the paragraph you wish to adjust—you don't need to highlight the entire paragraph.

You enter values in the Paragraph palette as you do in other palettes and dialog boxes. Simply highlight the value you want to edit and then type in the value you want. Remember, you can press the Tab key to move forward through the available values boxes, and you can press Shift+Tab to move backward through the values boxes.

TIP Paragraph formatting affects all text between one paragraph return and the next. If you ever want to break a line without creating a new paragraph, press Shift as you press Enter. This action enters a *soft return*, which breaks the line but doesn't start a new paragraph.

Setting Alignment

Paragraph alignment refers to how the text in a paragraph conforms to the columns and margins of its text frame. For example, as shown below, the text in some paragraphs is even along one side, but uneven, or ragged, along the other side, while the text of some paragraphs is even on both sides, with the last line allowed to remain short and to the left. The seven alignment formats available in InDesign are:

Flush Left/Ragged Right   Lines of type are even along the left side and uneven on the right.

> Back in the old days, when type was set by hand from big, divided drawers that contained one size of one type face and style, a font was the term used to designate that one set of type.

Centered   Lines of type are centered between the column sides or margins.

> Back in the old days, when
> type was set by hand from big,
> divided drawers that contained
> one size of one type face and
> style, a font was the term used
> to designate that one set of
> type.

Flush Right/Ragged Left Lines of type are even along the right side and uneven on the left.

> Back in the old days, when
> type was set by hand from big,
> divided drawers that contained
> one size of one type face and
> style, a font was the term used
> to designate that one set of
> type.

Justified Lines of type are even on both sides and the last line is allowed to end short of the right side.

> Back in the old days, when type
> was set by hand from big, divided
> drawers that contained one size
> of one type face and style, a font
> was the term used to designate
> that one set of type.

Center Justified Lines of type are even on both sides and the last line is centered.

> Back in the old days, when type
> was set by hand from big, divided
> drawers that contained one size
> of one type face and style, a font
> was the term used to designate
> that one set of type.

Right Justified Lines of type are even on both sides and the last line is moved to the right side.

> Back in the old days, when type
> was set by hand from big, divided
> drawers that contained one size
> of one type face and style, a font
> was the term used to designate
> that one set of type.

Justify All/Force Justified All of the lines of type are even on both sides, including any short last lines, which are then stretched (sometimes awkwardly) across the width of the column.

> Back in the old days, when type was set by hand from big, divided drawers that contained one size of one type face and style, a font was the term used to designate that one set of type.

To apply an alignment option, first choose the Text tool and select a text frame. Place the text insertion point anywhere in a paragraph or select a block of paragraphs. Then access the Paragraph palette, shown in Figure 9.7, by choosing Type ➢ Paragraph or by pressing Ctrl/Cmd+M.

Now simply click on one of the alignment option buttons to apply that option to the selected paragraph or paragraphs.

Alternately, you can use the keyboard shortcuts listed in Table 9.4 to apply an alignment option.

TABLE 9.4: PARAGRAPH ALIGNMENT KEYBOARD SHORTCUTS

Paragraph Format	Keyboard Shortcut
Flush Left/Ragged Right	Shift+Ctrl/Cmd+L
Centered	Shift+Ctrl/Cmd+C
Flush Right/Ragged Left	Shift+Ctrl/Cmd+R
Justified Left	Shift+Ctrl/Cmd+J
Full Justified/Force Justified	Shift+Ctrl/Cmd+F
Justified Right	Shift+Alt/Option+Ctrl/Cmd+R
Justified Center	Shift+Alt/Option+Ctrl/Cmd+C

 TIP You can actually apply both left justification and right justification to a single line of text so that you can spread out words or characters with empty space between. Simply apply left justification to the line, then enter a Tab character between the words you want to spread and then apply right justification. The line will retain its left justification, but any type after the tab will align right.

Optical Margin Alignment

In addition to the other alignment options, InDesign offers *optical margin alignment*, also called *hanging punctuation*, which aligns the text in a paragraph along one edge, but allows any punctuation that winds up at the margin edge to intrude into the gutter or margin. This feature can be useful for some design applications, but it applies to all paragraphs in an entire story and even hyphens will hang over, so you'll want to be careful about applying it. Text must be aligned right, left, centered, or justified. An example of optical margin alignment is shown in Figure 9.8.

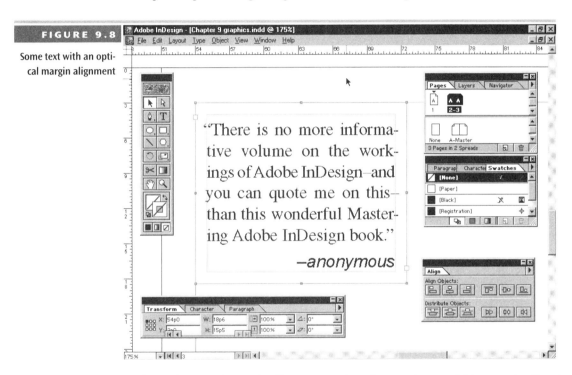

FIGURE 9.8

Some text with an optical margin alignment

To apply optical margin alignment, select the text frame which contains the story to which you want to apply the feature. (You don't actually have to use the Text tool for this selection.) Now choose Type ➢ Story to open the Story palette, shown below.

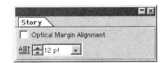

Click the Optical Margin Alignment checkbox. The value box at the bottom specifies the amount of overhang and you may need to experiment with the various values to decide which works best. The optimum value may be the same amount as the point size of the type.

Using Tabs and Indents

As you probably know, *tabs* allow you to specify where certain text will align along a horizontal line of type. You can specify tabs that will align text from that tab to the right, tabs that will align text from that tab to the left, tabs that will center text on that tab, and tabs that will align text along a decimal point or other character you specify. You can also fill tabbed spaces with a character to create dot leaders or other design effects. Setting a tab applies that tab to the entire selected paragraph.

Tab characters, entered by pressing the Tab key, can be entered in the text either before or after setting the tabs.

Indents are different from tabs—they only allow you to move text in from the edges of a frame or to indent the first line of a paragraph.

TIP Don't use tabs when you really should use indents. For example, paragraphs should be indented, not tabbed. Use the First Line Left Indent setting for paragraph indents. Tabs should be used between indents when you want to align text vertically, for example, in a table. Too many tabs can create formatting problems when you have to go back through and remove them.

If someone gives you a text file that has been tabbed for its paragraph indents, you can quickly remove these tabs without harming any other tabs by using the Find/Change command. Choose the Text tool and select all of the text that contains the unwanted tabs. Then choose Edit ➢ Find/Change or press Ctrl/Cmd+F to open the Find/Change dialog box. Open the Special Characters option menu at the right of the Find What text area, then select End of Paragraph. Alternately, you can just enter "^p" in the Find What text entry area. Then select Tab Character from the Special Characters option menu or enter "^t". In the Change To text area, either enter "^p" or select End of Paragraph from the Special Characters option menu. This action will remove all tabs that occur immediately after a paragraph return and replace them with a paragraph return. Now you need to specify the First Line Indent, which is presented below.

Setting Tabs

By default, InDesign automatically sets tabs at 3 pica/.5 inch increments. To set your own tabs, choose the Text tool and select the text to which you want to specify tabs. Then choose Type ➢ Tabs or press Shift+Ctrl/Cmd+T to open the Tabs palette, shown next.

SETTING PARAGRAPH SPECIFICATIONS

The default version of the Tabs palette floats in the InDesign work area and displays only a portion of the tab ruler. This may work okay for you, but if you're like me, you want to see the tab ruler aligned with and associated with the text to which you are applying tabs. To get the Tabs palette to align with the text, scroll the page view to show the top of the text frame on which you are working, then click the Magnet icon on the right side of the Tabs palette. This action will snap the Tabs palette to the text frame and display the tab ruler associated with the available text area, as shown below.

NOTE If you are a QuarkXPress user, you will notice how inconvenient this default Tabs palette is. I hope that future versions of InDesign won't require you to scroll to the top of a text frame to snap the Tabs palette to the text. This may cause a lot more work when trying to add tabs only to a small portion of a longer story. For now, if you want the tab ruler to be closer to the portion of the text for which you are actually setting the tab or tabs, go ahead and scroll up to the top of the text frame, align the Tabs palette by clicking the Magnet icon, then scroll the page view back to where you want it.

InDesign offers four different tab-alignment options.

Left-Justified Tab This is the most commonly used tab setting, used when you want words to line up on the left side of a tab stop.

Center-Justified Tab Often used in tabular material, this tab aligns text around the center of tab stop so the text looks (surprise!) like it's centered.

Right Justified-Tab Most commonly used to align numbers in tabular material, this setting aligns text on the right side of a tab stop.

Align to Decimal (or Other Specified Character) Tab You can use this tab to produce lists of numbers that line up neatly on the decimal point, but you can also create leadered entries in tables of contents using any leader character you wish.

To set a tab, choose the Text tool and position the text insertion point anywhere in the paragraph for which you want a tab or tabs. You can also select an entire story by choosing Edit ➢ Select All or pressing Ctrl/Cmd+A.

Now open the Tabs palette by choosing Type ➢ Tabs or by pressing Shift+Ctrl/Cmd+T. Select the tab-alignment option you want by clicking the appropriate button. Once you have done this, you can set a tab by clicking anywhere in the area just above the ruler, where you can see the triangular indent icons, as shown below.

Alternately, you can enter a tab by typing in its X value, which defines its position across the horizontal line. You'll notice that the X value appears whenever you click to create a tab, or whenever you select a tab for editing. You must press Tab, Enter, or Return to set the value.

TIP If you aren't exactly sure where you want your tab set, but you do want it to be positioned with some numerical exactitude, try this: Go ahead and click to set a tab in the Tabs palette, at the approximate position you want the tab. Then go to the X: value box and refine the position. For example, after clicking you see that the tab is set at the 1.2678" position. You could enter "1.25" in the X value to set it at a more "even" position.

You can repeat this operation for as many tabs as you want, as long as they are separated by at least one point. Once they are set, you can refine their positions down to 0.01 points.

If you are entering multiple tabs that are equidistant apart, just set the first one and then choose Repeat Tab from the Tabs palette menu, shown below.

To set a tab that aligns on decimal points (perhaps for dollar amounts), or any other character, select the decimal tab-alignment button. Then set the tab as you would any other tab. Enter a period or any other character in the Align On value box.

Editing Tabs

Once you have set a tab, you can alter its position or change its tab type.

To change the position of a tab, click on its tab stop marker above the ruler in the Tabs palette to select it. You can then drag it to another position, or you can enter a new value in the X value box and press Tab, Enter, or Return.

To change a tab from one type to another, click on its tab stop marker above the ruler in the Tabs palette to select it. Then click on any of the tab-alignment buttons or press Alt/Option and click the tab stop marker to cycle through the tab-alignment options.

Removing Tabs

To remove one tab, select its tab stop marker and drag it away from the tab ruler. To remove all the tabs, choose Clear All from the Tabs palette menu.

Setting Fill Characters

Those cute little dotted lines that cross from one tabbed text to another are called *leaders*, because they *lead* your eye across an otherwise empty space. You can use any one character or a pattern of up to eight characters for the fill.

To set the fill character, set and select any tab. Enter a character or characters in the Leader value box of the Tabs palette, shown below.

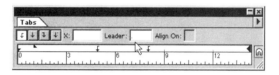

The font that is used for the leader characters can be any font you choose. To change the font, simply select the tab character in the text frame, then specify a type family, style, and/or size of the character in the Character palette or Type menu, as described earlier in this chapter.

Setting Indents

Once again, indents are the feature you use to specify your first line indents for paragraphs, as well as for any other time when you wish to set your text in from the edges of the text frame or text frame inset. (Text frame insets are discussed later in this chapter.) You can set indents either via the Paragraph palette or the Tabs palette.

InDesign provides three indent options: first line left indent, left indent, and right indent.

To set indents for your text using the Paragraph palette, choose the Text tool and select the paragraph to which you want to apply the indent. Then enter a value in the value box for the indent option you want.

To set indents for your text using the Tabs palette, choose the Text tool and select the paragraph to which you want to apply the indent. Choose Type ➢ Tabs or press Shift+Ctrl/Cmd+T to open the Tabs palette, shown next.

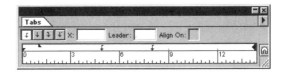

The indents are represented by the solid triangle to the far right of the tab ruler and the split triangle to the left, as shown below. If there is a first line left indent set, the two halves of the split triangle on the left will be separated, with the position of the top half indicating the first line left indent.

To change the indents from the Tab palette, simply drag the triangle indent markers to the positions you want. Notice that when you drag the bottom half of the split triangle, the top half moves with it, retaining its first line left indent amount. But if you drag the top half of the split triangle, you adjust the amount of first line left indent only.

Alternately, you can select one of these split triangle halves or the right-side indent marker and enter values for them in the X value box. The numerical value of whichever marker is selected appears in the X value box.

Setting Hanging Indents

A *hanging indent* is when the first line of a paragraph is actually to the left of the following lines of text. You can set a hanging indent in the Tabs palette by dragging the top half of the split triangle to the left of the bottom half.

You can set a hanging indent in the Paragraph palette by entering a negative value, such as "-.25", in the First Line Left Indent value box.

If you are formatting a bulleted list and you want the bullet to be to the left of all the text and have the text aligned on the left, follow these steps:

1. Type a bullet (Alt/Option+8), then a tab character, followed by your list entry.
2. Access the Tabs palette by choosing Type ➢ Tabs or pressing Shift+Ctrl/Cmd+T.
3. Drag both halves of the split triangle to the position where you want the text aligned on the left.
4. Drag the top half of the split triangle to the position where you want the bullet to align.
5. Set a left-aligned tab stop right on top of the bottom half of the split triangle. You can do this visually or by comparing their values in the X value box. Now your type will start and align on that tab.

Automatically Adding Space before and/or after a Paragraph

Don't use extra paragraph returns to add space between paragraphs. When you use extra paragraph returns, the space between paragraphs will be governed by the leading of the extra returns, which might be more or less than you really want. If you have a whole bunch of extra returns and you want to reduce or increase the space between paragraphs, think of how tedious it would be to go through and select and change each one. You wouldn't be able to change them all at once without also changing the leading of the text between them. Using the Space Before and Space After options allows you to select all the text at once and swiftly change the amount of space between the paragraphs.

Creating Drop Caps

This paragraph begins with a *drop cap*, sometimes called an *initial cap*. InDesign will typeset these features for you at the beginning of any and all paragraphs you select. Drop caps can be one or more characters. Drop caps can be pretty much any number of lines that you want for the height of the character or characters, but you don't want to overdo it. As you can see below, you can create many different looks for drop caps.

This paragraph begins with a *drop cap*, sometimes called an *initial cap*. InDesign will typeset these features for you at the beginning of any and all paragraphs you select. Drop caps can be one or more characters. Drop caps can be pretty much any number of lines that you want for the height of the character or characters, but you don't want to overdo it. As you can see below, you can create many different looks for drop caps.

This paragraph begins with a *drop cap*, sometimes called an *initial cap*. InDesign will typeset these features for you at the beginning of any and all paragraphs you select. Drop caps can be one or more characters. Drop caps can be pretty much any number of lines that you want for the height of the character or characters, but you don't want to overdo it. As you can see below, you can create many different looks for drop caps.

This paragraph begins with a *drop cap*, sometimes called an *initial cap*. InDesign will typeset these features for you at the beginning of any and all paragraphs you select. Drop caps can be one or more characters. Drop caps can be pretty much any number of lines that you want for the height of the character or characters, but you don't want to overdo it. As you can see below, you can create many different looks for drop caps.

To set drop caps, choose the Text tool and select one or more paragraphs. Access the Paragraph palette by choosing Type ➢ Paragraph or by pressing Ctrl/Cmd+M.

Enter a value in the Drop Cap Number of Lines value box, shown below, for the number of lines tall you want the drop cap character to appear.

Now enter a value in the Drop Cap One or More Characters value box, shown below, for the number of characters you want to make up the drop cap.

You can format a drop cap just as you can any other type character to adjust its size, style, and/or font.

Adding Rules to Text

Typeset *rules* are lines that are associated with particular paragraphs of type. These rules are *not* underlines. Rules can be placed above or below a paragraph, they can be of any weight you choose, and they can be moved up and down in relation to the baseline. You can even use a rule to create a colored background for type.

T I P Don't draw lines under your text when you want the lines to be associated with the text and move with the text as it reflows during editing. If you draw lines, you'll have to go back and find them, then move them accordingly. Rules always stay right with the text to which you originally applied them, no matter what the text does.

To set a rule or rules for a particular paragraph, choose the Text tool and select the paragraph to which you want to add a rule or rules. Choose Type ➢ Paragraph or press Ctrl/Cmd+M to open the Paragraph palette.

Now choose Paragraph Rules from the Paragraph palette menu, shown below, to open the Paragraph Rules dialog box, shown in Figure 9.9.

FIGURE 9.9

Paragraph Rules dialog box

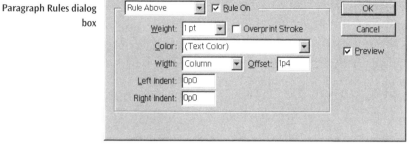

You access both the Rule Above and Rule Below options in the Paragraph Rules dialog box. Select one or the other from the option menu at the top of the dialog box. Both dialog boxes offer the same options and operate the same way. If you want to preview the rule before accepting it, click the Preview checkbox.

To turn on a rule, click the Rule On checkbox. Conversely, to turn off the rule, simply click the Rule On checkbox again.

WARNING Don't make the mistake of thinking that opening the Paragraph Rules dialog box and then clicking Cancel actually cancels the rule. That action only cancels and closes the dialog box. You must use the Rule On checkbox to turn rules on and off.

You specify the weight, or thickness, of the rule in the Weight value box. You can either enter a numerical value or open the option menu to select an offered value. When entering weight values for a rule above, the rule grows taller up from its bottom. When entering weight values for a rule below, the rule grows deeper down from its top.

The default color for a rule is the color of the text and is specified in the Color text area by (Text Color). You can change this color to any color currently listed in the swatches palette by opening the Color option menu and selecting a color. (Selecting colors is discussed in Chapter 12.)

The width of the rule refers to how wide it is in relation to the column of text. Selecting Text will draw the rule only as wide as the text in the column. Selecting Column will draw the rule the full width of the column, minus any text frame inset, which is also shown below. The Column option ignores any indents applied to the text.

The Offset value determines how far the rule will be drawn from the baseline of the first or last line of text in that paragraph. You can specify a numerical value down to 0.001.

You specify how much you may want to indent the rule by entering values in the Left Indent and Right Indent values boxes. These indent values will be subtracted from the width of the rule, whether you have selected Column or Text for the width. These values do not affect the type.

The Overprint Stroke option protects the rule in case the rule appears over another color. When printed with the Overprint Stroke option selected, the rule will be printed above any color background, protecting its print quality.

To use a paragraph rule as a background box for type, open the Paragraph Rules dialog box and apply either a rule above or rule below. Then enter negative values for the offset and positive values for the weight. A good rule of thumb for starting out is to use the same point values for the weight and offset, entering the offset value as a negative. Then experiment with the weight and offset to refine it. The example below was drawn with an offset of "-p28" and a width of "40 pts".

Mastering Adobe InDesign

Specifying a Text Frame Inset

A *text frame inset* moves text in from the outline of a text frame. A text frame inset is often used for margins when setting type in a colored or bordered box.

To specify a text frame inset, select any text frame with any selection tool. Choose Object ➤ Text Frame Options or press Ctrl/Cmd+B to open the Text Frame Options dialog box, shown in Figure 9.10.

FIGURE 9.10
Text Frame Options dialog box

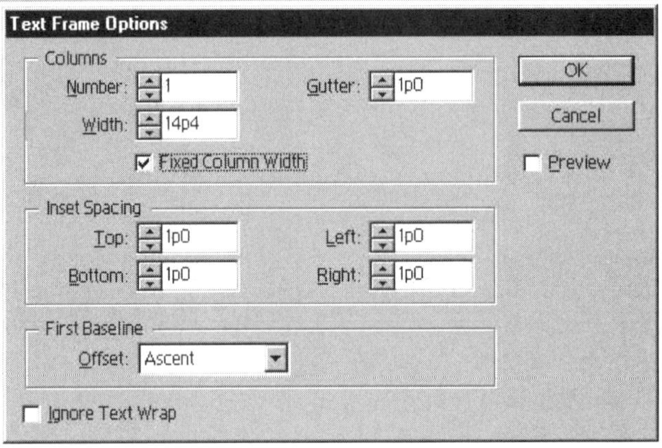

Specify text inset by entering values in the Inset Spacing value boxes or by clicking the up or down arrows at each box to raise or lower the currently specified value.

You can specify different text inset values for each of the four sides of a rectangular text frame, but only one value for irregular and polygonal text frames.

chapter 10

Saving Time with Type Styles

Featuring:

- *Defining styles* — *232*
- *Applying styles* — *249*
- *Modifying styles* — *251*
- *Importing styles* — *253*

Saving Time with Type Styles

One of the most tedious operations in desktop publishing can be type formatting. Just think of all the different text blocks and stories in a multi-page document, and how all of those text blocks and stories have text that must be formatted. You're spending a lot of time selecting text and applying all of those different type styles.

Not only that, but how about even after you've done all the original formatting? What about when someone suddenly decides that all of the subheads that you so carefully and individually formatted now need to be changed to reflect a new design effect? Now you must go through and tediously reformat each and every one of them.

Don't do either. In this chapter, I'll show you how to apply sweeping formatting changes to text using character and paragraph styles.

Styles are collections of type formatting that you define and then apply to text. They can apply any of the formatting options you can apply manually, and they do it all at once. When you update or change the style, the changes are automatically applied to all text in the document that has been assigned that style. Not only that, but you can set them so that when you're typing in a block of text that has been set with a style, you automatically go to another style of your choosing when you press Return.

You can create styles from scratch in a document or you can bring in styles from other documents.

You should use character styles when all you want is to apply font character formatting attributes. When you want to apply both character and paragraph formatting attributes, you should use paragraph styles.

Working with the Style Palettes

The Character Styles and Paragraph Styles palettes store the defined styles and provide the navigation and editing commands necessary to edit and import the various styles. As you'll see below, they look pretty much the same and work in the same ways.

The Character Styles Palette

Access the Character Styles palette shown in Figure 10.1, by choosing Type ➢ Character Styles, pressing Shift+F11, or clicking its tab in its palette group.

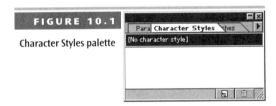

FIGURE 10.1
Character Styles palette

Access the Character Styles palette menu, shown in Figure 10.2, by clicking and holding the arrowhead to the right of the Character Styles palette tab.

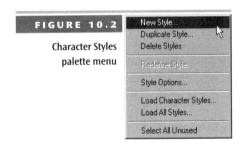

FIGURE 10.2
Character Styles palette menu

The Paragraph Styles Palette

Access the Paragraph Styles palette, shown in Figure 10.3, by choosing Type ➢ Paragraph Styles, pressing F11, or clicking its tab in its palette group.

FIGURE 10.3
Paragraph Styles palette

Access the Paragraph Styles palette menu, shown in Figure 10.4, by clicking and holding the arrowhead to the right of the Paragraph Styles palette tab.

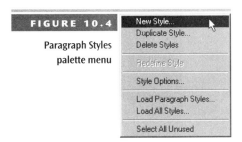

FIGURE 10.4
Paragraph Styles palette menu

Using the Character Styles and Paragraph Styles Palettes

As you can see in Figures 10.1 and 10.3, by default, no styles are defined until you create and define them.

Styles are listed alphabetically by their names. When you place the text insertion point in a text frame, the name of any style applied to that range of text will highlight in the two styles palettes. If no style is applied to that range of text, the [No Paragraph Style] bar will highlight. If more than one style is applied to that range of text, no styles will highlight.

If you apply a style to a range of text and then make some formatting changes to that text, a plus mark will appear after the style name, as shown below, indicating that the selected text has been formatted differently than the originally applied style.

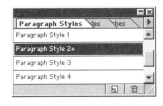

Imported styles will appear in the list with a small floppy disk icon, as shown below, indicating that they are imported.

When you have more styles than can be listed in the default palette, a scroll bar will appear on the right to allow you to navigate to the desired style, as shown in the examples above. When you select text that has a style applied to it that is not currently visible in the palette list, that name will highlight and the list will automatically scroll to show the name of the style.

From the palette menus, shown in Figures 10.2 and 10.4, you can perform operations ranging from creating new styles to duplicating, deleting, and importing styles.

Defining Styles

When creating new styles, you can create one that is based on selected text, without any changes and with a default name, or you can create one that is based on selected text and make changes to its formatting and/or give it a name before accepting it.

NOTE Character styles contain only character-level formatting attributes, but paragraph styles contain both character-level formatting attributes and paragraph-level attributes. So if you want to define a style that changes the font and size of selected text, but doesn't change the alignment or first line left indent of selected text, define and apply a character style. If you want to define a style that changes both the font and the alignment of the selected text, define and apply a paragraph style.

Defining a Style on a Range of Formatted Text, Without Changes

To define a new style without changing any formatting, choose the Text tool and select a range of text. Click the New Style button in either the Character Styles palette or the Paragraph Styles palette.

This action creates the new style immediately and names it according to its order in the style palette. For example, if the last style named by InDesign was "Character Style 2," the new style will be based on the selected text and given the name "Character Style 3."

After the new style is created, you can edit it as you would any other style, following the procedures for editing styles described later in this chapter.

NOTE If you create a new style while no text is selected, the new style will be based on the default type formatting attributes. The default formatting attributes are set when you specify formatting attributes with no text selected.

Defining a Style on a Range of Selected Text, with Changes

To make changes to a style's formatting and/or give it a name as you create it, choose the Text tool and select the text on which you want to base the style. Choose New Style from either the Character Styles palette or the Paragraph Styles palette to open the New Character Style dialog box, which is shown in Figure 10.5.

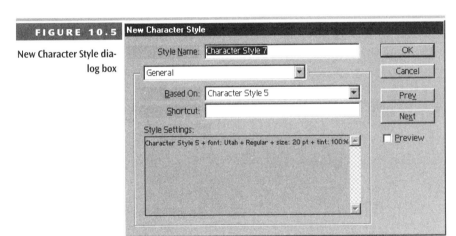

FIGURE 10.5

New Character Style dialog box

The New Character Style dialog box opens to the General options. The default name for the style is displayed in the Style Name text area and the formatting attributes from the selected text are displayed in the Style Settings box.

To see formatting changes applied to the selected text as you change them in the New Style dialog box, click the Preview checkbox.

Basing the New Style on an Existing Style

The Based On text area and option menu indicate what style, if any, that the new style will be based on. This feature creates a "parent/child" link between styles. When you change the formatting of the "parent" style, any formatting attributes that are common to the two styles are changed automatically in the "child." Formatting attributes that are unique to the individual styles are not changed. In other words, let's say you create Style 1, based on no styles, then duplicate that style and base the Style 2 on Style 1. Then you create Style 3, based on Style 2. From then on, all changes to Style 1 would be reflected in the formatting attributes in Style 1 that are also in Styles 2 and 3. Changes to Style 2 would be reflected in the common formatting attributes of Style 3, but not in Style 1.

Is that as clear as mud, or what? Take a look at Table 10.1 and the graphics beneath it. I'll use these to give you a more detailed explanation of how the Based On relationships work.

TABLE 10.1: SAMPLE STYLES

Style Name	Style Attributes
STYLE 1	Arial, 9 pt. size, 10 pt. leading, Left alignment, First Line Left Indent 1p0
STYLE 2	Based On: Style 1 + Center Alignment, First Line Left Indent 0p0
STYLE 3	Based On: Style 2 + 14 pt. leading

Lorem ipsum dolor sit amet, consectetuer adipiscing elit, sed diam nonummy nibh euismod tincidunt ut laoreet dolore magna aliquam erat volutpat. Ut wisi enim ad minim veniam, quis nostrud exerci tation ullamcorper suscipit lobortis nisl ut aliquip ex ea commodo consequat.

Lorem ipsum dolor sit amet, consectetuer adipiscing elit, sed diam nonummy nibh euismod tincidunt ut laoreet dolore magna aliquam erat volutpat. Ut wisi enim ad minim veniam, quis nostrud exerci tation ullamcorper suscipit lobortis nisl ut aliquip ex ea commodo consequat.

Lorem ipsum dolor sit amet, consectetuer adipiscing elit, sed diam nonummy nibh euismod tincidunt ut laoreet dolore magna aliquam erat volutpat. Ut wisi enim ad minim veniam, quis nostrud exerci tation ullamcorper suscipit lobortis nisl ut aliquip ex ea commodo consequat.

See how each paragraph contains the same text, but has different type formatting. Here are some facts you should see about the above styles and their paragraphs:

- Style 1 is set with Arial at 9 points, with 10 points of leading, left alignment, and a first line left indent of 1 pica.
- Because Style 2 is based on Style 1, it also has all of those attributes, but it is center aligned and has no first line left indent.
- Because Style 3 is based on Style 2, which is based on Style 1, Style 3 has all of the same attributes of Style 1, plus the attributes added by Style 2, plus leading of 14 points instead of 10.

Okay, so now I'm going to change the type face family in Style 1 to Times. The graphic below shows how that affects the three paragraphs.

Lorem ipsum dolor sit amet, consectetuer adipiscing elit, sed diam nonummy nibh euismod tincidunt ut laoreet dolore magna aliquam erat volutpat. Ut wisi enim ad minim veniam, quis nostrud exerci tation ullamcorper suscipit lobortis nisl ut aliquip ex ea commodo consequat.

Lorem ipsum dolor sit amet, consectetuer adipiscing elit, sed diam nonummy nibh euismod tincidunt ut laoreet dolore magna aliquam erat volutpat. Ut wisi enim ad minim veniam, quis nostrud exerci tation ullamcorper suscipit lobortis nisl ut aliquip ex ea commodo consequat.

Lorem ipsum dolor sit amet, consectetuer adipiscing elit, sed diam nonummy nibh euismod tincidunt ut laoreet dolore magna aliquam erat volutpat. Ut wisi enim ad minim veniam, quis nostrud exerci tation ullamcorper suscipit lobortis nisl ut aliquip ex ea commodo consequat.

See? They each changed to Times type family, but the formatting attributes that were unique to each one stayed the same.

TIP How can you tell if a style is a parent or child style? When you are in the New Style dialog box or the Modify Style Options dialog box, which is shown in Figure 10.21, you will know if you are in a "parent" style if [No Style] is listed in the Based On text area and you will know if you are in a "child" style if there is a style listed in the Based On text area.

By default, the text style, if any, that was applied to the text you selected before opening the New Style dialog box will appear in the Based On text area. You can base a style on any of the existing styles by either typing in the name for a style or by selecting a style from the Based On option menu.

Here are some guidelines for basing styles on other styles:

- You don't have to base a style on any other style.
- Whichever style you create first will not be based on any style.
- Any style that you base on another style can afterwards be "unbased" simply by selecting [No Style] in the Based On text area of the styles palette.
- A style cannot be based on any of its own child styles.
- The Based On option menu will only offer the available styles.

Assigning a Keyboard Shortcut to a Style

You can also apply a keystroke combination to a style so that you can apply a style to text with that keystroke.

While in the New Character Style dialog box, shown in Figure 10.5, you can define the keystroke combination for a style by pressing Shift+Alt+Ctrl in Windows or Shift+Option+Cmd on the Mac, then pressing any number key on the numeric keypad on the right side of your keyboard. In Windows, make sure Num Lock is turned on.

Pressing a key while holding down these modifiers will automatically enter the keystroke combination in the Shortcut text area of the New Character Style dialog box, as shown in Figure 10.6.

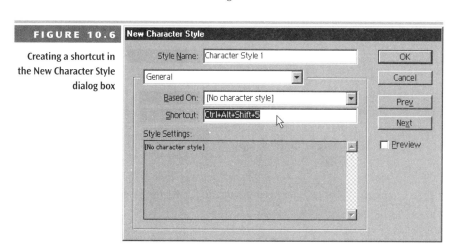

FIGURE 10.6

Creating a shortcut in the New Character Style dialog box

You cannot type in the Shortcut text area of the New Character Style dialog box. You must define the keystroke combination by the method described above.

Defining Styles in the Character Styles Palette

To create a new character style, you don't actually need to select any text, nor do you need to base the style on any particular text. You don't even need to select the Text tool or activate any text frame. You can create a style from scratch by defining it in the Character Styles palette.

To define a style from scratch, choose Type ➢ Character Styles or press Shift+F11 to open the Character Palette.

Now choose New Style from the Character Styles palette menu. This opens the New Character Style dialog box.

 WARNING If you perform this operation while text is selected, the new style will be based on the formatting of that text. If you want to start from scratch, make sure to click away from any text frames before opening the New Character Style dialog box.

As you can see in Figure 10.7, the main option menu lists the four formatting areas you can access to define a new character style. You can move to one of these areas by selecting one from this option menu, or by clicking the Prev or Next buttons in the New Character Style dialog box.

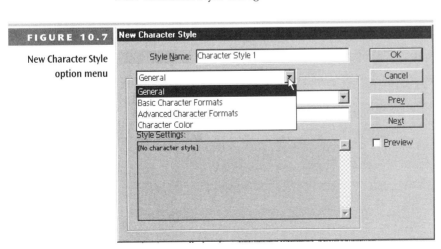

FIGURE 10.7

New Character Style option menu

As with many other dialog boxes, while working in any of the areas of the New Character Style dialog box, you can reset the values to their defaults by pressing Alt/Option to toggle the Cancel button to the Reset button.

Setting Basic Character Formats

Selecting Basic Character Formats or pressing the Next button will open the Basic Character Formats area of the New Character Style dialog box, as shown in Figure 10.8.

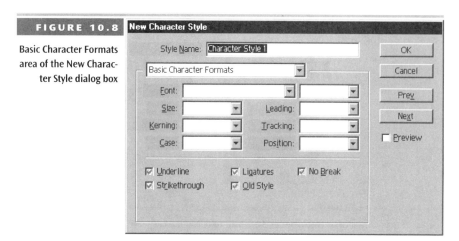

FIGURE 10.8

Basic Character Formats area of the New Character Style dialog box

As you can see, in this area you can define the following character attributes:

- Font (the type family)
- Style
- Size
- Leading
- Kerning
- Tracking
- Case (Normal, Small Caps, All Caps)
- Position (Normal, Superscript, Subscript)

Simply type in the values you want or choose values from the associated option menus.

The Type Style value box is not labeled, but it is the one immediately to the right of the Font value box.

You can also turn on the attributes from the following list by clicking their checkboxes:

- Underline
- Strikethrough
- Ligatures
- Old Style
- No Break

Setting Advanced Character Formats

Selecting Advanced Character Formats or pressing the Next button will open the Advanced Character Formats area of the New Character Style dialog box, as shown in Figure 10.9.

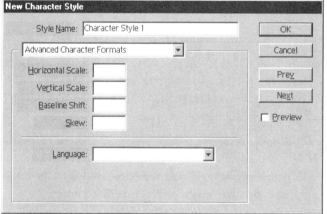

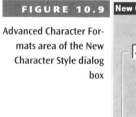

FIGURE 10.9

Advanced Character Formats area of the New Character Style dialog box

As you can see, in this area you can define the following character attributes, which are described in detail in Chapter 14:

- Horizontal Scale
- Vertical Scale
- Baseline Shift
- Skew
- Language

For Horizontal Scale, Vertical Scale, Baseline Shift, and Skew, type in the values you want. For Language, type in a value or select one from the option menu.

Setting Character Color

Selecting Character Color or pressing the Next button will open the Character Color area of the New Character Style dialog box, as shown in Figure 10.10.

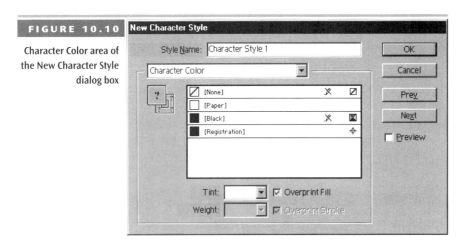

FIGURE 10.10

Character Color area of the New Character Style dialog box

All colors currently available in the Swatches palette appear in the color name display area. (The Swatches palette and selecting and applying color is discussed in Chapter 12.) If you have more colors in the Swatches palette than will display in the color name display area, scroll bars will appear.

 WARNING You won't be able to access the Swatches palette while in the New Character Styles dialog box, so make sure you have selected all the colors you want for your style before you open the New Character Styles dialog box.

You can apply a fill and/or stroke color to the text. Click on either the Fill Color icon or the Stroke Color icon, shown below, to select one.

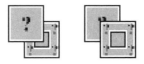

As you can see above, when you open the New Character Style dialog box without selecting any text, these Fill and Stroke Color icons are grayed out and have questions marks in them. If you don't select a color here in the New Character Style dialog box or you select [No Color], black will be applied automatically as a fill color to text to which this new Character Style is applied. In addition, a plus symbol (+) will appear next to the style's name in the Character Styles palette.

To specify a color for either the stroke or the fill, click on its icon and then click on one of the available colors. The name of the color will highlight and the color will appear in the respective color icon, as shown in Figure 10.11.

FIGURE 10.11

New Character Style dialog box with selected color

To remove a color, click on either the Fill Color or Stroke Color icon and then click on [No Color].

In the Tint value box, you can specify a percentage of the color you want applied. Alternately, you can select one of the offered percentages from the Tint option menu.

You can adjust the thickness of the outer stroke by entering a value in the Weight value box or selecting an offered value from the Weight option menu.

You can select Overprint Fill or Overprint Stroke by clicking in their respective checkboxes. Overprint Fill and Overprint Stroke are advanced printing operations, covered in Chapter 18.

Defining Styles in the Paragraph Styles Palette

Just as when creating new character styles, when creating a new paragraph style, you don't actually need to select any text, nor do you need to base the style on any particular text. You don't even need to select the Text tool or activate any text frame. You can create a style from scratch by defining it in the Paragraph Styles palette.

To define a style from scratch, choose Type ➢ Paragraph Styles or press F11 to open the Paragraph Palette.

Now choose New Style from the Paragraph Styles palette menu, as shown below.

This action opens the New Paragraph Style dialog box, shown in Figure 10.12.

WARNING   If you perform this operation while text is selected, the new style will be based on the formatting of that text. If you want to start from scratch, make sure to click away from any text frames before opening the New Paragraph Style dialog box.

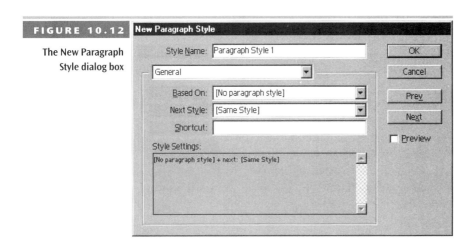

FIGURE 10.12

The New Paragraph Style dialog box

NOTE   The four formatting areas of the New Character Style dialog box: General, Basic Character Formatting, Advanced Character Formatting, and Character Color, all appear here in the New Paragraph Style dialog box. The only difference between those in the New Character Style dialog box and these in the New Paragraph Style dialog box is that the General area has the additional option of New Style.

As you can see in Figure 10.13, the main option menu lists the same formatting areas available in the New Character Styles dialog box, plus the seven additional paragraph formatting areas you can access to define a new paragraph style.

FIGURE 10.13

New Paragraph Style option menu

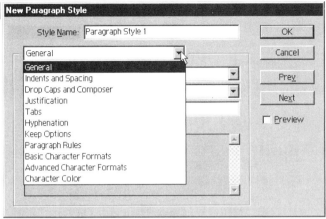

You can move to one of these areas by selecting one from the option menu, as shown above, or by clicking the Prev or Next buttons in the New Paragraph Style dialog box.

While working in any of the areas of the New Paragraph Style dialog box, you can reset the values to their defaults by pressing Alt/Option to toggle the Cancel button to the Reset button.

Setting a Next Style

The Next Style value box that you can see in Figure 10.12 allows you to specify a style to which InDesign will automatically switch when you enter a paragraph return while entering text. For example, you might type a headline or subhead with Style 1 applied to it, then when you enter a paragraph return, InDesign automatically switches to Style 2, which is for body text.

Unlike the Based On option described earlier in this chapter, the Next Style option doesn't limit your choices. You can follow any style with any other style.

Apply a next style by selecting a style from the Next Style option menu.

As you can see in Figure 10.12, one of the possible selections is [Same Style]. You should use this selection when you are entering body text or other styles that won't usually be immediately followed by a change of style.

The [No Paragraph Style] selection also leaves the formatting the same, just as the same thing as the [Same Style] selection, except that it also removes any style link.

Setting Indents and Spacing

Selecting Indents and Spacing or pressing the Next button will open the Indents and Spacing area of the New Paragraph Style dialog box, as shown in Figure 10.14.

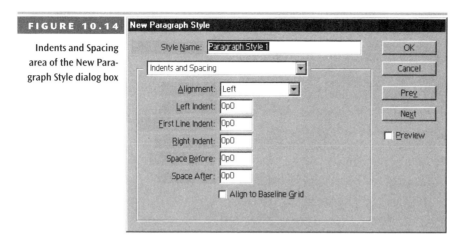

FIGURE 10.14

Indents and Spacing area of the New Paragraph Style dialog box

As you can see, in this area you can define the text alignment by selecting an offered alignment option from the Alignment option menu.

You can also define the following paragraph attributes by entering values in their respective value boxes:

- Left Indent
- First Line Indent
- Right Indent
- Space Before
- Space After

If you want to align the text to the baseline grid, click the checkbox of that name. (Aligning text to the baseline grid is described in Chapter 14.)

Setting Drop Caps and the Composer

Selecting Drop Caps and Composer or pressing the Next button will open the Drop Caps and Composer area of the New Paragraph Style dialog box, as shown in Figure 10.15.

As you can see, in this area you can create a drop cap by entering values in the Lines and Characters value boxes. (Drop caps are discussed in Chapter 9.)

In this area you can also specify the Composer to apply to this style by selecting an offered selection from the Composer option menu. The Composers are explained in Chapter 14.

Setting the Justification

Selecting Justification or pressing the Next button will open the Justification area of the New Paragraph Style dialog box, as shown in Figure 10.16.

DEFINING STYLES 245

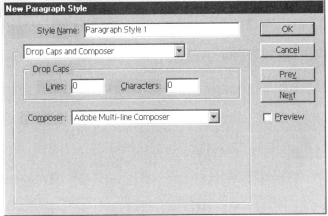

FIGURE 10.15

Drop Caps and Composer area of the New Paragraph Style dialog box

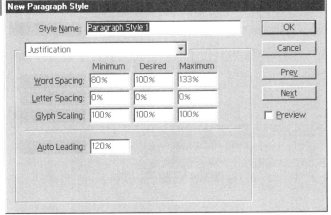

FIGURE 10.16

Justification area of the New Paragraph Style dialog box

As you can see, in this area you can define the values to be used for justification control. (Justification is discussed in Chapter 14.) You can enter Minimum, Desired, and Maximum values for these options:

- Word Spacing
- Letter Spacing
- Glyph Scaling

You can specify a new percentage for InDesign's automatic leading by entering a value in the Auto Leading value box. (Auto leading is discussed in Chapter 9.)

Setting Tabs

Selecting Tabs or pressing the Next button will open the Tabs area of the New Paragraph Style dialog box, as shown in Figure 10.17.

As you can see, in this area you can set the tabs you want for this particular style. (Tabs are discussed in Chapter 9.)

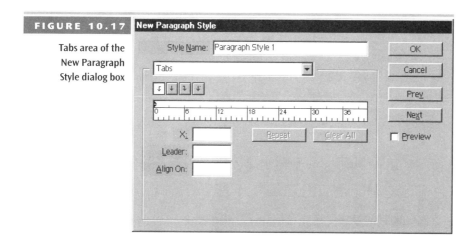

FIGURE 10.17

Tabs area of the New Paragraph Style dialog box

Setting the Hyphenation

Selecting Hyphenation or pressing the Next button will open the Hyphenation area of the New Paragraph Style dialog box, as shown in Figure 10.18.

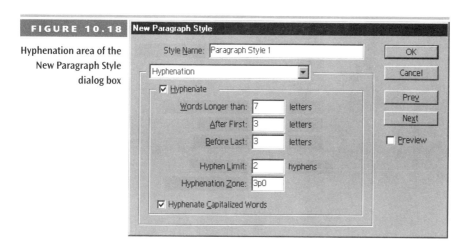

FIGURE 10.18

Hyphenation area of the New Paragraph Style dialog box

As you can see, in this area you can control the hyphenation of this style. (Hyphenation is discussed in Chapter 14.)

If you don't want this style to be hyphenated at all, simply click the Hyphenate checkbox to remove the checkmark.

If you do want this style to be hyphenated, click the Hyphenate checkbox and specify values for the following options:

- Words Longer Than
- After First
- Before Last
- Hyphen Limit
- Hyphenation Zone

You can also elect to stop the hyphenation of capitalized words by clicking the Hyphenate Capitalized Words checkbox.

Setting the Keep Options

Selecting Keep Options or pressing the Next button will open the Keep Options area of the New Paragraph Style dialog box, as shown in Figure 10.19.

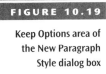

FIGURE 10.19

Keep Options area of the New Paragraph Style dialog box

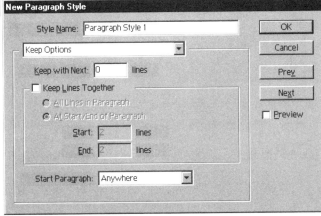

In this area you can control the composition of paragraphs when automatic page breaks occur within the paragraph. (Keep options are discussed in Chapter 14.)

To specify the number of lines from a following paragraph that InDesign will force this style to stay with, enter a value in the Keep with Next value box.

If you want to keep together all of the lines in a paragraph or a specific number of lines in the paragraph, click the Keep Lines Together checkbox to activate the checkmark, then click one of the following options:

- All Lines in Paragraph
- At Start/End of Paragraph

If you select At Start/End of Paragraph, you also need to specify values in the Start and End value boxes.

You can also tell InDesign whether you want this style's paragraph to begin where it naturally occurs, in the next column, or on the next page, by selecting one of the options from the Start Paragraph option menu.

Setting Paragraph Rules

Selecting Paragraph Rules or pressing the Next button will open the Paragraph Rules area of the New Paragraph Style dialog box, as shown in Figure 10.20.

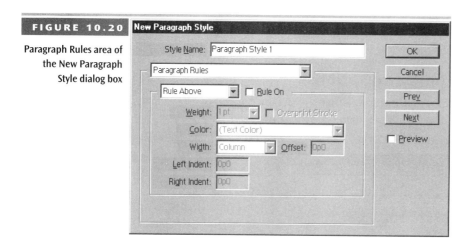

FIGURE 10.20

Paragraph Rules area of the New Paragraph Style dialog box

As you can see, in this area you can create horizontal rules that accompany paragraphs of type. (Rules are discussed in Chapter 9.) Turn rules on and off by clicking the Rule On checkbox. You have the option of specifying a rule above or a rule below the paragraph by selecting one of those options from the option menu just beneath the Paragraph Rules option menu.

For either option, you can specify values for the following options:

- Weight
- Color
- Width
- Offset
- Left Indent
- Right Indent

Remember that to specify a color for the style, you must have selected a color in the Swatches palette.

You can choose the Overprint Stroke option by clicking its checkbox.

Applying Styles

Once you have created a style or styles, you can apply them to text easily by selecting a range of text and then clicking on the name of the style in the appropriate style palette.

Applying Character Styles

Remember that when applying a character style, you are only applying the four formatting option groups that are available in a character style. In other words, when you apply a character style, only character-level attributes are applied to the text and any paragraph-level attributes you may have applied to the text are not affected.

Those four option groups, as described in the section on defining character styles earlier in this chapter, are the following:

- General
- Basic Character Formats
- Advanced Character Formats
- Character Color

To apply a character style to existing text, choose the Text tool and select a range of text. Then choose Type ➢ Character Styles or press Shift+F11 to open the Character Styles palette.

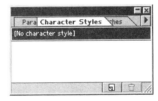

Click on the name of a style to apply it to the text.

To apply a character style to text as you type, choose the Text tool and then choose Type ➢ Character Styles or press Shift+F11 to open the Character Styles palette. Click on the name of a style to select that style, then start typing. The style will be applied to the text as you type.

For either of these options, you can also select a character style by pressing the keystroke combination you may have specified when you created a new style or edited an existing style, as described earlier in this chapter. Remember that in Windows you have to make sure that Num Lock is on.

Applying Paragraph Styles

If you are applying both character-level formatting attributes and paragraph-level attributes, you should use a paragraph style. When applying a paragraph style, you

can apply all 11 of the formatting option groups that are described in the sections on defining character styles and paragraph styles earlier in this chapter.

The formatting option groups available through paragraph styles are the following:

- General
- Indents and Spacing
- Drop Caps and Composer
- Justification
- Tabs
- Hyphenation
- Keep Options
- Paragraph Rules
- Basic Character Formats
- Advanced Character Formats
- Character Color

To apply a paragraph style to existing text, choose the Text tool and select a range of text. Then choose Type ➤ Paragraph Styles or press F11 to open the Paragraph Styles palette.

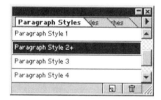

Click on the name of a style to apply it to the text.

To apply a paragraph style to text as you type, choose the Text tool and then choose Type ➤ Paragraph Styles or press F11 to open the Paragraph Styles palette. Click on the name of a style to select that style, then start typing. The style will be applied to the text as you type.

For either of these options, you can also select a paragraph style by pressing the keystroke combination you may have specified when you created a new style or edited an existing style, as described earlier in this chapter. Remember that in Windows you have to make sure that Num Lock is on.

While applying a paragraph style to selected text, you can completely remove any currently applied formatting attributes in that text by pressing Alt/Option when you click the name of the paragraph style in the Paragraph Styles palette. This option assures that the selected paragraph style is the only style applied to that text.

TIP If you have already specified character formatting attributes to a range of selected text and want to apply only the paragraph-level formatting attributes of an existing paragraph format, press Shift+Alt in Windows and Shift+Option on the Mac when you click the name of the paragraph style in the Paragraph Styles palette. This option protects the character-level formatting attributes currently applied to the text and applies only the paragraph-level formatting attributes of the selected paragraph style.

Modifying Styles

Once you have created and defined a style, you can modify that style either by opening its Modify Style Options dialog box, or by reformatting a range of text to which that style has been applied and then automatically redefining that style according to those formatting changes.

When you modify a style, all text—anywhere within the document—to which that style has been applied will be changed to reflect the changes to the style. You can see how this can save you time. You can apply a formatting style throughout your document, then you can change every occurrence of that style all at once.

To modify a style by editing the values in the Modify Style Options dialog box, double-click the name of the style in its style palette or select Style Options from the style's palette menu.

This action opens the Modify Character/Paragraph Style Options dialog box, shown in Figure 10.21, which offers the same options that are described in the previous sections of this chapter on defining new styles.

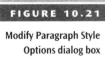

FIGURE 10.21
Modify Paragraph Style Options dialog box

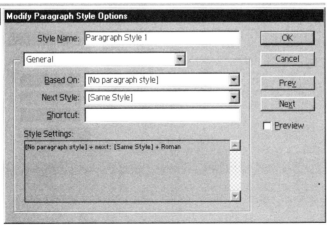

Navigate through the different formatting option areas by selecting one from the option menu directly beneath the Style Name text area or by clicking the Prev or Next button. When you are satisfied with the changes, click OK to accept the changes and apply them to all type throughout the document to which that style has been applied.

TIP You might think that you must select a range of text to which the style you want to modify has been applied, but you don't. If you want to edit a style that is different than the one applied to any text that you may have selected, just press Ctrl in Windows or Cmd on the Mac when you double-click the style's name in the style palette. This action simply opens the Modify Character/Paragraph Style Options dialog box of that style without applying the style to the selected text.

Alternately, you can modify a style by selecting a range of text to which that style has been applied and making the formatting changes that you want. When you do this, a plus symbol (+) will appear next to the name of the style in the style palette, as shown below, to indicate that the selected text has been altered from that style.

Once you have made all of the formatting changes to the text, choose Redefine Style from the style's palette menu, shown below.

This action automatically applies to the style all of the changes you made to the text. All text to which that style has been applied will reflect the changes.

Duplicating Styles

You can create a copy of any style by selecting that style in the Style palette and choosing Duplicate Style from the style palette menu.

This action opens the Duplicate Character/Paragraph Style dialog box, shown in Figure 10.22, which is the same dialog box as the New Character/Paragraph Style and Modify Character/Paragraph Style dialog boxes, which are discussed in previous sections of this chapter.

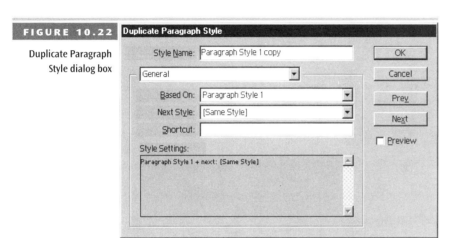

FIGURE 10.22

Duplicate Paragraph Style dialog box

By default, the duplicate style is the same as the original style and InDesign adds "copy" to the name of the original style and displays it in the Style Name text area. You can leave it with that name or give it an entirely different name by typing in what you want.

You can then navigate through the formatting option areas by selecting them from the option menu directly beneath the Style Name text area.

Click OK to accept the duplicate style.

The new style is added to the style palette, but the original style remains applied to its ranges of text.

Importing Styles from Another Document

You can import (load or append) styles from one InDesign document into another. You can import the character styles, the paragraph styles, or both.

WARNING   This is not the procedure for importing styles from a document saved in another application. Placing a document from another application, using the File≻Place command, automatically imports all of the styles of that document. Styles imported in this fashion are indicated in the Character Styles palette and Paragraph Styles palette with a little disk symbol to the right of their names.

To import styles from one document to another, go to the document into which you want to load the styles. Then open the palette menu and choose Load Character Styles or Load Paragraph Styles, whichever is appropriate. To load both styles, choose Load All Styles, which appears in both of the styles palettes.

These actions open the Open a File dialog box, shown in Figure 10.23.

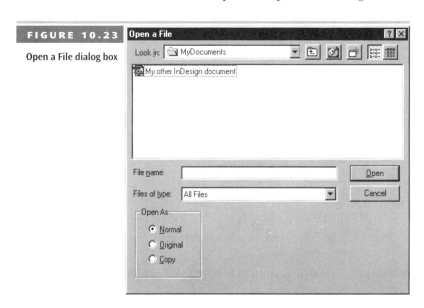

FIGURE 10.23
Open a File dialog box

All you have to do now is select a file and click Open. The styles in that document will be imported into your active document.

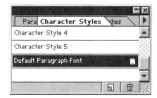

NOTE When you import styles from another document, all of the styles from that other document are imported. As a result, you may have unused styles that you want to delete; this process is described in the "Removing Unused Styles from the Styles Palette" section below.

Avoiding Mistakes When Importing Styles

Be careful when importing styles. If any of the imported styles share the same name with any of the existing styles in your active document, the new, imported styles will strip the old style's formatting from all of the text in the document and replace it with the new, imported style. If that happens, don't panic—you can fix it without having to go back and re-link all the text to another style. Without changing anything else, do this:

1. Select the style's name in the styles palette.
2. Choose Duplicate Style from the styles palette menu.
3. Give the duplicate style a name in the Duplicate Character/Paragraph Style dialog box and click OK. This will become the new name for the imported style.
4. Select the original style's name in the styles palette (the same one you selected in Step 1).
5. Reapply the text formatting attributes to one paragraph of the text. This action should cause a plus symbol (+) to appear next to the style's name.
6. Choose Redefine Style from the styles palette menu.

These steps move the imported style to its own named style and restore the formatting to the text that already had the original style applied to it.

Removing a Style from Text

Once you have applied a style to text, you can "unapply" that style by breaking the link between the style and the text. The formatting of the text remains the same, but you will no longer be able to automatically make changes to that text by making formatting changes to that style. You can also break the link between text and a style while removing all of the style's formatting attributes from that text.

To remove a style from text, choose the Text tool and select the text from which you want to remove the style.

If you now click [No Character Style] or [No Paragraph Style] in the styles palette, as shown below, you remove the link between the text and the style. The text does not change appearance at all, but changes to the style will no longer affect this text.

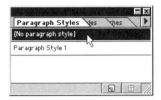

Now, if you actually want to remove the formatting attributes of the style from the text, press Alt/Option while you click [No Character Style] or [No Paragraph Style]. This removes the formatting of the text and the link to the style. The appearance of the text doesn't change, but the link to the style will have been broken. Consequently, any changes you later make to the style will not affect this text.

Deleting Styles

To delete a style from your document with approval, simply select the name of the style in its particular style palette and click the Trash button in the palette. InDesign will prompt you to approve the deletion, as shown below.

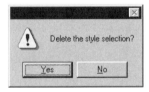

To delete a style from your document without approval, select the name of the style in its particular style palette and choose Delete Styles from the palette menu. Alternately, drag the style to the Trash button in the palette.

Removing Unused Styles from the Styles Palettes

Sometimes you may wind up with more styles in your styles palettes than you are using in the document. This often happens when you import styles from another document just so you can use a few of them. (Remember that when you import styles from another document, *all* of the styles from that other document are imported.)

To clean up your styles palettes and remove all of the unused styles, simply choose Select All Unused from the style palette menu, as shown below.

This action highlights all of the unused styles in the styles palette. To delete them, choose Delete Styles from the styles palette menu.

chapter 11

Storing Elements in Object Libraries

Featuring:

- Navigating the Object Library palette 262
- Creating an object library 266
- Opening an object library 268
- Adding and removing objects from a library 268
- Placing objects from an object library into a document 275
- Copying objects from other libraries 276
- Moving objects between libraries 279
- Cataloging the contents of object libraries 280
- Searching for objects in object libraries 281
- Closing an object library 285
- Deleting an object library 285

CHAPTER 11

STORING ELEMENTS IN OBJECT LIBRARIES

O bject libraries are high-level time-savers. You can store regularly used objects—including placeholders, shapes, graphics or text frames, entire pages, even ruler guides and grids—that you can then quickly find and place in any open InDesign document.

You should be storing any elements that you use regularly from one project to the next. These elements could be as complex as entire page layouts or as simple as the individual logos you may use on regular features. Of course, you could also save and place these objects by opening a document that contains them, but object libraries offer cataloging and control features that an ordinary document does not. By storing the elements in an object library, you can put everything you use into one place, rather than having to search through an open document—or several open documents—to find one little element. You can sort elements by type or name, and you can search for only the element or elements you want.

Essentially, object libraries are documents. But instead of being documents that have a page layout, they are documents that store objects.

Object libraries are created, saved, and opened as are other InDesign documents. You can have open as many libraries as your system's RAM will support.

Object libraries also perform like the publish and subscribe features available on other Mac applications. Placing an object in a library preserves a link between the object in the library and the original object. If that original object is edited or changed, the object in the library reflects those changes—everywhere you have placed it. In fact, this protection feature goes as deep into the saved object as necessary. For example, if you've saved a page to a library and that page has a properly-linked graphic in it, even changes to the original graphic will be reflected in the object in the library.

You can even preserve the original layering of an object saved in a library, so that you can edit those individual layers in any InDesign document where you place the object.

Navigating the Object Library Palette

Object libraries appear in the Object Library palette. The name of the library appears as the name of the tab for that library, as shown in Figure 11.1. If you have opened six libraries, you'll see six tabs, each named for its library.

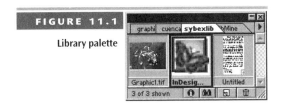

FIGURE 11.1
Library palette

To select an object library, click on its tab in the palette. By default, the objects currently in the library are displayed individually in the palette as thumbnail images. You can change this display to a listing of the objects in the library, as shown below.

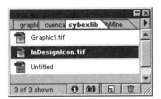

As you can see, the library objects are listed by name, along with icons that identify their type. To change the display of the objects to a list, choose List View from the Object Library palette. To change the display to show the thumbnails, select Thumbnail View.

NAVIGATING THE OBJECT LIBRARY PALETTE 263

If you don't have more library objects in an object library than will display on your screen, you can see them all by choosing Show All from the Object Library palette menu.

When you have a bunch of library objects, you can sort them so that they display by their names, their types, or their relative ages. To change the sorting of the objects in the Object Library palette, choose Sort Items from the palette menu and then choose one of the sorting options, as shown below.

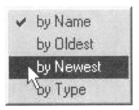

When you have multiple object libraries in an Object Library palette, you can drag any of them out of that palette group to create a new, individual Object Library palette, or you can add that object library to any other palette group.

You can also sort objects by keywords in their descriptions. For more information on cataloging your library objects, see the "Cataloging Objects in an Object Library" section later in this chapter.

To create a new Object Library palette for an individual object library, simply click and hold on the object library's tab and drag it to an area of the desktop where there are no other palette groups, as shown in Figure 11.2.

Release the mouse button to place that object library in that spot, in a new Object Library palette, as shown in Figure 11.3.

If you want to place an Object Library palette into another palette group, drag the object library from its palette group and drop it onto another palette group, as shown in Figure 11.4.

When you drop the object library, it will be added to the other palette group, as shown in Figure 11.5.

FIGURE 11.2

Dragging an object library out of a palette

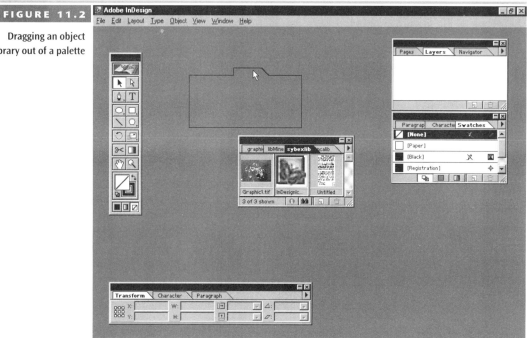

FIGURE 11.3

A new Object Library palette

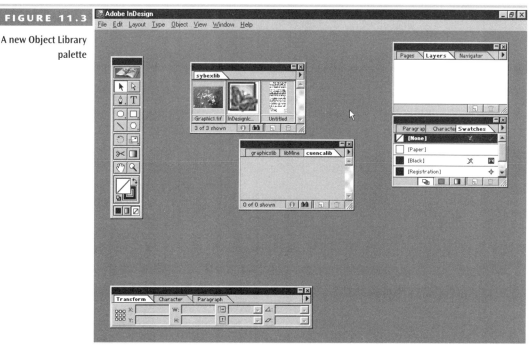

FIGURE 11.4

Dragging an object library onto another palette group

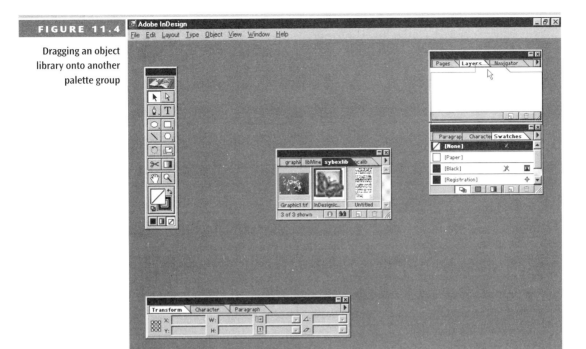

FIGURE 11.5

Object library in another palette group

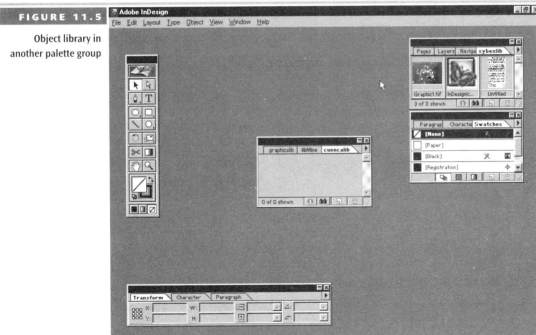

The display in the lower left corner of the Object Library palette lists the number of objects displayed out of the entire number of objects in the object library. If you want to display more objects in the palette, you can resize the Object Library palette by pulling the window borders to the size and shape you want. You can minimize or close the palette by clicking the Minimize or Close buttons at the top right of the palette.

When you activate an object by clicking on it once, you can view its item information by clicking the Library Item Information button. (For more information about item information, see the "Cataloging the Contents of an Object Library" section later in this chapter.)

You can also view the item information by double-clicking the object's thumbnail or text listing.

Clicking the Show Library Subset button is like clicking a search button—it begins the searching process. (See the "Searching for Objects in an Object Library" section later in this chapter.)

Clicking the New Library Item button will add any object(s) you have selected to the library. (See the "Adding Objects to an Object Library" section later in this chapter.) You can also add an object by dragging it onto the New Library Item button.

When an object is selected in the library, clicking the Trash button will delete that object. (See the "Removing Objects from an Object Library" section later in this chapter.) You can also delete an object from the library by dragging it onto the Trash button.

Creating an Object Library

As I mentioned earlier in the chapter, an object library is essentially a document file, but a document file that is a bit different than other document files. Even though you open them through a different command, object libraries are like other documents in that they are created, saved, and opened.

To create a new object library, choose Window ➢ Libraries ➢ New. This action opens the New Library dialog box, shown in Figure 11.6.

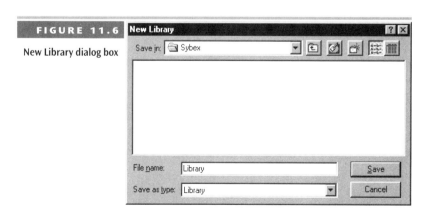

FIGURE 11.6

New Library dialog box

In the New Library dialog box, navigate through your directory structure to where you want to save the library.

Enter a name for the library and click Save.

Some Naming Tips for Libraries

How you name your libraries can make finding them easier or harder. You should consider naming your libraries with a name that tells you that it is a library. Even though when you reopen your library, the Open a Library dialog box will only show you the available libraries, you may at some time need to move or copy a library and it will make it easier to find if you use something like "lib" in the name.

Also, because of how InDesign displays the names of each open library in the Object Library palette as its tab name, you may want to consider using something like "lib" as the first part of the name. As shown below, when you have several libraries open, you only see the last part of their name from behind the other tabs. All you can see of the libraries named "something-lib" is the last part of their name: "lib."

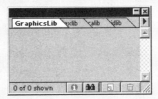

So if you call a file "libMine," you'd see the "Mine" part more easily, as shown below.

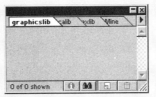

This practice will not only make it easier to read the remainder of the library's name behind the other tabs, it will also keep all of your libraries grouped together in their folder.

Another consideration is the length of the libraries' names. Since the name will be displayed in full as the tab name in the Object Library palette, you should try to keep the names succinct, so that the tabs won't be too large in the palette. This may not make much difference if you only have one or two libraries open, but it will make a big difference if you have three or more open.

TIP If you already have at least one other library open and can see the Object Library palette, you can access the New Library dialog box by choosing New Library from the Object Library palette menu.

Opening an Object Library

Once you have created a library, you can open it for the first time by choosing Window ➢ Libraries ➢ Open, or by pressing Shift+Ctrl+Alt+L in Windows or Shift+Cmd+Option+L on the Mac. This action opens the Open a Library dialog box, shown in Figure 11.7.

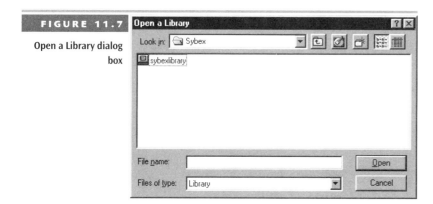

FIGURE 11.7

Open a Library dialog box

By default, the Open a Library dialog box displays only the available InDesign libraries in a given folder. You can also select All Files from the Files of Type option menu to display all of the files in a folder, but that will only make your search more tedious if there are a lot of files in that folder.

To open a library, select it in the list of displayed files or type its name in the File Name text entry area. Then click Open.

Opening a library in this way also opens or focuses the Object Library palette. (*Focus* is a computing term for bringing a window to the front, so that you can see it. The opposite is *blur*.)

Showing an Object Library That Is Already Open

As with most palettes, you can choose to hide or show the Object Library palette. If you hide the Object Library palette, you don't close the open object libraries. The object libraries that you have created or opened since you first launched InDesign will remain open until you actually close them. As long as they are open, their names are displayed in the Window ➤ Libraries pull down menu, as shown in Figure 11.8.

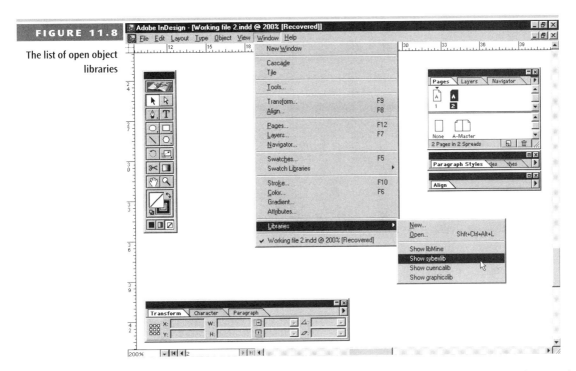

FIGURE 11.8

The list of open object libraries

Selecting one of the displayed names in this menu opens the Object Library palette and focuses that library.

Hiding and Showing the Object Library Palette

InDesign's handling of open object libraries and the Object Library palette is sort of goofy on the one hand, but sensible on the other. As you learned in the previous sections, all of the open libraries are displayed in the Object Library palette. You can select one of these libraries merely by clicking its tab in the Object Library palette. What's goofy about the whole thing is that when you choose Window ➤ Libraries, the menu displays all the open libraries, and if you select one of them, they all "show" in the Object Library palette. So why not just have a single command: Window ➤ Libraries ➤ Hide/Show Object Library palette?

You might not see the sensibility of this configuration until you open more than about four or five object libraries. With that many tabs in a little palette, you're unlikely to be able to see the names on the tabs. Rather than clicking on each tab until you get to the one you want, you can simply choose Window ➢ Libraries ➢ Show *such-and-such*, as shown in Figure 11.8. I think this makes sense, but it also seems that it would be quicker if that sort of library list was available actually in the Object Library palette.

So when you have selected an object library—either by choosing it from the Window ➢ Libraries menu or by clicking on its tab in the Object Library palette—that library's name in the Window ➢ Libraries menu changes from "Show such-and-such" to "Hide such-and-such," as shown below. If you select "Hide such-and-such," it not only hides that object library, it hides the whole Object Library palette! (Goofy again.)

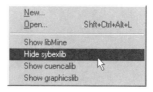

So in other words, you really can't hide an object library without actually closing it and you can't hide or show the Object Library palette without showing all of the open object libraries.

Adding Objects to an Object Library

Once you have created an object library you can begin to add items to it. You can add individual shapes, frames, placeholders, pages, graphics, text frames, and ruler guides—even grouped objects.

NOTE When you drag an object to the Object Library palette, it may appear that you are moving the object on the page. Don't worry. As soon as you let go of the object in the Object Library palette, the original object will pop back into its original position. However, if you do let go of the object before you reach the Object Library palette, you will indeed move it on the page.

If you want to catalog your objects as you add them to an object library, press Alt/Option when following any of the steps described in this section. This action will open the Item Information dialog box, where you can edit the objects' Item Information. (See the "Cataloging Objects in an Object Library" section later in this chapter.)

Adding Shapes, Frames, Placeholders, and Graphics

To add any shape, frame, placeholder, or graphic, simply select that object with any selection tool and then perform one of these operations:

- Drag the item into the Object Library palette.
- Click the New Item button in the Object Library palette.
- Choose Add Item from the Object Library palette menu, shown below.

Adding Groups of Objects

To add a group of objects, first select all of the objects, then perform one of these operations:

- Drag the group of items into the Object Library palette.
- Click the New Item button in the Object Library palette.
- Choose Add Item from the Object Library palette menu.

 TIP Why add a group of objects to an object library? If you regularly use a logo or some other standing element on your pages and that element is made up of more than one object, such as a text frame and a graphic, you obviously want to add them to the library together. Anytime you want to preserve the arrangement of multiple objects that you use regularly, adding them as a group makes sense.

The selected objects don't have to be grouped already to be added as a group. In other words, you can simply select two or more objects, then add them to the object library. When you place them from the object library into a document, they are placed together, in the arrangement in which they were added to the library. (Grouping objects is covered in Chapter 15.)

Of course, you can also go ahead and group them and then add the group to the library.

When you add a group of objects that are not grouped to an object library and then place them from the object library to a page, they will be in their original arrangement and will all be selected so that moving one will move them all in unison. However, if you click away from any of them, then click back on one of them and move it, you'll only be moving that one element. So be sure that you don't accidentally disturb their arrangement. If that arrangement is critical, you should consider grouping them before adding them to the library.

Another thing to consider when adding a group of multiple objects is that you may have more than one type of object, but InDesign doesn't provide a way for you to catalog objects as a group or multiple categories. What this means is that you might have a group containing a graphic and text. Unfortunately, when you catalog the item in its Item Information dialog box, you can select Image or Text for the Object Type, but not both. Nor is there a Group object type. (See the "Cataloging Objects in an Object Library" section later in this chapter.)

Adding Text Frames

You can add text to an object library, but you can only add it as the contents of a text frame. In other words, if you want to add to an object library only a small portion of text from a longer story, you should copy or cut that selected text from its text frame and then paste it into an empty text frame before adding it to an object library.

Any text formatting that you have applied to the text in the text frame will be preserved.

Beware of formatting, though, because any character or paragraph styles that are applied to the text in that text frame will be saved with the object when it is added to the object library. Then, when you add that text frame to another document, those character and/or paragraph styles will be added to the new document. If the new document already contains styles with the same names as some of the styles you are adding with the library object, then the formatting attributes of the styles in the new document will be applied to the text in the library object you are importing. So, let's say you added some text with formatting, which you applied to the text as "Style 1," to an object library. You should make sure you don't place that text into a new document that also has a "Style 1" with different formatting. If you do, the original formatting that you wanted may be overwritten with a completely different style.

Once you have a text frame filled with only the text you want to add to an object library, select that text frame with any selection tool and then perform one of these operations:

- Drag the text frame into the Object Library palette.
- Click the New Item button in the Object Library palette.
- Choose Add Item from the Object Library palette menu.

Adding Pages

You can add an entire page of objects to an object library. However, you are adding them as a group of individual objects, rather than as a page. This distinction is important because once you place the group of objects onto another page, you could inadvertently move one or more of the objects if you don't first group them.

TIP If you are thinking of adding a "page" of objects that includes only one or two actual objects, you might consider adding them to an object library individually. Unless, of course, you want to preserve the arrangement of the objects on the page. In that case, adding them to an object library together makes sense.

To add a page to an object library, you can simply choose Add All Items on Page from the Object Library palette, as shown below.

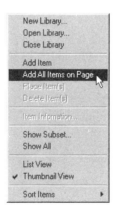

As with other grouped objects, if your primary motivation for adding a page of objects to an object library is to preserve the arrangement of the objects on the page, you should consider grouping them first, so that you won't inadvertently disturb that arrangement. So, if you want to first group the objects on a page, you should select them all and group them, then perform one of these operations:

- Drag the group into the Object Library palette.
- Click the New Item button in the Object Library palette.

Adding Ruler Guides

To add a ruler guide or a grid of ruler guides to an object library, select one guide or press Shift and then select multiple ruler guides. Then perform one of these operations:

- Click the New Item button in the Object Library palette.
- Choose Add Item from the Object Library palette menu.

NOTE   You cannot drag guides to the Object Library palette.

Removing Objects from an Object Library

If you add an object to the library, you can remove it when you no longer want it there.

To delete an object from the object library, select that object in the Object Library palette, then perform one of the following operations:

- Drag the object to the Trash button in the Object Library palette.
- Click the Trash button in the Object Library palette.
- Choose Delete Item(s) from the Object Library palette menu, as shown below.

Placing Objects from an Object Library into a Document

Once you have created an object library and added objects to it, you can begin placing those objects into any InDesign documents.

To place library objects from an object library into a document, select an object in the Object Library palette and then do one of the following:

- Drag the object into a document.
- Choose Place Item(s) from the Object Library palette menu, as shown below.

Placing Library Objects with Their Layering Intact

If you created any library objects in a document that had multiple layers and you want to preserve the layering of the objects as you place them, follow these steps:

1. Open the Layers palette, shown below, of the document into which you want to place the library objects by choosing Window > Layers, pressing F7, or clicking the Layers palette tab in its palette group.

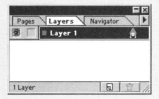

Continued on next page

> ### Placing Library Objects with Their Layering Intact *(continued)*
>
> 2. Open the Layers palette menu and check to see if Paste Remembers Layers option is selected, as shown below. If the option has a checkmark next to it, it is selected. If it does not, select it and release the mouse to activate the option.
>
>
>
> 3. Place the library object into the document. The Layers palette will reflect the addition of the layering from the library object, as shown below.
>
>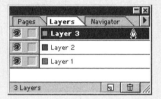
>
> For more information about layers, see Chapter 13.

Copying Objects from Other Object Libraries

You can copy objects from one object library to another using a simple drag–and-drop method. But you must be able to see both of the object libraries at the same time. How can you see them both at the same time, if they're both in the same palette, with one hidden behind the other? Simple. You just drag one object library out of the palette and either into another palette or into a palette of its own.

To isolate two object libraries, select one of them and drag it out of the Object Library palette, as shown in Figure 11.9.

Let go and the object library will open alone in a new Object Library palette, as shown in Figure 11.10. Of course you could also drag the object library onto another palette group, thereby adding it to that palette group.

COPYING OBJECTS FROM OTHER OBJECT LIBRARIES 277

FIGURE 11.9

Dragging an object library out of palette

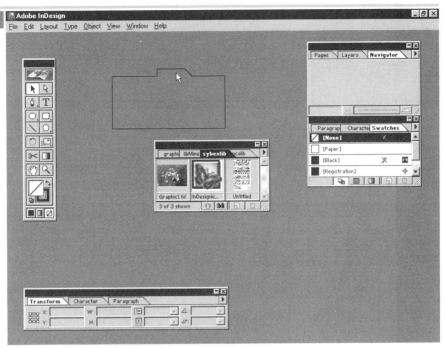

FIGURE 11.10

New Object Library palette

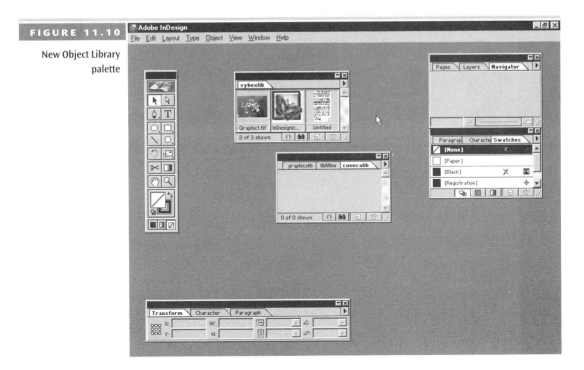

Then click the tab of the object library into which you want to add the library object, as shown below, so that it focused in the palette.

Now, to copy an object from one library to the other, simply drag and drop the object as shown in Figure 11.12.

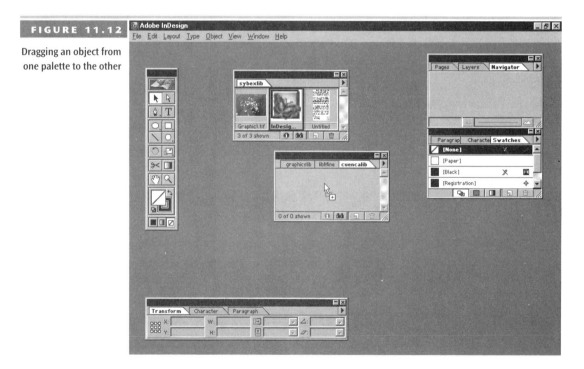

FIGURE 11.12

Dragging an object from one palette to the other

As you can see, the plus symbol (+) appears with the cursor to indicate that you will be adding the object to the other object library.

When you drop the object into that other object library, it is added to that object library, as shown in Figure 11.13. The original item in the other Object Library palette remains undisturbed.

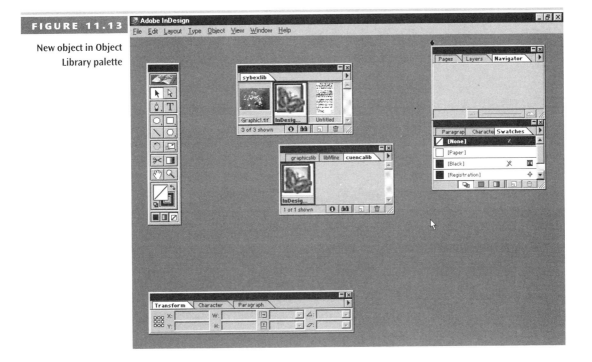

FIGURE 11.13

New object in Object Library palette

Moving Objects between Object Libraries

You can also copy an object from one object library to another and delete the library object from its original object library at the same time, which is called *moving*. You should be careful that you really want to do this, because the original will be deleted. Of course, if you do this accidentally, you can always just copy the library object back to the original object library as described in the previous section.

To perform a move, rather than a copy, when adding a library object from one object library to another, first isolate the two object libraries as described in the previous section.

Then hold down Alt/Option as you drag an object from one object library to the other. When you drop the library object into the new object library, the original library object is deleted from its object library.

Cataloging Objects in an Object Library

Cataloging the objects in your object libraries allows to sort more quickly and more efficiently through large object libraries. You can sort the objects by several criteria and display only a few of the objects at a time, in what are called *subsets*.

Cataloging your library objects is easy. You merely need to specify information about them in their respective Item Information dialog boxes, as shown in Figure 11.14.

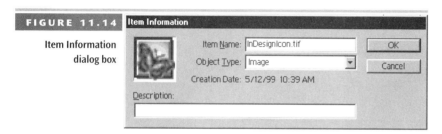

FIGURE 11.14

Item Information dialog box

To access the Item Information dialog box for an object, select an object in the Object Library palette, then either double-click on it, click the Item Information button, or choose Item Information from the Object Library palette menu, shown below.

The Item Information dialog box displays the current values specified for the object's name, type, creation information, and description. You can change the name of the object if you wish. You can select or change its Object Type and you can write a description of the object.

By default, InDesign will give graphics—including EPS and PDF files—their filename. You can change this, or you may feel it makes sense to leave it that way. Shapes, frames, placeholders, and text files are given numbered "Untitled" names, which you should change to a name that helps you identify the object.

The object types that are available in the Object Type option menu are shown in Figure 11.15.

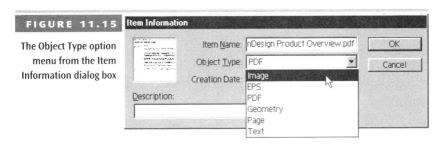

FIGURE 11.15
The Object Type option menu from the Item Information dialog box

The types of objects and how InDesign categorizes them are:

Image Graphics files other than PDF and EPS files

EPS Encapsulated PostScript files

PDF Adobe Portable Document Format files

Geometry Shapes, placeholders, and frames

Page Objects added to the object library with the Add All Items on Page command

Text Simple text

By default, the Description area is blank. Here you can type in a description for the object of up to 100 characters. The description can be used later for sorting and searching, so give careful consideration to what you enter. For example, don't waste your allotted description space with unnecessary words.

Try to use keywords that you can apply to other objects that you would want to search for together later. You might want to keep a list of some common keywords you're using for various objects, so that you can later call them up together. For example, enter something like "subhead logo small section 1." For another object, you might enter "subhead logo large section 1." Later, when sorting your objects, you could search for "subhead," "section 1," or "logo," to retrieve only those subheads, logos, or other objects you might want for a particular section.

Searching for Objects in an Object Library

InDesign allows you to search through your object libraries to retrieve only certain library objects. As your object libraries become larger, you may not want to sort through even all of the graphics objects or text objects. You can sort them down to even smaller *subsets*. When you search for objects in an object library, you generate a subset of library objects. Only those objects retrieved into this subset will be displayed in the Object Library palette. Subsets can contain as few as one object, or all the objects in the object library.

If you have carefully considered the organization of your object libraries and have written keyword descriptions that will produce the results you want, you could generate subsets that retrieve only those objects you want displayed at that time. This can speed your work, eliminating some of the time you would otherwise need to sort through the object library.

Even if you haven't entered keywords for your objects, you can still show subsets based on the image name, object type, and creation date.

To show a subset of library objects, open an object library and click the Show Library Subset button, or choose Show Subset from the Object Library palette menu, shown below.

These actions open the Subset dialog box, shown in Figure 11.16.

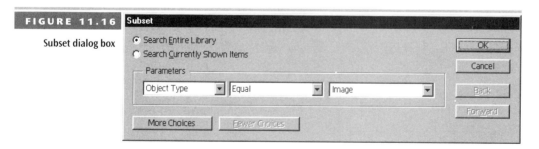

FIGURE 11.16

Subset dialog box

In the Subset dialog box, you can elect to search the entire library or to perform a second search on the currently-displayed subset by clicking one of the radio buttons at the top of the dialog box.

In the Parameters area, you specify the criteria by which you want to sort the library objects. If you want to narrow the search by including more than one criteria, you click the More Choices button to expand the dialog box to add additional criteria, as shown in Figure 11.17.

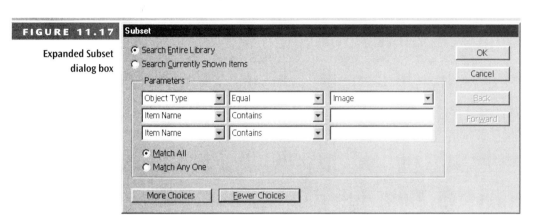

FIGURE 11.17
Expanded Subset dialog box

Once you add criteria, you can then click the Fewer Choices button to remove those additional criteria.

You can also specify whether you want InDesign to match all or any of the criteria by clicking the Match All or Match Any One radio buttons.

The search criteria and their conditions are:

Item Name If you select Item Name, shown below, you can look for objects that contain or do not contain a word in their name. When you select Item Name from the first option menu, the second option menu automatically offers Contains or Doesn't Contain. You then enter the word to use in the third value box.

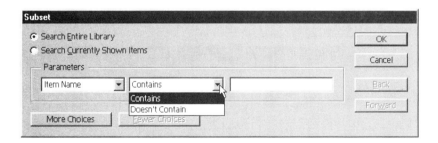

Creation Date If you select Creation Date, you can search for objects using Greater Than, Less Than, Equal, or Not Equal, as shown next. By default, the current day's date is entered and you can edit it as necessary.

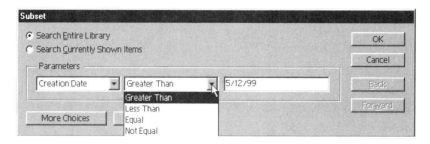

Object Type   Selecting Object Type allows you to search for objects of a specific type. Once you select Object Type in the first option menu, the second option menu offers Equal or Not Equal for the search modifiers. The third option menu then offers the image types, as shown below.

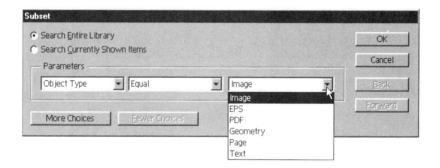

Description   If you have entered keywords or any other text in the Description area of the Item Information dialog box, presented in the previous section, you can search for objects that contain or do not contain specific words in their descriptions. Choosing Description from the first option menu offers Contains/ Doesn't Contain from the second option menu, as shown below. You then type a word in the third value box.

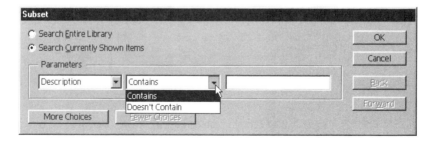

Once you have performed a search and have produced a subset, you can choose Show All from the Object Library palette menu to once again display all of the objects in that object library.

If you perform a search that still produces too many results, you may choose to go ahead and search again through only those objects produced in the first search. To do this, click the Search Currently Shown Items radio button in the Subset dialog box, and once again specify the parameters you want.

Closing an Object Library

To close a library, click its tab in its palette group or choose its name in the Window ➢ Libraries submenu, as shown below.

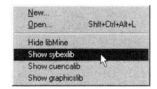

Then choose Close Library from the Object Library palette menu, shown below.

Remember that closing a library does not delete the library. It merely closes it during that particular InDesign work session.

Deleting an Object Library

To delete a library, you actually have to go out to Windows Explorer or the Mac Finder, locate the library you want to delete in whatever folder you saved it and then manually delete it by using one of the operating system's methods, such as right-clicking and choosing Delete from the Windows context menu or by dragging it to the Mac trash can icon.

chapter 12

SELECTING AND APPLYING COLOR

Featuring:

- Basic desktop color theory — 290
- Defining color from the Toolbox — 296
- Using the Swatches palette — 297
- Using the Colors palette — 309
- Defining tints and gradients — 314
- Applying color, tints, and gradients to paths and frames — 318
- Applying color, tints, and gradients to type — 324

CHAPTER 12

SELECTING AND APPLYING COLOR

There's a lot more to using color effectively in desktop publishing than just saying "I want blue here and red there." You must understand the basic difference in how color is presented both on the computer screen and on paper. You must understand the capabilities and compatibility of different color models and color modes. These things aren't difficult to grasp, even though they may seem confusing at first.

After I present these color theory basics, I'll then get into selecting colors in InDesign and applying them to the objects on an InDesign document page. Advanced printing topics, such as color trapping, are presented in Chapter 18. Color calibration is covered in Appendix C.

Understanding Basic Desktop Color Theory

Okay. Let's dive into this color theory stuff. We must always remember that there are two very important differences between how we perceive the colors we see on our computer and how those colors will be created when we print them on paper:

- A computer monitor or television screen produces the colors we see by shining light at our eyes. Three different colors—red, green, and blue—are shined out at us in different mixtures, producing different colors. These three colors of light are added together to create all the different combinations of colors we see on the screen.

- Colors are printed on paper by mixing inks of different colors. The inks are actually translucent, which means that some light is transmitted through them, like a stained glass window. When light from the sun or an electric light passes through the translucent ink, the ink acts as a filter, absorbing some of the color in the light and reflecting some of the color back out at our eyes. The colors of the inks are subtracted from each other to create the different combinations of colors.

What you've just read is the difference between *additive color* and *subtractive color*. The RGB colors are the primary additive colors, resulting in white when mixed together equally at full strength. As you can see in the Figure 12.1, when three spotlights are shined together and one is red, one is blue, and one is green, different colors are produced where they overlap. Where they all three overlap, they *add* together to create white. Where they overlap in twos, they actually create the subtractive primary colors, discussed below.

FIGURE 12.1

The additive color wheel

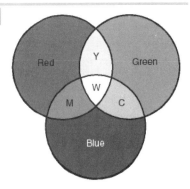

Notice in Figure 12.1 that where the red and blue overlap they create magenta (M), where red and green overlap they create yellow (Y), and where blue and green overlap they create cyan (C). These three colors—cyan, magenta, and yellow—are the *subtractive* primary colors. When these three colors are mixed, they actually absorb light—they *subtract* light—resulting in black when mixed together equally at full strength, as shown in Figure 12.2. When these three colors are mixed at different strengths, many other colors can be reproduced.

FIGURE 12.2

The subtractive color wheel

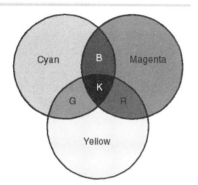

In reality, when we use translucent inks of these three subtractive colors and mix them equally, we wind up with a muddy brown color. So when we print ink on paper, we add black ink for the true black. We use cyan, magenta, yellow, and black to print full color on paper. Those are the *process colors*: cyan, magenta, yellow, and black, which we refer to as CMYK. ("K" is used for black, rather than "B", so that it won't be confused with blue.)

TIP   Here's a tip for remembering the difference between additive and subtractive color models: think of adding light and subtracting light. If you add light, things get lighter—or whiter. If you subtract light, things get darker—or blacker. So the three additive colors add light to create white and the subtractive colors subtract light to create black.

TIP   Here's a tip for remembering which of the two types of models creates white—constituting the additive colors—and which creates black—constituting the subtractive colors. Just remember that in the two models, black is with the colors that create it. So, CMYK is the subtractive color model.

Color Gamuts

When we open our eyes upon waking, we perceive the world around us in different colors. The total range of colors and shades of colors that we can see is called a *gamut*. The gamut is the total amount of color difference that can be perceived or reproduced by different means. Our eyes have the widest gamut, that is, they can see the most colors. Printing color inks on paper produces the narrowest gamut.

Gamuts are also called *color spaces*. The simplest way to think of a gamut is as a container of color. The number of colors that a certain device can produce is that device's gamut or color space. It's that simple.

As you can see in Figure 12.3, various gamuts overlap, but some gamuts fall way short of containing all the colors that other gamuts contain.

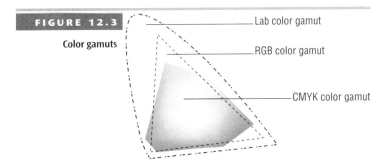

FIGURE 12.3
Color gamuts

As you work in the RGB gamut of your computer monitor, you are limited to how many of the colors of nature you can output. If you are planning to print your project on a printing press, you'll be printing in the CMYK gamut, which is even more limited. When you define a color in InDesign that cannot be reproduced via the four process colors of CMYK printing, that color is referred to as being *out-of-gamut*, meaning it does not fall within the container of colors possible with CMYK printing.

When working in either the LAB or RGB color modes and you define a color that cannot be printed via CMYK—an out-of-gamut color—InDesign notifies you of this by displaying the gamut alert icon, which is a triangle with an exclamation point in it, as shown in the Color palette below.

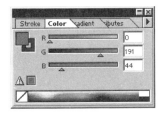

The little color swatch next to the gamut alert icon shows you the closest CMYK color to the color you have selected. If that color is acceptable to you, you can click on the little color swatch to select that color. When you do, the respective color values will be automatically defined in the Color palette and the gamut alert icon will disappear, as shown below.

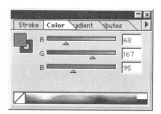

NOTE If you are working on a project that will not be printed on a printing press, perhaps intended for the Web or other electronic display, you need not worry about out-of-gamut colors. You can define any RGB color you want and you'll be fine.

Color Models

When we first set out to describe a range of colors in a gamut, we must use a *color model*. A color model is a method of describing color objectively so that it can be generally reproduced on a monitor or on paper. In other words, we need someway to say "I want that apple to be red," so that a computer, which thinks only in terms of numbers, can understand.

InDesign uses three color models: RGB, CMYK, and L*a*b.

The RGB Color Model

RGB is the color model that is universal to color computer monitors and television screens. The primary additive colors of red, green, and blue (RGB) are shined together—added—to create all the colors we see on the screen. When all three of them are shined together equally at full brightness, we see white. When all three of them are dimmed to zero brightness, we see black. When we mix them in varying brightnesses, we see all kinds of colors. When two additive colors mix, they create one of the subtractive primary colors, either cyan, magenta, or yellow.

The CMYK Color Model

CMYK is the color mode used by commercial printers to create colors with ink on paper. C stands for cyan, M for magenta, Y for yellow, and K for black. The reason that four colors are used, rather than just the three complementary colors, is that when they are mixed together equally at full strength they create a muddy brown, rather than black. So a black ink is added. This is called four-color process printing.

Cyan, magenta and yellow are the subtractive primary colors and absorb color rather than adding it. When two of these subtractive primaries are added, they create an additive primary color, either red, green, or blue.

The L*a*b model

The CIE L*a*b color model is an international standard for creating consistent color across all device platforms. It supposedly contains every color visible to the human eye.

L*a*b color is defined by its luminance (L) value—think of this as its brightness—and two color values: *"a"*, which defines its green-to-red color component and *"b"*, which is its blue-to-yellow color component.

The internal color mode used by InDesign to convert colors from one mode to another is the LAB mode, based on the L*a*b color model, because all of the colors contained in the RGB and CMYK gamuts fall within the L*a*b model. Because of this use by InDesign of the LAB mode, many professionals define colors in the LAB mode, described in the next section, because the colors they choose in the LAB mode don't have to be converted into another mode before being converted to CMYK.

Color Modes

Now that we have color models to describe the colors we need to produce, we need another system to reproduce the colors of the color models. We need *color modes*. A color mode is a numeric system used by an application for reproducing a specific color model. For example, when we define colors using the RGB color mode, telling our computer to shine its monitor's lights in various numerical combinations of those three colors, we can reproduce specific colors of a color mode.

The RGB Mode

On the computer, each individual pixel comprising the monitor's screen display is assigned a color value. The RGB values are described as a number from 0 to 255 (256 colors). When all three color values are zero, the result is black. When all three color values are 255, the result is white. Medium gray would be R, G, and B values of 127.

You might choose to define your colors via RGB mode if your project will only be displayed on a computer screen.

The CMYK Mode

The CMYK mode is based on the CMYK color model. So when defining colors in InDesign via the CMYK mode, you specify a percentage of ink for each of the four colors. The four color values are entered as percentages of 100, with less ink providing less color. In other words, the higher the percentages, the darker the colors.

WARNING Remember that your computer monitor relies on the three-color RGB model and that CMYK is a four-color model. Consequently, you will never see an absolutely true screen representation of CMYK colors on the computer screen. For precision when producing documents that will be printed on paper by a printing press, you should use a color book filled with swatches of printed colors, defined by their four CMYK percentages. That way, you'll get the colors you mean to get when the project is printed.

Since ink-on-paper color printing presses are the only four-color output devices, there is really no reason to define colors in the CMYK mode for documents that will not eventually be printed on a color printing press.

The LAB Mode

LAB mode is often used by professionals because of its color range, and the fact that the L*a*b color model is designed to produce accurate colors on any device. You can print LAB mode documents to PostScript Level 2 and 3 printers.

TIP Because the L*a*b model separates color values from their luminance value, the LAB mode can be useful for adjusting colors without affecting their brightness or for adjusting the brightness of a color without affecting its hue.

The luminance, or lightness, component value is entered as a number from 0 to 100. The color components *A* and *B* can be entered as values from +120 to -120.

TIP As I mentioned earlier, some professionals prefer defining colors in LAB mode because it is InDesign's internal color mode, covering all the colors available in the other color modes.

Spot Color

When I described the process of printing full-color documents on a printing press with the four subtractive primaries of cyan, magenta, yellow, and black, I talked about how you can define all the colors in the CMYK gamut by setting various values for each ink. When you do this, you are actually printing an illusion of specific colors. Those other colors aren't really on the paper, but the properties of the translucent inks and the printing press make it look like they are. This printing process is referred to as *4-color process printing* and the CMYK colors are referred to as *process colors*.

However, you can print specific colors by selecting an ink that is actually that color. This is called *spot color*. You could print a document using all spot colors, if you

wanted, but that could get expensive if you choose a lot of them. Each spot color will need a printing plate of its own and will have to have one press ink well devoted to that color.

Also, you can't print full-color photographs with spot colors. Think of the number of inks that might require.

You can choose to apply only one spot color, along with black, for a document, or you can add a spot color or two to the four process colors.

Spot colors are most useful for applying precise color—perhaps for a corporate logo or other identifying color—or for adding color to a document that might otherwise be printed only with black.

Ink manufacturers supply books and charts that show all of their colors of inks, defined by their proprietary names. You use these books and charts to select the color you want. InDesign supports several of these color-matching schemes, allowing you to select colors by the manufacturer's names.

Often, spot colors aren't colors at all, but are applied as shiny varnishes or clear protective coatings.

InDesign's Color Scheme

In order to apply color to objects in InDesign, you must understand how InDesign is set up to handle the selection, storage, and application of color.

InDesign is not a painting program like Photoshop, nor is it a drawing program like Illustrator. Primarily, you can apply colors to objects as strokes, or outlines, and as fill, or background colors. You can apply gradients, which are smooth transitions between colors. But you can't grab a tool and paint a new rendition of the Mona Lisa. (Somebody probably could, but it would be really painstaking.)

The three main color controls in InDesign are the Toolbox, the Color palette, and the Swatches palette.

- Through the Toolbox, you can apply color to objects.
- In the Color palette, you can specify and apply colors.
- In the Swatches palette, you can specify, store, and apply colors.

WARNING It is important to note the difference between InDesign's *None* or *No color* and white. As far as InDesign is concerned, white is an opaque color. It is not the color of the paper, showing through. In other words, if you have an object filled or stroked with white, nothing underneath that object's fill or stroke will show through. If you want an object to be "transparent" you must apply *None* or *No color*.

Selecting Colors in InDesign

When specifying colors in InDesign, you have two options:

- You can create a color on the run in the Color palette, after which that color is not stored or linked to its occurrences in other objects.
- You can create a color in the Swatches palette, which you can then name and link to all its occurrences throughout a document.

Naming and saving colors in the Swatches palette is like using character and paragraph styles for text formatting, as presented in Chapter 10. Once you create a color and apply it to several objects, you can edit that color in the Swatches palette and the changes will be reflected throughout the document. If you apply all of your colors through the Color palette, you may not wind up with the same degree of consistency throughout the document, nor will you be able to apply sweeping changes to colors easily.

In addition, named colors in the Swatches palette are the only colors available in many of the dialog boxes, such as the Character Color area of the Character Styles dialog box. In other words, you won't be able to apply color through these dialog boxes until you have defined and saved the colors you want in the Swatches palette.

For these reasons, you are better off working through the Swatches palette, rather than the Color palette. Of course, there may be times when you are doing something very simple and don't need a lot of colors. In those cases, you may find working through the Color palette sufficient for your needs.

Navigating the Swatches Palette

The Swatches palette is by far the most powerful of the InDesign color controls. In the Swatches palette you can create, name, and save colors and gradients. You can then easily apply those saved colors and gradients to objects throughout a document. When you edit or change a named and saved color or gradient, the changes are reflected in every object to which that color or gradient has been applied.

Access the Swatches palette, shown in Figure 12.4, by choosing Window ➢ Swatches, by pressing F5, or by clicking the Swatches tab in its palette group.

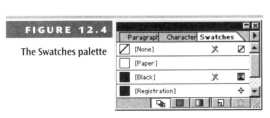

FIGURE 12.4

The Swatches palette

As you can see, the colors of the swatches are displayed to the left of their names. The None swatch shows the white swatch with the red bar, as shown below.

Color swatches show their colors, as shown below.

Gradient swatches show the actual gradient and its color in its swatch, as shown below.

In each swatch's bar, you see other icons that indicate its type and other properties. The special icons and their meanings are shown in Table 12.1.

TABLE 12.1: ICONS IN THE SWATCHES PALETTE

Icon	Name	Description
✗	No Edit	Neither the None swatch nor the Black swatch can be edited.
⊘	None	This symbol is universal in InDesign to indicate that there is no color applied.
✚	Registration	The color of registration marks, which is usually black, is indicated by this symbol.
◩	CMYK color	If a color has been defined in the CMYK mode, its swatch displays this symbol.
▮	RGB color	If a color has been defined in the RGB mode, its swatch displays this symbol.
▰	LAB color	If a color has been defined in the LAB mode, its swatch displays this symbol.
▦	Process color	If a color is created to match a specific process color, this icon appears with it.
◉	Spot color	If a color is based on a spot color, this icon appears with it.
New Color Swatch 71%	Color tint	If you have defined a color that is only a tint, or percentage, of another color, that percentage is shown in the swatch.

The buttons across the bottom of the Swatches palette, from left to right, are shown in Table 12.2.

TABLE 12.2: BUTTONS ON THE SWATCHES PALETTE

Button	Name	Description
	Show All Swatches	Click this button to display all of the colors saved as swatches.
	Show Color Swatches	Click this button to display only the color, spot color, and tint swatches.
	Show Gradient Swatches	Click this button to display only the gradient swatches.
	New Swatch	Click this button to create a new swatch. (Creating swatches is covered later in this section.)
	Trash	You can delete swatches by dragging them onto this button or by selecting them and then clicking this button.

The four colors shown in the Swatches palette pictured in Figure 12.4 are the default swatches and cannot be removed. These four swatches are:

None   You can remove color from an object by using this swatch. It cannot be edited or removed from the Swatches palette. It is always displayed, regardless of which display button you may have clicked.

Paper   You can use the Paper swatch for two operations. You can apply it to object that you want not to print, sort of like reversing type. For example, when you print your document, any objects to which the Paper swatch has been applied will not print—nor will any object directly underneath that object—allowing the paper to show through. Also, using the Paper swatch, you can simulate the appearance of the color of your paper stock. In other words, you can edit the Paper swatch to approximate the color of your paper stock, then create a frame the size of your document and apply the Paper swatch to that as fill. Then when you layout your document, you can see on-screen how the color of the paper might affect the appearance of the surrounding colors of your document.

Black   If printing on a printing press, objects to which the Black swatch has been applied would print with 100% black ink. You cannot edit or remove this swatch from the Swatches palette. By default, this color overprints all other colors unless you deselect Overprint Black in the File ➢ Preferences ➢ General dialog box. (Overprinting black is covered in the advanced printing topics in Chapter 18.)

Registration   Registration marks are the little targets, crosshairs, and trim marks that print outside the document dimensions. These registration marks enable the press operators to align, or register, the four different color plates so that they print properly. Trim marks show where the document should be cut to size. When you apply this color to an object, it will print on all four color separations. You can edit this color, but you can't remove the Registration swatch from the Swatches palette. (Printing color separations and registration marks are covered in Chapter 18.)

Creating Swatches

Before you create a new color swatch, you can select the color you want for the swatch. The color that is currently displayed in the Fill Color box or the Stroke Color box of the Toolbox, shown below, is the color for which the new color swatch is created.

If you want to base the new swatch on a color already applied to an object, either as a fill or a stroke, select that object and then click on either the Fill Color box or the Stroke Color box of the Toolbox. Then, to create a new swatch, you either click the New Swatch button in the Swatches palette or choose New Color Swatch from the Swatches palette menu, as shown below.

If you click the New Swatch button, the current color of the currently-selected color box in the Toolbox will be automatically created and given a numerically consecutive name, such as "New Color Swatch 1," "New Color Swatch 2," and so on.

If you wish to edit the color of the new swatch as you create it, or if you want to give the new color swatch a particular name, press Alt/Option as you click the New Swatch button, or choose New Color Swatch from the Swatches palette menu. This opens the New Color Swatch dialog box, as shown in Figure 12.5.

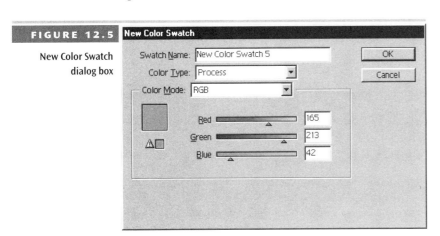

FIGURE 12.5
New Color Swatch dialog box

As you can see, the New Color Swatch dialog box allows you to specify a name for the new swatch by typing it in the Swatch Name text area.

You can select Process or Spot from the Color Type option menu. From the Color Mode option menu, you can choose LAB, CMYK, or RGB. Depending on which you choose, the Color Mode area changes to offer the respective color component controls.

The color component controls for RGB are shown in Figure 12.5 and the color component controls for LAB and CMYK are shown in Figures 12.6 and 12.7.

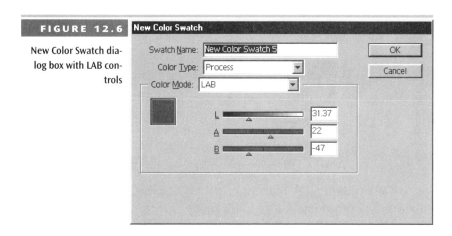

FIGURE 12.6

New Color Swatch dialog box with LAB controls

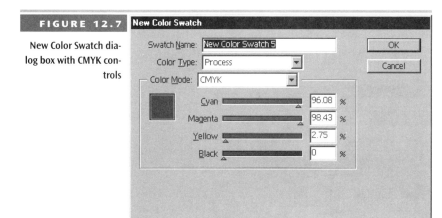

FIGURE 12.7

New Color Swatch dialog box with CMYK controls

You can edit any of these color component controls by dragging the sliders under the color bars. The color display to the left will change to reflect the edits.

TIP If the out-of-gamut alert icon, shown in Figure 12.5, appears when you create a color swatch, you have created a color that can not be printed via the CMYK process. The color swatch that appears next to the alert icon is the closest in-gamut color to the one you defined. You can click that little swatch to select that in-gamut color.

When you click OK, the new color swatch will take its place in the Swatches palette, as shown below.

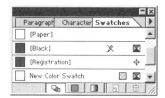

Editing Swatches

To edit a swatch, you must first select it by clicking it in the Swatches palette or by selecting an object in the document to which that swatch has been applied.

WARNING Be careful. If you select a swatch while any object or objects in the document are selected, the color of that swatch will be applied to the selected object(s).

Once you have selected a swatch, either double-click the swatch's name or choose Swatch Options from the Swatches palette menu, shown below. These actions open the Swatch Options dialog box, shown in Figure 12.8.

As you can see, the Swatch Options dialog box offers the same options as the New Color Swatch dialog box. By altering any of these values, you can rename the swatch or change its type or color. Click the Preview checkbox to view changes before accepting them.

WARNING If you have applied a swatch to objects in your document and then edit the swatch, the color changes will be reflected in all occurrences of that color, throughout the document. If you don't want that to happen, you should probably duplicate the swatch, as described in the next section, and then edit the duplicate.

FIGURE 12.8

Swatch Options dialog box

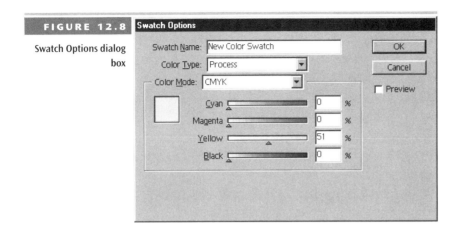

Duplicating Swatches

If you want to duplicate a swatch, perhaps to create one similar to it, first select that swatch by either clicking it in the Swatches palette or by selecting an object in the document to which that swatch has been applied. Then you can either choose Duplicate Swatch from the Swatches palette menu, as shown below, or you can simply drag a swatch to the New Color Swatch button.

These operations automatically duplicate the swatch, naming it after the original, with "copy" appended to the name. You can then edit the swatch normally.

Deleting Swatches

To delete a swatch from your document, you must first select it. You can select multiple swatches for deletion by pressing Shift and clicking their names in the Swatches palette. You can delete a selected swatch or swatches from your document in one of three ways:

- Click the Trash button.
- Drag the selected swatch or swatches to the Trash button.
- Choose Delete Swatch from the Swatches palette menu, as shown next.

ADDING COLORS FROM SWATCH LIBRARIES

After you perform any of these operations, InDesign will prompt you with the Delete Swatch dialog box, shown in Figure 12.9.

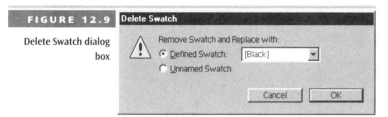

FIGURE 12.9
Delete Swatch dialog box

The purpose of this dialog box isn't clear, so don't be fooled by what it does. See where it says "Remove Swatch and Replace With"? That does not refer to replacing the swatch in the Swatches palette. It refers to replacing the color of the swatch in all its occurrences throughout the document.

For example, let's say you have been using a swatch called "My Swatch" for a bunch of objects throughout the document and you decide to delete that swatch. If you select Defined Swatch and select one of the available swatches from the Defined Swatch option menu, all objects in the document that have had My Swatch applied to them will be changed to whatever swatch you choose in the Defined Swatch option menu. Be careful. You could turn a bunch of objects into a color you don't really want them to be.

If you select Unnamed Swatch, all of those occurrences will remain the same color, but they won't be associated with any swatch.

In either case, the selected swatch or swatches will be removed from the Swatches palette.

Adding Colors from Swatch Libraries

Manufacturers of inks and other color systems publish books, charts, and computer applications that give examples of their products so designers and production artists can effectively select and apply desktop colors that will reproduce as intended. You can obtain these publications and select colors from them, then enter the manufacturer's specific name for the color in InDesign. When the colors are separated for printing, you supposedly get what you wanted. In practice, this does work very well.

Some designers use these color systems primarily to select spot colors, those specific inks that are of the single color they want. But using them to assure the printing of a specific process color makes sense, too. Color systems such as Pantone, Trumatch, and Focoltone show the CMYK equivalents for producing various colors, on both uncoated and coated paper stocks.

TIP Selecting colors from a color system is only part of the process of obtaining final printed copy that appears as you intend. Color calibration of your system is also important and it is covered in Appendix C.

Using Commercial Color Systems

InDesign supports several of the more popular color selection systems. You can use them to apply color to your documents. To access the list of supported color systems, choose Window ➢ Swatch Libraries. The list of color systems appears as a submenu, as shown below.

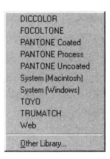

The color systems supplied with InDesign are the following:

DIC Color   1280 CMYK spot colors widely used in Japan, from the *DIC Color Guide*, from Dainippon Ink & Chemicals, Inc.

Focoltone   763 CMYK colors, including overprint examples, used primarily in the United Kingdom.

PANTONE Coated   Examples of spot color inks available from PANTONE, as they appear on coated paper stock.

PANTONE Process   Examples of CMYK process colors generated with common printing inks used in the United States.

ADDING COLORS FROM SWATCH LIBRARIES

PANTONE Uncoated Examples of spot color inks available from PANTONE, as they appear on uncoated paper stock

System (Windows) The 256 RGB colors of the default 8-bit color palette of the Windows operating system.

System (Mac OS) The 256 RGB colors of the default 8-bit color palette of the Mac operating system.

Toyo Color Finder 1050 More than 1000 colors widely used in Japan.

Trumatch More than 2000 colors, tints, and four-color grays that have been specified on computer and then separated and printed.

Web The palette of 216 colors that are supposedly the safest for use on the various browsers and computer platforms of the World Wide Web.

To select a color from one of these systems and add it to your Swatches palette, follow these steps:

1. Refer to a color book and select the color you want.
2. Choose Window ➢ Swatch Libraries ➢ [*Your color system selection*] to open the palette of that particular color system, as shown below.

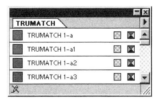

3. Sort through the swatches and select the color you want.
4. Either double-click the color or choose Add to Swatches from the color system's palette menu.

This process will add the color swatch to your Swatches palette. The new swatch will be named exactly as it appeared in the color system's swatch library.

Once you add these colors to your Swatches palette, you can edit them as you would any other color. They will be also saved with your document.

 WARNING Don't edit color system colors if you plan on getting the results you intended when you selected them. Also, if you choose spot colors and then edit them, the spot color ink that is used won't match the color you created by editing the original. If you ever do want to use one for a starting point for a custom color, just be sure to rename it so that you don't confuse it with an authentic color.

Importing Colors from Other Files

Anytime you copy or drag-and-drop an object from another document into your open InDesign document, you also import any color swatch that may be applied to that object.

You can also copy or drag-and-drop colors and gradients directly from Adobe Illustrator. You should use global process colors in Illustrator for any colors you intend to export to InDesign.

You can also import the entire swatch library of documents from the following document types:

- Adobe InDesign documents (.INDD)
- Adobe InDesign templates (.INDT)
- Adobe Illustrator documents (.AI)
- Adobe Illustrator EPS documents (.EPS)

To import the color swatches from another document, choose Window ➢ Swatches Library ➢ Other Library.

This action opens the Select a Library to Open dialog box, shown in Figure 12.10.

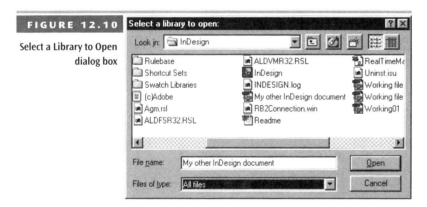

FIGURE 12.10

Select a Library to Open dialog box

Locate the other file you want to open, then click Open. InDesign opens the swatches of the other document in a new palette, as shown below.

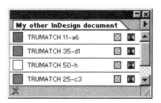

You can now add any of these other swatches to your document by double-clicking them or by selecting one or more and choosing Add To Swatches from the palette menu.

Alternately, you can import swatches from one document to another by opening another document and dragging swatches from its swatches library onto the window of the other document.

Defining Colors in the Colors Palette

You can use the Colors palette to define and apply colors, but you can't name and save the colors. This means that you can apply a color to an object, but if you want to apply that color to another object, you'll have to write down the color component values and enter them again for the other object.

Access the Color palette, shown below, by choosing Window ➢ Color, by pressing F6, or by clicking the Color tab in its palette group.

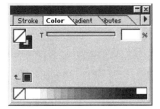

If this is the first time you will be defining a color for the document you have open, the Color palette will open to the default grayscale values of the Fill and Stroke colors.

As you can see, the Color palette offers the Fill/Stroke color boxes in the upper left. By clicking one of these, you can choose the color for it. Whatever color is currently defined for each of them is currently displayed in them.

The bar with a T before it is the Tint color value slider. You won't actually see a slider under the bar until you click somewhere along the bar or in the Tint Ramp, which is the color bar at the bottom of the Color palette. Once you click somewhere in either of those bars, the grayscale ramp appears in the Tint color value slider and the base color and its equivalent Color mode values are displayed beneath it, as shown below. The Tint Ramp changes to the Color Spectrum of the color mode you have selected.

What you can see in the Color palette shown previously is that the color selected for the fill color is 79% of black in the CMYK color mode. You can quickly select colors from one of the three color modes by choosing the appropriate selection in the Color palette menu, shown below.

Once you select one of the color modes, the color components for that particular color mode are displayed, as shown below in the Color palette for the RGB mode.

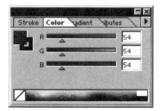

What you can see in the Color palette above is that the tint of Black that was selected in the grayscale values is now shown as the equivalent color of RGB. If you had selected LAB, the color values for that tint of black would have appeared as the LAB values, as shown below.

You can quickly select colors for either the fill color or the stroke color by clicking on their respective color box at the upper left and then performing one of the following operations:

- Click somewhere in the Color Spectrum bar at the bottom of the Color palette.
- Enter numerical values in the text entry areas to the right of each color component slider.
- Drag the sliders under each color component slider.

To apply no color for either the fill or stroke color, click on the None icon at the left of the Color Spectrum. To apply full white or full black, click on the white or black swatches at the right of the Color Spectrum.

If, after editing a color, the out-of-gamut alert icon appears in the lower left of the Color palette, as shown below, it means that you have defined a color that is not printable on a four-color printing press. The little color swatch next to the out-of-gamut alert icon is the closest color that is printable. You can select that color by clicking the little swatch.

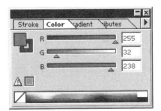

You can define a color in the Color palette and then name and save it in the Swatches palette. Once you define the color you want, access the Swatches palette by choosing Window ➢ Swatches, pressing F5, or by clicking the Swatches tab in its palette group. Select New Color Swatch from the Swatches palette menu and follow the steps described earlier in this chapter for naming and saving the color in the Swatches palette.

You can use the Color palette to access and edit colors that you named in the Swatches palette by clicking on a color in the Swatches palette. The color will appear in the Color palette for you to edit. However, changes you make in the Color palette to named colors from the Swatches palette are not reflected in the color in the Swatches palette. You must edit named colors in the Swatches palette, as described earlier in this chapter. You might choose to edit a named color in this fashion to derive and apply a variation of a named color. Of course, you could then save and name that color as a color in the Swatches palette, as described above. But if that's your intention, you might as well do that in the Swatches palette.

You can choose to display only the Color Spectrum of the selected color in a specific color mode by choosing Hide Options from the Color palette menu. This action shrinks the Color palette to display only the color spectrum, as shown below.

You can still change the color mode by selecting an alternative from the Color palette menu, as described above.

Tinting Colors

Once you have a color defined, you can use a lighter shade of that color, called a *tint*. If you're using a spot color or two on a project because you can't afford four-color process printing, you might find tinting to be a great way to give those one or two colors a lot more variety. You can also use tinting if you have created a four-color process color and just want to use a lighter version of that color, without changing its hue.

You can name and save tints, but you don't have to. You can also tint only named colors.

NOTE If you edit a named color, any tints based on that named color will be changed accordingly, but the tint percentages will be preserved.

To create a tint, you must first select a color in the Swatches palette. Open the Swatches palette by choosing Window ➢ Swatches, by pressing F5, or by clicking the Swatches tab in its palette group.

Once you select a named color in the Swatches palette, you can create a new tint swatch or you can simply apply an unnamed tint to an object. If you create a new tint swatch, you can edit it later by double-clicking it or by choosing Swatch Options from the Swatches palette menu, as described earlier in this chapter.

Creating a Tint Swatch Using the Color Palette

Open the Color palette by choosing Window ➢ Color, by pressing F6, or by clicking the Color tab in its palette group. When you select a named color in the Swatches palette, the Color palette shows the color and the Tint slider, as shown below.

When it first opens, the Color palette will show the selected color at 100 percent tint. You can change this percentage by dragging the tint slider, entering a numerical value to the right of the slider, or by clicking somewhere in the Tint Ramp at the bottom of the Color palette. As you alter the tint, the original named color in the Swatches palette will remain unchanged.

To save the tint as a named color, click the New Swatch button in the Swatches palette. The new tint swatch is named after the original named color, with the tint percentage appended to the name, as shown in Figure 12.11.

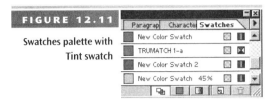

FIGURE 12.11
Swatches palette with Tint swatch

Creating a Tint Swatch Using the Swatches Palette

Select a named color in the Swatches palette and choose New Tint Swatch from the Swatches palette menu, as shown below. This action opens the New Tint Swatch dialog box, shown in Figure 12.12.

As you can see, you can't alter the name of the original named color, nor can you edit its color values. But down there at the bottom of the dialog box, you can drag the Tint slider or enter a numerical value for the tint.

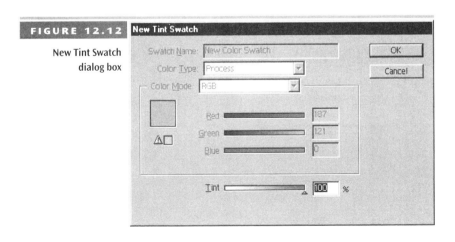

FIGURE 12.12
New Tint Swatch dialog box

Click OK to save the tint as a new tint swatch. The new tint swatch will be named after the original named color, with the tint percentage appended to the name, as shown in Figure 12.11.

Tinting an Object Without Saving the Tint Swatch

Of course, you can tint an object or objects to which a named color has been applied without saving the tint as a tint swatch.

Start by selecting an object or objects to which a named color has been applied, which will highlight the named color's swatch in the Swatches palette.

Now access the Color palette by choosing Window ➢ Color, by pressing F6, or by clicking the Color tab in its palette group. When the Color palette opens to the Tint slider, as shown below, simply drag the slider, enter a numerical percentage value, or click in the Tint Ramp at the bottom of the palette.

Now if you move on to other operations, the selected object or objects will reflect the tinted color, but the tint will not have been saved as a tint swatch. Nor will the original named color be affected.

If you change the original named swatch to another color, the object or objects to which you applied the unsaved tint will also reflect that color change, at the percentage you applied as a tint.

Defining Gradients

A *gradient* is a gradual transition from one color to another. InDesign allows you to create both linear and radial gradients, as shown in Figure 12.13.

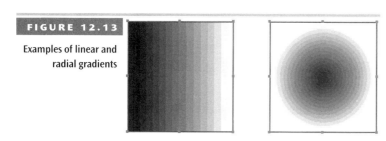

FIGURE 12.13

Examples of linear and radial gradients

InDesign offers several gradient features:

- You can apply a gradient to either just one object or to several objects.
- You can apply a gradient to the fill or the stroke of an object, or to both the fill and the stroke of an object.
- You can define gradients that transition only once between only two colors, or several times between two colors. You can also define gradients that transition several times between multiple colors.
- Although you can define gradients in any color mode, you should define them in CMYK if you will be printing your document on a printing press. This is because the necessary conversion of gradients created in other color gamuts to CMYK may produce undesirable color shifts.
- You can define gradients in either the Swatches palette or the Gradient palette. Just as with solid colors and tints, working in the Swatches palette allows you to save the gradient as a swatch. You can also define a gradient in the Gradient palette and then save it as a swatch.
- You apply gradients basically the same way as you apply color. If you select an object prior to defining a gradient, that gradient will be applied to the selected object.
- You can use the Gradient tool on the Toolbox to adjust the angle and the length of an applied gradient.

Navigating the Gradient Palette

Whether you are working in either the Gradient palette or the Swatches palette, the basic steps for defining a gradient are the same. However, starting the operation is slightly different between the two.

Before starting to define a gradient, you should be familiar with the components of a gradient, as shown in the Gradient palette below.

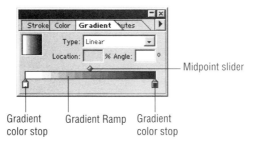

As you can see, the Gradient itself is displayed in the swatch at the upper left. The type is displayed in the Type option menu. The location percentage refers to the positions of the *stops*, which are the little boxes that look like houses under the Gradient

Ramp at the bottom of the palette. The stops define where one color is at 100 percent, falling off to either side. The little diamond above the Gradient Ramp is the midpoint, which indicates where the two colors will each be at 50 percent of their full color. When you click on one of the stops or a midpoint, its location relative to the full length of the Gradient Ramp is displayed in the Location value box, as shown above. The Angle value represents the rotation of the gradient from the horizontal.

Creating a New Gradient Swatch in the Swatches Palette

To create a new gradient swatch, access the Swatches palette by choosing Window ➢ Swatches, by pressing F5, or by clicking the Swatches tab in it palette group.

Choose New Gradient Swatch from the Swatches palette menu, as shown below.

This action opens the New Gradient Swatch dialog box, shown in Figure 12.14.

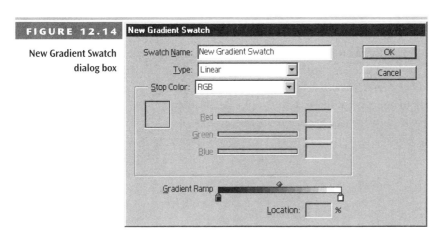

FIGURE 12.14
New Gradient Swatch dialog box

You can give the swatch a name other than the default name by typing it in the Swatch Name text area. You select either Linear or Radial from the Type option menu.

Click on one of the color stops under the Gradient Ramp at the bottom of the dialog box. The Stop Color option menu, shown next, offers the three color modes, plus the Named Color option.

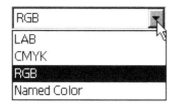

The Stop Color display area will change according to which color mode you select, displaying the respective color components. If you select Named Color from the Stop Color option menu, you will be presented with the list of colors from the Swatches palette, as shown in Figure 12.15, from which you can select a named color.

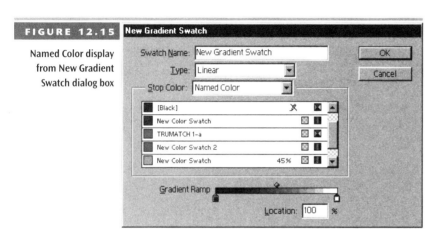

FIGURE 12.15
Named Color display from New Gradient Swatch dialog box

To define the color of a stop, click that stop and then either define the color in the LAB, CMYK, or RGB color mode or select a named color from the Swatches palette.

Once you define or select colors for both of the stops, you will see the transition displayed in the Gradient Ramp. You can drag the midpoint to change the transition or you can click the midpoint and enter a percentage value in the Location text area.

You can add additional color stops by clicking at a point beneath the Gradient Ramp. For each color stop you add, InDesign will automatically add another midpoint between that new color stop and the next one. You can define or select colors for the new color stops just as you did the original stops.

Click OK to save the new gradient swatch.

Defining a Gradient in the Gradient Palette

You can also define new gradients or edit applied gradients in the Gradient palette. If you define a new gradient in the Gradient palette, it won't be saved unless you make a new gradient swatch for it. If you use the Gradient palette to edit the gradient of an object to which a named gradient has been applied, you will *not* affect the named gradient. But, conversely, any changes you make to the original named gradient in the Swatches palette will affect the edited gradient.

Applying Color, Tints, and Gradients to Paths and Frames

Once you have defined a color, a gradient, or a tint, you can apply it to an object. If you have selected an object prior to defining these color options, you will automatically apply that color option to that object, depending on whether you select the Fill or Stroke color box in the Color palette or Toolbox.

If you already have colors, gradients, or tints defined, or if you defined them without selecting an object, you can apply them to objects through the Toolbox, the Colors palette, or the Swatches palette.

NOTE Although the following three sections refer to applying color, the procedures for applying tints are the same as those described.

Applying Color from the Toolbox

Using the toolbox, you can only apply whatever color, gradient, or tint was last selected or defined in the Color palette, Gradient palette, or Swatches palette.

The tools for applying color from the Toolbox are shown below.

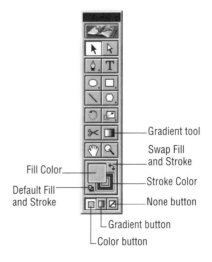

The two large color boxes represent the fill color and the stroke color. The color in the Fill Color box will be applied to the contents of an object. The color in the Stroke Color box will be applied to the outline, or stroke, of an object. You determine which will be applied by clicking one or the other to bring it to the front. Unless you are working with selected text, you can toggle between the two by pressing X on the keyboard.

Click the Swap Fill and Stroke icon to switch the colors of the two boxes. If you have an object selected—but not text—you can switch the colors of the object between the two colors currently selected in the Fill and Stroke color boxes by pressing Shift+X.

Click the Default Fill and Stroke icon to automatically change the colors to None for fill and black for stroke.

The Color button applies the last-selected color from the Color palette or Swatches palette to a selected object's fill or stroke, depending on whether the Fill color box or the Stroke color box is in front. The keyboard shortcut for applying solid color to selected objects—but not selected text—is the comma (,). This tool only works on selected objects to which color has not already been applied.

The Gradient button applies the last-selected gradient from the Gradient palette to a selected object's fill or stroke, depending on whether the Fill Color box or the Stroke Color box is in front. In other words, once you use the Gradient tool to apply a gradient, that gradient is stored in memory and can be automatically applied to other objects with the Gradient button. The keyboard shortcut for applying the gradient to selected objects—but not selected text—is the period (.).

The None button applies no color to a selected object's fill or stroke, depending on whether the Fill Color box or the Stroke Color box is in front. The keyboard shortcut for applying None to selected objects—but not selected text—is the slash (/).

It is important to note that the "last selected color" used by these tools in the Toolbox is actually the current color—if any—that has been applied to an object. When you select an object to which color has already been applied, its fill and stroke colors are automatically shown in the Color palette and those colors also become the color in the Color button. If an object has a gradient applied, the gradient becomes the gradient in the Gradient button.

What's this mean to you? If you select an object that has a gradient applied, you will see the last selected color from the Color palette or Swatches palette in the Color button and you can apply that to the selected object. If you select an object that has a solid color applied, you will see the last selected gradient from the Gradient palette in the Gradient button and you can apply that to the selected object. However, you can't change an object's applied color to another color with the Color button, nor can you change an object's applied gradient to another gradient with the Gradient button. So, unless an object has no color selected, you still have to select and apply a new color from the Color, Gradient, or Swatches palette.

Applying Color from the Color Palette

Anytime you select an object and then define a color in the Color palette, you will be applying the colors you select in the Color palette for fill and stroke. So, to apply a color to an object from the Color palette, simply select that object, click on either its Fill Color box or its Stroke Color box, and then open the Color palette and define the color you want for the object's fill and/or stroke.

Anytime you click the Fill Color box or the Stroke Color box in the Color palette, that color box is brought to the front in the Toolbox. Conversely, anytime you click the Fill Color box or the Stroke Color box in the Toolbox, that color box is brought to the front in the Color palette.

When you select an object to which color has already been applied, you see its fill and stroke colors in the Fill Color box and the Stroke Color box in both the Color palette and the Toolbox.

Applying Color from the Swatches Palette

To apply color to an object from the Swatches palette, you must first select either the Fill Color box or the Stroke Color box in the Toolbox or the Color palette. Then, when you open the Swatches palette and select one of its named colors, that color will be applied to whichever color box you selected in the Toolbox or Color palette.

When you select an object to which a named color has already been applied and select either its Fill Color box or its Stroke Color box, that named color is highlighted in the Swatches palette.

Anytime you select an object and then select an existing named color or create and define a new named color in the Swatches palette, you will be applying the named color from the Swatches palette to that selected object. So to apply a color to an object from the Swatches palette, simply select that object, click either its Fill Color box or Stroke Color box, and then open the Swatches palette and define the color you want for the object's fill and/or stroke.

Applying Gradients to an Object

To apply a gradient to an object, follow these steps:

1. Select an object to which you want to apply the gradient. Click either its Fill Color box or its Stroke Color box in the Toolbox.
2. Open the Gradient palette by choosing Window ➢ Gradient or by clicking the Gradient tab in its palette group.
3. Select either Linear or Radial from the Type option menu.

4. To define the colors of the stops for the gradient, click on one of the color stops beneath the Gradient Ramp.

5. You can now select one of the color swatches in the Swatches palette by pressing Alt/Option and clicking a swatch in the Swatches palette. Or you can define a color by opening the Color palette, as shown below.

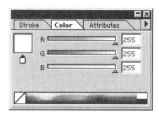

As you can see, when you click on a color stop and then access the Color palette, the color stop icon appears beneath the color swatch in the Color palette. You can now define the color as you would any other color, as described earlier in this chapter.

You can add additional color stops by clicking anywhere beneath the Gradient Ramp.

Applying Gradients with the Gradient Tool

Once you have defined and applied a gradient to an object, you can use the Gradient tool to adjust its rotation or its length, or to apply the gradient to multiple objects.

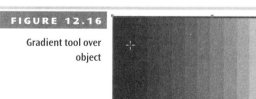

To adjust a gradient with the Gradient tool, select an object to which a gradient has been applied. Select the Gradient tool.

The cursor changes to the crosshair icon, as shown in Figure 12.16. Position the crosshair at the point where you want the gradient to begin. The beginning of the gradient is the point at which there is solid color behind the point and the gradient in front of the point, or toward the end of the gradient.

FIGURE 12.16

Gradient tool over object

Now press the mouse button and drag the Gradient tool in the direction and for the length of the gradient you want, as shown in Figure 12.17. If you press Shift as you drag, the line will be constrained to multiples of 45 degrees.

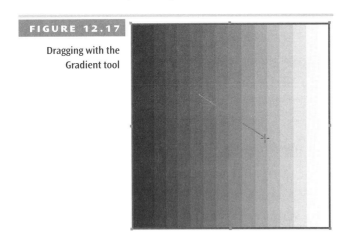

FIGURE 12.17

Dragging with the Gradient tool

As you can see in Figure 12.18, when you let go, the gradient will be drawn between the first point where you started dragging, and the second point, where you let go. On either side of the gradient, solid colors will fill the areas outside the gradient.

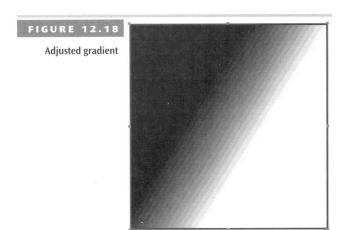

FIGURE 12.18

Adjusted gradient

You can perform this operation with either radial or linear gradients.

To apply a gradient to multiple objects, you must first apply a gradient to each object. Then select all of the objects to which you want to apply the single gradient, as shown in Figure 12.19.

Now select the Gradient tool and position it where you want the gradient to begin. Drag it to where you want the gradient to end, as shown in Figure 12.20. If you press Shift as you drag, the line will be constrained to multiples of 45 degrees.

APPLYING COLOR, TINTS, AND GRADIENTS TO PATHS AND FRAMES 323

FIGURE 12.19

Selected multiple objects with gradients

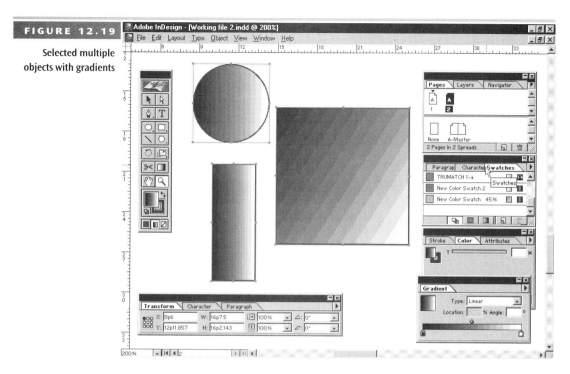

FIGURE 12.20

Dragging Gradient tool across multiple objects

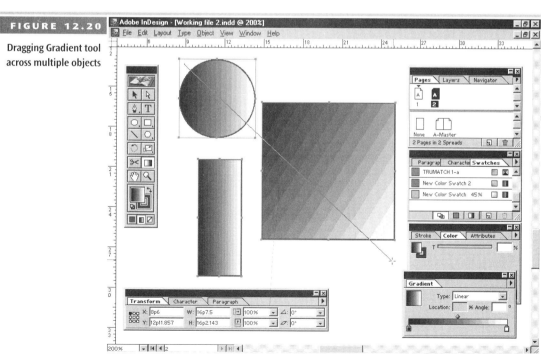

When you let go, the gradient will be drawn across the selected objects, as if they were transparent and the gradient was beneath them, as shown in Figure 12.21.

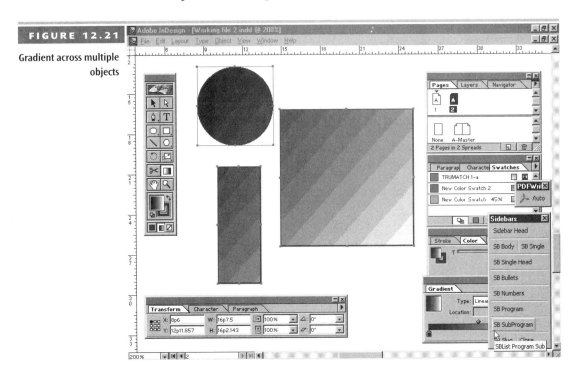

FIGURE 12.21
Gradient across multiple objects

Applying Color and Tints to Type

In InDesign, you can fill or stroke type with color just like you do with paths and frames. You can even apply different colors, tints, and gradients to different selected text within the same text frame.

Applying color or tints to the fill and stroke of selected text is done just as it is with other objects. Simply select a range of text and then click either its Fill Color box or Stroke Color box in the Toolbox or the Color palette and define a color.

Applying gradients to text, however, requires some additional consideration.

Applying Gradients to Type

When you apply a gradient to text, you are applying the gradient "underneath" the entire text frame. So the text at the top of the text frame will be filled or stroked with one part of the gradient and the text at the bottom of the text frame will be filled or stroked with another part of the gradient, as shown next. When the text is edited and reflowed, the text you originally selected may have moved in relation to the gradient and its appearance may change.

If this is not the effect you want, there are several ways you can alter the gradient in text. First, you can alter the gradient itself, so that its range of color spans only the length of the text to which you want to apply it, as shown below. However, this method does not protect you from losing contact between the gradient and the specific text you want if the text is reflowed.

You can also apply multiple gradients within the same text frame. Select a range of text and apply a gradient. Then select another range of text and apply another gradient. With this method, there still remains the possibility that reflowing the text will mess with your text and gradient relationship.

The only way to apply a gradient to text and have that gradient move with the text if it is reflowed, is to select a range of text, convert it to outlines, and then apply a gradient to it, as shown below. (Converting text to outlines is covered in Chapter 17.)

 NOTE Of course, much of the danger of having a gradient and selected text lose their selected appearance is eliminated when using small blocks of type, such as headlines. In those cases, it is unlikely that editing will change much about the text's alignment with its gradient.

chapter 13

Understanding Layers

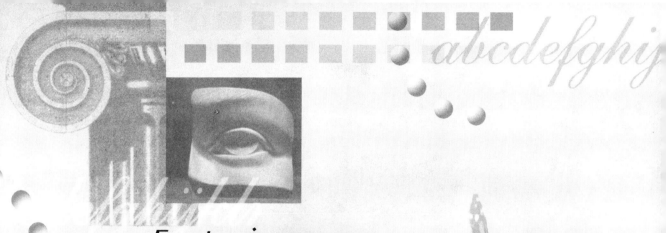

Featuring:

- Understanding the difference between layers and the object stack ... 330
- Using the Layers palette ... 334
- Working with layers ... 343
- Managing layers ... 352

CHAPTER 13

UNDERSTANDING LAYERS

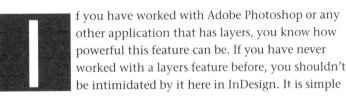

f you have worked with Adobe Photoshop or any other application that has layers, you know how powerful this feature can be. If you have never worked with a layers feature before, you shouldn't be intimidated by it here in InDesign. It is simple and easy to understand.

In fact, from the moment you launched InDesign and created or opened a document file, you have been working with layers. InDesign automatically creates one layer when a document is created. So everything you've done in InDesign so far was on that one layer. Now you'll learn how to add additional layers and take much more control over your document layout.

Using layers, you can experiment with different layouts within one document. You can create a stacking order that allows you to set objects on top of each other, overlapping them to create a three-dimensional appearance. You can create different versions of a layer that enable you to create different looks for one document. You can easily separate text objects, graphics, and other objects into dedicated layers, making it easier to locate, select, and edit them.

When you use layers, you can hide the contents of some layers, while showing the contents of other layers, making it easier to see the displayed objects. You can also lock layers so that you don't accidentally move or change its contents.

Understanding the Difference between Layers and the Object Stack

It is important for you to understand the distinction between the layers feature and the natural stacking of objects on a layer as you add objects to a document. This stacking of objects, the *object stack*, occurs whether you use layers or not and you must understand this to utilize features such as text wrapping. Layers, on the other hand, enable you to take more control over the building of a document.

Even though these concepts are similar in that they involve the vertical positioning of objects on a document page, they differ in how much control you have over how the objects behave.

Let's look at how InDesign "thinks" about how you go about laying out objects in its documents.

First off, you must begin to think of the vertical position screen on your computer monitor as being a desktop pasteboard or drawing board that has been tilted up from its horizontal orientation to a vertical orientation, as in the illustration below. The laws of gravity have been suspended, because the objects that you place on this now-vertical pasteboard stay where you place them; they don't all fall down to the bottom of the screen.

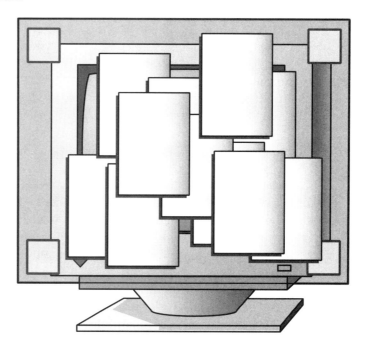

But now let's take a step back. Let's lay that pasteboard back down so that we can examine the principles of paste-up in InDesign.

How the Object Stack Works

Each time you draw, place, or paste a new object onto the InDesign pasteboard, that object is positioned on top of all the other objects on that pasteboard, as shown below.

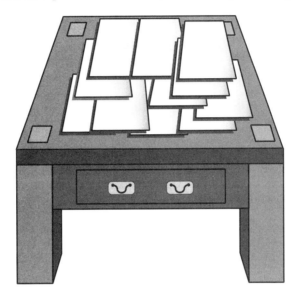

That's all the object stack really is. It's the "vertical" arrangement of the objects on a pasteboard. Think of taking a deck of cards and placing them on the pasteboard one at a time, with at least a part of one card on top of another. Each time you laid down a new card, that card would automatically, naturally, be on top of the other cards.

That's how InDesign does it, too. If you draw one object, then draw another object, that second object will automatically be placed "on top" of the other.

Even though this stacking is really coming out at you from the vertical position of the computer monitor's screen, it works just the same way as if it were on a horizontal table. It's just that you have to think now of things being "in front," or "behind," rather than "on top" or "under."

Now, just as you could pull out one card from the stack and tuck it into another place in the stack, you can rearrange the objects in your InDesign document, moving them up (forward) or down (backward) in the stacking order. This is important to understand because of how you must arrange objects for text wrap, among other things. (Arranging objects is discussed in Chapter 15.)

What you *can't* do with the object stack is selectively hide and display the objects. You have to delete an object to hide it.

How Layers Work

Now you should understand how that object stack works. Layers work the same way, except that you now pretend that between objects you place a transparent sheet of plastic or film onto which you place objects. If that piece of plastic were lying there with objects on it, you could pick it up by the edges and move it out of the way, leaving undisturbed the objects on other sheets of plastic. You could rearrange the sheets, so that the one on the bottom is moved to the top, revealing more of its contents. You could place certain objects on one sheet and other objects on a second sheet, then alternately view how the two different sets of objects look when placed individually on top of the other sheets.

On each layer, you can have an object stack of however many objects you need. You could have one object or you could have fifty.

Layers cover the entire document. In other words, if you create an additional layer, you can have some objects on it on page 2 and other objects on it on page 46.

When you first create a new document, it automatically contains one layer.

Figure 13.1 shows a document with four layers. Notice that they are currently all visible. Each object is on a separate layer. Now in Figure 13.2 let's hide Layer 4—which contains the rectangle with the text inside it—so we can see how the objects underneath are layered.

What we can see now is that the rectangle with the gradient in it is on top of both the ellipse and the rectangle. Consequently, we know that the gradient rectangle must be on Layer 3. Let's test it by hiding Layer 3 in Figure 13.3.

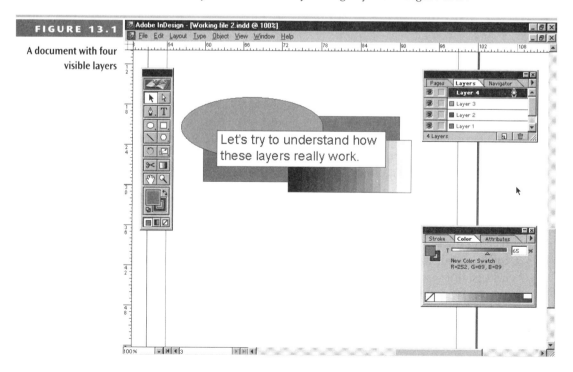

FIGURE 13.1

A document with four visible layers

UNDERSTANDING THE DIFFERENCE BETWEEN LAYERS AND THE OBJECT STACK 333

FIGURE 13.2

The same document with Layer 4 hidden

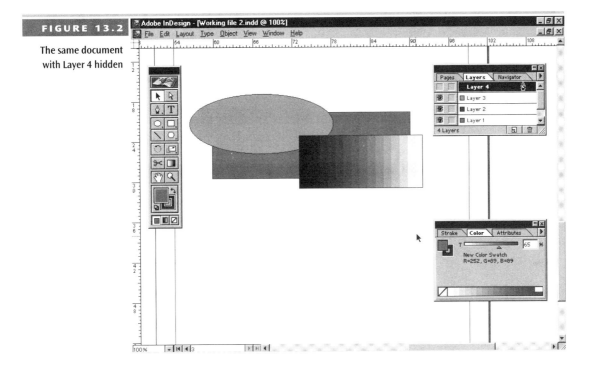

FIGURE 13.3

The same document with Layers 3 and 4 hidden

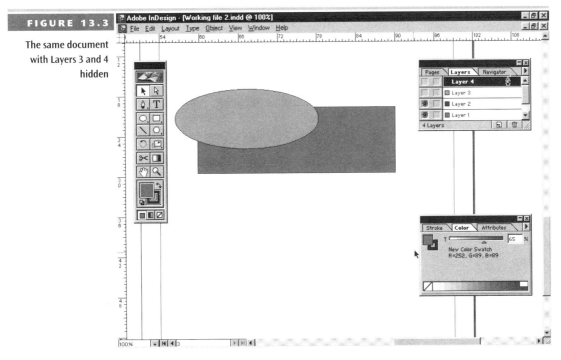

Yep, we were right. Now let's go ahead and show all the layers again, but this time we'll move Layer 2, which contains the ellipse, up above Layer 4. See Figure 13.4.

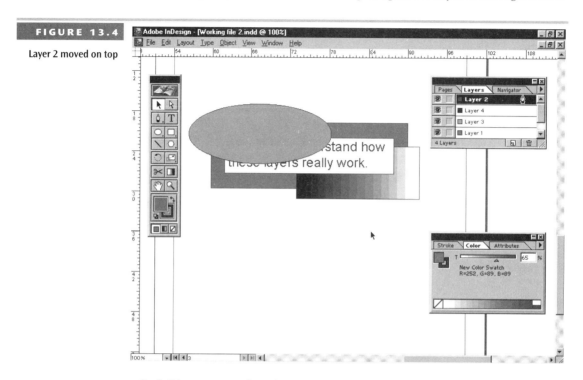

FIGURE 13.4

Layer 2 moved on top

See? We can move these layers around and quickly show and hide them to get a different view of the document. We can actually do a lot of really neat things with layers.

Using the Layers Palette

Layers are created, edited, and controlled from the Layers palette, shown in Figure 13.5. Open the Layers palette by choosing Window ➢ Layers, pressing F7, or by clicking the Layers tab in its palette group.

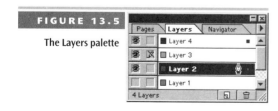

FIGURE 13.5

The Layers palette

"Reading" the Layers Palette

What you see in that Layers palette shown in Figure 13.5 is four layers, with Layer 4 being the layer "on top" of the others. Existing layers and their names are displayed according to their position in the stack of layers. The topmost layer listed in the Layers palette is the topmost layer on the stack of layers.

Layers 2, 3 and 4 are visible, as indicated by the eyeball icon to the left of their names.

Layer 3 is locked to editing, as indicated by the no editing icon to the left of its name.

Layer 2 is the selected layer, indicated by its layer name being highlighted. The selected layer is the layer which will be affected by the next layer command. You can have more than one selected layer.

Layer 2 is also the target layer, as indicated by the pen icon to the right of its name. The *target layer* is the layer onto which you will place a pasted or newly drawn object. You can have only one target layer.

Layers 2 and 4 contain objects in the document that are currently selected, as indicated by the little color dot to the right of their names.

Selecting and Targeting Layers in the Layers Palette

In order to select and work on the contents of a layer, that layer must be selected. Selected layers are highlighted in the Layers palette. You automatically select a layer when you select the contents of that layer. You can also select a layer by clicking its name in the Layers palette.

You can select consecutive multiple layers by pressing Shift and clicking the layers. You can select non-consecutive multiple layers by pressing Ctrl/Cmd and clicking the layers.

The target layer is the layer onto which objects will be positioned. When you draw a new object; import, place, or paste objects; or move objects from another layer, they will be positioned on the target layer. You define the target layer by clicking its name in the Layers palette. You can only have one target layer at a time.

If you have selected multiple layers, you can click between them to move the target layer, but if you then click on a layer that is not selected, all the layers but that one will be deselected.

To understand the distinction between selected layers and the target layer, let's do a little exercise.

Figure 13.6 shows the same four objects on four layers used earlier in the chapter. I have selected all of the objects by pressing Ctrl/Cmd+A. I have also highlighted both Layer 2 and Layer 3.

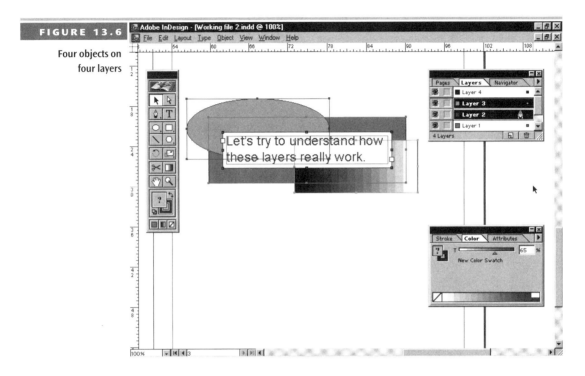

FIGURE 13.6
Four objects on four layers

Now I'll choose Delete Layers from the Layers palette menu.

InDesign then warns me that the selected layers contain objects and asks for approval of the deletion operation.

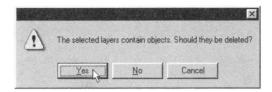

As you can see in Figure 13.7, InDesign only deleted the two objects that were on the two layers selected in the Layers palette. The objects on the other two layers were unchanged.

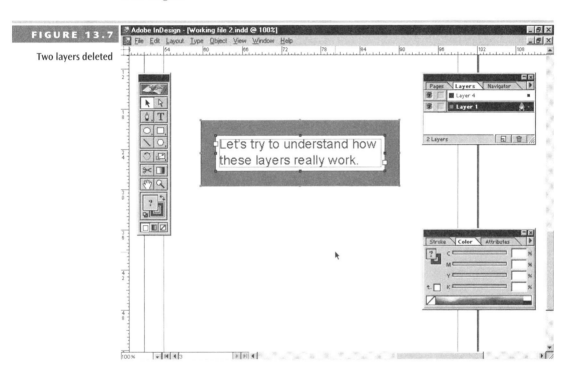

FIGURE 13.7

Two layers deleted

Now let's go back to the original four objects on four layers shown in Figure 13.6. This time, all four objects are still selected and two layers are selected. The target layer, identified by the pen icon to the right of its name, is Layer 2. Now I'll paste an object that I copied to the clipboard (see Figure 13.8). Notice that the pasted object is behind the gradient rectangle, which is on Layer 3. Because Layer 2 was the target layer, the object was pasted to Layer 2, even though both Layer 2 and Layer 3 were selected.

So you see, the target layer will be the layer to which new objects are pasted, drawn, imported, and so on. Selected layers are the layers to which layers commands are applied.

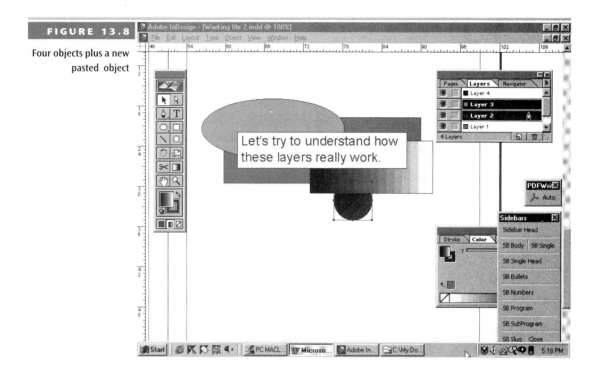

FIGURE 13.8
Four objects plus a new pasted object

Hiding and Showing Layers

Layers 2, 3, and 4 in Figure 13.9 are visible, as indicated by the eyeball icon to the left of their name. Clicking this eyeball icon on and off hides and shows the layer's contents. Layer 1 in Figure 13.9 is hidden, as indicated by the absence of an eyeball icon on its layer.

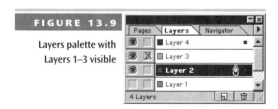

FIGURE 13.9
Layers palette with Layers 1–3 visible

You can choose Hide Others from the Layers palette menu, as shown next, to display the contents of only the selected layer.

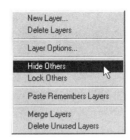

If you have one or more layers selected while any of the document's layers are hidden, you can choose Show All Layers from the Layers palette menu, as shown below, to display the contents of all the layers.

Creating Layers

As I mentioned earlier, when you create a new document, you automatically have one layer. You can add as many layers as your computer's RAM will support.

When creating new layers, you have several options:

- You can click the New Layer button of the Layers palette to create a layer that is automatically placed at the top of the Layers palette display.

- You can select a layer and then press Ctrl/Cmd and click the New Layer button of the Layers palette to create a layer that is automatically placed immediately above a selected layer.

- You can choose New Layer from the Layers palette menu, as shown below, to specify a new layer's options, such as its name, identifying color, and so on, as you create the new layer.

- You can press Alt/Option and click the New Layer button from the Layers palette to specify a new layer's options, such as its name, identifying color, and so on, as you create the new layer.

When you use the New Layer button of the Layers palette, as described above, you will create a layer to which the default options will be applied.

The default options for a new layer are:

- A consecutive number name, such as "Layer 2"
- The next unused identifying color from the list of colors offered in the Color option menu of the Layer options menu
- Show Layer
- Show Guides

Specifying Layer Options

As described above, you can specify the layer options for a new layer by either choosing New Layer from the Layers palette menu or by pressing Alt/Option and clicking the New Layer button in the Layers palette.

Alternately, you can specify the layer options for an existing layer by selecting that layer in the Layers palette and then choosing Layer Options for "Layer *X*" from the Layers palette menu, as shown below.

Either of these methods opens the Layer Options dialog box, shown in Figure 13.10.

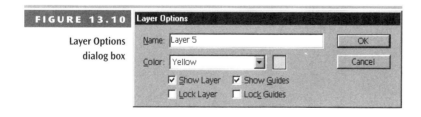

FIGURE 13.10
Layer Options dialog box

The layer options are the following:

Name As long as you don't have more than one layer selected, you can specify a new name for the layer. Type in the name.

Color You can select an identifying color by choosing one of the offered colors in the Color option menu, shown in Figure 13.11. You can select duplicate identifying colors for layers, but then you won't be able to quickly see which layer an object is on.

You can also select a color of your own choosing by selecting Other from the bottom of the Color option menu. This option opens the color picker of the operating system of your computer, where you can define a new color.

FIGURE 13.11

Color option menu from Layer Options dialog box

Show Layer This option toggles the layer's visibility, just like clicking the little eyeball icon in the Layers palette.

Show Guides Any ruler guides that you have placed on a layer can be hidden or shown with this option. This option only affects the ruler guides on the selected layer.

Lock Layer You can prevent any editing or changes to a layer by selecting this option, which is the same as clicking the pencil icon on and off in the Layers palette. (See the next section for more information on locking layers.)

Lock Guides You can lock the positions of any ruler guides on the selected layer with this option.

Locking Layers

If you want to prevent any changes or editing to the contents of a layer, you can lock it by clicking the little box immediately to the left of the layer's name and identifying color swatch, as shown below.

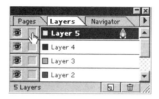

 Clicking this box will lock the layer, displaying the no editing pencil icon in the box. Alternately, you can lock a layer by selecting it and either double-clicking it or choosing Layer Options from the Layers palette menu to access the Layer Options dialog box, shown in Figure 13.10. Simply click the Lock Layer checkbox and click OK to lock the layer

You can choose Lock Others from the Layers palette menu, as shown below, to lock all of the unselected layers.

If any layers are locked and you select a layer or layers, you can select Unlock All Layers from the Layers palette menu, as shown below.

Working with Layers

As you build your document layouts, you can add new objects to layers, you can copy objects from one layer to another, and you can move objects from one layer to another.

Placing Objects on Layers

To add an object to a layer, you can create a brand new object, you can paste an object from the clipboard, or you can place text or graphics.

You shouldn't have any trouble adding objects to layers. You don't really do anything different than you have been doing with that one layer automatically created for you by InDesign when you first created your document. That layer is just like all other layers and everything you've learned so far about laying out and designing a document works just the same.

The only thing you need to do differently is to make sure that you are working on the layer you want to be working on. That's simple. Just click on the name of the layer in the Layers palette.

When you click on any one layer in the Layer's palette, that layer automatically becomes the target layer. The target layer is the layer on which you will be adding objects. The target layer is indicated in the Layers palette by the pen icon. In the example below, Layer 4 is the target layer. As you draw, copy, place, or paste objects or text, they will be placed on that layer.

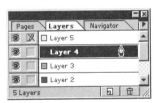

Even if you select more than one layer in the Layers palette, as shown below, which you can do by pressing Shift or Ctrl/Cmd as you click on the names of the layers, you can still have only one target layer. The target layer can be any one of those selected layers and you can click from one to the other of those selected layers to designate a different layer as the target layer. If, however, you click any layer that is not one of the selected layers, that layer becomes selected and it becomes the target layer. All of the other layers become deselected.

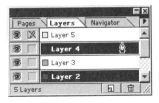

You can't add new objects to a layer that is locked or hidden.

Drawing New Objects on a Layer

To draw a new object on a layer, select the layer in the Layers palette. Then choose a drawing tool, such as the Rectangle tool, and draw the object. Again, nothing is any different about the actual drawing of the object than when you were working with that one original layer. Just make sure that you are working on the layer you really want.

Pasting Objects or Text on a Layer

Once you cut or copy an object or text from somewhere in InDesign or another application, that object or text is stored in your computer's clipboard. When you choose Edit ➢ Paste or press Ctrl/Cmd+V, you paste that stored object or text to the current document.

Now that you're working with layers, nothing about that changes. Again, just make sure you select the layer you really want.

Copying Objects from One Layer to Another

Copying objects from one layer to another is just as simple as cutting or copying objects and then pasting them somewhere else. It may even be more simple. It's definitely more efficient because you don't have to go through the usual cut-and-paste operation.

Just remember that the stacking order of the layers could affect the visibility of objects or text that you copy from one layer to another.

Let's go back to our four objects on four layers, as shown in Figure 13.12. In this example, I've already selected the ellipse.

Notice that Layer 2 is now highlighted in the Layers palette. That's because the ellipse is on Layer 2.

NOTE Notice that a little red square has appeared next to the pen icon on the right of the layer's name in the Layer's palette. That little red square tells you that there are objects on that layer that have been selected. If you select other objects on other layers, then little colored dots will show by those layers' names, as well.

To copy the selected ellipse to another layer, all I have to do is press Alt/Option and drag that little colored dot from Layer 2 to another layer.

WARNING You must press Alt/Option as you drag the dot or you will be *moving* the selected object or objects, deleting them from the original layer.

FIGURE 13.12

Four objects on four layers with the ellipse selected

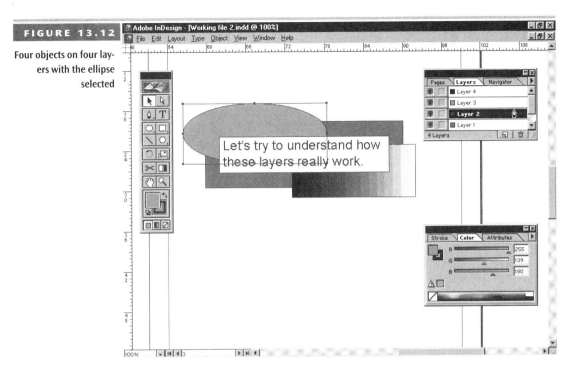

In this case, I'll press Alt/Option and drag the little dot from Layer 2 to Layer 4, as shown below. As you can see, the plus symbol (+) is added to the cursor, which indicates that the selected objects will be copied.

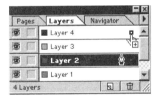

When I let go, the pink ellipse will have been copied from Layer 2 to Layer 4, as shown in Figure 13.13.

How can we tell if the pink ellipse was actually "copied" to Layer 4, and not just moved? Click the eyeball icon by Layer 4 in the Layers palette to hide Layer 4. As you can see in Figure 13.14, the original pink ellipse is still on Layer 2.

346 CHAPTER 13 • UNDERSTANDING LAYERS

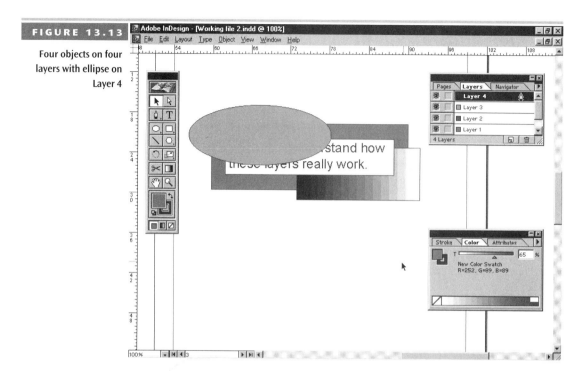

FIGURE 13.13

Four objects on four layers with ellipse on Layer 4

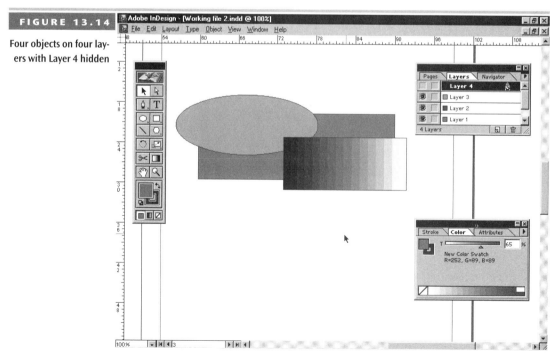

FIGURE 13.14

Four objects on four layers with Layer 4 hidden

The great thing about this is that the relative position of the pink ellipse on the page did not change. If we had gone through the whole cut-and-paste operation, the ellipse would have been pasted to the center of the screen and we would have had to reposition it.

And even though you can't add new objects to a hidden or locked layer, you can copy objects from an unlocked, visible layer to a locked and/or hidden layer by pressing Ctrl+Alt in Windows or Cmd+Option on the Mac as you drag the little dot to the layer that is hidden and/or locked.

Moving Objects from One Layer to Another

Actually moving objects from one layer to another, where the object is deleted from the original layer, is done the same way as copying between layers, except that you don't press any modifier keys as you drag the little dot.

So, to *move* the selected pink ellipse to another layer, all I have to do is drag that little colored dot from Layer 2 to another layer.

First you select an object or objects on one or more layers, as described in the previous section. This time, I'll just drag the little dot from Layer 2 to Layer 4, as shown below, without pressing any other keys. As you can see, the hand cursor doesn't have a plus symbol (+), which indicates that the selected objects will be moved, rather than copied.

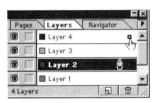

When I let go, the ellipse will have been moved from Layer 2 to Layer 4, as shown in Figure 13.15. This time, however, the original ellipse has been deleted from Layer 2, as you can see in Figure 13.16, when Layer 4 is hidden. Once again, the great thing about this is that the relative position of the ellipse on the page did not change.

If you want to move objects from an unlocked, visible layer to a locked and/or hidden layer, simply press Ctrl/Cmd as you drag the little dot to the layer that is hidden and/or locked.

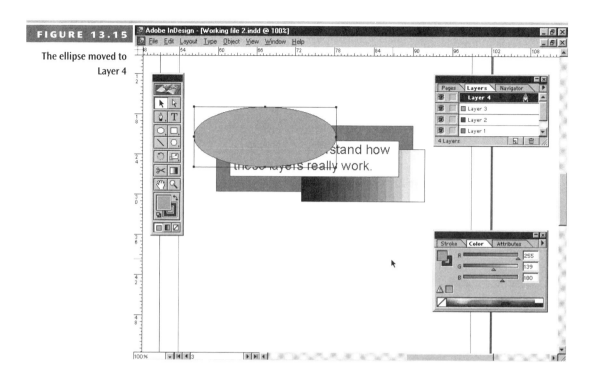

FIGURE 13.15

The ellipse moved to Layer 4

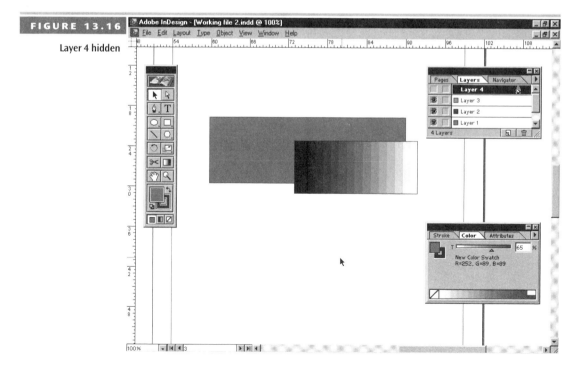

FIGURE 13.16

Layer 4 hidden

Preserving the Layering of Objects When You Copy or Move Them

When you copy or paste multiple objects from one layer to another or from several layers to another, or when you paste layered objects to another document, you risk losing the relative positions of the objects in their layering or stacking order.

There are two ways to prevent this loss of positioning:

- When moving multiple objects from one or more layers to another, be cautious about the order in which you move or copy the objects in order to preserve their layering or stacking order positions.
- If you select the Paste Remembers Layers option from the Layers palette menu, as shown below, you can preserve the layering and stacking of the objects when you copy and paste them.

To show you how this works, I'll perform a couple of examples. For the first one, I'll show you how to preserve the stacking order of objects that you move or copy from one or more layers to another. I'll start with the original four objects on four layers that we've been using throughout this chapter.

First, I'll select all four of the objects. I can do this by drawing a marquee around them all with the Selection tool or I can select them individually while pressing Shift. Once they're all selected, you'll see the little colored dots in each of their layers in the Layers palette, as shown below.

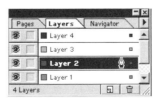

I want to move them all to Layer 1, but I want to preserve their stacking order so that the text remains on top. If I just start dragging their little colored dots in a random order, I will mess up my layering. For example, if I start by dragging the object from Layer 4, then follow with Layer 2, then follow with Layer 3, I will have positioned the object from Layer 4—the text—near the bottom, under the other two objects, as shown in Figure 13.17.

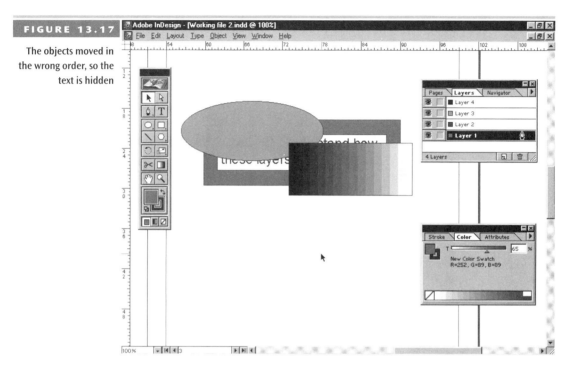

FIGURE 13.17

The objects moved in the wrong order, so the text is hidden

In order to preserve their relative stacking order, I must add them to Layer 1 in the order I want them to be positioned, starting with the bottom-most object first. In other words, I'll want to start with the object from Layer 2, then move the object on Layer 3, then the object on layer 4. If I do it that way, they will retain their relative position in the stack, and they will all be on Layer 1, as shown in Figure 13.18.

To preserve the layering of objects, you can use the Paste Remember Layers option. You should use this option if you are copying and pasting layered objects:

- From one layer to another
- From one place to another in a document
- From one document to another document

For example, let's go back to the four objects on four layers that we have been using throughout this chapter. If we now select all four objects and copy them to another document, we get the result shown in Figure 13.19.

WORKING WITH LAYERS 351

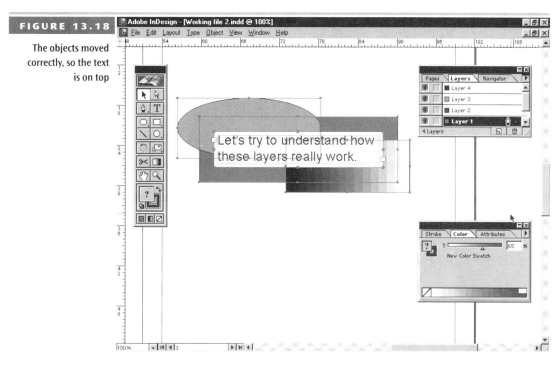

FIGURE 13.18

The objects moved correctly, so the text is on top

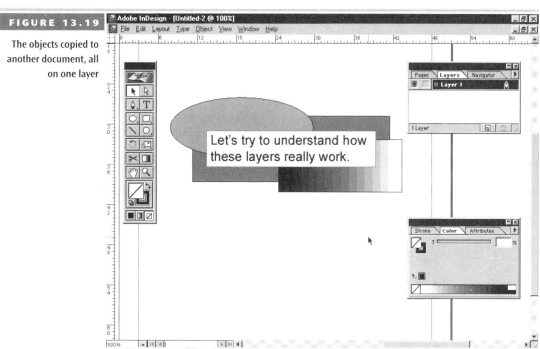

FIGURE 13.19

The objects copied to another document, all on one layer

We've lost the layering that we built in the first document. All of the objects were pasted to the existing Layer 1. To preserve the original layering of the objects, we should choose Paste Remembers Layers from the Layers palette menu before we perform the pasting operation.

This option preserves the layering of objects when we paste the layered objects and adds new layers to the new document as needed, as shown in Figure 13.20.

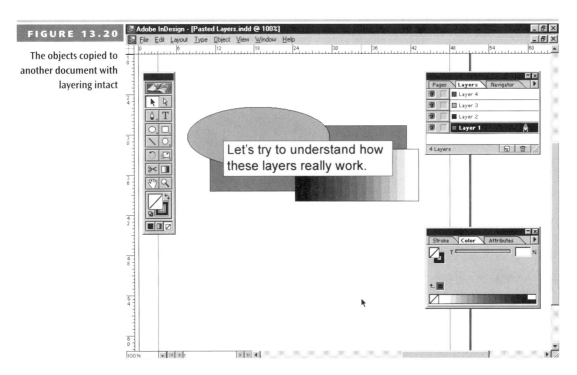

FIGURE 13.20

The objects copied to another document with layering intact

One thing you must be careful of when you use Paste Remembers Layers, however, is the names of layers on both the original and the new document. For example, if both documents contain layers named Layer 1, Layer 2, Layer 3, and Layer 4, and you paste the four objects on four layers to the new document, the objects will be included on the layers that have the same name as their layer in the original document. This might cause you to mix objects on layers in the new document. You might want to rename some of the layers if you want to paste the objects into individual layers of their own in the new document.

Managing Layers

InDesign's Layers palette offers several ways that you can manage layers to help you work more efficiently.

Identifying Layers with Color

One of the coolest features of InDesign's layers is the color-coding you can do with layers and the objects on them. For example, look back at Figure 13.18. You can see that each layer in the Layers palette has a colored box immediately to the left of its name. If you look at the objects selected on the page, you can see that the bounding box of each one is also colored. (This is difficult to see because this book isn't printed in color, but trust me, they're colored.) The colors of the bounding boxes match the colors of the layers on which the objects are positioned.

This is a great feature. You can select multiple objects on a page and immediately identify which layer they belong to.

To change the colors of a layer, select a single layer in the Layers palette and either double-click it or choose Layer Options for "Layer X" from the Layers palette menu. The Layer Options dialog box will open and you can select a color from the Color option menu. The layer's color is both listed in the option menu and displayed in the swatch to the right.

If you want to use a color other than those offered in the Color option menu, select Other from the bottom of the Color option menu, as shown in Figure 13.21, which will open your operating system's color picker.

FIGURE 13.21

Color option menu from Layer Options dialog box with Other

Changing the Stacking Order of Layers

You can also move the layers up and down in their stacking or layering order. You might need to do this to change the overlapping or visibility of some objects, for instance.

To rearrange the layers in the Layers palette, simply select a layer or layers in the Layers palette and drag it or them up or down. As you do, a heavy line will appear between other layers, as shown below, to indicate where the layer(s) will be positioned if you let go there.

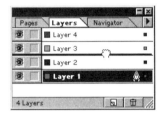

Deleting Layers

When you no longer need a layer, you can delete it. You should be cautious that you aren't deleting something on a layer that you have forgotten, perhaps on another page of the document. You can always check by hiding all of the other layers and looking at each individual page or spread to see if anything you don't want to delete appears.

You can delete one layer at a time by selecting only one layer in the Layers palette, or you can delete multiple layers by pressing Shift or Ctrl/Cmd as you select the layers. Once you have selected the layer or layers you want to delete, you can delete the layer(s) in one of three ways:

- Drag the layers to the Trash button in the Layers palette.
- Click the Trash button in the Layers palette.
- Choose Delete Layer "Layer *X*" or Delete Layers from the Layers palette menu, as shown below.

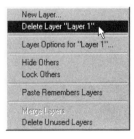 

You can also clean up your Layers palette by using the Delete Unused Layers command from the Layers palette menu.

TIP If you make it a practice to use only the Delete Unused Layers command to delete layers, you will never risk accidentally losing any objects.

Merging Layers

At times, you may feel that you have arranged objects on two or more layers in a way that you wish to preserve, or you may need to reduce the number of layers for efficiency. In those cases, you could choose to *merge* multiple layers into one.

When you merge layers, the contents of the selected layers are merged into the selected target layer. The target layer remains in the document, but the other merged layers are deleted from the document.

To merge layers, select two or more layers in the Layers palette. Click on one of the selected layers to define it as the target layer. The pen icon is displayed in the target layer.

Choose Merge Layers from the Layers palette menu, as shown below.

You should understand how merging layers affects the stacking of objects. In the Layers palette below, Layers 1 and 4 will be merged. Layer 4 is defined as the target layer.

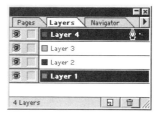

When you choose Merge Layers, the objects on Layer 1 will move up through the layering stack to be added to Layer 4 and Layer 1 will be deleted. This movement will place the objects on Layer 1, in this case the rectangle, in front of the contents of Layers 2 and 3, as shown in Figure 13.22.

Conversely, if the same two layers are to be merged, but Layer 1 is defined as the target layer, the contents of Layer 4 will be merged downward to Layer 1. The contents of Layer 4 will now be behind the contents of Layers 2 and 3, as shown in Figure 13.23.

FIGURE 13.22

Layer 1 merged into Layer 4

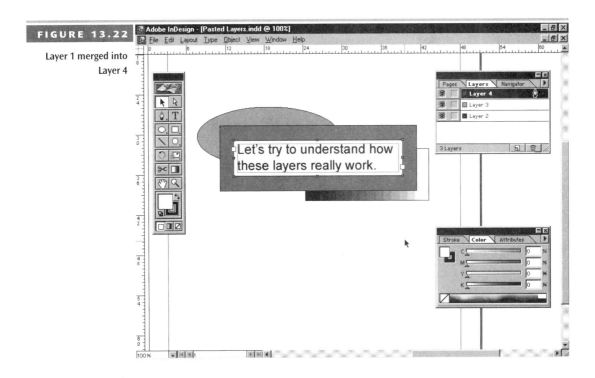

FIGURE 13.23

Layer 4 merged into Layer 1

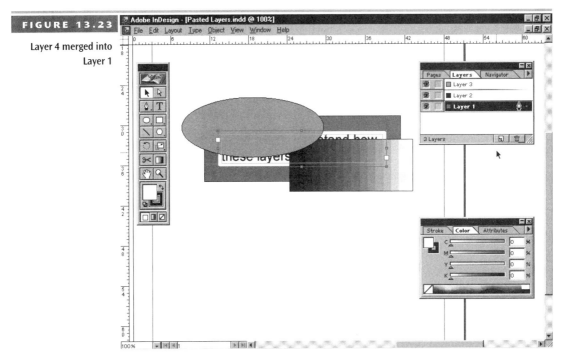

Consequently, be cautious as you merge layers. Don't inadvertently rearrange the stacking order of your layered objects.

Flattening All Layers in a Document

Unlike Adobe Photoshop, InDesign does not have a dedicated command for *flattening* a document. Flattening a document merges all of its layers into one single layer.

To flatten a document, simply select all of its layers and then choose Merge Layers from the Layers palette menu.

PART III
JOGGING

chapter 14

Advanced Type Control

Featuring:

- Controlling the flow of text — 363
- Threading text through linked text frames — 363
- Setting columns — 377
- Type fitting with scaling — 382
- Using a baseline grid — 383
- The paragraph Keep Options — 387
- Raising and lowering type on the baseline — 389
- Special type features — 392
- InDesign's composition options — 398
- Hyphenation and justification — 400

CHAPTER 14

ADVANCED TYPE CONTROL

In Chapters 5 and 9 we covered the basics of entering text on a page and formatting type. Now we can get down to really controlling the appearance of text in your InDesign documents.

InDesign thinks of one contiguous block of text as a *story*, whether it is in one text frame or linked through 20 text frames, whether it contains one actual "story" or ten little "stories." You can have as many stories in a document as you wish.

In this chapter, we'll look at how to "continue" stories from one text frame to another, how to define columns in text frames, and how to fit type to a specific space.

Threading Text through Linked Text Frames

You've got all that text and just one little text frame on page one. How do you get that text to continue on other pages, in other text frames? That's what we're going to do right now: flow the text.

As you learned in Chapter 5, you must place or enter all text in text frames. Any shape, frame, or placeholder can become a text frame. You just select it with the Text tool, shown below, and start typing or entering text.

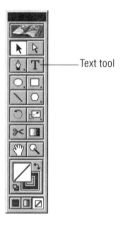

You can also automatically create text frames by using the File ➢ Place command, which was also covered in Chapter 5.

Once you enter text in a shape, frame, or placeholder, it becomes a text frame. You can distinguish text frames from other objects by their *in ports* and *out ports,* as shown below.

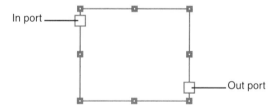

When you have text in a text frame, the in port and out port will display icons indicating the status of the text. You can see at a glance if there is additional text in that story, if that story flows to another text frame, or if the story ends with that text frame.

The in port and out port of the text frame below shows that this is the first text frame for this particular story, and that it ends in this text frame. You see that because the in port is empty and the out port is empty.

THREADING TEXT THROUGH LINKED TEXT FRAMES

> Lorem ipsum dolor sit amet, consectetuer adipiscing elit, sed diam nonummy nibh euismod tincidunt ut laoreet dolore magna aliquam erat volutpat. Ut wisi enim ad minim veniam, quis nostrud exerci tation ullamcorper suscipit lobortis nisl.

We can see from the in port and out port of the text frame below that this is the beginning of this particular story and that there is additional text in the story, but that it does not link to any other text frame. This is indicated by the empty in port and the plus symbol (+) in the out port.

> Lorem ipsum dolor sit amet, consectetuer adipiscing elit, sed diam nonummy nibh euismod tincidunt ut laoreet dolore magna aliquam erat volutpat.
> Ut wisi enim ad minim veniam, quis nostrud exerci tation ullamcorper suscipit lobortis nisl. aliquip ex ea com-

In the text frame below, we see that this text frame contains a story that began in another text frame and continues on to another text frame. The little arrowhead icons in the in port and out port show that the text came in from elsewhere and flows out to somewhere.

> modo consequat.
> Duis autem vel eum iriure dolor in hendrerit in vulputate velit esse molestie consequat, vel illum dolore eu feugiat nulla facilisis at vero eros et accumsan et iusto odio dignissim qui blandit praesent luptatum zzril delenit

In the text frame below, we can see by the arrowhead in the in port and the empty out port that the story came in from elsewhere, buts end in this text frame.

augue duis dolore te feugait nulla facilisi.

Lorem ipsum dolor sit amet, consectetuer adipiscing elit, sed diam nonummy nibh euismod tincidunt ut laoreet dolore magna aliquam erat volutpat.

See how easy it is to "read" those text frames? Now we'll take a look at getting the text to flow through the text frames the way we want. First, though, we need to look at how the cursor changes to indicate what we are doing with our text.

Automatically Flowing Text as You Enter or Place It

If you have "loaded" the cursor with text from the out port of a text frame, which we will discuss later in this section, or if you have chosen the File ➢ Place command and selected a text file for importing, or placing, your cursor will change to indicate what you are about to do with the text.

WARNING   If you have any object selected when you use the File ➢ Place command, the imported text will be flowed into the selected object and you won't get a Loaded Text icon.

When your cursor is loaded with text, it changes to the Loaded Text icon.

NOTE   Even though Adobe refers to these next steps as "manual" flowing of text, I think it's really doing a lot of automatic flowing, as you will see, so I have included it in this section.

Flowing Text One Text Frame at a Time

When the Loaded Text icon is showing, you can click at a point outside any objects to automatically create one new text frame, filled with the text that is loaded in the cursor. From the point where you click, InDesign will create a text frame that is the width of the page margins, filling down to the bottom of the page margins.

If you position the cursor over an empty shape, frame, or placeholder, the cursor changes again, as shown below.

If you click within that shape, frame, or placeholder, InDesign will change it to a text frame and automatically flow that text into it—and into any text frames to which it may be linked. (We'll discuss linking text frames later in this section.)

If that frame or placeholder has been divided into columns, as has the one shown in Figure 14.1, InDesign will flow the text into the columns beginning at the top left of the left-most column, regardless of where you click in the frame.

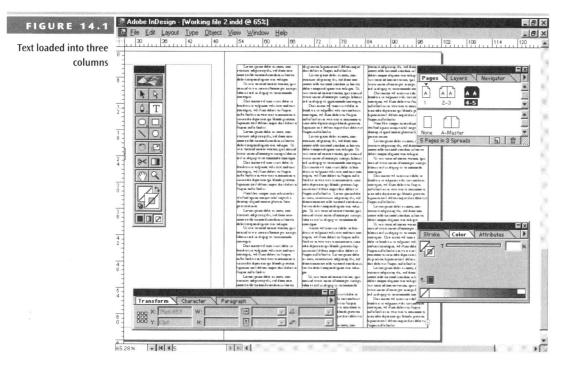

FIGURE 14.1

Text loaded into three columns

When the Loaded Text icon is showing, you can also click and drag, as shown next, to create the text frame that will be filled with the loaded text.

Flowing Text and Automatically Loading the Cursor with the Overflow Text

When the Loaded Text icon is showing, you can press Alt/Option while the cursor is positioned over an empty area of the page or over any shape, frame, or placeholder to change the cursor to the Semi-Autoflow icon.

When you click with the Semi-Autoflow icon, the loaded text is flowed into the frame and then any overflow text is automatically loaded into the Loaded Text icon, ready to be flowed into another text frame.

Flowing Text and Automatically Adding Text Frames and Pages for the Entire Story

If you press Shift when the Loaded Text icon is showing, InDesign will create a new text frame and as many new text frames on as many new pages as necessary to flow the entire story.

When you press Shift with the Loaded Text icon showing, the icon changes to the Autoflow icon. If you click with this Autoflow icon in a page column, InDesign will automatically create a text frame the width of that column, fill it with the text, and then automatically create new text frames and new pages until the entire story is flowed. Just as with other loaded text icons, the text frame will be drawn from the point where you click downward to the bottom page margin. Subsequent frames will be automatically drawn from the top page margin to the bottom page margin.

Remember that Master Text Frames option in the New Document dialog box, described in Chapter 2? If you selected that option, InDesign automatically creates text frames on each page that are the size of the margins on the page. If you click with the Autoflow icon in one of those master text frames, InDesign will fill that frame with the text and then automatically create new pages—with master text frames—and flow the story until it runs out.

NOTE It doesn't matter to InDesign if you click the Autoflow icon over any shapes, frames, or placeholders on a page. It will draw new text frames anyway, right over the other objects on the page or pages.

Manually Threading Overflow Text to Other Text Frames

If you have entered text into a frame and there is overflow text, as indicated by the plus symbol (+) in the out port of a text frame, as shown below, you need to *thread* that text into one or more additional text frames.

Lorem ipsum dolor sit amet, consectetuer adipiscing elit, sed diam nonummy nibh euismod tincidunt ut laoreet dolore magna aliquam erat volutpat. Ut wisi enim ad minim veniam, quis nostrud exerci tation ullamcorper suscipit lobortis nisl. aliquip ex ea com-

When you thread text from one text frame to another, it can flow through the separate text frames as if they were just one text frame. In other words, the text continues on unbroken as if it had just moved over to a new column or page. The beauty of this is that you don't have to cut and paste little bits of text to fill separate text frames with the continuation of a story, which could lead to real problems if the text is changed.

Once the text is threaded, it can reflow as often and as much as necessary as a result of editing or type formatting changes. It will reflow through the additional text frames as if they were all one text frame.

This is really a pretty simple process. If you want to see a graphic representation of the connecting lines between linked text frames, as shown in Figure 14.2, simply choose View ➢ Show Text Threads or press Ctrl+Alt+Y in Windows or Cmd+Option+Y on the Mac.

Threading Text from One Frame to Another

To thread text from one frame to another, select the Selection tool. Now click with the Selection tool in the out port of a text frame that shows the arrowhead icon in it, as shown in Figure 14.3.

This action loads the cursor, as indicated by the cursor changing to the Loaded Text icon.

N O T E   Once you load text into the cursor in this way, that text remains loaded until you either click with the Loaded Text icon or click on any tool in the Toolbox. If you save the document while the cursor is loaded, you can close the document, or even quit InDesign and reopen it, and the text will still be loaded in the cursor.

370 CHAPTER 14 • ADVANCED TYPE CONTROL

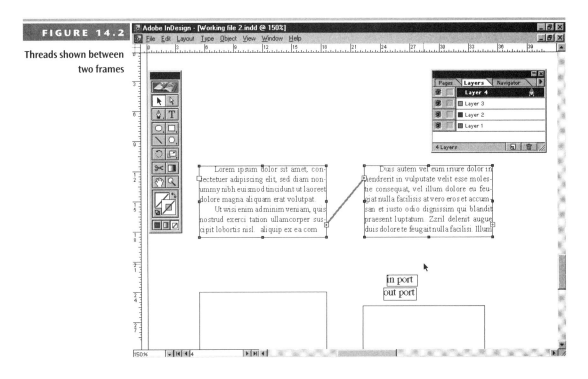

FIGURE 14.2

Threads shown between two frames

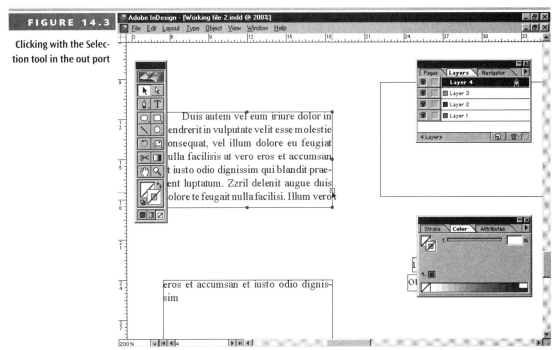

FIGURE 14.3

Clicking with the Selection tool in the out port

Now, when you position the Loaded Text icon over another shape, frame, or placeholder, you see the Thread icon, as shown in Figure 14.4.

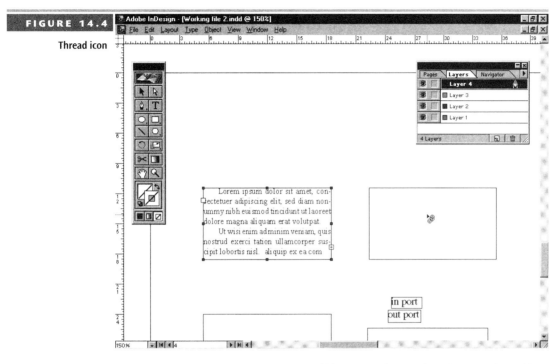

FIGURE 14.4
Thread icon

If you click now, the loaded text will be entered into this object and it will become a text frame, as shown in Figure 14.5. If you have selected View ➢ Show Text Threads, you will see a connecting line from the first text frame to the added text frame, no matter how many pages away it may be. If there is additional text, it will be indicated by the plus symbol (+) in the out port.

If you click where there is no other object, InDesign will draw a new text frame from that point down to the bottom page margin. If your page is divided into columns, the text frame will be the width of one column. You can also drag with the Loaded Text icon to draw a new text frame yourself.

You can repeat the threading operation as many times as you need to flow the story to its end.

Adding a New Text Frame between Two Threaded Text Frames

If you have already threaded text between two frames, you can easily "insert" an additional text frame between the two original text frames.

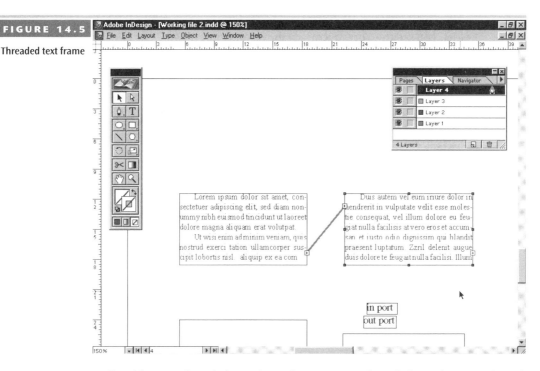

FIGURE 14.5

Threaded text frame

To add a new threaded text frame between two threaded text frames, select the Selection tool and click the out port of the text frame immediately "upstream" from where you want the new text frame to be threaded, as shown in Figure 14.6.

Now position the cursor over the new text frame in the thread. You'll see the Thread icon. When you click with the Thread icon in this new text frame, the story will be threaded through this new text frame and it will be automatically linked to both the text frame immediately before it and immediately after it, as shown in Figure 14.7.

The new text frame does not have to be drawn already for you to insert a new text frame. Let's go back to the original two threaded text frames, as shown in Figure 14.8. Notice that this time there is no object between them.

I'll click the out port of the text frame on the left to load the cursor. Then, with the Loaded Text frame, I'll drag to draw a new text frame between the original two, as shown in Figure 14.9.

As you can see, the Loaded Text icon changes to the crosshair as you draw the new object. Once you release the mouse, the new text frame is drawn and filled with the threaded text.

THREADING TEXT THROUGH LINKED TEXT FRAMES

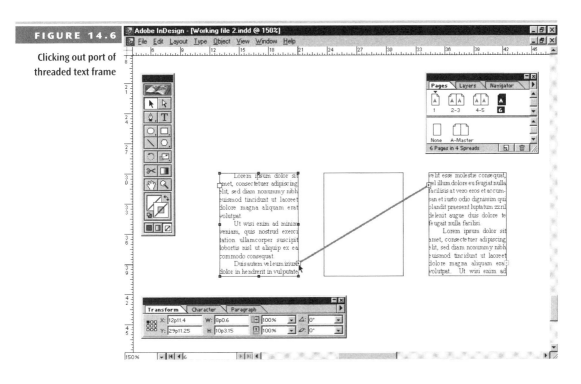

FIGURE 14.6
Clicking out port of threaded text frame

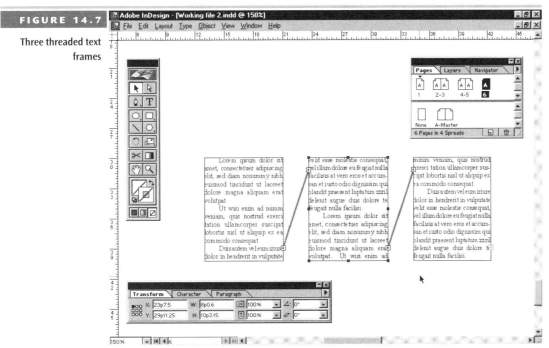

FIGURE 14.7
Three threaded text frames

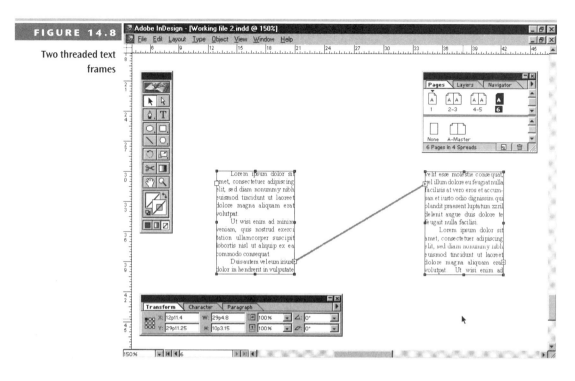

FIGURE 14.8

Two threaded text frames

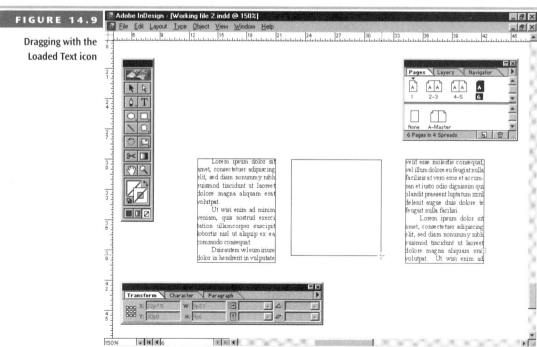

FIGURE 14.9

Dragging with the Loaded Text icon

TIP You don't have to worry about positioning the new text frame exactly between two threaded text frames. As long as you load the cursor with text from the upstream text frame, you can click anywhere in the document and the new text frame will be threaded between the upstream and downstream text frames.

Of course, you can also simply click anywhere. You don't need any object. If you click where there is no object, InDesign will draw the new text frame from that point to the bottom page margin, at the width of the page columns (if there are any).

Unthreading Text Frames

If you want to disconnect the thread between two threaded text frames, select the Selection tool and then just double-click on either the out port of the upstream text frame or the out port of downstream text frame to sever the thread.

If you click only once, you load the cursor with text. The cursor will then change to the Unthread icon when you position it over any text frame currently linked to that thread.

Clicking with this Unthread icon will sever the thread between the two text frames.

Deleting a Threaded Text Frame

If you want to delete one or more threaded text frames, click the Selection tool and then select one or more threaded text frames. Press Shift as you click to select multiple text frames. In Figure 14.10, I have selected the middle text frame.

Once you select the text frame(s) you want to remove from the thread, choose Edit ➢ Cut, or press Ctrl/Cmd+X, to delete the selected frame(s). The text in the thread is untouched. It merely reflows between the existing upstream and downstream text frames, as shown in Figure 14.11.

Since you used the Edit ➢ Cut command, you copied the selected text frame(s) to the clipboard. And get this: you also copied the text that appeared in the cut text frame(s). In other words, you copied a snapshot of how that threaded text frame looked in the thread. If you paste the contents of the clipboard, you'll see the same text frame, with the same text in it, as shown in Figure 14.12. But that text is no longer threaded to the original story; it has become a little island of a piece of the original story. Nor was any of the threaded text in the original story cut out. The original story remains intact. Kind of strange, eh?

You can paste the text frame(s) anywhere you want. You can leave that piece of the original story in the frame(s) or you can delete it.

376 CHAPTER 14 · ADVANCED TYPE CONTROL

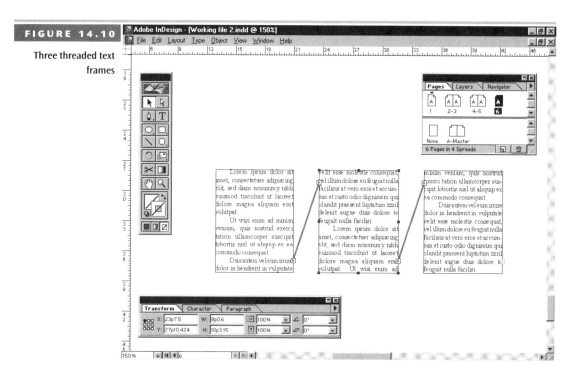

FIGURE 14.10

Three threaded text frames

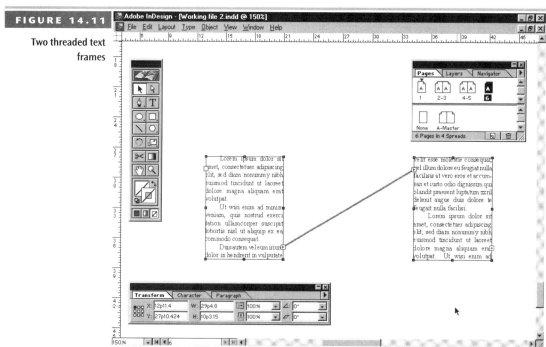

FIGURE 14.11

Two threaded text frames

SETTING COLUMNS

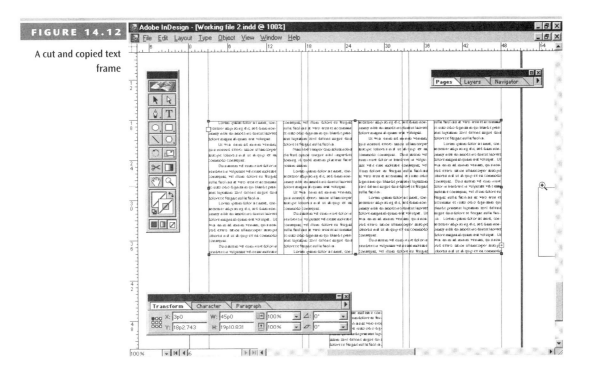

FIGURE 14.12

A cut and copied text frame

Setting Columns

You can divide your text frames into columns of text. And as you learned in Chapter 2, you can easily add page columns to your document when you create it. You can also adjust these page columns or add page columns to an existing page. (Changing the page margins and columns is covered in Chapter 16.)

The thing is, don't confuse page margins with text frame columns. They are completely separate, even though they can match. In other words, you might have your document set for three equal page columns, and you could have a three-column text frame that spans those three page columns, but you could also have a text frame with four columns that spans those three page columns, as shown in Figure 14.13.

You should not use separate text frames for each column of text you want on the page columns. That's a waste of energy. Just use one text frame, drag it across the width of the page and then divide it into the number of columns you want. If the text frame is the same size as the area inside the page margins and you divide the text frame into the same number of columns as the page columns, your text frame columns will match the page columns, as shown in Figure 14.14.

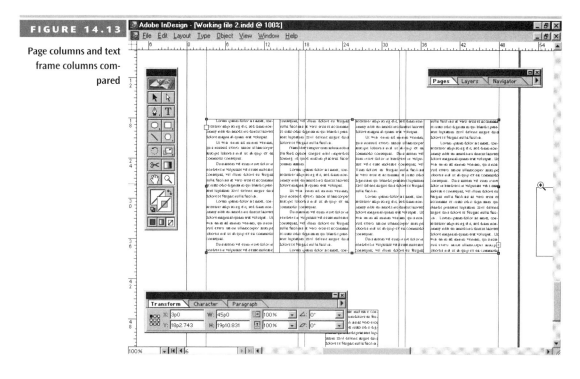

FIGURE 14.13

Page columns and text frame columns compared

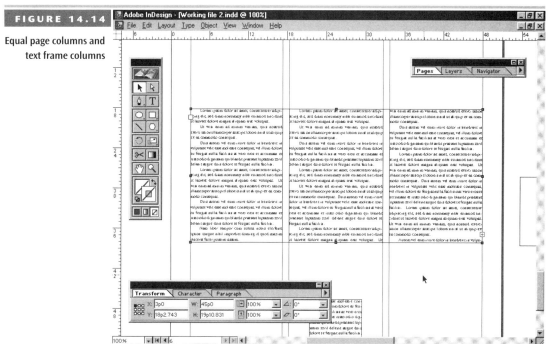

FIGURE 14.14

Equal page columns and text frame columns

The columns in a text frame are always equal in width. You specify the number of columns you want and InDesign divides the text frame equally. You can also specify the amount of space between the columns.

To specify the number of columns in a text frame, select a text frame with the Selection tool, the Direct Selection tool, or the Text tool. Choose Object ➢ Text Frame Options or press Ctrl/Cmd+B to open the Text Frame Options dialog box, shown in Figure 14.15.

Specify a number of columns in the Number text area or click the up or down arrow to raise or lower the number. If you click the Preview option checkbox, you can watch the column changes before accepting them.

You can specify the amount you want for a gutter, which is the amount of space between the columns. Traditionally, this has been one pica, but some contemporary designers will specify another number. Enter a number or click the up or down arrow.

Now, as I mentioned above, the columns must be of equal width because they are equal divisions of the text frame. So why does InDesign offer an option for the width? Actually, I'm not sure. And, combined with the Fixed Column Width option, it can do some weird things to your text frames.

For example, look at the text frame and the associated Text Frame Options dialog box shown in Figure 14.15.

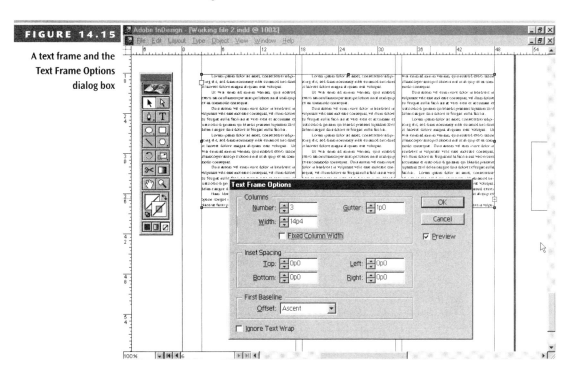

FIGURE 14.15

A text frame and the Text Frame Options dialog box

What you can see is that the text frame has three columns and gutters of one pica. The column width is 14p4, which has been automatically determined by InDesign, based on the width of the text frame, the number of columns, and the gutter width.

If I now start clicking the up arrow of the Width option, the whole text frame starts getting wider, as shown in Figure 14.16.

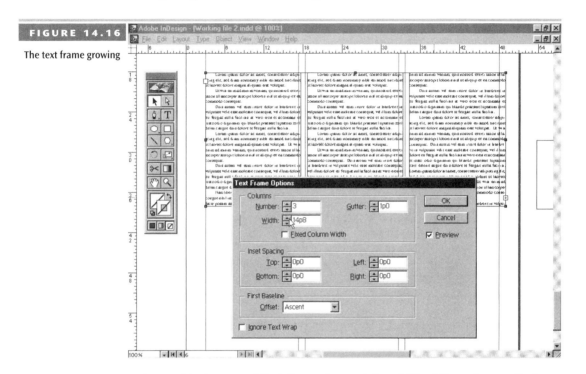

FIGURE 14.16

The text frame growing

I guess I just assumed that if you changed the width of the columns, that InDesign would automatically adjust the width of the gutters and that the width of the columns would be limited to what could be derived from the existing area inside the text frame. But InDesign is preserving the gutter width and changing the width of the text frame. This could be a problem if your text frame is to be fixed to a certain page column width.

Okay, then. That's weird, but this next option is really pretty cool. If you check the Fixed Column Width checkbox, InDesign will only let you increase or decrease the size of the text frame by the width of the columns. To see what I mean, look at the text frame shown in Figure 14.17.

As you can see, this is a two-column text frame across two page columns. The Fixed Column Width option has been selected for this text frame. I'm now going to drag the right-side handle of the text frame's bounding box just to the right of the gutter.

SETTING COLUMNS

FIGURE 14.17

Text frame with two columns on a three-column page

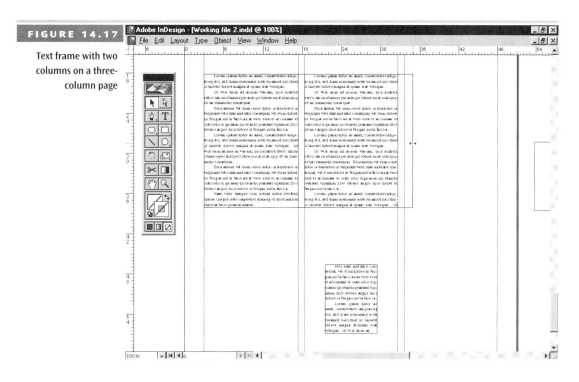

FIGURE 14.18

Expanding the text frame

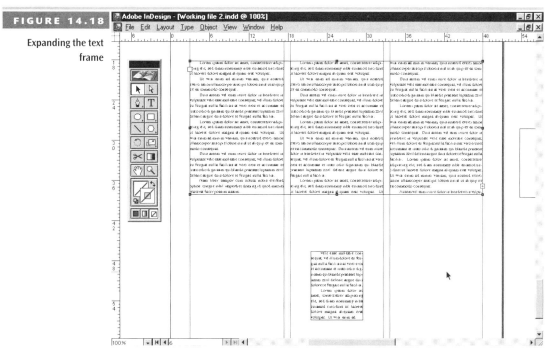

When I let go anywhere across the gutter to the right, InDesign will automatically draw the text frame to the exact width necessary for one more column and then fill that new column with the flow of text, as shown in Figure 14.18. Cool, eh? If you are designing on columns that remain fixed in width, you can adjust the widths of your text frames—and have the number of columns automatically adjusted—without having to open up the Text Frame Options dialog box to manually reset the number of columns.

Type Fitting with Scaling

Okay, so you're tooling along, slapping together the last few pages of your document, when you realize that your text is running a few inches too long. What do you do? Edit the text? Maybe. How about *scaling* the type? By scaling the type down a little bit, you might be able to squeeze that text into the available space. On the other hand, if you're text is too short, you could scale the type up.

Scaling refers to altering the size of the type. Figure 14.19 shows the effects of scaling on type. You can scale type vertically, that is, make its apparent height larger or smaller, and you can scale type horizontally, which alters its width. Notice that if you apply both horizontal and vertical scaling equally, it appears as if you increased or decreased the point size of the type.

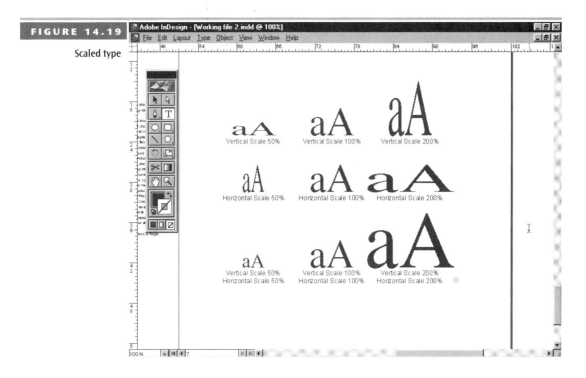

FIGURE 14.19

Scaled type

If you are trying to fit type into a specific space, try vertically scaling the type a bit. As a rule, you should not vertically scale more than about 97% or 103%, because you'll start to change the color of your type blocks and it will be obvious you have altered the scale. But even that little three percent, throughout the course of an entire story, can make a big difference in the eventual length of the story.

Using a Baseline Grid

You can also lock the lines of type to an invisible, underlying grid called the *baseline grid*. This can help you horizontally align the lines at the tops and bottoms of the columns in one or more text frames.

To use the baseline grid, you must first define the spacing of the grid. Once a paragraph of type is locked to this baseline grid, the value entered for the leading in the Character palette will not matter. The type will lock to the spacing of the baseline grid.

You can show or hide the Baseline Grid by choosing View ➢ Show Baseline Grid or by pressing Ctrl+Alt+apostrophe (') in Windows or Cmd+Option+apostrophe (') on the Mac.

Setting the Baseline Grid Options

To specify the spacing of the baseline grid, choose File ➢ Preferences ➢ Grids to open the Preferences dialog box to the Grids options, as shown in Figure 14.20.

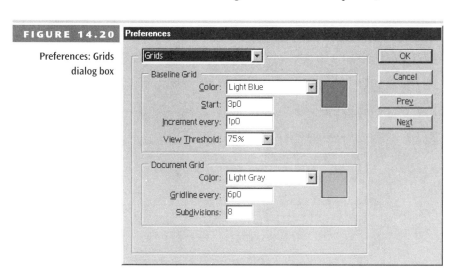

FIGURE 14.20
Preferences: Grids dialog box

As you can see, you can choose a color for the baseline grid from the Color option menu.

The Start value determines where on the page the first line of the grid will be positioned. For example, if you enter 3p0, the first line of the grid will be positioned three picas from the top margin.

The Increment Every option is like the leading of the baseline grid. This is the value you specify that determines how far apart the lines of the grid will be.

The View Threshold value specifies the page view magnification at which the baseline grid will be visible. At magnifications below this percentage, you won't see the grid.

Here are some important concepts to remember about the baseline grid:

- The baseline grid is specified once for an entire document. You can't have different baseline grids for different pages or text frames. The text in every paragraph you lock to the baseline grid, in every text frame in the document, will be locked to the same grid. For the most part, this is a good thing. This enables you to align the text of different text frames to the same grid, producing a more precise and consistent look to your document.

- Text that has been locked to the baseline grid will be allowed enough vertical space to accommodate its point size, then the next line will be positioned on the next available increment of the grid. What this means is that if you have 12 point type locked to a 10 point grid, each line will actually spread over two baselines, as shown in Figure 14.21.

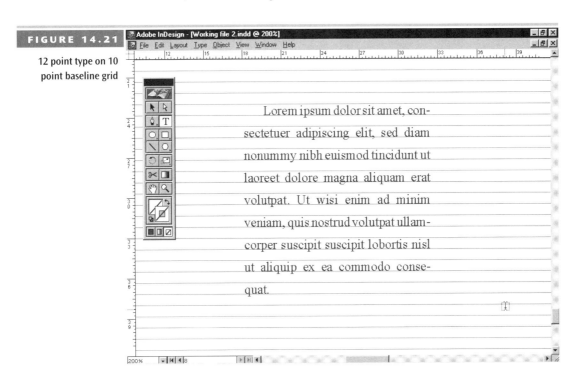

FIGURE 14.21

12 point type on 10 point baseline grid

- Even text that is the same point size as the incremental value of the baseline grid will bump down to the second available line, as if it were larger than the incremental value of the baseline grid.
- You do not have to lock every paragraph in a document or text frame to the baseline grid. You can lock one or ten or all of them.

It's important to understand that whatever value you enter for the Increment Every option will be the vertical spacing of the lines in the paragraphs you lock to the baseline grid—regardless of the leading you specify for those paragraphs. The lines of type will ignore any leading value you specify in the Character palette and will lock to the next baseline grid line. Consequently, you should enter a value that is the same as the leading you want for the type or a value that can be multiplied or divided evenly to produce that leading you want. You might have to consider it carefully to come up with a baseline grid increment that will accommodate all the different leading and spacing you might use in a particular document.

For example, let's say you have 10 point type on 12 points of leading. You could simply specify a baseline grid increment of 12 points. But what if you wanted to have six points of extra space between every paragraph? If you specified a Space Before value of six points, that would cause the next paragraph to skip a line, which would result in actually having 12 points of extra space, as shown in Figure 14.22.

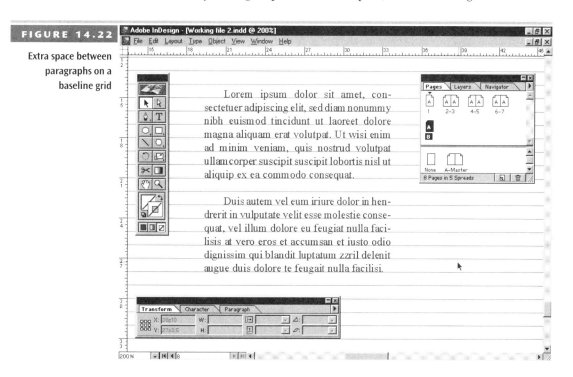

FIGURE 14.22

Extra space between paragraphs on a baseline grid

But if you were to specify an incremental value of 6 points for the baseline grid, your lines of type could lock to the grid naturally, even if you added 6 points of space between paragraphs, as shown in Figure 14.23.

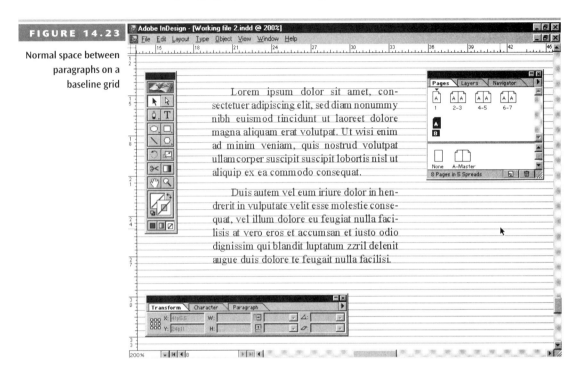

FIGURE 14.23
Normal space between paragraphs on a baseline grid

Locking Text to the Baseline Grid

To lock a paragraph to the baseline grid, select the Type tool and position the text insertion point at a point in a single paragraph or select a range of text in multiple paragraphs.

Click the Align to Baseline Grid button in the Paragraph palette. It's right next to the Do Not Align to Baseline Grid button, as shown below.

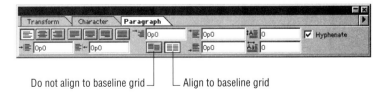

Do not align to baseline grid — — Align to baseline grid

To unlock text from the Baseline Grid, select the paragraph or paragraphs you want to unlock and then click the Do Not Align to Baseline Grid button.

Using the Paragraph Keep Options

In typography, a *widow* is a short line of type or an individual word that winds up being alone at the end of a paragraph. Sometimes these widows occur at the top of a page or column.

A typographic *orphan* occurs when the first line of a paragraph is at the end of a page or at the bottom of a column. This could also be a headline or subhead that gets separated from the first paragraph following it, as shown in Figure 14.24.

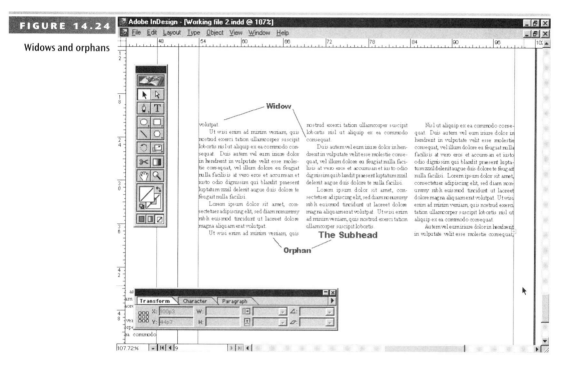

FIGURE 14.24

Widows and orphans

Widows and orphans can be controlled using the paragraph Keep Options, which allow you to specify how many lines must remain together at the end of a paragraph and/or before a column break or page break.

NOTE If you're wondering why they're called *Keep Options*, it's because they are a group of options that allow you to specify how many lines of a paragraph to keep together.

To specify the Keep Options for a paragraph, select the Text tool and select a paragraph or paragraphs, or a paragraph style. Open the Paragraph palette and choose Keep Options from the Paragraph palette menu, as shown next.

This opens the Keep Options dialog box, shown in Figure 14.25.

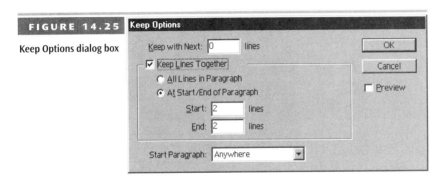

FIGURE 14.25

Keep Options dialog box

The following are the Keep Options:

Keep with Next   You can specify how many lines of the following paragraph must be included with the selected paragraph before a column or page break. For example, if you enter a "2", then no page break or column break would occur until after the first two lines of the following paragraph.

Keep Lines Together   By selecting this option, you can choose All Lines in Paragraph to keep all the lines in a paragraph together. This would prevent the paragraph from being broken at all by a column or page break. Or you can select At Start/End of Paragraph to specify how many lines at the beginning and end of a paragraph must be kept together before a break.

Start Paragraph   You can specify what InDesign will do with a particular paragraph by selecting either Anywhere, In Next Column, or On Next Page from the Start Paragraph option menu. If you select In Next Column, the selected paragraph would automatically be jumped to the top of the next column, regardless of whether it is at the bottom of the column. Similarly, if you select On Next Page, the paragraph is automatically jumped to the next page.

The Keep Options are best used for keeping heads and subheads with the paragraphs that follow, so that you don't wind up with stranded heads and subheads. Applying Keep Options to an entire story can cause problems.

For example, if you specify Keep Options for a paragraph, you may wind up with columns that are not even at the bottom, as shown in Figure 14.26.

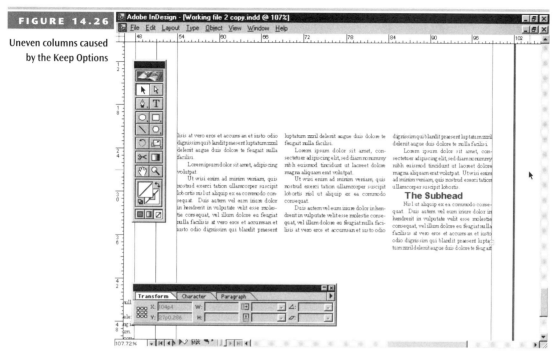

FIGURE 14.26

Uneven columns caused by the Keep Options

This happens because you have told InDesign that it can't break the column where it would naturally occur. You've specified that a certain number of lines of a paragraph must be kept with a certain number of lines of the following paragraph. Consequently, InDesign may be forced to break the column or page and send several lines to the next column or page, even if it means leaving a gap at the bottom of the previous column or page.

What this means is that if you are setting type in columns that must be a certain depth, you should not apply the Keep Options to the entire story.

Raising and Lowering Type on the Baseline

The *baseline* of type is the invisible line upon which it rests, as shown in Figure 14.27. As you can see, the "bodies" of the type rest on the baseline. All of the features of the type that hang down below the baseline are called *descenders*. All of the features that rise above the bodies of the type are called *ascenders*.

FIGURE 14.27 A baseline

You can raise and lower type in relation to this baseline by applying Baseline Shift, as shown in Figure 14.28.

In this illustration, a Baseline Shift value of 5 points has been applied to the "i" character. A Baseline Shift value of –5 points has been applied to the "n" character. As you can see, positive numerical values raise the characters above the baseline and negative numerical values lower the character below the baseline.

You can use Baseline Shift to create your own fractions, to set footnote numbers, or when creating special typographic designs.

To apply Baseline Shift to type, select the Text tool and then select the character or characters you want to adjust. Open the Character palette as shown below. In the Baseline Shift value box, either click on the up or down arrow or enter a numerical value to set the amount of baseline shift to apply to the character(s).

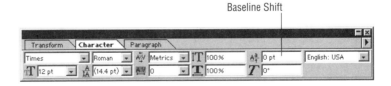

Enter positive numerical values to raise the character(s) above the baseline and negative numerical values to lower the character(s) below the baseline.

FIGURE 14.28

Applying a baseline shift

When clicking the up or down arrow, the amount of baseline shift applied is set by the value entered in the Baseline Shift value box of the File ➢ Preferences ➢ Units & Increments dialog box, shown in Figure 14.29.

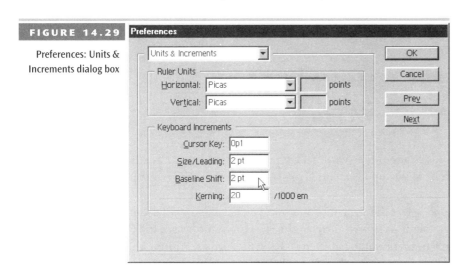

FIGURE 14.29

Preferences: Units & Increments dialog box

If you press Shift as you click the up or down arrow, the incremental amount of increase or decrease of the value is greater.

Using Special Type Features

In addition to those advanced typography and typesetting features discussed previously in this chapter, you can adjust the appearance of your individual characters of type in many other ways. Some designers rarely use these additional features, while others use them regularly.

Skewing

Skewing type distorts it as if you could grab hold of the top of a letter and pull it horizontally to the left or right while the base stayed in place, as shown in Figure 14.30.

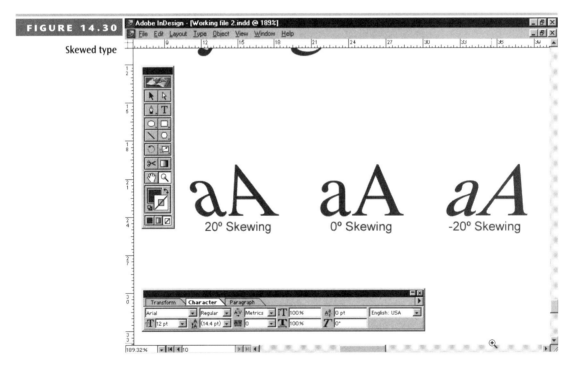

FIGURE 14.30
Skewed type

Don't confuse skewed type with italic type. Italic type is type that has been designed specifically to appear slanted or skewed. Skewed type is just plain old distorted type.

To skew type, select the Type tool and select a character or characters of type. Open the Character palette as shown next. In the Skewing value box of the Character palette, enter a numeric value between –85 and 85 degrees. Positive values skew the type to the left and negative values skew the type to the right.

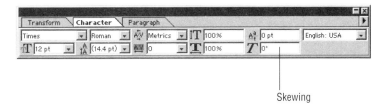

Skewing

Subscript and Superscript

Subscript and superscript characters are most often used to create fractions, footnotes, and so on. These features apply both baseline shift and a specified type size reduction to selected type. Figure 14.31 shows some subscript and superscript characters.

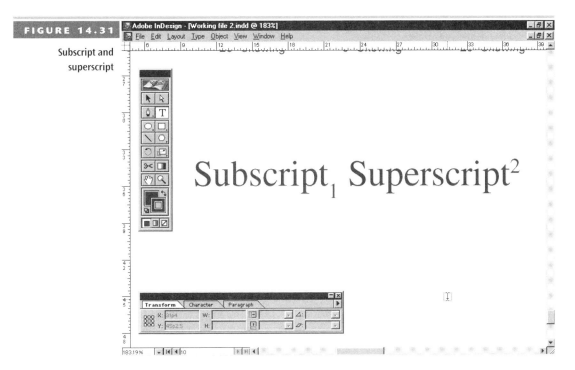

FIGURE 14.31
Subscript and superscript

To apply Subscript or Superscript to type, select the Type tool and select a character or characters. Open the Character palette and choose either Subscript or Superscript from the Character palette menu, as shown next.

You can adjust the automatically applied amount of baseline shift and size reduction by choosing File ➢ Preferences ➢ Text to open the Text options of the Preferences dialog box, as shown in Figure 14.32.

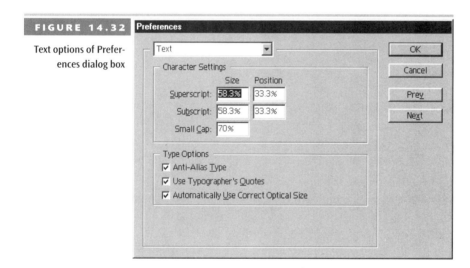

FIGURE 14.32

Text options of Preferences dialog box

To alter the size reduction amount, enter a numerical value in the Size value box for either Superscript or Subscript.

To alter the baseline shift amount, enter a numerical value in the Position value box for either Superscript or Subscript.

Small Caps

Some designers utilize the Small Caps feature to help draw attention to type. The Small Caps feature turns all selected type characters into capital letters. If the letter was entered as a capital letter, by pressing Shift as it was typed, that letter remains a normal capital letter. If the letter was entered as a lower case letter, that letter becomes a smaller capital letter, as shown in Figure 14.33.

FIGURE 14.33

Small caps

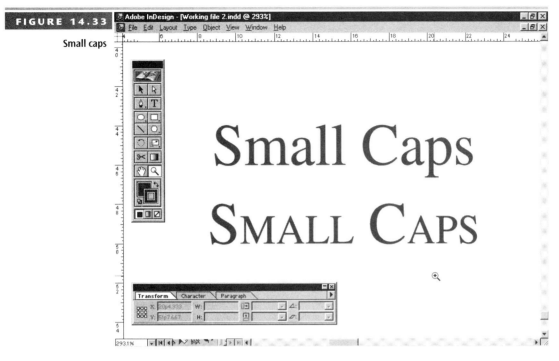

To apply the Small Caps feature to type, select the Type tool and select a character or characters. Open the Character palette and choose Small Caps from the Character palette menu, as shown below.

You can change the size percentage automatically applied to selected text by choosing File ➢ Preferences ➢ Text to open the Text options of the Preferences dialog box, as shown in Figure 14.32.

To alter the size percentage amount, enter a numerical value in the Small Cap value box.

Old Style Numerals

Old Style numerals, as shown below, are included in the data files of many Open Type fonts.

123456789

123456789

123456789

You can apply the Old Style feature to selected type by selecting the Type tool and selecting a numerical character or characters. The typeface you are using must be an Open Type font. Then open the Character palette and choose Old Style from the Character palette menu.

Alternately, if the font features Old Style numerals, you can select Old Style from the Type Style option menu of the Character palette, as shown below.

Language

InDesign's Language option affects the hyphenation of words based on their different syllable breaks in different languages.

You can apply different language dictionaries to a range of type as small as one character, or to an entire story.

To apply a specific Language to type, select the Type tool and select a range of text. Open the Character palette and choose a language from the Language option menu.

Underline and Strikethrough

Back when all printed documents were printed from little pieces of metal type that were gathered together individually, there was no such thing as underlined type or strikethrough type in a book or other printed document. There was no way to produce all those individual pieces of type with little underlines under the type or lines drawn through the characters, and there was no way to have those underlines and strikethroughs always line up perfectly and without breaking the line.

Both underlining and strikethrough, shown in Figure 14.34, were originally features of typewriters, which didn't have bold or italic type to emphasize certain characters. Underlining was used as an alternative to both bold and italic type. Strikethrough was used to indicate deletions.

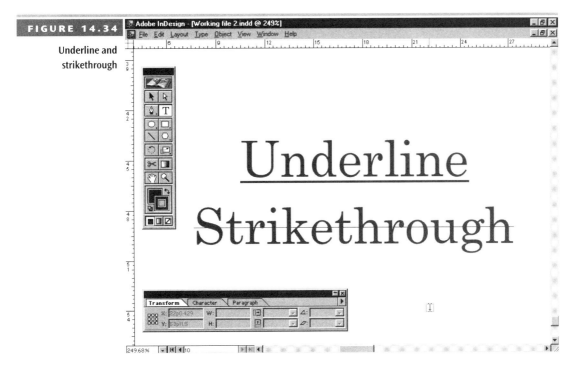

FIGURE 14.34
Underline and strikethrough

This is why many older typographers (like that old geezer Mike Cuenca) and other traditionally-trained typographers despise both underline and strikethrough. We feel that there is no place for them in typography. Unfortunately, they have become common anyway, because of the widespread use of the computer by designers and typographers who don't know any better.

So if you still want to apply underline or strikethrough to your type, select the Type tool and select a character or characters. Open the Character palette and choose Underline or Strikethrough from the Character palette menu, as shown next.

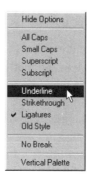

The weight of the underline is based on the size of the text and the strikethrough line is always one-half point.

InDesign's Composition Options

As you know, when text is set in a document, words are often broken into syllables and hyphenated. To assure a pleasing visual appearance of columns of text, this hyphenation should happen as infrequently as possible. When text is justified, the spaces between words are varied to help avoid awkward hyphenation. InDesign offers two different options for determining how the lines of text in a document will be broken by hyphenated words. These two options are the Adobe Multi-Line Composer and the Adobe Single-Line Composer. These composition options define how much space can be set between words and letters, how much scaling can be used, and where lines can be broken to optimize the appearance of the text.

By default, InDesign uses the Adobe Multi-Line Composer. This option allows you to specify a range of lines that will be included in the composition considerations. Compared to using only one line of text, this use of multiple lines of text increases the likelihood that the Composer will be able to eliminate unnecessary word breaks and uneven word spacing. The Composer has more options for spacing out the words on each line, selecting optimum word breaks, and so on.

In contrast, the Adobe Single-Line Composer evaluates the possible word spacing, word breaks, and glyph scaling of only one line, which decreases its options for optimizing the composition.

NOTE A *glyph* is a character of type. *Glyph scaling* is the changing of the width of an individual character of type.

These two composition options use different rankings of composition options as they consider the possible compositions of the text. If you are aware of how they consider these criteria, you can more effectively specify the composition options for optimum text appearance.

The Adobe Multi-Line Composer compares the different composition possibilities for the included lines and evaluates these possibilities, assigning a ranking of "good" possibilities and "bad" possibilities. The Composer then attempts to use the best combination of these possibilities to produce the most pleasing result. The Composer evaluates the possibilities according to the following two pretty simple principles:

- Evenness of letter and word spacing is good.
- Hyphenation is bad.

The Adobe Single-Line Composer sets type the way it has been set by computers in the past, one line at a time. It evaluates the words in a single line and then determines how much word spacing and letter spacing will be necessary to break the line optimally.

The Adobe Single-Line Composer, by default, prefers to adjust word spacing over hyphenation, prefers hyphenation over letter spacing, and prefers compressed word and letter spacing over expanded word and letter spacing.

You can select either multi-line or single-line composition for individual paragraphs. You can set them all to one or the other, or you can set some to one and some to the other composition option.

To specify which composition option to use for a paragraph, select the Text tool and select a paragraph or paragraphs. Open the Paragraph palette and choose Adobe Multi-Line Composer or Adobe Single-Line Composer from the Paragraph palette menu, as shown below.

You can adjust the settings for the Adobe Multi-Line Composer by choosing File ➤ Preferences ➤ Composition to open the Preferences: Composition dialog box, shown in Figure 14.35.

You can specify the number of lines to include in the comparison by entering a numerical value in the Look Ahead value box. The greater the number of lines included, the slower the composition speed.

You can specify the number of possible break points to consider for each line by entering a numerical value in the Consider up To value box. (The Highlight options are discussed in the "Highlighting Composition Problems" section at the end of this chapter.)

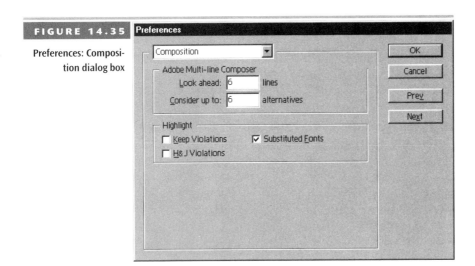

FIGURE 14.35

Preferences: Composition dialog box

Hyphenation and Justification

As discussed in the previous section, optimum hyphenation is important for producing the most pleasing appearance of columns of text. You want to avoid series of hyphens in multiple lines, to avoid words that are hyphenated poorly, and to avoid awkward word and letter spacing.

Justification is the alignment of text in columns. Traditionally, *justified* referred to text that was set to be evenly aligned on both sides of a column. Today, many people refer to justification when they really mean *alignment*. Alignment is the choice you make about how you want the lines of text to be set in the columns. Remember the alignment choices presented in Chapter 9?

In InDesign, the justification options apply to each of the alignment options, determining how much word and letter spacing is allowable and how much, if any, glyph scaling is allowed.

InDesign allows you a great deal of control over the hyphenation and justification of your text blocks. You can request hyphenation of words at specific syllables, you can turn automatic hyphenation on and off, you can specify minimums and maximums for word and letter spacing, and so on.

Hyphenating Manually

Really, the only way to hyphenate manually would be to turn off automatic hyphenation and then go through the text line-by-line and enter hyphens and returns to break the lines. This would not be fun in a long document.

InDesign allows you to "request" the breakpoint you want for particular words by entering what is called a *discretionary hyphen*. If all of the other considerations used by automatic hyphenation combine to produce a hyphen in that word, InDesign will break the word only at that point.

NOTE By default, InDesign won't break words at any em dashes, en dashes, or thin spaces. If you want InDesign to consider breaking words at those characters, enter a discretionary hyphen immediately after an em dash, en dash, or thin space.

To enter a discretionary hyphen, select the Text tool and click at the point in a specific word where you want the word to break. Then simply press Ctrl+Shift+hyphen (-) in Windows or press Cmd+Shift+hyphen (-) on the Mac.

Alternately, access the context menu for type by right-clicking in Windows or by pressing Ctrl when clicking with the Mac mouse. Then select Insert Special Character ➢ Discretionary Hyphen as shown below.

Turning Automatic Hyphenation On and Off

If you're setting headlines, subheads, or other lines that you don't want broken by hyphens, you can turn off automatic hyphenation simply by selecting a paragraph or paragraphs and then deselecting the Hyphenate checkbox in the Paragraph palette, shown below.

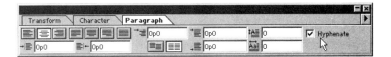

Specifying Automatic Hyphenation Options

You can adjust the automatic hyphenation options for individual paragraphs. So even if you have automatic hyphenation turned on for an entire document, you could still go through paragraph-by-paragraph and specify different hyphenation options for each paragraph.

To adjust the hyphenation options for a paragraph or paragraphs, select a paragraph or paragraphs and then open the Paragraph palette. Choose Hyphenation from the Paragraph palette menu, as shown below.

This action opens the Hyphenation dialog box, shown in Figure 14.36.

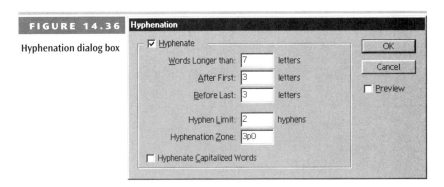

FIGURE 14.36

Hyphenation dialog box

The Hyphenate checkbox at the top of the Hyphenate dialog box is the same as the Hyphenate checkbox shown earlier in the Paragraph palette. It turns automatic hyphenation on and off.

If a checkmark is in the checkbox, automatic hyphenation is on and you can specify the following options:

Words Longer Than   Enter a numerical value to specify a minimum number of letters that a word must contain before it is considered for a hyphenated breakpoint.

After First   Enter a numerical value to specify how soon in a word a hyphen may be inserted. In other words, the number of letters in a word that must be included on a line before a hyphen is inserted.

Before Last   Enter a numerical value to specify how late in a word a hyphen may be inserted. In other words, the number of letters in a word that must be left over for the next line after a hyphen is inserted.

Hyphen Limit   Enter a numerical value to specify how many consecutive lines can have hyphens.

Hyphenation Zone   Enter a measurement for how far from the end of a line a word can go before being hyphenated or moved down to the next line. This option is used only with the flush left, centered, and flush right alignment options, and only when Adobe Single-Line Composer is selected.

Hyphenate Capitalized Words   Click this option on or off depending on whether or not you want capitalized words, such as proper names and acronyms, to be hyphenated.

Setting Words so They Won't Break

You can specify certain words or even a range of words that you don't want hyphenated under any circumstances.

To prevent the hyphenation of a word or words, select the Text tool and then select the word(s) you want to protect from hyphenation.

Open the Character palette and choose No Break from the Character palette menu, as shown below.

Alternately, you can simply enter a discretionary hyphen just before the first letter of a single word to prevent hyphenation of that word. Enter the discretionary hyphen as described earlier in this section.

Entering Hyphens and Spaces that Won't Break

If you don't want two hyphenated words, such as "paste-up," to be broken at that hyphen, you can enter a nonbreaking hyphen. If you don't want a space between two words to be the end of a line, you can enter a nonbreaking space.

NOTE By default, InDesign won't break words at any em dashes, en dashes, or thin spaces. If you want InDesign to consider breaking words at those characters, enter a discretionary hyphen immediately after an em dash, en dash, or thin space.

Entering a Nonbreaking Hyphen

To enter a nonbreaking hyphen between two words, select the Text tool and click at the point between the two words or select the hyphen that is already there. Press Ctrl+Alt+hyphen (-) in Windows or press Cmd+Option+hyphen (-) on the Mac.

Alternately, open the context menu for type by right-clicking in Windows or by pressing Ctrl when clicking with the Mac mouse. Choose Insert Special Character ➢ Nonbreaking Hyphen as shown below.

Entering a Nonbreaking Space

To enter a nonbreaking space between two words, select the Text tool and click at the point between the two words or select the space that is already there. Then simply press Ctrl+Alt+X in Windows or press Option+spacebar on the Mac.

Alternately, open the context menu for type by right-clicking in Windows or by pressing Ctrl when clicking with the Mac mouse. Choose Insert Special Character ➢ Nonbreaking Space.

Setting Justification options

You can adjust the values that InDesign uses to determine optimum justification of lines of type for individual paragraphs or entire stories.

To adjust the justification options for a paragraph or paragraphs, select a paragraph or paragraphs and then open the Paragraph palette and choose Justification from the Paragraph palette menu, as shown below.

This action opens the Justification dialog box, shown in Figure 14.37.

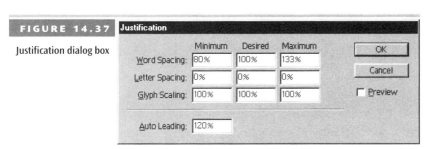

FIGURE 14.37

Justification dialog box

As you can see, you can set Minimum, Desired, and Maximum values for these three options:

Word Spacing The amount of space between words. You can enter numerical values from 0% to 1000%.

Letter Spacing The amount of space between letters, including tracking and kerning values. You can enter numerical values from -100% to 500%.

Glyph Scaling The percentage of change to the width of individual characters of type. If you select a range of text that is not justified, entering any value other than 100% in this value box horizontally scales the selected text.

For justified type, InDesign uses all three values: Minimum, Desired, and Maximum. The Desired value is always sought, but the range of percentages between the minimum and maximum values determines how much latitude InDesign is allowed when adjusting spacing to optimize justification. Narrow ranges are best for the Adobe Single-Line Composer and wider ranges are better for the Adobe Multi-Line Composer.

For the flush left, centered, and flush right alignment options, only the Desired value is used.

Entering a Flush Space

At some point, you have probably noticed in books or magazines the little icon that indicates you have reached the end of a story. The variable space that is between the last word of the line and the little end-of-story icon is called a *flush space*. This flush space automatically adjusts to move the end-of-story character or icon to the far right of the last line of a paragraph that has the Justify All Lines alignment option applied to it.

You can use any alpha-numeric character for the end-of-story icon, or you can use special characters or specially-designed icons.

To enter a flush space between the last word of a paragraph and the end-of-story character, select the Text tool and click at the point between the last word in the paragraph and the end-of-story character. Open the context menu for type by right-clicking in Windows or by pressing Ctrl when clicking with the Mac mouse. Choose Insert Special Character ➢ Flush Space as shown below.

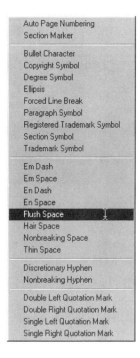

Now make sure that you have applied the Justify All Lines alignment option to that paragraph. Choose the Text tool and select the paragraph. Then open the Paragraph palette and click the Justify All Lines button, as shown below.

Highlighting Composition Problems

If you want to see the "problem" lines of type that have been necessarily composed outside the preferences you have specified in the Hyphenation and Justification dialog boxes, choose File ➢ Preferences ➢ Composition to open the Preferences/Composition dialog box, shown in Figure 14.38. Click the H&J Violations checkbox.

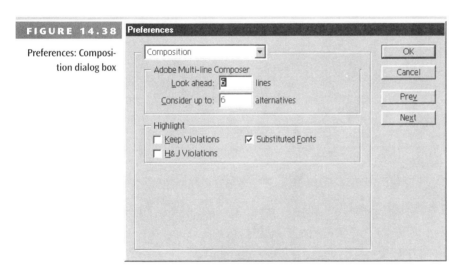

FIGURE 14.38
Preferences: Composition dialog box

To have InDesign highlight lines that violate the Keep Options you may have specified, as described earlier in this chapter, check the Keep Violations option.

The Substituted Fonts option will highlight any fonts that may have been substituted for the original fonts because the fonts were not on your system. InDesign highlights the problem lines in three shades of yellow according to their respective importance, with the darkest yellow indicating the most serious problems.

chapter 15

Transforming, Placing, and Aligning Objects

Featuring:

- **Transform palette basics** — 412
- **Determining the point of origin** — 417
- **Duplicating objects** — 420
- **Positioning, scaling, and reflecting objects** — 423
- **Rotating and distorting objects** — 428
- **Duplicating objects as you transform them** — 430
- **Aligning and distributing objects** — 432
- **Grouping and ungrouping objects** — 435
- **Understanding the object stack** — 437

CHAPTER 15

TRANSFORMING, PLACING, AND ALIGNING OBJECTS

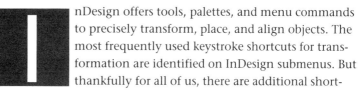

nDesign offers tools, palettes, and menu commands to precisely transform, place, and align objects. The most frequently used keystroke shortcuts for transformation are identified on InDesign submenus. But thankfully for all of us, there are additional shortcuts for object editing and a listing can be found in Appendix E or from the Edit Shortcuts dialog box. To open the Edit Shortcuts dialog box, select File ➢ Edit Shortcuts. When the dialog box opens, select Object Editing from the Product Area pulldown menu. (You will have to scroll down in the menu to locate Object Editing; it is listed at the top of the second group of products.)

Whether you transform a single selected object, several selected objects, a selected group or several selected groups of objects, InDesign characterizes them all as a single unit. When you assign a value or drag the selection, any change in position, orientation, size, or scale will be applied to all the objects in the current selection. To transform an object that is part of a group, you first have to ungroup the selection. Then you select the individual object and transform it. After the transformation is complete, you can regroup the objects. Some more things to consider when transforming objects:

- Type selected with the Text tool cannot be transformed.
- If you select a frame with the Selection tool, you can transform both the frame and its contents as a single unit.

• When you use the Direct Selection tool, you can transform either the frame or its contents separately.

Transform Palette Basics

The Transform palette contains several commands that permit you to view or specify any selected object's geometric information. Additional commands are available in the Transform palette menu.

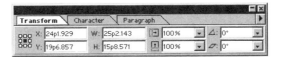

The options for the Transform palette are as follows:

Proxy for Origin The individual points, called *proxy points*, that make up the Proxy for Origin icon are each selectable. Rather than using your pointer to click and move the *point of origin* (the reference point for all transformations), you can simply click a proxy point to move the point of origin for the object. The box in the top left-hand corner corresponds to the top left corner of the object's bounding box anchor point. A solid black box in the icon represents the selected point of origin. If you look at Figure 15.1, you will see the point of origin positioned in the center of the selected object and the center proxy point of the Proxy for Origin icon selected and solid black. For more information, see the "Determining the Point of Origin" section later in this chapter.

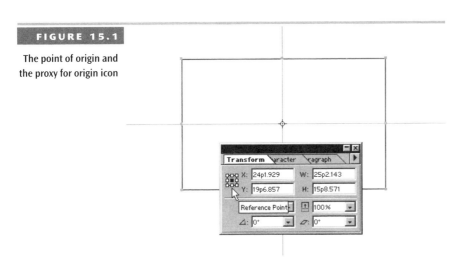

FIGURE 15.1

The point of origin and the proxy for origin icon

TRANSFORM PALETTE BASICS 413

Horizontal (X) and Vertical (Y) Position The X and Y geometric coordinates represent the position of the selected object's designated reference point. In Figure 15.2, you will see the following settings:

- The Proxy for Origin reference point set to the upper left-hand corner box.
- The horizontal and vertical positions of the bounding box's upper left-hand corner anchor point set to X: 12p0 and Y: 12p0.
- The ruler guides intersecting at the X: 12p0 and Y: 12p0 geometric coordinates.

NOTE How to enter or change a numeric entry in an InDesign palette is discussed in Chapter 3.

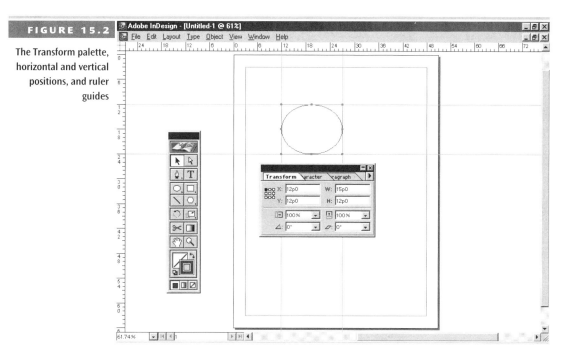

FIGURE 15.2

The Transform palette, horizontal and vertical positions, and ruler guides

TIP Before changing an object's position in a layout or using any of the other Transform palette's options, you'll find it helpful to first place ruler guides, even temporarily. The ruler guides will make it easier to precisely position or transform objects. Ruler guides can provide a frame of reference for an object's original position on the pasteboard or in a nested object before scaling, rotating, etc. How to use ruler guides is covered in Chapter 3.

Width and Height The Width and Height boxes give the dimensions, in current units, of the selected object. In Figure 15.2, the selected object has a width of 15p0 and a height of 12p0.

Rotation Angle Use the Transform palette to enter or select an angle of rotation rather than visually rotating the chosen object using your mouse or other pointing tool. You can either type in a number or select an angle from the option menu, as shown in Figure 15.3.

TIP Choosing the Rotate, Scale, or Shear tool opens the Transform palette (if it's not open already). The Transform palette will focus on the option of the selected tool. You can now enter a numeric value or select from the option's pull-down menu.

WARNING Selecting or deselecting the Transformations Are Totals option from the Transform palette menu influences the value of the Rotate Angle option. For further details, see the "Rotating and Distorting Objects" section later in this chapter.

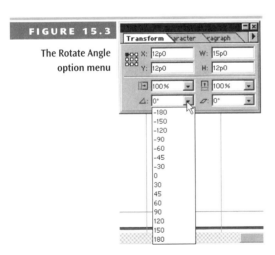

FIGURE 15.3
The Rotate Angle option menu

Scale X Percentage Use this Transform palette option to change an object's X-coordinate dimension by a fixed percentage of the object's width. Enter a numeric value or select from the pull-down menu to increase or decrease by a fixed percentage an object's width.

Shear Angle This option functions in a similar way to the Rotate Angle option. Enter a value or select from the option menu.

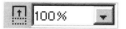**Scale Y Percentage**   Use this Transform palette option to change an object's Y-coordinate dimension. Works like the Scale X Percentage option, but increases or decreases by a fixed percentage an object's height.

From the Transform palette menu, shown below, you have a different set of options.

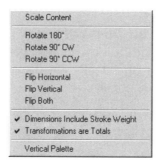

The Transform palette menu options are:

Scale Content   When the Scale Content option is selected, you can scale the content of a graphics or text frame as you change the dimensions of the frame using only the Transform palette commands. You cannot use the Scale Content command when you scale an object by dragging.

WARNING   Scaling a frame and its content in only one dimension will distort the content.

Rotate 180°, or 90°CW, or 90°CCW   Menu shortcuts for rotating an object 180 degrees, 90 degrees clockwise, or 90 degrees counter clockwise.

Flip Horizontal, or Vertical, or Both   Changes the orientation of the selected object.

Dimensions Include Stroke Weight   Selecting this option changes the height and width measurements. See the "Stroke Weight and Object Dimensions" sidebar below for more information.

NOTE   A frame's stroke weight builds from the center reference of the stroke. Objects outlined with wide strokes will grow in size and may need to have alignments adjusted. For more information about frame and stroke basics, see Chapter 4.

Transformations Are Totals   This option controls the reference orientation for nested objects. When you select this option, transformation information is displayed for nested objects relative to the pasteboard. If this option is deselected, transformation information is relative to the parent object. The size of the angle of rotation will be different because of the following:

- When the Transformations Are Totals option is selected, the angle is calculated from a pasteboard baseline set at zero degrees rotation.
- If the option is not active, the rotation angle is calculated from the bottom edge of the parent object, which can be set at any angle of rotation.

Horizontal/Vertical Palette   Change the display orientation of the palette. The identifying option name changes when the alternate palette format is the current selection. If you're using the horizontal palette, then this line will be labeled vertical palette and vice versa.

Stroke Weight and Object Dimensions

Selecting the Dimensions Include Stroke Weight option from the Transform palette menu will change the values seen in the Width and Height boxes of the Transform palette. This may not be critical for object's outlined with 1 point or smaller rule, but for larger object outlines this dramatically changes an object's dimension measurements. Always confirm this option's setting before transforming any object. In the first graphic below, this option is not selected and the Width and Height values are both set to 4p2 for a rectangle outlined with a 10-point rule. In the second graphic, Dimensions Include Stroke Weight have been selected, increasing the Width and Height to 5p0.

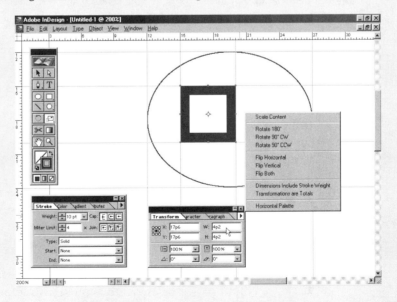

Continued on next page

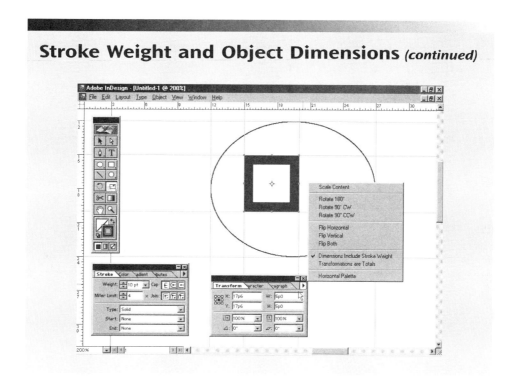

Stroke Weight and Object Dimensions *(continued)*

Determining the Point of Origin

When you select the Rotate, Scale, or Shear tools, an icon will appear indicating the point of origin. This point of origin is the reference point for all transformations. (When you change tools, the point of origin resets to its default position for that tool.) Reposition the point of origin by placing the tool cursor on the point of origin and then dragging it to the new coordinates. You can also reset the point of origin by changing the proxy point in the Transform palette (see the previous section). Figure 15.4 shows the point of origin being moved by dragging. Refer back to Figure 15.1 to see the proxy on the Transform palette.

Some basics about the point of origin:

- The upper left corner is the default point of origin for most objects, except:
  - Lines: midpoint of the line
  - Inline graphic: center point of graphic. This point cannot be moved.
- For objects like circles, ellipses, polygons, and any shape other than a rectangle or square, the point of origin may fall outside the edge of the object. See Figure 15.5 for an example of a selected polygon and its rotation point of origin.

FIGURE 15.4

Dragging the point of origin

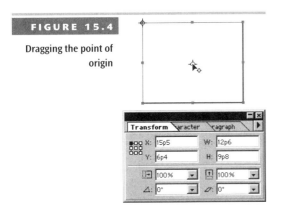

FIGURE 15.5

A polygon and its point of origin

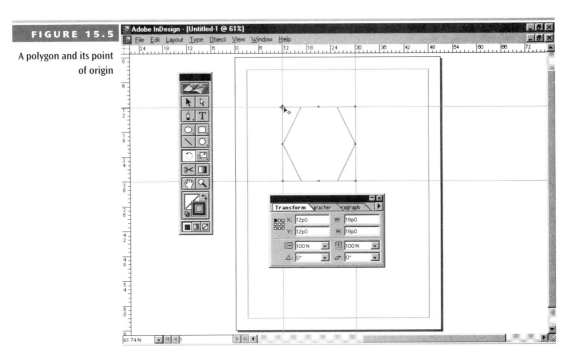

> **WARNING** Where the Transform palette's X and Y coordinates meet is the point of origin for determining an object's position in the document or pasteboard. When the point of origin is moved to a position outside the area defined by a bounding box or selected path, the X and Y (horizontal and vertical) values no longer represent the exact position of the selected object.

Positioning Objects

We each have our preferred techniques for comping out ideas during a creative brainstorming session or quickly laying out production-ready pages. To accommodate individual preferences, InDesign offers different techniques for positioning objects. For those of you who need to cut back on the time spent mousing, you'll find keyboard shortcuts for the fast placement of objects. The following sections highlight the different techniques.

Dragging Objects

You can drag an object to a new position with the Selection tool. Follow these steps:

1. Choose the Selection tool from the toolbox, or press V to activate the tool.
2. Select the object using your mouse or other pointer tool. Refer to the "Understanding the Object Stack" section later in this chapter for more details about the object selection shortcuts.
3. Drag the object to its new location. Press the Shift key as you drag to constrain the object to multiples of 45 degrees.

Using the Transform Palette

In the palette, enter a new value for either the X (horizontal) or Y (vertical) or both positioning options. To accept the new value(s), press Enter (Windows) or Return (Macintosh).

Moving or Copying to Another Layer or Page Spread

You have the option of choosing from the menu or using the keystroke shortcuts.

1. Cut the object or copy the object to the clipboard by using the old familiar menu commands: choose either Edit ➢ Cut or Edit ➢ Copy. Or you can use the workhorse keyboard shortcuts: press Ctrl+X (Windows) or Cmd+X (Macintosh) to cut a selection. Press Ctrl+C (Windows) or Cmd+C (Macintosh) to copy a selection.
2. Select the destination layer or page spread.
3. Choose Edit ➢ Paste. The object appears in the center of the target page or spread. Another option is the Edit ➢ Paste Into an object command. Use Paste Into when you're inserting an image into a text outline or adding a clipping path to an image. You can also press Ctrl+V (Windows) or Cmd+V (Macintosh) to paste the selected object in the center of the target spread or page. To paste into an object, press Ctrl+Alt+V (Windows) or Opt+Cmd+V (Macintosh).

Using the Arrow Keys

You can use your keyboard's arrow keys to reposition objects on the spread. There are three techniques:

- Press the ↑ (Up), ← (Left), ↓ (Down), or → (Right) arrow key to move an object one unit.

NOTE   Cursor key behavior (setting the size of one unit) is controlled in the Preferences: Units & Increments dialog box. Appendix B reviews the Units & Increments preferences options.

- When you press the Shift with an arrow key, the object moves 10 times the unit set in the Preferences: Units & Increments dialog box.
- To move continuously, keep holding down an arrow key. Don't use this technique when moving over larger areas of the layout. How quickly you can move the object is a factor of how fast your computer can process the data. You'll find it much more productive to turn on the Snap to Guides command: press Shift+Ctrl+; (Windows) or Shift+Cmd+; (Macintosh), drag a ruler guide to help position the object, and then drag the object in place.

TIP   Keep the Navigator palette open when positioning objects. Use the slider bar in the Navigator palette to quickly change views.

Duplicating Objects

Duplicating an object is quick and easy in InDesign. Just choose an object and then select Edit ➢ Duplicate. A copy of your selected object appears offset to the right and slightly down from the original, as shown in Figure 15.6. To make things even quicker, use the keystroke shortcut Ctrl+Alt+D (Windows) or Opt+Cmd+D (Macintosh).

FIGURE 15.6

Duplicating objects

Duplicating Objects with the Step and Repeat Commands

This is yet another method for duplicating objects: the Step and Repeat command. Use this command to position a series of boxes or rules when you're designing forms. Or for printing jobs where you need to set up duplicates, such as mailing labels or business cards. Just step and repeat your master design. Then edit individual copies to create labels and cards for your client's different locations or employees. To step and repeat duplicate objects, follow these directions:

1. Select Edit ➤ Step and Repeat or press Shift+Ctrl+V (Windows) or Shift+Cmd+V (Macintosh).

2. The Step and Repeat dialog box opens as shown below.

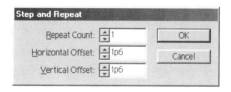

3. In the dialog box, which functions like QuarkXpress's Step and Repeat command, you can set the following options:

    Repeat Count Enter a value to specify the number of duplicates you want. Don't include the original in your value.

    Horizontal and Vertical Offset Use these options to determine how far to move and position each new duplicate. To set up duplicate objects in a horizontal or vertical row, set the offset value to 0 (zero).

WARNING When setting the offset value, you must add the original object's width plus the space between each duplicate object or the original object's height plus the space between each object to set the correct offset value. Otherwise your duplicates will overlap. If you step and repeat rule lines, don't forget that the line width will affect how many lines you can duplicate in an area.

TIP Before setting step and repeat values, it pays to do a little simple measuring. To quickly measure an area that you want to fill with duplicates, select the Rectangle tool and draw a frame to the size of the area. With the temporary frame selected, look at the Transform palette's Width and Height object measurements. You now know the maximum length for each dimension. If you would like to use the Transform palette to help calculate offsets, see Chapter 3.

Creating a Full Page of Duplicates

If you would like to create a full page of duplicates, follow these directions:

1. Select and position your original object at the top left corner of your page margins. For my example I will be duplicating rules. (For any other object, the steps are the same. Just substitute the appropriate values that you need.) My rule line is set to Length: 14p (picas) and Width: p2 (points). I will create three columns of rules and 46 rules in each column. The gutter between each column of rules is 1p6. The area that the duplicates will fill is 45p wide × p720 column depth. (I changed the vertical ruler to points to make it easier to calculate how many rules can fit in each column.)

2. Press Shift+Ctrl+V (Windows) or Shift+Cmd+V (Macintosh) to open the Step and Repeat dialog box.

3. To create my first column of rules, the values I entered were Repeat Count 45, Horizontal Offset 0p, Vertical Offset 16 pt (points). Click OK to accept step and repeat values. You can see the results in Figure 15.7.

NOTE If you enter a repeat count value that creates too many duplicates (exceeds the size of the pasteboard), a warning alert will appear on screen requesting that you change the value to a smaller number.

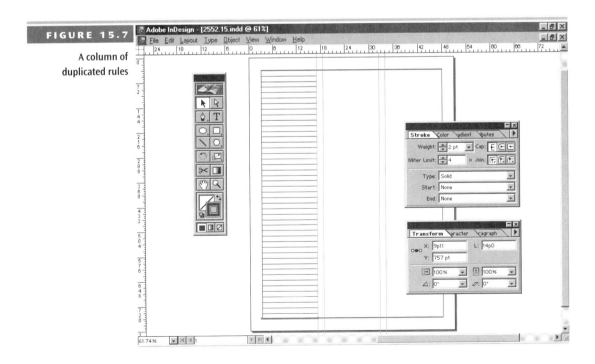

FIGURE 15.7

A column of duplicated rules

4. Now you need to select all the rules in the first column and make them into a group. Press Ctrl+G (Windows) or Cmd+G (Macintosh) to create a group.

5. Now you need to duplicate the group. Press Shift+Ctrl+V (Windows) or Shift+Cmd+V (Macintosh) to open the Step and Repeat dialog box again.

6. Enter the second set of step and repeat values. Repeat Count: 2, Horizontal Offset: 15p6 (rule length plus the width of the gutter), and Vertical Offset 0 pt. In Figure 15.8 you can see a page filled with equally spaced two-point rules.

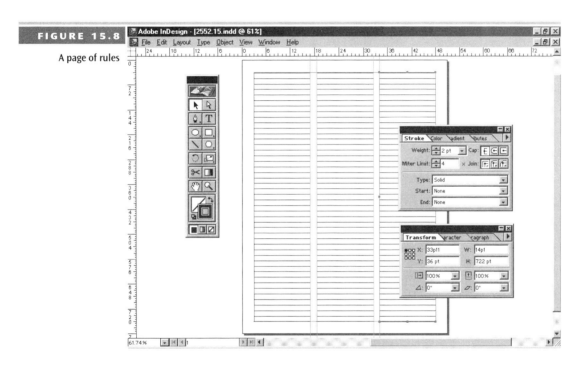

FIGURE 15.8

A page of rules

Scaling Objects

You can change the proportions of objects by dragging the object or by changing the values in the Transform palette. When you scale an object, you are increasing or decreasing an object's size along either its horizontal (X) axis, vertical (Y) axis, or both axes (X and Y). Keep in mind that the scaling percentage is measured relative to the specified point of origin.

WARNING Watch out when scaling type with the Scale tool. Before scaling text frames, open both the Character and Transform palettes. They contain valuable information to help you correctly measure scaled text. When you scale a text frame box using the Scale tool, the point size of the type is no longer correctly reported in the Character palette. To find the actual point size of the scaled text, multiply the original point size indicated in the Character palette by the Scale Y percentage noted in the Transform palette. Reference the total if you need to match the type specifications. When working with paths instead of text, open the Stroke palette rather than the Character palette. Use the same method as for type when calculating the weight of scaled paths.

Scaling an Object by Dragging

Again InDesign provides a choice of tools to complete a task. You can use either the Selection or the Scale tool to resize an object by scaling. The following sections show you how to scale objects with each tool.

Scaling with the Selection Tool

To scale an object using the Selecting tool, follow these steps:

1. Choose the Selection tool from the Toolbox or press V.
2. Select the object.
3. Select the bounding box handle you want to drag from.
4. To maintain the original proportions, press Shift (Windows and Macintosh) as you drag from any handle. The handle you select will determine in which direction(s) the object will grow. In Figure 15.9 a Webdings-type dingbat is scaled using the Selection tool. Notice the absence of a point of origin.

Scaling with the Scale Tool

To scale and object with the Scale tool, follow these steps:

1. Choose the Scale tool from the Toolbox or press V.
2. Select the object.
3. Set the point of origin.
4. Position the Scale tool away from your defined point of origin. The larger the distance between the tool cursor and the point of origin when dragging begins, the greater the Scale tool precision.
5. Drag the Scale tool along either the horizontal (X) or vertical axis (Y) to resize only one dimension of the object. Drag between axes to scale both X and Y dimensions.

FIGURE 15.9

Scaling with the Selection tool

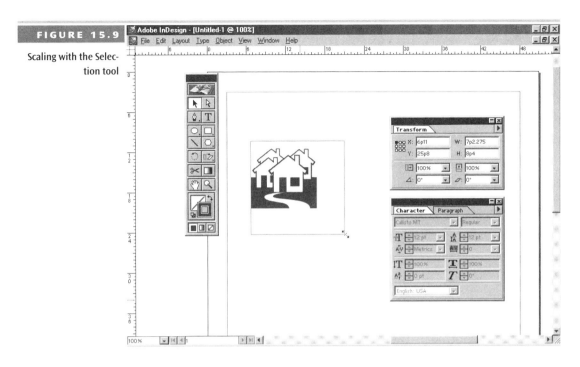

TIP It's helpful when scaling both dimensions to place the point of origin on a corner anchor point. As you drag from the opposite corner point, press the Shift key to scale the selected object proportionally.

Figure 15.10 shows the Scale tool resizing a Webdings-type dingbat by dragging. Note the presence of a point of origin and a tool cursor that is different from the Selection tool cursor used when dragging.

Using the Transform Palette to Scale an Object

If you would like to scale an object by a specific percentage, the Transform palette provides several options. You can enter a numeric value for Width (W:), Height (H:), Scale X Percentage, or Scale Y Percentage. Press Enter (Windows) or Return (Macintosh) to apply the value.

NOTE To preserve the proportions of the original object, press Ctrl+Enter (Windows) or Cmd+Return (Macintosh) to set the other dimension when entering a value in the Transform palette.

FIGURE 15.10

Resizing with the Scale tool

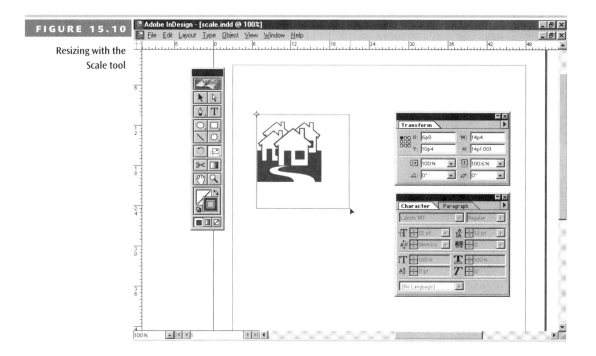

 TIP Remember to select or deselect the Scale Content option in the Transform palette menu before scaling a frame filled with content.

If you'd like to quickly change one dimension of an object, you can select from the Scale X Percentage or Scale Y Percentage option menus. Drag down to make your selection. The preset percentages are 25, 50, 75, 90, 100, 110, 125 175, and 200. Reducing an object below 25% or enlarging an object above 200% will require you to enter a value in the Transform palette or drag it to scale.

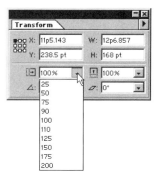

Reflecting Objects

In addition to the easily accessible reflecting options in the Transform palette menu (Flip Horizontal, Flip Vertical, and Flip Both), you can flip objects (across an invisible axis at the point of origin setting) applying the following methods:

- With the Selection tool, pull one side of an object's bounding box past the opposite side. Be careful when using this tool to reflect an object because as you pull past the opposite side of the object, you can change the dimensions of the object. Try placing ruler guides first to indicate the correct size of the reflected object. The guides will provide a visual reference as you pull the object's bounding box with the Selection tool, as seen in Figure 15.11. The gray ellipse in the figure represents the original position of the object.

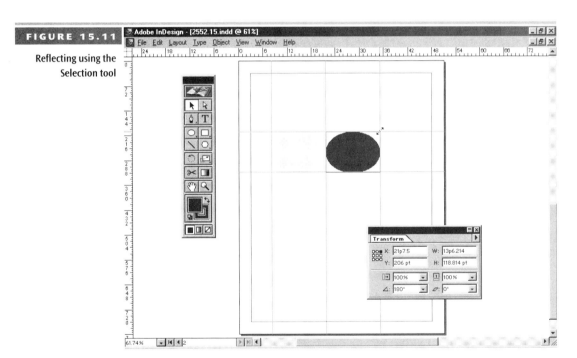

FIGURE 15.11

Reflecting using the Selection tool

- In the Transform palette, enter a negative value for either the Scale X Percentage or Scale Y Percentage option. Press Enter (Windows) or Return (Macintosh), or click your mouse button to apply the new value.

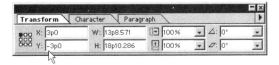

TIP If you press Ctrl+Enter (Windows) or Cmd+Return (Macintosh) to apply the negative value for flipping, InDesign will scale the object in both dimensions and reflect the object on both the horizontal and vertical axes (a 180 degrees rotation).

WARNING To position the point of origin for reflecting, first select one of the transform tools: Rotate, Shear, or Scale. Then select a flipping option from the Transform palette menu or enter a negative scale value in the Transform palette.

- Rotate an object first if you want to reflect an object at an angle other than those preset in the Transform palette. Remember to check and reposition, if necessary, the point of origin after rotating the object.

Rotating and Distorting Objects

If you're like me and love to create shaped typography in different isometric projections or add cast shadows to text or graphics, the Rotating and Shear tools are frequently used friends. If you've worked with these tools before in Photoshop or Illustrator, you'll find yourself in a very familiar environment. For those of you who haven't worked with these Adobe graphics programs, here's the lowdown on Rotate and Shear.

TIP If you can't find the Shear tool icon on the toolbox, it's hidden. Click the triangle on the Scale tool or type "S" to reveal and select the tool.

If you've been trying out the previously discussed Scale tool, then you're more than halfway there in learning how to use the Rotate and Shear tools. Just like the Scale tool, you can:

- Set the point of origin.
- Use the Transform palette to rotate or skew by a preset measurement (see the "Transform Palette Basics" section earlier in this chapter).
- Enter a custom value in the Transform palette.
- Quickly pick preset measurements from the Transform palette menu.
- Constrain tool behavior by pressing the Shift key when dragging the selected object (multiples of 45 degrees).
- For tighter control of the tool, position the cursor as far away from the point of origin as you can.

When specifying a precise measurement in the Transform palette, keep the following in mind:

Rotate To rotate selected objects clockwise, enter a positive angle like 55°. To rotate selected objects counterclockwise, enter a negative value like ×55°. If you'd like to use the Transform palette to calculate a new rotation angle, enter a mathematical expression, such as 55° + 9, to rotate the object another 9 degrees clockwise or ×55° + 9 to change the angle of rotation to ×46°. To apply the newly entered values, press Enter (Windows) or Return (Macintosh).

NOTE There's more about entering numeric values in palettes in Chapter 3.

Shear To quickly slant any frame, enter a positive or negative value in the Transform palette. Press Enter (Windows) or Return (Macintosh) to apply the new value. Remember the angle of the slant is calculated from the current angle of the frame. Make use of mathematical expressions like those examples cited for the Rotate tool. It's an easy way to finely adjust a frame to fit customized content or a text wrap.

In Figure 15.12, an ellipse was distorted by applying new rotation and shearing values. The gray ellipse represents the original object.

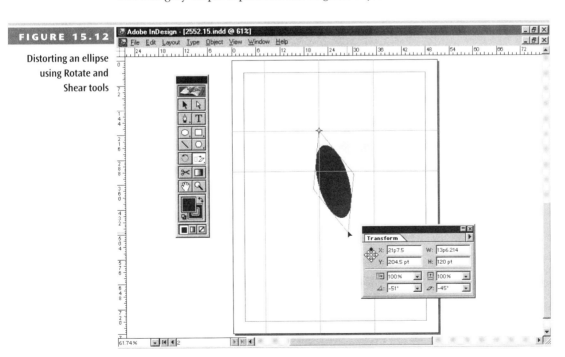

FIGURE 15.12
Distorting an ellipse using Rotate and Shear tools

Duplicating Objects as You Transform Them

Here's an InDesign option where you can have lots of fun creating logos and other artwork. As you duplicate objects, you can transform the duplicate by rotation, shearing, changing proportions and placement. You have three techniques to choose from:

Dragging plus shortcut keys Choose either the Selection, Rotate, Scale, or Shear tool. Press Alt (Windows) or Option (Macintosh) to generate and transform the duplicate when dragging. If you want to constrain the duplicate transformation, press Alt+Shift (Windows) or Option+Shift (Macintosh) instead as you drag. The transformed duplicate should appear after you've dragged a short distance.

TIP It may take some practice to get the hang of things. Watch out for duplicates that haven't been transformed stacking in front of the original object.

Transform palette plus shortcut keys After entering the value in the Transform palette, press Alt+Enter (Windows) or Option+Return (Macintosh).

Arrow keys plus shortcut keys When pressing arrow keys to reposition objects, press Alt (Windows) or Option (Macintosh) if you want to generate and position a duplicate.

Here's an example of how a text character was specified, duplicated, and transformed to create a graphic element.

1. To begin the process, open the Character and Paragraph palette group and the Transform palette (if they're not open already).
2. Select the Text tool and create a text frame.
3. Choose the font and specify point size (in this example: Webdings at 200 pt) in the Character palette. Center-align the text frame by selecting the option in the Paragraph palette. (Duplicating and transforming text is easier to control when the text is centered in the paragraph.)
4. Enter text. As shown in Figure 15.13, the lower case j was typed to generate the Webdings airplane.
5. Select the Rotate tool and then select the text frame. Drag the frame to reorient the object away from the text baseline (see Figure 15.14).
6. With the Rotate tool and original object still selected, move the point of origin away from the object's bounding box.

DUPLICATING OBJECTS AS YOU TRANSFORM THEM 431

FIGURE 15.13

Entering text to be used for duplicating and transforming

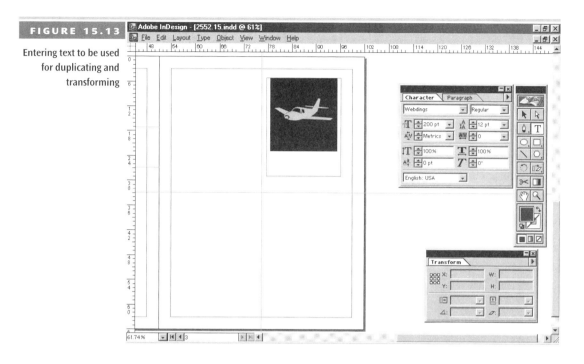

FIGURE 15.14

Using the Rotate tool

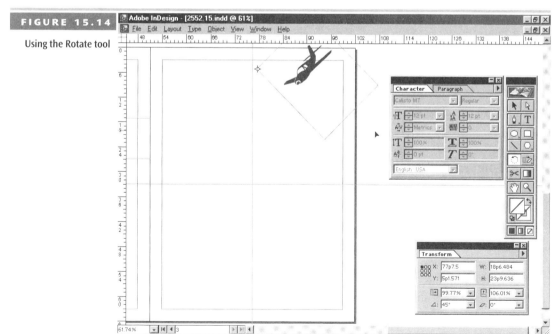

7. Press Alt (Windows) or Option (Macintosh) to generate and rotate the duplicate when dragging as seen in Figure 15.15.

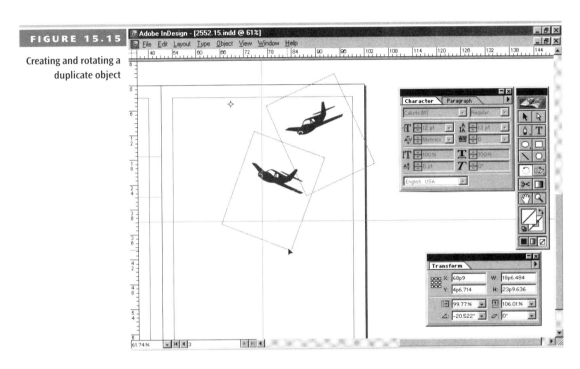

FIGURE 15.15
Creating and rotating a duplicate object

8. For this example, I generated a second duplicate using the procedures described in Steps 6 and 7. For your own project, you can create as many variations you need.
9. I then selected each airplane in turn with the Text tool and filled it with a gradient. The direction of the gradient was angled to match the path of the airplane with the Gradient tool.
10. Using the Selection tool, I finalized the position of each airplane. See Figure 15.16 to see the completed example.

Aligning and Distributing Objects

When you want to align and distribute objects, open the Align palette by selecting Window ➢ Align or pressing F8. After the Align palette opens, click the palette menu triangle (right side of the palette) to show the Distribute Spacing options, if they are not already visible.

FIGURE 15.16

Completed version of duplicating and rotating example

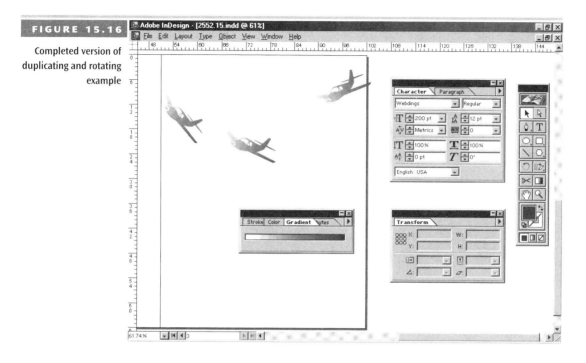

WARNING   The Align palette does not affect locked position objects.

WARNING   You can change the alignment of a text *frame* with an Align palette option, but not the alignment of a text *paragraph*. For example, you cannot use the Align palette to change the justification of a paragraph from flush left to flush right. To change the paragraph click one of the Paragraph palette's alignment buttons. For more on text composition basics, see Chapter 9.

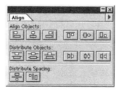

Setting the Align Objects Options

The Align palette offers the following choices for aligning objects:

Horizontal Align Left   Using the left edge of the object furthest to the left as the line of reference, this command aligns two or more objects along a common axis.

Horizontal Align Center   InDesign measures the distance from the left edge of the furthest selected object on the left to the right edge of the furthest selected object on the right and divides by two to find the alignment axis. All selected objects are center aligned to this vertical axis.

Horizontal Align Right   Using the right edge of the object furthest to the right as the line of reference, this command aligns two or more objects along a common axis.

Vertical Align Top   All selected objects align at their top edge. The top edge of the topmost chosen object determines the alignment axis position.

NOTE   Objects positioned along the same vertical axis will stack one in front of the other when vertically aligned top, center, or bottom. To learn more about accessing individual objects in a stack, see "Understanding the Object Stack" later in this chapter.

Vertical Align Center   InDesign measures the distance from the top edge of the topmost selected object to the bottom edge of the furthest selected object on the bottom and divides by two to find the alignment axis. All selected objects are center aligned to this horizontal axis.

Vertical Align Bottom   All selected objects align at their bottom edges. The bottom edge of the bottommost chosen object determines the alignment axis position.

Setting the Distribute Objects Options

Distributed objects are spaced evenly along a horizontal or vertical axis. To distribute objects you *must* select minimally three objects.

Vertical Distribute Top   InDesign evenly positions objects by measuring from the top edge of the topmost object to the top edge of the next object to the top edge of the next object and so on, for all objects chosen for vertical distribution.

GROUPING AND UNGROUPING OBJECTS 435

Vertical Distribute Center InDesign positions objects by measuring off the same distance between the horizontal center lines of all selected objects.

Vertical Distribute Bottom Functions the same way as the Vertical Distribute Top option, except that InDesign measures the distances using the bottom edge of each object as the reference line.

WARNING If you are distributing objects of unequal dimensions, the space between the bottom or right side of an object and the top or left side of the next object will not be the same for each object selected for distribution. Some objects will be unevenly spaced. If you want the space between the objects to be the same measurement for all objects, use the Distribute Spacing options instead.

Horizontal Distribute Left Using a horizontal axis, objects are evenly spaced from the left edge of one selected object to another.

Horizontal Distribute Center InDesign positions objects in the same way as the Vertical Distribute Center option, except that the program measures from the vertical center line of each selected object.

Horizontal Distribute Right Objects are evenly spaced along the horizontal axis using the right edge of each selected object as the line of reference.

Setting the Distribute Spacing Options

The Align palette offers the following choices for spacing objects:

Vertical Distribute Space This option evenly spaces all objects, regardless of dimensions, along a vertical axis.

Horizontal Distribute Space Whatever their dimensions, all objects are evenly spaced along a horizontal axis.

NOTE Objects placed on different named layers can be aligned, distributed, and spaced using the Align palette options.

Grouping and Ungrouping Objects

Grouping and ungrouping objects is a fast and easy way to move or transform several objects within your layout. Each object in the group retains its original attributes and position relative to other objects in document. You can place objects in one group and in turn combine that subgroup with other groups to create a parent group.

You'll want to create a group when you need to globally change the solid color or gradient for several objects. You will also find grouping handy when you want to apply a corner effect to several graphic or text frames.

WARNING You cannot group locked and unlocked objects in the same group. If you attempt to combine unlocked and locked objects in the same group, a Group Alert appears on screen. The alert prompts you to Lock All or Unlock All objects, or Cancel the Group command.

NOTE If you place a subgroup into a larger parent group, you are creating a nested group. Chapter 6 reviews nested objects.

Grouping or Ungrouping Objects

When you want to group or ungroup multiple objects follow these steps:

1. Choose the Selection tool, and as you select each object press the Shift key. If you select part of an object, such as its anchor point, you add the entire object to the group you are creating.

2. Choose Object ➢ Group or press Ctrl+G (Windows) or Cmd+G (Macintosh) to combine the objects into the group. When creating groups using objects that are on different named layers, all objects get moved to the same frontmost layer. See the next section for more details.

3. If you need to ungroup objects, choose Object ➢ Ungroup, or press Shift+Ctrl+G (Windows) or Shift+Cmd+G (Macintosh). This disassembles the chosen group into selectable subgroups or individual objects.

NOTE To determine if an object is part of a group, use the Selection tool to select it and then check to see if the ungroup command is available. If the command is not dimmed, then the object is part of a group. A quick way to access the ungroup command is to use a context menu. Chapter 3 discusses how to work with context menus.

Creating Groups from Objects on Different Named Layers

You can create groups using objects positioned on different named layers. Consider working with this option when you're overlaying text placed on one layer with a photograph or graphic located on another layer. The objects in these groups have the following properties:

- All the objects in the group will move to the frontmost layer from which you selected an object.
- When you select the group, the bounding box will be identified by the frontmost layer's color.
- If you hide the layer on which the group is located, all objects in that group will not be visible. When you hide a layer that's not the group layer, the object originally selected from that layer remains visible in the group because the object now exists only on the group layer. Any ungrouped objects that are on the original layer will be hidden from view. This holds true even if the group is moved to the pasteboard.
- If you ungroup the objects, all objects in the group will continue to be part of layer they were moved to when the group was formed.

Consider carefully before creating any groups with some objects but not all objects in a stack of overlapping objects located on one layer. For example, on Layer1 is a logo composed of three stacking objects: a background circle with a line of text and a glyph, which is in front of the text. The stack is ungrouped. Positioned on Layer2 is the corporate name. In error only the background circle and the corporate name was selected and grouped. Because of grouping rules, the background circle is now on the frontmost layer, Layer2. The logo text and glyph are no longer visible. When the group doesn't work, select the Undo command and try again. To fix this problem, all of Layer1's objects were grouped first, and then combined with the single object on Layer2 to form a larger group. All the objects are now positioned on Layer2 and visible in correct stacking order.

TIP If it's important to also retain the original object to layer positioning, then save a back-up version of the file before grouping objects placed on different layers.

Understanding the Object Stack

All the objects in your document are not stacked like one continuous deck of cards. It's important to remember that each named layer can have its own separate stack. To access all the objects stacked in the document, you have to select each layer individually, and then select an object from that layer's stack.

NOTE Chapter 13 has more information about layers.

Here are things to consider when working with object stacks:

- Objects are stacked in the order that you create or import them. Even if you switch between layers as you make or import objects, InDesign will still maintain a separate stacking order for each layer. When there are no named layers in a document (the Layers palette lists only Layer1), the document has only a single stack of objects.
- As each object is created or imported, it displays in front of all existing objects on that layer
- If two objects overlap, the object created last is positioned in front.

WARNING Grouping and ungrouping of objects may alter an object's placement within a stacking order.

- If you need to amend a layer's object stacking order, select Object ➢ Arrange and then choose one of the Arrange submenu commands: Bring to Front, Bring Forward, Send to Back, and Send Backwards. The Arrange submenu commands are also accessible as a context menu.

chapter 16

DOCUMENT MANAGEMENT

Featuring:

- **Managing documents with the Pages palette** — 442
- **Adding and deleting pages** — 447
- **Using master pages** — 454
- **Numbering pages** — 461
- **Overriding master objects** — 468
- **Changing margin and column settings in an existing document** — 469
- **Adjusting a layout** — 470

CHAPTER 16

DOCUMENT MANAGEMENT

As you learned in Chapter 2, InDesign documents are composed of pages, spreads, and master pages. A *page* is a single sheet or leaf of a document; a *spread* is comprised of two pages displayed side by side; and a *master page* (or sometimes just *master*) is a page that you can apply to other pages and spreads. You'll do most of your work manipulating pages, spreads, and master pages with the Pages palette. In this chapter, I'll show you how to use the Pages palette and its menu, specify island spreads, add and delete pages or spreads, number pages, create and assign master pages, change margins and columns in existing documents, and adjust document layout.

For this chapter, you'll probably want to display your InDesign document as a spread. If you didn't select the New Document dialog box's Facing Pages option to arrange pages in spreads, then select File ➢ Document Setup to reset your open document's specifications. The keystroke shortcuts are Ctrl+Alt+P (Windows) or Opt+Cmd+P (Macintosh). Click OK to accept the changes. In Figure 16.1, the Facing Pages option was selected and the number of pages were increased to four in the Document Setup dialog box. (When the number of pages increases, the pages are automatically added after the selected page.)

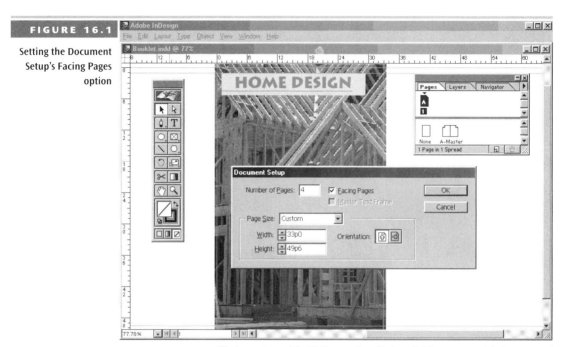

FIGURE 16.1

Setting the Document Setup's Facing Pages option

Photo courtesy of Corbis Images (royalty-free division www.corbisimage.com)

Managing Documents with the Pages Palette

If the Pages palette is not already open, select Window ➢ Pages, or press F12 (Windows/Macintosh).

As you can see in Figure 16.2, the Pages palette is divided into two parts. The top half (above the horizontal double line) shows the page icon (selected). In the center of a page icon, you'll see a letter (prefix), which indicates the master assigned to the page. Below the page icon is its page number. The inverted triangle above the page one icon is the section indicator. (There's more about Section options later in this chapter.) A right-hand (recto) page's icon will have its top-right corner folded down, and the left (verso) page, its top-left corner folded down. For spreads that have more than two pages, the pages in the center will be represented by a rectangle.

The master icons appear below the horizontal double line. By default, you'll see an icon for None and A-Master when you first open the Pages palette for your new document. A name and a prefix identify each master. The prefix is used to label icons of pages, thereby allowing you to verify which master was applied to individual pages, spreads, or masters.

MANAGING DOCUMENTS WITH THE PAGES PALETTE   443

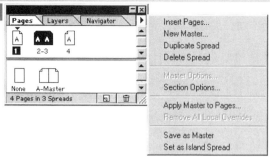

FIGURE 16.2

The Pages palette and its menu

If you are working with a very large document with multiple masters and/or lots of pages, use the scroll bars on the right to find the master or page/spread icons you need. When you change the palette's dimensions by dragging any corner of the palette (Windows) or dragging from the bottom right corner (Macintosh), more area is added to the Pages section. If you want to assign more area to the Masters section instead, select the horizontal double line in the palette and drag to a new position.

N O T E Because of European language page numbering conventions, first and last pages are each shown as a single page by default. See the "Creating Island Spreads" section in this chapter to learn how to change this default.

The Pages palette also has a menu that you can access by clicking the triangle in the upper-right-hand corner. As shown in Figure 16.2, there are palette menu commands for working with selected pages or spreads. Others are activated if you first selected a master page icon.

W A R N I N G Select all pages in a spread if you want to use the Spread options in Pages palette menu.

Selecting and Targeting Spreads

Depending on whether you want to affect a page/spread or an object, you can select or target a spread. Selected and targeted pages or spreads are indicated differently in the Pages palette.

Selecting When you select a page or spread, it will be changed by your next action in InDesign. Setting new page dimensions is one example. Changing margins is another. In the Pages palette, the highlighted page icon(s) identifies the selected spread(s) by changing from white to another color. Single-click a page icon (not the page number) to select it as illustrated in Figure 16.3. Note that when you make a selection, in this case page 3 of the document, the view doesn't change. The highlighted page number (1) identifies the page currently on view in the document window.

Press the Shift key as you click to choose multiple contiguous pages or spreads. Press the Control key as you click to choose multiple noncontiguous pages or spreads. A spread is selected when all its pages are highlighted in the Pages palette. You can also select an entire spread by single-clicking its page range number, i.e., 2–3.

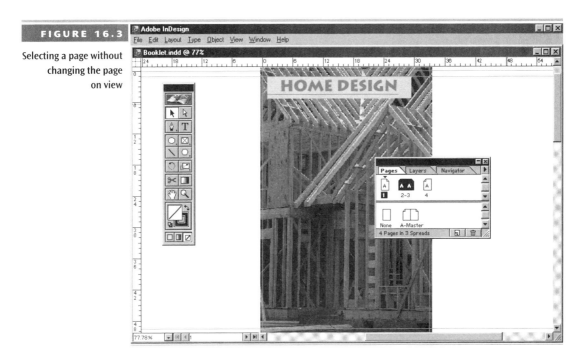

FIGURE 16.3
Selecting a page without changing the page on view

Targeting When you want to see the object that you will create or modify, target the object's spread. You are limited to only one targeted spread at a time.

As shown previously in Figure 16.3, the highlighted page number identified the targeted page on view. If you want to target a spread, choose one of these options:

- In the Pages palette, double-click the page numbers or the page/spread icons. The new targeted page/spread will appear centered in the document window.
- In the document window, change any object on a spread or its pasteboard, or click a spread or its pasteboard.

Table 16.1 shows five helpful shortcuts for changing the spread on view in the document window:

TABLE 16.1: SPREAD SHORTCUTS

Command	Windows	Macintosh
First Spread	Shift+Alt+Page Up	Opt+Shift+Page Up
Last Spread	Shift+Alt+Page Down	Opt+Shift+Page Down
Next Spread	Alt+Page Down	Opt+Page Down
Previous Spread	Alt+Page Up	Opt+Page Up
Cycle through Previously Selected Spreads	Ctrl+Page Up or Ctrl+Page Down	Cmd+Page Up or Cmd+Page Down

Creating Island Spreads

Island spreads are spreads that can contain up to a maximum of 10 pages. Create island spreads when you want to see more than two pages at a time on a single pasteboard. Before we get started creating island spreads, here are some basics:

- Island spreads can be used to lay out gatefold or accordion foldout brochures or inserts.
- You can arrange, add, or delete pages before or after an island spread without affecting its content.
- When you set four pages, for example, as island spreads, they will display two at a time per pasteboard unless the pages are physically dragged into a double spread.
- You can only set even number island spreads from the Pages palette menu.
- To create an uneven numbered spread, i.e., a 3-fold document, you will need to drag the single page to the island spread in the Pages palette.

NOTE Odd-numbered first and last pages are not considered island spreads.

To create an island spread, press Shift as you select the pages included in the spread from the Pages palette. After you've made your selection, choose Set as Island Spread from the Pages palette menu. The new island spread is identified in the Pages palette by the square brackets before and after the page number, as shown below. (If you want to add pages to an island spread, refer to the "Adding Pages" section in this chapter.)

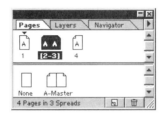

Clearing Island Spreads

If you need to clear an island spread, first select the island spread in the Pages palette. Next choose Clear Island Spread from the Pages palette menu. When you clear an island spread, all the pages that were in the spread are redistributed to match the Facing Pages setting selected previously in either the New Document or Document Setup dialog boxes. Make note of potential content organization problems as discussed in the following section.

NOTE If your document does not contain an island spread, the Clear Island Spread option is not visible in the Pages palette menu. You will see the Set as Island Spread option instead.

Arranging Pages and Spreads

There will be times when you will need to reorder the sequence of pages in your document, such as when copy is cut from a magazine article or three more graphs are added to the report to the shareholders. You can arrange pages and spreads in InDesign by using the drag-and-drop method in the Pages palette. Simply select a page or spread icon in the Pages palette and drag it to where you want it to be placed. As you drag, the hand icon appears and a vertical bar indicates the new position of the page or spread (see Figure 16.4). Release the mouse button to drop the page or spread. (Remember to first select all the pages in a spread before moving an entire spread.)

When dragging a page or spread to a new position in the Pages palette, keep the following in mind:

- If the vertical bar touches an island spread, the page you are dragging will be added to the island spread.

- The Facing Pages setting of the New Document or Document Setup dialog boxes determines the distribution of the arranged pages when it is active. When the sequence of pages is changed, content spread across several pages may need to be repositioned. Content may end up not on a page, but extend onto the pasteboard. Or you may see a blank page between content that is supposed to cross a binding gutter.
- Threads between text blocks on pages that were added, arranged, or deleted are preserved.

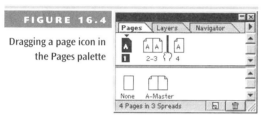

FIGURE 16.4

Dragging a page icon in the Pages palette

TIP Remember to proofread the newly arranged pages to determine if the copy still makes sense. Also watch out for photos or other artwork that may not be accurately positioned with their captions or body text.

Adding Pages

In the New Document or the Document Setup dialog box, you specified the number of pages in a document. For existing or open documents, you could add more pages by opening the Document Setup dialog box again, or use one of the following methods to add pages:

Pages palette MSClick the New Page button located at the bottom of the palette to add a single page after the last page or spread. This new page will be assigned the same master as the last page in the current document. If you select all the pages of an island spread, clicking the New Page button will still add only one new page. Use the next option to add as many pages as needed.

Pages palette menu When you want to add multiple pages anywhere in the document or assign a specific master to the new pages, follow these steps:

1. Select Insert Pages from the Pages palette menu.
2. The Insert Pages dialog box opens. Enter the number of new pages that will be added to the document.

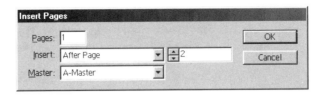

3. Choose the place of insertion in the document from the Insert option menu: After Page, Before Page, At Start of Document, or At End of Document.

4. To identify the point of reference for the Insert option, type a page number in the box to the right of the Insert menu.

5. From the Master option menu, select the master you want to assign to the inserted pages. If you don't want to assign any of the choices listed as masters, then cancel the page insertion. Create a new master and then insert the pages. Or use the layout created on the new inserted pages as the model for a new master. (More details are found in the "Creating and Assigning Master Pages" section later in this chapter.)

NOTE When text autoflows into a frame, InDesign can generate new pages as needed. For more information about text flow and connecting text blocks see Chapter 14.

Inserting Pages in Island Spreads

When you want three or more pages in a spread, you need to create an island spread (see the "Creating Island Spreads" section earlier in this chapter). Once created, you can add pages to the island spread (not to exceed a total of 10 pages) using one of the following options:

Pages palette   Drag an existing page icon until it touches the island spread. Wherever you touch (release the mouse button) will be the point of insertion for the added page. For example, if you touch the outer left edge of an island spread, the added page becomes the first page in the island spread, as seen in Figure 16.5. The figure illustrates how the first page (the cover) of a three-page document was dragged to the island spread. This action overrides the first page as a single-page spread default setting. Figure 16.6 shows the end result—a three-page spread for an accordion folded brochure that will be printed on one side.

In looking at Figures 16.5 and 16.6, you may have noticed that after the first page was added to the island spread, the two pasteboards were combined into one. The Pages palette document status line (bottom left) reflects this change: "3 Pages in 2 Spreads" became "3 Pages in 1 Spread." For complex documents where you can't see all the page or master icons at one time in the Pages palette, the status line becomes an important asset for monitoring how a document is set up.

Pages palette menu If you would like to add a new page to an island spread, select Insert Pages from the Pages palette menu. In the open Insert Pages dialog box, set the specifications for the page(s) insertion.

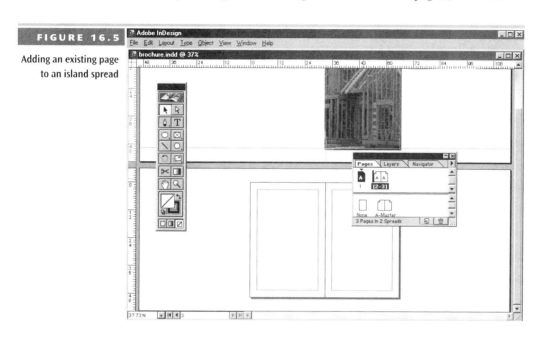

FIGURE 16.5

Adding an existing page to an island spread

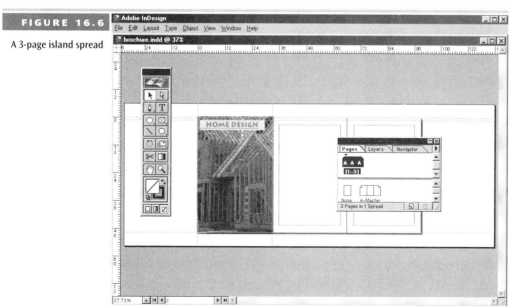

FIGURE 16.6

A 3-page island spread

Just For Fun: Using Island Spreads to Create a 4-Page Gatefold Book Insert

If you'd like to change the 3-page spread for an accordion folded brochure from the example above to a 4-page gatefold book insert (outside left and right pages fold in toward the center) do the following:

1. In the Pages palette, select the A-Master icon, and then choose Master Options from the palette menu. (There's more about masters later in this chapter.)
2. In the Master Option dialog box, change the Number of Pages to 4. Click OK.
3. In the Pages palette, select the island spread. Click the New Page button on the Pages palette. Page 4 is added to the document.
4. Select and drag page 4 until the bar touches the island spread. Page 4 is now included in the island spread.
5. Select the first page of the island spread that contains the cover artwork and typography.
6. Drag the first page of the island spread until the bar touches the right edge of the current third page. Release the mouse button to drop the page. (When changing the arrangement of pages, you have to touch the right edge of a page to position a page after it.)

7. As shown next, the front cover is now correctly positioned for printing a gatefold insert. Also added in this example: A flipped copy of the cover photo was placed on island spread's second page to create a back cover for the 4-page gatefold insert. (Chapter 15 has more info on transforming images and graphics.)

Continued on next page

Just For Fun: Using Island Spreads to Create a 4-Page Gatefold Book Insert *(continued)*

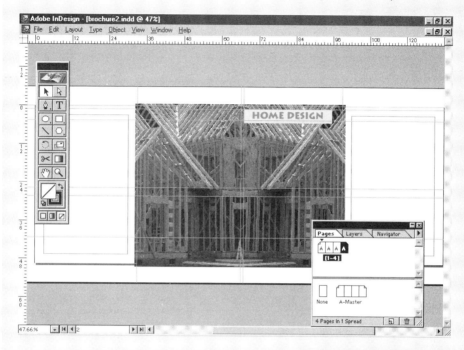

You want to avoid butting page edges into folds of other pages. To create a 4-page gatefold brochure that folds flat, make the far left and far right pages narrower in width than the two center pages of the island spread. It's a good idea to create a paper dummy of your project so you can test folds, diecuts (if any), postal weight, and how the paper handles in use. Contact your local paper merchant or your printer's paper supplier to arrange for free samples.

The direction of the paper grain (alignment of fibers) influences folding. To avoid cracking and wrinkles in folds, plan your design so that the binding or spine runs parallel to the paper grain. Consult with your printer or binder for projects that contain complex folds or folds that are against grain direction (90 degrees).

Duplicating Pages

If you need to re-create pages that contain custom ruler guides or objects, duplicating pages can be a very helpful, time-saving technique. When you duplicate a spread, you also duplicate all the objects on that spread.

WARNING   Text threads within the duplicated spread remain intact, but text threads from the duplicated spread to other spreads will be broken. There is no change to the original spread's text threads. Always proofread your document after duplicating pages. See Chapter 14 for more details about text threads and linking text.

Using the Pages palette, you can duplicate a selected spread by dragging a page numbers range like [1–4] or 4–5 to the New Page button.

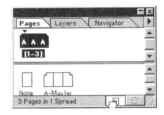

As shown in Figure 16.7, the duplicate spread is inserted at the end of the document, in this case the 3-page accordion brochure. You can also use the Duplicate Spread option from the Page palette menu to insert a spread at the end of a document.

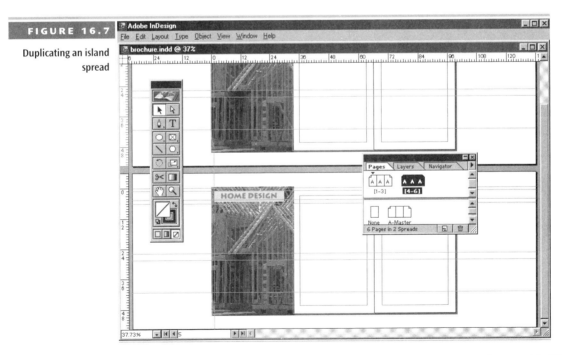

FIGURE 16.7

Duplicating an island spread

If you'd like to use your mouse and keyboard to duplicate a spread, press Alt (Windows) or Option (Macintosh) as you drag the page range numbers of a spread to a new position in the Pages palette.

Deleting Pages

When you want to delete a page or spread from the document, you have the following options:

Pages palette   You can drag a page/spread icon or page range numbers to the Trash button located at the bottom of the palette. Or choose a page/spread icon and then click the Trash button. If you want to delete more than one page at a time from the Pages palette, press the Shift key when selecting pages or spreads.

Pages palette menu   After you selected the pages or spreads that you want to delete, select Delete Page or Delete Spread from the menu. (Which one you see depends on which one you selected.)

There are a couple things to watch out for when deleting pages or spreads. If your pages have different settings for inside and outside margins, you could have a major problem when deleting or removing an odd number of pages in a spread. Objects originally on a left page may be repositioned relative to the margin if the page becomes a right page after you deleted the pages. See Chapter 14 for more details about flowing text.

Problems also can exist when removing or deleting pages that are the first page in a section. Page numbering can be affected. To avoid this problem, reassign the first page in a section to another existing page or the substitute you're adding in, and then delete or remove the original section opener.

Reorganizing Spreads

Using the Pages palette, you can decrease the number of pages in an island spread by dragging a page out of the spread. Move the vertical bar until it is no longer touching any page icons in the spread. Remember to select only the page you want to remove from the spread. Otherwise you'll see a warning icon (circle with diagonal line through it) signaling that the action can't be done. Also after removing the page, don't forget to change the master to match the new island spread.

Using Master Pages

Let's assume for a moment that your client just walked in with their last small change—the CEO didn't like the graphic element you placed with the page number. He wants the corporate logo. Not a problem if the document's an 8-page booklet. The courier will not be arriving for another hour and there's still time to make the change on each page. But what if you're not designing an 8-page booklet—instead it's a 296-page catalog. Is it your version of the latest horror movie? Not a chance! The document was designed using master spreads. You open the file in InDesign, make the change in the parent master spread, save the changes, and close the file. Crisis averted.

Learning how to design with master pages may save you time not only in crisis situations, but in regular production cycles where objects or layouts are used repeatedly. It's also a great way to build a library of templates that can facilitate creative brainstorming. In addition to page numbers and repeating graphic elements that appear in the same position on many pages, apply masters when defining margins and columns, guidelines, and headers or footers. Consider the following when building your document with master spreads:

- Think of organizing your masters like a family tree starting from a parent master, which sets the foundation. For example, use the parent master to define page-numbering placement or headers and footers, elements that are found on almost every page. Then base additional masters (second generation) on this parent when you define an individual section's margins and columns. Or use one of the children (second generation) to create another variation, such as section openers where you have to break the grid, use custom guidelines, or place the same artwork.

NOTE When you update the parent master, then all its children masters are automatically changed. A prefix will identify which master is its parent (Based on Master:) in the center of the master page icon.

- Remember that masters cannot contain sections. Specify where a section begins and ends in a document using the Pages palette menu's Section Options. Where a section starts is indicated by the inverted triangle above a page icon.

- If you're defining a master for a 4-page island spread, then use a 4-page master. Do this even if individual master pages don't contain objects on them and the layouts are okay as is. The general rule of the thumb is this: a master should contain the same number of pages as the page spread it's defining. If you vary the page spread, then make a variation of the applied master. (There's more info later in this section on how to create a master from a page spread.)

- A new master uses a default prefix and name when you don't identify a custom name or prefix, and you set the Based on Master option to None. See the next section for more details.

TIP Choose Layout ➤ Layout Adjustment to check out the options for layout adjustment. How you use this feature can affect how a master is applied in your layout and how objects are positioned in that layout. For more details see the "Adjusting Your Layout" section at the end of this chapter.

- A master can have layers. On which master's layer an object is placed will affect its stacking order and where that object will appear in the document.
    - If the document has only one layer, its objects will appear behind other objects on the page. For documents that have masters and pages with multiple layers, the master's objects will appear behind the page objects on the corresponding layer level.
    - To make a master's object appear in front of other objects on the page, place it on a higher layer in the master.

NOTE See Chapter 13 for more detailed information about working with layers.

Creating a New Master

Depending upon whether you want to create a master from scratch or base the new master on an existing master, page, or spread, you have various options.

To create a brand-new master, select New Master from the Pages palette. This opens the New Master dialog box, in which you can specify the Prefix (limited to one character), Name, Based on Master, and Number of Pages in your new master (maximum of 10). Pressing Ctrl+Alt (Windows) or Cmd+Opt (Macintosh) as you click the New Page button also opens the New Master dialog box.

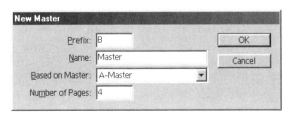

TIP InDesign will automatically update the default prefix to next available prefix by tracking the number of masters assigned to a document. If you attempt to use an existing prefix and name combination, you will see a warning on screen prompting you to type another one. When you click OK to close the message box, InDesign will automatically change the name displayed in the New Master dialog box. The suggested new name is based upon the default master naming system. You can use that name or type one of your own choosing.

When you want to base a new master on an existing master, select a master from the Pages palette and then choose Duplicate Master Spread *"Master Name"* from the palette menu. See Figure 16.8.

 NOTE This option is only available after you're selected a master. Otherwise you will see Duplicate Spread as the listed option in the palette menu.

FIGURE 16.8

Duplicating a master

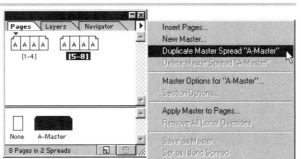

You can create a new master automatically by selecting an entire spread and then choosing the Save a New Master option from the Pages palette menu, as shown in Figure 16.9. No dialog box opens with this command. If you selected the wrong page spread as the source for the new master, use the Edit ➢ Undo command, and then select again.

You can also create a master from a selected page spread using the drag-and-drop method. In the Pages palette, select the source (page spread) for the new master. Next, drag the cursor until it crosses the horizontal double line into the bottom half of the palette. As you can see in Figure 16.10, a hand icon with a black outline surrounding the entire bottom half of the Pages palette appears when you drag the selected spread from the top half of the Pages palette. Release the mouse button to complete the action.

USING MASTER PAGES   457

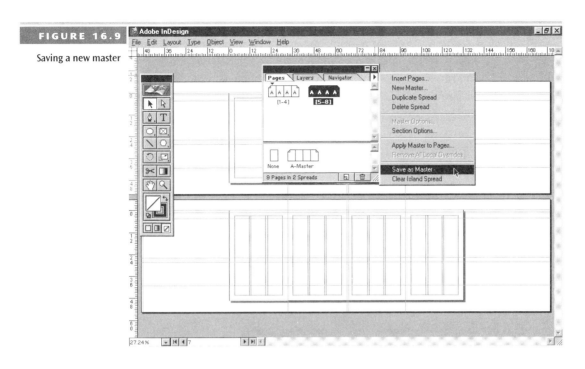

FIGURE 16.9

Saving a new master

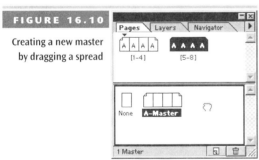

FIGURE 16.10

Creating a new master by dragging a spread

Applying a Master to a Spread

Figure 16.11 shows the results of creating a master from a page spread. When you look at the figure, make note of the spread used as the source for new master. The spread's prefix is still A, representing its currently assigned master. Although you used this spread as the source for a new master, its assigned master does not change as part of the creation process. If you want the new master to be applied to its source spread, select the spread and choose Apply Master from the Pages palette menu. Use this option any time you want to apply a master to a spread in the document. In the Apply Master dialog box, shown in Figure 6.12, select which master you want to apply and the page(s) to which it should be applied. Click OK. In Figure 16.13, you can see how the prefix changed for the second island spread [5-8] to B. B-Master is now assigned to this island spread.

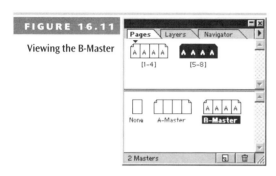

FIGURE 16.11

Viewing the B-Master

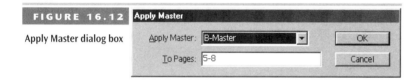

FIGURE 16.12

Apply Master dialog box

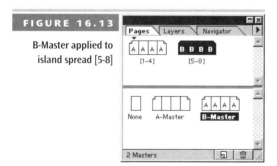

FIGURE 16.13

B-Master applied to island spread [5-8]

The drag-and-drop method can also be used to apply a master to a spread. Select a master from the bottom half of the Pages palette, and drag it to the page numbers of the chosen spread in the top half of the palette. When you see a black rectangle surround all the pages you are applying the master to, release the mouse button. (See Figure 16.14, left example). The prefix will change in the spread's icons, confirming completion of the action. If all the spread's pages are not changed to meet your specifications, then select Edit ➢ Undo and try again.

You also can apply the master to only one page of the spread. The black rectangle in this case will surround only that single page. See the right example in Figure 16.14 where a third master (C-Master) was applied to the fourth page of the island spread [1-4]. This page represents the first left-hand page that you see when the insert is opened; its layout is a variation of the B-Master.

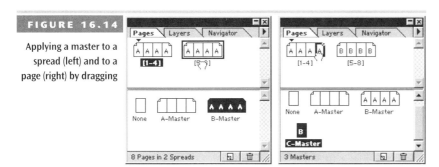

FIGURE 16.14

Applying a master to a spread (left) and to a page (right) by dragging

Applying a Master to Another Master

As you saw in Figure 16.14, you can apply a master to a spread. You can also change which master is applied or which master is the basis of another master. When you want to apply one master to another master, you could do this by choosing one of the following:

- Using the same dragging technique discussed previously for applying a master to a spread, you can apply an existing master to another master. In this case, select the master and drag until you see the rectangle surround the master pages that you want to reassign.

WARNING You can't apply a master variation (child) to its parent. A warning message will appear and the action will be voided.

- Using the Master Options "*Master Name*" option from the Pages palette menu, you can open the Master Options dialog box and change the Prefix (limited to one character), Name, Based on Master, and Number of Pages (maximum of 10) assigned to an existing master. See Figures 16.15 and 16.16.

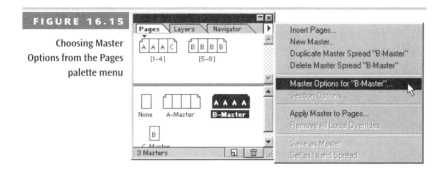

FIGURE 16.15
Choosing Master Options from the Pages palette menu

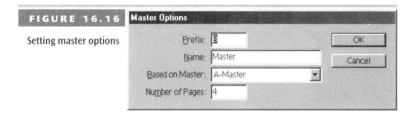

FIGURE 16.16
Setting master options

Deleting a Master

To delete a master(s) from the document, select the master you want to delete and then press the Trash button, or select Delete Master *"Master Name"* from the Pages palette menu. If you attempt to delete a master currently assigned to a page or spread, the following message will appear asking you to confirm or cancel the deletion.

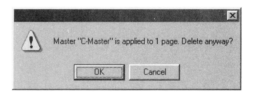

Copying a Master from One Document to Another Document

If you'd like to copy a master from one document to another document, do the following:

1. Open both documents by selecting File ➢ Open, or by pressing the shortcut Ctrl+O (Windows) or Cmd+O (Macintosh). (Open multiple document windows when you want to duplicate one master to several different documents.) Have the Pages palette on view.

2. Select Window ≻ Tile so that you can view the open documents on the screen side-by-side.
3. Choose the window of the document whose master you will be applying to another master.
4. In the Pages palette of the selected document, choose the master you want to copy to another document.
5. Drag the selected master until you are in the window of another document. The Hand icon and a black outline framing the second document window will be visible. (See Figure 16.17.) Release the mouse button to complete the process. The copied master will come into view in its new document window.
6. Repeat Steps 4 and 5 as needed.
7. Edit (as required) the copied master and assign to page spreads.

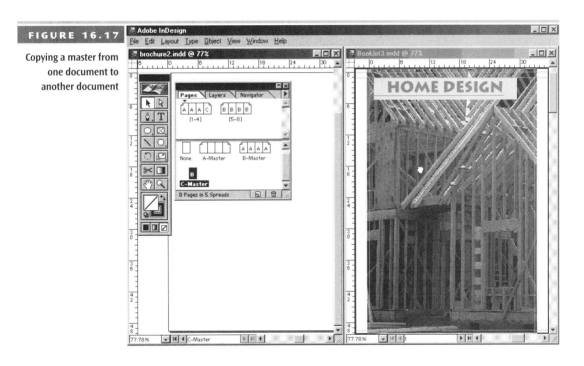

FIGURE 16.17
Copying a master from one document to another document

Numbering Pages

InDesign allows you to assign a page number to a page or a master that can be automatically updated. To save production time, place the page number on the parent master. (See the previous section for more info about masters.) How a document is numbered is controlled by the numbering preference, the sections you assign to your document, and your section preferences. Some facts about numbering documents in InDesign:

- Each document can have up to 9,999 pages.
- When multiple documents are used to create one publishing project, page numbers can go as high a 99,999.
- By default, the first page is a right (recto) page and is numbered 1. Odd-numbered pages are always right-hand pages. If you move the first page into an island spread, the first page becomes a left (verso) page. (See the Pages palette in Figure 16.6.) If the page number of the first page is changed from an odd to an even number, the page will change from a recto to verso page.

Setting Numbering Preferences

Numbering preferences are set in the Preferences: General dialog box. Select File ➢ Preferences ➢ General to open the dialog box. The shortcut is Ctrl+K (Windows) and Cmd+K (Macintosh). You can choose between absolute and section numbering. Absolute numbering uses one numbering style for the entire document—1,2,3, or a,b,c, for example. If you want to mix numbering styles, such as Roman numerals for a book's front matter and Arabic numerals for the other pages, choose section numbering as your preference.

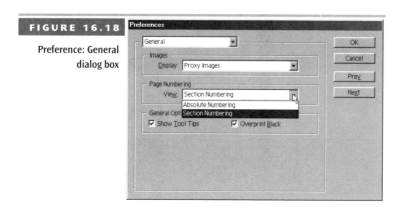

FIGURE 16.18

Preference: General dialog box

NOTE Appendix A discusses InDesign's preferences options.

Assigning an Automatically Updated Page Number

In this section, I will show you how to specify page numbers with graphic elements using masters. If you want to specify a page number on a page, start the process by selecting the specific page instead of a master. What I will be creating is a header for a book that includes a page number, the document title, and a paragraph rule below. My document has 88 pages on 45 spreads, not including the cover and inside flyleaf. There will be multiple sections in the document

1. In the Pages palette, double-click the A-Master. The A-Master will be the parent of all the other masters I will create later for this document. As shown in Figure 16.19, the A-Master is now on view and ready for placing a text frame.

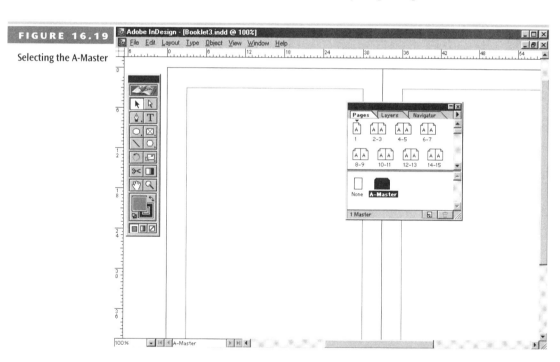

FIGURE 16.19
Selecting the A-Master

2. Select the Type tool from the toolbox. Open the Transform/Character/Paragraph palette group by selecting Type ➤ Character or by pressing Ctrl+T (Windows) Cmd+T (Macintosh).

3. Set your type specifications in the Character/Paragraph palettes. For my example, I selected Adobe Garamond Bold and used the group palette default settings. In

the upper-left corner of the left page, drag to create a new text frame. Make the text frame large enough to contain the header text and the page number.

NOTE For more information about text composition see Chapters 5, 9, 10, and 14.

4. The insertion point in the new text frame is flashing. Because you are creating a header for a left page, you will insert the page number first. Choose Layout ➢ Insert Page Number, or press Ctrl+Alt+N (Windows) or Cmd+Opt+N (Macintosh). As shown in Figure 16.20, the prefix A appears in the text box. When you insert a page number in a text box that's on a master page, you will see the prefix letter of the master instead of a page number. When viewed, the pages (applied to the master) will automatically display the page number using the character specifications that you selected at the time of insertion.

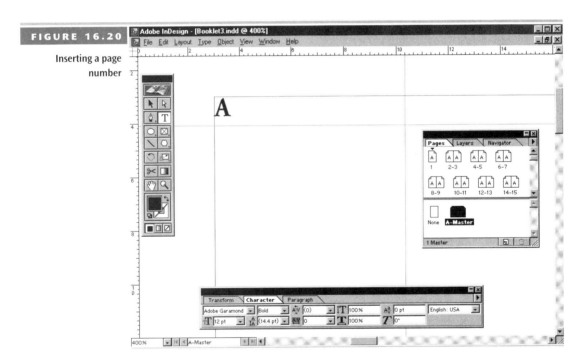

FIGURE 16.20
Inserting a page number

5. In the text box, you'll want to insert an en space between the page number and the document title. To save time, open a context menu by clicking the right mouse button (Windows) or press the Control key as you hold down the mouse button (Macintosh). From the context menu, select Insert Special Characters ➢ En Space.

6. In the text box, type the title of your document (see Figure 16.21).

FIGURE 16.21

Adding the title of the document

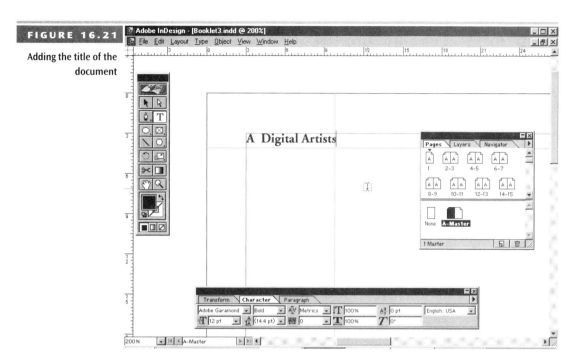

7. If you'd like to add a rule below your header, click the Paragraph palette's tab to display the Paragraph palette. Select Paragraph Rules from the Paragraph palette menu.

8. In the Paragraph Rules dialog box, select the Rule On checkbox to activate the dialog box.

9. Choose Rule Below from the main option menu.

10. Select the rule's Weight, Color, Width, Offset and Indents (if any). Figure 16.22 shows the settings for my example. The completed header is shown in Figure 16.23.

FIGURE 16.22

Creating a paragraph rule

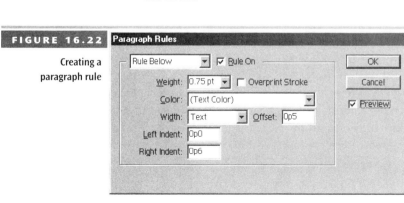

TIP If you want the paragraph rule to extend across the full width of the page, make the page-number text frame also the full width of the page. Then set Width: Column in the Paragraph Rules dialog box.

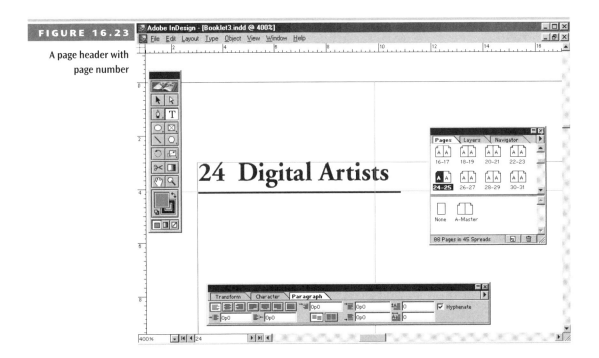

FIGURE 16.23
A page header with page number

11. To create the header for the right page, follow Steps 1–10, except set the paragraph column to flush right in the Paragraph palette before inserting the page number.

Assigning Sections to a Document

When you want to assign different sections to a document, do the following:

1. Duplicate the A-Master to create A-Master copy. Use the Master Options dialog box to change the prefix and name to B-master. (See the "Creating a New Master" section earlier in this chapter.) Each master will be assigned to a section. The B-Master defines the front matter pages 1–10 and has a Roman-numeral numbering system.

NUMBERING PAGES

2. Define the first page of the A-Master defined section by selecting the first page in the Pages palette; in the example it's page 11.

3. Select Section Options from the Pages palette menu. The New Section dialog box opens as shown in Figure 16.24. (If an existing section was selected in the Pages palette, then the dialog box that opens will be titled Section Options.)

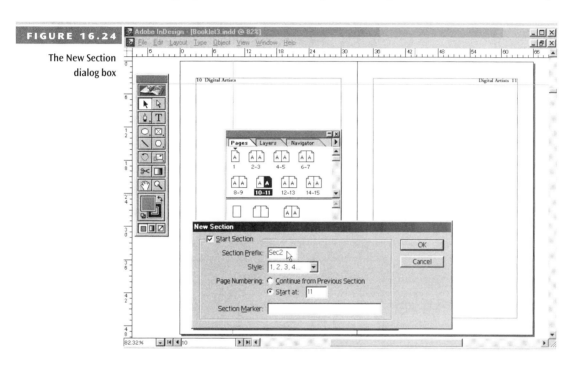

FIGURE 16.24
The New Section dialog box

4. Set the following options in the Section Options dialog box as required, and click OK:

   Section Prefix   Figure 16.25 shows that InDesign automatically updated the section prefix to Sec1, the default. If you want to assign a custom label, type up to five characters in the Section prefix box. The custom section prefix name will appear in the page box, which is in the lower left corner of the document window. (Chapter 2 reviews document window organization.)

   Section Marker   If you'd like to label a section on the page, type your description in the Section Marker box. To learn how to place the description you typed in the Section Marker box into the page-numbering text frame, see the next section, "Inserting a Section Marker."

Style Choose the page numbering style from the Style option menu. In Figure 16.25, Roman numerals were assigned to the B-Master pages (Sec1).

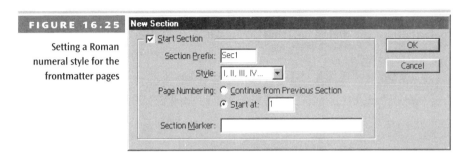

FIGURE 16.25

Setting a Roman numeral style for the frontmatter pages

Page Numbering Select either Continue from Previous Section or Start At. For my example, I selected Start At because I was using two different numbering styles as shown in Figures 16.24 and 16.25. Even if you select a non-Arabic numbering style, like Roman numerals, always use an Arabic number (1) when defining the start of a section.

If you want to end a section, you need to start another section. The last-defined section in the sequence of pages defines the page numbering until the end of the document.

Inserting a Section Marker

After you complete setting and applying Section Options, go to the master (or page) where you set the text for your header or footer. Select the page number text frame and then, instead of selecting the en space as we did before, choose Insert Special Character ➢ Section Marker from the context menu. When you insert the word "Section" into the page number text frame or any other text frame on a master page, the description you typed into the Section Options dialog box will be automatically inserted on each page the master was assigned to.

Overriding Master Objects

Master objects are objects that are placed on master pages. Because they are part of a master page, these objects will appear on all pages and spreads that the master was applied to. You may want to override master objects in certain situations. For example, when designing layouts, such as section openers, you can use the override option to remove unnecessary page numbering. Depending on your specific needs, there are several methods for overriding master objects. To confirm which objects are master objects in a page spread, target a spread by double-clicking its page number, and then select View ➢ Display Master Items.

When you want to override a master object on a document page, press Ctrl+Shift (Windows) or Command+Shift (Mac) as you select the master object(s)s applied to that page. You can now change the object using the transform tools or delete the object from the page. Once a spread is targeted, you can do the following:

- Choose Remove Selected Local Overrides from the Pages palette menu. This action removes master overrides from one or more objects on a document spread.

- If you want to remove all master overrides from a spread, first target the spread where you want to remove all master overrides. Next, choose Edit ➢ Deselect All to confirm all objects on the spread are deselected. Lastly, select Remove All Local Overrides from the Pages palette menu.

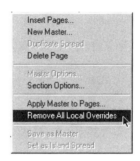

Changing Margin and Column Settings in an Existing Document

Here's how to modify margins and columns in an existing master:

1. Select a master page or master page spread you want to change.
2. Choose Layout ➢ Margins and Columns to open the Margins and Columns dialog box.
3. Modify your margins and columns settings as desired. Click OK.
4. As shown in Figure 16.26, the right page columns were changed from one to three columns with a one-pica gutter. Keep in mind that all pages assigned to the B-Master will be automatically changed. If you want to change only one page, then use the override techniques discussed in the previous section in this chapter.

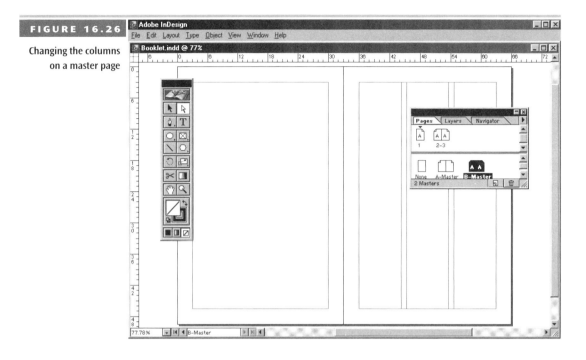

FIGURE 16.26

Changing the columns on a master page

Creating Uneven Columns

As shown in Figure 16.27, you can select and drag any page column line to a new position on either a page or master in the document. If you make the change on a master, the change will affect all the pages assigned to that master.

NOTE Columns, which are specified in text frames, will always have the same column width. InDesign does not allow for uneven text frame columns.

Adjusting Your Layout

There might be times when you'll want to adjust your layout globally because you need to rearrange objects to fit a new layout and don't want to change each object one at a time. For example, you're preparing a printed document for Web publishing and need to change page size to fit within a Web-defined frame. If you enable layout adjustment and select the appropriate adjustment options, the objects on the page will be fitted to the new layout size.

FIGURE 16.27

Creating an uneven column by dragging

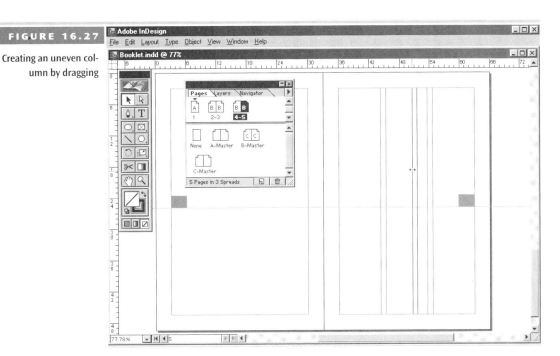

Choose Layout ➢ Layout Adjustment to open the Layout Adjustment dialog box shown in Figure 16.28. The layout adjustments options are as follows:

Enable Layout Adjustment Turns layout adjustment on or off.

NOTE Layout adjustment is triggered by modifications to page size, orientation, margin, or column settings, but not by dragging column guides.

Snap Zone During layout adjustment, this option determines how close an object needs to be to a margin guide, column guide, or page edge to align with it. Enter a value based on how you originally set up your document's guides. Watch out for problems with multiple column documents that have very small gutters.

Allow Graphics and Groups to Resize Because this options allows rescaling of graphics, frames, and groups during layout adjustment, be careful when enabling this option. If you're changing the proportional ratio of height to width when you resize the document, you will distort the objects if this option is enabled. Proceed with caution.

Allow Ruler Guides to Move When this option is enabled, ruler guides may be repositioned during layout adjustment.

Ignore Ruler Guide Adjustments Choose this option when ruler guides are freely placed and don't follow a tightly set-up framework. Objects aligning to page edges and column and margin guides are not affected by this option.

Ignore Object and Layer Locks Choose this option when you want to override individually locked objects or objects on locked layers.

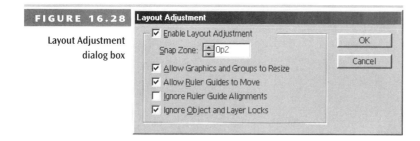

FIGURE 16.28

Layout Adjustment dialog box

NOTE Consult Chapter 7 to learn how to undo mistakes.

TIP Before repurposing an existing document for another publishing format, always save a copy of the document and its linked objects. Work with the copy when reformatting layouts.

PART IV
SPRINTING

chapter 17

Drawing and Editing Freeform Frame Shapes

Featuring:

- Path anatomy — 478
- Bézier curves theory — 481
- Drawing and editing paths — 486
- Combining multiple paths into compound paths — 515
- Editing text shapes — 519
- Drawing and exporting clipping paths — 520

CHAPTER 17

Drawing and Editing Freeform Frame Shapes

ven though Adobe InDesign is not a drawing program like Adobe Illustrator, nor a painting program like Adobe Photoshop, you can do some drawing in InDesign. Remember, the foundation of InDesign's layout operations is the *object*. As presented in Chapter 4, objects can be simple rectangular, elliptical, and polygonal shapes, frames, and placeholders. All of these objects are used as containers of text, graphics, and color. And all of these objects are made up of *paths*.

Paths can be extremely simple or extremely complex. A path might be a simple straight line between two points that you stroke and use as a graphic element. Or a path might be a complex combination of straight and curved lines that combine to create a unique frame shape that can be stroked and/or filled with color, text, and graphics.

Even those simple shapes that you draw with the drawing tools of the Toolbox, such as ellipses, rectangles, and polygons, are essentially paths. In fact, you can edit the paths of these simple shapes to radically modify their appearance.

Alternately, you can create new, complex shapes by drawing with the Pen tool. When you draw with the Pen tool, you draw one path or a series of path segments that you can then modify or alter almost infinitely. Shapes drawn with the Pen tool can be made up of straight, curved, or a combination of straight and curved path segments.

Paths are common to Adobe's InDesign, Photoshop, and Illustrator applications and can be dragged-and-dropped and/or copied and pasted between these applications.

Understanding Path and Shape Anatomy

Like those simple objects drawn with the Ellipse tool, the Rectangle tool, and the Polygon tool, objects drawn with the Pen tool can be *closed* frames or shapes intended as containers of color, text, and/or graphics. A closed shape is one that is made up of paths that connect all the way around, like a rectangle, a circle, or a star, as shown in Figure 17.1.

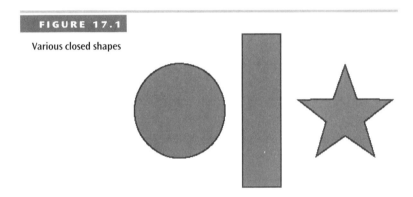

FIGURE 17.1

Various closed shapes

However, unlike those other objects drawn specifically as frames, paths can remain *open*, meaning that they can be just a simple line, as shown in Figure 17.2.

FIGURE 17.2

An open shape with stroke color only

In Chapter 4, we talked about how you can fill and stroke objects. You can choose to apply only a stroke color to an open shape, as shown in Figure 17.2, which preserves its appearance as a line. Or you can choose to apply a fill color also, which automatically closes the concave shapes of the path, as you can see in Figure 17.3. Filling an open path does not close the path, it just fills it.

FIGURE 17.3

An open shape with stroke and fill color

Of course, you can also apply only a fill color, also, as shown in Figure 17.4.

FIGURE 17.4

An open shape with fill color only

You can also fill an open shape with text or graphics, as shown in Figure 17.5.

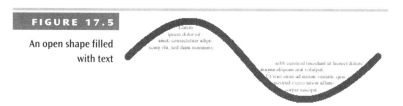

FIGURE 17.5

An open shape filled with text

Paths can consist of a single line between two points, or they can consist of lines between multiple points. The multiple lines that make up one path are called *segments*.

Segments can be either straight or curved, as shown in Figure 17.6. As you can see, paths can consist of both straight and curved segments. The points at the ends of the path are called *anchor points*.

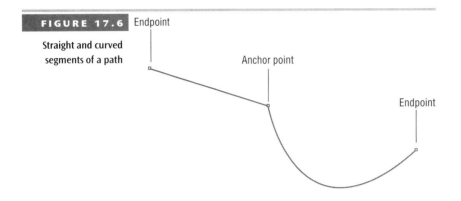

FIGURE 17.6

Straight and curved segments of a path

In the case of open paths, like the one shown in Figure 17.6, the anchor points at each end are called *endpoints*. Anchor points (including endpoints) can be one of two types: corner points and smooth points. A *corner point* is a point that creates an angle, as do all of those in the shape shown in Figure 17.7.

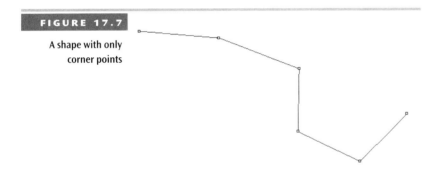

FIGURE 17.7

A shape with only corner points

Corner points can join both straight and curved segments, as shown in Figure 17.8.

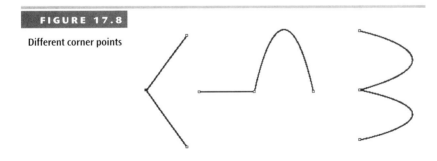

FIGURE 17.8

Different corner points

A *smooth point* is a point that creates an arc, as do all of those in the shape shown in Figure 17.9. Smooth points can connect only curved segments.

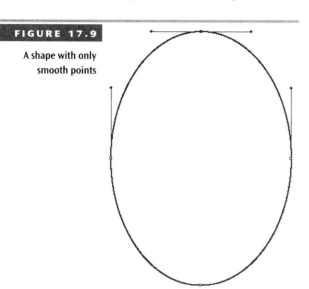

FIGURE 17.9

A shape with only smooth points

Anchor points become corner or smooth points as you draw with the Pen tool. Any anchor point can be changed from a corner point to a smooth point after drawing.

Understanding Bézier Curves Theory

The path and point basics described in the previous section are the basics of drawing with the Pen tool in Adobe InDesign and are also the foundation of Bézier curves theory.

Bézier curves are common to many graphics programs on the desktop and are named for the French mathematician who developed the system thirty years ago. Bézier curves are actually defined by the anchor points described in the previous section. When an anchor point is selected with the Direct Selection tool, direction lines, tipped with direction points, extend outward from the anchor point as shown in Figure 17.10.

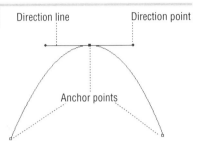

FIGURE 17.10

Anchor points, direction lines, and direction points

These direction lines and direction points determine the direction of the curve that extends from an anchor point and how much of an arc it may have. They are only visible when an anchor point is selected with the Direct Selection tool, and they do not print.

Perhaps the most important thing to remember about using Bézier curves is to use as few anchor points as possible to draw your shapes. Not only will this reduce the amount of editing required to alter your shapes, but it will reduce the sizes of your files and make them easier to display and print. Every anchor point requires disk storage space and memory, so the more anchor points used to create your shapes, the larger the file will be and the more memory-intensive the file will be to display and print.

For example, look at the three shapes shown in Figure 17.11.

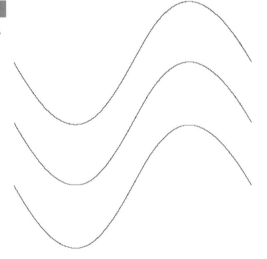

FIGURE 17.11

Three different shapes

They are each exactly the same, right? Well, no, not actually. The top shape was drawn with two anchor points, the middle shape was drawn with three anchor points, and the bottom shape was drawn with five anchor points, as shown in Figure 17.12.

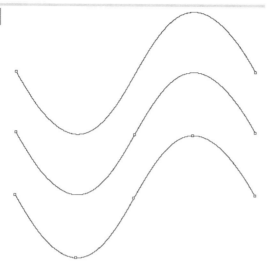

FIGURE 17.12

Three different shapes with anchor points showing

As you can see, you can accomplish the exact same shape with just two points, instead of three or even five. You can greatly reduce the number of points necessary in your documents if you try to understand how Bézier curves work, so that you can create the shapes you want in the most efficient way possible.

In Figure 17.13, notice how the direction point on the left has risen and the curve extending to the left from the anchor point is now more sweeping. Because this particular anchor point is a smooth point and can connect only smooth curves, the direction point on the right has moved downward proportionally and the curve extending from the right of the anchor point is now less curved. What this really means is that the lines extending from a smooth point must appear as if they were one smooth, unbroken line laid on top of the anchor point, even if that line happens to be curving at the anchor point.

FIGURE 17.13

The direction line changed

Now watch what happens when we drag the direction points farther away from the anchor point, as shown in Figure 17.14.

FIGURE 17.14

The direction points moved

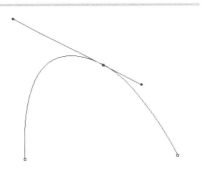

See how the curve extending from the left of the anchor point bulged when we dragged the direction point farther from the anchor point? Notice also that we can drag either of the direction points separately from the other, even on a smooth point.

Right now, the top point in this path is a smooth point, while the endpoints on this path are corner points. The lines extending from corner points will be angled in relation to each other, as you can see on the path in Figure 17.15 that is made of only corner points. Even if one or both of them are curved lines, they can appear as if they are two separate lines that each begin at that anchor point.

FIGURE 17.15

Corner points with different angles

See how each of those corner points can have a line extending from it in an arbitrary direction? One line can be a curved line and the other can be straight, or they can both be curved lines, or they can both be straight lines. Unlike the direction points of a smooth point, you can drag the direction points of a corner point separately from each other, as shown in Figure 17.16.

FIGURE 17.16

Corner points with direction lines dragged in different directions

If a straight path segment extends from one side of an anchor point and a curved path segment from the other, the anchor point may have a direction line and direction point only for the curved segment, as shown in Figure 17.17.

FIGURE 17.17

A corner point with only one direction line

Direction lines and direction points extend in each direction from the anchor point. The direction lines indicate the angle of the curves as they extend out from the anchor points. If a direction line is long, the curve for that direction line will be more curved. If the direction line is shorter, the curve extending from the point will be less curved, as demonstrated in Figure 17.18.

FIGURE 17.18

A shallow curve

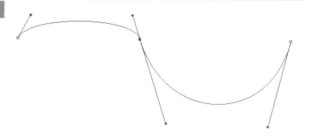

Even if you draw a straight line with the Pen tool, you have still drawn a Bézier curve. It's just that you have drawn a Bézier curve with no curve in it. You can create a straight segment between two segments when the direction lines between two corner points are both either tucked away inside their respective corner points, or pointed directly at each other, as shown in Figure 17.19.

FIGURE 17.19

A straight segment

In case you're wondering how two points can make two separate arcs, check out Figure 17.20, which shows these same three shapes from the beginning of this section, with the anchor points, direction lines, direction points selected for the top shape.

FIGURE 17.20

Three different shapes with direction lines showing

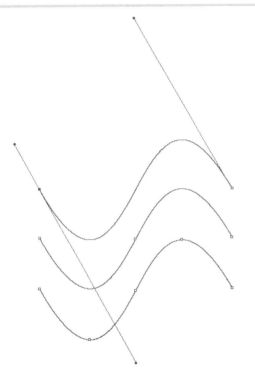

If the direction lines between two points both point up, they will produce one arc, upward. If the direction lines between two points both point down, they will produce one arc, downward. But if one direction line points up and the other points down, they will produce two separate arcs.

Drawing Paths

Drawing paths is actually pretty easy. Once you get the hang of it, you can do it quickly and efficiently.

To draw paths, you use the Pen tool. Use the tip of the pen icon as the positioning point. When you click with the Pen tool, it changes to an arrowhead to indicate that you are drawing.

If you click and let go, you will place an anchor point at that position. If you have clicked at a spot you don't want, continue to press the mouse button and also press the spacebar and drag to reposition the arrowhead.

If you draw paths while no default fill or stroke colors are defined in the Toolbox, you won't see the path when it is deselected or when you are drawing new path segments. Even if you aren't sure what colors you may want for a path's object, you might want to go ahead and at least apply a stroke to the path, so you can see it. You can always change the colors after you've drawn the path. (Selecting and applying colors is discussed in Chapter 12.)

If, while drawing a path segment, you don't like the results of an operation, you can return to the starting point by selecting Edit ➤ Undo or by pressing Ctrl/Cmd+Z.

Drawing Straight Segments

You can draw shapes that are made up completely of straight path segments if you wish, or you can draw straight path segments that can be part of a shape made up of both straight and curved path segments.

To draw straight path segments, follow these steps:

1. Select the Pen tool.

2. Place the tip of the pen icon at the point where you want the straight segment to begin and click. Be careful not to drag with the mouse as you click. The first anchor point is placed at that point. Don't worry, you aren't supposed to see the line yet.

3. Move to the place where you want the straight segment to end. Click here, again without dragging. If you want to constrain the path segment to 45 degree angles, press Shift as you position the pen point. The second anchor point will be placed at this point, and this time you should see the line drawn between the two points, as shown below. The first anchor point is now displayed as a hollow square and the second anchor point is now displayed as a filled square, indicating it is the selected point.

4. If you intend to continue drawing a shape made up only of straight path segments, continue to position and click at the points you need to complete your shape.

5. If you want to draw a shape that remains open, simply click on any other tool in the Toolbox, press Ctrl/Cmd and click anywhere in the window where there are no other objects. You can also simply choose Edit ➤ Deselect All.

6. If you want to close the shape, position the pen point over the first anchor point. A small circle will appear next to the pen icon, as shown below, to indicate that you have reached the original anchor point and will be closing the shape.

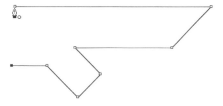

7. Click at this point, when the pen point icon has the little circle, to close the shape, as shown below.

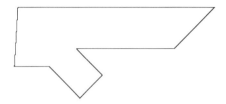

Drawing Curved Segments

You draw curved path segments in much the same way as straight path segments, only this time you drag with the Pen tool to shape the curve as you position the anchor point.

To draw curved segments, follow these steps:

1. Select the Pen tool.

2. Place the tip of the pen icon at the point where you want the curved segment to begin. Press the mouse button and hold it down. Once again, the pen icon will change to the arrowhead.

3. While continuing to hold down the mouse button, drag the arrowhead to create a smooth point. Drag the arrowhead in the general direction that you want the new curve path segment to arc and about as much as you think you want the arc to curve, as shown below. Let go when you think you have a good estimation of the new curved segment. Once again, you won't see this curved segment until you create the second anchor point.

4. Now move to where you want this curved segment to end. Click and drag again to complete the arc of the curved segment. As long as you hold down the mouse button, you can experiment with the curve to draw it the way you want. If you drag the direction point in the same direction that you dragged the direction point of the first anchor point, you will draw an "S"-shaped curve, as shown next.

If you drag the new direction point in the opposite direction that you dragged the direction point of the first anchor point, you will draw a "C"-shaped curve, as shown below.

5. If you intend to continue drawing a shape made up only of straight path segments, continue to position, click, and drag at the points you need to complete your shape.

6. If you want to draw a shape that remains open, simply click on any other tool in the Toolbox, press Ctrl/Cmd and click anywhere in the window where there are no other objects. You can also choose Edit ➢ Deselect All.

7. If you want to close the shape, position the pen point over the first anchor point. A small circle will appear next to the pen icon, as shown in Figure 17.21, to indicate that you have reached the original anchor point and will be closing the shape.

FIGURE 17.21

Closing a shape

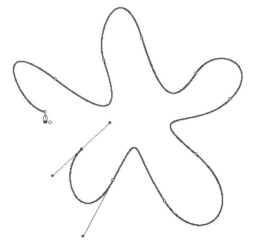

8. Click and drag at this point, when the pen point icon has the little circle, to close the shape, as shown in Figure 17.22.

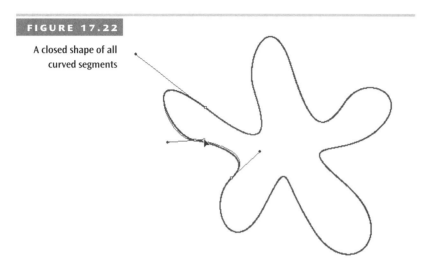

FIGURE 17.22

A closed shape of all curved segments

Combining Corners, Curved Segments, and Straight Segments As You Draw

You don't have to draw only straight segments in a shape, nor do you have to draw only curved segments in a shape. You can easily draw a combination of straight and curved segments, extending from a combination of smooth points and corner points.

Drawing a Straight Segment Followed by a Curved Segment

As described in the previous section, when you draw curved segments, you drag with the Pen tool as you place an anchor point. However, when you do this, you are automatically creating a smooth point. And a smooth point would alter your straight segment, turning it into a curved segment, as shown below.

What you really want there is a corner point, as shown next, so that you don't disturb the straight segment.

If you are drawing a straight segment and want to follow that straight segment with a curved segment, without changing the straight segment to a curved segment, follow these steps:

1. Select the Pen tool.
2. Place the tip of the pen icon at the point where you want the straight segment to begin and click. Be careful not to drag with the mouse as you click. The first anchor point is placed at that point. You won't see the line yet.
3. Move to the place where you want the straight segment to end. Click here, again without dragging. If you want to constrain the path segment to 45 degree angles, press Shift as you position the pen point. The second anchor point will be placed at this point, and this time you should see the line drawn between the two points, as shown below. The first anchor point is now displayed as a hollow square and the second anchor point is now displayed as a filled square, indicating it is the selected point.

4. Now place the Pen tool over the second anchor point. The Convert Direction Point icon will appear with the little pen icon, as shown below.

5. While keeping the Pen tool positioned over the second anchor point, so that you continue to see the Convert Direction Point icon, click and drag to pull out the direction point from the anchor point, as shown below. As you can see, the Pen tool icon changes once again to the arrowhead as you drag.

6. When you let go, you'll see the original straight segment with a single direction line extending from it, as shown below. You won't see the curved segment until you place the next anchor point.

7. Now move to the position where you want the next anchor point. Click and drag as you would to draw a smooth point, as shown below.

8. Now you'll have the straight segment, a corner point, and then the curved segment, as shown below.

Drawing a Curved Segment Followed by a Straight Segment

Okay, so now let's say you want to follow that curved segment by a straight segment. You've already drawn a smooth point, so if you were to place the next anchor point—even if you just click as if you were drawing a straight segment—you would be drawing another curved segment, as shown below.

You have to convert that smooth point to a corner point if you want to follow with another straight segment. To follow a curved segment with a straight segment, follow these steps:

1. Select the Pen tool.

2. Place the tip of the pen icon at the point where you want the curved segment to begin. Press the mouse button and hold it down. The pen icon will change to the arrowhead.

3. While continuing to hold down the mouse button, drag the arrowhead to create a smooth point. Drag the arrowhead in the general direction that you want the new curve path segment to arc and about as much as you think you want the arc to curve, as shown below. Let go when you think you have a good estimation of the new curved segment. Once again, you won't see this curved segment until you create the second anchor point.

4. Now move to where you want this curved segment to end. Click and drag again to complete the arc of the curved segment, as shown below. Let go when you have drawn the arc you want.

Now you have a curved segment with smooth points at each end. To follow with a straight segment, you need to convert that second smooth point to a corner point.

5. Place the Pen tool icon over the second point. The Convert Direction Point icon will appear next to the Pen tool icon, as shown below.

6. Click the second anchor point to convert it to a corner point. One of the direction lines will disappear, as shown below.

7. Now move to the position where you want the next, straight segment to end and click, as shown below. You will have created a straight segment after the original curved segment.

Drawing Two Curved Segments Connected by a Corner Point

We have drawn curved segments following straight segments and straight segments following curved segments. In each case, we had to convert smooth points to corner points. Obviously, we would never need to connect two curved points with a corner point, right?

Wrong. Take a look at the illustration below.

See? If you want two consecutive curved segments that both have arcs on the same side of the anchor points, you must connect them with a corner point. To draw two curved segments connected by a corner point, follow these steps:

1. Select the Pen tool.
2. Place the tip of the pen icon at the point where you want the first curved segment to begin. Press the mouse button and hold it down. The pen icon will change to the arrowhead.
3. While continuing to hold down the mouse button, drag the arrowhead to create a smooth point.

4. Now move to where you want this curved segment to end. Click and drag again to complete the arc of the curved segment, as shown next. Let go when you have drawn the arc you want.

5. Now press Alt/Option and grab the direction line for the next curve. If you are pressing Alt/Option, you will be able to split the direction lines of that smooth point, as shown below. Drag the direction line to set the direction of the next curved segment.

You just converted that smooth point to a corner point.

6. Move to where you want the next curved segment to end. Click and drag to shape the curve, as shown below.

You have just connect two curved segments with a corner point, as shown below.

Editing Paths

Once you have drawn a path you are not stuck with it. You can freely edit any path you have drawn. You can move or delete the original anchor points, add new anchor points, convert anchor points, open and close paths, reshape the curved segments, or connect two or more separate paths.

Anchor points are the keys to editing paths. By editing the anchor points, you can make a lot of changes to your paths.

Selecting Paths and Anchor Points

In order to edit your paths, you must first select them. To select paths, you need to use the Direct Selection tool. You can select it by clicking its icon in the Toolbox or by pressing "A" while no text is selected.

As you may remember from Chapter 3, when you select an object with the Selection tool, you see its bounding box, as shown in Figure 17.23. When you see an object's bounding box, you can move it and edit its size and proportions, but you can't edit its path.

FIGURE 17.23

Selected object with bounding box

When you select an object with the Direct Selection tool, you see its anchor points, as shown in Figure 17.24. When you can see its anchor points, you can edit its path.

FIGURE 17.24

Selected object with anchor points

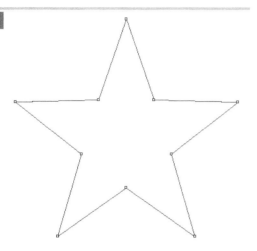

To select a path, click its shape with the Direct Selection tool. If you have not applied a fill or stroke color to an object and can't see it, draw a marquee with the Direct Selection tool around the area where you think it is.

To select an anchor point, click it with the Direct Selection tool. A selected anchor point is indicated by a filled square.

You can also manipulate anchor points using the Pen tool. With the Pen tool, you can select the anchor point that was last drawn by clicking it. However, if you position the Pen tool over the anchor points of a closed shape or the anchor points that are not endpoints of a shape, the Pen tool will change to the Delete Anchor Point tool and you will delete that anchor point if you click it. If you position the Pen tool over the anchor point that was the first anchor point drawn for an open shape, the Pen tool will change to the Close Shape tool and you will close the shape. In any case, selecting an anchor point with the Pen tool will not allow you to edit that anchor point. You will only be able to continue the existing path.

Moving Anchor Points

You can move any anchor point by selecting it with the Direct Selection tool and then dragging it, as shown in Figure 17.25.

FIGURE 17.25

Dragging anchor point with Direct Selection tool

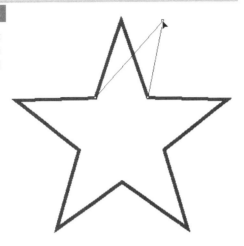

As you can see, when you click and hold with the mouse, the Direct Selection tool changes to the arrowhead. When you release the mouse, the path will change to reflect the repositioning of the anchor point, as shown in Figure 17.26.

FIGURE 17.26

The altered shape

Moving the anchor point between two segments will change both segments. Naturally, if you move the anchor point between two curved segments, you will alter the shapes of those curves, as shown in Figure 17.27.

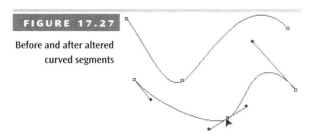

FIGURE 17.27

Before and after altered curved segments

Adding Anchor Points

You are not stuck with the number of anchor points that you place when you originally draw a path. You can add any number of points to a path, but remember that as a rule of thumb you should keep your paths as simple—using as few anchor points—as possible.

You can add anchor points to a path using either the Pen tool or the Add Anchor Point tool. When you add a new anchor point, InDesign automatically creates a corner point or a smooth point, depending on which is necessary to create the existing shape at that new point. In other words, InDesign sticks in a new point that is already adjusted to create the shape of the path at that point.

You can choose the Add Anchor Point tool in one of the following methods:

- Click the Pen tool, or whatever Pen tool is displayed in the Toolbox, and hold down the mouse button to display the hidden tools. Slide over to the Add Anchor Point tool to select it.
- Press the plus symbol (+) on the keyboard to choose the Add Anchor Point tool. (Don't press Shift.)
- Press Shift+P to cycle through the hidden Pen tools.
- Press Alt/Option and click on the Pen tool icons to cycle through the hidden Pen tools.

To add an anchor point to a path using the Add Anchor Point tool, follow these steps:

1. Select the Direct Selection tool.
2. Select the path.
3. Select the Add Anchor Point tool.
4. Position the Add Anchor Point tool over the path at the point where you want to add a new anchor point.
5. Click to add a new anchor point.

To add an anchor point to a path using the Pen tool, follow these steps:

1. Select the Direct Selection tool.
2. Select the path.
3. Select the Pen tool.
4. Position the Pen tool over the path at the point where you want to add a new anchor point. When you are over the path, the Pen tool changes to the Add Anchor Point tool, as shown in Figure 17.28.

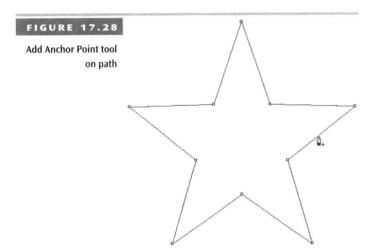

FIGURE 17.28

Add Anchor Point tool on path

5. Click to add a new anchor point.

Deleting Anchor Points

You can just as easily remove anchor points from an existing path. However, you must consider what removing the point might do to the shape of your path. Unlike adding points, where InDesign automatically preserves the existing path shape, removing points can drastically alter the path. In Figure 17.29, the original star shape path on the left was drastically altered by the removal of just three anchor points from the copy of the star shape path on the right.

You can delete anchor points from a path using either the Pen tool or the Delete Anchor Point tool.

WARNING You must use the Delete Anchor Point tool to delete anchor points. Even if you have selected just an anchor point, if you press Delete, Backspace, Clear, or choose Edit ➢ Cut or Edit ➢ Clear, you delete the entire path.

FIGURE 17.29

Two stars, with and without anchor points removed

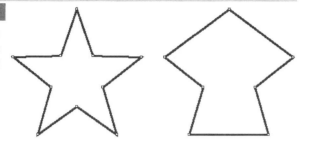

You can choose the Delete Anchor Point tool in one of the following methods:

- Click the Pen tool, or whatever Pen tool is displayed in the Toolbox, and hold down the mouse button to display the hidden tools. Slide over to the Delete Anchor Point tool to select it.
- Press the hyphen symbol (-) on the keyboard to choose the Delete Anchor Point tool.
- Press Shift+P to cycle through the hidden Pen tools.
- Press Alt/Option and click on the Pen tool icons to cycle through the hidden Pen tools.

To delete an anchor point from a path using the Delete Anchor Point tool, follow these steps:

1. Select the Direct Selection tool.
2. Select the path.
3. Select the Delete Anchor Point tool.
4. Position the Delete Anchor Point tool over the point you want to delete.
5. Click to delete the anchor point.

To delete an anchor point from a path using the Pen tool, follow these steps:

1. Select the Direct Selection tool.
2. Select the path.
3. Select the Pen tool.
4. Position the Pen tool over the existing point you want to delete. When you are over an existing point, the Pen tool changes to the Delete Anchor Point tool, as shown in Figure 17.30.
5. Click to delete the anchor point.

FIGURE 17.30

Delete Anchor Point tool on an anchor point

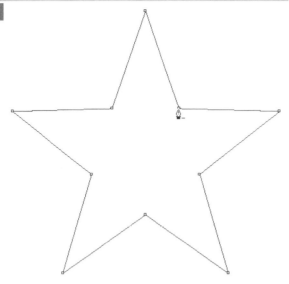

Converting Anchor Points

Once you have drawn a path, you can convert the existing anchor points from smooth point to corner points and from corner points to smooth points. Once again, you should be prepared for these conversions to drastically alter the appearance of the existing shape.

The conversion of all anchor points is accomplished with the Convert Direction Point tool. The Convert Direction Point tool is selected by one of the following methods:

- Click the Pen tool, or whatever Pen tool is displayed in the Toolbox, and hold down the mouse button to display the hidden tools. Slide over to the Convert Direction Point tool to select it.
- Press the hyphen symbol (-) on the keyboard to choose the Convert Direction Point tool.
- Press Shift+P to cycle through the hidden Pen tools.
- Press Alt/Option and click on the Pen tool icons to cycle through the hidden Pen tools.

- While using the Pen tool, you can temporarily switch to the Convert Direction Point tool by pressing Alt/Option.
- While using the Direct Selection tool, you can switch to the Convert Direction Point tool by pressing Ctrl/Alt in Windows and Cmd/Option on the Mac.

Converting a Corner Point to a Smooth Point or to a Corner Point with Independent Direction Lines

To convert a corner point to a smooth point or to a corner point with independent direction lines, follow these steps:

1. Select the Direct Selection tool.
2. Select the path.
3. Select the Convert Direction Point tool.
4. Place the Convert Direction Point tool over the corner point you want to convert.
5. Click and drag direction points out of the point, as shown in Figure 17.31.

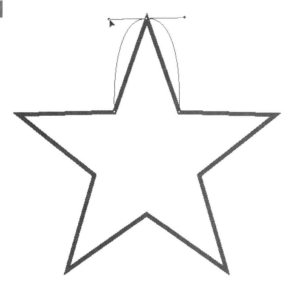

FIGURE 17.31

Dragging direction points out of a corner point

You now have a smooth point. If you now want to convert this smooth point to a corner point with independent direction points, simply stay with the Convert Direction Point tool and drag either of the new direction points, as shown in Figure 17.32.

FIGURE 17.32

Dragging direction points independently

Converting a Smooth Point to a Corner Point without Direction Lines

To convert a smooth point to a corner point without independent direction lines, follow these steps:

1. Select the Direct Selection tool.
2. Select the path.
3. Select the Convert Direction Point tool.
4. Place the Convert Direction Point tool over the smooth point you want to convert.
5. Click the smooth point. The smooth point will convert to a corner point, as shown in Figure 17.33.

Converting a Smooth Point to a Corner Point with Independent Direction Lines

To convert a smooth point to a corner point with independent direction lines, follow these steps:

1. Select the Direct Selection tool.
2. Select the path.
3. Select the Convert Direction Point tool.

EDITING PATHS 505

4. Place the Convert Direction Point tool over one of the direction points of the smooth point you want to convert.
5. Drag the direction point. The smooth point will convert to a corner point with independent direction lines, as shown in Figure 17.34.

FIGURE 17.33

Converting a smooth point to a corner point

FIGURE 17.34

Converting a smooth point to a corner point with independent direction lines

Continuing an Open Path

If you have drawn an open path and decide you need to continue, or extend, the path, you can add additional anchor points, just as if you had not stopped your original drawing. You can actually extend the path from either endpoint.

To continue an open path, follow these steps:

1. Select the Direct Selection tool.
2. Select the path.
3. Select the Pen tool.
4. Position the Pen tool over the endpoint from which you want to extend the path. A little slash will appear next to the pen tool icon, as shown below, indicating that you are about to select that endpoint.

5. Click to select that endpoint.
6. Now move to where you want the next endpoint and continue drawing the path as if you had never stopped. You can simply click to add a new corner point, or you can click and drag to create a new smooth point.

Closing a Path That Was Drawn Open

If you have an existing open path that you want to close, follow these steps:

1. Select the Direct Selection tool.
2. Select the path.
3. Select the Pen tool.
4. Position the Pen tool over one of the endpoints of the path. A little slash will appear next to the pen tool icon indicating that you are about to select that endpoint.
5. Click to select that endpoint.
6. Position the Pen tool over the other endpoint. The little open circle will appear next to the Pen tool, indicating that you are about to close the path, as shown in Figure 17.35.
7. Click the endpoint to close the path.

FIGURE 17.35

Pen tool with little circle

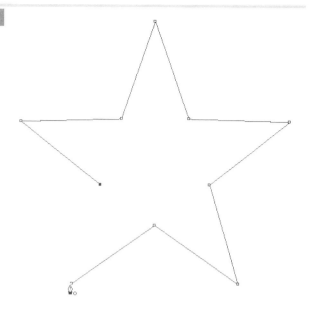

Opening a Closed Path

To open an existing closed path, follow these steps:

1. Select the Direct Selection tool.
2. Select the path.
3. Select the Scissors tool by clicking its icon in the Toolbox or by pressing "C."
4. When you select the Scissors tool, the cursor will change to a crosshair.
5. When you position this Scissors tool cursor over an anchor point, a small circle appears at the center of the cursor, indicating you have covered the anchor point.
6. Click that anchor point to split it into two anchor points. You won't notice any difference until you move one of the anchor points.
7. Now select the Direct Selection tool and click and drag the anchor point you just split, as shown in Figure 17.36. Don't worry about trying to figure out which segment you'll be moving, just grab the anchor point and drag.

When you let go, you will have opened the closed path, as shown in Figure 17.37.

FIGURE 17.36

Dragging a split anchor point with the Direct Selection tool

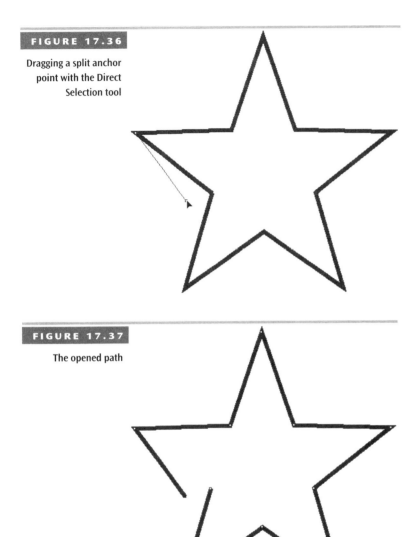

FIGURE 17.37

The opened path

Connecting Multiple Paths

If you have two or more paths that you want to connect, follow these steps:

1. Select the Direct Selection tool.
2. Select the path.
3. Select the Pen tool.

4. Position the Pen tool over the endpoint you want to connect with the other path. A little slash will appear next to the Pen tool icon, as shown in Figure 17.38, indicating that you are about to select that endpoint.

FIGURE 17.38

Pen tool with slash

5. Click to select that endpoint.
6. Now move over to the endpoint you want to connect to on the other path. This time, a little icon that looks like an anchor point, as shown in Figure 17.39, will appear next to the Pen tool icon.

FIGURE 17.39

Pen tool with anchor point icon

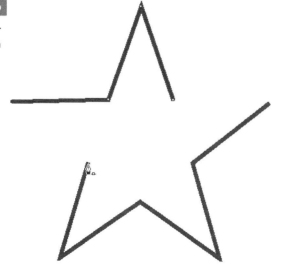

7. Click that endpoint. InDesign will automatically draw a straight segment between the two paths, as shown in Figure 17.40.

FIGURE 17.40

Connected paths

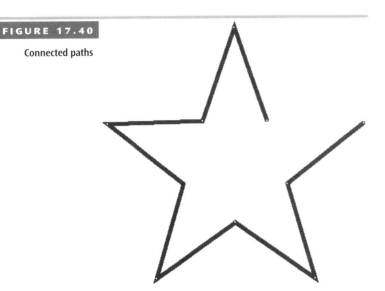

Changing Curved Segment Shapes by Dragging Their Direction Points

After you have drawn a path, you can adjust the curved segments as much as you need. As described earlier in this chapter, you can move the anchor point between two curved segments, which will alter the segments. And you can drag the direction points of an anchor point to alter curved segments.

NOTE While drawing a smooth point, its direction points are locked together and will move toward and away from the anchor point in unison. However, as soon as you have drawn a smooth point, you can drag either anchor point toward or away from the anchor point separate from the other.

Remember, the direction points and direction lines of a smooth point will always rotate in unison around their anchor point. The only way to separate them is to convert them to a corner point with independent direction lines, as described earlier in this chapter.

To alter a curved segment's shape, follow these steps:

1. Select the Direct Selection tool.
2. Select the path.

3. Select an anchor point to show its direction lines and direction points, as shown in Figure 17.41.

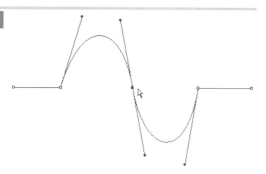

FIGURE 17.41

Selected anchor point with direction lines and direction points

4. Dragging the direction points of the anchor point in an "orbit" around the anchor point rotates the direction of the curve's exit from the anchor point, as shown in Figure 17.42.

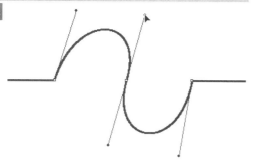

FIGURE 17.42

Dragging direction points in orbit

5. Dragging the direction points closer to the anchor point or farther away from the anchor point increases or decreases the sweep of the curved segments, as shown in Figure 17.43.

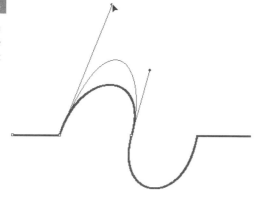

FIGURE 17.43

Dragging a direction point away from the anchor point

Splitting Paths and Frames with the Scissors Tool

You can "split" paths and frames, whether or not they are closed. You can use the Scissors tool to "cut" pieces out to delete them or move them to another location. You can cut them at anchor points, or at any spots on their paths.

Before you can split any path or frame, you must select it with the Direct Selection tool to activate its path.

NOTE You can't split a text frame filled with text. But you can empty the text frame, then split it.

As shown below, when you split an open path with the Scissors tool, you can simply split it and have two paths where before you had one. Or you can cut out a piece of the path.

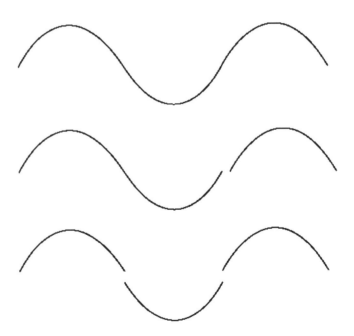

When you split a closed path with the Scissors tool, you can open the path or you can cut out a piece of the path.

EDITING PATHS

To split a path at an anchor point, follow these steps:

1. Select the Direct Selection tool.
2. Select the path or frame.
3. Select the Scissors tool. When you position the Scissors tool over the document window, it changes to the crosshair.
4. Position the Scissors tool over an anchor point. An open circle will appear in the center of the crosshair cursor of the Scissors tool, indicating that you are going to cut at that point.
5. Click. You have just split the path at that anchor point.
6. Now select the Direct Selection tool and select the anchor point where you just clicked with the Scissors tool.
7. Drag the anchor point away from the path, as shown in Figure 17.44.

FIGURE 17.44

Dragging away a newly-split anchor point

If you want to take out a piece of a path, go back and repeat Steps 4 and 5 for an additional anchor point.

You can then verify that you have split the path into two pieces by selecting the Selection tool and clicking one or both of the path pieces to display the paths' bounding boxes. If you select both paths, you should see two separate bounding boxes now, as shown in Figure 17.45.

You can also split a path or frame at any point on the path away from anchor points. Simply repeat the previous procedure, clicking with the Scissors tool on the path wherever you want to split the path. This time, however, you'll be creating a new endpoint for each side of the newly split path, as shown in Figure 17.46.

FIGURE 17.45

Two bounding boxes

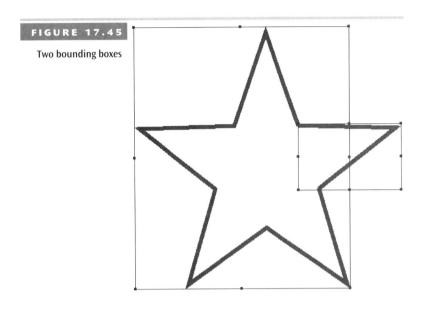

FIGURE 17.46

Splitting on a path, with two new endpoints

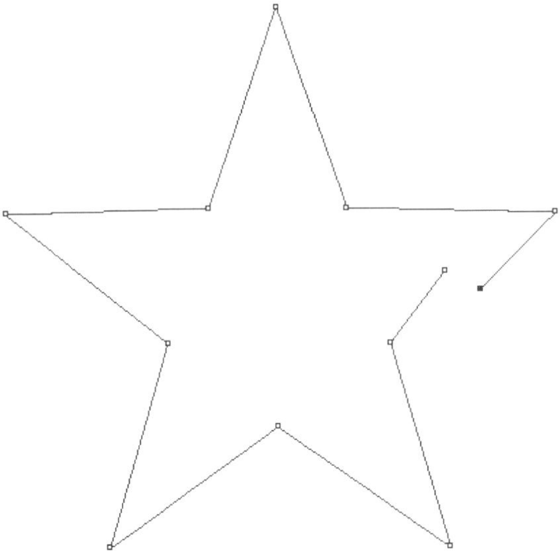

Anytime you split a path into pieces, the new pieces will share the same characteristics of the original path, such as stroke color and weight, fill color, and so on.

Splitting Graphics Frames

If you split a graphics frame that contains a graphic into two separate graphics frames, each of the two frames will contain the graphic. However, the graphic will only display in the "closed" portion of the new frame shapes, as shown below.

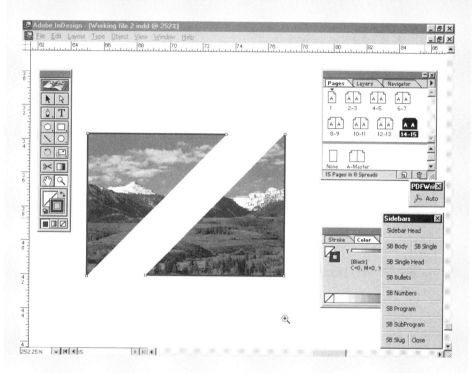

You can delete the image from one or the other of the two frames, or you can use them for special effects.

Combining Multiple Paths into Compound Paths

Compound paths are simply two or more paths that have been combined together into one object. The multiple paths of a compound path move together and share the same formatting attributes. You can use compound paths to create shapes that have "holes" in them, as shown in Figure 17.47. You can create compound paths from either closed or open paths.

FIGURE 17.47

Compound path on graphic image

When you create paths from text characters, any characters with "holes" in them, such as "o," "a," "g," and "d" are automatically created as compound paths.

As with all paths, complex paths with a lot of anchor points can cause printing problems for some printers. Remember to keep your paths as simple as possible.

Creating Compound Paths

When creating compound paths, the bottom-most path in the stacking order becomes the "parent" in a sense, passing on to the other paths in the compound path all of its formatting attributes, such as stroke fill and color. Once you create the compound path, all of the original paths become *subpaths*.

After you create a compound path, all formatting attributes made to the compound path will apply to all of the subpaths in it.

TIP If you are creating a graphic or other object out of multiple paths and you want each of those paths to retain individual formatting attributes, you may want to group them, rather than combine them into a compound path.

To create a compound path, follow these steps:

1. Select the Selection tool or the Direct Selection tool.
2. Select one path and then select at least one more path, as shown in Figure 17.48, by pressing Shift as you select the additional paths.
3. Choose Object ➢ Compound Paths ➢ Make.

FIGURE 17.48

Two paths selected over image

The resulting compound path will have a "hole" where the two paths overlap. In other words, any place where one path is on top of another, there will be a hole, as shown in Figure 17.47.

Editing Compound Paths

Even after being combined into a compound path, subpaths can be edited with the Direct Selection tool and the Pen tool, as described earlier in this chapter. You can add new anchor points or select existing anchor points to move or delete them, or to adjust the shapes of segments, as shown in Figure 17.49.

FIGURE 17.49

An edited compound path

Reversing a Path

If you combine multiple paths into a compound path and don't see a hole where you expect it, you may need to reverse a subpath. The direction of a path—that is, the order in which its anchor points were drawn—determines whether that path is made into a subpath that is filled, meaning it will be opaque, or made into a subpath that becomes a transparent hole.

So if you combine two or more paths into a compound path and you get results like those shown in Figure 17.50, reverse one of the subpaths.

FIGURE 17.50

A compound path without a hole

To reverse a subpath, follow these steps:

1. Select the Direct Selection tool.
2. Select one anchor point on one subpath in the compound path, as shown in Figure 17.51.

FIGURE 17.51

An anchor point selected in subpath

3. Choose Object ➢ Reverse Path.

 TIP Don't worry about the direction of a path until you make a compound path and need to reverse the direction of a subpath. Even then, don't try to figure it out, just reverse a subpath.

Releasing a Path

Breaking up a compound path is referred to as *releasing* the path. When you release a subpath from a compound path, it retains the formatting attributes it got when you made it part of the compound path. It does not go back to what it may have been before.

You can't break up a compound path that is filled with text. You also can't break up a compound path that has been pasted into a frame.

To release a path, follow these steps:

1. Select the Selection tool or the Direct Selection tool.
2. Select a compound path.
3. Choose Object ➤ Compound Paths ➤ Release.

Editing Text Shapes

All text characters can be converted to paths and then edited, reshaped, filled, and so on. This feature can be great when you have special effects to create for large type, but not so great for body type because once you convert text to paths, you can no longer edit it as text. Nor can you simply resize the type by changing its point size in the Character palette. Basically, what happens is that the type becomes a shape or frame.

In fact, you can use these new shapes as graphics frames or text frames or you could create new type characters with them and/or fill them with color, as shown in Figure 17.52.

FIGURE 17.52

Text characters converted to paths and filled

You can select a range of text in a text frame to convert to paths, or you can select a text frame to convert the entire contents of the text frame to paths. If you select a range of text in a text frame and then convert that selected text to paths, the resulting shapes become inline graphics and move with the text as it reflows.

To convert text to paths, follow these steps:

1. Select the Text tool and select a character or characters of text, or select the Selection tool and select a text frame.
2. Choose Type ➤ Create Outlines.

To see the type outlines that have been created, select the Direct Selection tool and select the characters. You can now edit these type outlines just as you would any path.

NOTE If the font information necessary to create outlines is not available for a selected range of text, InDesign will alert you that it can't convert the text.

You can also automatically create paths from a copy of the selected text, which leaves the original selected text untouched. You can then select the outlines and move them away from the original, or leave them there.

To produce paths from a copy of selected text, follow these steps:

1. Select the Text tool and select a character or characters of text, or select the Selection tool and select a text frame.
2. Press Alt/Option as you choose Type ➢ Create Outlines.

This action creates paths that appear directly on top of the original. Using the Selection tool, you can move them if you wish.

Using and Creating Clipping Paths

A *clipping path* is basically a frame for a graphic image that exactly fits the image or some part of the image, hiding everything else. For example, if you have a picture of your dog sitting on the porch, you could make a clipping path that would hide everything in the picture but the dog. You can use images with clipping paths to simulate transparent backgrounds for images.

Images with clipping paths already defined and saved for them can be imported from other applications. You can also create clipping paths in InDesign manually or automatically. Whether a clipping path is imported or generated within InDesign, it is a path that can be edited just as can any other path in InDesign.

Importing Images with Clipping Paths

By default, when you place an image for which a clipping path has been saved, InDesign automatically imports the clipping path and creates a graphics frame that is the shape of the clipping path. You can turn off this feature by selecting the Show Import Options option in the File ➢ Place dialog box and then deselecting the Create Frame From Clipping Path option.

NOTE Importing images with the File ➢ Place command is discussed in Chapter 6.

Image file types that support clipping paths include EPS, TIFF, and Photoshop.

Drawing a Clipping Path Manually

A clipping path can be any drawn shape or path. You make it a clipping path by pasting a graphic inside the shape or path with the Edit ➤ Paste Into command.

To place an image into a shape or path that will become the clipping path for the image, follow these steps:

1. Draw a shape or path with any drawing tool. In Figure 17.53, I've drawn that familiar star.

FIGURE 17.53

Drawing a star shape

2. Cut an image from any graphics frame.
3. Select the shape or path that you want to use as the clipping path and choose Edit ➤ Paste Into. The result should look something like Figure 17.54.
4. Select the image with the Direct Selection tool and drag it around in the new clipping path to position it as you want.

FIGURE 17.54

Image pasted into star shape

To manually draw a clipping path for an image, follow these steps:

1. Place the image in a graphics frame, as shown in Figure 17.55.

FIGURE 17.55

Image in a graphics frame

2. Select the Pen tool.
3. Draw a path around the area of the image you want to be visible, as shown in Figure 17.56.

FIGURE 17.56

Path drawn on an image

4. Cut the image from the graphics frame.
5. Select the path, as shown in Figure 17.57.

FIGURE 17.57

The selected path

6. Choose Edit ➢ Paste Into. The result should look something like Figure 17.58.

FIGURE 17.58

Image pasted into path

7. Select the Direct Selection tool and select the image contents. Drag to position the image so that it appears through the clipping path.

Once you position the image to fit the shape, you can use this new clipping path to mask the other areas of the image. As you can see in FIgure 17.59, you can then use the image as a graphic with text wrapping around the clipping path.

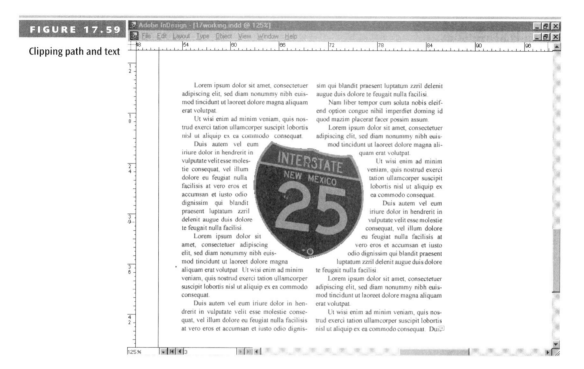

FIGURE 17.59
Clipping path and text

Generating a Clipping Path Automatically

You can also automatically generate a clipping path with the Object ➢ Clipping Path command. The Clipping Path command compares light and dark areas of an image to generate the clipping path according to parameters you define. Consequently, images that are dark on light backgrounds are best for automatic generation of clipping paths.

Even if you automatically generate a clipping path, once it is generated, you can manually edit the path as much as you need.

To automatically generate a clipping path, first select a placed image. Then choose Object ➢ Clipping Path to open the Clipping Path dialog box, shown in Figure 17.60.

FIGURE 17.60

Clipping Path dialog box

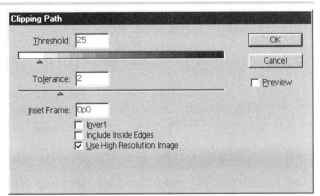

You can select the Preview option to see how your settings will affect the clipping path.

For optimum results, specify the following parameters:

Threshold Specifies how dark a pixel must be to be included within the clipping path. You can enter a numerical value in the Threshold value box or drag the slider to set the value.

Tolerance Specifies how close to or far from the specified threshold a pixel can be to be included in the clipping path. You can enter a numerical value in the Tolerance value box or drag the slider to set the value.

Inset Frame This frame is like a border around the pixels selected by the Threshold and Tolerance values. If you want no visible border around the image, set a low number, if you want more of a visible border set a higher number. You enter a numerical measurement amount in the Inset Frame value box.

Invert Reverses the path to hide the area within the clipping path and show the area outside the clipping path. This option can be useful if you have a light image on a dark background.

Include Inside Edges This option can be either helpful or disastrous, depending on the image. It includes the pixels inside the clipping path that are under the specified threshold. In other words, you might wind up with a clipping path with holes in it. On the other hand, if you're creating a clipping path for a picture of a donut, you might want that.

Use High Resolution Image Looks at the actual, high resolution image for the image when generating the clipping path. Although this method is the most precise, it is also the slowest. If you figure you're going to have to manually adjust the clipping path anyway, you might deselect this option to quickly generate a clipping path that you can then begin editing.

The image shown in Figure 17.61 was generated from the same image used above, with settings of 138 for the Threshold and 4 for the Tolerance.

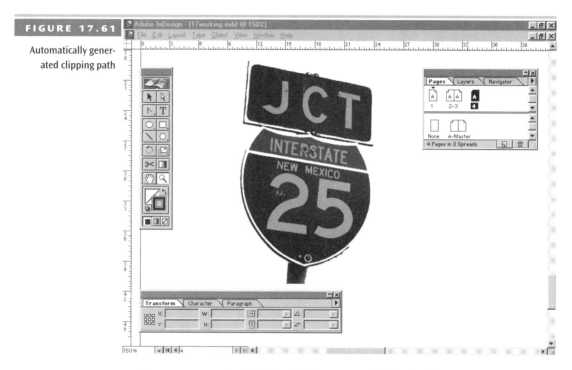

FIGURE 17.61

Automatically generated clipping path

As you can see, the Clipping Path command did a fairly good job of isolating the darker areas from the lighter areas. However, to get this kind of separation, the lighter grays are also masked. If this works for your image, fine. Otherwise, once you generate the clipping path, you can always edit the path as you would any other path.

chapter 18

Advanced Printing Options

Featuring:

- *Scaling and tiling your printed documents* ... 532
- *Printing thumbnails* ... 535
- *Printing graphics and fonts* ... 538
- *Creating color separations* ... 544
- *Printing page marks* ... 557
- *Trapping color* ... 561
- *Preflighting your document* ... 565
- *Packaging files for service providers* ... 575
- *Exporting to a Prepress file* ... 578

ADVANCED PRINTING OPTIONS

This chapter continues the discussion of the InDesign printing options introduced in Chapter 8. In this chapter, I'll explain the printing options for scaling and tiling documents, printing thumbnail versions of document pages, specifying graphics and font processing, creating color separations, printing documents with page marks, trapping color, preflighting, packaging files for service providers, and exporting to a Prepress file. While reading this chapter, you may find it useful to reference Appendix C, *Color Management and Calibration,* and Chapter 12, *Selecting and Applying Color.*

To print a document, choose File ➢ Print or press Ctrl+P (Windows) or Cmd+P (Macintosh). This opens the Print dialog box, shown in Figures 18.1 and 18.2. To set page options, click the Properties button in the Print dialog box (Windows) or choose File ➢ Page Setup (Macintosh) before selecting the print command. The Macintosh Page Setup shortcut is Shift+Cmd+P.

Here are two undocumented features for Macintosh users:

- Press Cmd+Shift as you select File ➢ Print to restore a document's Print dialog box settings to the default set.

- Press Option as you click the OK button to save the current settings in the Page Setup dialog box as the new defaults.

You can cycle through the options in the Print dialog box by clicking the appropriate tab (Windows) or selecting from the option menu below the printer's name (Macintosh). This action will bring those options to the front. For example, Figures 18.1 and 18.2 show the Scale and Fit options in frontmost view.

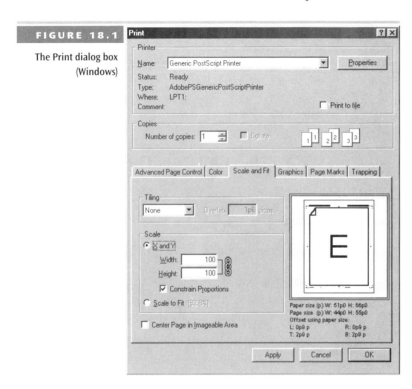

FIGURE 18.1

The Print dialog box (Windows)

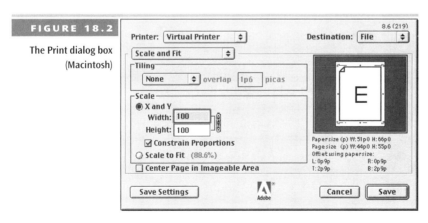

FIGURE 18.2

The Print dialog box (Macintosh)

ADVANCED PRINTING OPTIONS

WARNING Don't forget to read the InDesign ReadMe file for the latest information about how InDesign works with other prepress products.

Background Printing with the Mac

If you're using a Macintosh, you also can enable or disable background printing. When you activate this option, you can continue working in InDesign while your document is printing. Because the entire document is first spooled to your hard disk, you may run out of storage space if your document has a large number of high-resolution images. In that case, disable background printing, but remember that you can't use InDesign until the job has finished printing. (Your pages may print faster when background printing is disabled.) To enable or disable background printing, select File ➢ Print and choose Background Printing from the Printer option menu. Specify your choice by clicking on the radio button, as seen in the following graphic.

WARNING Blank pages or misprinting pages can occur with some printers if you attempt to print a watermark using the AdobePS 4.3 driver on Windows 98.

Scaling and Tiling Your Printed Documents

When you need to print an oversized document on a smaller sheet of paper, select from the Print: Scale and Fit options. You can choose to scale at a document's current proportions, set different scaling values for width and height, scale or tile automatically, or tile manually. If necessary, you can also set the page to center in the imageable area when scaling and/or tiling. InDesign allows you to scale a document from 25% to 400%.

If you scale a document beyond the dimensions of the selected paper size, the upper left part of the image area is printed. To print a very large document or to enlarge a smaller document to fit a larger area, you can, if needed, specify both scaling and tiling values.

The Scale and Fit options include a preview window, as seen in Figures 18.1 and 18.2. This same preview window also appears in the Print: Page Marks options shown later in Figures 18.17 and 18.18. In the preview window you'll see the paper area and document outlines, polarity (negative or positive), page marks, emulsion side information, and page information. Below the preview window you'll see the numerical offset values, which will appear in red if the document page is too large for the selected paper size. You can also find information about current selected options, i.e. number of tiling pages. The page marks shown in the preview window are identified in Figure 18.19. See the "Generating Film Negatives or Positives" section later in this chapter to learn how to set polarity and emulsion settings.

WARNING InDesign uses the selected PPD's offset and paper information to create the preview. If the PPD does not match the capabilities of your selected printer, then the preview may be inaccurate.

NOTE The maximum page size printable from a Windows system is 129 x 129 inches or 10.75 x 10.75 feet.

Scaling a Document to Fit a Paper Size

InDesign allows you to scale your document to fit a wide range of pages. If you look again at Figure 18.1 or 18.2, you'll see that the Scale options are set to the default settings: the Width and Height values are set at 100%, the Constrain Proportions checkbox is selected, and the Link icon is visible. (Tiling is set to None.) When Constrain

SCALING AND TILING YOUR PRINTED DOCUMENTS 533

Proportions is selected, you only need to enter a scaling value once in either the Width or Height box. The value is entered automatically in the other box, and the document is scaled using current document proportions.

When you want to scale the document at another proportional ratio, deselect Constrain Proportions. The Link icon will no longer be visible. The document can be scaled at a different value for each dimension. Don't forget to consider that changing the page proportions will distort the objects found in the document.

TIP You may need to scale in only one direction to compensate for stretching of the plate in flexographic (rotary letterpress method) printing. Consult with your printer to confirm the correct scaling value.

WARNING Scaling can be set in both the InDesign Print: Scale and Fit dialog box and in the PostScript driver's Advanced (Windows) or Page Attributes (Macintosh) dialog box. InDesign ignores driver settings for scale. When scaling your document, always specify percentages in the Print: Scale and Fit dialog box. There's no need to duplicate the setting in the driver.

Applying the Scaling to Fit Option

InDesign will automatically calculate a scaling value if you select the Scale to Fit option. If you'd like to scale a document with its page marks positioned, first set your printer's marks in the Page Marks options, and then choose the Scale to Fit option.

Setting Tiling Options

When you apply the tiling option to an oversized document page, as shown in Figure 18.3, it is divided into segments. Each segment of the document page is then printed on its own page. After the tiles are printed, you assemble the document by overlapping page edges and matching crop marks.

InDesign has three tiling options: None, Auto, and Manual. When you select Auto from the Tiling option menu, seen in Figure 18.4, you can enter an Overlap value, which must be greater than the minimum nonprintable margins for the printer. The largest value you can set for overlap is equal to 50% of the shortest side of the document. For example, if your paper size is 8.5 inches × 11 inches (215.9 mm × 279.4 mm), the maximum amount of overlap that you can set is 4.25 inches (107.95 mm). Remember to also check that Crop Marks is selected from the Print: Page Marks options. (See "Printing with Page Marks" later in this chapter.)

FIGURE 18.3

Tiling a document page

Oversized document page divided into segments

Printed Tiles assembled

 WARNING When tiling documents on a Macintosh, avoid using the US Letter (Small) default setting if you're printing on letter-sized paper. Instead, specify US Letter, which has the narrower printer margin setting, as your paper size. You'll be less likely to clip the crop marks that are necessary for aligning the overlapping tiles. To change the paper size, choose File ➢ Page Setup ➢ Page Attributes, and then select US letter from the option menu.

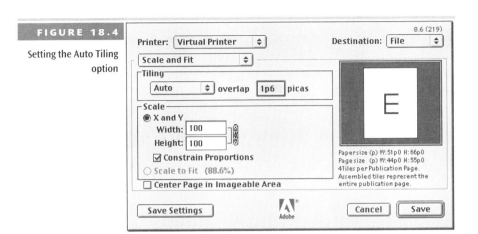

FIGURE 18.4

Setting the Auto Tiling option

When you select Manual as your tiling option, the Overlap option is dimmed. Follow these steps to manually set overlap:

1. Set up your document for printing by selecting your printer, paper size, and orientation. Also, select Crop Marks from the Print: Page Marks options.
2. Print the first tile.
3. Reset the ruler's zero point reference. When you change the setting, the position of the zero point relative to the top left corner of the page changes. When you print a page, the output device uses the new reference as its starting position. (See Chapter 3 for more details about setting the zero point reference.)
4. Print the second tile.
5. If necessary, change the zero point reference and print again. For each tile that you print, you'll need to first reposition the zero point reference.

Printing Thumbnails

When you print thumbnail versions of your document to your local printer, you can quickly view how content, graphics, and other page elements flow from one page to the next. These prints can also be a useful tool when designing a Web site. For example, you can mark up each page with callouts to organize a site map, designate image maps, and link between different page elements or pages. (Chapter 20 reviews repurposing print documents for Web distribution.) See the following instructions to print thumbnails using the Macintosh and Windows 98 and NT operating systems. Don't forget to correctly set paper size and page orientation before printing.

WARNING Never use the thumbnails N-up printing settings when printing color separations or reader's spreads. Otherwise, you'll produce output ready to dump in the recycling bin. When printing color separations or reader's spreads, always select the One Page per Sheet option.

Printing Thumbnails with Windows 98

To print thumbnails using Windows 98, set the paper and Advanced Page Control options and then do this:

1. Select File ➢ Print.
2. When the Print dialog box opens, click the Properties button.
3. Click the Graphics tab.
4. Choose a setting from the Layout option menu, and then click OK to close the Properties dialog box.

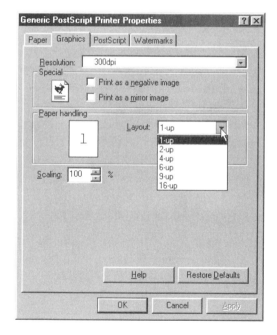

5. In the Print dialog box, click OK or press Enter to print the document.

Printing Thumbnails with Windows NT

To print thumbnails using Windows NT, set the paper and Advanced Page Control options and then do this:

1. Select File ➢ Print.
2. When the Print dialog box opens, click the Properties button.
3. Click the Advanced tab.
4. Scroll down and click the + (plus sign) next to Document Options.
5. Choose Page Layout (N-up). Select an option from the list that appears in the bottom half of the dialog box.
6. Click OK to accept the new setting and to close the Properties dialog box.

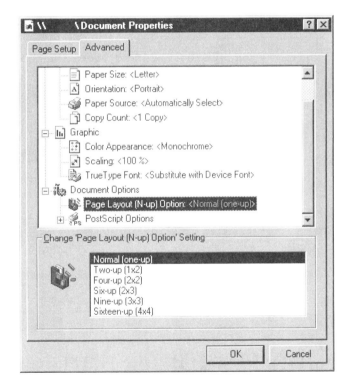

7. In the Print dialog box, click OK or press Enter to print the document.

Printing Thumbnails with Macintosh

To print thumbnails using a Macintosh, set the Page Setup options and other Print dialog box options and then do this:

1. Select File ➤ Print.
2. In the Print dialog box, choose Layout from the option menu under the printer name.
3. Select a Pages per Sheet setting from the option menu. Note that the preview window changes to reflect the chosen layout setting.
4. Choose a Layout Direction setting. Click on either icon to determine how InDesign positions the thumbnail versions of your document pages on the sheet of paper.
5. To specify a thin or hairline, single or double line border around each thumbnail page, make a selection from the Border option menu. (The default is None.)
6. Click OK to print your document pages as thumbnails.

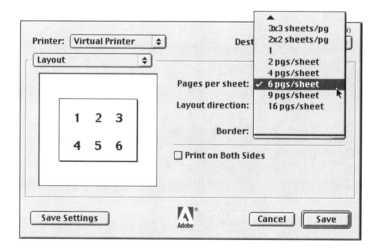

Printing Graphics and Fonts

When your document includes high-resolution images or placed PDF/EPS graphics, you can tailor your printing settings to match your needs. For example, you might want to set fast proofing for comps or preparing color separations. Which options you choose in the Print: Graphics dialog box, shown in Figures 18.5 and 18.6, will determine the file size and processing time of the PostScript file when you click the Print button.

PRINTING GRAPHICS AND FONTS 539

 WARNING Although the Windows version of InDesign can print to non-PostScript printers, you cannot print EPS graphics correctly. EPS graphics print at the on-screen preview image resolution.

FIGURE 18.5

Print: Graphics options (Windows)

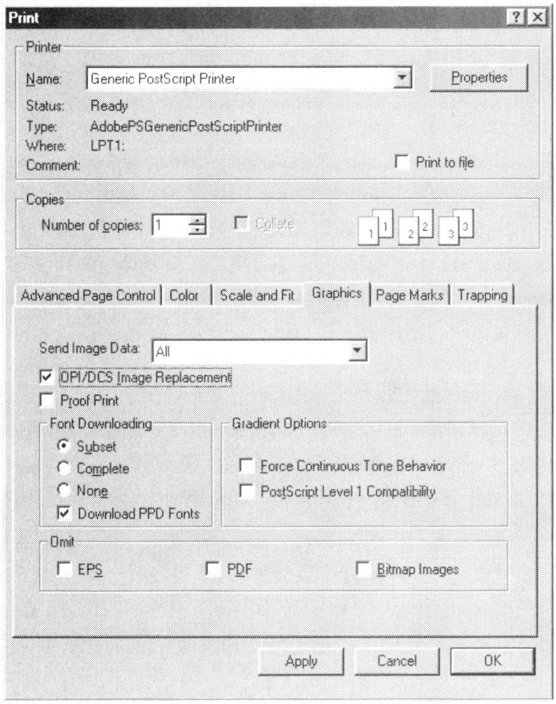

FIGURE 18.6

Print: Graphics options (Macintosh)

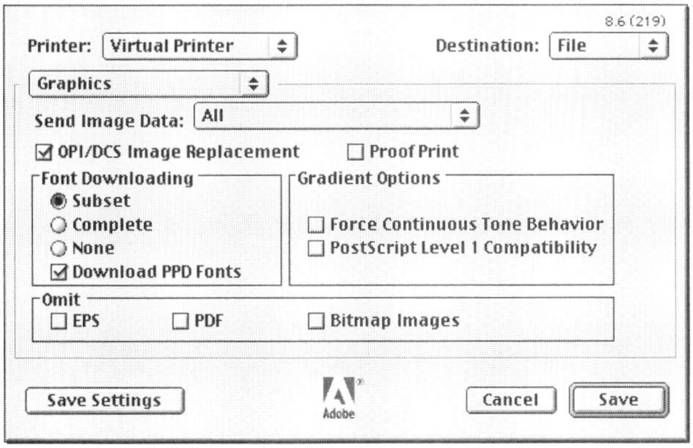

Setting Graphics Printing Options

The Print dialog box has the following Graphics options for controlling how image data is processed:

Send Image Data You can choose one of three settings: All, Optimized Subsampling, and Low Resolution (72 dpi). When you select All, the full-resolution data for all graphics is sent to the printer. Use this option for any high-resolution output to imagesetters or when preparing color separations. Also use this option when printing jobs containing black and white text and spot colors.

TIP When printing a PostScript file with high-resolution images, confirm that your printer memory and disk storage can handle large PostScript jobs. You don't want to be in a crunch situation and discover that you've maxed out your system's capabilities and can't print the file. If you're caught in a bind, try reducing the number of pages you're sending at any one time to the printer, and turn off background printing if you're using a Mac.

When you select Optimized Subsampling, InDesign sends only as much data as needed to print the graphic at the output device's highest resolution. (Make sure that the output device is set to its highest resolution settings.) This setting is recommended when proofing documents containing high-resolution images to a desktop printer.

For fast proofing of your document, select Low Resolution (72 dpi). Use this option in conjunction with the OPI/DCS Image Replacement option to substitute screen resolution for high-resolution graphics imaging in your output.

OPI/DCS Image Replacement This option functions similarly to the Perform OPI Replacement option available when exporting to a PDF, EPS, or Prepress file. If you select this option, high-resolution versions of images replace low-resolution (proxies) linked using OPI (Open Press Interface) comments when you print the document. (File formats, including DCS, are defined in Chapter 1.)

NOTE Specify low-resolution (proxies) in the Preference: General dialog box. Choose File ≻ Preference ≻ General, and then select Proxy Images from the Images Display option menu.

Proof Print When your document contains large image files, you may want to select this option to quickly proof document text and typographic settings. In a proof print, graphics frames with *X*s in them replace the graphics contained in the document. The graphics frames resemble the Rectangle, Ellipse, and Polygon frame tool icons that appear in the Toolbox. Because the graphics frames retain the dimensions of the imported graphics, you can also use this option to check page layouts.

Specifying How Fonts Will Be Downloaded

You can store Type 1, TrueType, and bitmap fonts on your computer and in your printer's memory. Fonts stored in the printer's memory are called *printer-resident fonts*. If you specify printer-resident fonts, you don't need to download fonts to your printer. But if you specify the printer-resident fonts, make sure that these fonts have exactly the same character set as the fonts on your system. Otherwise, the printed document may be missing upper ASCII characters, such as currency symbols. The Download PPD Fonts checkbox is selected by default in the Font Downloading section of the Print: Graphics dialog box.

NOTE When you use Type 1 PostScript fonts, the document usually prints faster. But the same document printed from different output devices may look different. When you use TrueType fonts instead, your document usually prints slower, but output from different devices generally will look identical. But watch out when using the AdobePS 4.3 driver and TrueType fonts to create a PDF file. Your fonts may not convert correctly when viewed in Adobe Acrobat Distiller.

Proofing with Desktop Inkjet Printers

If you're interested in proofing using your desktop ink jet printer, you'll need to install an Adobe PostScript 3-supported RIP on your system. (RIP is the acronym for Raster Image Processor.) You may want to check out the RIPs from Birmy Graphics Corporation and Adobe Systems. You can find out more about Birmy's products–PowerRIP, Press Proof, and PowerRIP Pro—at their Web site (www.birmy.com), or by calling (407) 768-6766 or faxing (407) 768-9669. At the Web site you'll find a list of supported printers from companies such as Epson, ALPS, and Canon. There's information about Adobe PressReady at www.adobe.com/prodindex/pressready/main.html; you can also call your local Adobe dealer. For the first release of PressReady, Adobe announced driver support for the Canon BJC-8500; Epson printers 800, 850, 1520, and 3000; and HP (Hewlett Packard) printers 895C, 1120C, and 2000.

WARNING Bear in mind that some RIPs are set up to substitute PostScript fonts for TrueType variations. Check with your service provider to determine if this is the case. Because of potential differences in the character sets, the document text may reflow causing problems in pagination and ragged right or left text margin.

When the Download PPD Fonts option is selected, all fonts that you used in the document will be downloaded, even if those fonts exist as printer-resident fonts. Selecting this option guarantees that InDesign uses the font outlines on your computer for printing. This will help to avoid problems with differences in font character sets between the computer and output device. Your printer can also reference the same outlines used when setting trapping values. If you did not use extended character sets in your document, you can deselect this option when desktop draft printing.

NOTE Before printing, don't forget to preflight your document to check font status. See the "Checking the Status of Fonts Used in a Document" section later in this chapter for more details. You also find more information about packaging fonts for service providers in the section "Assembling the Package," also in this chapter.

WARNING InDesign will ignore the PostScript driver settings for font downloading. Set your font downloading specifications in the InDesign Print: Graphics dialog box.

The Font Downloading options are as follows:

Subset When you choose Subset, the InDesign Font Downloading default, only the characters (glyphs) used in the document are downloaded to the output device. Glyphs are downloaded once per page. Watch out when using this option. The document may require editing by your service provider, and necessary characters could be missing from the font set. This could create post-production delays until you send another file for processing. If this may be a possibility, then choose the complete downloading option.

Complete Select this option to download all fonts once per page.

None Use this option when you're specifying printer-resident fonts in your document. Only the references to the fonts are downloaded, which may speed up file processing and printing.

WARNING Bitmapped fonts cannot be trapped. If you want to trap text, specify Type 1 PostScript or TrueType fonts.

WARNING You cannot correctly display or print PDFs created in InDesign in Illustrator 8.1 or earlier.

Controlling Gradient Behavior

There are two gradient options in the Print: Graphics dialog box:

Force Continuous Tone Behavior Use this option when you're printing to a device that does not use halftone or stochastic screening. For example, select this setting when proofing to dye-sublimation, continuous tone color laser, and inkjet printers.

PostScript Level 1 Compatibility If you're a Windows user and substituted an older PostScript Level 1 driver for the PostScript driver shipped with InDesign, you'll need to select this option. (Macintosh users can ignore this option.)

 NOTE Some of the options in the Print: Colors dialog box also affect how gradients are printed; see the "Gradients and the Print: Color Options" sidebar later in this chapter.

When you want to speed up the processing and printing of files you can choose to omit specific graphic files from the printed document. When using the OPI setting in Print: Graphics panel, click the appropriate checkbox(es) when you want to omit a specific graphics file format in the image data that's sent to a printer or file. Choose EPS, PDF, Bitmap Images, or all three. The OPI links (comments) will be retained in the file, and the printed file displays omitted graphics as a gray box.

 WARNING When applying an OPI workflow, keep in mind that the Omit options can be specified only for linked graphics. If the graphic was embedded in the InDesign document, then the OPI comments are no longer retained with the file.

Creating Color Separations

When planning for post-production processing and printing, bear in mind that InDesign's Color and Trapping options in the Print dialog box need to be viewed in the larger context of what other equipment and software will be used by your vendors. Each job will be unique. Your job specifications will not only be influenced by the selection of a service provider and printer, but also by, among other things, layout and artwork, papers, inks, vendor equipment, and—let's not forget—the job budget.

As concept-production-printing workflows continue to change, reflecting the further integration of digital processes and color management standardization, it's more important than ever for designers and graphics arts professionals to meet as early as possible in the process to plan and determine project specifications. For example, instead of using your software application at your computer (host) to specify color separation data for trapping or color values, which is then processed by the output device, you opt for In-RIP separations. With In-RIP separations you can choose, as one example, to apply auto-trapping using data based upon the color management profiles embedded into the document and the CRD (color rendering dictionary) of the output device.

With that decision made to use In-RIP separations, you'll need any PostScript 3 output device to process the files. But if your vendor does not have a PS3 device, then you have to find out if they have a PostScript Level 2 device and a RIP that supports In-RIP separations. The second configuration may work just fine—that is, if you're not creating duotones in Photoshop 5 or later. Then you're back to requiring a PostScript 3 device for In-RIP separations. As you can see, things can get a bit confusing, so don't be afraid to bring your InDesign comps to service providers and printers. And most of all, remember that InDesign version 1 will be as new to them as it is to you.

TIP Want to learn more about InDesign from the emerging user group or share your tips and tricks? Join the InDesign Talk mailing list. Sign up and get more information at: http://www.blueworld.com/lists/

WARNING Don't forget to preflight a document before preparing color separations.

Choosing Composites or Color Separations

InDesign offers you a choice of printing your file as a composite or color separation; an example of each is shown in Figure 18.7. If you want to follow a traditional host-based preseparated workflow, you can use InDesign to prepare color separations to output from your in-house or local service bureau's imagesetter or proofing printer. But if your prepress service provider is using one of the newer In-RIP separation workflows to create separations, do trapping, and perform other post-processing tasks, then you can use InDesign's Composite PostScript file option instead. This is useful because a Composite PostScript file size is smaller, so there's less data that needs to be transmitted to the output device, or via the Internet to a service provider's FTP site.

Although Figure 18.7, as well as Figures 18.10 and 18.11, only show the four process colors—cyan (C), magenta (M), yellow (Y), and black (K)—you can have additional spot color and varnishes as well. (See Figure 18.8.) When you look at Figures 18.7 and 18.8, note that the order for listing the process colors reflects the sequence in which they are actually printed—yellow first, then magenta, then cyan, and finally black. When the colors are not printed in the correct sequence, skin tones, for example, will be inaccurate.

NOTE InDesign always displays the process colors in the panel window, even if you only use spot colors in your document. If your document ink color is only black, InDesign will only send a single page for processing.

FIGURE 18.7

A composite page and 4-color separations

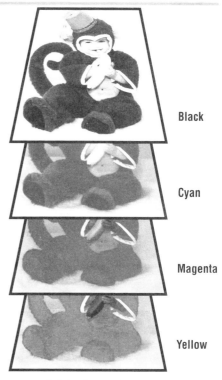

Composite   4-Color Separation

FIGURE 18.8

Separating process colors, spot colors, and varnish

A. Process Colors

B. Process + Spot

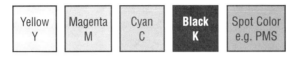

C. Process + Spot + Varnish

When working with either composites or separations, you'll need to understand how line screens, halftone dots, and printer dots differ. (See Figure 18.9.) The line screen consists of dots, either as a halftone (based on a grid) or a stochastic pattern (variable placement and dot size determined by an algorithm using a fixed set of parameters). The individual screen dots are built from the printer dots. The fewer the printer dots in a halftone or stochastic dot, the lighter the value or shade of gray. The finer the screen, or higher the screen frequency number, the smaller the dot. But remember that because each dot represents a spot of ink, your choice of paper, inks, and kind of press used and other variables like temperature and humidity will impact how your printed piece will finally look.

Table 18.1 shows Adobe's recommendations for output device resolution and maximum line screen necessary for halftone dots to retain all 256 levels of gray. Use InDesign's Color options in the Print dialog box to set your line screen specifications. Table 18.2 shows how screen frequency and printing application compare. Screen frequency is represented as a value of *lpi* (lines per inch).

NOTE Adobe recommends applying a custom screen instead of the settings in Table 18.1 when using a device that supports PostScript 3 with smooth shading.

WARNING You want to avoid using unnamed colors in your document. If you need to correct color, you'll have to change each instance one by one, a potentially tedious and expensive situation. InDesign 1 doesn't globally change unnamed colors.

CREATING COLOR SEPARATIONS

FIGURE 18.9
Line screen, halftone dots, and printer dots

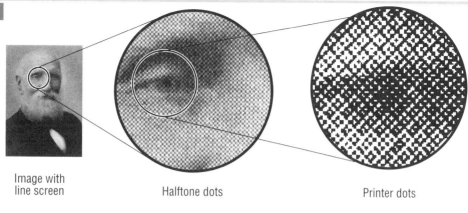

Image with line screen | Halftone dots | Printer dots

TABLE 18.1: OUTPUT DEVICE RESOLUTION AND MAXIMUM LINE SCREEN FOR HALFTONE DOTS TO RETAIN ALL 256 LEVELS OF GRAY

Final Output Device Resolution	Maximum Line Screen to Use
300	19
400	25
600	38
900	56
1000	63
1270	79
1446	90
1524	95
1693	106
2000	125
2400	150
2540	159
3000	188
3252	203
3600	225
4000	250

TABLE 18.2: SCREEN FREQUENCY

Screen Frequency	Printing Usage
65 lpi	Newsletters and grocery coupons
85 lpi	Newspapers
120 lpi	Low end offset printing, uncoated papers
133 lpi	4-color magazines
150 lpi	Brochures or other marketing materials
177 lpi	Annual reports and images in art books

Setting Composite Printing

To set composite printing, click the Composite radio button in the Print: Color dialog box, shown in Figures 18.10 and 18.11. A file prepared for composite printing may be requested by your printer or service provider when they want to apply the automated processing features of PostScript 3. Consult with your vendor to determine how they want the file prepared for processing with their software and equipment.

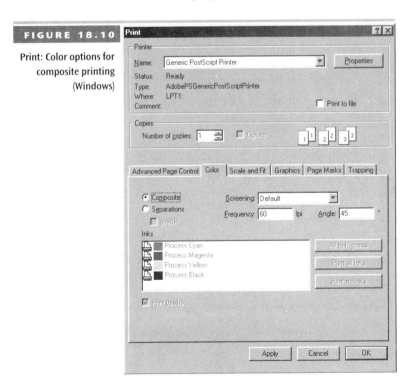

FIGURE 18.10

Print: Color options for composite printing (Windows)

CREATING COLOR SEPARATIONS   549

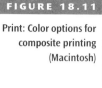

FIGURE 18.11

Print: Color options for composite printing (Macintosh)

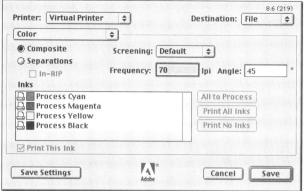

Turning On the In-RIP Separation Option

In the Print: Color dialog box, as shown in Figure 18.12, you can also activate the Adobe In-RIP option. If you want to enable In-RIP Trapping as well, go to the Trapping options in the Print dialog box. (The Print: Trapping options are reviewed in the "Trapping Color" section later in this chapter.)

Adobe In-RIP Trapping requires the following hardware and software:

- Adobe PostScript printer driver version 5.1 or later (Windows NT), version 4.3 or later (Windows 98), or version 8.6 or later (Mac OS). The driver ships with InDesign and is available on the CD-ROM.

- A PPD (PostScript Printer Description) that supports Adobe In-RIP Trapping. Don't forget to select this PPD using the Adobe PS printer driver.

- An Adobe PostScript 3 output device whose RIP supports Adobe In-RIP Trapping. Check with the manufacturer and/or service provider to see if the output device supports PostScript 3 features.

 WARNING   When printing from devices that do not support Adobe In-RIP Trapping, any traps set automatically will not be included in the output. Only traps for individual objects that were set manually will be retained.

 WARNING   When printing In-RIP separations from a Macintosh, always specify one sheet only as the Pages per Sheet setting in the Print: Layout dialog box. If you don't, you'll end up with unnecessary blank pages.

Determining Color Separation Specifications

When you select InDesign's Separations option, the All to Process, Print All Inks, and Print No Inks buttons become active, as shown in Figure 18.12. You can use these buttons to help determine how each ink color will be printed.

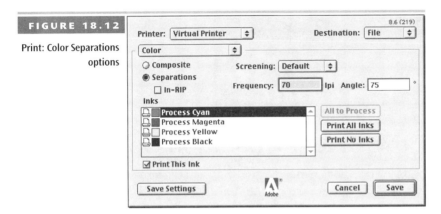

FIGURE 18.12

Print: Color Separations options

When you select each ink color, you will see the information change for the Screening, Frequency, and Angle. To prevent moiré patterns (undesirable patterns that distort image clarity and quality), the screen angle for each color in the document needs to be correctly specified. When setting screen angles, also watch out for images that contain gradients or stripes. Overlaying a halftone screen on these images areas may produce moiré patterns as well. Consult with your printer or prepress provider to minimize these problems on press.

You can also select or deselect inks by clicking the Print This Ink checkbox or by double-clicking the printer icon next to the color name. When you deselect this option, a large "X" appears on top of the printer icon, as shown below. When you see this "X" it means the color will not be printed. To change the setting, just click again on the Print This Ink checkbox.

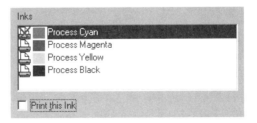

CREATING COLOR SEPARATIONS 551

When you click the Print No Inks button, an "X" will appear on all the printer icons in this panel window. You can use this button when you want to print one or two inks. First, click the Print No Inks button to deselect all inks. Then, double-click the crossed-out printer icon to select the color you want to print.

If you use an unnamed color or spot color in your page design, i.e. PANTONE Coated or Uncoated color, the All to Process button becomes active in the Print: Color dialog box. When you click the All to Process button, any spot color you've specified will be printed in its closest process color simulation. The Color panel shows the changes by graying out or dimming the spot color names, and changing the All to Process button to the Revert to Spot button once the conversion is completed. To restore the document's spot colors, click the Revert to Spot button.

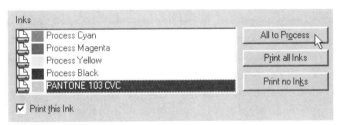

Here are some items to keep in mind when specifying the All to Process option:

- When applying the All to Process option to placed PDF files that contain LAB and RGB colors, you need to create In-RIP separations if you want to convert the LAB and RGB colors to CMYK.

- When applying the All to Process option to a placed duotone EPS file, you also need to turn on the In-RIP option if you want the file to separate correctly. (Watch out for limitcheck errors on some In-RIP devices.) If you don't want to use the In-RIP option, you'll have to deselect the All to Process option.

 NOTE For best results when printing separations, create PDFs in CMYK color mode, and avoid using spot colors, raster images, and mesh shading.

 NOTE Any page containing a placed PDF file will always generate Cyan, Magenta, Yellow, and Black plates. This holds true even if the objects in the PDF document are not made with all the process colors.

Gradients and the Print: Color Options

Here are some other things to keep in mind about gradients:

- When specifying a gradient between two spot colors, avoid assigning the same screen angle to both spot colors. If both spot colors have the same screen angle, the colors will overprint each other. Which screen angles you select depends on the other colors that will be separated. Consult with your service provider before setting screen angles.
- If you created gradients in InDesign composed of both spot and process colors, you will not be able to separate them. If that's the case, click the All to Process button to convert all the gradient's spot colors to process equivalents. Also bear in mind that spot-to-process gradients created in Illustrator will not separate correctly from InDesign. In Illustrator, change the gradient to either spot-to-spot or process-to-process color, save the file, and import again to InDesign.
- To correctly separate a placed PDF file that includes a gradient fill or duotone EPS, select the In-RIP option in the Print: Color dialog box.
- Gradients created with a Black swatch will ignore the Overprint Black preference setting and knockout objects below it. To overprint type or gradient filled objects, you will have to apply the Overprint Fill or Overprint Stroke setting using the Attributes palette. (For more details, see "Overprinting Strokes, Fills, or Text" later in this chapter.)
- PostScript 3 output devices are capable of producing smoother gradients.

Generating Film Negatives or Positives

When your printer requires film instead of the digital files, you'll need to specify the film polarity and emulsion when you process the digital files. (*Emulsion* is the film's photosensitive substance.) Figure 18.13 shows how an image looks on a film positive, negative, and negative with emulsion-side down. (Negative/emulsion down is also called *negative/wrong reading* or *negative/mirror print*.)

WARNING Because polarity and emulsion settings can be set in both the PostScript RIP and in an imagesetter, it is crucial that this setting is set only once. If you set negative polarity and emulsion-side down both in the PostScript RIP and the imagesetter, then you'll end up with positive film/emulsion-side up.

Before sending the files for processing, check with your service provider to determine the capabilities of their imagesetters. The imagesetter may offer enhanced processing features, such as more dot reproduction in the shadow areas or pre-compensated halftone screens for negative and positive output. If that's the case, then you'll forego setting polarity and emulsion in your host computer, and request in your instructions for processing that the imagesetter features be applied.

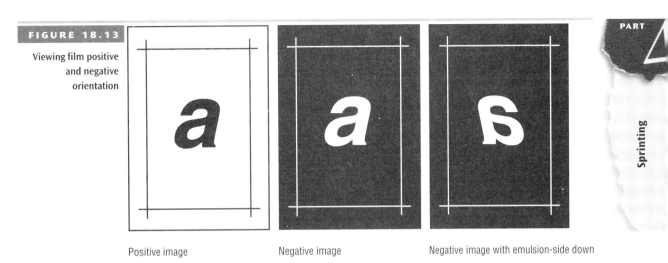

FIGURE 18.13
Viewing film positive and negative orientation

Positive image   Negative image   Negative image with emulsion-side down

Using Windows 98

Windows 98 users should follow these steps to specify emulsion and polarity for a document:

1. Select File ➢ Print to open the Print dialog box.
2. Click the Properties button, and then click the Graphics tab, as shown in Figure 18.14.

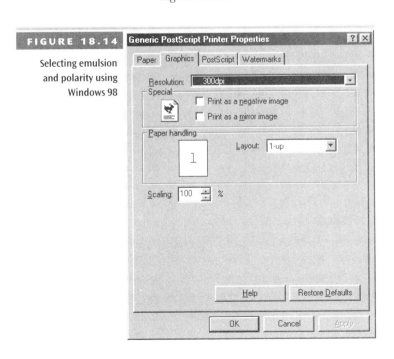

FIGURE 18.14
Selecting emulsion and polarity using Windows 98

3. Click the Print as a Negative Image checkbox to print negative pages. If you want to print positive pages, deselect the option.

4. Click Print as a Mirror Image to print emulsion-side down. Deselect the option to print emulsion-side up.

5. After completing the selection process, click OK to close the Properties dialog box.

Using Windows NT

If you're using Windows NT, follow these steps to specify emulsion and polarity for a document:

1. Choose File ➢ Print and then click Properties.
2. Click the Advanced tab to view Document Options.
3. Click the + (plus sign) next to Document Options to see the PostScript Options. Click the + (plus sign) next to PostScript Options to view Mirrored and Negative Output, as shown in Figure 18.15.

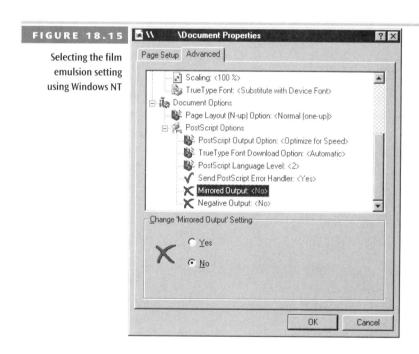

FIGURE 18.15

Selecting the film emulsion setting using Windows NT

4. Choose Mirrored Output, and then click either Yes to print emulsion-side down or No to print emulsion-side up.

5. To specify negative or positive pages, select Negative Output. Choose Yes to print negative pages or No to print positive pages.

6. Click OK to close the Properties dialog box.

Using a Macintosh

If you're using a Macintosh, follow these steps to specify positive or negative printing (polarity) and emulsion side:

1. Select File ➢ Page Setup to open the Page Setup dialog box.

2. Select PostScript Options from the option menu under the printer name.

3. Under the Visual Effects heading in the PostScript Options dialog box, shown in Figure 18.16, do the following:

    - To print emulsion-side up, deselect Flip Horizontal and Flip Vertical.
    - To print emulsion-side down, select either Flip Horizontal or Flip Vertical, depending on the orientation of the document.
    - To print positive pages, deselect Invert Image.
    - To print negative pages, select Invert Image.

4. After completing your selections, click OK to close the dialog box.

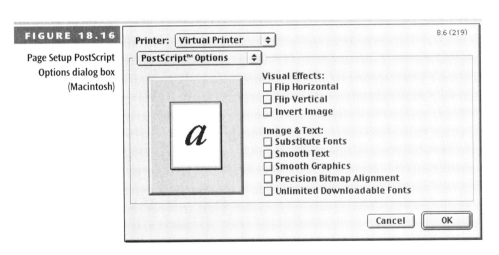

FIGURE 18.16

Page Setup PostScript Options dialog box (Macintosh)

Learning More about Electronic Prepress and Printing

If you'd like to polish your prepress production skills and learn more about the technical aspects of printing, here are two resources that offer training.

GATF/PIA

The GATF/PIA (the Graphic Arts Technical Foundation consolidated with the Printing Industries of America and its 31 local affiliates) offers workshops, seminars, and conferences about printing and preproduction. GATF/PIA also publishes advanced technical references about electronic prepress, the lithographic printing process, and industry trends. Their Web site has links to schools, vendors and suppliers, associations and GATF/PIA affiliates, trade magazines and publishers, printers, and other service providers. The Web site address is http://www.gatf.lm.com/ or http://www.gatf.org/. Contact information is as follows:

Graphic Arts Technical Foundation
200 Deer Run Road
Sewickley, PA 15143-2600 USA
Phone: (412) 741-6860 or 1-800-910-GATF
Fax: (412) 741-2311
e-mail: info@gatf.org

T&E Center of Rochester Institute of Technology (RIT)

RIT's T&E Center (Technical and Education Center of the Graphic Arts and Imaging) provides training in traditional and digital technologies for designers, managers, and graphic arts industry professionals. Their workshops, seminars, and classes are held in comprehensive prepress and press labs, as well as state-of-the-art imaging facilities. Visit the RIT Web site at www.rit.edu for more information about T&E Center programs. You can also contact the center at:

Rochester Institute of Technology
Technical and Education Center of the Graphic Arts and Imaging
66 Lomb Memorial Drive
Rochester, NY 14623-5604
Phone: 1-800-724-2536, ext. 815
Phone: Outside the Continental U.S.: (716) 475-7090, ext. 815
Fax: (716) 475-7000
e-mail: webmail@rit.edu

Printing with Page Marks

When you need to add *page marks* or *printer's marks*, open the Print: Page Marks dialog box shown in Figures 18.17 and 18.18. Click the various checkboxes for the different kinds of marks. You use page marks to align separation films, trim film or press sheets to size, align tiled pages, measure output for correct calibration and dot density, to name a few examples. Keep in mind that you can also set page marks in the Export PDF: and Export Prepress: Pages and Page Marks dialog boxes. Chapter 19 discusses PDF files (.pdf), and the "Exporting to a Prepress File" section later in this chapter reviews the .sep file format.

WARNING If you're using ScenicSoft's Preps trapping software, check the InDesign ReadMe file for more details about the Pages and Page Marks settings that you'll need to use.

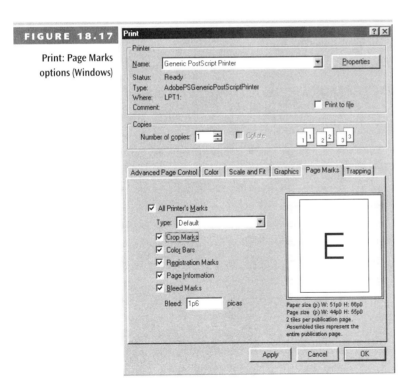

FIGURE 18.17

Print: Page Marks options (Windows)

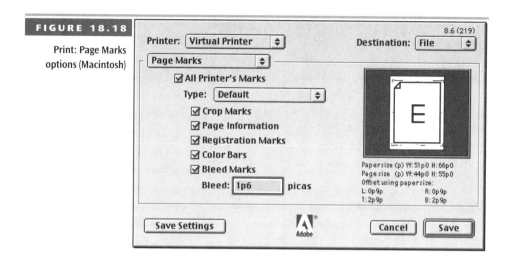

FIGURE 18.18
Print: Page Marks options (Macintosh)

Selecting Page Marks

You can set the following options in the Print: Page Marks dialog box:

All Printer's Marks   Choose this option when you want to use all the page marks.

Type   You can choose default page marks or custom marks. Custom marks are an InDesign option for third party plug-ins, such as those needed for specifying page marks for Asian pages.

Crop Marks   These are horizontal and vertical hairline rules that define the edge of the page. Also called *trim marks*. To help register one sheet of film to another sheet, select Crop Marks when specifying color separations.

Page Information   Select this option to print the filename, page number, current date and time, and color separation name. They are printed in either in 8-point Arial (Windows) or 8-point Helvetica (Macintosh). Figure 18.19 shows the page information at the bottom of the sheet of paper. To print page information, you need 0.5 inches (13mm) along the horizontal edge. Remember to use this measurement when calculating the correct paper size for printing.

Registration Marks   Registration marks are small targets, usually a circle with cross hairs. InDesign places registration marks at mid-point of the width and height outside the page area of the document. You need to specify registration marks when creating color separations.

Color Bars   Color bars represent the CMYK inks and tints of gray (in 10% increments). Your service provider measures these small squares of color to determine what adjustments, if needed, are made to ink density on the printing press or proofing specifications.

Bleed Marks Defines the area that is assigned to the page bleed. It's marked off by hairline rules. Be careful not to confuse bleed marks with crop marks when trimming documents.

Bleed Enter a value in this field to define the extra amount added to the image area outside the defined page area. Setting this value to zero causes InDesign not to print anything beyond the edge of the page. Consult with your service provider to determine if they require a minimum bleed measurement. Also, make sure when extending images or other objects beyond page boundaries that they are correctly sized and positioned to compensate for bleed.

WARNING If you enter a bleed value with an uppercase letter, such as for 1P6 instead of a lowercase letter as in 1p6, and then click Apply (Windows) or Save Settings (Macintosh), you'll see the Bleed value is out of range or invalid alert. You'll need to enter all measurement units in lowercase, such as p (picas) or mm (millimeters).

TIP When placing large graphics, the page size edge may no longer be visible on the pasteboard. Before positioning artwork, you may find it useful to position ruler spread guides to mark off page and bleed areas on the pasteboard. If you do this on the parent master page, these guides will appear on every document page. See Chapter 16 to learn more about using master pages.

Choosing a Paper Size to Match Page Mark Specifications

When you select a page mark option, the boundaries of the page are expanded to accommodate the page marks. If your selected paper size is no longer large enough to accommodate the document page plus page marks, you'll see the offset values shown below the preview window turn red. Printing the document with these offset values will give you unsatisfactory results. Some (if not all) of the page marks will not appear on the resulting output. To correct this situation, you can choose from these options:

- Change the paper size, as previously discussed in Chapter 8. If you change paper size, confirm that your targeted output device can handle the new paper size specification. When you output to a remote printer, make sure that the paper size is in stock and loaded into a cassette. Or set a time when the production assistant or operator can manually load your selected paper into the printer.

WARNING When proofing, always check that the printer's color management settings match your document's specifications. Beware of printer override options that can cause shifts in document color specifications.

- Scale the document. Before attempting to scale film output, always check with your service provider to see if the resized document will be acceptable. For more information about scaling, refer to the "Scaling and Tiling Your Printed Documents" section earlier in this chapter.

- Scale and tile the document. You should avoid using this option when processing film output. In most cases, the resulting film will be unacceptable.

The InDesign defaults for drawing page marks are 3 points from the edge of the trimmed page or 3 points from the edge of a specified bleed. (There's more about bleeds in the following section.) Figure 18.19 shows a document with page marks positioned.

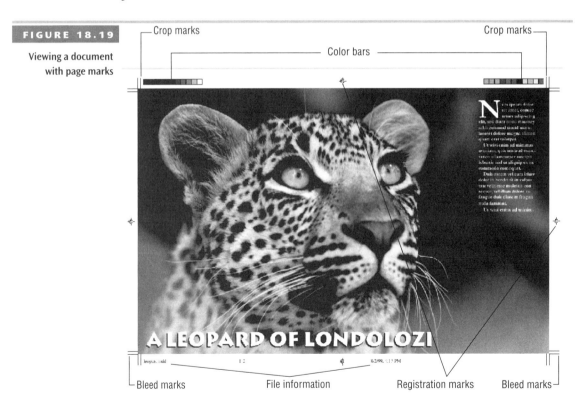

FIGURE 18.19

Viewing a document with page marks

Photo courtesy of Corbis Images (royalty-free division www.corbisimage.com)

Trapping Color

Trapping is used to correct for ink misregistration in press prints when you're printing several inks on the same sheet of paper, as shown in Figure 18.20. You can choose to use process colors that don't need trapping, overprint with black, manually over-trap strokes or fills, or use Adobe In-RIP trapping. But trapping is both an art and a science, and requires an understanding of how ink interacts with paper and other techniques for aligning or registering plates on press. If you're unfamiliar with how to set the trapping values, it's better to keep hands off the Print: Print Trapping dialog box shown in Figures 18.21 and 18.22, and leave trapping to your printer or service provider. They have expert software, from companies like ScenicSoft, which may do a much better job of setting traps. If you use the wrong trapping settings, you could create a larger, more noticeable problem on the printed sheet than what the trapping was supposed to correct.

WARNING If you're planning to use TrapWise 2.3.6 from ScenicSoft, Inc., don't forget to read the "About PostScript Levels" information in the InDesign ReadMe file. Because TrapWise 2.3.6 uses non-Adobe emulation of PS Level 1, you may have difficulty in correctly imaging InDesign files. Also refer to the ScenicSoft Web site for more information about current products and future updates: www.scenicsoft.com.

FIGURE 18.20

Trapping to correct for ink misregistration

 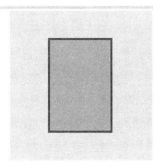

Ink misregistration   Trapping applied

NOTE When you select two process colors that contain a color in common and place them next to each other, you don't need to trap those colors.

There will be situations where if you look at a document with an untrained eye, it may not be obvious where trapping is needed. This is a good reason to leave trapping to the printer. In addition, printers can use a technique on press called *wet ink trapping* to control how one color overprints onto another. If your press proof has uneven,

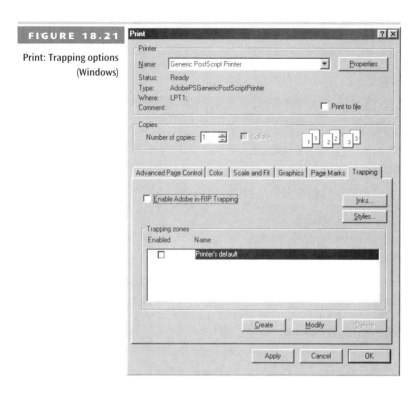

FIGURE 18.21

Print: Trapping options (Windows)

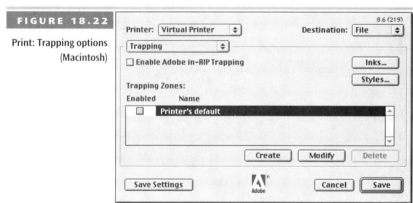

FIGURE 18.22

Print: Trapping options (Macintosh)

mottled, or splotchy colors, then it could be a problem with incorrect ink tack (stickiness). Each printing ink has a tack rating, and the ink with the highest tack rating is printed first, with any other ink printed in descending order. But press conditions can change influence tack, and it is important to do densitometer readings of the color bars during the printing process. When selecting any newly released paper stock, it may be a good idea to consult with your paper merchant and with your printer's customer service representative to find out when the paper is not a suitable option. Or you will discover that there will be additional charges to set up the press properly. (To learn how to place color bars on your printed sheet, see the "Selecting Page Marks" section earlier in this chapter.)

There's another issue you need to note. InDesign's trapping options are manually set, and do not support the automated trapping features of PostScript 3 In-RIP trapping. Check the Adobe Web site for further developments of an automatic trapping plug-in, or set up Adobe Online to receive updates. (Appendix A and B review Adobe Online options.)

Overprinting Strokes, Fills, or Text

You can use the Attributes palette to select paths for overprinting. But keep in mind that setting overprinting in the Attributes palette overrides all trapping options chosen in the Print: Color and Trapping dialog boxes. Your monitor will not display the effects of overprinting, but you can check overprinting by printing a proof on most PostScript Level 2 and PostScript 3 devices. When selecting overprinting options, consult with your vendor(s) to see if their equipment and software support overprinting options.

When manually overprinting black text, consider the following Adobe guidelines:

- In the Stroke palette, set the stroke weight measurement to equal the required trap width. Use this method when applying a spread, and not a choke. *Spreads* are traps where the edges of an object are enlarged slightly outward, and compensate for misregistration on-press by overlapping one color or tint on another. *Chokes* are another method for creating overlaps for trapping, such as when you want to overprint a light-colored background on darker colored type. Always consult with your prepress service provider or printer before setting any spreads or chokes.

- You commonly apply the lighter color to the stroke and overprint the stroke when a stroke is used to trap two spot colors or a spot and a process color.

- Overprinting is not necessary when using a stroke to trap two process colors. To create a CMYK stroke color, pick the higher value that either process color shows for cyan, magenta, yellow, and black.

When you want to overprint a stroke or fill, do the following:

1. Choose text characters with the Type tool, or one or more paths with the Selection or Direct Selection tool.
2. If the Attributes palette is not in view, choose Window ➢ Attributes.
3. In the Attributes palette, do one or both of the following:
    - To overprint the fill of selected objects or to overprint unstroked type, choose Overprint Fill.
    - To overprint the stroke of selected objects, choose Overprint Stroke.

When you want to overprint a paragraph rule, do the following:

1. Confirm that a swatch exists for your overprint color.
2. Using the Type tool, click an insertion point in a paragraph.
3. In the Paragraph palette, choose Paragraph Rules from the Paragraph palette menu. The Paragraph Rules dialog box opens as shown in Figure 18.23.
4. From the Paragraph Rules option menu at the top of the dialog box, choose the paragraph rule you want to overprint.
5. Click the Overprint Stroke checkbox and then click OK.

FIGURE 18.23

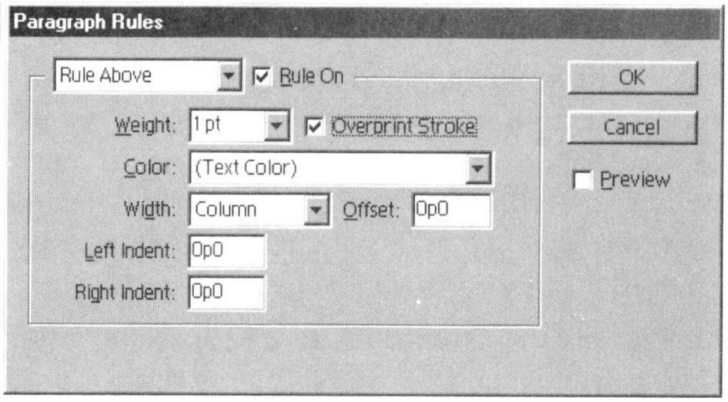

Paragraph Rules dialog box

NOTE The Overprint Stroke option in the Paragraph Rules dialog box can be part of a Paragraph Style.

Because overprinting some or all instances of black ink is a common practice in commercial printing, InDesign sets Overprint Black as a default preference in the General Options dialog box. Overprinting black helps prevent misregistration of small black type and colored areas outlined with black lines. When this option is selected, all black strokes, fills, and type characters of any size is overprinted. If you disable Overprint Black, all instances of black knock out as underlying ink is removed. Select File ➤ Preferences ➤ General to open the dialog box to change the Overprint Black setting.

Preflighting Your Document

You'll sometimes need to perform a quality control check of the document before sending the document to an outside vendor or exporting to another file format. InDesign includes the preflight feature for this purpose, which allows you to check for missing links and images, fonts, color management profiles, and hidden layers (but *not* for pasteboard content). After completing the preflighting process, InDesign generates an on-screen report, which can be saved and printed as a text file.

Before beginning the preflight process, you should double-check your document's color settings. Choose File ➤ Color Settings ➤ Document Color Settings. These settings are included in the Adobe InDesign Preflight Report. In the Document Color Settings dialog box shown in Figure 18.24, the Source Profile for CMYK is Kodak SWOP Proofer CMYK–Coated Stock. (To learn more about the SWOP standard, see the "Learning about Specifications for Web Offset Publications (SWOP)" sidebar below.)

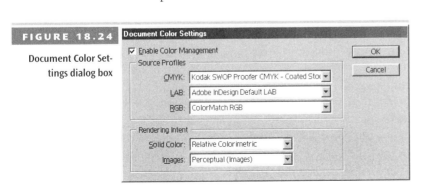

FIGURE 18.24

Document Color Settings dialog box

Learning about Specifications for Web Offset Publications (SWOP)

SWOP, founded in the late 1980s and incorporated as a not-for-profit in 1988, issues and regularly updates specifications and guidelines for web production printing. Web printing, which is also called *roll-fed printing*, uses continuous rolls of paper rather than the flat sheets of paper that are fed into a sheet-fed press. Magazines and newspapers are, for example, printed on web presses.

With a board of directors that includes representatives of the American Association of Advertising Agencies (AAAA), the Magazine Publishers of America (MPA), the International Prepress Association (IPA), and the Web Offset Association of the Printing Industries of America, SWOP has been developing and promoting a certification standard for web offset printing.

To learn more about the SWOP specifications, guidelines for web production printing, SWOP products, and other information (including samples of the forms for the Off-Press Proof Application Data Sheet and the Standard Inspection Report for Supplied Advertising Material), contact SWOP at:

SWOP, Inc.
60 East 42nd Street, Suite 721
New York, NY 10165
Phone: (212) 983-6042
Fax: (212) 983-6043
e-mail: swopinc@aol.com
URL: www.swop.org

In addition to the above named material and other useful information, the Web site has links to companies that support the SWOP standard including Heidelberg USA, Xerox, Eastman Kodak Company, DuPont, and other printing/prepress associations. You'll want to check the Web site to keep abreast of the revisions to the SWOP specifications and guidelines. The targeted date of publication for the revised guidelines and specifications is early 2000.

Viewing the Preflight Summary Information

To open the Preflight dialog box, select File ➤ Preflight or press Shift+Ctrl+Alt+F (Windows) or Opt+Shift+Cmd+F (Macintosh). It will open to the Summary options as shown in Figures 18.25 and 18.26. The information appearing in the panel includes the status of fonts, links, graphics, and other information relating to color management. Figure 18.27 shows the sample project that was used to create the information found in the Windows Preflight dialog box. In this sample, fonts and links were correctly applied in the document. In the Macintosh sample (not shown), there were uninstalled font and missing placed files. This results in alert icons, which appear in the Macintosh Preflight dialog box in Figure 18.26. An alert icon will mark each instance of a problem in the document.

If you want to see information about hidden layers and their content, click the Show Data for Hidden Layers checkbox at the bottom of the Summary panel. If you want to go directly to a problem area, select the option from the menu at the top of the dialog box. You can click the Next button to navigate to the Fonts dialog box, or click Previous to view the Print Settings panel.

At any time during your review of current preflight data, you can generate a report, which is saved as a text file. For more details, see "Creating and Printing a Preflight Report" later in this section.

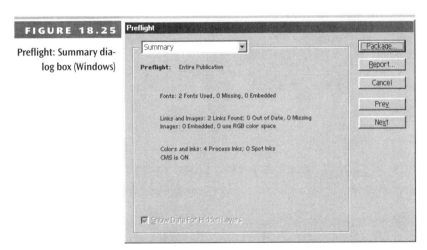

FIGURE 18.25

Preflight: Summary dialog box (Windows)

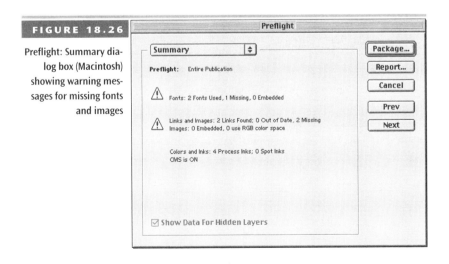

FIGURE 18.26

Preflight: Summary dialog box (Macintosh) showing warning messages for missing fonts and images

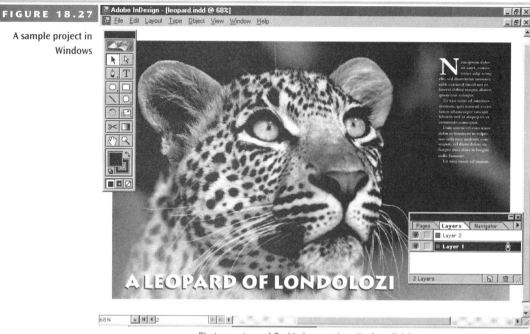

FIGURE 18.27

A sample project in Windows

Photo courtesy of Corbis Images (royalty-free division www.corbisimage.com)

Checking the Status of Fonts Used in a Document

The Preflight: Fonts dialog box, shown in Figures 18.28 and 18.29, provides information about all fonts used in a document. The information displayed tells you about:

- Fonts specified with InDesign's Type commands
- Fonts embedded in EPS files
- Fonts contained in Adobe Illustrator files
- Fonts contained in placed PDF pages
- Fonts used in the document, but not installed on your computer

 NOTE There's more about text formatting in Chapter 9, and placed graphics in Chapter 8.

FIGURE 18.28

Preflight: Fonts dialog box (Windows)

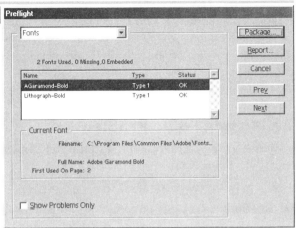

FIGURE 18.29

Preflight: Fonts dialog box (Macintosh) showing missing fonts

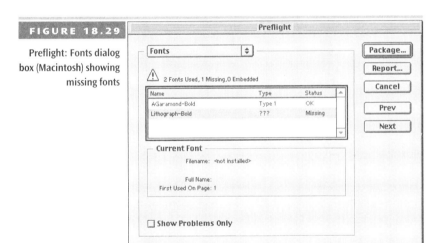

Above the font list, in which you'll find the name, type, and status of each font used in the document, is a comment line summarizing font usage. In Figure 18.29, you'll see the alert icon because a font is not installed on the computer. The listing for Lithograph Bold indicates question marks under Type and the Status is identified as Missing. Because Lithograph Bold was selected when I clicked on the listing, Current Font (below the font list) shows that the font was not installed on the computer. In addition to the page where the font was first used, the Current Font area provides the full name of the font. In Figure 18.28, for example, Adobe Garamond Bold was selected as the current font.

NOTE You can click the Show Problems Only checkbox, located at the bottom of the dialog box, to view only problem fonts in the Preflight: Font dialog box. If this option is selected, the Preflight: Summary dialog box will only list problem fonts. You can also choose to activate this option in the Preflight: Links and Images dialog box. As in the case with fonts, only problem links and images will appear in the information listings.

Correcting the Missing Fonts Problem

To fix the problem of missing fonts, click Cancel to exit the Preflight dialog box, and then do one or several of the following:

- Install the missing fonts on your computer
- Select a PPD (PostScript Printer Description file) with the needed fonts
- Replace the missing font in the document with a font installed on your system

WARNING The initial release of InDesign cannot globally replace fonts as you can in QuarkXPress. To replace a font, you have to locate and change each usage one by one.

- If fonts that appear in placed graphics are not available for installation on your computer, open the placed graphic in its native program and replace the missing font there. Save the revised graphic. Using InDesign, remove the originally placed graphic, import the revision, and save the updated document. Start the Preflight process again.

NOTE Missing font names are listed in the Type ≻ Font menu under the heading "Missing." In the Character palette, they appear at the bottom of the typeface family list, and are identified by open and closed brackets [*Font name*]. These font lists may not be updated when changes are made in the document, such as when pasting or placing text with missing fonts. To make sure that these menus are correct and up to date, press Ctrl+Alt+Shift+/ (Windows) or Cmd+Option+Shift+/ (Macintosh).

Preflighting Links and Images

The Preflight: Links and Images dialog box, shown in Figures 18.30 and 18.31, has a similar user interface as the Fonts options—with an important exception. Unlike the Preflight: Fonts dialog box, you don't have to exit the dialog box to make necessary repairs.

You can check this dialog box for information about embedded profiles. If None appears under the ICC Profile heading, then no profile has been applied to the imported file. Files with embedded profiles that were not installed on the computer, placed in the wrong folder, or named incorrectly will be listed under the ICC profile heading as Missing. Consult Appendix C for more information about ICC profiles and other color management issues.

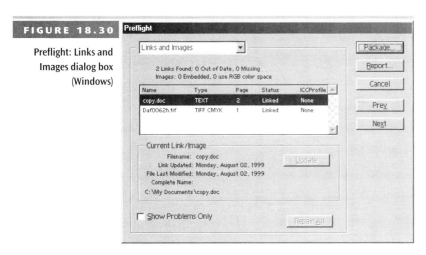

FIGURE 18.30

Preflight: Links and Images dialog box (Windows)

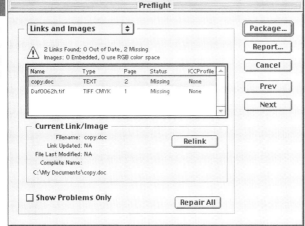

FIGURE 18.31

Preflight: Links and Images dialog box (Macintosh) showing Relink and Repair All options activated

One more item to look at in Figures 18.30 and 18.31. Notice the comment in the status line (above the Links and Images list) concerning RGB images: "0 use RGB color space." For print applications, bear in mind that an RGB image may not separate properly unless color management is turned on and an ICC profile is correctly embedded in the file. Don't leave the processing of RGB images to chance. It's a good idea to consult with your service provider or printer before sending any files. Some vendors may not accept RGB files for processing. When sending RGB image files, it's important to provide vendors with detailed instructions and accurate proofs for color matching.

When you click on a problem link or image, as shown in Figure 18.31, Relink (Macintosh) and Repair All buttons become activated. Clicking either button opens a dialog box for finding the missing link or image, as shown in Figure 18.32. (The Relink button is named Update in the Windows version of InDesign. See Figure 18.30.)

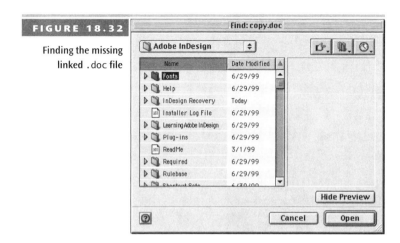

FIGURE 18.32

Finding the missing linked .doc file

After locating and selecting the correct image files or other placed importable files, click Open (Windows) or Choose (Macintosh) to make the repair. The information appearing in the Preflight: Summary, Links and Images, and Print Settings dialog boxes will be updated.

If the newly placed images contained fonts, you may want to click Previous to double-check font status. Otherwise, click Next to move to the Preflight: Colors and Inks dialog box.

Checking for Duplicate Spot Colors

Figure 18.33 shows the Preflight: Colors and Inks dialog box. The list contained in the dialog box is generated from the document's print settings and ink list. Use this list to check for duplicate spot colors, such as swatches selected from the PANTONE Coated or Uncoated library. When the document file is processed, each spot color produces a separation plate—even if it's a duplicate color. To avoid any additional fees for processing any unnecessary separation plates, delete any duplicate colors from the Swatches palette.

To correct ink problems, exit the Preflight dialog box by clicking Cancel. Select and delete the duplicate color from the Swatches palette. While you're at it, it may be a good idea to remove any unused colors from the Swatches palette. Doing this housekeeping will help to avoid incorrectly assigned colors if the service provider needs to edit the document. (Chapter 12 goes into detail about the Swatches palette.)

Because no spot colors were used in my sample project, Figure 18.33 shows only the Process colors: Cyan, Magenta, Yellow, and Black. Note that the listing also includes valuable information about the halftone screen and screen angle, which was assigned to each color in the Print: Color dialog box. See the "Creating Color Separations" section earlier in this chapter for more information.

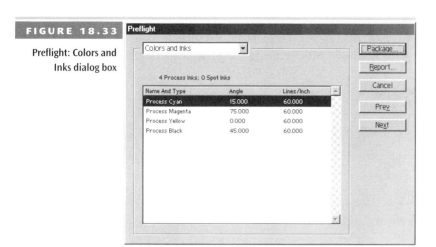

FIGURE 18.33

Preflight: Colors and Inks dialog box

Click Next to move on to the Preflight: Print Settings dialog box.

Viewing Print Settings

Use the scroll bar in the Print Settings panel to view all of the document's current print settings, as shown in Figure 18.34.

FIGURE 18.34

Preflight: Print Settings dialog box showing an on-screen report

Printing the Preflight Report

To create a text file of the report for printing, click the Report button in the Preflight dialog box. InDesign automatically places the text file in the same folder as its pre-flighted document. If you would like to print a copy of the report, find the file on your computer and double-click the listing to open the .txt file. The text file either opens in Windows Notepad (Figure 18.35) or Macintosh SimpleText (Figure 18.36). Because the text file uses a screen font, you'll need to assign a printer font in whichever program you're using before printing the report.

FIGURE 18.35

Adobe InDesign Preflight Report opened in Windows Notepad

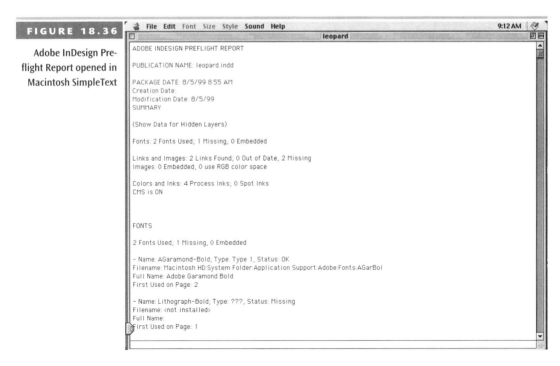

FIGURE 18.36

Adobe InDesign Preflight Report opened in Macintosh SimpleText

Packaging Files for Service Providers

The Packaging command makes it easy to gather files that you need to send off to your service provider including fonts, linked graphics, and ICC profiles. When you want to package files you can do one of the following:

- In Preflight dialog box, click the Package button
- Select File ➢ Package
- Press Shift+Ctrl+Alt+P (Windows) or Opt+Shift+Cmd+P (Macintosh)

InDesign will prompt you to save the file before opening the Package dialog box. If there were changes to the file since your last preflight check, or if you did not do a preflight check, InDesign automatically checks the document. An alert will appear if there are problems with the file. Click View Info to open the Preflight dialog box. Use the information in the Preflight dialog box to diagnose the problem, and then make any repairs as needed. (In the alert dialog box you can also click Continue, but if there are problems with the document it makes no sense to continue the packaging process.) Once the repairs have been made, start the packaging process again.

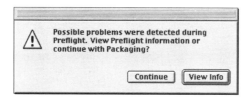

Creating Instructions for Service Providers

When the preflight process is completed and everything checks out okay, the Printing Instructions dialog box opens, as shown in Figure 18.37. Fill in each field of the dialog box by typing the information. The words "instructions.txt" appears as the filename at the top of the dialog box. Change the word "instructions" to better reflect the name of the InDesign file, but don't overtype the file extension. This Printing Instructions report will be stored in the same folder as the other packaging files. When you've completed the instruction form, click Continue to proceed to the Package Publication dialog box (Windows) or the Create Package Folder (Macintosh).

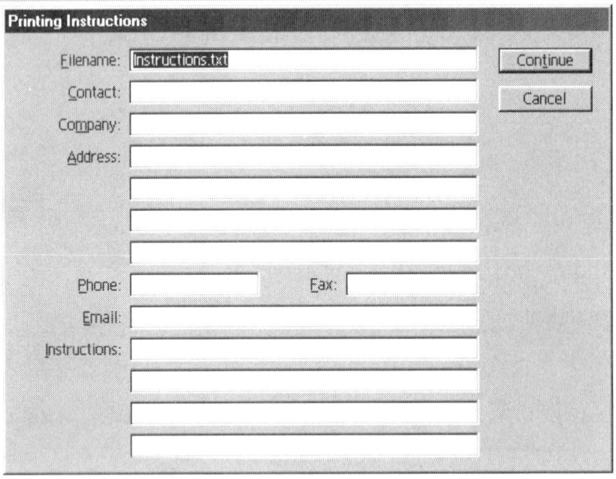

FIGURE 18.37

Printing Instructions dialog box

Assembling the Package

In the Package Publication or Create Package Folder dialog box, shown in Figures 18.38 and 18.39, do the following:

1. Select the location of the saved package files.

2. Type a name for the Package folder, which will contain any folders and files created during the packaging process.

3. Customize the package by selecting from the following options (the names differ depending on platform; the Windows names are shown here):

    Copy Fonts Allows you to copy only the necessary fonts, but not the entire font family. This is a default setting.

    Copy Linked Graphics Another default setting. When this option is selected, all graphics files are copied. Even if you deselect this option, linked text will still be copied to the package folder.

    Update Graphic Links Leave this default selected. You want to update the graphics links to the location of the package folder. To update text links, you will have to do so manually. Check the document for any problems with text flow and formatting. See Chapter 5 for more details about linking imported text.

    Include Fonts and Links from Hidden Layers You can select this option if you want to package objects on hidden layers.

View Report If you choose this option, the Printing Instructions report will automatically open after packaging is completed. When you want to edit this document prior to completing the packaging process, click the Instructions button on this dialog box.

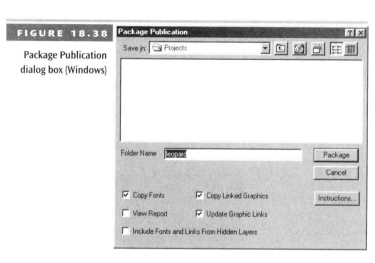

FIGURE 18.38

Package Publication dialog box (Windows)

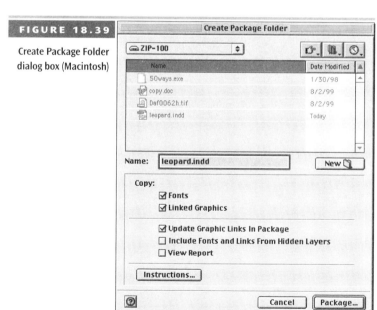

FIGURE 18.39

Create Package Folder dialog box (Macintosh)

When you've completed your selections, click the Package button. Figures 18.40 and 18.41 show the package created for the sample project illustrated in Figure 18.27.

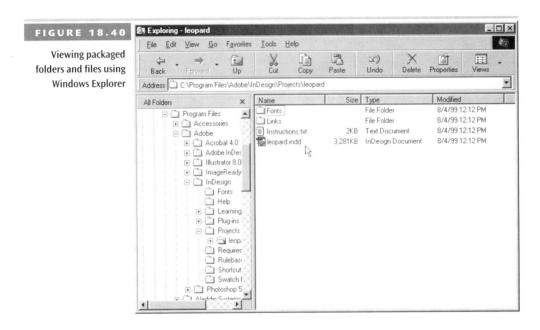

FIGURE 18.40

Viewing packaged folders and files using Windows Explorer

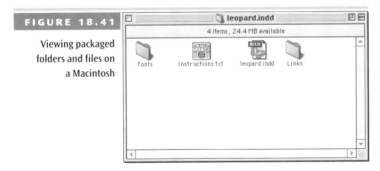

FIGURE 18.41

Viewing packaged folders and files on a Macintosh

Exporting to a Prepress File

In addition to exporting a document to EPS, PDF, and HTML, you can also export a document as a Prepress file. The Export EPS option creates a standard `.eps` file (see Chapter 2). The Prepress file, the second PostScript file format you can create in InDesign, is optimized for post-processing procedures such as trapping and page imposition. Because all device and driver dependencies are removed, you'll find it easier to print to most output devices. The Prepress file has a `.sep` file extension.

WARNING Remember to save the Prepress file to your hard drive first before transferring to other storage media or uploading to a network. Because transfer times for PostScript files is often very slow, you want to guard against lost or corrupt data.

WARNING When printing an EPS or a Prepress file, InDesign does not check for missing fonts that are contained in placed Vector EPS files or native Illustrator files (.ai). Because InDesign allows placement of these files even if their fonts are not loaded on the system, you should consider selecting File ➢ Preflight before printing the document.

To export an InDesign document to a Prepress file, do the following:

1. Select File ➢ Export or press Ctrl+E (Windows) or Cmd+E (Macintosh). The Export dialog box opens, as shown in Figures 18.42 and 18.43.

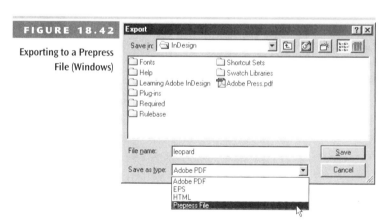

FIGURE 18.42

Exporting to a Prepress File (Windows)

2. Choose Prepress File from the Save as Type (Windows) or Formats (Macintosh) option menus.

3. When the Export Prepress File dialog box opens, view the Prepress Options, as shown in Figure 18.44. If you don't see these options, then select Prepress Options from the menu at the top of the dialog box or click the Next button. The Prepress Options include: Encoding, PostScript, Embed Fonts, Color, Images, Omit, and Perform OPI Replacement. Go to Chapter 2's section "Exporting EPS Files" to read more about these options.

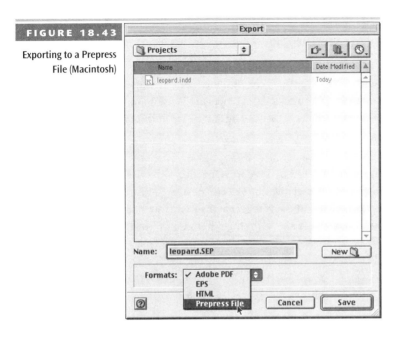

FIGURE 18.43

Exporting to a Prepress File (Macintosh)

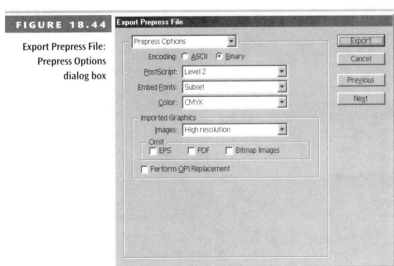

FIGURE 18.44

Export Prepress File: Prepress Options dialog box

4. After selecting your Prepress Options, click Next to move on to the Pages and Page Marks options shown in Figure 18.45.

5. Set your Pages and Page Marks options. (The Pages and Page Marks options for setting All Pages, Ranges By Section, and Reader's Spreads are also covered in Chapter 2's section "Exporting EPS Files." Specifying Page Mark options was discussed earlier in this chapter.)

EXPORTING TO A PREPRESS FILE 581

FIGURE 18.45

Export Prepress File: Pages and Page Marks dialog box

WARNING In exported EPS, Prepress, or PDF files, don't give spot colors the RGB or CMYK ink names—red, green, blue, cyan, magenta, and yellow. It will confuse everyone, and may lead to problems later when checking proofs or film. (Black cannot be recreated as a spot color.) EPS or PDF files using these names will not print correctly.

chapter 19

Exporting Documents in PDF Format

Featuring:

- Preparing files for PDF export — 586
- Exporting a document to PDF — 589
- Setting PDF options — 592
- Setting image compression — 595
- Specifying pages for export — 600
- Applying security controls — 602

Exporting Documents in PDF Format

Chapter 2 provided an introduction to PDF file basics, and in Chapter 6 you learned about placing PDF files as graphics. This chapter continues the discussion by showing you how to prepare InDesign files for PDF export and how to configure the Export PDF dialog boxes for different distribution technologies, such as high-resolution composite printing and on-screen viewing. When the InDesign export process is completed, the resulting PDF file can be viewed on any platform and from any Web browsers that support Adobe Acrobat Reader 4 or later. The PDF export file will print as viewed on-screen.

NOTE A copy of Acrobat Reader 4 is available for installation from the InDesign CD-ROM or can be downloaded free from the Adobe Web site at www.adobe.com.

When incorporating PDF file creation into your workflow, remember that InDesign's PDF export feature is not as robust as that of Adobe Acrobat 4, the full-featured program for creating PDF files. InDesign does not support the following Acrobat 4 features: annotations, movies, sound, hypertext links, form fields, and bookmarks. InDesign also does not support Acrobat plug-ins from other vendors, such as tools for preparing separations, trapping, and imposition of PDF files. If you want to add these extra features or others to your InDesign-generated PDF files, the files have to be opened and changed in Adobe Acrobat 4 or a PDF editing program.

NOTE Several of the Adobe Acrobat plug-ins developers will be offering similar tools to expand the functionality of the InDesign PDF export feature. In Chapter 3 you can learn more about these companies and their products.

TIP If you intend to have both InDesign and Acrobat open at the same time on your computer, check your available memory to head off any system crashes. Adobe recommends 32 MB for the Windows and 12 MB for the Macintosh versions of Acrobat 4.

Preparing Files for PDF Export

Before preparing your InDesign document for PDF export, you need to ask yourself how the document will be distributed and printed. For example, is the document part of a high-resolution composite printing workflow? Or are you publishing the PDF file to the World Wide Web for downloading and printing to a desktop printer? Or are you including the PDF files on a CD-ROM? And for those situations where you're using several distribution methods, plan to export the document more than once, using different settings to fit each technology's requirements. As you will see in this chapter, how the PDF document will be distributed and used influences Adobe's recommended settings.

Using PDF Files in High-Resolution Composite Printing

When you export your document to a composite PDF file in InDesign, you're creating a *digital master*, which should include all the essential information for correctly processing and printing the document. Using Adobe Acrobat or a PDF editor, the digital master can be viewed, edited, combined with other PDF files, and proofed in your studio or by your service provider. Using software tools especially created for the commercial printing market, the service provider also can perform preflight checks, set traps and page imposition, and generate color separations. Consider the following when preparing InDesign documents for high-resolution PDF export:

- When using PDF files in high-resolution printing, always confirm the requirements for file preparation and for setting PDF export options with your printer, prepress, or service bureau provider. You should also request their policies and procedures for color management profile settings. This will allow you to correctly embed any color profiles in your image files or InDesign documents and avoid additional charges that can occur when your vendor corrects files or replaces incorrectly processed proofs or imagesetter output. (Appendix C reviews color management and calibration.)

- You want to avoid potentially conflicting trapping commands from being applied to the file during post-processing. Before trapping any images or other graphics (prior to placement in your InDesign document), or trapping any artwork or typography created in InDesign, confirm whether your service provider accepts trapped files from customers. Some vendors may have post-processing workflows that use In-RIP Trapping as supported by Adobe PostScript 3 technology or special trapping applications like TrapWise. A quick call to your vendor may save valuable production time or prevent additional vendor charges for removal of your traps from the files. (Chapter 18 discusses InDesign's trapping feature in more detail.)

- Always perform a preflight check of the InDesign document prior to exporting as a PDF file. (See Chapter 18 for more information about preflight checking of your document before printing and other advanced printing topics.)

- Select the appropriate high-resolution images to match the final output size. Watch out for an image labeled "high-resolution" but whose file size and pixel resolution may be too small for poster-sized or larger reproduction. When resampling and compressing scanned images to alleviate storage problems or to make files smaller for transmission to a service provider's FTP site, preview PDF files to confirm image quality before sending files out for processing. Zoom in at 400% or greater magnification to check that the smallest details in the image file are not distorted.

- If printing the PDF file as a four-color process job, use CMYK images for the best results. You can convert RGB images, which are not placed PDF files, to CMYK when you select CMYK from the Color option menu in the Export PDF: PDF Options dialog box. But always check the PDF files for potential problems in color shifting, banding, and other image distortion problems. You'll find better results if you do the color conversion in an image-editing program, and then place the CMYK file in your InDesign document. (See the "Setting PDF Options" section later in this chapter.)

- If you placed Photoshop 5.02 or earlier DCS files, colorized TIFF images, or duotone EPS files in your InDesign document, you should check to see if your service provider is processing the file using a PostScript Level 2 RIP. If they are, you can't create composite PDF files that include the necessary information for color separations. The black plate will contain all the colors. To work around this problem, substitute graphics produced in Photoshop 5.5 or create a preseparated PostScript file. Create the PDF file from this PostScript file.
- When printing from a Macintosh computer, limit the document dimensions to no more than 200 × 200 inches.

WARNING Watch out for potential numbering changes between the original version of an InDesign document and its PDF variation. The physical page numbers on the InDesign pages may not correspond to the page numbers Acrobat uses to move through the document. By default InDesign assigns numbers (integers) to the PDF file, beginning with page 1 of the document. The export algorithm ignores any sections such as front-matter, which are numbered with Roman numerals. To fix this problem, open and renumber the PDF export file in Adobe Acrobat 4.

Using PDF Files in Web and CD-ROM Applications

When exporting documents for distribution on the Web, it's important to consider the filenames and file sizes of your PDF documents. You want to make your files easy to find using a Web search engine, browser, server, or versions of Microsoft Windows. Make the filenames relevant to the content of the document, no more than eight characters long, and include the .pdf file extension. (Some Web server and network applications truncate filenames longer than eight characters.)

Also consider dividing a large document into a collection of smaller PDF documents. Links between the InDesign-exported PDF files can be added later in Adobe Acrobat 4 or in an HTML editor. Smaller documents download faster, and each of these documents can have a targeted name appropriate to its content. This may increase the probability that your PDF document will be returned as a listing in Web search engine results.

Don't forget to perform a quality control review of any PDF files that you are distributing via the Web or a CD-ROM. You can never predict where software conflicts may occur. Here's a series of questions that you can use as a checklist:

- Have you downloaded the PDF file from a Web server using different browsers and computer systems? Did all files and content download correctly and reasonably fast?

- Can you access, read, install, or copy the file from the CD-ROM (as defined by assigned security settings)?
- Are all pages correctly inserted, sequenced, numbered, and in the proper orientation?
- Are all layouts complete?
- Does the artwork look good on screen? Are any of the images blocky or lacking in detail? (If so, then you'll need to change the compression settings.)
- Is the text correct, legible, and the fonts properly assigned?
- Is security set to the required level of access?
- Are any other enhancements that you added in Acrobat 4 or a PDF editor correctly positioned and functioning?
- Did you print (in color and black-and-white) the PDF files to different printer models to check that the output is OK?

As part of your InDesign and Acrobat 4 workflow, you may assign security settings in Acrobat and not in InDesign, unless required otherwise. Neither InDesign nor Acrobat keeps a record of any passwords that you assign to the document. If you don't remember the passwords, you will not be able to override any restrictions that you set when the file was exported. Acrobat or PDF editor tools or menu items that relate to the restricted features will be dimmed. The security settings for placed PDF pages in your InDesign document can also be problematic if set to a tighter level of security. (See Chapter 6 for more information about placing PDF files in an InDesign document.) See the "Applying Security Controls" section later in this chapter for more information.

Exporting a Document to PDF

When you're ready to export your document to PDF, do the following:

1. Select File ➢ Export, or press Ctrl+E (Windows) or Cmd+E (Macintosh). The Export dialog box opens, as shown in Figures 19.1 and 19.2.
2. Choose PDF from the Save as Type (Windows) or Formats (Macintosh) option menus.
3. Type a filename (no more than eight characters long, with no special characters or spaces between the letters for Web usage or use with Windows systems). Select a location and file folder where you plan to store the PDF file. If you're a Macintosh user, remember to add the file extension to the filename.

4. Click Save. The Export PDF dialog box opens, as shown in Figure 19.3. You're now ready to choose your export options. There are four different areas: PDF Options, Compression, Page and Page Marks, or Security. Each is addressed in turn in the following sections.

5. When you're finished, click Export. Your InDesign document will be exported as a PDF file and placed in the folder that you designated in the Export dialog box.

You can view the PDF file using Acrobat Reader 4, as shown in Figure 19.4. Figure 19.5 shows the same PDF file open in Acrobat 4 (Macintosh). (In Chapter 20, I will show how the same InDesign document was also prepared and exported to HTML.)

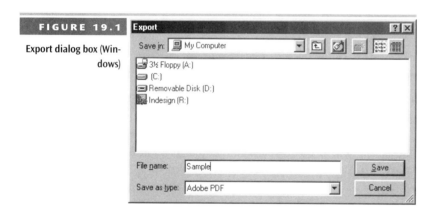

FIGURE 19.1
Export dialog box (Windows)

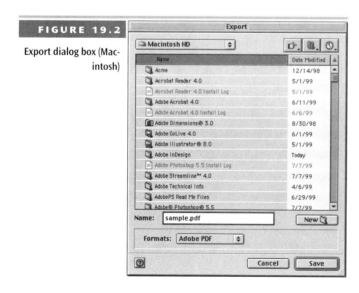

FIGURE 19.2
Export dialog box (Macintosh)

EXPORTING A DOCUMENT TO PDF 591

FIGURE 19.3

Export PDF: PDF Options dialog box

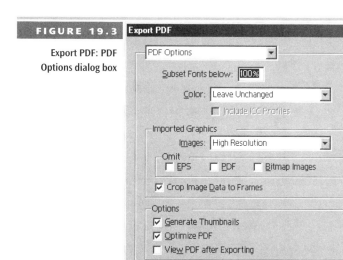

FIGURE 19.4

Using Acrobat 4 Reader to view an InDesign exported PDF file

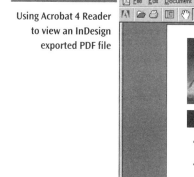
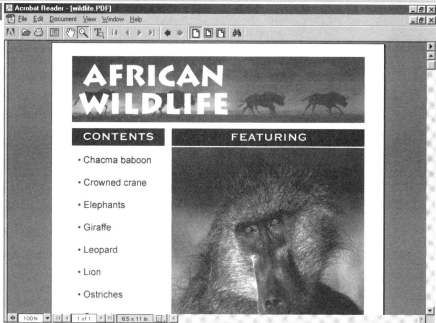

Photos courtesy of Corbis Images (royalty-free division) www.corbisimages.com

FIGURE 19.5

Using Acrobat 4 to open an InDesign exported PDF file

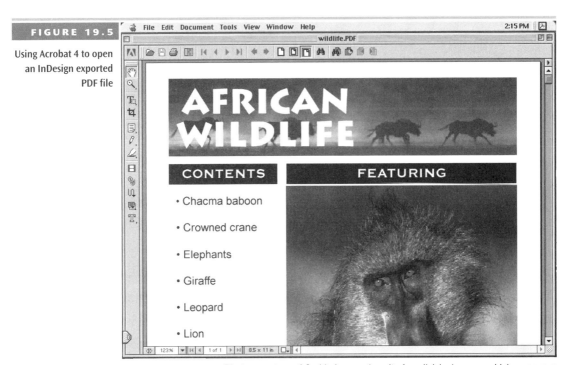

Photos courtesy of Corbis Images (royalty-free division) www.corbisimages.com

 WARNING   The PDF export filter does not support a separated document-to-printer workflow. The PDF file prints only as a composite document. If you want to print color separations of the PDF file, open the InDesign PDF in Adobe Acrobat 4 and apply Acrobat 3 or 4 compatibility settings. Then, print the PDF file separations to your selected output device. For more details about InDesign's advanced printing options, see Chapter 18.

Setting PDF Options

In the Export PDF: PDF Options dialog box, shown in Figure 19.3, you set the options for fonts, color, images, and display for the exported PDF file.

The first group of options are:

Subset Fonts Below   The value you enter in the threshold percentage field determines the percentage of characters that are embedded into the document. If you're not sure how the document will be used later, then keep the setting at 100% (default).

Color When you choose Leave Unchanged, RGB, or CMYK from the Color option menu, you specify how color information is represented in the exported PDF file. When you select Leave Unchanged, each image in the file will retain its original color space. Only select RGB when your PDF file will be viewed on-screen. Use CMYK for four-color printing applications, such as inkjet printers, color lasers, and commercial printing presses.

If you use the color settings defaults and had previously selected Enable Color Management (File ➢ Color Settings ➢ Document Color Settings), you will have calibrated color output. But if you use InDesign's internal RGB-to-CMYK conversion and had previously *de*selected the Enable Color Management option, the color output will be uncalibrated.

During color conversion, all spot color information is preserved. Only the process color equivalents convert to the selected color space during the conversion process. Consult your prepress vendor if you are not sure as to which settings to choose.

Color spaces in a placed PDF file cannot be converted. You have two choices when you want to color-separate a PDF file that has placed PDF files with RGB graphics:

- Modify the placed PDF file in its original application by converting the RGB graphics to CMYK. Then delete and replace the originally placed PDF file in your document with the edited version. Export the PDF file. Open and color separate the PDF file in Acrobat 4.

    or

- In Acrobat, you could turn color management on and specify to process RGB PDF files in the document. Make sure the output device supports In-RIP separations. The first choice may yield better results.

NOTE Remember that InDesign only supports composite PDF printing. To color-separate the PDF file, use Adobe Acrobat 4.

Include ICC Profiles If you enabled color management before you began the export process, then choosing this option will embed color profile information into the PDF file. When your PDF file is viewed or printed, the application or output device will use the profile information to translate colors into another color space (if needed).

Setting Imported Graphics Options

The second group of options in the Export PDF: PDF Options dialog box allow you to set the resolution of the placed bitmapped image, omit image formats from file data, and crop image data to the visible portion of the frame.

The options are as follows:

Images   This option determines how much image data will be included in the exported PDF file. Select High Resolution (the default setting) when printing your file on a high-resolution output device. The file will contain all available image data. When you choose Low Resolution, the PDF file contains only the screen-resolution (72 dpi) versions of placed bitmap images. Use this option when your PDF file will be seen on the Web or used with other on-screen applications, or in conjunction with the OPI/DCS Image Replacement option in the Print dialog box.

Omit   When using OPI, click the appropriate checkbox(es) when you want to omit a specific graphics file format in the image data that's sent to a printer or file. Choose EPS, PDF, Bitmap Images, or all three. The OPI links (comments) will be retained in the file, and the exported file displays omitted graphics as a gray box when viewed. (Chapter 6 contains more information about graphics basics.)

Crop Image Data to Frames   When attempting to reduce file size, you can choose this option to reduce image data to reflect only that portion that is visible within the frame. Avoid selecting this option when your document contains images that bleed or that will be repositioned later.

Setting Thumbnails, File Optimization, and Viewing Options

This is the last group of options that you can set in the Export PDF: PDF Options dialog box:

Generate Thumbnails   Click this checkbox when you want to produce a thumbnail for each exported page. If Reader's Spreads is also selected in the Pages and Page Marks dialog box (see Figure 19.10 later in this chapter), you can generate one thumbnail for each reader spread in the PDF file.

Optimize PDF   When you want to speed up access and viewing when downloading the PDF file from the Web or a network, click this checkbox. Optimizing the PDF file reduces file size by removing repeated background images, text, and line art, and replacing each repeated object with a pointer to its first occurrence.

If the document is multi-paged, the file is set up to download one page at a time from Web servers.

View PDF After Exporting When you choose this option, the PDF file will open in Acrobat Reader 4 or another application that you (or an installer) designated for your operating system.

The comment at the bottom of the dialog box ("Note: All fonts used in publication will be embedded.") reminds you that fonts will be embedded into the PDF file. For any fonts used in the document, check with the type supplier(s) to determine if you can distribute their fonts within PDF files.

When you've completed your review or selection of options in PDF Options dialog box, click Next to go to the Export PDF: Compression dialog box.

Setting Image Compression

The compression options in the Export PDF: Compression dialog box, shown in Figure 19.6, allow you to reduce the PDF file size, but also enable you to ruin image quality if you are not careful. At the end of this section are Adobe's recommended compression settings for high-resolution and on-screen applications. To avoid problems, it may be a good idea to check with your service provider to learn their recommended procedures and settings for compressing and resampling of files.

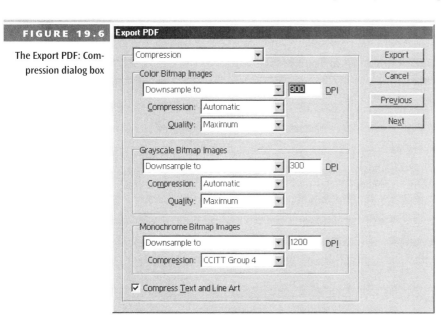

FIGURE 19.6

The Export PDF: Compression dialog box

Resampling Your Image Files

InDesign allows you to resample color, grayscale, and monochrome bitmap images. When you downsample or subsample a bitmap image, you're reducing the amount of data in an image. By adjusting these settings, you can set the amount of image data at the level needed by the device to correctly process the file. For example, if you forget to change the default compression settings (which are for high-resolution applications) to the recommended settings for on-screen viewing, your PDF file will take longer to download from the Web server. (The recommended settings are shown later in this chapter in Figures 19.7–19.9.)

Don't overlook the fact that InDesign does *not* resample document images to a higher resolution. You cannot reprocess a 72dpi image to 300 dpi, for example. Resampling an image to a higher resolution has to be carefully done in an image-editing program to avoid losing image sharpness. If that solution is not an option, then you will have to rescan the source image transparency or print at the correct resolution and image dimensions. (For more information about placing graphics in your InDesign document, see Chapter 6.)

To resample an image, choose a resampling method from the appropriate option menu (either Color, Grayscale, or Monochrome Bitmap Images), and enter a resolution above which InDesign will apply resampling in the DPI field. As a rule of thumb, the resolution setting for color or grayscale images is 1.5 to 2 times the screen frequency at which the PDF file will be printed of viewed. So if the printer resolution is 2400 dpi (dots per inch) for an imagesetter and the line screen is 150 lpi (lines per inch), then you enter 300 in the DPI field. Because InDesign has a sampling threshold of 1.5, the program will not resample an image whose resolution does not exceed the value you enter by 1.5 times.

For monochrome images, the resolution that you enter should match the output device, but should not exceed 1500 dpi. Settings beyond 1500 dpi have no effect on the image other than increasing file size.

You can choose one of the following resampling methods:

Downsample To   *Downsampling* uses pixel averaging in a sample area to reduce pixel dimensions (height and width of a bitmap image), thereby reducing image file size.

Subsample To   Using a pixel in the center of the sample area and applying the specified resolution, *subsampling* replaces the sample area with the pixel. Because the selected pixel may have a different tonal setting from other pixels in the sample area, the resulting image may appear too flat and missing critical detail. Subsampling is not recommended for commercial printing applications.

No Sample Change   If you don't want to resample the images in the PDF file, select No Sampling Change from the option menu.

 WARNING   If you select Subsample To, you may lose image display when resampling monochrome images. If this happens, trash the PDF file and export the document again, but select instead either Downsample To or No Sampling Change as your setting.

Setting Image Compression

In addition to resampling, you can also apply image compression to color, grayscale, and monochrome bitmap images in order to reduce file size. When you compress color or grayscale images, your options on the Compression option menu are None, Automatic, JPEG, or Zip. (Compression methods are covered in the next section.) If you select Automatic, InDesign examines the file and determines the compression method that it will automatically apply to each image. In most cases, the results will be OK, but check the resulting PDF file to be sure.

You also choose a Quality setting when you set image compression. The quality settings for Automatic and JPEG are Minimum, Low, Medium, High, and Maximum. Automatic and Maximum are the default settings, and are used for high-resolution printing applications. Zip compression has two quality settings: 4-bit and 8-bit.

 WARNING   Don't use the 4-bit Zip compression quality setting with 8-bit image files. Data will be lost and the image will be unusable.

Your menu option choices for monochrome bitmap compression are None, CCITT Group 3, CCITT Group 4, Zip, and Run Length. These options are covered in the next section.

InDesign's Compression Methods

InDesign can apply one of the following compression methods:

Zip   Use Zip compression for image files that contain large areas of solid colors or repeating patterns. Because this method is lossless (data is not removed to reduce file size), you can choose to apply Zip compression to 2-, 4-, and 8-bit grayscale images; 4-bit color images; indexed 8-bit color images; and 16- and 24-bit color images containing contrasting colors.

JPEG   This compression method creates smaller file sizes by removing data from the file. The quality of the compressed file can be influenced by the content and color gamut of the uncompressed image. Settings may work fine in one image but not in another because of a difference in tonal range or detail. Don't apply JPEG compression in this dialog box if your PDF image files are in the JPEG file format and were previously compressed. You may end up with strange artifacts in the image that distort content.

CCITT   InDesign provides two CCITT (International Coordinating Committee for Telephony and Telegraphy) compression methods that can be used with black-and-white digital paintings or 1-bit scanned images. They are

CCITT Group 3   The monochrome bitmaps are compressed one row at a time. This is the compression method used by most fax machines. Avoid using for commercial printing applications.

CCITT Group 4   The better choice for compressing monochrome images. It's the default setting.

Run Length   If your images contain large areas of flat black or white shapes and solid lines, this lossless compression method may be a good choice.

Compressing Text and Line Art

If you want to reduce file size, click the Compress Text and Line Art checkbox. InDesign applies the Zip method of compression, which does not affect quality.

Adobe's Recommended Compression Settings

Figures 19.7 shows Adobe's recommended compression settings for high-resolution printing. These are the default settings in the Export PDF dialog box.

Figures 19.8 and 19.9 illustrate Adobe's recommended settings for on-screen viewing.

FIGURE 19.7

High-resolution compression settings

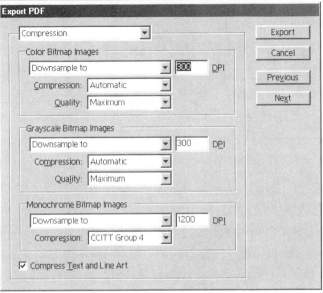

FIGURE 19.8

On-screen viewing recommended settings (PDF Options)

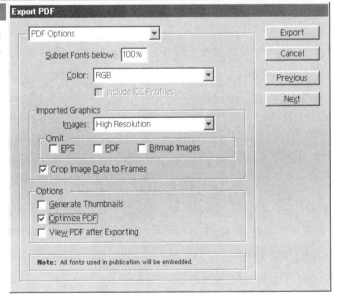

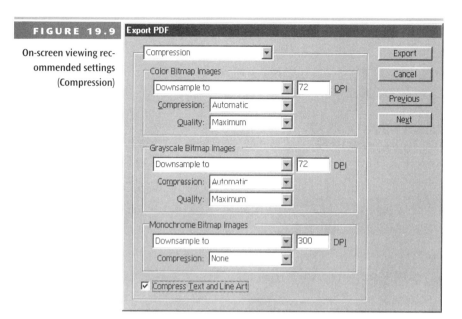

FIGURE 19.9

On-screen viewing recommended settings (Compression)

When you've completed your review or selection of options in the Compression dialog box, click Next to view the Export PDF: Pages and Page Marks dialog box.

Specifying Pages for Export

In the Export PDF: Pages and Page Marks dialog box, shown in Figure 19.10, you can select which document pages will be contained in the PDF export file. At the bottom of this dialog box are the Page Marks options that you can place on the page when printing the PDF file.

The options for assigning pages are:

All Pages Click the radio button to export a PDF file that contains all the pages of the document. This is the default setting.

Ranges Click the radio button to select this option for the current document. You can identify which range of pages are exported by typing a hyphen between page numbers such as 12-15, or by placing commas between page numbers such as 5, 12, 21.

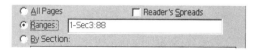

SPECIFYING PAGES FOR EXPORT   601

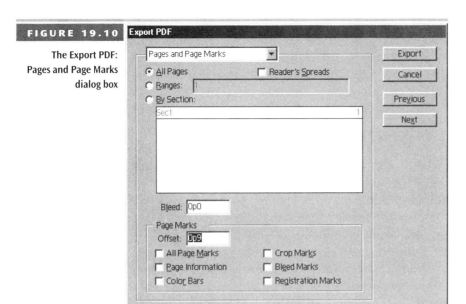

FIGURE 19.10

The Export PDF: Pages and Page Marks dialog box

By Section   This option allows you to select entire sections to export. Click the radio button to turn on the option, and click on a section name to make a selection. Press the Shift key as you click section names to make a multiple selections. To choose nonconsecutive sections, hold down the Ctrl key (Windows) or the Cmd key (Macintosh) instead during the selection process.

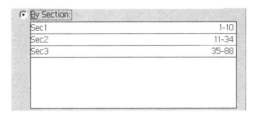

Reader's Spreads   When you want to export all the pages in the spread as if they were printed on the same sheet, choose this option. Chapter 18 has more about reader's spreads.

WARNING   Don't send reader's spreads for prepress setup or printing. Your printer cannot use these spreads for press imposition. Pages would appear in the wrong position on the press sheet.

You can also set page mark options for bleed, page mark offset, and select a variety of markings that print on the press sheet outside the boundary of the page bleed.

When you choose any of these options, the PDF file boundary increases to fit the positioning of the page marks or a specified bleed. For more information about these page mark options, see Chapter 18.

After completing your review or selection of Page and Page Marks options, click Next to view the Export PDF: Security dialog box.

Applying Security Controls

In the Export PDF: Security dialog box, shown in Figure 19.11, you can adjust the various security settings for exporting PDFs. Click the Use Security Features checkbox to activate the PDF export security control options. Adobe uses the RSA Corporation's RC4 method of security to secure PDF documents. By typing in passwords and making menu selections, you set your file access and usage restrictions.

The security settings that you choose in this dialog box only apply to the current document. This eliminates any problems with unwanted passwords and usage restrictions in other InDesign documents. However, you may have problems exporting the document correctly if you used placed PDF pages in the document. When a placed PDF has tighter security restrictions than the InDesign exported PDF document, the placed PDF file will export as a gray box. To override this problem, request the passwords for the placed PDF file. Using Adobe Acrobat 4, change the security settings to match the settings that will be assigned to the InDesign PDF export file. Substitute the modified PDF file for the originally placed PDF file.

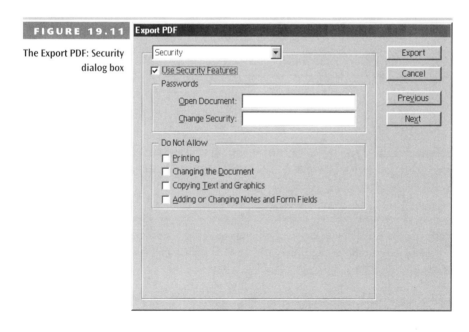

FIGURE 19.11

The Export PDF: Security dialog box

Setting Passwords and Preventing Unauthorized Usage

InDesign, like Acrobat, provides for a double password security access: *open* and *owner*. The Open Document password that you type in the menu field gives authorized users access to open the document in a PDF viewer or editor. Any restrictive features activated in the PDF Export: Security dialog box's Do Not Allow area determine the level of user access to the document.

The password you type into the Change Security menu field sets the *owner* password. Authorized users of the owner password have unrestricted access to the PDF file and can set or change security settings. When a PDF file is assigned both an open and owner password, either password can open the document. When setting passwords, it's a good idea to follow these guidelines:

- You can enter up to 32 characters to create a password, including letters, numerals, or punctuation marks.
- If you set any restrictions in the Do Not Allow area, be sure to assign an owner password. Otherwise, your restrictions can be overridden in Adobe Acrobat. If the user attempts to change the document in a PDF editor, any tools and menu items relating to the restrictive features will be dimmed (not available to use).
- *Do not* type the same password in both the Open Document and Change Security menu fields. If the passwords are the same, users with access to the open password will be able to set or change security options. Users will then gain unrestricted access to the PDF document.
- InDesign creates *no* record of any assigned passwords. Forgotten passwords cannot be recovered from the document. Always make a copy of assigned passwords and store in a secure location. Also consider storing passwords in another secure location off-site.
- When working in teams or workgroups, determine security policies and file access rights as they relate to design and production workflows. Distribute security guidelines to all members of the team.

Selecting Security Options

The options selected from the Do Not Allow area determine the level of security access for the exported PDF file. The more security options that you choose to assign to the PDF file, the more limited the user access. You can set the following security options:

Printing Selecting this option prohibits users from printing the PDF file.

Changing the Document Prevents users from making any changes to the document. Don't select this option when adding a form (in Acrobat) to the exported PDF file that users will fill in and return. If this creates a security problem, create a separate PDF file in Acrobat that contains only the form.

Copying Text and Graphics This option will prevent unauthorized copying of text and graphics to another PDF document or program file using Acrobat or a PDF editor's tools and menus.

Adding or Changing Notes and Form Fields When you want to prevent Acrobat or PDF editor users from adding or modifying notes or form fields, choose this security option.

chapter 20

EXPORTING DOCUMENTS TO THE WORLD WIDE WEB

Featuring:

- Designing for the Web   607

- Preparing documents for HTML export   611

- Setting HTML options   618

Exporting Documents to the World Wide Web

Using InDesign's Export: HTML (Hypertext Markup Language) feature, you can create HTML pages that can be published to the World Wide Web. In this chapter, I will discuss how InDesign fits into a Web page design workflow, how to prepare documents for HTML export, and how to set HTML options in the Export HTML dialog boxes. At the end of this chapter are figures that show how a sample document I exported looks when viewed with different browsers and applications. Also shown is the HTML code that InDesign generated when the document was exported.

Designing for the Web

The HTML files that you create using the Export command (File ➤ Export) can be opened in a browser, an HTML editor, or a Web site development program like Adobe GoLive. When you generate HTML pages in InDesign, keep in mind that there are limitations to what can be achieved with this feature. (More on this later in this chapter.)

Web publishing is a dynamic environment where content is updated frequently, and where the site visitor is an active participant in defining how a Web page will look on screen. Web designers determine (among other things) which graphics and other visual elements, text, and forms appear on screen when a visitor clicks different links or accesses Web page content. A print document has a defined beginning and end, but a document on the Web may be modified with a simple click of a mouse. When repurposing a printed document for the Web, consider the larger context: How can I create an integrated design solution that works well in different publishing channels? In this ever-changing environment, take some time to evaluate and plan how your InDesign documents will best fit within a print + Web publishing workflow.

For example, consider this scenario. You've designed an annual report or other document that includes many pages of financial data. It's critical that all the tabular figures, including the dollar signs, correctly align vertically when viewed on a Web page. But HTML has its limitations for defining spaces between characters, such as $525.00. And there's no avoiding the fact that a site visitor's choice of monitor, computer, operating system, browser, and browser's preferences (including default text styles) will ultimately determine how the document will appear on screen. Because the browser—and not InDesign—determines the hyphenation and justification rules, the browser and the size of the browser window controls where text lines break.

As a solution, you could publish the document as a PDF file that a visitor can download from the client's Web site and print using a desktop or network printer. Or you could divide the original document into several documents. The front section, which may include a marketing overview or letter from the management, can be exported as an HTML file. The financial data and accompanying notes are still exported as a PDF file because this will guarantee that the layout will appear and print as designed. A Web site design program or HTML editor is then used to add the other needed elements or links to publish either solution to the Web.

Using HTML

When you build a Web site, you use HTML to format text, insert images into Web pages, and define layout grids, tables, clickable image maps, horizontal lines, horizontal/vertical/block spacers, links and anchors, comments, and line breaks. HTML markup instructions are enclosed in angle brackets such as `<TITLE>wildlife</TITLE>` or `<BODY bgcolor="#FFFFFF">`. These instructions are called *tags*.

In the first example above, the tag tells the browser to display the text "wildlife" in the browser's title bar. The second example tells the browser that the text color is white. The #FFFFFF is an example of hexadecimal code, which is used in HTML to describe color. (There is more about Web color and hexadecimal code in the "Converting from Print to Web Colors" section later in this chapter.)

Text that appears formatted in your browser must be enclosed between the *start tag* `<TITLE>` and the *end tag* `</TITLE>`. You can tell the difference between the pair of tags by looking for the "/" that always appears in an end tag. A basic HTML page includes a title <TITLE>, which appears in the browser's title bar, a header <HEAD>, and a body text section <BODY>. In this basic structure only the contents between the <BODY> tags will appear on the Web page. The text in the header section is invisible. The header can contain information or comments about how the HTML code was generated and what Cascading Style Sheets, if any, were used. (See the next section for more information on Cascading Style Sheets.)

You don't format text in HTML as you would text in a traditional print document, i.e., by specifying a font in an exact point size. Instead, you specify different levels in a hierarchy, such as <H1> for a main (first-level) header, through <H6> for the smallest subheader.

Using Cascading Style Sheets and Other Web Design Tools

If you look at the InDesign-generated HTML code at the end of this chapter, you'll notice that it contains Cascading Style Sheets (CSS-1). InDesign supports the HTML 4 standard, which is why the document contains Cascading Style Sheets specifications. Cascading Style Sheets are a standard developed by the World Wide Web Consortium (see the sidebar below), in an effort to provide Web developers with tools to improve Web design and make it easier to describe the overall layout of a Web page when viewed with different browsers. CSS-1 consists of style definitions or style rules that apply to specific page elements or entire pages. It's identified within the <STYLE> tag, as shown in the following example: <STYLE type="text/css">. Browsers that support the CSS-1 standard include Microsoft Internet Explorer 3 and 4, and Netscape's Navigator 4 and Communicator 4. Even if a browser supports the standard, however—each browser still has its own idiosyncrasies—there is no guarantee that your Web page will look the same when viewed with different browsers (see Figures 20.21–20.25).

Some of the other tools that you can use to build a Web site include:

- JavaScript, a scripting language used to define advanced tags for specifying flashing buttons, button rollovers, and hit counters
- Java Applets, which can be used to add, among other things, interactivity or animations to a Web site
- Plug-ins, such as Macromedia Shockwave for viewing animations or Acrobat Reader for viewing PDF files
- Dynamic HTML, whose basic objects include date and time stamps, button images, URL popup, and action items

For a more detailed discussion about Web site design, HTML, and other Web-related topics, check out the following Sybex titles:

- *Mastering HTML 4 Premium Edition*, by Deborah S. Ray and Eric J. Ray
- *Mastering Photoshop 5 for the Web*, by Matt Straznitskas
- *The Complete Website Upgrade and Maintenance Guide*, by Lisa Schmeiser
- *Mastering JavaScript and JScript*, by James Jaworski

Setting Web Standards

Since its founding in October 1994, the World Wide Web Consortium (W3C) has been providing leadership in the development of common protocols that promote the full potential of the Web. The W3C is an international industry consortium with more than 330 member organizations. The W3C is jointly hosted by the Massachusetts Institute of Technology Laboratory for Computer Science (MIT/LCS) in the United States; the Institut National de Recherché en Informatique et en Automatique (INRIA) in Europe; and the Keio University Shonan Fujisawa Campus in Japan. Tim Berners-Lee, creator of the Web, is the Consortium's director, and Jean-François Abramatic is the chairman.

The W3C provides a repository of information about the Web for developers and users, reference code implementations to embody and promote standards, and various prototype and sample applications to demonstrate use of new technology. The Consortium also issues technical reports with specifications that include recommendations, working drafts, and notes.

You'll find a wealth of information at the W3C Web site about user interface domain issues including standards regarding HTML, Style Sheets (both CSS and XSL), Synchronized Multimedia, and Graphics. You may want to closely follow XSL development and its application by browser developers. Extensible Stylesheet Language (XSL) is a language for expressing stylesheets, and is currently integrated into Internet Explorer 5's Microsoft XML (Extensible Markup Language) processor. Other topics of interest to designers include electronic commerce, privacy, and the Web Accessibility Initiative. As designers, you may want to pay particular attention to the Web Accessibility Initiative (WAI), which the W3C is developing in coordination with industry, disability organizations, research centers, and governmental agencies. WAI's goal is to reduce the barriers on the Web for people with visual, hearing, physical, and cognitive disabilities.

The World Wide Web Consortium (W3C) Web site address is www.w3.org.

Preparing Documents for HTML Export

Before exporting a document to HTML, you should save a copy of the document. Select File ➢ Save a Copy, or type Ctrl+Alt+S (Windows) or Opt+Cmd+S (Macintosh). Give the file a new name. You may want to set up a naming convention for your records or file library that helps identify those documents that are the source for the HTML files. It will make them easier to track later if you need to update or modify the documents.

Close the original document file. Select File ➢ Open, or press Ctrl+O (Windows) or Cmd+O (Macintosh) to access the Open a File dialog box. Select the copy of the document you created, and click OK. Now you prepare this document for exporting to HTML. Here's a list of tasks that you may have to do, before you begin the export process in InDesign.

Document Dimensions and Page Layout   Before exporting to HTML, consider how the document will be viewed from a browser. Will a document page be seen on a full-size Web page (1:1), or will it instead be placed into a frame whose dimensions are smaller than a full-size Web page? (Browser windows can be subdivided into several independent windows or frames.) If you're using frames in your Web site, determine what percentage of the document first appears in its frame and how much scrolling is needed both horizontally and vertically to read the document. If it's hard to follow the content, you may have to change the document's dimensions and reorganize the page layout before exporting to HTML.

NOTE   Document management is covered in Chapter 16.

Fonts   Identify all fonts in use in headlines. If it's important to maintain a specific font style, size, and text color, (and avoid browser font substitutions), then create each head in an image-editing program as a GIF file. Swap these GIF files in the document for its corresponding headline text. You'll also need to do this if you want anti-aliased text. *Anti-aliased text* appears smooth-edged on-screen because averaged pixels were added to the edge of each text character. The averaged pixels are calculated from the color of the text and the background. InDesign does not create anti-aliased text from outlines when exporting documents to HTML.

TIP When you create anti-aliased text headings in an image editing program, make sure that the background color is the same color as the Web page background or graphic that the text will appear in front of. Otherwise, your anti-aliased text will have an annoying halo. You can, if necessary, set the background color to be transparent when exporting the image file to GIF.

Text Underlined text is used to identify links on a Web page. For any body text that will be a link in the HTML document, change the font style to underline. Use the Type tool to select the text copy. Then choose Underline from the Character palette menu. For faster productivity, use the shortcut Shift+Ctrl+U (Windows) or Shift+Cmd+U (Macintosh) to apply underline to the selected text. You may want to change the text color, too. It's easier to identify a text link if its color is different from the surrounding text. See the next section to learn more about Web color.

You will need to resolve any problems with missing fonts, keep violations, and H&J violations before exporting the document to HTML. Otherwise, the pink and yellow colors used to highlight these problems in the InDesign document may appear in the HTML file. This is particularly a problem when a text frame that has been rotated or otherwise transformed is exported (transformed text frames are converted to a GIF file). If you cannot resolve the problem before exporting, then *dis*able the Highlight options in the Preferences: Composition dialog box (File ➢ Preferences ➢ Composition).

WARNING Text frames should not be grouped if you want the resulting HTML text to be searched and edited.

WARNING Don't use paragraph rules below text to identify links. Paragraph rules are lost when the document is exported to HTML.

Images If you're using CMYK or separated image files, remove these files from your document and substitute JPEG files that are in sRGB color mode. *sRGB* was developed as color standard for Windows-based computers. Although its color gamut cannot render as many different tonal variations of colors as other RGB models like Adobe RGB (1998), it's become the best choice for cross-platform Web authoring. When viewed on the Web, sRGB images appear brighter and have better contrast than images assigned other RGB color models. CYMK files do not translate well and image quality will be poor when viewed in a browser. Don't convert the CMYK file back to RGB. The results will be unsatisfactory, because RGB has a larger color gamut. Rather begin with a LAB or RGB image file and convert to sRGB.

NOTE Chapter 6 reviews graphics basics.

Check the file sizes of all images and other artwork. You'll want to use the smallest possible file size while still optimizing image quality. Keep in mind that Web images are seen at screen or low resolution (72 or 96 dpi). High-resolution image files needed for print applications are overkill on the Web. In addition, visitors to your designed Web pages will be turned off if image downloads times are too slow. To batch process image files for the Web, consider using Adobe ImageReady 2 (Windows and Macintosh), or Equilibrium DeBabelizer Pro 4.5 (Windows) or DeBabelizer 3 (Macintosh).

NOTE See the "Converting Graphics in Your HTML File" section later in this chapter for more details on how InDesign exports different image file formats.

Animations You can place animated GIFs in an InDesign document. Before exporting to HTML, position any animation that you'd like to view on a Web page.

WARNING Grouped objects are converted to GIF or JPEG files. You should ungroup objects when those image formats are not the right specification. Check each ungrouped object to determine if you need to re-create any of them in an image editing program.

Converting from Print to Web Colors

Before exporting a document to HTML, it's a good idea to convert your solid print-based colors (other than black or white) to the nearest Web color library swatch. Doing this conversion will allow your document's colors to be displayed consistently across Windows and Macintosh systems. To convert from print to Web-safe colors, do the following:

1. If they're not already in view, open the Swatches and Color palettes. Also select the Web color option from the Swatches Library menu list. After InDesign loads

the Web color swatches, the palette tab will be labeled "Web." (Chapter 12 reviews Color and Swatch palette basics.) InDesign's Web palette is consistent with Photoshop and Illustrator's Web-safe color palette.

2. In the Swatches palette, select the color swatch that will be edited. In Figure 20.1, Trumatch color 1-a5 was selected as the example.

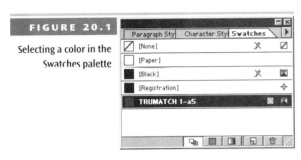

FIGURE 20.1

Selecting a color in the Swatches palette

3. Next, select RGB from the Color palette menu. You'll now see the RGB values for the CMYK Trumatch color.

4. In the Web color library palette, scroll down until you find the nearest RGB value to the selected print-based color. As shown in Figure 20.2, you can see a comparison of the RGB value of the existing color in the Color palette and its nearest Web color. In the Web color palette, double-click the Web color to place the swatch in the Swatches palette.

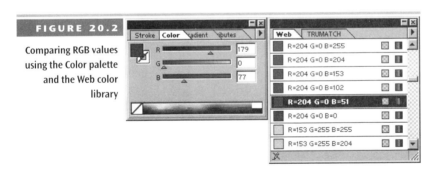

FIGURE 20.2

Comparing RGB values using the Color palette and the Web color library

You may notice that the same numbers are used over and over again as the color values in Figure 20.2. This is because Web-safe palette colors are represented in RGB color mode using combinations of the following values: 0, 51, 102, 153, 204, and 255. Each Web color corresponds to a specific hexadecimal code used to describe color in HTML. There's more about Web color and hexadecimal codes in the "Formatting Your InDesign HTML File" section later in this chapter.

 TIP If your document will be distributed via both print and the Web, do a color test early in the concept stage to pick the optimal color palette for both distribution channels. Keep in mind that substituting colors can greatly alter the appearance of a document. Check out the colors used in Figure 20.2 on your own machine. Comparing these two colors clearly demonstrates the problems when selecting a Web color palette for your document late in the production process. It's hard to find a close color match that will maintain the overall color appearance of a document.

5. Select the original color (Trumatch 1-a5 in my example). Choose Delete Swatch from the Swatches palette menu.

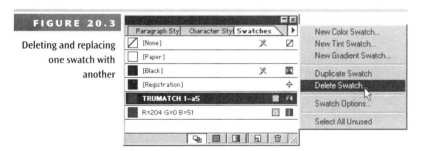

FIGURE 20.3

Deleting and replacing one swatch with another

6. In the Delete Swatch dialog box, select the Defined Swatch option and the Web color (labeled using its RGB values) from the drop-down menu list. Click OK. This action will globally replace the original print-based color with the new Web-safe color. (Ignore the Out-of-Gamut warning that appears in the Delete Swatch dialog box. It's for CMYK applications.) See Figure 20.4 to see the final result: the new list of swatches in the Swatches palette.

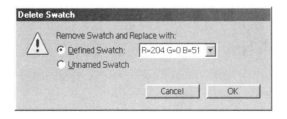

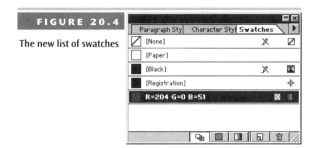

FIGURE 20.4
The new list of swatches

Naming Your HTML File

Even if you're using the Macintosh version of InDesign, you should follow these file naming conventions:

- Limit filenames to no more than eight characters, and follow the filename with a file extension. This will enable your files to work correctly with UNIX servers and networking software that shorten or truncate long filenames.

- The file extension for HTML files is .html or .htm. Check with the Web server or network administrator to determine which extension they recommend that you use. (The Windows version of InDesign automatically adds .html to the filename.)

- Because some browsers cannot recognize path names that include special characters like question marks (?), asterisks (*), or spaces between the letters in a filename, avoid using them in filenames. Refer to an HTML editing guide for more information about file naming conventions.

WARNING Before exporting to HTML, make sure that paragraph and style names consist solely of the characters a–z or A–Z (no bullet points). Otherwise, you may have a problem with some browsers correctly recognizing the style name. If that happens, the browser's default style is applied instead of your specified style.

InDesign Attributes Kept When Exporting to HTML

When InDesign exports a document to HTML, the following document attributes are retained in the HTML file:

Character specifications:
- Font style
- Font size

- Leading
- Underline
- Strikethrough
- Font color

NOTE Don't forget to test your Web pages using different browsers. Although InDesign may retain the attribute, the browser may not recognize and display that attribute correctly. You may have to edit the HTML to restore the attribute to the Web page.

Paragraph specifications:
- Alignment
- Indents
- Space before and space after paragraphs

InDesign Attributes Lost When Exporting to HTML

The following InDesign document attributes are *not* retained when you export your document to HTML. Use an HTML editor to fix problems with positioning of text and to add rules to your HTML file.

- Baseline shift
- Ligatures
- Old Style attributes
- Tracking
- Kerning
- Paragraph rules (both above and below)
- Hyphenation and Justification (H&J)
- No-break settings
- Keep Options
- Tab positions

NOTE The browser controls where hyphenation and justification line breaks occur. If flow of text is critical for presenting the content, consider saving the document as a PDF file that you upload to the Web site.

Converting Text to a GIF File

If you want to use text that has nonstandard attributes, set the export HTML formatting option to Maintain Non-Standard Text. (See the next section in this chapter.) If you need anti-aliased text, re-create the text as a GIF file in a program like Photoshop. Then, replace the InDesign nonstandard text with its graphics version before exporting to HTML.

The nonstandard text attributes are:

- Text with gradient applied
- Frame background
- Frame stroke
- Text containing inline graphics
- Text in a nonrectangular, skewed, rotated, or scaled frame

Setting HTML Options

After you've prepared your document for export to HTML, you're ready to start the export process. To export an InDesign document to HTML, do the following:

1. Select File ≻ Export, or press Ctrl+E (Windows) or Cmd+E (Macintosh). The Export dialog box opens, as shown in Figures 20.5 and 20.6.

2. Choose HTML from the Save as Type (Windows) or Formats (Macintosh) option menus.

3. Type a filename of no more than eight characters with no special characters or spaces between the letters. Select a location and file folder where you plan to store the HTML file and its image files. If you're a Macintosh user, remember to add the file extension to the filename.

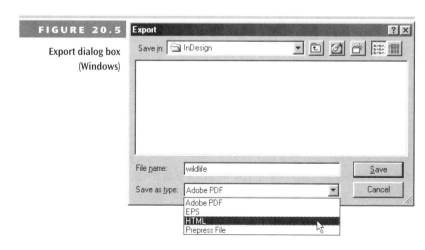

FIGURE 20.5

Export dialog box (Windows)

SETTING HTML OPTIONS 619

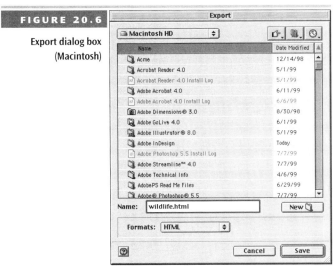

FIGURE 20.6

Export dialog box (Macintosh)

4. Click Save. The Export HTML dialog box opens, as shown in Figure 20.7. You're now ready to choose your export options.

To navigate through the Export HTML dialog boxes, click the Previous or Next buttons or select one of the following from the drop-down menu: Documents, Formatting, Layout, or Graphics.

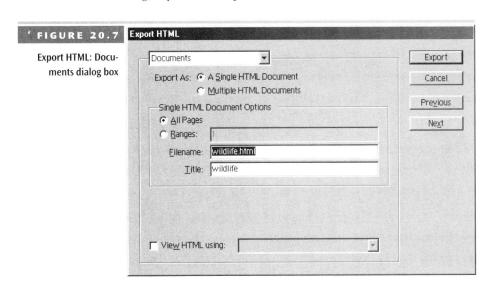

FIGURE 20.7

Export HTML: Documents dialog box

Choosing Your Document Export Options

The options that are set in the Export HTML: Documents dialog box will affect the entire document. You can choose to export a document as either a single HTML document or as multiple HTML documents. If you have a multi-page InDesign document, and use the Single HTML Document default setting, you will create only one Web page that runs on endlessly. (Each document page displayed by the browser is separated by a rule.) It is not recommended that you use this setting for a document with a range of pages. Instead, you should click the radio button next to the Multiple HTML Document listing and activate the option. The dialog box changes as shown in Figure 20.8.

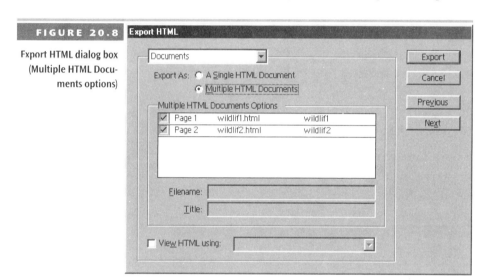

FIGURE 20.8

Export HTML dialog box (Multiple HTML Documents options)

In the Multiple HTML Documents Options box, you'll see an individual HTML file for each page in the document. InDesign's default naming convention for HTML files in the list is based on the filename you assigned when saving the HTML file. InDesign applies a number at the end of the filename that corresponds to the source document's page numbering. As you can see in Figure 20.8, the filename with the added number still equals only eight characters. The "e" was dropped from the name to compensate for the added numeral. Using a numbering sequence as part of the filename helps to track pages when placed on the Web server. It's a quick way to identify if content is missing or out of sequence. If you would like to modify the list you can do any of the following:

Remove a page The checkbox to the left of the page number is a toggle switch. If the checkbox is empty, the page is removed from the list (the listing is still visible). Click the box again to restore the HTML page to the list.

Change the filename and title   To modify the HTML filename and title, select the page by clicking on the listing. The name and title will appear in the Filename and Title boxes below the page list. You can now enter or edit the filename and title. To avoid confusion later when working with the files, use a filename and title that are similar.

A navigation bar is added to your Web pages when you Export as Multiple HTML Documents (see Figure 20.9). You set the placement of the navigation bar in the Export HTML: Layout dialog box. (See Figure 20.18 later in this chapter.) If you want to use a different navigational element, you will have to edit the HTML document.

FIGURE 20.9
Multiple document navigation bar

Viewing Your HTML File

It's often a good idea to view your new HTML file immediately after you export it. To do so, simply select the View HTML Using option in the HTML Export: Documents dialog box. Then choose a browser or HTML editing program from the View HTML Using option menu. (InDesign will automatically list your computer's default browser.) After you click the Export button in the dialog box, the HTML document is displayed automatically using the browser or HTML editing program that you selected. As you can see in Figure 20.10, the Windows version of InDesign lists all browsers and other HTML programs by their filename followed by the .exe file extension. InDesign's Macintosh version lists browsers and other applications by the program name, as shown in Figure 20.11.

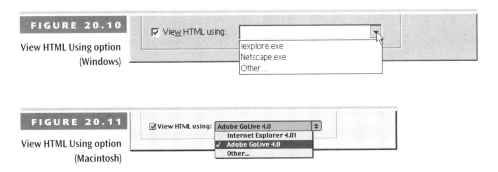

FIGURE 20.10
View HTML Using option (Windows)

FIGURE 20.11
View HTML Using option (Macintosh)

If you'd like to assign another browser or HTML editor to the View HTML Using option menu, select Other from the menu list. This opens the Locate Browser dialog box. On the Windows platform, do the following:

1. Locate and select the .exe file of the browser or program you want to assign to the View HTML Using list.

2. Click Open to assign the program to the View HTML Using option menu. InDesign automatically returns to the Export HTML: Document dialog box. Figure 20.12 shows how the .exe file for FrontPage Express was located in the Program Files/FrontPage Express/Bin folder.

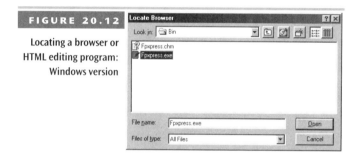

FIGURE 20.12

Locating a browser or HTML editing program: Windows version

On the Macintosh platform, do the following:

1. Locate the folder of the program or browser you want to add to the View HTML Using menu list. Select the program name or icon.

2. Click Open to assign your selection to the list. InDesign automatically returns to the Export HTML: Document dialog box. Figure 20.13 shows Adobe GoLive 4 selected.

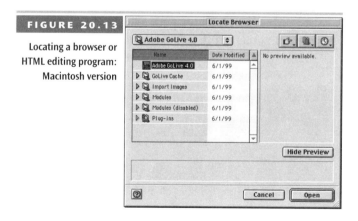

FIGURE 20.13

Locating a browser or HTML editing program: Macintosh version

Formatting Your InDesign HTML File

The Export HTML: Formatting dialog box shown in Figure 20.14 allows you to set options for text and page backgrounds.

FIGURE 20.14

Export HTML: Formatting dialog box

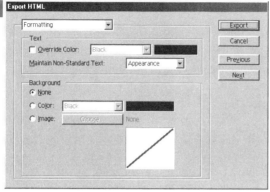

Setting Text Options

The Maintain Non-Standard Text option menu offers two settings for formatting text in your HTML file: Appearance (default) and Editability. If you select Appearance, InDesign will convert text to a graphics file. (Attributes that apply are listed in the "Converting Text to a GIF File" section earlier in this chapter.) The resulting graphics file will retain the visual appearance of the original text (no anti-aliasing), but you will not be able to edit the text. On the other hand, choosing Editability will allow editing of the text, but attributes such as gradient applied or skewing will be lost. You should remember that this option applies only to InDesign text composition and not to any typographic elements that you may have imported from programs like Illustrator. (How placed graphics are managed is set in the Export HTML: Graphics dialog box, discussed in the "Converting Graphics in your HTML File" section later in this chapter.)

When you select the Override Color checkbox, you can choose one color to replace all the text color specified in your document with the following exception: Text created using nonstandard text attributes, which may become a graphic (GIF file) in the HTML conversion process, are not affected by the Override Color option. The nonstandard text will retain the original specified color.

T I P Use the Override Color of text with caution. If you want to replace several text colors consistently throughout the document, consider using the technique described in the "Converting from Print to Web Colors" section earlier in this chapter.

If you decide to use the Override Color option, you can select a Web-safe color from the option menu or double-click the color box to open a color picker. Choosing Custom from the option menu (at the bottom of the list) also opens the color picker. (See Table 20.1 in the "Setting Background Options" section later in this chapter for a listing of the RGB values and the hexadecimal code for all the color names in the Override Color option menu.)

TIP If the Override Color or Background Color option is selected and the option menu is still not accessible, try deselecting the color option and selecting it again.

Using the Color Picker

The Windows and Macintosh versions of InDesign use different color pickers. Here's how to use each one.

Windows To create a new color using the color picker, click on an empty Custom colors box or on an existing Custom color as seen in Figure 20.15. (If all the Custom Colors boxes are defined, the Define Custom Colors button is unavailable as an option.) When this happens, you can define a custom Web-safe color by typing values (0, 51, 102, 153, 204, or 255 only) in the Red, Green, and Blue boxes. Then click Add to Custom Colors. Click OK to make the new Web-safe color the selection and to return to the Export HTML: Formatting dialog box. Continue to choose or review your HTML export specifications.

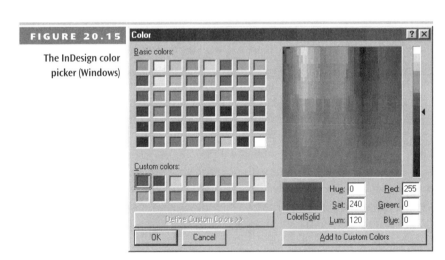

FIGURE 20.15

The InDesign color picker (Windows)

Macintosh The color picker available in the Macintosh version of InDesign, shown in Figure 20.16, offers an easier-to-use interface for creating a new Web-safe color. From the scroll-down menu on the left, choose the HTML Picker. In the HTML Picker, turn on the Snap to Web color option by clicking on the box next to the option listing. To change colors, move any or all of the sliders bars for R: (Red), G: (Green), or B: (Blue). The picker shows the Original and New color, as well as the HTML hexadecimal code for the new color. After creating the color you'd like to use, click OK to apply the new color and to return to the Export HTML: Formatting dialog box. Continue to choose or review your HTML export specifications.

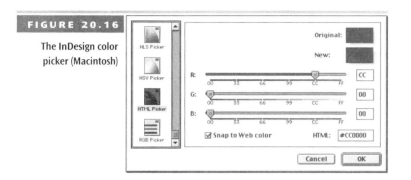

FIGURE 20.16

The InDesign color picker (Macintosh)

Setting Background Options

In the Export HTML: Formatting dialog box, you have three choices for specifying the background of your Web page. You can select one of the following by clicking its radio button:

None   This is the default option. When selected, the background of your Web page defaults to the preferences set in the site visitor's browser.

Color   You can assign a Web-safe color as your Web page background. To select the color, use the same process as described in the previous section for the Override Color option. See Table 20.1 below for a listing of the RGB values and the hexadecimal code for all the color names listed in the Background: Color option menu.

Image   InDesign allows you to assign a graphic to tile as a textured background for your Web page. When you want to assign a graphic to a background, click the Choose button to open an Image File dialog box. (The Files of Type option defaults to GIF Files in the Windows version of InDesign.) Select a GIF file that you'd like to use, and then click Open to automatically apply the graphic as the HTML document's background. As shown in Figure 20.17, the word "None" (to the right of the Choose button) changed to the filename and file extension of the applied graphic, and the red diagonal line was replaced by a thumbnail of the graphic in the Image box.

TIP To create faster download times of your Web page background image, set your graphic's dimensions to about 96 x 96 pixels at 72 dpi.

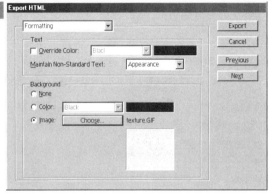

FIGURE 20.17

The updated Export HTML: Formatting dialog box

TABLE 20.1: RGB AND HEXADECIMAL VALUES FOR CUSTOM COLORS

Custom Color	Red, Green, Blue (RGB)	Hexadecimal Code
Red	255, 0, 0	FF0000
Cherry Red	204, 0, 0	CC0000
Peach	255, 204, 153	FFCC99
Dusty Rose	204, 153, 153	CC9999
Maroon	153, 51, 153	993399
Orange	255, 153, 0	FF9900
Mustard	255, 204, 0	FFCC00
Yellow	255, 255, 0	FFFF00
Gold	204, 204, 0	CCCC00
Olive Green	102, 102, 0	666600
Lime	0, 255, 0	00FF00
Green	0, 204, 0	00CC00
Forest Green	0, 102, 51	006633
Teal Green	0, 102, 102	006666
Ocean Blue	0, 102, 153	006699
Turquoise	0, 153, 153	009999
Cyan	0, 255, 255	00FFFF
Blue	0, 0, 255	0000FF

Continued on next page

TABLE 20.1: RGB AND HEXADECIMAL VALUES FOR CUSTOM COLORS (continued)

Custom Color	Red, Green, Blue (RGB)	Hexadecimal Code
Royal Blue	0, 0, 153	000099
Sky Blue	204, 255, 255	CCFFFF
Violet	153, 102, 255	9966FF
Dark Purple	102, 0, 102	660066
Magenta	255, 0, 255	FF00FF
Beige	204, 204, 153	CCCC99
White	255, 255, 255	FFFFFF
Light Gray	204, 204, 204	CCCCCC
Dark Gray	102, 102, 102	666666
Black	0, 0, 0	000000

As you look at Table 20.1, keep in mind that hexadecimal codes contain zeros and not capital "O"s. Avoid typing a capital "O" when specifying a color in HTML. Hexadecimal codes are described using combinations of CC, FF, and numerals: 00, 33, 66, 99.

Specifying Your HTML File Layout

The Export HTML: Layout dialog box options, shown in Figure 20.18, are for setting the page layout specifications of your Web page, including the margins and navigation bar (if needed). Each option offers the following choices:

Positioning   The default setting is Best (CSS-1). (CSS or Cascading Style Sheets are discussed at the beginning of this chapter.) If you select None, or if the browser used to view your Web page does not support HTML 4 and the CSS standard, the HTML document that InDesign generates will present the content as one continuous column of information (see Figure 20.27). Even if a browser supports the CSS standard, there is no guarantee that the Web page will be viewed as designed (see Figures 20.24–20.25).

InDesign Margins   You can choose to set your Web page margins to match its source InDesign document. Select Maintain, the default setting, if you want this layout specification. When you choose None, the browser of the site visitor will apply its own default margins to your Web page.

NOTE   If your document is used within a Web site that you did not design, check with the Webmaster to determine if there are design standards that you need to follow. You may have to reset your document's margins to match the Web site's existing pages.

Navigation Bar This is where you turn on and set the placement of the navigation links for Multiple HTML files (specified in the Export HTML: Document dialog box). The links are shown as the words "Next" and "Previous." (See Figure 20.9.) You can position the navigation bar at the Top, Bottom, or Both on the Web page. To change the style of the navigation bar, you'll need to open the HTML files in an HTML editing program. If there is another navigation bar that you plan to add later using the HTML editing program, select None. InDesign will forego the creation of a navigation bar when you export the document.

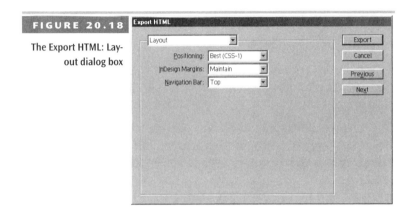

FIGURE 20.18

The Export HTML: Layout dialog box

Converting Graphics in Your HTML File

When exporting to HTML, you decide how InDesign will manage your document's graphics and/or images in the Export HTML: Graphics dialog box, shown in Figure 20.19. The settings are for Save Image As, Use Images Sub-Folder, Palette, Color Depth, Interlace, Image Quality, and Format Method.

WARNING A cropped image which appears on only one page but is specified to span multiple pages (part of the image is hidden by the frame) will not export correctly to HTML. Before exporting, open the image in Photoshop or another image editing program and crop to the exact size needed. Replace the original version of the image in the InDesign document and then export to HTML.

Converting Image Formats to GIF or JPEG

When setting your Save Images As preference (Automatic, GIF, or JPEG), consider the following information about how InDesign's conversion algorithm manages image files in the document. Keep in mind that GIF, animated GIF, JPEG, and PNG are the image formats supported by HTML.

SETTING HTML OPTIONS

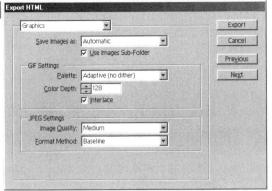

FIGURE 20.19

The Export HTML: Graphics dialog box

When you choose Automatic, InDesign normally exports RGB, CMYK, LAB, and grayscale images as JPEGs. But if the image has any of the following specifications, it is exported as a GIF instead:

- Transparency or assumed transparency via an alpha channel
- A linked image already in GIF format
- Black and white image with 1 bit/pixel (assumed transparency)
- Images that were cropped, skewed, or rotated (an implied transparency)
- Placed PDF, EPS, DCS, WMF, or PICT files
- Graphics containing splines (circle, rectangle, lines, etc.)
- Rasterized image containing text

NOTE The conversion algorithm is not foolproof. There may be an alpha channel that doesn't cause transparency, but Adobe wanted to be sure that if an image has transparency it's not exported as a JPEG file. JPEG images partially hidden from view by the frame are considered cropped, and will be exported as a GIF file.

WARNING When exporting to HTML and using Best (CSS-1) as your positioning Layout setting, InDesign may create 1K GIF files for images that don't exist. These files can be removed from the HTML document.

Some other things to consider are:

- Indexed-color images are converted to GIF.
- Nonstandard text is converted to GIF. Nonstandard text with inline images is converted to JPEG.
- With any of the settings selected (Automatic, GIF, or JPEG), linked images already saved as GIF or JPEG with a resolution of 72 dpi are exported without

conversion. Because of this option, any GIF animations or GIFs with transparency applied will be retained. InDesign will not add any additional lossy compression to JPEG files that have these specifications.

- If you select the GIF or JPEG setting, then GIF, JPEG, or PNG files that have embedded images are converted to your chosen setting.

If you choose the Use Images Sub-Folder option, InDesign creates and places the converted images into a new subfolder within the HTML file folder when you export to HTML. If you deselect the option, InDesign will place the image files in the same folder as the HTML file.

Setting Your GIF File Options

You can set the following options for your GIF files:

Palette Pick the option that will manage the color in your GIF files. Choose one of the following, but keep in mind that you're working to optimize image quality while minimizing download times. GIF files can contain a maximum of 256 colors, which are in the Indexed Color palette. Don't confuse the Indexed Color palette with the Web-safe color palette. The Web palette has a maximum of 216 colors (system colors common to both Windows and Macintosh computers).

- **Adaptive (No Dither)** This option creates a representative sample of colors in the file without using dithering (simulation of additional colors using existing colors in the file). This is the default option applied to GIF files exported using the Automatic setting. Use this option when converting images that have more than 256 colors.

- **Web** Use for graphics where there are solid colors in the image, such as logos, line drawings, or cartoons. The colors in this palette are a subset of the Windows and Mac OS system colors and are common to both palettes.

- **Exact** Apply this setting when graphics contain less than 256 colors. Use Exact instead of the Web palette to create smaller file sizes.

- **System (Win) or System (Mac)** Not recommended as a palette selection. Because the system palettes are not the same, using either setting will create color distortions in your image files when viewed on the other system using an 8-bit display.

TIP When you're not sure which setting will work best, use an image-editing program to create sample test files applying the InDesign options. This will help you to set a standard for your images or graphics. If you're using a variety of image files that require different palette settings, consider editing the files in your image editing program and then placing them in the document. Remember that the files must be 72 dpi if you want them exported without conversion by InDesign.

Color Depth This option can be used only with the Adaptive or Exact color palettes. You can specify the maximum number of colors allowed for each GIF file when you export to HTML (up to 256). It is not recommended that you adjust color depth to a lower setting when converting a variety of image files. You may find that the results are unsatisfactory. If you want to adjust color depth, you'll find better results when you edit using Photoshop or another image editing program. This will allow you to adjust for the best presentation of image content at viewing size.

Interlace When this option is chosen, GIF images will display gradually in increasing detail as the images files download to the site visitor's Web browser.

Setting Your JPEG File Options

You can globally set the JPEG options for each image in your HTML file. Your Image Quality options are Low, Medium, High, or Maximum. The lower the image quality the smaller the file size. Medium is the default setting.

The Format Method option you select—either Progressive or Baseline—controls how quickly the JPEG file downloads to the browser. If you choose Progressive, the JPEG files will gradually display in the browser. It's better to choose Baseline because Progressive files are slightly larger and require more RAM on your site visitor's computer. If they have not allocated enough RAM to their browser, you may crash the browser. Baseline JPEG images display a placeholder on the Web page until the entire JPEG file has completely downloaded from the Web server.

NOTE There's more about JPEG files in Chapters 1 and 8.

Exporting Your Document

Once you've prepared your document in InDesign and set all your layout options, the lion's share of your work is done. Just click Export in the Export HTML dialog box and your InDesign document will be exported as a Web page. The resulting HTML document and its image files are placed in the folder that you specified in the Export dialog box. (See Figures 20.5 and 20.6.)

Keep in mind that InDesign can create HTML documents, but to actually publish those documents on the Web and make them available to Web browsers, you have to place those documents on a Web server.

NOTE Unfortunately, the InDesign-to-HTML process is a one-way street: there is no HTML Import filter in InDesign.

Checking Your Files after Exporting to HTML

To fully test Web pages created by InDesign, install as many different browsers as you can on your computer. It's important to test all Web pages before uploading the files to the Web server. You should also run tests by downloading the pages from the Web server using different browsers. You'll want to do some quality control checks on the coding, links, and download times for each browser, and discover if any artwork or other content is missing, of poor quality, or incorrectly positioned.

Figure 20.20 shows the sample InDesign file used to create the HTML examples that appear in the rest of this section. The default settings I used included setting Layout Positioning to the Cascading Style Sheet option (CSS-1) and the Save Images As option to Automatic.

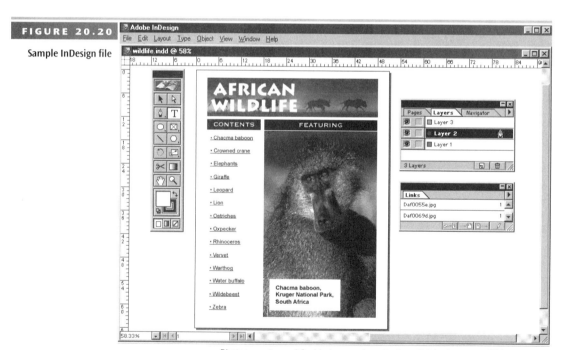

FIGURE 20.20

Sample InDesign file

Photos courtesy of Corbis Images (royalty-free division) www.corbisimages.com

The following figures show sample results when viewed with different browser and HTML editing programs (using default settings).

Figures 20.21 and 20.22 show the HTML document viewed using Internet Explorer 4 on a Windows 98 machine. The resulting HTML file most accurately displays the original InDesign document, which was created using the same computer system.

CHECKING YOUR FILES AFTER EXPORTING TO HTML 633

FIGURE 20.21

The top of the HTML file viewed using Internet Explorer 4

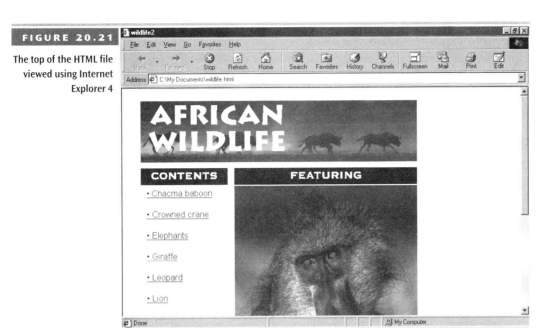

Photos courtesy of Corbis Images (royalty-free division) www.corbisimages.com

FIGURE 20.22

The bottom half of the HTML page viewed using Internet Explorer 4

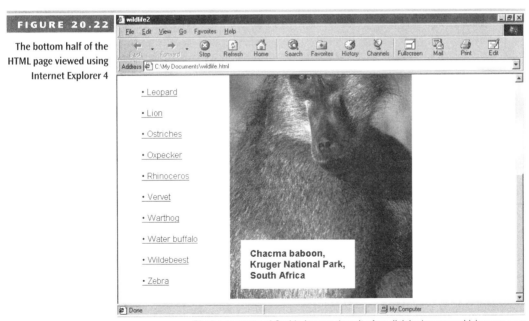

Photos courtesy of Corbis Images (royalty-free division) www.corbisimages.com

NOTE   The main heading text in Figure 20.21 is not anti-aliased.

TIP Because of features that your Web site may offer, you can recommend to visitors that they use a specific browser or plug-in when viewing the Web site. If you do make a recommendation, provide a link to a Web page where visitors can download the browser or plugin (if needed).

Figure 20.23 shows the HTML page with the source code displayed in the Notepad window. To display source code in Internet Explorer 4, select View ➢ Source. Notepad opens and displays the code for the HTML file. At the end of this chapter you can see all the code that appeared in the Notepad window.

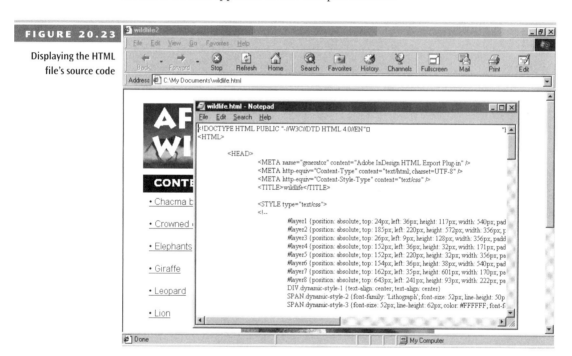

FIGURE 20.23

Displaying the HTML file's source code

Figures 20.24 and 20.25 show the HTML page when viewed with Netscape Navigator 4 on a Windows 98 computer. Notice the problems with maintaining the text attributes for leading in both the main headline and the list of animal names.

WARNING Netscape 4–4.5.1 (Macintosh) displays the Netscape preferences default font rather than the fonts you specified in the InDesign HTML file. This problem may or may not be fixed in later versions of Netscape.

CHECKING YOUR FILES AFTER EXPORTING TO HTML   635

FIGURE 20.24

Viewing the top half of the HTML file with Netscape Navigator 4

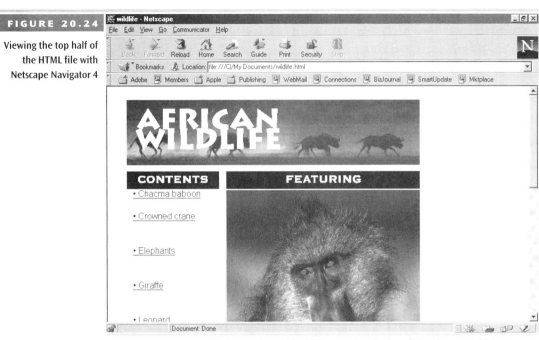

Photos courtesy of Corbis Images (royalty-free division) www.corbisimages.com

FIGURE 20.25

Viewing the bottom half of the HTML file with Netscape Navigator 4

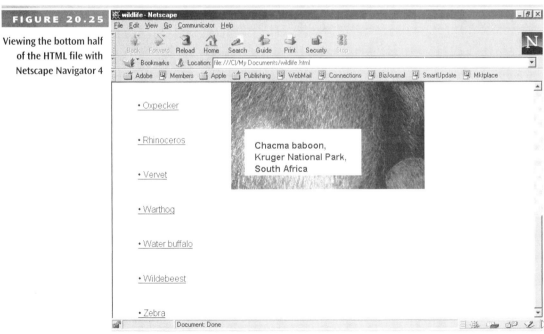

Photos courtesy of Corbis Images (royalty-free division) www.corbisimages.com

Figure 20.26 illustrates the HTML file generated by InDesign when opened in the Macintosh version of Adobe GoLive 4. Because fonts were missing on the Macintosh, a GIF file created in Photoshop was substituted for the headline "African Wildlife," and the subheads set in Lithograph Bold were changed to Helvetica Black. Notice also how the body text (list of animals) changed from Ariel to Courier. Font substitution will be a problem when viewing HTML files using browsers that don't have the fonts you specified installed on its computer. If you need to maintain design standards, create headlines as GIF files and select a font for body text that will be available on Macintosh, Windows, UNIX, and other operating systems. Look for the lowest common denominator. For body text that has to follow a corporate identity standard, consider using PDF files for those documents.

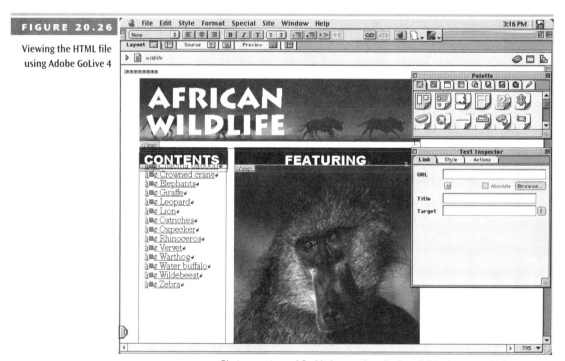

FIGURE 20.26

Viewing the HTML file using Adobe GoLive 4

Photos courtesy of Corbis Images (royalty-free division) www.corbisimages.com

Figure 20.27 shows the HTML file when viewed using Microsoft's HTML editor, FrontPage Express, on a Windows 98 machine. Look at the figure and notice how the layout changed because FrontPage Express does not support Cascading Style Sheets (CSS-1). You will see similar results when viewing the HTML file using a browser that does not support HTML 4 and the CSS-1 standard. This is one of the reasons why some Web sites do not use CSS, but offer documents for downloading that were saved as PDF files.

FIGURE 20.27

Viewing the HTML file using FrontPage Express

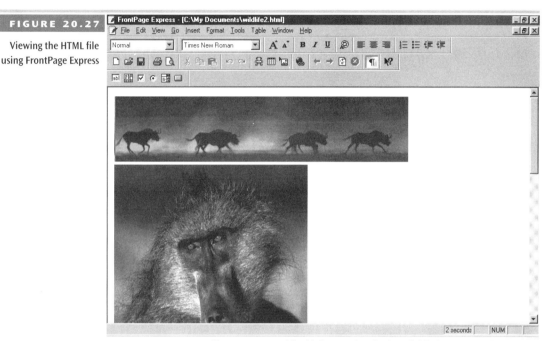

Photos courtesy of Corbis Images (royalty-free division) www.corbisimages.com

Conclusion

You've now reached the end of the main body of this book. Congratulations! You've entered a new era in desktop publishing and cross-platform content development. As you continue to work with InDesign, and to discover its strengths and weaknesses, don't forget to provide Adobe with your feedback. User comments from the field will help to target further development of the program. And remember to set up Abobe Online to keep abreast with the latest features updates and bug fixes, and join the InDesign Talk e-mail discussion list managed by Blue World Communications, Inc. for Adobe. Sign up and get more information at `www.blueworld.com/lists/`.

Sample HTML Code Generated after Exporting a Document in InDesign

The following code was created when the document illustrated in Figure 20.5 was exported using the default settings. This code was copied from the Notepad file shown in Figure 20.23. If you're familiar with HTML, you'll be able to scan the code and see how InDesign codes its documents when exporting to HTML.

```
<!DOCTYPE HTML PUBLIC "-//W3C//DTD HTML 4.0//EN"
            "http://www.w3.org/TR/REC-html40/strict.dtd">
<HTML>

    <HEAD>
        <META name="generator" content="Adobe InDesign HTML Export Plug-in" />
        <META http-equiv="Content-Type" content="text/html; charset=UTF-8" />
        <META http-equiv="Content-Style-Type" content="text/css" />
        <TITLE>wildlife</TITLE>

        <STYLE type="text/css">
        <!-
            #layer1 {position: absolute; top: 24px; left: 36px; height: 117px; width: 540px; padding: 0px; margin: 0px; z-index: 1}
            #layer2 {position: absolute; top: 185px; left: 220px; height: 572px; width: 356px; padding: 0px; margin: 0px; z-index: 2}
            #layer3 {position: absolute; top: 26px; left: 9px; height: 128px; width: 356px; padding: 0px; margin: 0px; z-index: 3}
            #layer4 {position: absolute; top: 152px; left: 36px; height: 32px; width: 171px; padding: 0px; margin: 0px; z-index: 4}
            #layer5 {position: absolute; top: 152px; left: 220px; height: 32px; width: 356px; padding: 0px; margin: 0px; z-index: 5}
            #layer6 {position: absolute; top: 154px; left: 36px; height: 38px; width: 540px; padding: 0px; margin: 0px; z-index: 6}
            #layer7 {position: absolute; top: 162px; left: 35px; height: 601px; width: 170px; padding: 0px; margin: 0px; z-index: 7}
            #layer8 {position: absolute; top: 643px; left: 241px; height: 93px; width: 222px; padding: 0px; margin: 0px; background-image: url(Images/Image30.gif); z-index: 8}
```

Continued on next page

Sample HTML Code Generated after Exporting a Document in InDesign *(continued)*

```
        DIV.dynamic-style-1 {text-align: center; text-align: center}

        SPAN.dynamic-style-2 {font-family: 'Lithograph'; font-size: 52px;
line-height: 50px; color: #FFFFFF; font-weight: bold; font-family:
'Lithograph'; font-size: 52px; line-height: 50px; color: #FFFFFF; font-
weight: bold}

        SPAN.dynamic-style-3 {font-size: 52px; line-height: 62px; color:
#FFFFFF; font-family: 'Times'; font-size: 52px; line-height: 62px; color:
#FFFFFF}

        DIV.dynamic-style-4 {margin-left: 12px; margin-left: 12px; text-
align: left}

        SPAN.dynamic-style-5 {font-family: 'Arial'; font-size: 16px; line-
height: 19px; font-family: 'Arial'; font-size: 16px; line-height: 19px;
color: #000000}

        SPAN.dynamic-style-6 {font-family: 'Arial'; font-size: 16px; line-
height: 19px; text-decoration: underline; font-family: 'Arial'; font-size:
16px; line-height: 19px; color: #000000; text-decoration: underline}

        SPAN.dynamic-style-7 {font-family: 'Arial'; font-size: 17px; line-
height: 40px; text-decoration: underline; font-family: 'Arial'; font-size:
17px; line-height: 40px; color: #000000; text-decoration: underline}

        DIV.dynamic-style-8 {margin-left: 18px; margin-right: 18px; margin-
left: 18px; margin-right: 18px; text-align: left}

        SPAN.dynamic-style-9 {font-family: 'Arial'; font-weight: bold;
font-family: 'Arial'; font-size: 12px; line-height: 14px; color: #000000;
font-weight: bold}

        SPAN.dynamic-style-10 {font-family: 'Arial'; font-size: 18px; line-
height: 21px; font-weight: bold; font-family: 'Arial'; font-size: 18px;
line-height: 21px; color: #000000; font-weight: bold}

        DIV.DefaultParaStyle {text-align: left}

        SPAN.DefaultParaStyle {font-family: 'Times'; font-size: 12px; line-
height: 14px; color: #000000}


    -->
    </STYLE>
```

Continued on next page

Sample HTML Code Generated after Exporting a Document in InDesign *(continued)*

```html
    </HEAD>

    <BODY bgcolor="#FFFFFF">

        <DIV id="layer1">
            <IMG height="117" width="540" src="Images/Image25.gif" alt="Image25.gif" />
        </DIV>

        <DIV id="layer2">
            <IMG height="572" width="356" src="Images/Image26.gif" alt="Image26.gif" />
        </DIV>

        <DIV id="layer3">

            <DIV class="dynamic-style-1">
            <SPAN class="dynamic-style-2">African<BR></SPAN>
            </DIV>

            <DIV class="dynamic-style-1">
            <SPAN class="dynamic-style-2">Wildlife</SPAN><SPAN class="dynamic-style-3"><BR></SPAN>
            </DIV>

        </DIV>

        <DIV id="layer4">
            <IMG height="32" width="171" src="Images/Image27.gif" alt="Image27.gif" />
        </DIV>
```

Continued on next page

Sample HTML Code Generated after Exporting a Document in InDesign *(continued)*

```
      <DIV id="layer5">
           <IMG height="32" width="356" src="Images/Image28.gif" alt="Image28.gif" />
      </DIV>


      <DIV id="layer6">
           <IMG height="38" width="540" src="Images/Image29.gif" alt="Image29.gif" />
      </DIV>


      <DIV id="layer7">


        <DIV class="dynamic-style-4">
        <SPAN class="dynamic-style-5"><BR></SPAN>
        </DIV>


        <DIV class="dynamic-style-4">
        <SPAN class="dynamic-style-6">â_¢ </SPAN><SPAN class="dynamic-style-7">Chacma baboon<BR></SPAN>
        </DIV>


        <DIV class="dynamic-style-4">
        <SPAN class="dynamic-style-7">â_¢ Crowned crane<BR></SPAN>
        </DIV>


        <DIV class="dynamic-style-4">
        <SPAN class="dynamic-style-7">â_¢ Elephants<BR></SPAN>
        </DIV>


        <DIV class="dynamic-style-4">
        <SPAN class="dynamic-style-7">â_¢ Giraffe<BR></SPAN>
```

Continued on next page

Sample HTML Code Generated after Exporting a Document in InDesign *(continued)*

```
</DIV>

<DIV class="dynamic-style-4">
<SPAN class="dynamic-style-7">â_¢ Leopard<BR></SPAN>
</DIV>

<DIV class="dynamic-style-4">
<SPAN class="dynamic-style-7">â_¢ Lion<BR></SPAN>
</DIV>

<DIV class="dynamic-style-4">
<SPAN class="dynamic-style-7">â_¢ Ostriches<BR></SPAN>
</DIV>

<DIV class="dynamic-style-4">
<SPAN class="dynamic-style-7">â_¢ Oxpecker<BR></SPAN>
</DIV>

<DIV class="dynamic-style-4">
<SPAN class="dynamic-style-7">â_¢ Rhinoceros<BR></SPAN>
</DIV>

<DIV class="dynamic-style-4">
<SPAN class="dynamic-style-7">â_¢ Vervet<BR></SPAN>
</DIV>

<DIV class="dynamic-style-4">
<SPAN class="dynamic-style-7">â_¢ Warthog<BR></SPAN>
</DIV>
```

Continued on next page

Sample HTML Code Generated after Exporting a Document in InDesign *(continued)*

```
        <DIV class="dynamic-style-4">
        <SPAN class="dynamic-style-7">â_¢ Water buffalo<BR></SPAN>
        </DIV>


        <DIV class="dynamic-style-4">
        <SPAN class="dynamic-style-7">â_¢ Wildebeest<BR></SPAN>
        </DIV>


        <DIV class="dynamic-style-4">
        <SPAN class="dynamic-style-7">â_¢ Zebra<BR></SPAN>
        </DIV>


    </DIV>

    <DIV id="layer8">


        <DIV class="dynamic-style-8">
        <SPAN class="dynamic-style-9"><BR></SPAN>
        </DIV>


        <DIV class="dynamic-style-8">
        <SPAN class="dynamic-style-10">Chacma baboon, Kruger National Park,
South Africa <BR></SPAN>
        </DIV>


    </DIV>

  </BODY>
</HTML>
```

appendix A

INSTALLING INDESIGN

INSTALLING INDESIGN

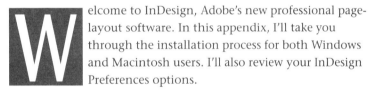

elcome to InDesign, Adobe's new professional page-layout software. In this appendix, I'll take you through the installation process for both Windows and Macintosh users. I'll also review your InDesign Preferences options.

What's Inside the Package

Included in the box with Adobe InDesign are sample files, multimedia tutorials, white papers, support information, and other bonus content:

- Adobe Acrobat Reader 4 software for viewing Portable Document Format (PDF) files
- The latest Adobe PostScript printer driver for Windows or the Macintosh, as well as a comprehensive set of PostScript Printer Description (PPD) files (optional installation)
- Adobe technical information about Adobe InDesign SDK, scripting, and tagged text
- PDF brochures describing third-party plug-ins
- Training and support materials
- Adobe Illustrator 8 and Photoshop 5 tryouts, and Adobe product brochures

Adobe also provides Adobe Online for setting up a link to the Adobe Web site. To use Adobe Online you need to have an Internet connection. Adobe Online can be set to periodically check the Adobe Web site. At the Web site, you can find an assortment of product support materials and the latest news about InDesign.

TIP See the ReadMe First! file on the CD for a complete listing of all the contents. You should also open each folder on the CD to see that folder's ReadMe file.

Hardware and Software Requirements

Here are the InDesign hardware and software requirements for both Windows and Macintosh computers.

Windows Systems Requirements

Adobe InDesign 1 for Windows *requires* the following hardware and software:

- An Intel® Pentium® II or faster processor.
- Windows 98, Windows NT 4 Workstation with Service Pack 4, or later.
- A hard disk with at least 74MB of free space.
- At least 48MB of random-access memory (RAM)
- A CD-ROM drive
- 256-color (8-bit) at 800 × 600 monitor resolution video display card.
- For PostScript® printing devices, Adobe PostScript Level 2 (or higher) printer driver.

For best performance, Adobe Systems *recommends* the following hardware and software:

- Pentium II® 300Mhz or faster Intel® processor.
- 64MB or more of RAM.
- High resolution (24-bit super VGA or greater) video display card.
- Adobe Postscript Level 2 (or higher) printer.
- An Internet connection.

Macintosh OS system requirements

Adobe InDesign 1 for Macintosh *requires* the following hardware and software:

- PowerPC® 604 processor or greater.
- Mac OS 8.5 or later.
- A hard disk with at least 130MB of free space at the time of installation. Installation also requires free disk space on the startup drive for temporary files and items added to the system folder (even if InDesign is installed on another drive).

NOTE Check the InDesign 1 ReadMe file for more information about protective shutdowns and limited disk space (Miscellaneous section).

- At least 48MB of random access memory (RAM) (virtual memory on) or 96 MB RAM (virtual memory off).
- A CD-ROM drive.
- Monitor resolution of 832 × 624 pixels.

WARNING If you have a ATI graphics card installed in your computer, refer to InDesign's ReadMe file for more details about system lock-up problems when panning with the InDesign grabber hand (Miscellaneous section).

- Adobe PostScript Level 2 (or higher) printer.

For best performance, Adobe Systems *recommends* the following hardware and software:

- PowerPC® G3 processor.
- 128MB or more of physical RAM. There's detailed information about optimizing InDesign performance in the "In Depth-Performance.pdf" document. The PDF file is in the More About Adobe InDesign / Learning Adobe InDesign folder on the CD-ROM.
- High resolution 24-bit screen display.
- An Internet connection.

WARNING Check the ReadMe file for the latest information on InDesign's hardware and software requirements. If you plan to have several software programs or utilities open at the same time, add up the individually recommended memory and hard disk needs. These totals will help you to determine the minimum baseline requirements for configuring your system.

Checking Your Computer System

InDesign is a resource-intensive software application. It is important to check your computer system before installing InDesign. You want to determine if your currently configured system will support your workflow requirements. Print a copy of your system configuration and the installed application software. Reference this document when you are selecting your InDesign installation options and preferences.

TIP Don't forget that you will be setting your InDesign color workflow requirements too. See Chapters 12, 18, and Appendix C for more information on this topic.

Here's how to find your Windows 98, Windows NT, and Macintosh OS system information.

Windows 98

On your Windows 98 computer you can quickly find out about your system. Select Start ➢ Programs ➢ Accessories ➢ System Tools ➢ System Information. When the Microsoft System Information window opens, you see a table of contents on the left and in a second frame a general summary of your system configuration, as shown in Figure A.1. For more detailed information, click on a category listing in the table of contents. You can choose to read a topic's basic information, advanced information or history. To save, export, or print the screen information, use the File menu commands.

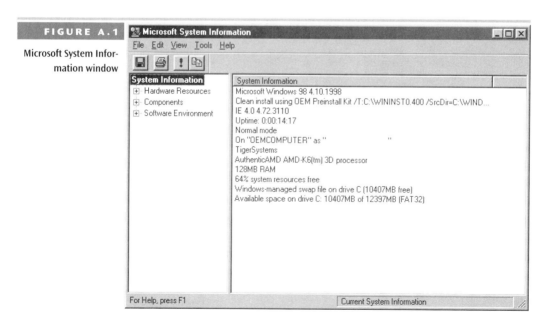

FIGURE A.1

Microsoft System Information window

Windows NT

Here are two ways to check your Windows NT system configuration.

- Open My Computer. Right-click inside the window. From the menu, choose Properties. You'll get the screen showing system properties, shown in Figure A.2, which provides basic information. Click on different tabs to find more specific information. Press Print Scrn to print a copy of the information.

or

- Go to Start ➢ Programs ➢Administrative Tools (Common) ➢ Windows NT Diagnostics. The screen shows system diagnostics, with tabs identifying different sets of information, as shown in Figure A.3. Click on different tabs to separately check each specification; this is the more detailed display of information. Select from the menu File ➢ Print to create a paper copy of the screen information.

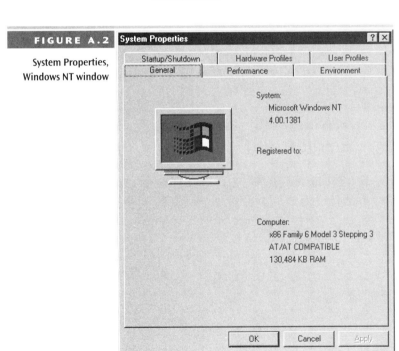

FIGURE A.2

System Properties, Windows NT window

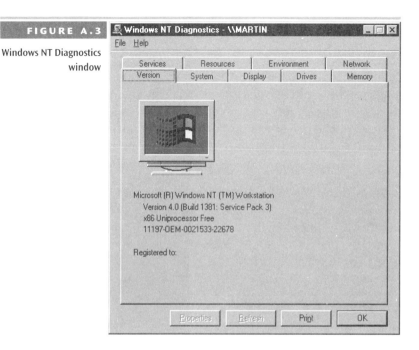

FIGURE A.3
Windows NT Diagnostics window

Macintosh

Apple displays your Macintosh computer setup information in the Apple System Profiler. This information includes your system software version, how many and what kinds of drives are connected to your computer, and what installed applications are on your computer. To open the Apple System Profiler, choose Apple System Profiler from the Apple menu. With the Profiler open, as shown in Figure A.4, click on the arrows in the left-hand margin or click on the tabs to see more detailed information. To create, print or save a report follow these instructions:

1. From the Apple menu, select File ➢ New Report.
2. When the dialog box appears, select the items you want in your report. Click OK to accept your list of items. The report appears.
3. Open the Apple File menu again. This time choose the Print or Save commands.

Installing InDesign

Start first by checking for any potential software conflicts. Read all the ReadMe files for the application, drivers, or utilities that you're installing. Before beginning the installation process disable your virus protection software. Close any programs you have running.

FIGURE A.4

Apple System Profiler window

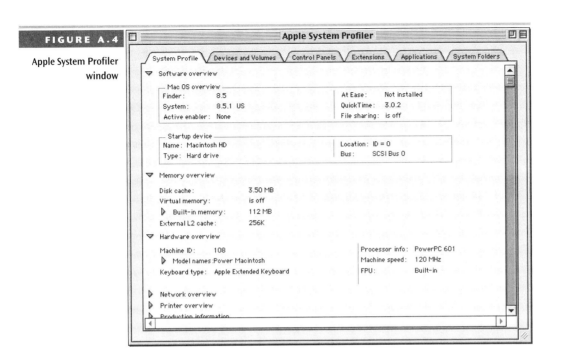

 WARNING   Before installing any new software application, driver or utilities, remember to back up your system and your work.

InDesign must be installed from the Adobe InDesign CD onto your hard disk drive. The application cannot run from the CD. Have your serial number accessible before beginning the installation process. The serial number is found on the CD sleeve or on the registration card. Just in case the registration card or CD sleeve becomes lost or stolen, make a copy of the registration card. Store the copy in another place that's safe.

Starting the Installation

To install InDesign, place the CD in your computer's CD drive. Your computer will read the CD and automatically open the Adobe InDesign AutoPlay screen (Windows) or a window displaying the CD's contents (Macintosh). Before installing, explore the contents on the CD to decide what you would like to install.

Here's how to start the installation process: right-click the Adobe InDesign AutoPlay screen Install button (Windows) or click the InDesign Install icon (Macintosh). An Adobe Set-up Wizard program opens. You will respond to a series of on-screen questions to complete the installation. If you have an Internet connection and a browser installed on your system, the installation process can help you to set up

Adobe Online. If you don't have an Internet connection and/or a browser, then skip these steps.

NOTE During the installation process, you specify which language version of InDesign you want to install. The selected language determines the application's default settings for the spelling and hyphenation dictionary, unit of measure and page size. See the "Setting Preferences" section in this Appendix for more information about changing your document's dictionary.

There are two installation options: Typical and Custom. Choose Typical to install the most common components that Adobe recommends for most users. This install includes the Learning InDesign folder, which contains tutorials and accompanying files. If you have a shortage of hard drive storage space, you may not want to install this folder on your hard drive.

The Custom install, which is recommended for advanced users, allows you to select those components that you want to install. Use Custom install, for example, if you already have the current or later version of the Kodak Color Management Profiles on your system.

WARNING The Kodak CMM version 2.6.3, which is included with Apple ColorSync 2.6.1 may cause pages within a Macintosh InDesign document to fail to display. Later versions solve the problem. Download an update from Kodak's Web site: www.kodak.com/go/getKodakColorProcessor

Installing Other Components

The CD also includes separate installation processes for installing the PostScript Driver and Adobe Acrobat Reader 4. Before installing the PostScript driver, check the release level. If you previously installed that release or a later version on your computer, you can skip the PostScript driver installation.

The PDF files on the InDesign CD need Adobe Acrobat 4 Reader to be read. If you have Adobe Acrobat 3, the full-blown application and not the Reader on your system, upgrade now to version 4. When you install the Adobe Acrobat 4 Reader, the setup Wizard (Windows) looks for older versions of the files and removes them. Adobe Acrobat Exchange, Catalog, and Distiller are not available to use any more. On the Macintosh, the system defaults to the version 4 Reader and opens it, not Adobe Acrobat Exchange 3.

WARNING When printing from InDesign on a Macintosh, you must specify "PostScript 2 Only" or "PostScript 3 Only" in the printer driver's PostScript Settings dialog box. The driver's "PostScript 1, 2, and 3 Compatible" option amounts to support for Level 1, which does not meet InDesign's PostScript Level 2 requirement.

Don't forget to register your software. You have to be a registered user to have access to Adobe technical support.

Launching InDesign

InDesign starts like any other software application on Windows or Macintosh computers. On Windows, choose Start ➤ Programs ➤ Adobe ➤ Adobe InDesign to launch the program. On Macintosh, open the folder where you placed the InDesign application and double-click the Adobe InDesign program icon. The program window appears. You can begin working by creating a new document or opening an existing one. To learn about setting InDesign preferences, see the next section.

TIP Creating or opening InDesign files are covered in Chapter 2.

Setting Preferences

Select File ➤ Preferences from InDesign's Menu Bar and choose from the options on the Preferences submenu to access various dialog boxes for customizing InDesign's operations. Adobe has closely followed the Photoshop GUI (graphical user interface) in building InDesign. You'll discover that InDesign settings are changed using similar methods, such as pull-down menus, check-off boxes, and direct numeric entry. When no documents are open, changing settings will globally modify new documents defaults. If you decide to change settings when a document is open, then only that document's defaults are affected. When you're done making changes, click OK to accept.

You can navigate from one Preferences dialog box to another by using the following methods:

- Choose from the Preferences submenu list
- Select a new dialog box from the top-left pull-down menu, which identifies the current Preferences dialog box

- Click on the Prev (Previous) or Next buttons.

If you would like to restore all preferences and default settings, see the following instructions:

1. If InDesign is running, close the program. Choose File ➢ Exit (Windows) or File ➢ Quit (Macintosh).
2. Next, choose Start ➢ Find ➢ Files or Folders (Windows) or Open the InDesign Folder (Macintosh).
3. Now, go to the InDesign Defaults:
    - Windows: Type **"InDesign Defaults"** in the Named text box. Remember to put quotes around the phrase, or the Find command finds only files containing InDesign, ignoring everything after the space. Click Find Now. From the list that appears, select the InDesign Defaults file. You have the option of either renaming or deleting the file. Do this also for the InDesign Saved-Data file.
    - Macintosh: With the InDesign Folder open, select the InDesign Defaults file. Rename or delete the file. Repeat this procedure for the InDesign Saved-Data file.
4. When you restart InDesign, a new InDesign Defaults file and InDesign Saved-Data file will be created.

General

In the Preferences: General dialog box, you can choose your images display, page numbering view, and general options. (See Figure A.5.) The Display option menu offers three choices: proxy images (for position only), full resolution images, and gray out images. Page numbering can be set up for a whole document or for an individual section. Using a checkbox, you can turn on or off tool tips and overprint black options.

NOTE See Chapter 18 for more information about printing options.

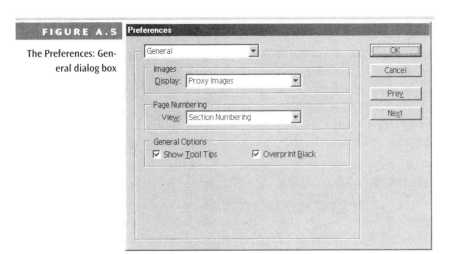

FIGURE A.5
The Preferences: General dialog box

Text

The Preferences: Text dialog box contains the character settings for superscript, subscript, and small cap letters, as shown in Figure A.6. Using the percentage settings, InDesign generates these pseudo-characters from the selected typeface's full-size characters and numerals. You may want to adjust these percentages when working with decorative or extremely proportioned typefaces or fonts. Other dialog box options include setting anti-alias type, typographer's quotes, and automatically using correct type optical size.

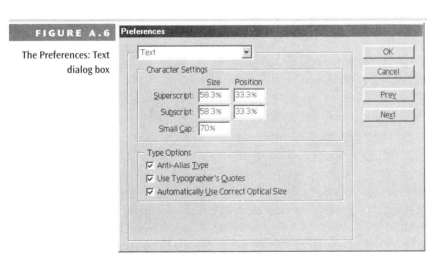

FIGURE A.6
The Preferences: Text dialog box

Composition

The Preferences: Composition dialog box modifies the Adobe Multi-line Composer's operation. In this dialog box, shown in Figure A.7, you determine how many lines ahead and how many alternatives will be considered when composing text. By changing the settings in this dialog box, you manipulate the look and feel of your copy blocks. Also available are options to turn on or off font substitution, keep violations, and H&J (hyphenation and justification) violations.

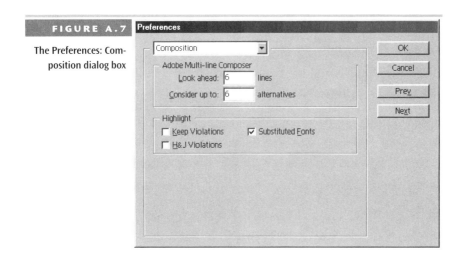

FIGURE A.7
The Preferences: Composition dialog box

NOTE Get more details about text composition in Chapters 5, 9, and 10.

Units & Increments

In the Preferences: Units & Increments dialog box, you choose the unit of measurement for InDesign's on-screen rulers. (See Figure A.8.) Using the option menus, the horizontal and vertical on-screen rulers can be set to the same or different units of measurement. The measurement units that you can select from are points, picas, inches, inches decimal, millimeters, centimeters, cicero, and custom. If you pick custom, you can set you own special tick marks for the on-screen ruler. This can be particularly useful when you want your vertical on-screen ruler tick marks to match your baseline gridlines.

In this dialog box you can also set the keyboard units. Enter a measurement unit in each of the dialog box fields to set the behavior of the cursor key, size/leading changes, baseline shift, and kerning. Kerning (the adjustment of the space between individual letters, numerals or punctuation), is measured as a value of /1000 em units.

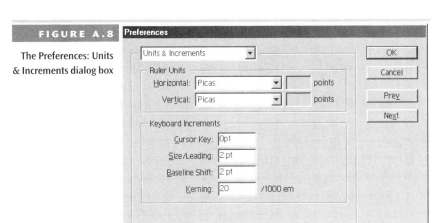

FIGURE A.8

The Preferences: Units & Increments dialog box

NOTE   For more info about using rulers and keyboard shortcuts, see Chapter 3.

Grids

Working with customized grids can speed up object placement in a document. Use the Preferences: Grids dialog box to edit InDesign's baseline and document grids, as shown in Figure A.9. You can set the gridline color, start point, the amount of leading between the baselines, and the view threshold for the baseline grid. The Document Grid settings are for gridline color, distance between gridlines, and the number of subdivisions in the grid. Light blue and light gray are the default colors.

To change colors, double-click on the color chip box. The system color picker opens. You can choose one of the preset colors or choose to create another custom color.

TIP   To make gridlines standout from your layout objects, select a color that highly contrasts with your document color palette.

NOTE   See Chapter 3 to learn more about using the InDesign desktop.

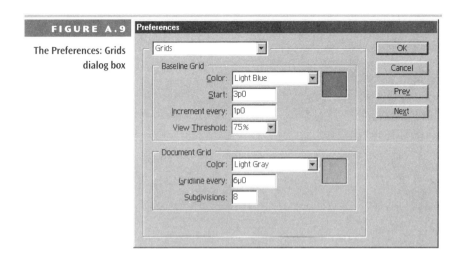

FIGURE A.9
The Preferences: Grids dialog box

Guides

The Preferences: Guides dialog box is where you set the color of a document's margins and columns. (See Figure A.10.) Magenta and violet are the default colors. Color selection methods are the same as for grids. (See the previous section.) A checkbox for defaulting guides to black and setting the Snap to Zone are other guide option choices in this dialog box.

Ruler guides settings are not specified in the Preferences: Guides dialog box. Instead, choose Layout ➢ Ruler Guides to open the Ruler Guides dialog box.

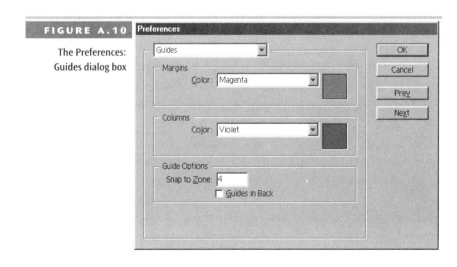

FIGURE A.10
The Preferences: Guides dialog box

NOTE Working with guides is covered in more detail in Chapter 3.

Dictionary

The spelling and hyphenation rules applied in text composition are controlled by which dictionary you choose in this Preferences dialog box, as shown in Figure A.11. Remember to recompose all text when adding or changing a document's user dictionary.

In addition to identifying language, you can also designate the vendor of the Hyphenation and Spelling component. Proximity is Adobe's vendor, but you can install and use components from other vendors. Once installed, these components can be selected from the Preferences: Dictionary dialog box.

 WARNING Always confirm that everyone in your workgroup has and is using the same customized user dictionary for the document or project. The system Find command can be used to locate and copy user dictionary files from one computer to another.

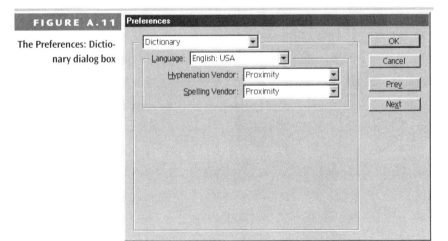

FIGURE A.11
The Preferences: Dictionary dialog box

 NOTE See Chapters 5, 9, 10, and 14 for more info about composing text.

Online Settings

If you skipped the Adobe Online set-up when you installed InDesign or want to reconfigure your settings, use the Adobe Online Preferences dialog box. (See Figure A.12.) Click the Wizard button to open a series of step-by-step installation screens. If you'd rather not use the Wizard, then enter your information in the dialog box fields and check off your preferences on both pages. Click on the tab to switch between pages, as seen in Figure A.13. You can also access the Adobe Online Preferences dialog box by selecting File ➢ Adobe Online, and then clicking the Preferences button on the Adobe Online splash screen.

 WARNING Adobe Online requires an Internet connection and a browser installed on your system.

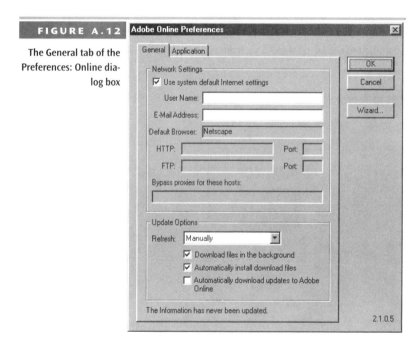

FIGURE A.12

The General tab of the Preferences: Online dialog box

SETTING PREFERENCES 663

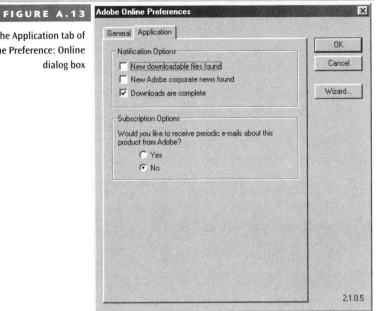

FIGURE A.13

The Application tab of the Preference: Online dialog box

appendix B

THE INDESIGN DESKTOP

THE INDESIGN DESKTOP

If you're a Photoshop or Illustrator user, you'll discover a familiar environment when you explore InDesign, Adobe's publishing and layout application. Adobe worked hard to seamlessly integrate InDesign with both graphics applications. In this appendix, I'll review InDesign's document display windows, the Toolbox, the menus, and the palettes.

Document Display Windows

In addition to Zoom In and Zoom Out commands, InDesign's View menu lists four options for displaying documents:

- Fit Page in Window
- Fit Spread in Window
- Actual Size
- Entire Pasteboard

Keep in mind that monitor and window dimensions affect what you see in each view. If you choose Fit Page in Window, for example, you'll find that a 15-inch monitor, with the InDesign window maximized, will display a 69.23% reduction of the document. On the other hand, a 20-inch monitor will show an 81% reduction of the document page for the same command.

Fit Page in Window

Even if a page is part of a multi-page spread, the Fit Page in Window command creates a single page document view. Select View ➢ Fit Page in Window to activate this command. Created from a 15-inch monitor screen capture, you can see in Figure B.1 that InDesign shows a 69.23% reduction of the single page.

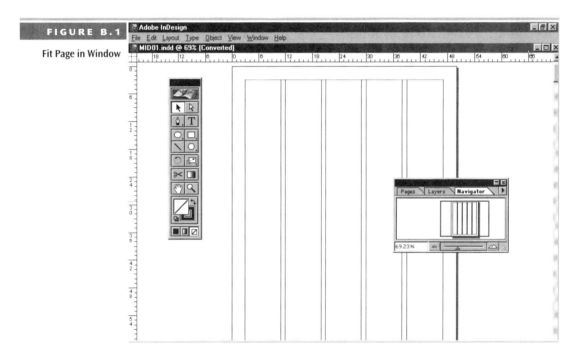

FIGURE B.1

Fit Page in Window

Fit Spread in Window

When you want to view more than one page at a time, select the Fit Spread in Window command from the View menu. Again using a 15-inch monitor for the screen capture, you can see in Figure B.2 that InDesign calculates the same reduction percentage for Fit Spread in Window as it did for the Fit Page in Window command. In this case it was 69.23%.

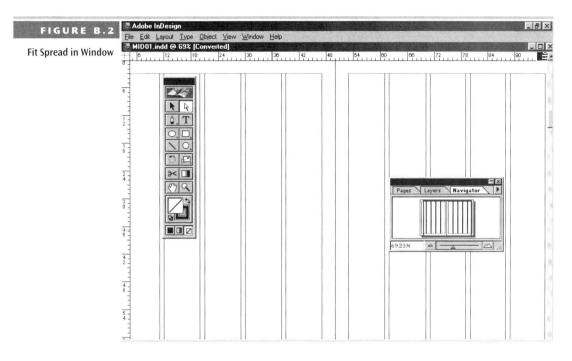

FIGURE B.2
Fit Spread in Window

Actual Size

The Actual Size command displays the document at 100%. Figure B.3 shows how much of the document can be seen at the 100% view on a 15-inch monitor.

TIP Working with a small monitor will increase the amount of time you spend scrolling, and opening and closing palettes. If your budget doesn't allow for the purchase of a larger monitor, consider adding a second small monitor to your computer configuration. The first monitor will display the InDesign tools and palettes that you need. The second will show your document.

Entire Pasteboard

To facilitate the give-and-take of the creative process, Adobe identified an area outside an InDesign page or spread where objects can be placed prior to positioning them on the page. This area is called the *pasteboard* and can be accessed by selecting View ➢ Entire Pasteboard. Figure B.4 shows multiple spreads and their pasteboards.

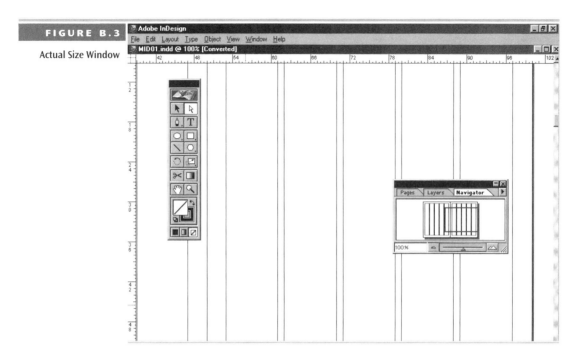

FIGURE B.3
Actual Size Window

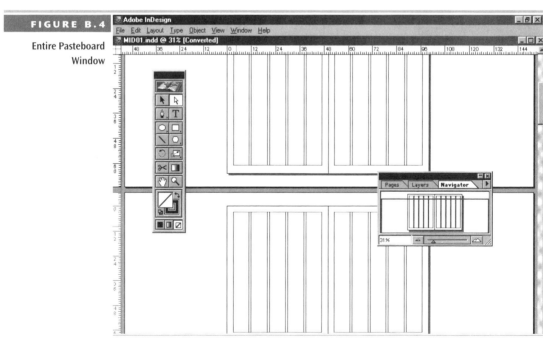

FIGURE B.4
Entire Pasteboard Window

TIP Check the pasteboard area to see how far objects placed on the page *bleed*, or extend, past the edge of the page.

The InDesign Toolbox

InDesign's Toolbox, shown in Figure B.5, contains the tools you use to manipulate objects on the desktop, such as the Selection tool, Pen tool, Rotate tool, etc. The Toolbox also contains the Adobe Online icon, the Fill/Stroke Color Indicator, and the fill color options. If a small triangle appears in a tool icon's lower right-hand corner, you can click that triangle to open additional tool options.

FIGURE B.5

The InDesign Toolbox

Adobe Online

When you click the book with butterfly graphic at the top of the toolbox, Adobe Online launches your installed browser and logs on to your default Internet network. You can download the latest InDesign updates and news from Adobe.

Selection and Direct Selection Tools

Use the Selection and Direct Selection tools to choose any object or group of objects on any layer. Once selected, an object can be modified or moved. The appearance of the bounding box changes when you switch between the Selection and Direct Selection tools.

The Selection tool works well for general layout activities, such as positioning and sizing objects. When an object is selected with this tool, you see an object bounded by a box rectangle with eight handles.

The Direct Selection tool is used for drawing and editing paths, frames, and frame contents, and for moving anchor points on a path. When drawing with the Pen tool, press Ctrl (Windows) or Command (Macintosh) to temporarily activate the Direct Selection tool to edit the path. .

 NOTE Want to find out about actions that use selection tools? See Chapters 4, 6, 15, and 17.

Pen and Type Tools

The Pen and Type tools are used for drawing and editing paths and creating text.

InDesign's Pen tool operates like the pen tools in Adobe Illustrator and Photoshop. InDesign has four tools for drawing and editing one path or a series of path segments: Pen, Add Anchor Point, Delete Anchor Point, and Convert Direction Point. Use the Pen tool to create complex paths that combine straight lines and precise curves.

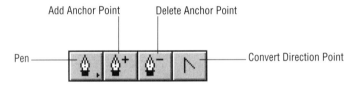

 NOTE See Chapter 17 to learn more about drawing and editing paths.

 Select the Type tool for entering or editing text in a frame. Keep in mind that all InDesign text is contained within a frame.

 NOTE You can find more about type basics in Chapter 5.

Ellipse, Rectangle, Line, and Polygon Tools

These tools allow you to create basic shapes and lines. It's helpful to have the Transform palette open when drawing. You could quickly edit the size, orientation, and skew of any shape.

The Ellipse tool offers two options. You can draw a simple path shape or use the Ellipse frame tool to define a layout placeholder. To create a circle, press the Shift key as you drag your mouse.

The Rectangle tool, which draws outlined or filled boxes and defines layout placeholders, is great for developing layout sketches. You can quickly block out major areas of pages and spreads to test ideas. To draw a square, press the Shift key as you drag your mouse.

When you're drawing only straight lines, the Line tool makes a great substitute for the more complex Pen tool. Before you begin drawing, open the Strokes palette to set weight, miter limit, etc. by double-clicking on the Line tool icon. To constrain a line to 45 degree angles, press the Shift key as you drag.

Create hexagonal (six-sided) shapes or layout frame placeholders with the Polygon tool or double-click the Polygon tool icon to open the Polygon Settings dialog box. In the dialog box, you can determine the number of sides and star inset of the polygon. You can change the length of the line segments using the Direct Selection tool.

NOTE Drawing with geometric shapes and lines is covered in Chapter 4.

Rotate, Scale, and Shear Tools

Use these tools to visually change orientation, size, and proportions. If the Transform palette is open, you'll see the measurement units changing in the palette as you move the tool. The further the tool cursor is from the point of origin, the finer your control of that tool.

When you drag the Rotate tool, you reorient objects to a defined point of origin. Press Shift as you drag to move objects by multiples of 45 degrees.

From your defined point of origin, drag the Scale tool to visually resize objects. The Shear tool slants, or skews, an object along a horizontal axis. To constrain shearing to 45-degree increments, press Shift as you drag.

NOTE See Chapter 15 for a guide to transforming, placing, and aligning objects.

Scissors and Gradient Tools

The Scissors and Gradient tools are used to customize paths, frames, and shapes.

Employ the Scissors tool if you want to split a path, graphics frame, or empty text frame at any anchor point or along any segment. Be aware of the restrictions Adobe sets for working with scissors. For example, you can't split a frame containing text. Or this example: you must slice a path in two places if you want to split a closed path into two open paths. Refer to the InDesign Help menu for a list of other restrictions and the workarounds.

NOTE   Cut to Chapter 17 to learn about editing paths and shapes.

The Gradient tool works like Adobe Illustrator's Gradient tool. Select the Gradient tool when you want to apply a gradient to an object. (See the "The Apply Color/Apply Gradient/Apply None Swatch" section later in this appendix.) How your gradient will flow depends on where you place the start point and which direction you drag to. If you would like to create a new gradient, select the New Gradient Swatch option from the Swatches palette menu. Use the New Gradient Swatch option dialog box to define the color stops in the gradient. Double-click the Gradient tool icon to open the Gradient palette.

NOTE   Check out Chapter 12 for more info about gradients.

Hand and Zoom Tools

The Hand and Zoom tools, along with the Zoom commands and the Navigator palette, let you see different parts of a spread at various magnifications.

Change the view of your document by dragging the Hand tool. It's helpful to have the Navigator palette open when you do this.

You select the Zoom tool and click to magnify the view. Click again to continue magnifying the view (maximum view is 4,000%). If you press Alt (Windows) or Option (Macintosh) as you click, the view is reduced.

Fill/Stroke Color Indicator

The Fill/Stroke Color Indicator functions like Adobe Illustrator's indicator. The frontmost icon (choose either Fill Colors or Stroke Colors) is the active selection and its specifications can be changed. An object drawn with a stroke color assigned and fill color set to None will have a transparent fill.

Fill Colors   This icon, the square box, represents the active fill color. If the box is white with a red diagonal line through it, then no fill color is assigned (None).

Stroke Colors   This icon, an outlined box, shows whether or not a stroke color was specified. A red diagonal line through the box means None or no stroke color assigned.

Swap Fill/Stroke   To switch between fill and stroke as the active selection, click on the icon located in the upper right-hand corner.

Default Fill/Stroke   Located in the lower left-hand corner, click this icon to apply the default fill and stroke.

The Apply Color/Apply Gradient/Apply None Swatch

You can use these tools to apply a color, gradient, or none to selected objects.

WARNING   You can't assign a tint or gradient to an imported image. The None swatch can't be applied to a grayscale or 1-bit image.

Click the Apply Color button to assign the last selected solid color or double-click the Apply Color button to open the Color palette. Use the Color or Swatches palette to make another color the active selection.

Click the Apply Gradient button to apply the last selected gradient. If you want to change gradients, double-click the button to open the Gradient palette.

TIP   Before you work with the Gradient tool discussed earlier, you have to first assign a gradient to an object using the Apply Gradient button.

Click the Apply None button to remove an object's fill or stroke color.

The InDesign Menus

Adobe InDesign has nine menu bar options:

- Adobe InDesign icon
- File
- Edit
- Layout

- Type
- Object
- View
- Window
- Help

Below each menu option there is a list of commands or other options. When you make a menu selection, you will either apply a command or open a dialog box, submenu, palette, or new window. If a shortcut key is available for that action, it will appear in the right-hand column. Triangles on the right side of the menu identify the location of submenus. Figure B.6 shows the InDesign main menu for Windows; Figure B.7 shows the InDesign main menu for Macintosh.

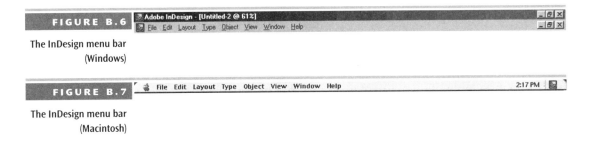

FIGURE B.6
The InDesign menu bar (Windows)

FIGURE B.7
The InDesign menu bar (Macintosh)

 NOTE Chapter 3 has more information about working with menus.

Adobe InDesign Icon (Windows)

These are the options available from the Windows Adobe InDesign icon:

Restore   Brings back your window to its original state.

Move   Repositions the application window on your desktop.

Size   Changes the size of your document window.

Minimize   Collapses a window to the title bar only. It's a great way to conserve space on the desktop while having several applications open at the same time.

Maximize   Makes your program window fill the monitor screen from edge to edge or maximizes the size of the document window in the program window.

Close   Closes the document window.

Next Go to the next open document window.

Adobe InDesign Icon (Macintosh)

These are the options available from the Macintosh Adobe InDesign icon:

Hide InDesign Conceals InDesign's application window.

Hide Others Conceals from view the windows of any other open applications.

Show All Shows all open application windows.

Finder Lets you access the desktop. Applications listed below the Finder are open. Click on the program name to show the window.

File Menu

The File menu contains commands for creating, managing, and saving InDesign documents; importing, linking, and exporting files; setting your application, color, and keyboard shortcut preferences; accessing Adobe Online; and closing down InDesign. Figure B.8 shows the File menu for Windows; Figure B.9 shows the File menu for Macintosh.

New The New document command opens a dialog box where you specify the number of pages, page size dimensions and orientation, margins, columns, and turn on facing pages and master text frame options.

Open Select this command to open InDesign document or template files, and Adobe PageMaker 6.5, Quark XPress 3.3–4, and Adobe PDF files.

Close Closes your current open document. A screen prompt appears if didn't save your changes to the document. Select Save or Don't Save changes. The Cancel option voids the Close command.

Save You can save an InDesign document or template. If you are saving a new, untitled document, this command opens the Save As dialog box.

Save As/Save a Copy In the Save As dialog box, you determine the storage drive, file folder, filename, and whether you are saving an InDesign document or template file.

FIGURE B.8

The File menu (Windows)

New...	Ctrl+N
Open...	Ctrl+O
Close	Ctrl+W
Save	Ctrl+S
Save As...	Shft+Ctrl+S
Save a Copy...	Ctrl+Alt+S
Revert	
Place...	Ctrl+D
Links...	Shft+Ctrl+D
Export...	Ctrl+E
Document Setup...	Ctrl+Alt+P
Preflight...	Shft+Ctrl+Alt+F
Package...	Shft+Ctrl+Alt+P
Print...	Ctrl+P
Preferences	▶
Color Settings	▶
Edit Shortcuts...	Shft+Ctrl+Alt+K
1 wildlife2.indd	
Adobe Online...	
Exit	Ctrl+Q

FIGURE B.9

The File menu (Macintosh)

File	
New...	⌘N
Open...	⌘O
Close	⌘W
Save	⌘S
Save As...	⇧⌘S
Save a Copy...	⌥⌘S
Revert	
Place...	⌘D
Links...	⇧⌘D
Export...	⌘E
Document Setup...	⌥⌘P
Page Setup...	⇧⌘P
Preflight...	⌥⇧⌘F
Package...	⌥⇧⌘P
Print...	⌘P
Preferences	▶
Color Settings	▶
Edit Shortcuts...	⌥⇧⌘K
Adobe Online...	
Quit	⌘Q

NOTE For much more info on creating and managing files, see Chapter 2.

Revert Use the Revert command when you want to quickly comp out or mock up different layout concepts. As long as you don't save your changes, you can go back to your last-saved version.

Place The Place command is used for importing files into the InDesign workspace. In the Place dialog box, select and preview your file, pick your import and retain format options, and decide whether to convert quotes from "typewriter" to typographic style.

NOTE Learn more about working with graphics in Chapter 6.

Links You select this command to show the Links palette.

Export Choose to export your InDesign document either as an Adobe PDF, EPS, HTML, or Prepress file format.

NOTE Exporting documents are covered in Chapters 2, 18, 19, and 20.

Document Setup The Document Setup command opens a dialog box where you can change the current active document's page count, page size, dimensions, and orientation. There is a checkbox for selecting the facing pages option.

Page Setup (Macintosh) Page Setup displays a dialog box in which you can select your Adobe supported printer, page attributes, paper size, orientation, N-up printing, printer driver's PostScript settings, and booklet printing option.

TIP Windows users click the Properties button in the Print dialog box to access Page Setup.

Preflight The Preflight command performs a quality-control check of the document before you send the document to a service provider or printer. You can check for missing links and images, fonts, color management profiles, and hidden layers, but not for pasteboard content. The Preflight command generates an on-screen report, which can be saved or printed using Windows Notepad or Macintosh SimpleText.

Package The Package command collects files for handing off to third parties, including fonts, linked graphics, ICC profiles, and printing instructions. This feature is a great asset for documenting projects.

Print The Print command opens a dialog box where your choose your printer, destination, and printer settings. You can send the files to the printer or save your settings (for a virtual printer).

NOTE Chapter 18 is the place to go for more information about preflighting and printing options

Preferences The Preferences command opens a submenu where you can select eight different dialog boxes for customizing InDesign.

Color Settings This command opens a submenu where you select either the Application Color Settings or Document Color Settings dialog box. Correctly setting color profiles is critical to the success of your project. Before finalizing your document color settings, verify the color profiles of all imported files to find any incompatibilities.

TIP Don't forget to consult with your service provider or printer early on in the design phase to short circuit any potential color workflow production problems

NOTE See Appendices A and C for more details about setting preferences.

Edit Shortcuts The Edit Shortcuts command shows a dialog box where you can edit existing shortcuts sets, create new sets, and select another set to use with your document or the application. Before editing a set, print a copy of all the assigned shortcuts and unassigned items like fonts listed on screen. You'll gain a better perspective of what you can do.

NOTE Cut to Chapter 3 for more info about editing shortcuts. Check out Appendix E for a comparison list of InDesign, QuarkXPress, and PageMaker shortcuts.

Adobe Online The menu command to access Adobe Online. See the Toolbox listing in this appendix for more details.

Exit (Windows)/Quit (Macintosh) The menu command to close the application. If there are any open InDesign documents or templates with unsaved changes, a screen prompt will appear. Decide if you want to Save or Don't Save these changes before the document or template is closed. Select Cancel to void the Exit/Quit command.

Edit Menu

The Edit menu provides commands such as undo and redo of actions, cut, copy and paste using the Clipboard, clear, duplicate objects, step-and-repeat, and text and dictionary editing.

Undo/Redo Your creative brainstorming gets a big boost from the multiple Undos and Redos allowed by InDesign. If you're working quickly, don't worry, InDesign records your last action (Undo) and last undo (Redo) next to the command name. If you save or close a document, or exit InDesign, the program discards the action information.

N O T E Using InDesign's multiple undos and the Revert command are covered in Chapter 7.

Cut, **Copy**, **Paste**, and **Paste Into** These menu commands are similar to those in Photoshop and Illustrator. They all use the Clipboard, which allows you to transfer objects between InDesign layers, pages/spreads, and documents. You can also utilize the Clipboard to transfer objects between InDesign and open documents in other programs.

Clear Deletes the current selection. Use Undo if you clear the wrong selection.

N O T E Basic desktop functions are discussed in Chapter 3.

Duplicate This command creates a copy of your current selection on the same layer.

Step and Repeat You'll discover this command makes designing forms a lot easier. In the dialog box, set the number of duplicates you want of the selected object. Also enter the vertical and horizontal offsets for positioning the duplicates. If you want to keep the same vertical or horizontal alignment as the original, enter 0 as the measurement unit.

Select All/Deselect All Globally select and deselect multiple document objects.

Find/Change The Find/Change command opens a dialog box. Select the criteria and words that InDesign will use for searching and replacing text in your current document. Click the More button in the Find/Change dialog box to view Find/Change Style Settings options. Click the Format button to view a series of dialog boxes for changing Style Options, Indents and Spacing, Drop Caps and Composer, Keep Options, Basic Character Formats, Advanced Character Formats, and Character Color. To navigate between Find/Change Format Settings dialog boxes, click the Previous or Next buttons or select an option from the menu at the top of the dialog box.

Find Next Select Find Next instead of Find/Change if you want to continue looking for the previously searched word or phrase.

NOTE Go to Chapter 5 for more information about text entry and editing.

Check Spelling This command activates InDesign's spelling checker. Which language rules are applied is controlled by the dictionary you picked in the Preferences dialog box.

Edit Dictionary The Edit Dictionary command opens a dialog box where you can add, remove, or manually hyphenate words in the current dictionary.

WARNING Remember to distribute custom dictionaries to the entire workgroup.

Layout Menu

The Layout menu contains commands for the setup of the document, guides, and rulers; for navigating from one page to another; and for setting page numbering.

Margins and Columns Use the Margins and Columns command to set or change the default layout settings for all new documents or the current open document.

Ruler Guides   In the dialog box that displays with this command, set the ruler guides' view threshold (magnification below which rulers are not displayed) and line color.

Create Guides   In the Create Guides dialog box, you set the number of rows and columns, gutter size, as well as other options for placing, removing, or previewing guides.

Layout Adjustment   Select this menu command to turn Enable Layout Adjustment on or off.

NOTE   See Chapters 2 and 3 for more details about document setup.

First Page/Previous Page/Next Page/Last Page/Go Back/Go Forward
These are page navigation commands.

TIP   Use the Edit Shortcuts command to set your own keystroke commands. The Edit Shortcuts keystroke command is Shift+Ctrl+Alt+K (Windows) or Opt+Shift+Cmd+K (Macintosh).

Insert Page Number   Set your page numbering in the dialog box that opens with this command.

WARNING   Remember to confirm absolute or section numbering for your pages. See File ≻ Preferences ≻ General dialog box.

Type Menu

The Type menu displays commands used for composing text, opening palettes, creating character outlines, and replacing and showing characters.

Font This command displays the list of typefaces or fonts installed on your system. "Missing" (not installed on your system) fonts that are specified in an open document will also appear in the font listing.

Size The menu option for setting the point size of your text. Choose a preset point size or other to enter a custom point size in the Character palette.

Character/Paragraph/Tabs/Story/Character Styles/Paragraph Styles The menu commands for showing palettes that you use when composing text.

Create Outlines Create outlined type from bitmapped characters.

TIP When creating outlines, remember to leave ample space inside characters (counters). It will help prevent filled-in characters during the printing process.

Insert/Replace Characters This is another method for editing composed text and inserting special characters or symbols.

Show Hidden Characters Shows or hides invisible or nonprinting characters.

NOTE Learn how to format text in Chapter 9.

Object Menu

The Object menu contains commands that can help you to arrange objects, create groups, ungroup objects, lock or unlock the position of elements, change text frames, manipulate content, set image color settings, and edit paths.

Arrange The Arrange command provides access to the Bring to Front, Bring Forward, Send Backward, and Send to Back submenu commands.

Group The Group command combines several selected objects into a single unit. This new combined unit can be moved or transformed without affecting the original positioning of one object to another or their attributes.

Ungroup The Ungroup command voids a previous Group command.

Lock Position/Unlock Position The two commands work as a toggle switch to prevent or to allow the moving of an element.

NOTE Because these menu commands relate to an active tool or selection, they are often found on context menus. See Chapter 3 for more info on context menus.

Text Frame Options Displays a dialog box where you can modify the selected text frame's specifications such as column width or gutter.

Fitting The Fitting menu command provides access to the Fit Content to Frame, Fit Frame to Content, Center Content, and Fit Content Proportionally submenu commands.

Content The Content menu command provides access to the Graphic, Text, and Unassigned submenu options.

NOTE Find more about placing graphics in InDesign documents in Chapter 6.

Text Wrap The Text Wrap command shows a palette.

TIP Combine the Text Wrap palette with the Transform, Character, and Paragraph palette group to speed up text specification. See Chapter 3 for more information about palette basics.

Corner Effects Select the size and effect applied to a corner of a frame or object.

Clipping Path InDesign supports EPS, TIFF, and PSD images that contain clipping paths. The clipping paths are used to define a transparent background for the image. Clipping paths are not created in InDesign, but are made in an image-editing program. (See Chapter 17 for more information about clipping paths.)

WARNING InDesign cannot import alpha-channel information from a TIFF image.

Image Color Settings Shows a selected image's color settings in a dialog box. You can enable color management and select a color profile or rendering intent. The dialog box will also display a warning when color management is turned off for the document.

Compound Paths Choose to Make or Release a compound path.

Reverse Path Changes the direction of a path.

NOTE Learn more about drawing and editing paths in Chapter 17.

View Menu

Change your InDesign's document window display with View menu commands such as Zoom In, Zoom Out, Fit Page in Window, Fit Spread in Window, Actual Size, and Entire Pasteboard. See the "Document Display Windows" section earlier in this appendix for a more detailed review of InDesign's document window options.

NOTE For more information about changing window views and other desktop basics, see Chapter 3.

The View menu also offers standard Show/Hide toggle switch commands for such program features as text threads, frame edges, rulers, guides, and baseline and document grids. There are toggle switch commands to Lock/Unlock Guides, Snap to Guides, Snap to Document Grid, and Display Master Items as well.

NOTE Go to Appendix A to find out more about grid and guides preference options.

Window Menu

The New Window, Cascade, and Tile commands on the Window menu allow you to manage the InDesign desktop. When you select Cascade, all your open windows are stagger-stepped so that you can see each windows title bar. The Tile command places open windows side by side on the program desktop.

The Window menu also lists commands for opening palettes such as Tools, Transform Align, Pages Layers, Navigator Swatches, Swatch Libraries, Stroke, Color, Gradient, Attributes, and Libraries.

Help Menu

Access the Help menu, shown in Figures B.10 and B.11, when you want to use the online help instead of the manual. Options include About InDesign (Windows), About Balloon Help (Macintosh), Show Balloons (Macintosh), Help Topics, and How to Use Help. Other commands—such as Top Issues, Downloadables, and Adobe Corporate News—provide access to Adobe technical papers, product information, and updates. If you want to register your copy of InDesign online, there is a command for that too.

FIGURE B.10
The Help menu (Windows)

FIGURE B.11
The Help menu (Macintosh)

Context Menus

Work with context-sensitive menus to quickly apply commands that relate to the active tool or selection. Most context menus can be accessed simply by right-clicking on the desktop (Windows) or by pressing the Control key as you hold down the mouse button (Macintosh). The following graphic is an example of a context menu.

NOTE Menus are placed in context in Chapter 3.

The InDesign Palettes

Commands to open palettes are found under the File, Type, Object, and Window headings on the main menu. InDesign has lots of palettes, 20 different kinds if you're not counting each item in the Library or Swatch Library. They are:

Pages	Color
Layers	Gradient
Navigator	Attributes
Transform	Align
Character	Tabs
Paragraph	Story
Paragraph Styles	Text Wrap
Character Styles	Links
Swatches	Library
Stroke	Swatch Library

Some palettes are grouped and others are not. You have the option to reorganize them to suit your needs.

Pages Palette

The Pages palette allows you to control pages, spreads, master pages, and master spreads. Page icons, with the page number indicated below the icon, appear in the top half of the palette. The master pages or spreads assigned to the document are shown in the bottom half of the palette.

NOTE   Find out about document management in Chapter 16.

Layers Palette

The Layers palette, at the heart of Adobe Photoshop and Illustrator, is also an integral part of InDesign. Working with the Layers palette, you can create, edit, lock, and delete layers. You can rearrange the order in which layers appear and move an object from its current layer to a different layer. The frontmost layer appears at the top of the Layers palette list. Toggle layer visibility by clicking on the eye icon in the left-hand column.

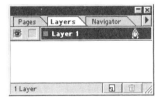

NOTE   See Chapter 13 to discover how to build a document using layers.

Navigator Palette

The Navigator palette is a blessing for finding your way around large documents. Use this palette to quickly change a document view. The palette features a thumbnail view, a view box that you move to change view locations, a magnification text box, zoom out and zoom in buttons, and a zoom slider bar. The Navigator palette menu commands permit you to assign a palette color to the view box and to view all spreads.

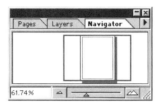

 NOTE Travel to Chapter 3 to learn how to navigate in the InDesign work area.

Transform Palette

With the Transform palette you can inspect or assign values for position, size, rotation, and shearing for any selected object. The Transform palette menu commands offer shortcuts for rotating or flipping (reflecting) objects. View the Transform palette in either horizontal or vertical format.

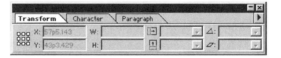

Character Palette

You assign your type specifications with the Character palette. Select your font family, type style, font size, leading, tracking, and fine-tune letter spacing (kerning), horizontal scale, skew, and language. Your chosen language affects the rules applied by the spelling checker and how text hyphenates and justifies. The palette can be seen in either a horizontal or vertical format.

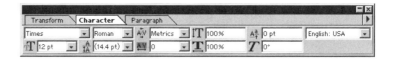

Paragraph Palette

The Paragraph palette is used to apply attributes to an entire paragraph. The *paragraph* is composed of a range of text with a carriage return at the end. In this palette you can define the left indent, the first line left indent, space before, the number of lines for a drop cap, hyphenation, alignment and justification, right indent, alignment to a baseline grid, space after the paragraph, and drop cap for one or more characters. The palette can be displayed in either a horizontal or vertical format.

 NOTE See Chapter 9 for more information about text composition.

Paragraph Styles Palette

Click on an insertion point or select text if you want to activate the Paragraph Styles palette. This palette displays information about the applied style: style name, style with additional formatting (overrides), and imported style. Lines of text with multiple assigned styles do not have a style highlighted in the Paragraph Styles palette.

Character Styles Palette

The Character Styles palette is nearly identical in appearance to the Paragraph Styles palette. You use this palette to assign a character style to the selected characters.

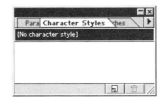

NOTE   Learn how to work with Styles palettes in Chapter 10.

Swatches Palette

This is your indispensable palette for color specification. Select the Swatches palette to create and name any color. Use this palette to edit any named color. New colors or gradients made and stored in the Swatches palette are only assigned to the current document. Different sets of swatches can be stored in the Swatches palette for each document.

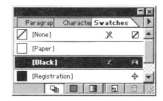

Stroke Palette

The Stroke palette sets the characteristics of a path: weight, cap style, miter limit, join style, dashed or solid line, start point, and end point.

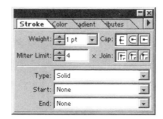

Color Palette

The Color palette can be used to mix colors and functions much like Adobe Illustrator's Color palette. The Color palette displays a fill box, stroke box, out-of-gamut alert, nearest color in the CMYK gamut, color spectrum, and color value slider. Adobe recommends mixing colors with the Swatches palette. Any time you want, you can move the current Color palette color to the Swatches palette.

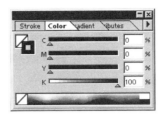

Gradient Palette

The Gradient palette, similar to the Adobe Illustrator Gradient palette, works well for making a rarely used unnamed gradient. Adobe recommends using the Swatches palette for creating and storing gradients.

 NOTE Learn how to select and apply color to type and objects in Chapter 12.

Attributes Palette

To overprint a stroke or fill, you use the Attributes palette. Select your object first, before you click an overprint attribute box.

 NOTE Advanced printing options are covered in Chapter 18.

Align Palette

The Align palette helps you to precisely line up selected objects along a horizontal or vertical axis. Objects can also be distributed evenly along a horizontal or vertical axis.

The Align palette doesn't affect locked objects and doesn't change the alignment of text paragraphs.

 NOTE See Chapter 15 to learn about precision object placement.

Tabs Palette

The Tabs palette allows you to set the indent markers for an entire paragraph. In the Tabs palette, you specify the tab style, tab position, tab leader box, and align on or off. The Tabs palette can be snapped to a frame by clicking on the Magnet icon, which is located to the right of the tab ruler.

 NOTE Formatting text using tabs and indents are discussed in Chapter 9.

Story Palette

Select and set the optical margin alignment (hanging punctuation) in the Story palette.

Text Wrap Palette

There are five options for wrapping text on the Text Wrap palette: wrap around bounding box, wrap around object shape, jump object, jump to next column, and no wrap. In this palette, you can also set the wrap-offset values.

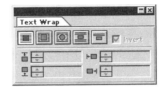

NOTE Wrap around Chapter 14 for more details about advanced type composition.

Links Palette

The Links palette is used to identify, select, monitor, and update images or text that are linked to external files.

NOTE See Chapter 7 for more information about importing, exporting, and managing graphics.

Library Palette

The Library palette displays information about the current object library and each item that is stored in that library. You can identify, search, sort, and display subsets of library items. Manage your digital assets by creating new libraries, adding or removing objects from existing libraries, selecting individual page elements, or all the elements on a page between the document and the object library. The object library is saved as a named file on your disk.

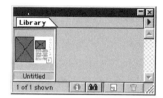

NOTE Browse through Chapter 11 for more info about storing elements in object or asset libraries.

Swatch Library Palette

Here's how to see a Swatch Library palette. When you select Window ➢ Swatch Libraries from the main menu, a submenu appears with the following options: DIC-COLOR, FOCOLTONE, PANTONE (Coated, Process, and Uncoated), System (Macintosh), System (Windows) TOYO COLOR FINDER, TRUMATCH, and Web. The Other Library option is used to import swatches from Adobe Illustrator documents. The Illustrator format is read and the selected swatch palette is opened. The palette will display information about the current available colors in that swatch. The following graphic is an example of a Swatch Library palette group.

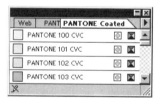

NOTE See Chapter 12 for more details about selecting color.

appendix C

COLOR MANAGEMENT AND CALIBRATION

COLOR MANAGEMENT AND CALIBRATION

In this appendix, I will review managing color in InDesign and calibrating and profiling your monitor and printer for consistent color reproduction.

Managing Color in InDesign

If you've worked with the color management tools in Photoshop 5 and Illustrator 8, you'll find yourself in familiar territory in InDesign. InDesign shares the same core Adobe technologies, such as Rainbow Bridge, Adobe CMS, Adobe Graphics Manager, Cool Type, and the Adobe PDF library. As with other aspects of InDesign, the color management tools can be modified and extended to fit specific company, client, or project workflows.

Color Management Terminology and Theory

Adobe's color management tools include the Adobe Color Management System (CMS) and the Adobe Gamma utility for calibrating and characterizing your monitors. These tools are ICC compliant. ICC stands for International Color Consortium, which in 1993 established an industry-standard format for describing the gamut (tonal range of colors) and unique characteristics of different devices, such as scanners, digital cameras, monitors, and proofing printers. Because the consortium includes major companies like Adobe Systems, Agfa-Gevaert N.V., Apple Computer, Eastman Kodak Company, Microsoft Corporation, and others, the use of ICC profiles for managing color is gaining widespread adoption in the desktop color market. This includes support at the system-level with applications such as Microsoft's Image Color Matching (ICM) 2 and Apple's ColorSync 2 and later. There's more info about ColorSync in the "About ColorSync" sidebar later in this appendix.

Here are some terms that you'll often find in color management:

Calibration *Calibration* allows you to set a device to known color conditions. Devices such as monitors and scanners can change color frequently. Because a monitor's phosphors lose brightness as they age, the color you see on screen shifts. A flatbed scanner's CCD (charge-coupled device) array will degrade from use, and over time this causes color shifts in the scanned files. The rule of thumb is to calibrate before you build a device color profile. If you do, the resulting profile will accurately represent the current color conditions of the device.

Characterization Each device has its own way of describing its color *characteristics*. When you create a profile (after calibrating a device), you are describing or characterizing those qualities unique to that device in specific situations. For example, changes in toner or ink, paper, screening, or the temperature and humidity in the room can affect a proofing printer's color profiles. For each change in variable, you would want the profile to reflect how that device was performing under those unique conditions.

Clipping When you're creating an image using Adobe RGB (1998), for example, and then change its RGB setup to sRGB, the color space becomes *clipped*. This happens because sRGB's color gamut cannot render as many different tonal variations of colors as Adobe RGB (1998). Your four variations of blue could become three, and the overall color shifts to reflect the more limited palette. Decreasing the tonal range of a color space can cause flattening of midtones or loss of highlight or shadow details in images.

CMM The abbreviation for *Color Matching Model* or *Color Management Module*. CMM is another name used for the Color Engine. The module, a CMS software component, uses the ICC device profiles to calculate the color space conversion from one device to another. For example, a desktop printer's CMYK profile was embedded in a document and proofed in-house. It was then outsourced for an Iris-generated proof. Because each printer's technology maps colors differently, the service provider used a CMM to change from the desktop printer's CMYK device profile to the Iris's CMYK device profile. Otherwise, the resulting color in the Iris proof would not accurately reflect the color space of the Iris printer.

CRD The abbreviation for *Color Rendering Dictionary*. Each output device has a built-in CRD. To override the default CRD, you have to download a new CRD to the output device. There's more about CRD's in the "Document Color Settings" section later in this appendix.

Gamma *Gamma* represents a monitor's intensity characteristics. Gamma settings influence how a monitor gradates the entire range of tonal values from black to white. Red, green, or blue gamma values can range from values of 0.75 to 3.75, according to Adobe Gamma. There are different gamma settings for Macintosh and PC monitors.

ICC Device Profile *Profiles* are used to perform color transformations from one device to another, and also to describe how each device reproduces its color space. You can obtain generic profiles from device manufacturers and other graphic arts industry suppliers, but they will not be appropriate for all your color workflows. When generic profiles can't handle the job, use device-profiling software and a color-measuring device like a colorimeter or spectrophotometer to create custom profiles. For a list of companies offering custom profiling products or measuring devices, see Table C.1 later in this appendix.

Phosphors A monitor's *phosphors* create a gamut of colors when they are charged by electrons at different voltages. As phosphors age, the tonal range of the colors that they produce will shift. Some monitors have an internal calibration system, which will adjust the factory-set standard for color to compensate for monitor deterioration.

Rendering Intents Adobe InDesign supports four methods for mapping or converting colors from one device's gamut to another device's gamut (tonal range of colors). They are Perceptual (Images), Saturation (Graphics), Relative Colorimetric, and Absolute Colorimetric.

NOTE Illustrator and PageMaker call perceptual and saturation rendering intents by a different name. Although called Image and Graphics, respectively, they accomplish the same results.

White Point *White point* is a required reference point used in device calibration and profile characterization. For example, in the Absolute Colorimetric mode rendering intent, white point represents paper color in digital soft proofing. The colorcast of the white point, i.e., is it shifting to yellow or blue or another color, becomes an important factor in the overall appearance of color on screen. It determines whether or not the on-screen representation will accurately reflect what happens on press or within other hard-copy output.

Adding Device Profiles to InDesign's CMS

When you installed InDesign, you selected device profiles that represented equipment you or your vendors are using. If you have a device for which Adobe did not supply a profile, you should contact the equipment manufacturer or locate the company's Web site. There may be generic profiles available as free product updates at their Web site or ftp address. If you obtain a generic profile from a manufacturer or create you own custom profile, you can add those profiles to your system. Choose one of the following methods:

- Copy profiles into the `WinNT\System32\Color` folder (Windows NT).
- Copy profiles into the `Windows\System\Color` folder (Windows 98). See Figure C.1 to view a list of profiles.
- Copy profiles into the `System\ColorSync Profiles` folder (Mac OS 8.5 or later and ColorSync 2.5 or later). If the profiles don't appear in the ColorSync control panel or plug-ins pop-up menus after installation and restarting of your computer, see the "About ColorSync" sidebar at the end of this section. Figure C.2 shows you the ColorSync 2.6.1 Control Panel.

Restart your computer after copying the profiles, regardless of which method you used.

NOTE Check with the instructions to see if you need to disable your virus protection software before you install a profile. If you do, remember to turn your virus protection software back on.

MANAGING COLOR IN INDESIGN 703

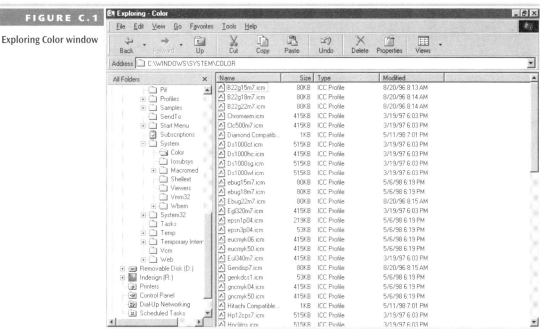

FIGURE C.1
Exploring Color window

Color Management and Calibration

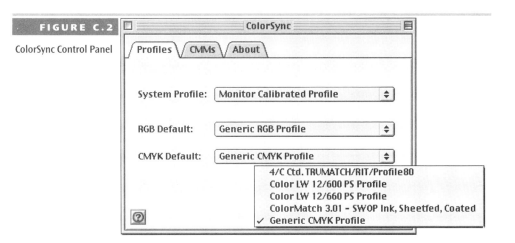

FIGURE C.2
ColorSync Control Panel

About ColorSync

ColorSync, Apple's MacOS color management architecture, is an environment for device calibration, characterization, and profiling. Like Adobe's color management system, ColorSync supports the ICC (International Color Consortium) standard. More than 100 hardware and software products are now ColorSync savvy, and the list is growing. Apple hopes to establish ColorSync as the industry standard for managing color and cross-platform color transformations.

Working as a faceless background application, you can use ColorSync to get detailed information about profiles placed in the ColorSync Profiles folder, profiles associated with displays, and profiles embedded within images. This is particularly helpful when your color workflow includes products and software from vendors other than Adobe.

Here are some trends in ColorSync's development:

- ColorSync 2.6.1, compatible with Adobe Separation Tables (creates link between CMYK and ICC device-independent color), will be updated to version 3 in early fall 1999.
- Macintosh users: Kodak CMM version 2.6.3, which is included within ColorSync 2.6.1 may cause pages within an InDesign document to fail to display. Also, if you're using the Agfa ColorSync CMM version 3.0.9, you'll need to update the component. See the InDesign ReadMe file for more details.
- Apple is also working on ColorSync for Windows, which was introduced to developers at Apple's 1999 World Wide Development conference.
- Apple is partnering with paper companies to create profiles of specific ink and paper combinations. These profiles are used in remote and soft proofing approval cycles where you need to simulate on screen the effect of different press conditions on a document.

If you're a Mac OS user, these ColorSync's options may help you to manage your color workflow better:

AppleScript support   Scripts supplied by Apple include options for building a table of images and profile data into a Web page for remote proofing, removing a profile from an image, mimicking a PC monitor, proofing to chosen profiles, and proofing to specific profiles. You can also add your own custom scripts to the AppleScripts folder located in the `Apple Extras/ColorSync Extras` folder.

Photoshop Plug-in   The Photoshop-compatible plug-in fully supports 16-bit color. If you're using several different image applications and they support Photoshop plug-ins, you can consistently apply the same profiles to each application's graphic file.

Profile First Aid   This utility, sometimes used in conjunction with the ColorSync Rename AppleScript, can verify and repair any noncompliant profiles that no longer show up in the ColorSync control panel or plug-ins pop-up menus.

Continued on next page

> **About ColorSync** *(continued)*
>
> An excellent online resource for learning the latest information about trends in color management is Apple's ColorSync User Group list. List members run the gamut from beginners to seasoned graphic arts and publishing professionals. Apple's ColorSync team monitors the discussions, which are not limited to Apple-related topics, and include helpful tips for working with other manufacturers' products. The posts are archived, enabling you to search for topics of interest from previous discussions.
>
> Sign up to become a list member at the Apple Color Sync Web site at www.apple.com/colorsync. The ColorSync Web page also has links for downloading updates, product news, technical support, and other color management resources.

Color Workflows

InDesign supports many different color management workflows, including a CMYK-press-oriented workflow, a hybrid CMYK+RGB+L*a*b workflow, and an RGB+L*a*b workflow. Within those basic workflows, changing a single factor, such as which ink sets you selected for your job, can influence color management decisions. Printing in only PANTONE® Match Colors or TOYO® inks, or adding these solid colors to a four-color process job, or specifying the PANTONE Hexachrome® (CMYK+Orange and Green) ink set, will produce very different results from the same document files.

Another, more contemporary challenge to the old standard of scanning in CMYK and printing in CMYK-oriented workflow is the increasing need to distribute information via several different media, including print, the Web, and CD-ROM or DVD formats. In this situation, long-standing processes that began with scanning to CMYK no longer are feasible. To convert a CMYK scan back to RGB for conversion to the Web's Indexed color model is a no-no since the color gamut of CMYK is much smaller than RGB. Lost colors cannot be regained by changing to a larger color space model. In addition, Photoshop doesn't allow conversion from CMYK directly to the Indexed color space model. The option just doesn't exist. The images will have to be rescanned from the originals, which may take time from already tight schedules or add additional overhead to a project's budget. In worst case scenarios, the originals are no longer available, and you're forced to schedule a new photo shoot. More and more you will see companies following the lead of publishers like Time Inc., whose magazines are now adopting scanning and archiving to RGB workflows. Apple Computer has been citing case studies like *People* magazine to promote the adoption of RGB-based ColorSync workflows throughout the communications community.

Ultimately there are no right or wrong workflows, but unique factors in each project that have to be acknowledged as part of your color management decision-making process. Consider these questions when determining which workflow to choose:

- What hardware and software will be used in the project?
- What are your scheduling milestones for concept development, artwork and copy creation, page assembly, proofing, creating final output, and distribution?
- What is the overall project budget?
- What is the color expertise of team members (including vendors and contractors)?
- Will schedules allow for training of team members?
- What is the current color-management policy, both in-house and at your prepress service provider or printer? How much of a seismic change will be required to adopt another color workflow process?
- Is the project goal the multi-platform distribution of the final product?
- Is your client willing to let you experiment with new processes?
- Can you set up a test project to work out the kinks without impacting everyday creation, assembly, production, and distribution cycles in your firm?

Selecting Color Settings

Here are some helpful suggestions to consider before choosing your application and document color settings:

- Before setting InDesign's application and document color specifications, schedule a production meeting with all team members to establish the color standards for the project. Do this as early in the design proposal phase as possible. Your discussion should include color settings for other software and hardware, such as scanners, digital cameras or desktop printers, that will be used in the project.
- Consult with your prepress provider or commercial printer to discover any potential red herrings that could become costly reworks on press. Don't be afraid to raise questions about color workflows and profile usage when asking for bids or estimates from service providers or printers. As the trend for the adoption of nonproprietary prepress processes increases, you will want to find out if your vendors can easily support ICC device-independent color management.
- Distribute application and color settings to all team members to help avoid problems when proofing or processing files for final output.
- Keep a record of the project's color specifications and history on file for future reference. Don't forget to update your records if changes are made during the actual production process.

- If this whole process seems overwhelming, give a color management consultant a call. If you don't know whom to call, check Adobe's InDesign or Apple Color-Sync Web pages. They list consultants who may be able to help you. For more local help, call or e-mail members of your professional society chapter to find a recommendation. Ask any consultant you're considering to present a portfolio and provide references that demonstrate knowledge in your industry niche (such as newspapers vs. magazines vs. annual reports). If they can't provide this information, you may want to keep looking.

- Take a class or workshop in color management at a local school or training facility, publishing conference, or university that targets designers or other publishing professionals. You can also search the Web for corporate-sponsored training programs or workshops.

Application Color Settings

The Application Color Settings apply to all open InDesign documents and are saved with InDesign—they're not saved with document or template files. To open the Application Color Settings dialog box, shown in Figure C.3, select File ➢ Color Settings ➢ Application Color Settings.

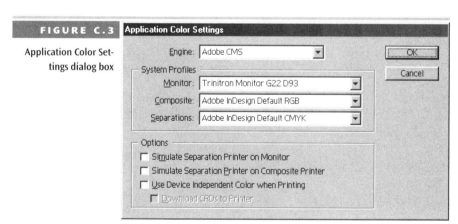

FIGURE C.3
Application Color Settings dialog box

WARNING If you're planning to use Photoshop 5 (or later) and Illustrator 8 with InDesign, check and confirm the color settings for those programs (or others) before setting InDesign's application and document settings. Your settings need to be consistent across all programs. To check Photoshop settings, select File ➢ Color Settings ➢ RGB Setup\CMYK Setup\Grayscale Setup\Profile Setup to open each of the dialog boxes. To check Illustrator's settings, select File ➢ Color Settings to choose which profiles to embed in each graphic.

In the Application Color Settings dialog box, you can make the following selections.

Engine

The color workflow you set up, as well as the requirements of hardware, software, utilities, and drivers that you're using, will help determine which engine is the better choice. Once you decide which CMS you'll be using, apply its application consistently across all platforms. InDesign offers two default choices for color management systems (CMS). They are:

- Adobe CMS
- Kodak Digital Science ICC CMS

NOTE Macintosh users working with ColorSync 2.6.1 will also see the Apple ColorSync, Agfa CMM, and the Heidelberg CMM in the InDesign Engine option menu. If you want to use another color engine or CMS with InDesign, it must be ICC compliant.

System Profiles

Change these system profiles any time you change or recalibrate monitors or output devices.

Monitor Choose the device profile for your monitor. The option menu, shown in Figure C.4, lists generic monitor profiles, including the Adobe InDesign Default RGB, several generic gamma monitors, different products models from companies such SONY, NEC, DiamondTron, and Hitachi, and any custom monitor profiles that you created and installed.

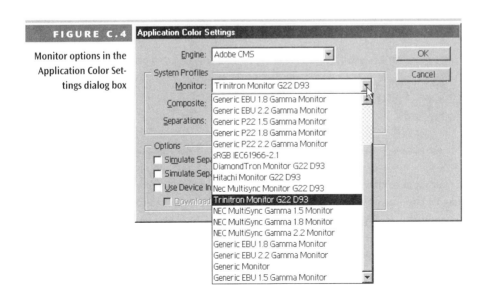

FIGURE C.4

Monitor options in the Application Color Settings dialog box

Composite From this option menu, shown in Figure C.5, choose the generic device profile that characterizes your color output, such as a color laser or non-Postscript ink jet printer. If one is available, select the custom profile that was made for your current in-house proofing printer.

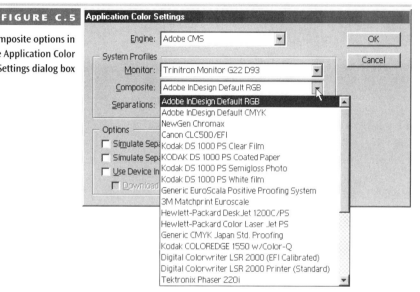

FIGURE C.5

Composite options in the Application Color Settings dialog box

Separations This profile represents your final CMYK press output, such as for your imagesetter or SWOP (Specifications for Web Offset Publications) standard. (Chapter 18 has more information about the SWOP standard.) Check with your prepress service provider and/or printer. They may have press or device profiles that they recommend and distribute to their clients. Install the profile following the instructions reviewed previously in this appendix.

(Color Settings) Options

The color settings in the Options area are used to apply soft proofing, remote proofing, and printer specifications.

Simulate Separation Printer on Monitor Select this option when you want to use your monitor as a soft-proofing device. To create your document's on-screen proof, InDesign displays the press colors described in your chosen Separations system profile within your Monitor profile's color gamut.

 WARNING Choose a rendering intent from the Document Color Settings dialog box that relates results closest to your output requirements.

Simulate Separation Printer on Composite Printer Another proofing option that uses your chosen Separations profile. In this case, the press colors are reproduced as closely as possible on output from your composite-proofing device. Any differences in print head technology, inks, paper stock, and coatings used on papers will decrease the accuracy of the composite printer simulation. For the best results, work with your vendors to calibrate your composite printer to your final press standard. There's more information about calibrating printers in the "Customizing a Printer Profile" section later in this appendix. (This option is not available when you turn on Use Device Independent Color When Printing option.)

TIP The InDesign manual notes that you can also use your composite printer profile as your separation profile. When you do this, your monitor can be used to soft proof the composite device's output. Apply this option in situations where the composite color printer can be, for example, a networked Xerox color document printer, film recorder, or wide-format ink jet printer.

Use Device Independent Color when Printing Choose this option for printing with a PostScript device-independent color.

WARNING Only select this option if your printer supports PostScript device-independent color.

Download CRDs to Printer Some facts about this option:

- To use this option, the Use Device Independent Color when Printing option must also be selected.
- It builds a Color Rendering Dictionary (CRD) based on the Separations profile you selected in this dialog box. InDesign will download this custom CRD as a substitute for your output device's built-in CRD.
- Use with caution. This option is best left for use by expert color workflow specialists. Working with incorrectly built custom CRDs can create major headaches when ripping or processing files to devices such as imagesetters or digital presses.

Document Color Settings

Document Color Settings only apply to the open InDesign document. To open the Document Color Settings dialog box, shown in Figure C.6, select File ➢ Color Settings ➢ Document Color Settings.

When you click on the Enable Color Management checkbox, located at the top of the Document Color Settings dialog box, several things happen:

- All of InDesign's color management options are activated.
- Source Profile and Rendering Intent settings are saved with the document.

You should keep in mind that each document can have its own custom CMS specifications. You can also enable color management for one document but not for another, if necessary.

WARNING Don't Enable Color Management if you're only guessing when selecting source profiles and rendering intents. Your prepress service provider and/or printer can embed the correct profiles for you. If you do embed profiles, have your vendor confirm that your settings were correctly selected.

NOTE If you don't enable InDesign's CMS, the program will still embed the default CMYK, LAB, and RGB profiles into a document.

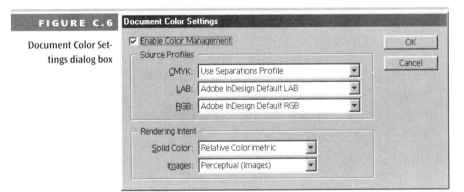

FIGURE C.6
Document Color Settings dialog box

The following options are available from the Document Color Settings dialog box.

Source Profiles

The source profiles you select serve several functions:

- They instruct InDesign's color engine or CMS on how to interpret color generated by different input devices like digital cameras or programs like Photoshop or CorelDRAW!
- They apply a profile to any artwork created with InDesign's drawing tools.
- They apply a profile to any artwork that was imported *without* an embedded profile.

Overriding Embedded Profiles InDesign's source profiles don't affect images imported with embedded profiles. If you want to override or ignore a placed image's profiles:

1. Select Object ➢ Image Color Settings to open the Image Color Settings dialog box. The default shortcuts are Shift+Ctrl+Alt+D (Windows) or Opt+Shift+Cmd+D (Macintosh).

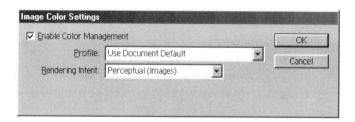

2. Select a new profile and rendering intent. Click OK to accept your changes.

WARNING InDesign only color manages bitmapped images. When working with a vector graphic image, embed the profile using the program of origination, i.e. Illustrator. For InDesign to color manage the file, you must convert the graphic to a bitmapped file format (like TIFF) before placing it in a document.

You can also use a context menu to access the Image Color Settings dialog box. To do this:

1. Select the image.
2. Right-click your mouse button (Windows) or press the Control key as the mouse button is held down (Macintosh) to open the context menu.
3. Select Graphics ➢ Image Color Settings.
4. Select your override profile or rendering intent as above, and then click OK to accept your changes.

TIP You can also use a ColorSync AppleScript to remove an embedded profile from an image file. (Macintosh)

Selecting a Source Profile Select a source profile from the CMYK, LAB, and RGB option menus. Adobe offers these suggestions:

- For each color model (CMYK, LAB, RGB), select a profile that best reflects the most common source for the images placed in your InDesign document.

- For CMYK, use the same Separations Profile that you selected in the Applications Color Settings dialog box.
- Choose the Adobe InDesign default LAB profile, which is equivalent to Photoshop's LAB profile. (In Photoshop 5 select File ➢ Color Settings ➢ Profile Setup.) If your team uses another LAB illuminant, select that custom profile instead for all programs.
- Select the RGB profile created when you calibrated your monitor, unless you're importing lots of scanned images (with no embedded profiles) made with a different monitor. Then, choose the profile that describes that source instead. (See Figure C.7.)

WARNING Avoid selecting sRGB for any print applications, particularly if you're a Macintosh user. sRGB, based on a PC monitor standard, has a limited tonal range of colors and will cause Macintosh-based graphics and documents to color shift when printed. Many imaging and graphics applications now default to sRGB. Don't forget to reset their RGB settings too.

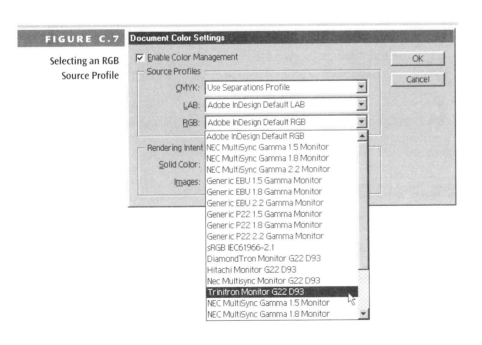

FIGURE C.7

Selecting an RGB Source Profile

Rendering Intent

When you choose your rendering intents, you're deciding how best to handle out-of-gamut colors. Out-of-gamut colors occur when you convert from larger color spaces like RGB to smaller ones like CMYK. InDesign allows you to specify default Solid Color and Images rendering intents. Choose a Solid Color setting for non-photographic InDesign artwork drawn with tools such as the Rectangle, Polygon, Pen, and Type tools. Use the Images options, shown in Figure C.8, to choose a placed images (photographs and illustrations) rendering intent. For each rendering intent you have the same four options:

Relative Colorimetric   Apply when color matching logos and other graphics to corporate graphic standards. Uses a monitor's characteristics (like white point) when translating color gamuts.

Perceptual (Images)   Works best for an image because the compressed color space retains the visual color appearance. Preserves the lightness or tonal relationships in the gamut when out-of-gamut colors shift to in-gamut colors.

Saturation (Graphics)   Retains color saturation at the expense of exact color matching. An out-of-gamut color will be mapped to the nearest in-gamut color. Consider using this intent with Illustrator or 3D computer graphics images.

Absolute Colorimetric   For color matching in absolute CIE (International Commission on Illumination) parameters. Doesn't use the white point monitor characteristic when translating gamut color.

NOTE   The Solid Color default rendering intent is Relative Colorimetric. The Images default rendering intent is Perceptual (Images).

FIGURE C.8
Rendering Intents

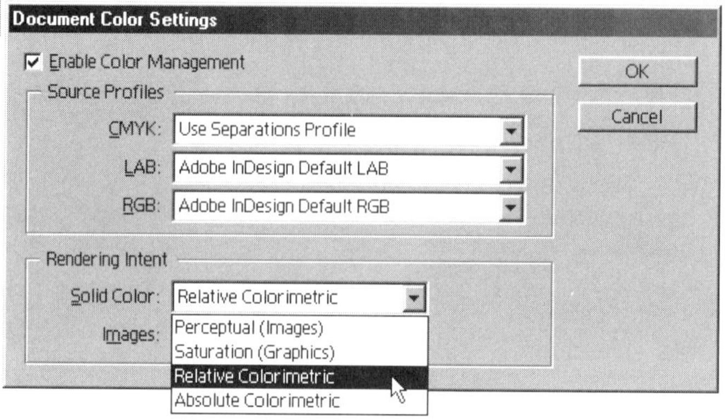

Calibrating Your Monitor

To set up a good color management workflow, you need to calibrate and profile your monitor on a regular basis. If your monitor was recently calibrated and profiled, skip this process when you launch InDesign. Instead, select that monitor profile in InDesign's color settings dialog boxes.

For the most accurate monitor calibration, measurement, and profiling, use a hardware device like a CIE-based colorimeter and calibrating and profiling software. The colorimeter attaches directly to the screen using suction cups or is supported by your hand. The instrument measures the monitor's color parameters such as gamma and shadow control. (See Figure C.9 for an example of a colorimeter from X-Rite.) The monitor's settings are then adjusted, documented, and converted into a grayscale or RGB display profile by the software. InDesign users, who don't have a monitor-measuring device, can use the Adobe Gamma utility supplied with the program. For more information about the utility, see the "Adobe Gamma Utility" section later in this appendix.

FIGURE C.9

X-Rite's Monitor Optimizer

X-Rite Monitor Optimizer
Photo courtesy of X-Rite, Incorporated

The Work Environment

The workroom environment affects monitor viewing conditions. Lighting conditions, the color of walls and ceilings, and placement of the monitor in a room impact how you perceive colors on screen. It is important to

- Create consistent lighting and viewing conditions throughout the day by controlling the flow of sunlight into the room and the intensity of artificial lighting.

- Avoid placing a monitor in front of a window, or in a location where direct spotlighting shines into the monitor screen. If necessary, place a hood on your monitor to reduce reflective glare on-screen.
- Eliminate the color cast from artificial lighting by turning off fluorescent lighting or replacing bulbs with D50 (5,000 degree Kelvin) lighting fixtures.
- Paint walls and ceilings a neutral gray color. Any bright colors in the room, including the clothing you wear, will be reflected in the monitor screen. That also goes for bright and busy computer desktop wallpaper.

TIP Confirm the requirements for contract proofs and your client's expectations for color matching.

Adobe Gamma Utility

You can use the Adobe Gamma utility to calibrate your monitor and create a monitor profile. The Adobe Gamma utility comes with InDesign and programs like Photoshop 5 and Illustrator 8. If you previously installed the utility with Photoshop 5 or Illustrator 8, you don't need to reinstall the utility to use it again with InDesign.

NOTE A Windows 98 user's ability to calibrate monitor settings with Adobe Gamma depends upon the installed video card and video driver software. For Windows NT, Adobe Gamma can characterize, but not calibrate monitors.

Preparing for Monitor Calibration

Follow these steps to prepare for monitor calibration.

1. Turn on and warm up your monitor for minimally a half-hour. This allows the monitor to stabilize.
2. Adjust room lighting to working conditions.

3. Change your computer's desktop wallpaper or background to a solid light gray color with no visible patterns. Follow the instructions for your operating system.

4. Turn up your monitor's brightness and contrast controls to their maximum settings.

WARNING Don't change brightness and contrast settings unless you are updating a monitor profile. Any adjustments nullify the currently used monitor profile.

Using the Adobe Gamma Utility

To open the Adobe Gamma utility, do one of the following:

- Windows: select Settings ➢ Control Panel ➢ Adobe Gamma (Figure C.10).
- Macintosh: select Apple ➢ Control Panels ➢ Adobe Gamma (Figure C.11).

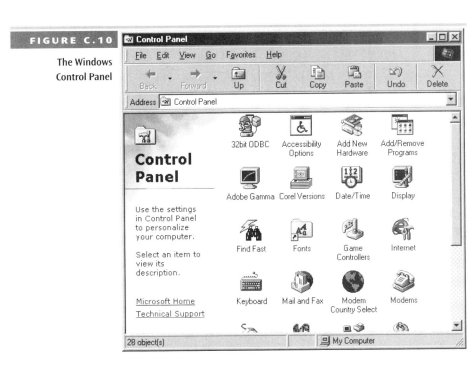

FIGURE C.10
The Windows Control Panel

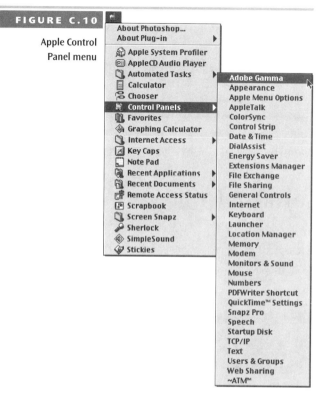

FIGURE C.10
Apple Control Panel menu

There are two versions of the utility that you can use, as shown in Figure C.12. If you're inexperienced in calibrating and profiling a monitor, select the Wizard (Windows) or Assistant (Macintosh) option. This option provides step-by-step instructions for choosing the reference monitor profile description, setting the optimum brightness and contrast range, describing the phosphors in use, calibrating the monitor's gamma and white point, and saving a profile. More experienced users can adjust settings in the Adobe Gamma utility control panel.

Begin the process by selecting your monitor's default profile if it's available. For either Adobe Gamma process, click the Load button if you need to select another monitor profile.

TIP It's useful to have your monitor's technical documentation or user guide on hand for easy reference. Consult the manufacturer if documentation is not available.

FIGURE C.12

Adobe Gamma opening screen

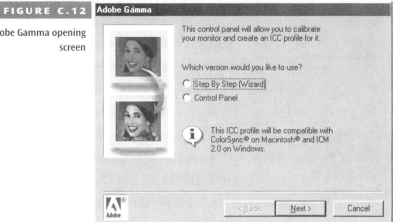

Adobe Gamma Control Panel

In the Adobe Gamma utility control panel, shown in Figures C.13 and C.14, select settings from option menus, turn on or off options with checkboxes, move sliders to adjust gamma settings, and click buttons to activate measuring tools and to load monitor profiles.

FIGURE C.13

Adobe Gamma Control Panel (Windows)

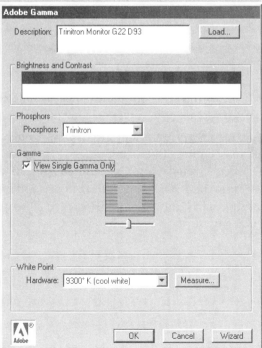

FIGURE C.14

Adobe Gamma Control Panel (Macintosh)

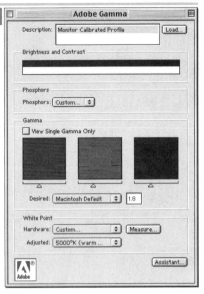

Do the following in the control panel:

Set Optimum Brightness and Contrast Range   Adjust the monitor's brightness control until the top bar's gray squares are as dark as possible (without matching the bar's black squares) while retaining a bright white bottom bar.

NOTE   The Wizard's brightness and contrast graphic is different from the Control Panel version. Follow the separate instructions for each version.

Select the Exact Phosphor Type   From the option menu, select your monitor's phosphor type. Consult manufacturer's documentation if you're not sure.

Calibrate the Monitor's Gamma   Adjust the gamma by moving the slider to correctly set how you monitor displays midtones. Drag the slider under each box until the center of the box fades into its patterned frame. If you select the View Single Gamma Only check box, then all the gammas will be combined into one reading, as shown in Figure C.14. Otherwise, you'll see separate Red, Green, and Blue gamma readings, as shown in Figure C.14.

WARNING   Use a light touch when making adjustments. Imprecise adjustments can create color-cast problems when printing.

Calibrate the Monitor's White Point Adobe Gamma provides these options for calibrating the white point of the current state:

1. Select your monitor's exact white point from the Hardware option menu. If you started the calibration process from a manufacturer-supplied profile, use its default white point value. When setting white point from a monitor's hardware controls, set the monitor first and then the Hardware menu to match.

TIP Remember generic manufacturer-supplied profiles reflect the condition of the phosphors when new.

2. Click the Measure button in the dialog box if you're not sure of the correct setting. A new screen with three squares appears, as shown in Figure C.15. Select the square that appears most neutral. Click the square you want to select. The screen returns to the Adobe Gamma control panel.

FIGURE C.15

Monitor calibration squares screen

On a Macintosh, you can also assign a target state by doing one of the following:

1. If you want to assign the current monitor white point, select Same as Hardware from the Adjusted option menu.

2. To calibrate a target value other than the current Hardware value, select another °K (degree Kelvin) setting from the Adjusted menu.

Saving the Monitor Profile

Follow these steps to save a new monitor profile in Windows:

1. Click the OK button at the bottom of the Adobe Gamma control panel.

2. The Save As dialog box opens as shown in Figure C.16. Rename the profile and select the destination folder, for example the System\Color.

3. Click Save to complete the process.

TIP Don't overwrite the original profile; use another name. Always keep copies of original profiles.

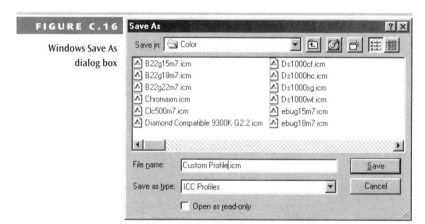

FIGURE C.16
Windows Save As dialog box

Follow these steps to save a new monitor profile in Macintosh:

1. Click the upper left-hand corner box to close the Adobe Gamma control panel.

2. A screen prompt appears requesting that you save changes before closing. Select Save.

3. The Save As dialog box opens as shown in Figure C.17. Rename the profile and select the destination folder—for example, the ColorSync Profiles folder.

4. Click Save to complete the process.

FIGURE C.17
The ColorSync Profiles Save As dialog box

Calibrating and Profiling Your Desktop Output Devices

Before you profile an output device, you will need to know that your printer is in good working order:

1. Follow the manufacturer's directions for installation and setup. Remember to remove any packing materials or tape from inside the printer. (If your printer is already installed, use this process to check your printer when you replace ink or toner cartridges.)
2. Check alignments of all moving mechanical parts, such as print heads in ink jet printers.
3. Print out the default test file pattern from the printer's control panel.
4. Check accessibility of all page setup dialog boxes that can change printer properties or determine advanced printing options.
5. Check for downloading of different file types (document, graphics, and images) from your computer to the printer, using different page setup specifications. This procedure is also another good test of print head alignment.
6. After you completed the installation and test process, you're ready to create a printer profile.

Customizing a Printer Profile

When you want to customize or create a new printer profile, you will need to do the following, as illustrated in Figure C.18:

1. Prepare a color target that contains color patches that can be measured. You can use profiling software tools or use standardized test targets such as the ANSI

IT8.7/3 target series or the GATF (Graphic Arts Technical Foundation) color triangle. (See Chapter 18 for contact information.) The IT8.7/3 target contains color patches that are used to measure ink density, dot gain, shadows, solid CMY colors, gray balance, saturated color with no black, and saturated color with 20% black.

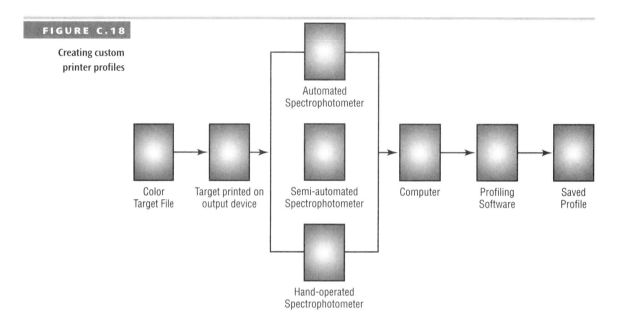

FIGURE C.18

Creating custom printer profiles

TIP When calibrating your scanner, you can use Kodak Professional Q-60 Color Input Targets for 35mm slide film, 4 x 5 inch Kodak Ektachrome film, and Kodak Ektacolor paper. They are ANSI IT8.7/1 compliant for transmission materials and It8.7/2 for reflection materials.

2. Print your color target on your desktop printer or other output device.

3. Measure the printed patterns that appear on the hard-copy output using either of the following:
   - A fully automated spectrophotometer
   - A semi-automated spectrophotometer
   - A hand-held spectrophotometer

In case you don't know what a spectrophotometer is, X-Rite's *Color Guide and Glossary*, available for downloading at their Web site (www.x-rite.com), defines it this way: "A spectrophotometer measures spectral data—the amount of light energy reflected from an object at several intervals along the visible spectrum."

Some of the newer measuring devices combine both a spectrophotometer and a densitometer in the same device. For the Web site addresses of companies offering measuring devices and profiling software, see Table C.1.

WARNING Creating custom printer profiles is not for neophytes. Accurately measuring patches for dot gain (the spread of tonal dots on press) and solid ink density can be difficult. For example, several ink jet manufacturers like Epson use micro-piezo ink jet technology. Prints are created by overlapping dots, and ink saturation coverage depends on the selected media type, i.e., high gloss coated vs. uncoated matte finish. The dot patterns are not like dot screen patterns traditionally used in offset printing.

4. Use profiling software to analyze the spectrophotometer color data and generate a printer profile.
5. Install the custom profile in your operating system's color profile folder.

TABLE C.1: MANUFACTURERERS OF HARDWARE AND/OR SOFTWARE FOR PROFILING DEVICES

Company	Web Site Address
Agfa Corporation	www.agfa.com/
BARCO Display Systems	www.barco-usa.com/
Color Savvy Systems Limited	www.colorsavvy.com/
Color Vision	www.colorpar.com/
Eastman Kodak Company	www.kodak.com/
GretagMacbeth	www.GretagMacbeth.com/
Heidelberg USA/Heidelberg CPS	www.Heidelbergusa.com/ www.linocolor.com/
ITEC, Inc. (Imaging Technologies Corp.)	www.color.com/ www.itec.net/
Imation Enterprises Corp.	www.imation.com/
Monaco Systems, Inc.	www.monacosys.com/
Pictographics International Corp.	www.picto.com/
Praxisoft	www.praxisoft.com/
Scitex America Corp.	www.scitex.com/
X-Rite, Inc.	www.x-rite.com/

TIP To find out more about the latest trends in publishing, visit the Seybold Seminars Web site: www.seyboldseminars.com. At the Web site, you'll find a listing of exhibitors and descriptions of their products.

appendix D

SCRIPTING IN INDESIGN

APPENDIX D

SCRIPTING IN INDESIGN

utomating many of InDesign's features can be accomplished via scripting. Scripting at its most basic implementation can be used to automate repetitive tasks. Applied imaginatively, scripting can support your efforts to build better workflow practices. Using scripts has an added bonus: Distributed scripts can help you maintain quality control standards across different projects, within workgroups, and when working with contractors and other vendors.

In this appendix, I'm not attempting to teach you scripting—the goal is to demonstrate how accessible InDesign is for writing scripts. The example script shows how a page containing headlines, body text, and images of different sizes can be created with scripting.

 NOTE Browse the *Adobe InDesign CD* and find the Scripting folder. The folder contains *The Adobe InDesign Scripting Guide*, a PDF file, and sample scripts. You should print these out, especially the guide, which includes the InDesign AppleScript (Macintosh) and Visual Basic (Windows) dictionaries or object libraries. When you script, you'll need to reference the dictionaries.

NOTE Unlike InDesign, QuarkXPress 4 doesn't support Visual Basic scripting.

Introduction

Scripting isn't only for programmers. Designers and other InDesign users can learn how to write InDesign scripts. Think about it this way. When you're writing scripts you're building a library of reusable digital assets such as templates, automated color workflows and style libraries, and other production shortcuts. If you're a small firm, having a library of scripts might just make it feasible for you to bid on larger, more complex projects.

Rather than repeat the introductory sample scripts provided in the guide (like `Hello World!`), I will show you how to build a basic page layout with image and text elements that have different specifications.

To avoid confusion, this appendix will now be divided into two parts: InDesign Scripting using Visual Basic and InDesign Scripting using AppleScript. For each part there will be an overview followed by step-by-step instructions for building a script.

InDesign Scripting Using Visual Basic

InDesign scripting in Windows requires Microsoft Visual Basic or an application that contains Visual Basic for Applications (VBA). Although InDesign supports VBA, it does not include VBA in the documentation. Adobe suggests using Microsoft Visual Basic "Learning Edition" if you don't already have a Visual Basic software package.

Visual Basic Overview

Visual Basic is a powerful language that simplifies the task of programming. When used with the InDesign object, it can automate and simplify many of the features of InDesign.

NOTE The Visual Basic programming topics, discussed in the following Overview, are only those that directly relate to the sample scripts in this appendix. For more in depth coverage of Visual Basic programming, check out *Mastering Visual Basic 6* by Evangelos Petroutsos (Sybex, 1998).

Objects

Visual Basic is an object-oriented programming language. Put simply, everything in Visual Basic revolves around objects. The window of an application is an object. Each button is an object. Menus and even toolbars are all objects. Consider the following screenshot of the Adobe InDesign Open a File dialog window as an example. Every element of this window is its own object. Everything from the drop-down Look In menu to the Open and Cancel buttons are objects. Even the area of the window that lists each of the files can be opened as an object.

Properties

Each of these objects has properties. Properties describe how the object looks and behaves within the application. For example, all buttons have height and width properties that control the size of the button. Buttons also have a caption property. The caption is the text that is displayed on a button. The Open button on the Open a dialog box is an example of a button that has its width set to be wider than its height. It also has the caption Open. This signifies that this button will open the selected document.

Options on the dialog box toolbar are actually small buttons. The height and width for toolbar buttons are set to be very small and use a picture property instead of the caption. The picture of the pencil and desk blotter is a button that accesses a view of your desktop when you click on it. It uses an image, instead of text, to indicate its function. This allows the button to be smaller, which leaves room in the window for other buttons.

The Language

Here's a simple example that demonstrates how to create an application that makes use of a button object. When clicked, this button will display a simple message to the user.

1. Launch Visual Basic and create a new project (a standard EXE).
2. Visual Basic automatically creates a blank form for you to start programming. If one does not appear, you can create one by selecting Add Form from the Project menu.
3. From the Visual Basic toolbox, select and draw a new button anywhere on the blank form.

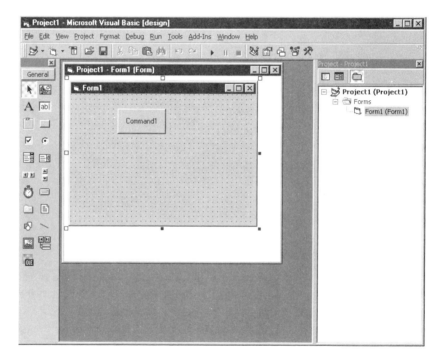

4. If you can see a window called Properties, skip to the next step. Otherwise, right-click on the new button and select Properties from the context-sensitive menu that appears.
5. Locate and click the property Caption in the Properties window.
6. Type in **Click Me** and press Enter.
7. Double click on the new button. A code window should appear.

Type the following lines into the code window (between the Private Sub Command1_Click() and End Sub lines).

```
'// This is example code demonstrating the use of a button.
'//
Dim myMessage as String

    MyMessage = "Congratulations, you've created a button object!"
    Msgbox myMessage
```

Comments   Comments are not required in a script, but they can be very helpful. These first two lines are comments because the lines begin with '//. All comments are noted in this way in the Visual Basic scripting code.

```
'// This is example code demonstrating the use of a button.
'//
```

Comments can be used to document who created the script or explain what the script is for. They can also be used to explain why a particular command was used. Comments are most useful when someone else needs to look at the script. There are often many ways to program the same task. Comments help others understand the reasoning behind the script. Comments are also helpful to the author of the script. After some time has passed the author may have forgotten why they wrote the script a particular way. Comments help to jog their memory.

NOTE   The program does not execute comments when it is run.

Variables

```
Dim myMessage as String
```

This is how a variable is declared in Visual Basic. A variable is a place in memory where information can be stored and retrieved at any time. Although it's not required, it's good programming practice to let Visual Basic know that you are going to use a particular variable. The Dim command lets Visual Basic know that it should set aside a place for a new variable.

Naming a Variable   Part of the variable declaration is its name. All variables have a name that is used to reference the information stored in it. Variable names can include any combination of letters and numbers up to 255 characters. Spaces or symbols cannot be used in the names of variables. Also, the first character of the variable must be a letter. In the sample code example for the button, the variable is called myMessage. This variable will hold the message that is displayed when the button is clicked.

Declaring the Type of Variable   The next part of the variable declaration tells Visual Basic what type of variable it is. There are many types of variables in Visual Basic. The most common types are Strings, Integers, and Doubles. Information that consists of any combination of characters, numbers, or symbols is called a String type. A number that represents a whole integer value is called an Integer type, while fractional numbers are called Single or Double types. The example, Dim myMessage as String, uses a String variable because it's storing a textual message that consists of characters and symbols.

Assigning the Message   The next part of the program code assigns the message that will be displayed to the variable just created.

    MyMessage = "Congratulations, you've created a button object!"

The left side of the equal sign is the variable, and the right side is the message. Notice that there are quotes around the message. This tells Visual Basic to treat the message as one long string.

Displaying the Message   The last statement in the program tells Visual Basic to display the message.

    Msgbox myMessage

Msgbox is a Visual Basic function that displays a box with a message in it. It also displays, by default, a button labeled "OK." If you've ever tried to exit any application without first saving your data, you've probably seen a message that asks if you are sure that you want to exit. That message was a Msgbox. In the example, myMessage was passed as a parameter to the Msgbox function.

Testing Your Script

After writing the button script, you'll need to test your code. Follow these steps:

1. Close the code window.

2. Select Start from the Run menu.

3. You will see a window with a single button on it with a caption that reads Click Me. Click on the button. A message appears on screen: Congratulations, you've created a button object!

4. Close the form by clicking on the "X" labeled button in the upper right hand corner of the window.

This example demonstrated how to use an object within Visual Basic, how to set a property (the caption), and how to specify what action occurs when the button is clicked.

When a button is clicked, a menu is selected, or anything at all happens within a Visual Basic program, an *event* is triggered. An event is the action that happens in response to interaction from the user. In the previous example, the event is called the *Click* event. Visual Basic executes the code that you typed in whenever the button is clicked.

Congratulations, you've created your first object-oriented application.

Scripting InDesign

Now that you've created your first Visual Basic application, you're ready to create an application that uses the objects provided by InDesign. The following example demonstrates how to create a single page layout in InDesign that contains a variety of elements.

1. Launch Visual Basic and create a new project (a standard EXE).
2. Select References from the Project menu.
3. Locate Adobe InDesign 1.0 Type Library and place a check in its checkbox. If you can't find the library, click the Browse button and locate the file scripting.rpln. The file is in the InDesign/Required folder on your hard drive.

WARNING Don't be confused by the use of the word "Type" in the Adobe InDesign 1.0 Type Library title. The word "Type" references a programming definition of the word and not the graphic arts industry use of the term. This library is not a font collection. Rather it is a file that contains information about exposed objects, properties, methods, and collections for use in a Visual Basic application.

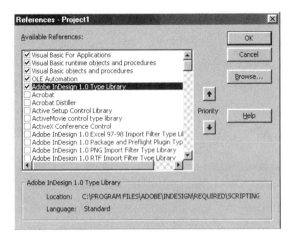

4. Click the OK button to close the References window.
5. Place a new button anywhere on the form. (You can set the caption property if you would like.)
6. Double-click the button to open the Code window.
7. Enter the following code into the Code window.

WARNING Comments are placed throughout the code to explain what to do next. Enter these instructions into the program that you are writing. They describe what the code is for or contain special instructions for entering the code.

WARNING Where the whole line of code doesn't fit on one line within the format of this book, you should type the code on one line and not match the book format.

```
Private Sub Command1_Click()
'// This function creates a sample InDesign page.
'//

'// Variable Declaration
'/
Dim myInDesign As InDesign.Application
Dim myDocument As InDesign.Document
Dim myFrame As InDesign.TextFrame
Dim myBounds As Variant
Dim myRectangle As InDesign.Rectangle
```

```
Dim myImage As InDesign.Image
Dim myParagraph As InDesign.Paragraph
Dim myLargeImage As String
Dim mySmallImage1 As String
Dim mySmallImage2 As String
Dim mySmallImage3 As String

'// Set variable references to the images that the page
'// will contain.
'// Variables are used to simplify the program.
'// If the image file names or locations need to be
'// changed, they can be changed here easily. You will
'// not have to hunt through the code to find out where to
'// change them.
'//
    myLargeImage = "C:\Corbis\Are0097d.jpg"
    mySmallImage1 = "C:\Corbis\Are0073e.jpg"
    mySmallImage2 = "C:\Corbis\Are0061e.jpg"
    mySmallImage3 = "C:\Corbis\Are0067e.jpg"
```

NOTE The four photos used to build the sample, scripted layout courtesy of Corbis Images (royalty-free division), www.corbisimages.com.

NOTE You should change the location and filename of the images to match graphics that you have and want to use.

Communicating with InDesign

```
'// In order to enable Visual Basic (VB) to to work with
'// InDesign, VB needs to know how to communicate with
'// InDesign. Creating a reference to the InDesign
'//.Application object accomplishes this.
'//
```

NOTE The following GetObject function instructs VB to access the InDesign Application object, which is external to VB.

```
    Set myInDesign = GetObject("", "InDesign.Application")
```

```
'// Images will be placed into the InDesign page
'// later in this program. By default as part of its
'// processing, the Place method displays a message
'// to prompt the user for information. This defeats
'// the purpose of automation, turn it off.
'// It is important however to turn the alerts back
'// on before the user is given control of the document.
'// This will be done later in the program.
'//
    myInDesign.UserInteractionLevel = idDontDisplayAlerts

'// Now that Visual Basic has a method of communicating
'// with the InDesign object (via the myInDesign
'// reference above), you can instruct the object to
'// Create a New Document.
'//
    Set myDocument = myInDesign.Documents.Add
```

Once you've created a new object in Visual Basic, you need a command to talk to that object, set its properties, and use its features. The Set command, used in the previous block of code, is how that is established. The InDesign object has a feature, which allows the creation of new documents. The function myInDesign.Documents.Add creates the new document and returns a reference to it. When you set myDocument equal to that reference, Visual Basic will know that you are referring to the new document whenever myDocument is used. Think of myDocument as an alias to the new document.

Placing and Fitting a Large Image

```
'// Place the large image on the page. To do this,
'// you'll create a rectangle that is sized to the
'// desired dimensions of the image.
'// Sizing the rectangle is done by setting its
'// GeometricBounds.
'// The coordinates of the GeometricBounds property are
'// listed in the order Y1, X1, Y2, X2.
'//
```

NOTE The GeometricBounds property expects the coordinates to be in an array. Arrays are another type of data (in addition to Strings, Integers, and Doubles). An array is very much like a table of rows and columns in a spreadsheet. The array function used here creates an array with four rows, one for each coordinate of the rectangle.

```
    myBounds = Array("3p0", "3p0", "63p0", "36p0")
    Set myRectangle = myDocument.Spreads.Item(1).Rectangles.Add
    myRectangle.GeometricBounds = myBounds

'// Now place the image inside the rectangle.
'//
    Set myImage = myRectangle.Place(myLargeImage)


'// When the image is placed within the rectangle, it may
'// not automatically size to fit within the bounds of
'// the rectangle.
'// To do this, you'll call the Fit function to make it
'// fit.
'//
    myImage.GeometricBounds = myRectangle.VisibleBounds
    myRectangle.Fit idContentToFrame
    myImage.GeometricBounds = myRectangle.GeometricBounds
```

See Figure D.1 to see how the script was implemented.

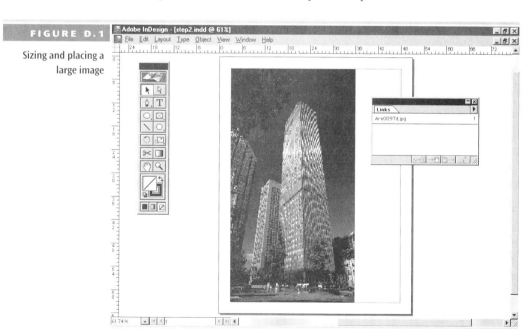

FIGURE D.1 Sizing and placing a large image

Placing and Fitting Three Smaller Images

```
'// Place three smaller images, overlapping the large image
'// on the bottom half of the page. With the exception
'// of the file name to place, and the coordinates of the
'// new photos, the steps are the same as for the large
'// image.
'//

'//
'// Smaller Image 1
'//

'// Set the size of the rectangle
'//
    myBounds = Array("24p0", "29p0", "34p0", "39p0")
    Set myRectangle = myDocument.Spreads.Item(1).Rectangles.Add
    myRectangle.GeometricBounds = myBounds

'// Place the image
'//
    Set myImage = myRectangle.Place(mySmallImage1)

'// Change the size of the image to match the size of the
'// rectangle
'//
    myImage.GeometricBounds = myRectangle.VisibleBounds
    myRectangle.Fit idContentToFrame
    myImage.GeometricBounds = myRectangle.GeometricBounds

'//
'// Smaller Image 2
'//

'// Set the size of the rectangle
'//
    myBounds = Array("37p0", "29p0", "47p0", "39p0")
    Set myRectangle = myDocument.Spreads.Item(1).Rectangles.Add
    myRectangle.GeometricBounds = myBounds

'// Place the image
'//
    Set myImage = myRectangle.Place(mySmallImage2)

'// Change the size of the image to match the size of the
'// rectangle
'//
```

```
        myImage.GeometricBounds = myRectangle.VisibleBounds
        myRectangle.Fit idContentToFrame
        myImage.GeometricBounds = myRectangle.GeometricBounds

'//
'// Smaller Image 3
'//

'// Set the size of the rectangle.
'//
        myBounds = Array("50p0", "29p0", "60p0", "39p0")
        Set myRectangle = myDocument.Spreads.Item(1).Rectangles.Add
        myRectangle.GeometricBounds = myBounds

'// Place the image.
'//
        Set myImage = myRectangle.Place(mySmallImage3)

'// Change the size of the image to match the size of the rectangle
'//
        myImage.GeometricBounds = myRectangle.VisibleBounds
        myRectangle.Fit idContentToFrame
        myImage.GeometricBounds = myRectangle.GeometricBounds
```

Figure D.2 illustrates the placement of all four images in the sample-scripted page.

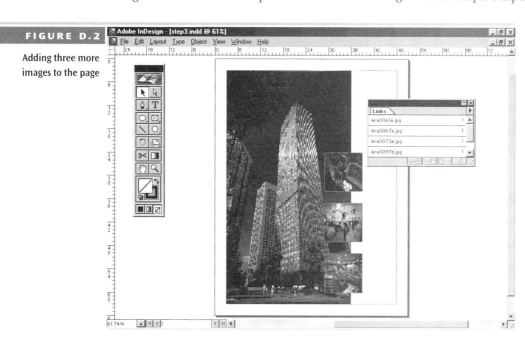

FIGURE D.2

Adding three more images to the page

Composing Text

```
'// Now that the images are placed, add some text to the
'// page.
'//

'// Top Text Frame (Small Heading)
'//
    myBounds = Array("3p0", "12p0", "5p0", "36p0")
    Set myFrame = myDocument.Spreads.Item(1).TextFrames.Add
    myFrame.FillColor = myDocument.Swatches("Paper")
    myFrame.GeometricBounds = myBounds
    myFrame.TextContents = "InDesign Scripting"


    With myFrame.Paragraphs.Item(1)
        .Font = "Arial Black"
        .PointSize = 24
        .Justification = idCenter
    End With
```

TIP Change the font if you want to use another character style. If no font is set, InDesign defaults to Times Roman.

TIP When the page is building, InDesign applies the Auto specification for leading if no leading value is set.

NOTE The text color default is black. To make the text more visible against the background, Figures D.3–D.6 were created with the Images Display preference set to Gray Out Images. When you run this sample script, the images will appear normally as in Figures D.1 and D.2. To reset the text color, use the color tools and commands in InDesign.

See Figure D.3 for an example of scripting for text composition.

FIGURE D.3

Composing a small heading

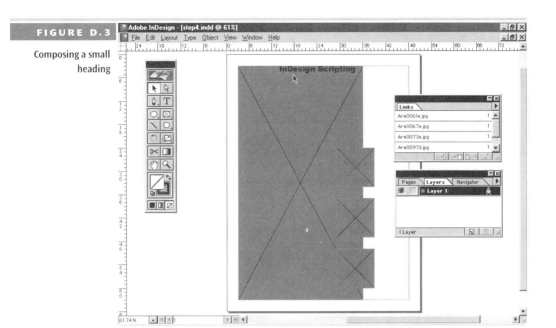

Title Headline

```
'// "Head Line"
'//
    myBounds = Array("51p0", "6p0", "54p0", "28p0")
    Set myFrame = myDocument.Spreads.Item(1).TextFrames.Add
    myFrame.FillColor = myDocument.Swatches("Paper")
    myFrame.GeometricBounds = myBounds
    myFrame.TextContents = "The Towers"

    Set myParagraph = myFrame.Paragraphs.Item(1)
    With myParagraph
        .Font = "Arial Black"
        .PointSize = 40
    End With
```

 TIP When the page is building, InDesign applies left justification if no value is set.

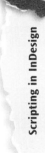

See Figure D.4 to view the results of the second text composition example.

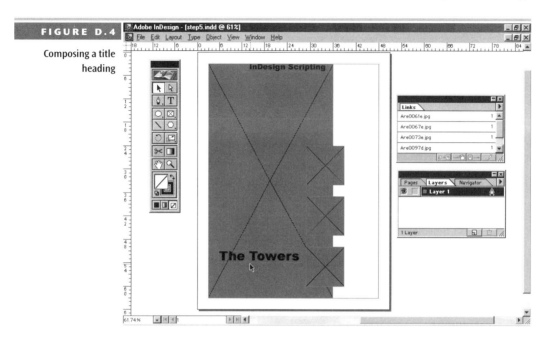

FIGURE D.4
Composing a title heading

Icon Element

```
'// "Icon Element"
'//
    myBounds = Array("7p0", "30p0", "12p0", "35p0")
    Set myFrame = myDocument.Spreads.Item(1).TextFrames.Add
    myFrame.FillColor = myDocument.Swatches("Paper")
    myFrame.GeometricBounds = myBounds
    myFrame.TextContents = "5"

    Set myParagraph = myFrame.Paragraphs.Item(1)
    With myParagraph
        .Font = "Arial Black"
        .PointSize = 82
    End With
```

Figure D.5 illustrates the positioning and fitting of an icon element.

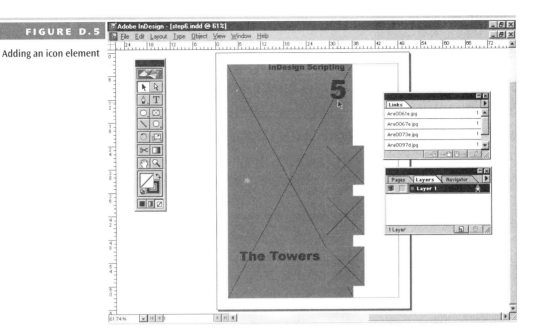

FIGURE D.5

Adding an icon element

Sub-headline

```
'// "Head Element"
'//
    myBounds = Array("4p0", "38p0", "8p6", "48p0")
    Set myFrame = myDocument.Spreads.Item(1).TextFrames.Add
    myFrame.GeometricBounds = myBounds
    myFrame.TextContents = "InDesign Scripting"

    Set myParagraph = myFrame.Paragraphs.Item(1)
    With myParagraph
        .Font = "Bookman Old Style"
        .FontStyle = "Bold Italic"
        .PointSize = 24
        .Leading = 24
        .Justification = idCenter
    End With
```

Body Text

```
'// "Body-Text" paragraph
'//
    myBounds = Array("8p6", "38p0", "21p0", "48p0")
    Set myFrame = myDocument.Spreads.Item(1).TextFrames.Add
    myFrame.GeometricBounds = myBounds
    myFrame.TextContents = " This layout was built by an Adobe InDesign
script. Don't shy away from using scripts. You'll discover how easy it is to
enhance creativity, build more predictable workflows, and develop a library
of digital assets."

    Set myParagraph = myFrame.Paragraphs.Item(1)
    With myParagraph
        .Font = "Arial"
        .PointSize = 12
        .Leading = 14
    End With
```

In Figure D.6, a Bookman Old Style Bold Italic heading and body text composed in Arial was added to the page layout.

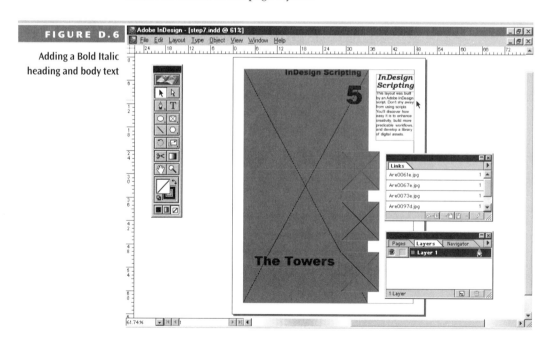

FIGURE D.6

Adding a Bold Italic heading and body text

Turning Alerts Back On

```
'// Turn the alerts back on.
'//
    myInDesign.UserInteractionLevel = idDisplayAlerts


'// Let the user know the program is done.
'//
    Msgbox "The document has been created."

'// Clean up the object references
'//
    Set myParagraph = Nothing
    Set myFrame = Nothing
    Set myImage = Nothing
    Set myRectangle = Nothing
    Set myDocument = Nothing
    Set myInDesign = Nothing
End Sub
```

TIP Although it is not required, it's a good idea to release all memory variables used in a program. Setting each variable to nothing does this.

To test this program, select Start from the Run menu. A form will be displayed with your button on it. When you click the button, InDesign will load (if it is not open already) and build the document. A message will be displayed to alert you when the document is finished.

InDesign Scripting Using AppleScript

To write InDesign scripts using the Macintosh OS, you need AppleScript (shipped with all Apple systems) and an AppleScript editor.

NOTE The AppleScript programming topics discussed in the following Overview are only those that directly relate to the sample scripts in this Appendix. For more in-depth coverage of AppleScript programming, check out the AppleScript Guide located in the AppleExtras folder/AppleScript folder. If you need the software, editor, or guide, you can download a copy from the Apple Web site www.apple.com.

AppleScript Overview

AppleScript is a tool that can simplify many tasks through automation. Its language breaks away from traditional programming languages by being more like a spoken language than a cryptic set of commands.

A Simple Example

Here is a simple example script that displays a dialog message to the user.

1. Launch the AppleScript Editor. It's in the Apple Extras folder/Apple Script folder. Double-click the Script Editor icon or list name.

2. The editor will automatically create a blank script for you to program.

3. Enter the following code:

```
-- This is an example script that demonstrates the use of a variable
-- and a message dialog.
Set myMessage to "Congratulations, this is your first AppleScript!"
display dialog myMessage
```

You continue by doing the following:

1. Select Run from the Controls window.

2. A dialog window should appear showing you the message "Congratulations, this is your first AppleScript!"

3. Click either the Cancel or OK buttons to close the window.

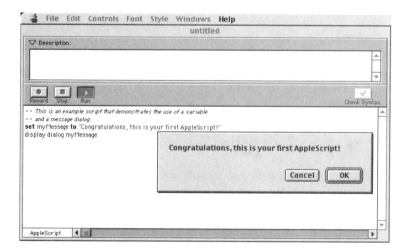

Comments This example demonstrates some simple features of an AppleScript. The first two lines (preceded by two dashes) are comments.

```
-- This is an example script that demonstrates the use of a variable
-- and a message dialog.
```

Comments are not required in a script, but they can be very helpful. Comments can be used to document who created the script or explain what the script is for. They can also be used to explain why a particular command was used. Comments are most useful when someone else needs to look at the script. There are often many ways to program the same task. Comments help others understand the reasoning behind the script. Comments are also helpful to the author of the script. After some time has passed the author may have forgotten why they wrote the script a particular way. Comments help to jog their memory.

TIP The program does not execute comments when it is run.

Variables The next line demonstrates the use of variables. A variable is a place in memory where information can be stored and retrieved at any time.

```
Set myMessage to "Congratulations, this is your first AppleScript!"
```

Naming a Variable All variables have a name that is used to reference the information stored in it. Variable names can include any combination of letters and numbers. Spaces or symbols cannot be used in the names of variables. Also, the first character of the variable must be a letter. In this example, the variable is called myMessage. This variable will hold the message that is displayed when the script is run.

String Variables There are many types of variables in AppleScript. The most common types are strings and integers. Information that consists of any combination of characters, numbers, or symbols is called a String. A number that represents a whole integer value is called an Integer (1, 2, 3, etc.). The sample script uses a String variable because it is storing a textual message that consists of characters and symbols.

The syntax for saving information to a variable is Set variable To information. This is where a variable is the name of the variable, and information is the data to be saved.

In the example, myMessage is the variable, and "Congratulations, this is your first AppleScript!" is the message. Notice that there are quotes around the message. This tells AppleScript to treat the message as one long string.

Display Dialog   The last statement in the program tells AppleScript to display the message.

```
display dialog myMessage
```

Display dialog is an AppleScript function that displays a box with a message in it. It also displays, by default, a button labeled "Cancel" and a button labeled "OK." If you've ever tried to exit any application without first saving your data, you have probably seen a message that asks if you are sure that you want to exit. That message was a display dialog.

In the example, `myMessage` was passed as a parameter to the display dialog function. Parameters are used to let the dialog function know what message it should display.

Congratulations, you have created your first AppleScript program!

Scripting InDesign

Now that you've created your first script, you're ready to create a script that uses the scripting features provided by InDesign. The following example demonstrates how to create a single page layout in InDesign that contains a variety of elements.

1. Launch the AppleScript Editor. It's in the Apple Extras/Apple Script folder. Double-click the Script Editor icon or list name.

2. The editor will automatically create a blank script for you to program.

3. Select File ➢ Open Dictionary… from the Script Editor menu. A dialog box opens.

4. Go to the Adobe InDesign/Required folder. Select and open Scripting.

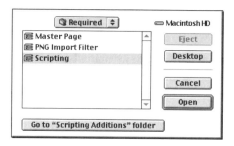

5. The Scripting Dictionary appears on screen. In the left-hand column, click a listing to see a definition. Use the dictionary to guide you when writing AppleScripts for InDesign.

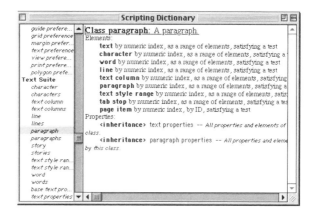

6. Enter the following code.

WARNING Comments are placed throughout the code to explain what to do next. Enter these instructions into the program that you are writing. They describe what the code is for or contain special instructions for entering the code.

WARNING Where the whole line of code doesn't fit on one line within the format of this book, you should type the code on one line and not match the book format.

Preparing InDesign to Receive Scripting Commands

```
-- The following tell command prepares InDesign to receive
-- scripting commands.
-- If InDesign is not already open, it will be opened.
--
tell application "InDesign"

-- Images are going to be placed into the InDesign page
-- later in this program.
-- By default, the Place command displays a message as part
-- of its processing to prompt the user for information.
-- This defeats the purpose of automation, so lets turn it
-- off.
--
```

```
-- It's important to remember to turn the alerts back on
-- before the user is given control of the document.
-- This will be done later in the script.
--

set user interaction level to never interact
```

Creating a New InDesign Document

```
-- The next command creates a new InDesign document
-- and opens up communication with that document by
-- using the tell command.
--

set myDocument to make document
tell myDocument

    -- Set variable references to the images that the
    -- page will contain.
    -- Variables are used to simplify the program. If the
    -- image file names or locations should ever need to
    -- be changed, they can be changed here easily without
    -- having to hunt through the script to find where
    -- they are used.
    --

    set myLargeImage to "Macintosh HD:Corbis:Are0097d.JPG"
    set mySmallImage1 to "Macintosh HD:Corbis:Are0073e.JPG"
    set mySmallImage2 to "Macintosh HD:Corbis:ARE0061e.JPG"
    set mySmallImage3 to "Macintosh HD:Corbis:ARE0067e.JPG"
    tell spread 1
```

NOTE The four photos used to build the sample scripted layout are courtesy of Corbis Images (royalty-free division), www.corbisimages.com.

WARNING You should change the location and filename of the images to match the images that you have and want to use. Colons should separate folders.

Placing and Fitting a Large Image on a Page

```
-- Place the large image on the page. To do this
-- you'll create a rectangle that is sized to the
-- desired dimensions of the image.
-- Sizing the rectangle is done by setting its
-- Geometric Bounds.
-- The coordinates of the Geometric Bounds property
-- are listed in the order Y1, X1, Y2, X2.
--
```

NOTE The Geometric Bounds property expects the coordinates to be in an array. Arrays are another type of data (in addition to Strings, Integers, and Doubles). An array is very much like a table of rows and columns in a spreadsheet. The array function used here creates an array with four rows, one for each coordinate of the rectangle.

```
set myRectangle to make rectangle
tell myRectangle
   -- Set the size of the rectangle to fill a
   -- large portion of the page
   --
   set geometric bounds to {"3p0", "3p0", "63p0", "36p0"}

   -- Now, place the image inside the rectangle
   --
   set myRectangle to myLargeImage
   place myRectangle

   -- When the image is placed within the
   -- rectangle, it may not automatically size
   -- to fit within the bounds of the rectangle.
   -- To do this, you'll call the fit command.
   --
   fit myRectangle given content to frame
end tell
```

WARNING The Adobe Scripting Guide example for the `fit` command is not correct. For the fit command to work correctly, you have to set your object and place your object as two separate command lines, as shown above. Don't set and place your object in the same scripting command, as shown on page 115 in the Adobe Scripting guide. It doesn't work.

See Figure D.7 to see how the script ran.

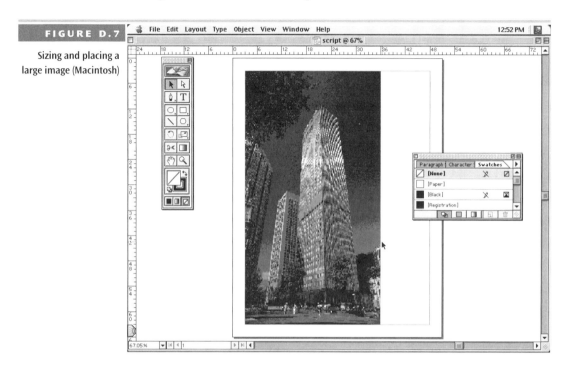

FIGURE D.7

Sizing and placing a large image (Macintosh)

Placing and Fitting Three Small Images on a Page

```
-- Place three smaller images, which will overlap
-- the larger image. With the exception of the
-- file name to place and the coordinates of the
-- images, the steps are the same as for the large
-- image.
--

-- Smaller image 1
--
set myRectangle to make rectangle
tell myRectangle
    -- Set the size of the rectangle
    --
    set geometric bounds to {"24p0", "29p0", "34p0", "39p0"}
```

```applescript
        -- Place the images
        --
        set myRectangle to mySmallImage1
        place myRectangle
        
        -- Change the size of the images to match the size of the rectangle.
        --
        fit myRectangle given content to frame
end tell


-- Smaller image 2
--
set myRectangle to make rectangle
tell myRectangle
        -- Set the size of the rectangle
        --
        set geometric bounds to {"37p0", "29p0", "47p0", "39p0"}
        
        -- Place the image
        --
        set myRectangle to place mySmallImage2
        place myRectangle
        
        -- Change the size of the image to match the size of the rectangle.
        --
        fit myRectangle given content to frame
end tell


-- Smaller image 3
--
set myRectangle to make rectangle
tell myRectangle
        -- Set the size of the rectangle
        --
        set geometric bounds to {"50p0", "29p0", "60p0", "39p0"}
        
        -- Place the image
        --
```

```
        set myRectangle to mySmallImage3
        place myRectangle

        -- Change the size of the image to match the size of the rectangle.
        --
        fit myRectangle given content to frame
    end tell
```

Figure D.8 illustrates the placement of all four images in the sample-scripted page.

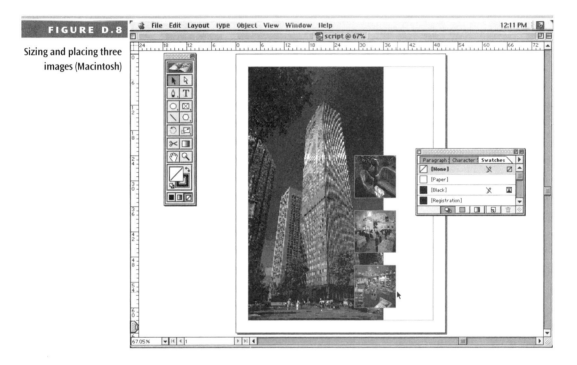

FIGURE D.8

Sizing and placing three images (Macintosh)

Composing Text

```
    -- Now that the images are placed, add some text to the page.

    -- Top Text Frame (Small Heading)
--

    -- Text is placed inside Text Frames - so create one for the Small
    -- Heading
    --
    set myFrame to make text frame
```

```
        tell myFrame
            -- Set the dimensions of the text frame to be located at the top
            -- of the page and only be one line tall.
            --
            set geometric bounds to {"3p0", "12p0", "5p0", "36p0"}

            -- Place the actual text within the text frame.
            --
            set text contents to "InDesign Scripting"

            -- Set myParagraph to Paragraph 1 so that we can manipulate the
            -- paragraph
            --
            set myParagraph to paragraph 1
            tell myParagraph
                -- Change the font, point size of the font to 24, and center
                -- the text
                --
                set font to "Arial Black"
                set point size to 24
                set justification to center
            end tell
        end tell
```

TIP Change the font if you want to use another character style. If no font is set, InDesign defaults to Times Roman.

TIP When the page is building, InDesign applies the Auto specification for leading if no leading value is set.

NOTE The text color default is black. To make the text more visible against the background, Figures D.9–D.12 were created with the Images Display preference set to Gray Out Images. When you run this sample script, the images will appear normally as in Figures D.7 and D.8. To reset the text color, use the color tools and commands in InDesign.

See Figure D.9 for an example of scripting for text composition.

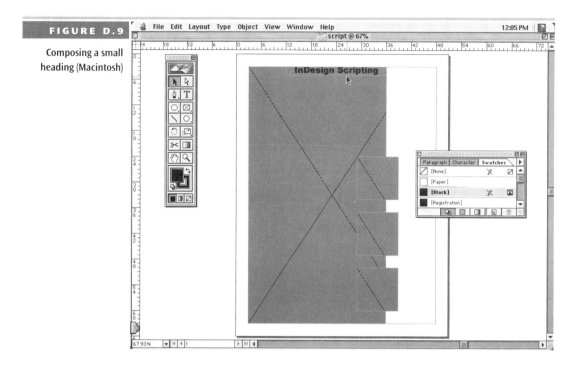

FIGURE D.9

Composing a small heading (Macintosh)

Title Headline

```
-- "Head Line"
--
set myFrame to make text frame
tell myFrame
   set geometric bounds to {"51p0", "6p0", "54p0", "28p0"}
   set text contents to "The Towers"
   set myParagraph to paragraph 1
   tell myParagraph
      set font to "Arial Black"
      set point size to 40
   end tell
end tell
```

 TIP When the page is building, InDesign applies left justification if no value is set.

See Figure D.10 to view the results of the second text composition example.

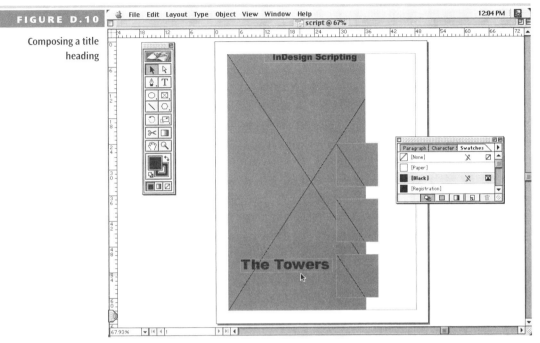

FIGURE D.10

Composing a title heading

Icon Element

```
-- "Icon Element"
--
set myFrame to make text frame
tell myFrame
    set geometric bounds to {"7p0", "30p0", "12p0", "35p0"}
    set text contents to "5"
    set myParagraph to paragraph 1
    tell myParagraph
        set font to "Arial Black"
        set point size to 82
    end tell
end tell
```

Figure D.11 illustrates the positioning and fitting of an icon element.

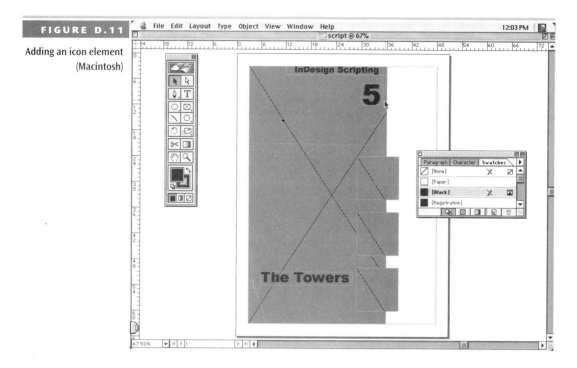

FIGURE D.11

Adding an icon element (Macintosh)

Sub-Headline

```
-- "Head Element"
--
set myFrame to make text frame
tell myFrame
   set geometric bounds to {"4p0", "38p0", "8p6", "48p0"}
   set text contents to "InDesign Scripting"
   set myParagraph to paragraph 1
   tell myParagraph
      set font to "Bookman Old Style"
      set font style to "Bold Italic"
      set point size to 24
      set leading to 24
      set justification to center
   end tell
end tell
```

Body Text

```
-- "Body-Text" paragraph
--
```

```
            set myFrame to make text frame
            tell myFrame
                set geometric bounds to {"8p6", "38p0", "21p0", "48p0"}
                set text contents to "This layout was built by an Adobe InDesign
script. Don't shy away from using scripts.  You'll discover how easy it is
to enhance creativity, build more predicable workflows, and develop a
library of digital assets."
                set myParagraph to paragraph 1
                tell myParagraph
                    set font to "Arial"
                    set point size to 12
                    set leading to 14
                end tell
            end tell

        end tell
    end tell
```

Figure D.12 shows a Bookman Old Style Bold Italic heading and body text composed in Arial ware added to the page layout.

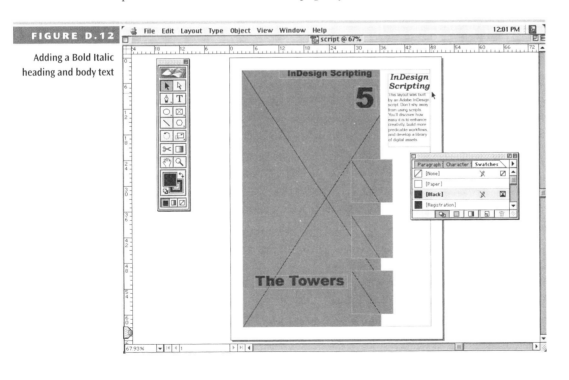

FIGURE D.12

Adding a Bold Italic heading and body text

Turning Alerts Back On

```
-- Turn the display alerts back on.
--
set user interaction level to interact with all
end tell


-- Let the user know the script is done.
--
display dialog "The document has been created."
```

Testing Your Script

To test this script, select the Run button in the Script Editor window. Once you've started the script, InDesign will load (if it is not open already) and create the document. A message will be displayed to alert you when the document is finished.

appendix E

Keyboard Shortcut Equivalents

KEYBOARD SHORTCUT EQUIVALENTS

This appendix contains the keystroke shortcuts for InDesign commands. To make searching the appendix easier, it's divided into two sections: Windows and Macintosh. The commands listed in the InDesign Default and QuarkXPress 4.0 sections are in the two shortcut sets that come with InDesign. Commands found under the PageMaker 6.5 heading are listed here for your convenience. To use the PageMaker command equivalents you need to create and apply a new shortcut set in the Edit Shortcuts dialog box. Select File ➢ Edit Shortcuts or type Shift+Ctrl+Alt+K (Windows) or Opt+Shift+Cmd+K (Macintosh) to open the dialog box.

For the sake of brevity, the menu command equivalent for Type ➢ Font lists only a single example: Times New Roman PS: Plain (none defined). In practice, all the typefaces that appear in your InDesign font list can be assigned a shortcut and are included in your version of the InDesign Default and QuarkXpress 4 command sets. If you change the list of fonts installed on your system, deactivate fonts, or find missing fonts, the shortcut you assign may be mapped to another font. Chapter 2 has more information about creating, editing, and removing shortcuts from In Design command sets.

InDesign Product Areas that can be assigned shortcuts are listed. If Adobe has not mapped a shortcut to a feature, the words "none defined" will be listed instead. Blank listings note non-functioning shortcuts—or as in the PageMaker examples—no similar defined task.

Quark users will find that not all QuarkXPress features are supported in InDesign or vice versa. Check the InDesign ReadMe file for more details.

In the following listings, if you see the words "by 5 times," that amount is set in File ➢ Preferences ➢ Units & Increments dialog box.

Windows

TABLE E.1: WINDOWS COMMAND EQUIVALENTS

InDesign Product Area	Command	InDesign Default	QuarkXPress 4	PageMaker 6.5
Edit Menu	Check Spelling…	Ctrl+I	Ctrl+Alt+W	Ctrl+L
Edit Menu	Clear	[none defined]	[none defined]	Del
Edit Menu	Copy	Ctrl+C	Ctrl+C	Ctrl+C
Edit Menu	Cut	Ctrl+X	Ctrl+X	Ctrl+X
Edit Menu	Deselect All	Shift+Ctrl+A	Shift+Ctrl+A	Shift+Ctrl+A
Edit Menu	Duplicate	Ctrl+Alt+D	Ctrl+D	
Edit Menu	Edit Dictionary…	[none defined]	[none defined]	
Edit Menu	Find Next	Ctrl+Alt+F	Ctrl+Alt+F	Ctrl+G
Edit Menu	Find/Change…	Ctrl+F	Ctrl+F	Ctrl+H
Edit Menu	Paste	Ctrl+V	Ctrl+V	Ctrl+V
Edit Menu	Paste Into	Ctrl+Alt+V	[none defined]	
Edit Menu	Redo	Shift+Ctrl+Z	Shift+Ctrl+Z	
Edit Menu	Select All	Ctrl+A	Ctrl+A	Ctrl+A
Edit Menu	Step and Repeat…	Shift+Ctrl+V	Ctrl+Alt+D	
Edit Menu	Undo	Ctrl+Z	Ctrl+Z	Ctrl+Z
File Menu	Adobe Online…	[none defined]	[none defined]	
File Menu	Close	Ctrl+W	Ctrl+W or Ctrl+F4	Ctrl+W
File Menu	Color Settings: Application Color Settings…	[none defined]	[none defined]	
File Menu	Color Settings: Document Color Settings…	[none defined]	[none defined]	
File Menu	Document Setup…	Ctrl+Alt+P	Shift+Ctrl+Alt+P	Shift+Ctrl+P

Continued on next page

TABLE E.1: WINDOWS COMMAND EQUIVALENTS (continued)

InDesign Product Area	Command	InDesign Default	QuarkXPress 4	PageMaker 6.5
File Menu	Edit Shortcuts…	Shift+Ctrl+Alt+K	Shift+Ctrl+Alt+K	
File Menu	Exit	Ctrl+Q	Ctrl+Q	Ctrl+Q
File Menu	Export…	Ctrl+E	Ctrl+Alt+E	
File Menu	Links…	Shift+Ctrl+D	Shift+F2	Shift+Ctrl+D
File Menu	New…	Ctrl+N	Ctrl+N	Ctrl+N
File Menu	Open…	Ctrl+O	Ctrl+O	Ctrl+O
File Menu	Package…	Shift+Ctrl+Alt+P	[none defined]	
File Menu	Place…	Ctrl+D	Ctrl+E	Ctrl+D
File Menu	Preferences: Composition…	[none defined]	[none defined]	
File Menu	Preferences: Dictionary…	[none defined]	[none defined]	
File Menu	Preferences: General…	Ctrl+K	Ctrl+Y	Ctrl+K
File Menu	Preferences: Grids…	[none defined]	[none defined]	
File Menu	Preferences: Guides…	[none defined]	[none defined]	
File Menu	Preferences: Online Settings…	[none defined]	[none defined]	
File Menu	Preferences: Text…	[none defined]	[none defined]	
File Menu	Preferences: Units & Increments…	[none defined]	[none defined]	
File Menu	Preflight…	Shift+Ctrl+Alt+F	Shift+Ctrl+Alt+F	
File Menu	Print…	Ctrl+P	Ctrl+P	Ctrl+P
File Menu	Revert	[none defined]	[none defined]	
File Menu	Save	Ctrl+S	Ctrl+S	Ctrl+S
File Menu	Save a Copy…	Ctrl+Alt+S	[none defined]	
File Menu	Save As…	Shift+Ctrl+S	Ctrl+Alt+S	Shift+Ctrl+S
Help Menu	About InDesign…	[none defined]	[none defined]	
Help Menu	Adobe Corporate News…	[none defined]	[none defined]	
Help Menu	Downloadables…	[none defined]	[none defined]	
Help Menu	Help Topics…	F1	F1	F1
Help Menu	How to Use Help…	[none defined]	[none defined]	
Help Menu	Online Registration…	[none defined]	[none defined]	
Help Menu	Top Issues…	[none defined]	[none defined]	
Layout Menu	Create Guides…	[none defined]	[none defined]	
Layout Menu	First Page	Shift+Ctrl+Page Up	Shift+Ctrl+Page Up	

Continued on next page

TABLE E.1: WINDOWS COMMAND EQUIVALENTS (continued)

InDesign Product Area	Command	InDesign Default	QuarkXPress 4	PageMaker 6.5
Layout Menu	Go Back	Ctrl+Page Up	Ctrl+Page Up	Ctrl+Page Up
Layout Menu	Go Forward	Ctrl+Page Down	Ctrl+Page Down	Ctrl+Page Down
Layout Menu	Insert Page Number	Ctrl+Alt+N	Ctrl+3	Ctrl+Alt+P
Layout Menu	Last Page	Shift+Ctrl+Page Down	Shift+Ctrl+Page Down	
Layout Menu	Layout Adjustment…	[none defined]	[none defined]	
Layout Menu	Margins and Columns…	[none defined]	[none defined]	
Layout Menu	Next Page	Shift+Page Down	Shift+Page Down	Page Down
Layout Menu	Previous Page	Shift+Page Up	Shift+Page Up	Page Up
Layout Menu	Ruler Guides…	[none defined]	[none defined]	
Object Editing	Apply default fill and stroke colors	D	D	
Object Editing	Select 1 object down from selection			
Object Editing	Select 1 object up from selection			
Object Editing	Select all guides	Ctrl+Alt+G	Ctrl+Alt+G	
Object Editing	Select through to bottom object			
Object Editing	Select through to next object			
Object Editing	Swap fill and stroke activation	X	X	
Object Editing	Swap fill and stroke colors	Shift+X	Shift+X	
Object Menu	Arrange: Bring Forward	Ctrl+]	Ctrl+F5	Ctrl+]
Object Menu	Arrange: Bring To Front	Shift+Ctrl+]	F5	Shift+Ctrl+]
Object Menu	Arrange: Send Backward	Ctrl+[	Shift+Ctrl+F5	Ctrl+[
Object Menu	Arrange: Send To Back	Shift+Ctrl+[	Shift+F5	Shift+Ctrl+[
Object Menu	Clipping Path…	[none defined]	Shift+Ctrl+F10	
Object Menu	Compound Paths: Make	Ctrl+8	Ctrl+8	
Object Menu	Compound Paths: Release	Ctrl+Alt+8	Ctrl+Alt+8	
Object Menu	Content: Graphic	[none defined]	[none defined]	

Continued on next page

TABLE E.1: WINDOWS COMMAND EQUIVALENTS (continued)

InDesign Product Area	Command	InDesign Default	QuarkXPress 4	PageMaker 6.5
Object Menu	Content: Text	[none defined]	[none defined]	
Object Menu	Content: Unassigned	[none defined]	[none defined]	
Object Menu	Corner Effects…	Ctrl+Alt+R	Ctrl+Alt+R	
Object Menu	Fitting: Center Content	Shift+Ctrl+E	Shift+Ctrl+M	
Object Menu	Fitting: Fit Content Proportionally	Shift+Ctrl+Alt+E	Shift+Ctrl+Alt+M	
Object Menu	Fitting: Fit Content to Frame	Ctrl+Alt+E	[none defined]	
Object Menu	Fitting: Fit Frame to Content	Shift+Ctrl+Alt+V	Shift+Ctrl+Alt+V	
Object Menu	Group	Ctrl+G	Ctrl+G	Ctrl+G
Object Menu	Image Color Settings…	Shift+Ctrl+Alt+D	Shift+Ctrl+Alt+D	
Object Menu	Lock Position	Ctrl+L	F6	Ctrl+L
Object Menu	Reverse Path	[none defined]	[none defined]	
Object Menu	Text Frame Options…	Ctrl+B	[none defined]	Alt+Ctrl+F
Object Menu	Text Wrap…	Ctrl+Alt+W	Ctrl+T	Alt+Ctrl+E
Object Menu	Ungroup	Shift+Ctrl+G	Ctrl+U	Shift+Ctrl+G
Object Menu	Unlock Position	Ctrl+Alt+L	Ctrl+Alt+L	Ctrl+Alt+L
Other	Close all	Shift+Ctrl+Alt+W	Shift+Ctrl+Alt+W	
Other	Close document	Shift+Ctrl+W	Shift+Ctrl+W	Ctrl+W
Other	Close document	Ctrl+F4	Ctrl+F4	
Other	Create outlines without deleting text	Shift+Ctrl+Alt+O	Shift+Ctrl+Alt+O	
Other	New default document	Shift+Ctrl+N	[none defined]	
Other	Next window	Ctrl+F6	Ctrl+F6	
Other	Previous window	Shift+Ctrl+F6	Shift+Ctrl+F6	
Other	Quit	Alt+F4 or Ctrl+Q	Alt+F4 or Ctrl+Q	
Other	Save all	Shift+Ctrl+Alt+S	Shift+Ctrl+Alt+S	
Other	Update missing font list	Shift+Ctrl+Alt+/	Shift+Ctrl+Alt+/	
Text Selection	Find Next	Shift+F2	[none defined]	Ctrl+G
Text Selection	Load Find and Find Next instance			
Text Selection	Load Find with selected text			
Text Selection	Load Replace with selected text			

Continued on next page

TABLE E.1: WINDOWS COMMAND EQUIVALENTS (continued)

InDesign Product Area	Command	InDesign Default	QuarkXPress 4	PageMaker 6.5
Text Selection	Move down one line	Down Arrow	Down Arrow	Down Arrow
Text Selection	Move to beginning of story	Ctrl+Home	Ctrl+Home	Ctrl+Page Up
Text Selection	Move to end of story	Ctrl+End	Ctrl+End	Ctrl+Page Down
Text Selection	Move to the end of the line	End	End	End
Text Selection	Move to the left one character	Left Arrow	Left Arrow	Left Arrow
Text Selection	Move to the left one word	Ctrl+Left Arrow	Ctrl+Left Arrow	Ctrl+Left Arrow
Text Selection	Move to the next paragraph	Ctrl+Down Arrow	Ctrl+Down Arrow	Ctrl+Down Arrow
Text Selection	Move to the previous paragraph	Ctrl+Up Arrow	Ctrl+Up Arrow	Ctrl+Up Arrow
Text Selection	Move to the right one character	Right Arrow	Right Arrow	Right Arrow
Text Selection	Move to the right one word	Ctrl+Right Arrow	Ctrl+Right Arrow	Ctrl+Right Arrow
Text Selection	Move to the start of the line	Home	Home	Home
Text Selection	Move up one line	Up Arrow	Up Arrow	Up Arrow
Text Selection	Replace with Change to text			
Text Selection	Replace with Change to text and Find Next			
Text Selection	Select one character to the left	Shift+Left Arrow	Shift+Left Arrow	
Text Selection	Select one character to the right	Shift+Right Arrow	Shift+Right Arrow	
Text Selection	Select one line above	Shift+Up Arrow	Shift+Up Arrow	
Text Selection	Select one line below	Shift+Down Arrow	Shift+Down Arrow	
Text Selection	Select one paragraph before	Shift+Ctrl+Up Arrow	Shift+Ctrl+Up Arrow	
Text Selection	Select one paragraph forward	Shift+Ctrl+Down Arrow	Shift+Ctrl+Down Arrow	
Text Selection	Select one word to the left	Shift+Ctrl+Left Arrow	Shift+Ctrl+Left Arrow	Shift+Ctrl+Left Arrow
Text Selection	Select one word to the right	Shift+Ctrl+Right Arrow	Shift+Ctrl+Right Arrow	Shift+Ctrl+Right Arrow

Continued on next page

TABLE E.1: WINDOWS COMMAND EQUIVALENTS (continued)

InDesign Product Area	Command	InDesign Default	QuarkXPress 4	PageMaker 6.5
Text Selection	Select to beginning of story	Shift+Ctrl+Home	Shift+Ctrl+Home	
Text Selection	Select to end of story	Shift+Ctrl+End	Shift+Ctrl+End	
Text Selection	Select to the end of the line	Shift+End	Shift+End	
Text Selection	Select to the start of the line	Shift+Home	Shift+Home	
Tools, Palettes	Activate last-used field in palette	Ctrl+`	Ctrl+`	
Tools, Palettes	Apply color	, (comma)	, (comma)	
Tools, Palettes	Apply gradient	. (period)	. (period)	
Tools, Palettes	Apply None	/	/	
Tools, Palettes	Direct Selection Tool	A	A	
Tools, Palettes	Ellipse Tool	L	L	Shift+F5
Tools, Palettes	Ellipse Tool (select hidden tools)	Shift+L	Shift+L	Shift+Alt+F5 [select ellipse frame tool]
Tools, Palettes	Gradient Tool	G	G	
Tools, Palettes	Hand Tool	H	H	
Tools, Palettes	Line Tool	E	E	Shift+F3
Tools, Palettes	Pen Tool	P	P	
Tools, Palettes	Pen Tool (select hidden tools)	Shift+P	Shift+P	
Tools, Palettes	Polygon Tool	N	N	Shift+F6
Tools, Palettes	Polygon Tool (select hidden tools)	Shift+N	Shift+N	
Tools, Palettes	Rectangle Tool	M	M	Shift+F4
Tools, Palettes	Rectangle Tool (select hidden tools)	Shift+M	Shift+M	Shift+Alt+F4 [select rectangle frame]
Tools, Palettes	Rotate Tool	R	R	Shift+F2
Tools, Palettes	Scale Tool	S	S	
Tools, Palettes	Scale Tool (select hidden tools)	Shift+S	Shift+S	
Tools, Palettes	Scissors Tool	C	C	
Tools, Palettes	Selection Tool	V	V	F9
Tools, Palettes	Toggle between Selection and Direct Selection tool		Ctrl+Tab	Ctrl+Tab or Shift+F8
Tools, Palettes	Toggle to add anchor point	= or Num +	= or Num +	

Continued on next page

TABLE E.1: WINDOWS COMMAND EQUIVALENTS (continued)

InDesign Product Area	Command	InDesign Default	QuarkXPress 4	PageMaker 6.5
Tools, Palettes	Toggle to delete anchor point	- or Num −	- or Num −	
Tools, Palettes	Type Tool	T	T	Shift+Alt+F1
Tools, Palettes	Zoom Tool	Z	Z	Shift+Alt+F7
Type Menu	Character Styles…	Shift+F11	Shift+F11	
Type Menu	Character…	Ctrl+T	Shift+Ctrl+D	Ctrl+T
Type Menu	Create Outlines	Shift+Ctrl+O	Shift+Ctrl+O	
Type Menu	Font: Times New Roman: Regular	[none defined]	[none defined]	
Type Menu	Insert Character…	[none defined]	[none defined]	
Type Menu	Paragraph Styles…	F11	F11	
Type Menu	Paragraph…	Ctrl+M	Shift+Ctrl+F	Ctrl+M
Type Menu	Show Hidden Characters	Ctrl+Alt+I	Ctrl+I	
Type Menu	Size: 10	[none defined]	[none defined]	
Type Menu	Size: 11	[none defined]	[none defined]	
Type Menu	Size: 12	[none defined]	[none defined]	
Type Menu	Size: 14	[none defined]	[none defined]	
Type Menu	Size: 18	[none defined]	[none defined]	
Type Menu	Size: 24	[none defined]	[none defined]	
Type Menu	Size: 30	[none defined]	[none defined]	
Type Menu	Size: 36	[none defined]	[none defined]	
Type Menu	Size: 48	[none defined]	[none defined]	
Type Menu	Size: 6	[none defined]	[none defined]	
Type Menu	Size: 60	[none defined]	[none defined]	
Type Menu	Size: 72	[none defined]	[none defined]	
Type Menu	Size: 8	[none defined]	[none defined]	
Type Menu	Size: 9	[none defined]	[none defined]	
Type Menu	Size: Other…	[none defined]	[none defined]	
Type Menu	Story…	[none defined]	[none defined]	
Type Menu	Tabs…	Shift+Ctrl+T	Shift+Ctrl+T	Ctrl+I
Typography	Align center	Shift+Ctrl+C	Shift+Ctrl+C	Shift+Ctrl+C
Typography	Align force justify	Shift+Ctrl+F	[none defined]	Shift+Ctrl+F
Typography	Align justify	Shift+Ctrl+J	Shift+Ctrl+J	Shift+Ctrl+J
Typography	Align left	Shift+Ctrl+L	Shift+Ctrl+L	Shift+Ctrl+L
Typography	Align right	Shift+Ctrl+R	Shift+Ctrl+R	Shift+Ctrl+R
Typography	Align to baseline grid	Shift+Ctrl+Alt+G	Shift+Ctrl+Alt+G	

Continued on next page

TABLE E.1: WINDOWS COMMAND EQUIVALENTS (continued)

InDesign Product Area	Command	InDesign Default	QuarkXPress 4	PageMaker 6.5
Typography	Apply all caps	Shift+Ctrl+K	Shift+Ctrl+K	Shift+Ctrl+K
Typography	Apply bold	Shift+Ctrl+B	Shift+Ctrl+B	Shift+Ctrl+B
Typography	Apply italic	Shift+Ctrl+I	Shift+Ctrl+I	Shift+Ctrl+I
Typography	Apply ligatures	[none defined]	[none defined]	
Typography	Apply no break	[none defined]	[none defined]	
Typography	Apply normal	Shift+Ctrl+Y	Shift+Ctrl+P or Shift+Ctrl+Y	Shift+Ctrl+Spacebar
Typography	Apply old style figures	[none defined]	[none defined]	
Typography	Apply small caps	Shift+Ctrl+H	Shift+Ctrl+H	
Typography	Apply strikethrough	Shift+Ctrl+/	Shift+Ctrl+/	Shift+Ctrl+/
Typography	Apply subscript	Shift+Ctrl+Alt+= or Shift+Ctrl+Alt+Num +	Shift+Ctrl+9 or Shift+Ctrl+Alt+= or Shift+Ctrl+Alt+Num +	Ctrl+\
Typography	Apply superscript	Shift+Ctrl+= or Shift+Ctrl+Num +	Shift+Ctrl+0 or Shift+Ctrl+Num +	Ctrl+Shift+\
Typography	Apply underline	Shift+Ctrl+U	Shift+Ctrl+U	Shift+Ctrl+U
Typography	Auto leading	Shift+Ctrl+Alt+A	Shift+Ctrl+Alt+A	Shift+Ctrl+Alt+A
Typography	Auto-hyphenate on/off	Shift+Ctrl+Alt+H	Shift+Ctrl+Alt+H	
Typography	Decrease baseline shift	Shift+Alt+Down Arrow	Shift+Ctrl+Alt+9 or Shift+Alt+Down Arrow	
Typography	Decrease baseline shift by 5 times	Shift+Ctrl+Alt+Down Arrow	Shift+Ctrl+Alt+Down Arrow	
Typography	Decrease kerning/tracking	Alt+Left Arrow	Shift+Ctrl+Alt+[or Alt+Left Arrow	
Typography	Decrease kerning/tracking by 5 times	Ctrl+Alt+Left Arrow	Shift+Ctrl+[or Ctrl+Alt+Left Arrow	
Typography	Decrease leading	Alt+Up Arrow	Shift+Ctrl+Alt+; or Alt+Up Arrow	
Typography	Decrease leading by 5 times	Ctrl+Alt+Up Arrow	Shift+Ctrl+; or Ctrl+Alt+Up Arrow	
Typography	Decrease point size	Shift+Ctrl+, (comma)	Shift+Ctrl+, (comma)	Ctrl+Shift+<
Typography	Decrease point size by 5 times	Shift+Ctrl+Alt+, (comma)	Shift+Ctrl+Alt+, (comma)	
Typography	Define character style	[none defined]	[none defined]	Ctrl+3
Typography	Define paragraph style	[none defined]	[none defined]	
Typography	Increase baseline shift	Shift+Alt+Up Arrow	Shift+Ctrl+Alt+0 or Shift+Alt+Up Arrow	

Continued on next page

TABLE E.1: WINDOWS COMMAND EQUIVALENTS (continued)

InDesign Product Area	Command	InDesign Default	QuarkXPress 4	PageMaker 6.5
Typography	Increase baseline shift by 5 times	Shift+Ctrl+Alt+ Up Arrow	Shift+Ctrl+Alt+ Up Arrow	
Typography	Increase kerning/ tracking	Alt+Right Arrow	Shift+Ctrl+Alt+] or Alt+Right Arrow	
Typography	Increase kerning/ tracking by 5 times	Ctrl+Alt+Right Arrow	Shift+Ctrl+] or Ctrl+Alt+Right Arrow	
Typography	Increase leading	Alt+Down Arrow	Alt+Down Arrow	
Typography	Increase leading by 5 times	Ctrl+Alt+Down Arrow	Ctrl+Alt+Down Arrow	
Typography	Increase point size	Shift+Ctrl+. (period)	Shift+Ctrl+. (period)	Ctrl+Shift+>
Typography	Increase point size by 5 times	Shift+Ctrl+Alt+. (period)	Shift+Ctrl+Alt+. (period)	
Typography	Insert bullet	Alt+8	Alt+8	Alt+8
Typography	Insert copyright symbol	Alt+G	Alt+G	Alt+G
Typography	Insert discretionary hyphen	Shift+Ctrl+- or Shift+Ctrl+Num −	Ctrl+-	Ctrl+Shift+-
Typography	Insert ellipsis	Alt+;	Alt+;	Alt+0133 (on numeric keypad)
Typography	Insert em dash	Shift+Alt+-	Shift+Alt+-	Alt+Shift+-
Typography	Insert em space	Shift+Ctrl+M	Shift+Ctrl+5	Ctrl+Shift+M
Typography	Insert en dash	Alt+-	Alt+-	Alt+-
Typography	Insert en space	[none defined]	Shift+Ctrl+ 6	Ctrl+Shift+N
Typography	Insert figure space	Shift+Ctrl+Alt+8	Shift+Ctrl+Alt+8	
Typography	Insert flush space	Shift+Ctrl+Alt+J	Shift+Ctrl+Alt+J	
Typography	Insert hair space	Shift+Ctrl+Alt+I		
Typography	Insert left double quote	Alt+[	Alt+[	Alt+Shift+[
Typography	Insert left single quote	Alt+]	Alt+]	Alt+[
Typography	Insert non-breaking hyphen	Ctrl+Alt+-	Ctrl+=	Ctrl+Alt+-
Typography	Insert non-breaking space	Ctrl+Alt+X	Ctrl+Alt+X or Ctrl+5	Ctrl+Alt+Spacebar
Typography	Insert paragraph symbol	Alt+7	Alt+7	Alt+7
Typography	Insert punctuation space	[none defined]	[none defined]	

Continued on next page

TABLE E.1: WINDOWS COMMAND EQUIVALENTS (continued)

InDesign Product Area	Command	InDesign Default	QuarkXPress 4	PageMaker 6.5
Typography	Insert registered trademark mark	Alt+R	Alt+R	Alt+R
Typography	Insert right double quote	Shift+Alt+[	Shift+Alt+[	Alt+Shift+]
Typography	Insert right single quote	Shift+Alt+]	Shift+Alt+]	Alt+]
Typography	Insert section name	Shift+Ctrl+Alt+N	Shift+Ctrl+Alt+N	
Typography	Insert section symbol	Alt+6	Alt+6	Alt+6
Typography	Insert thin space	Shift+Ctrl+Alt+M	[none defined]	Ctrl+Shift+T
Typography	Insert trademark mark	Alt+2	Alt+2	Alt+0153 (on numeric keypad)
Typography	Keep Options…	Ctrl+Alt+K	Ctrl+Alt+K	
Typography	Normal horizontal text scale	Shift+Ctrl+X	Shift+Ctrl+X or Ctrl+]	Shift+Ctrl+X
Typography	Normal vertical text scale	Shift+Ctrl+Alt+X	Shift+Ctrl+Alt+X	
Typography	Paragraph Rules…	Ctrl+Alt+J	Shift+Ctrl+N	
Typography	Recompose all stories	Ctrl+Alt+/	Ctrl+Alt+/	
Typography	Redefine character style	Shift+Ctrl+Alt+C	Shift+Ctrl+Alt+C	
Typography	Redefine paragraph style	Shift+Ctrl+Alt+R	Shift+Ctrl+Alt+R	
Typography	Reset kerning and tracking	Shift+Ctrl+Q	Shift+Ctrl+Q	Shift+Ctrl+Q
Typography	Switch composer	Shift+Ctrl+Alt+T	Shift+Ctrl+Alt+T	
Typography	Toggle Typographer's Quotes preference	Shift+Ctrl+Alt+'	Shift+Ctrl+Alt+'	
View Menu	Actual Size	Ctrl+1	Ctrl+1	Ctrl+1
View Menu	Display Master Items	Ctrl+Y	[none defined]	Alt+Ctrl+N
View Menu	Entire Pasteboard	Shift+Ctrl+Alt+0	Ctrl+Alt+0	Shift+Ctrl+0
View Menu	Fit Page In Window	Ctrl+0	Ctrl+0	Ctrl+0
View Menu	Fit Spread In Window	Ctrl+Alt+0	[none defined]	
View Menu	Show/Hide Guides	Ctrl+;	F7	Ctrl+;
View Menu	Show/Hide Rulers	Ctrl+R	Ctrl+R	Ctrl+R
View Menu	Lock Guides	Ctrl+Alt+;	Ctrl+Alt+;	Ctrl+Alt+;

Continued on next page

TABLE E.1: WINDOWS COMMAND EQUIVALENTS (continued)

InDesign Product Area	Command	InDesign Default	QuarkXPress 4	PageMaker 6.5
View Menu	Show/Hide Baseline Grid	Ctrl+Alt+'	Ctrl+F7	
View Menu	Show/Hide Document Grid	Ctrl+'	Ctrl+'	
View Menu	Show Frame Edges	Ctrl+H	Ctrl+H	
View Menu	Show Text Threads	Ctrl+Alt+Y	Ctrl+Alt+Y	
View Menu	Snap to Document Grid	Shift+Ctrl+'	[none defined]	
View Menu	Snap to Guides	Shift+Ctrl+;	Shift+F7	Shift+Ctrl+;
View Menu	Zoom In	Ctrl+=	[none defined]	Ctrl+=
View Menu	Zoom Out	Ctrl+=	[none defined]	Ctrl+-
Views, Navigation	100% size	[none defined]	[none defined]	Ctrl+1
Views, Navigation	200% size	Ctrl+2	Ctrl+2	Ctrl+2
Views, Navigation	400% size	Ctrl+4	Ctrl+4	Ctrl+4
Views, Navigation	50% size	Ctrl+5	[none defined]	Ctrl+5
Views, Navigation	Access page number box in document window	Ctrl+J	Ctrl+J	Ctrl+Alt+P
Views, Navigation	Access zoom percentage box	Ctrl+Alt+5	Ctrl+Alt+5 or Ctrl+Alt+V	
Views, Navigation	Change Image Display preference	Shift+Ctrl+F5	[none defined]	
Views, Navigation	First spread	Shift+Alt+Page Up	Shift+Alt+Page Up or Ctrl+Page Up	
Views, Navigation	Fit selection in window	Ctrl+Alt+=	Ctrl+Alt+=	
Views, Navigation	Force redraw	Shift+F5	Shift+Escape	
Views, Navigation	Go to first frame	Shift+Ctrl+Alt+Page Up	Shift+Ctrl+Alt+Page Up	
Views, Navigation	Go to last frame	Shift+Ctrl+Alt+Page Down	Shift+Ctrl+Alt+Page Down	
Views, Navigation	Go to next frame	Ctrl+Alt+Page Down	Ctrl+Alt+Page Down	Alt+Ctrl+]
Views, Navigation	Go to previous frame	Ctrl+Alt+Page Up	Ctrl+Alt+Page Up	Alt+Ctrl+[
Views, Navigation	Last spread	Shift+Alt+Page Down	Shift+Alt+Page Down	
Views, Navigation	Next spread	Alt+Page Down	Alt+Page Down	
Views, Navigation	Previous spread	Alt+Page Up	Alt+Page Up	

Continued on next page

TABLE E.1: WINDOWS COMMAND EQUIVALENTS (continued)

InDesign Product Area	Command	InDesign Default	QuarkXPress 4	PageMaker 6.5
Views, Navigation	Scroll down one screen	Page Down	Page Down	Page Down
Views, Navigation	Scroll up one screen	Page Up	Page Up	Page Up
Views, Navigation	Toggle between current and previous views	Ctrl+Alt+2	Ctrl+Alt+2	
Window Menu	Align…	F8	Ctrl+, (comma)	Shift+Ctrl+E
Window Menu	Attributes…	[none defined]	[none defined]	
Window Menu	Cascade	[none defined]	[none defined]	
Window Menu	Color…	F6	[none defined]	Ctrl+J
Window Menu	Gradient…	[none defined]	[none defined]	
Window Menu	Layers…	F7	[none defined]	Ctrl+8
Window Menu	Libraries: New…	[none defined]	Ctrl+Alt+N	
Window Menu	Libraries: Open…	Shift+Ctrl+Alt+L	Shift+Ctrl+Alt+L	
Window Menu	Navigator…	[none defined]	[none defined]	
Window Menu	New Window	[none defined]	[none defined]	
Window Menu	Pages…	F12	F4	Shift+Ctrl+8
Window Menu	Stroke…	F10	Ctrl+B	
Window Menu	Swatch Libraries: DICCOLOR	[none defined]	[none defined]	
Window Menu	Swatch Libraries: FOCOLTONE	[none defined]	[none defined]	
Window Menu	Swatch Libraries: Other Library…	[none defined]	[none defined]	
Window Menu	Swatch Libraries: PANTONE Coated	[none defined]	[none defined]	
Window Menu	Swatch Libraries: PANTONE Process	[none defined]	[none defined]	
Window Menu	Swatch Libraries: PANTONE Uncoated	[none defined]	[none defined]	
Window Menu	Swatch Libraries: System (Macintosh)	[none defined]	[none defined]	
Window Menu	Swatch Libraries: System (Windows)	[none defined]	[none defined]	
Window Menu	Swatch Libraries: TOYO COLOR FINDER	[none defined]	[none defined]	

Continued on next page

TABLE E.1: WINDOWS COMMAND EQUIVALENTS (continued)

InDesign Product Area	Command	InDesign Default	QuarkXPress 4	PageMaker 6.5
Window Menu	Swatch Libraries: TRUMATCH	[none defined]	[none defined]	
Window Menu	Swatch Libraries: Web	[none defined]	[none defined]	
Window Menu	Swatches...	F5	F12	
Window Menu	Tile	[none defined]	[none defined]	
Window Menu	Tools...	[none defined]	F8	
Window Menu	Transform...	F9	F9	

Macintosh

TABLE E.2: MACINTOSH COMMAND EQUIVALENTS

InDesign Product Area	Command	InDesign Default	QuarkXPress 4	PageMaker 6.5
Apple Menu	About InDesign...	[none defined]	[none defined]	
Edit Menu	Check Spelling...	Cmd+I	Opt+Cmd+L	Cmd+L
Edit Menu	Clear	[none defined]	[none defined]	
Edit Menu	Copy	Cmd+C	Cmd+C	Cmd+C
Edit Menu	Cut	Cmd+X	Cmd+X	Cmd+X
Edit Menu	Deselect All	Shift+Cmd+A	Shift+Cmd+A	Shift+Cmd+A
Edit Menu	Duplicate	Opt+Cmd+D	Cmd+D	
Edit Menu	Edit Dictionary...	[none defined]	[none defined]	
Edit Menu	Find Next	Opt+Cmd+F	Opt+Cmd+F	Cmd+G
Edit Menu	Find/Change...	Cmd+F	Cmd+F	Cmd+H
Edit Menu	Paste	Cmd+V	Cmd+V	Cmd+V
Edit Menu	Paste Into	Opt+Cmd+V	Opt+Cmd+V	
Edit Menu	Redo	Shift+Cmd+Z	Shift+Cmd+Z	
Edit Menu	Select All	Cmd+A	Cmd+A	Cmd+A
Edit Menu	Step and Repeat...	Shift+Cmd+V	Opt+Cmd+D	
Edit Menu	Undo	Cmd+Z	Cmd+Z	Cmd+Z
File Menu	Adobe Online...	[none defined]	[none defined]	
File Menu	Close	Cmd+W	Cmd+W	Cmd+W

Continued on next page

TABLE E.2: MACINTOSH COMMAND EQUIVALENTS (continued)

InDesign Product Area	Command	InDesign Default	QuarkXPress 4	PageMaker 6.5
File Menu	Color Settings: Application Color Settings…	[none defined]	[none defined]	
File Menu	Color Settings: Document Color Settings…	[none defined]	[none defined]	
File Menu	Document Setup…	Opt+Cmd+P	Opt+Shift+Cmd+P	Shift+Cmd+P
File Menu	Edit Shortcuts…	Opt+Shift+Cmd+K	Opt+Shift+Cmd+K	
File Menu	Export…	Cmd+E	Opt+Cmd+E	
File Menu	Links…	Shift+Cmd+D	Opt+F13	Shift+Cmd+D
File Menu	New…	Cmd+N	Cmd+N	Cmd+N
File Menu	Open…	Cmd+O	Cmd+O	Cmd+O
File Menu	Package…	Opt+Shift+Cmd+P	[none defined]	
File Menu	Page Setup…	Shift+Cmd+P	Opt+Cmd+P	
File Menu	Place…	Cmd+D	Cmd+E	Cmd+D
File Menu	Preferences: Composition…	[none defined]	[none defined]	
File Menu	Preferences: Dictionary…	[none defined]	[none defined]	
File Menu	Preferences: General…	Cmd+K	Cmd+Y	Cmd+K
File Menu	Preferences: Grids…	[none defined]	[none defined]	
File Menu	Preferences: Guides…	[none defined]	[none defined]	
File Menu	Preferences: Online Settings…	[none defined]	[none defined]	
File Menu	Preferences: Text…	[none defined]	[none defined]	
File Menu	Preferences: Units & Increments…	[none defined]	[none defined]	
File Menu	Preflight…	Opt+Shift+Cmd+F	[none defined]	
File Menu	Print…	Cmd+P	Cmd+P	Cmd+P
File Menu	Quit	Cmd+Q	Cmd+Q	Cmd+Q
File Menu	Revert	[none defined]	[none defined]	
File Menu	Save	Cmd+S	Cmd+S	Cmd+S
File Menu	Save a Copy…	Opt+Cmd+S	[none defined]	
File Menu	Save As…	Shift+Cmd+S	Opt+Cmd+S	Shift+Cmd+S

Continued on next page

TABLE E.2: MACINTOSH COMMAND EQUIVALENTS (continued)

InDesign Product Area	Command	InDesign Default	QuarkXPress 4	PageMaker 6.5
Help Menu	Adobe Corporate News…	[none defined]	[none defined]	
Help Menu	Downloadables…	[none defined]	[none defined]	
Help Menu	Help Topics…	Help	Help	
Help Menu	How to Use Help…	[none defined]	[none defined]	
Help Menu	Online Registration…	[none defined]	[none defined]	
Help Menu	Top Issues…	[none defined]	[none defined]	
Layout Menu	Create Guides…	[none defined]	[none defined]	
Layout Menu	First Page	Shift+Cmd+Page Up	Ctrl+Shift+A	
Layout Menu	Go Back	Cmd+Page Up	Cmd+Page Up	Cmd+Page Up
Layout Menu	Go Forward	Cmd+Page Down	Cmd+Page Down	Cmd+Page Down
Layout Menu	Insert Page Number	Opt+Cmd+N	Cmd+3	Cmd+Opt+P
Layout Menu	Last Page	Shift+Cmd+Page Down	Ctrl+Shift+D	
Layout Menu	Layout Adjustment…	[none defined]	[none defined]	
Layout Menu	Margins and Columns…	[none defined]	[none defined]	
Layout Menu	Next Page	Shift+Page Down	Ctrl+Shift+L	Page Down
Layout Menu	Previous Page	Shift+Page Up	Ctrl+Shift+K	Page Up
Layout Menu	Ruler Guides…	[none defined]	[none defined]	
Object Editing	Apply default fill and stroke colors	D	D	
Object Editing	Select 1 object down from selection			
Object Editing	Select 1 object up from selection			
Object Editing	Select all guides	Opt+Cmd+G	Opt+Cmd+G	
Object Editing	Select through to bottom object		[none defined]	
Object Editing	Select through to next object		[none defined]	
Object Editing	Swap fill and stroke activation	X	X	
Object Editing	Swap fill and stroke colors	Shift+X	Shift+X	
Object Menu	Arrange: Bring Forward	Cmd+]	Opt+F5	Cmd+]
Object Menu	Arrange: Bring To Front	Shift+Cmd+]	F5	Shift+Cmd+]

Continued on next page

TABLE E.2: MACINTOSH COMMAND EQUIVALENTS (continued)

InDesign Product Area	Command	InDesign Default	QuarkXPress 4	PageMaker 6.5
Object Menu	Arrange: Send Backward	Cmd+[	Opt+Shift+F5	Cmd+[
Object Menu	Arrange: Send To Back	Shift+Cmd+[	Shift+F5	Shift+Cmd+[
Object Menu	Clipping Path...	[none defined]	Opt+Cmd+T	
Object Menu	Compound Paths: Make	Cmd+8	Cmd+8	
Object Menu	Compound Paths: Release	Opt+Cmd+8	Opt+Cmd+8	
Object Menu	Content: Graphic	[none defined]	[none defined]	
Object Menu	Content: Text	[none defined]	[none defined]	
Object Menu	Content: Unassigned	[none defined]	[none defined]	
Object Menu	Corner Effects...	Opt+Cmd+R	Opt+Cmd+R	
Object Menu	Fitting: Center Content	Shift+Cmd+E	Shift+Cmd+M	
Object Menu	Fitting: Fit Content Proportionally	Opt+Shift+Cmd+E	Opt+Shift+Cmd+F	
Object Menu	Fitting: Fit Content to Frame	Opt+Cmd+E	[none defined]	
Object Menu	Fitting: Fit Frame to Content	Opt+Shift+Cmd+V	Opt+Shift+Cmd+V	
Object Menu	Group	Cmd+G	Cmd+G	Cmd+G
Object Menu	Image Color Settings...	Opt+Shift+Cmd+D	Opt+Shift+Cmd+D	
Object Menu	Lock Position	Cmd+L	F6	Cmd+L
Object Menu	Reverse Path	[none defined]	[none defined]	
Object Menu	Text Frame Options...	Cmd+B	[none defined]	
Object Menu	Text Wrap...	Opt+Cmd+W	Cmd+T	Opt+Cmd+E
Object Menu	Ungroup	Shift+Cmd+G	Cmd+U	Shift+Cmd+G
Object Menu	Unlock Position	Opt+Cmd+L	[none defined]	Opt+Cmd+L
Other	Close all	Opt+Shift+Cmd+W	Opt+Shift+Cmd+W	
Other	Close document	Shift+Cmd+W	Shift+Cmd+W	Cmd+W
Other	Create outlines without deleting text	Opt+Shift+Cmd+O	Opt+Shift+Cmd+O	
Other	New default document	Shift+Cmd+N	Shift+Cmd+N	
Other	Save all	Opt+Shift+Cmd+S	Opt+Shift+Cmd+S	

Continued on next page

TABLE E.2: MACINTOSH COMMAND EQUIVALENTS (continued)

InDesign Product Area	Command	InDesign Default	QuarkXPress 4	PageMaker 6.5
Other	Update missing font list	Opt+Shift+Cmd+/	Opt+Shift+Cmd+/	
Text Selection	Find Next	Shift+F2	Shift+F2	Cmd+G
Text Selection	Load Find and Find Next instance			
Text Selection	Load Find with selected text			
Text Selection	Load Replace with selected text			
Text Selection	Move down one line	Down Arrow	Down Arrow	Down Arrow
Text Selection	Move to beginning of story	Cmd+Home	Cmd+Home	Home
Text Selection	Move to end of story	Cmd+End	Cmd+End	End
Text Selection	Move to the end of the line	End	End	
Text Selection	Move to the left one character	Left Arrow	Left Arrow	Left Arrow
Text Selection	Move to the left one word	Cmd+Left Arrow	Cmd+Left Arrow	Cmd+Left Arrow
Text Selection	Move to the next paragraph	Cmd+Down Arrow	Cmd+Down Arrow	Cmd+Down Arrow
Text Selection	Move to the previous paragraph	Cmd+Up Arrow	Cmd+Up Arrow	Cmd+Up Arrow
Text Selection	Move to the right one character	Right Arrow	Right Arrow	Right Arrow
Text Selection	Move to the right one word	Cmd+Right Arrow	Cmd+Right Arrow	Cmd+Right Arrow
Text Selection	Move to the start of the line	Home	Home	
Text Selection	Move up one line	Up Arrow	Up Arrow	Up Arrow
Text Selection	Replace with Change To text			
Text Selection	Replace with Change To text and Find Next			
Text Selection	Select one character to the left	Shift+Left Arrow	Shift+Left Arrow	
Text Selection	Select one character to the right	Shift+Right Arrow	Shift+Right Arrow	

Continued on next page

TABLE E.2: MACINTOSH COMMAND EQUIVALENTS (continued)

InDesign Product Area	Command	InDesign Default	QuarkXPress 4	PageMaker 6.5
Text Selection	Select one line above	Shift+Up Arrow	Shift+Up Arrow	
Text Selection	Select one line below	Shift+Down Arrow	Shift+Down Arrow	
Text Selection	Select one paragraph before	Shift+Cmd+Up Arrow	Shift+Cmd+Up Arrow	
Text Selection	Select one paragraph forward	Shift+Cmd+Down Arrow	Shift+Cmd+Down Arrow	
Text Selection	Select one word to the left	Shift+Cmd+Left Arrow	Shift+Cmd+Left Arrow	Cmd+Shift+Left Arrow
Text Selection	Select one word to the right	Shift+Cmd+Right Arrow	Shift+Cmd+Right Arrow	Cmd+Shift+Right Arrow
Text Selection	Select to beginning of story	Shift+Cmd+Home	Shift+Cmd+Home	
Text Selection	Select to end of story	Shift+Cmd+End	Shift+Cmd+End	
Text Selection	Select to the end of the line	Shift+End	Shift+End	
Text Selection	Select to the start of the line	Shift+Home	Shift+Home	
Tools, Palettes	Activate last-used field in palette	Cmd+`	Cmd+`	
Tools, Palettes	Apply color	, (comma)	, (comma)	
Tools, Palettes	Apply gradient	. (period)	. (period)	
Tools, Palettes	Apply None	/	/	
Tools, Palettes	Direct Selection Tool	A	A	
Tools, Palettes	Ellipse Tool	L	L	Shift+F5
Tools, Palettes	Ellipse Tool (select hidden tools)	Shift+L	Shift+L	Shift+Cmd+F5
Tools, Palettes	Gradient Tool	G	G	
Tools, Palettes	Hand Tool	H	H	Shift+F7
Tools, Palettes	Line Tool	E	E	Shift+F3
Tools, Palettes	Pen Tool	P	P	
Tools, Palettes	Pen Tool (select hidden tools)	Shift+P	Shift+P	
Tools, Palettes	Polygon Tool	N	N	Shift+F6
Tools, Palettes	Polygon Tool (select hidden tools)	Shift+N	Shift+N	
Tools, Palettes	Rectangle Tool	M	M	Shift+F4

Continued on next page

TABLE E.2: MACINTOSH COMMAND EQUIVALENTS (continued)

InDesign Product Area	Command	InDesign Default	QuarkXPress 4	PageMaker 6.5
Tools, Palettes	Rectangle Tool (select hidden tools)	Shift+M	Shift+M	Shift+Cmd+F4
Tools, Palettes	Rotate Tool	R	R	Shift+F2
Tools, Palettes	Scale Tool	S	S	
Tools, Palettes	Scale Tool (select hidden tools)	Shift+S	Shift+S	
Tools, Palettes	Scissors Tool	C	C	
Tools, Palettes	Selection Tool	V	V	Shift+F1
Tools, Palettes	Toggle between Selection and Direct Selection tool	Ctrl+Cmd+ Down Arrow or Cmd+Tab	Shift+F8 or Cmd+Tab or Ctrl+Cmd+ Down Arrow	
Tools, Palettes	Toggle to add anchor point	+ or Num +	+ or Num +	
Tools, Palettes	Toggle to delete anchor point	- or Num −	- or Num −	
Tools, Palettes	Type Tool	T	T	Shift+Cmd+F1
Tools, Palettes	Zoom Tool	Z	Z	Shift+Cmd+F7
Type Menu	Character Styles…	Shift+F11	Shift+F11	
Type Menu	Character…	Cmd+T	Shift+Cmd+D	Cmd+T
Type Menu	Create Outlines	Shift+Cmd+O	Shift+Cmd+O	
Type Menu	Font: Times New Roman PS: Plain	[none defined]	[none defined]	
Type Menu	Insert Character…	[none defined]	[none defined]	
Type Menu	Paragraph Styles…	F11	F11	
Type Menu	Paragraph…	Cmd+M	Shift+Cmd+F	Cmd+M
Type Menu	Show Hidden Characters	Opt+Cmd+I	Cmd+I	
Type Menu	Size: 10	[none defined]	[none defined]	
Type Menu	Size: 11	[none defined]	[none defined]	
Type Menu	Size: 12	[none defined]	[none defined]	
Type Menu	Size: 14	[none defined]	[none defined]	
Type Menu	Size: 18	[none defined]	[none defined]	
Type Menu	Size: 24	[none defined]	[none defined]	
Type Menu	Size: 30	[none defined]	[none defined]	
Type Menu	Size: 36	[none defined]	[none defined]	
Type Menu	Size: 48	[none defined]	[none defined]	

Continued on next page

TABLE E.2: MACINTOSH COMMAND EQUIVALENTS (continued)

InDesign Product Area	Command	InDesign Default	QuarkXPress 4	PageMaker 6.5
Type Menu	Size: 6	[none defined]	[none defined]	
Type Menu	Size: 60	[none defined]	[none defined]	
Type Menu	Size: 72	[none defined]	[none defined]	
Type Menu	Size: 8	[none defined]	[none defined]	
Type Menu	Size: 9	[none defined]	[none defined]	
Type Menu	Size: Other…	[none defined]	[none defined]	
Type Menu	Story…	[none defined]	[none defined]	
Type Menu	Tabs…	Shift+Cmd+T	Shift+Cmd+T	Cmd+I
Typography	Align center	Shift+Cmd+C	Shift+Cmd+C	Shift+Cmd+C
Typography	Align force justify	Shift+Cmd+F	[none defined]	Shift+Cmd+F
Typography	Align justify	Shift+Cmd+J	Shift+Cmd+J	Shift+Cmd+J
Typography	Align left	Shift+Cmd+L	Shift+Cmd+L	Shift+Cmd+L
Typography	Align right	Shift+Cmd+R	Shift+Cmd+R	Shift+Cmd+R
Typography	Align to baseline grid	Opt+Shift+Cmd+G	Opt+Shift+Cmd+G	
Typography	Apply all caps	Shift+Cmd+K	Shift+Cmd+K	Cmd+Shift+K
Typography	Apply bold	Shift+Cmd+B	Shift+Cmd+B	Shift+Cmd+B
Typography	Apply italic	Shift+Cmd+I	Shift+Cmd+I	Shift+Cmd+I
Typography	Apply ligatures	[none defined]	[none defined]	
Typography	Apply no break	[none defined]	[none defined]	
Typography	Apply normal	Shift+Cmd+Y	Shift+Cmd+P	
Typography	Apply old style figures	[none defined]	[none defined]	
Typography	Apply small caps	Shift+Cmd+H	Shift+Cmd+H	Cmd+Shift+H
Typography	Apply strikethrough	Shift+Cmd+/	Shift+Cmd+/	Shift+Cmd+/
Typography	Apply subscript	Opt+Shift+Cmd++	Shift+Cmd+- or Opt+Shift+Cmd++	Cmd+\
Typography	Apply superscript	Shift+Cmd++	Shift+Cmd++	Cmd+Shift+\
Typography	Apply underline	Shift+Cmd+U	Shift+Cmd+U	Shift+Cmd+U
Typography	Auto leading	Opt+Shift+Cmd+A	Opt+Shift+Cmd+A	Shift+Opt+Cmd+A
Typography	Auto-hyphenate on/off	Opt+Shift+Cmd+H	Opt+Shift+Cmd+H	
Typography	Decrease baseline shift	Opt+Shift+Down Arrow	Opt+Shift+Cmd+- or Opt+Shift+Down Arrow	
Typography	Decrease baseline shift by 5 times	Opt+Shift+Cmd+Down Arrow	Opt+Shift+Cmd+Down Arrow	
Typography	Decrease kerning/tracking	Opt+Left Arrow	Opt+Shift+Cmd+[or Opt+Left Arrow	

Continued on next page

TABLE E.2: MACINTOSH COMMAND EQUIVALENTS (continued)

InDesign Product Area	Command	InDesign Default	QuarkXPress 4	PageMaker 6.5
Typography	Decrease kerning/tracking by 5 times	Opt+Cmd+Left Arrow	Shift+Cmd+[or Opt+Cmd+Left Arrow	
Typography	Decrease leading	Opt+Up Arrow	Opt+Shift+Cmd+; or Opt+Up Arrow	
Typography	Decrease leading by 5 times	Opt+Cmd+Up Arrow	Shift+Cmd+; or Opt+Cmd+Up Arrow	
Typography	Decrease point size	Shift+Cmd+, (comma)	Shift+Cmd+, (comma)	Cmd+Opt+<
Typography	Decrease point size by 5 times	Opt+Shift+Cmd+, (comma)	Opt+Shift+Cmd+, (comma)	
Typography	Define character style	[none defined]	[none defined]	
Typography	Define paragraph style	[none defined]	[none defined]	
Typography	Increase baseline shift	Opt+Shift+Up Arrow	Opt+Shift+Cmd+= or Opt+Shift+Up Arrow	
Typography	Increase baseline shift by 5 times	Opt+Shift+Cmd+Up Arrow	Opt+Shift+Cmd+Up Arrow	
Typography	Increase kerning/tracking	Opt+Right Arrow	Opt+Shift+Cmd+] or Opt+Right Arrow	
Typography	Increase kerning/tracking by 5 times	Opt+Cmd+Right Arrow	Shift+Cmd+] or Opt+Cmd+Right Arrow	
Typography	Increase leading	Opt+Down Arrow	Opt+Shift+Cmd+' or Opt+Down Arrow	
Typography	Increase leading by 5 times	Opt+Cmd+Down Arrow	Shift+Cmd+' or Opt+Cmd+Down Arrow	
Typography	Increase point size	Shift+Cmd+. (period)	Shift+Cmd+. (period)	Cmd+Shift+>
Typography	Increase point size by 5 times	Opt+Shift+Cmd+. (period)	Opt+Shift+Cmd+. (period)	
Typography	Insert discretionary hyphen	Shift+Cmd+-	Cmd+-	Cmd+Shift+-
Typography	Insert em space	Shift+Cmd+M	Opt+Shift+Space	Cmd+Shift+M
Typography	Insert en space	[none defined]	Opt+Cmd+Space	Cmd+Shift+N
Typography	Insert figure space	Opt+Shift+Cmd+8	Opt+Shift+Cmd+8	
Typography	Insert flush space	Opt+Shift+Cmd+J	Opt+Shift+Cmd+J	

Continued on next page

TABLE E.2: MACINTOSH COMMAND EQUIVALENTS (continued)

InDesign Product Area	Command	InDesign Default	QuarkXPress 4	PageMaker 6.5
Typography	Insert hair space	Opt+Shift+Cmd+I	Opt+Shift+Cmd+I	
Typography	Insert non-breaking hyphen	Opt+Cmd+-	Cmd+= or Opt+Cmd+-	
Typography	Insert non-breaking space	Opt+Cmd+X	Cmd+5 or Opt+Cmd+X	Opt+Space bar
Typography	Insert punctuation space	[none defined]	[none defined]	
Typography	Insert section name	Opt+Shift+Cmd+N	Opt+Shift+Cmd+N	
Typography	Insert thin space	Opt+Shift+Cmd+M	Opt+Shift+Cmd+M	Cmd+Shift+T
Typography	Keep Options	Opt+Cmd+K	Opt+Cmd+K	
Typography	Normal horizontal text scale	Shift+Cmd+X	Shift+Cmd+X	Shift+Cmd+X
Typography	Normal vertical text scale	Opt+Shift+Cmd+X	Opt+Shift+Cmd+X	
Typography	Paragraph Rules…	Opt+Cmd+J	Opt+Cmd+J	
Typography	Recompose all stories	Opt+Cmd+/	Opt+Cmd+/	
Typography	Redefine character style	Opt+Shift+Cmd+C	Opt+Shift+Cmd+C	
Typography	Redefine paragraph style	Opt+Shift+Cmd+R	Opt+Shift+Cmd+R	
Typography	Reset kerning and tracking	Shift+Cmd+Q	Shift+Cmd+Q	
Typography	Switch composer	Opt+Shift+Cmd+T	Opt+Shift+Cmd+T	
Typography	Toggle Typographer's Quotes preference	Opt+Shift+Cmd+'	[none defined]	
View Menu	Actual Size	Cmd+1	Cmd+1	Cmd+1
View Menu	Display Master Items	Cmd+Y	[none defined]	Opt+Cmd+N
View Menu	Entire Pasteboard	Opt+Shift+Cmd+0	Opt+Cmd+0	Opt+Cmd+0
View Menu	Fit Page In Window	Cmd+0	Cmd+0	Cmd+0
View Menu	Fit Spread In Window	Opt+Cmd+0	[none defined]	
View Menu	Hide Guides	Cmd+;	F7	Cmd+;
View Menu	Hide Rulers	Cmd+R	Cmd+R	Cmd+R
View Menu	Lock Guides	Opt+Cmd+;	Opt+Cmd+;	Opt+Cmd+;
View Menu	Show Baseline Grid	Opt+Cmd+'	Opt+F7	
View Menu	Show Document Grid	Cmd+'	Cmd+'	
View Menu	Show Frame Edges	Cmd+H	Cmd+H	
View Menu	Show Text Threads	Opt+Cmd+Y	Opt+Cmd+Y	

Continued on next page

TABLE E.2: MACINTOSH COMMAND EQUIVALENTS (continued)

InDesign Product Area	Command	InDesign Default	QuarkXPress 4	PageMaker 6.5
View Menu	Snap to Document Grid	Shift+Cmd+'	[none defined]	
View Menu	Snap to Guides	Shift+Cmd+;	Shift+F7	Shift+Cmd+;
View Menu	Zoom In	Cmd++	Cmd++	Cmd++
View Menu	Zoom Out	Cmd+-	[none defined]	Cmd+-
Views, Navigation	100% size	[none defined]	[none defined]	Cmd+1
Views, Navigation	200% size	Cmd+2	Cmd+2	Cmd+2
Views, Navigation	400% size	Cmd+4	Cmd+4	Cmd+4
Views, Navigation	50% size	Cmd+5	[none defined]	Cmd+5
Views, Navigation	Access page number box	Cmd+J	Cmd+J	
Views, Navigation	Access zoom percentage box	Opt+Cmd+5	Ctrl+V or Opt+Cmd+5	
Views, Navigation	Change Image Display preference	Shift+Cmd+F5	Shift+Cmd+F5	
Views, Navigation	First spread	Opt+Shift+Page Up	Opt+Shift+Page Up	
Views, Navigation	Fit selection in window	Opt+Cmd++	Opt+Cmd++	
Views, Navigation	Force redraw	Shift+F5	Opt+Cmd+. (period)	
Views, Navigation	Go to first frame	Opt+Shift+Cmd+Page Up	Opt+Shift+Cmd+Page Up	
Views, Navigation	Go to last frame	Opt+Shift+Cmd+Page Down	Opt+Shift+Cmd+Page Down	
Views, Navigation	Go to next frame	Opt+Cmd+Page Down	Opt+Cmd+Page Down	Opt+Cmd+]
Views, Navigation	Go to previous frame	Opt+Cmd+Page Up	Opt+Cmd+Page Up	Opt+Cmd+[
Views, Navigation	Last spread	Opt+Shift+Page Down	Opt+Shift+Page Down	
Views, Navigation	Next spread	Opt+Page Down	Opt+Page Down	
Views, Navigation	Previous spread	Opt+Page Up	Opt+Page Up	
Views, Navigation	Scroll down one screen	Page Down	Page Down	Page Down
Views, Navigation	Scroll up one screen	Page Up	Page Up	Page Up
Views, Navigation	Toggle between current and previous views	Opt+Cmd+2	Opt+Cmd+2	

Continued on next page

TABLE E.2: MACINTOSH COMMAND EQUIVALENTS (continued)

InDesign Product Area	Command	InDesign Default	QuarkXPress 4	PageMaker 6.5
Window Menu	Align...	F8	Cmd+,	Shift+Cmd+E
Window Menu	Attributes...	[none defined]	[none defined]	
Window Menu	Cascade	[none defined]	[none defined]	
Window Menu	Color...	F6	[none defined]	Cmd+J
Window Menu	Gradient...	[none defined]	[none defined]	
Window Menu	Layers...	F7	[none defined]	Cmd+8
Window Menu	Libraries: New...	[none defined]	Opt+Cmd+N	
Window Menu	Libraries: Open...	Opt+Shift+Cmd+L	Opt+Shift+Cmd+L	
Window Menu	Navigator...	[none defined]	[none defined]	
Window Menu	New Window	[none defined]	[none defined]	
Window Menu	Pages...	F12	F10	Cmd+Opt+8
Window Menu	Stroke...	F10	Cmd+B	
Window Menu	Swatch Libraries: DICCOLOR	[none defined]	[none defined]	
Window Menu	Swatch Libraries: FOCOLTONE	[none defined]	[none defined]	
Window Menu	Swatch Libraries: Other Library...	[none defined]	[none defined]	
Window Menu	Swatch Libraries: PANTONE Coated	[none defined]	[none defined]	
Window Menu	Swatch Libraries: PANTONE Process	[none defined]	[none defined]	
Window Menu	Swatch Libraries: PANTONE Uncoated	[none defined]	[none defined]	
Window Menu	Swatch Libraries: System (Macintosh)	[none defined]	[none defined]	
Window Menu	Swatch Libraries: System (Windows)	[none defined]	[none defined]	
Window Menu	Swatch Libraries: TOYO COLOR FINDER	[none defined]	[none defined]	
Window Menu	Swatch Libraries: TRUMATCH	[none defined]	[none defined]	
Window Menu	Swatch Libraries: Web	[none defined]	[none defined]	
Window Menu	Swatches...	F5	F12	
Window Menu	Tile	[none defined]	[none defined]	
Window Menu	Tools...	[none defined]	F8	
Window Menu	Transform...	F9	F9	

Index

Note to the Reader: Page numbers in **bold** indicate the principal discussion of a topic or the definition of a term. Page numbers in *italic* indicate illustrations.

Numbers and Symbols

4-color process printing, 295, 587
4-page gatefold book inserts, 450–451
^ (caret) in searches, 124–125
$ (dollar sign) in searches, 124–125
… (ellipses) in menu commands, 39
? (question mark) in searches, 124–125

A

Absolute Colorimetric option in Image Import Options dialog box, 139
Acrobat, 585–586
Acrobat Reader
  downloading, 585
  installing, 654
active document window, 38
Actual Size command in View menu, 669, *669*
Add Anchor Point tool, 499
adding. *See also* entering; importing
  anchor points, 499–500, *500*
  in AppleScript scripts
    body text, 760–761, *761*
    icon elements, 759, *760*
    sub-headlines, 760
  ICC Device Profiles, 702–705, *703*
  import filters, 23, 115, 120
  objects to layers, 343–344
  objects to object libraries, **270–274**
    groups of objects, 271–272
    overview of, 270
    pages, 273–274
    ruler guides, 274
    shapes, frames, placeholders, or graphics, 271
    text frames, 272–273
  pages
    to documents, 447–448
    to island spreads, 448–449, *449*
  when threading text between frames, 368, 371–375, *372, 373, 374*
  section markers to documents, 468
  to spelling dictionaries, 130, *130*, 682
  to Swatches palette
    from commercial color systems, 306–307
    from other files, 308–309, *308*
    from swatches libraries, 305–306
  text frames and pages when threading text between frames, 368, 371–375, *372, 373, 374*
  values in palettes, 148, 202
  in Visual Basic scripts
    body text, 746, *746*
    icon elements, 744, *745*
Adding or Changing Notes and Form Fields option in Export PDF: Security dialog box, 604
add-ins. *See* plug-ins
additive color, **290–291**, *290*
Adobe Acrobat. *See also* PDF files
  Adobe Acrobat Reader
    downloading, 585
    installing, 654
  overview of, 585–586
Adobe Composer
  Composer options in New Paragraph Style dialog box, 244, *245*
  highlighting composition problems, 407, *407*
  hyphenation options and, **398–399**, *400*
  justification settings and, 398, 407
Adobe Gamma utility, **716, 717–722**. *See also* calibrating monitors
  Calibrate the Monitor's Gamma option, 720
  Calibrate the Monitor's White Point option, 702, 721–722, *721*
  control panel, 719–722, *719, 720*
  defined, **716, 717–718**
  opening, 717, *717, 718*
  preparing for monitor calibration, 716–717
  saving monitor profiles, 722, *722, 723*
  Select the Exact Phosphor Type option, 701, 720
  Set Optimum Brightness and Contrast Range option, 720
Adobe Illustrator
  AI files, **12**
  Application Color Settings dialog box and, 707
  compatibility with InDesign, 8–9, 699
  dragging-and-dropping graphics into InDesign, 9
  vector graphics and, 11
Adobe InDesign, **5–6, 647–662**
  versus Adobe Acrobat, 585–586
  Adobe InDesign icon commands
    on Macintosh computers, 677
    in Windows, 676–677
  compatibility with Illustrator and Photoshop, 8–9, 699
  defined, **5–6**
  features, **5–6**
  installing, **647–655**
    ATI graphics cards and, 649
    contents of installation package, 647–648
    identifying Macintosh system configuration, 652, *653*
    identifying Windows 98 system configuration, 650, *650*
    identifying Windows NT system configuration, 651, *651, 652*
    installing Acrobat Reader, 654
    installing InDesign, **652–654**
    installing PostScript Driver, 654–655
    Macintosh system requirements, 649
    ReadMe files, 649, 652

registering InDesign software, 655
Windows system requirements, 648, 649
Preferences dialog box, **655–662**, 679
  Adobe Online Preferences dialog box, 662, *662*, *663*
  Composition options, 658, *658*
  Dictionary options, 661, *661*
  General options, 656, *657*
  Grids options, 58, 659, *660*
  Guides options, 660, *660*
  navigating, 655–656
  opening, 655, 679
  restoring default settings, 656
  Text options, 657, *657*
  Units & Increments options, 658–659, *659*
  starting, **655**
  with Acrobat Reader, 586
  supported file formats, **11–13**
  terms defined, **7**, *8*
  using QuarkXPress keyboard shortcuts, 6, 49, 52
Adobe Online
  Adobe Online command in File menu, 680
  Adobe Online Preferences dialog box, 662, *662*, *663*
  Adobe Online tool, 671
Adobe PageMaker
  importing files, 23
  Tagged Text filter, 120
Adobe Photoshop
  Application Color Settings dialog box and, 707
  compatibility with InDesign, 8–9, 699
  dragging-and-dropping graphics into InDesign, 9
  Macintosh ColorSync plug-in, 704
  Photoshop graphics in exported PDF files, 588
  PSD files, **12**
Adobe QuarkXPress
  importing QuarkXPress files, 23
  keyboard shortcuts in InDesign, 6, 49, 52
Adobe Web site
  connecting to, *636*, 648, 662, *662*

downloading Acrobat Reader, 585
plug-ins updates, 67
Advanced Character Formats option in New Character Style dialog box, 239, *239*
After First option in Hyphenation dialog box, 403
AI files, **12**
alerts
  in AppleScript, 762
  in Visual Basic, 747
Align palette, **432–435**, **693–694**
  alignment options, 434
  defined, **693–694**
  Distribute Objects options, 434–435
  Distribute Spacing options, 432, 435
  opening, 432
  paragraph alignment and, 433
Align to Baseline Grid option, 58, 386
alignment. *See also* justification settings
  aligning objects, 432–435
  defined, **200**, **400**
  keyboard shortcuts for aligning paragraphs, 216
  Paragraph palette options, 200, 214–216
  in paragraph styles, 244–245, *245*
  tab alignment options, 219
all caps type style, 203, 206, *206*
All Documents option
  in Check Spelling dialog box, 129
  in Find/Change dialog box, 123
All Pages option in Export EPS dialog box, 34
All Printer's Marks option in Print dialog box, 558
All to Process option in Print dialog box, 551
Allow Graphics and Groups to Resize option in Layout Adjustment dialog box, 471
Allow Ruler Guides to Move option in Layout Adjustment dialog box, 471
A Lowly Apprentice Production (ALAP) plug-ins, 67–68

anchor points, **7**, **77–78**, **479–482**. *See also* paths
  adding, 499–500, *500*
  Bezier curves and, 481–486
  converting, 502–505, *503*, *504*, *505*
  corner points and, **480**, *480*
  defined, **7**, **479–480**, *480*
  deleting, 500–501, *501*, *502*
  Direct Selection tool and, 77–78
  direction lines, direction points and, 481–486, *482*, *486*
  and editing paths, 496
  endpoints and, **480**, *480*
  moving, 497–498, *498*, *499*
  selecting, 496–497, *496*, *497*
  smooth points and, **481**, *481*
animations in HTML files, 613
anti-aliased text in Web pages, 612, 618
.APLN files, 67
AppleScript, **729–730**, **747–762**. *See also* Visual Basic
  comments, 749, 751
  display dialog statements, 570
  downloading, 747
  InDesign scripts, **750–762**
    adding body text, 760–761, *761*
    adding icon elements, 759, *760*
    adding sub-headlines, 760
    composing text, 756–757, *758*
    composing title headlines, 758–759, *759*
    creating InDesign documents, 752
    enabling alerts, 762
    overview of, 750–751
    placing and fitting large images, 753–754, *754*
    placing and fitting small images, 754–756, *756*
    preparing InDesign to receive scripting commands, 751–752
    testing, 762
  overview of, 747–748
  scripts
    overview of, 729–730
    simple example, 748–750
  string variables, 749
  variables, 749

Application Color Settings dialog
  box, **706–714**
  Composite options, 709, *709*
  defined, **707**, *707*
  Download CRDs to Printer
    option, 710
  Engine options, 708
  Illustrator and, 707
  Monitor options, 708, *708*
  Options area, 709–710
  Photoshop and, 707
  selecting color settings, 706–707
  Separations option, 709
  Simulate Separation Printer on
    Composite Printer option, 710
  Simulate Separation Printer on
    Monitor option, 709
  System Profiles options,
    708–709, *708*, *709*
  Use Device Independent Color
    When Printing option, 710
Apply Gamma Correction option in
  Image Import Options dialog box,
  140
applying
  arrowheads and other line end
    shapes, 96–97
  color, **85–88**, **91**, **296–297**,
    318–326
    Apply Color, Apply Gradient,
      and Apply None Swatch
      tools, 675
    with Color palette, 87–88, *87*,
      297, 320
    color and tints to type, 324
    gradients with Gradient
      palette, 320–321
    gradients with Gradient tool,
      321–324, *321*, *322*, *323*, *324*
    gradients to type, 324–326
    grayscales or shades, 86
    to lines and shape outlines, 91,
      91
    overview of, **296**, **318**
    to shapes, 85, *85*
    from Swatches palette, 297,
      320
    from Toolbox, 318–319
  corner effects, 94, 685
  gradients
    with Gradient palette, 89–90,
      89, 320–321
    with Gradient tool, 321–324,
      321, *322*, *323*, *324*, 673–674
    from Toolbox, 318–319
    to type, 324–326
  master pages to spreads,
    457–459, *458*, *459*
  paragraph attributes, 214
  strokes to graphic frames, 152
  styles, **249–251**
    changing formatting after
      applying styles, 231
    character styles, 249
    paragraph formatting without
      character formatting, 251
    paragraph styles, 249–251
    removing or unapplying styles,
      255–256
  tints
    from Color palette, 86
    from Toolbox, 318–319
    to type, 324
  type styles, 205–206, *205*, *206*
arranging objects, 54, *55*, 684
arrow keys, positioning objects
  with, 420
arrowheads, 96–97
ascenders, **389**, *390*
Ascent setting for text baselines, 107
assigning
  automatically updated page
    numbers, 463–466, *463*, *465*
  keyboard shortcuts to styles, 236,
    236
  messages in Visual Basic, 734
  sections to documents, 466–468,
    467
ATI graphics cards, 649
Attributes palette, **693**
automatic hyphenation options,
  402–403, *402*
automatic leading, 208–209
Automatic Recovery feature, **170**,
  172–173
automatically creating clipping
  paths, 524–526, *525*, *526*
automatically creating text frames,
  76, 104
automatically threading text
  between text frames, 366–368
automatically updated page
  numbers, 463–466, *463*, *465*

B

background options
  in Export HTML: Formatting
    dialog box, 625–627, *626*
  in Image Import Options dialog
    box, 139
background printing on Macintosh
  computers, 531
Based On option in New Character
  Style dialog box, 233–236
baseline grids, **58–60**, **383–386**. *See
  also* grids
  Align to Baseline Grid option,
    58, 386
  defined, **58**, **383**
  locking text to, 58, 386
  setting options, 383–386, *383*,
    384, *385*, *386*
  setting up, 58–60, *59*
baselines. *See also* formatting
  ascenders, descenders and, 389,
    390
  defined, **200**, **389**, *390*
  First Baseline option in Text
    Frame Options dialog box, 107
  keyboard shortcuts, 203
  raising and lowering text on,
    389–391, *389*, *390*, *391*
Basic Character Formats options in
  New Character Style dialog box,
  238–239, *238*
Before last option in Hyphenation
  dialog box, 403
bevel join effect for corners, 93
Bezier curves theory, 481–486, *481*,
  486
Birmy Graphics Corporation, 541
bitmap graphics. *See also* graphics;
  vector graphics
  BMP files, **12**
  defined, **10–11**, *10*
  dragging-and-dropping
    Illustrator and Photoshop
    bitmaps into InDesign, 9, 588
  resizing, 11
  resolution and, 11
  size of, 11
  versus vector graphics, 11
Black swatch, 300
Bleed and Bleed Marks options in
  Print dialog box, 559
Bleed option in Export EPS dialog
  box, 34

blur, **268**
BMP files. *See* bitmap graphics
body text
 in AppleScript, 760–761, *761*
 in Visual Basic, 746, *746*
bold type style, **200**, **203**, **205–206**, *205*, *206*
books
 4-page gatefold book inserts, 450–451
 about HTML and other Web topics, 610
borders for graphic frames, **152–154**
 applying strokes to graphic frames, 152
 floating graphics in larger frames, 153–154
 keylines, **152**
 nesting objects, 153, 154–155, 436
bounding boxes
 Bounding Box option in Text Wrap palette, 156, *157*
 defined, **7**, *8*
 Selection tool and, 77–78
breaking up compound paths, 519
brightness settings in Adobe Gamma utility, 720
butt cap for lines, 94
buttons in Swatches palette, 299
By Section option in Export EPS dialog box, 34

C

calibrating monitors, **8**, **700**, **715–722**
 Adobe Gamma utility, **716**, **717–722**
  Calibrate the Monitor's Gamma option, 720
  Calibrate the Monitor's White Point option, 702, 721–722, *721*
  control panel, 719–722, *719*, *720*
  defined, **716**, **717–718**
  opening, 717, *717*, *718*
  preparing for monitor calibration, 716–717
  saving monitor profiles, 722, *722*, *723*
 Select the Exact Phosphor Type option, 701, 720
 Set Optimum Brightness and Contrast Range option, 720
 colorimeters and, 715, *715*
 defined, **700**
 gamma, 140, **701**, 720
 in Illustrator, Photoshop, and InDesign, 8
 phosphors, **701**, 720
 white points
  calibrating, 721–722, *721*
  defined, **702**
 workroom environments and, 715–716
 X-Rite Monitor Optimizer, 715, *715*, 724, 725
calibrating and profiling output devices, **723–725**
 creating or customizing printer profiles, 723–725, *724*
 preparing to calibrate, 723
 Web sites about profiling devices, 725
Cap Height setting for text baselines, 107
caret (^) in searches, 124–125
carriage returns, 118
Cascading Style Sheets (CSS-1) in HTML files, 609, 616
Case Sensitive option in Find/Change dialog box, 124
cataloguing objects in object libraries, 280–281, *280*, *281*
CCITT option in Export PDF: Compression dialog box, 598
changing. *See also* editing
 active document window, 38
 Change the Filename and Title option in Export HTML: Document dialog box, 621
 Changing the Document option in Export PDF: Security dialog box, 604
 curved segment shapes by dragging direction points, 510–511, *511*
 effect of stroking on frames, 92
 formatting after applying styles, 231
 initial document settings, 21
 line end caps, 94–95
 margin and column settings in master pages, 469, *470*
margin settings, 21
number of columns, 21
numerical values in palettes, 46–47, *47*
orientation of palettes, 44
page dimensions, 21
page layouts, 470–472, *472*
stacking order of layers, 354
thickness of lines or shape outlines, 90–91, *91*
views in windows, 53, *54*
character formatting, **200–213**. *See also* fonts; formatting; styles
 baselines
  defined, **200**
  First Baseline option in Text Frame Options dialog box, 107
  keyboard shortcuts, 203
 character attributes, **200**
 Character palette, **201–203**, **211–213**, **690**
  Character palette menu, 201, *201*
  defined, **201–203**, *201*, **690**
  identifying tracking and kerning settings, 211–212
  Language option, 396, 654
  manually setting kerning, 212–213
  manually setting tracking, 212
 No Break option, 403
 Old Style numerals option, 396
 scaling text, 424
 skewing text, 392, *392*, *393*
 small caps option, 394–395, *395*
 strikethrough option, 397–398, *397*
 subscript and superscript options, 393–394, *393*, *394*
 switching between metric and optical kerning, 211
 underline option, 397–398, *397*
drop or initial caps, **223–224**
in exported HTML files, 612, 616–617
finding and replacing, 126–128, *127*, *128*
glyph scaling
 defined, **398**
 Glyph Scaling option in Justification dialog box, 405

importing, 115
Insert/Replace Characters command in Type menu, 684
kerning, **200**, **210–213**
  defined, **200**, **210–211**, *211*
  identifying settings, 211–212
  keyboard shortcuts, 203, 213
  metrics kerning, **211**
  optical kerning, **211**
  setting manually, 212–213
keyboard shortcuts, 203
leading, **200**, **207–210**
  automatic leading, 208–209
  defined, **200**, **207–208**, *208*
  inline graphics and, 160
  keyboard shortcuts, 203
  setting manually, 208, 209–210
  for text baselines, 107
ligatures, **200**
scaling text, 382–383, *382*, 424
special characters, **108–111**
  defined, **108**
  entering with context menus, 110–111, *110*
  entering with Insert Character dialog box, 108–109, *109*
  entering with keyboard shortcuts, 109–110
  finding and replacing, 125–126
  flush spaces, 406–407
  metacharacters, 125–126
terms defined, **200**
tracking, **200**, **210–212**
  defined, **200**, **210**, *210*
  identifying settings, 211–212
  keyboard shortcuts, 203
  setting manually, 212
type styles, **200**, 203, **205–206**, **393–398**
  all caps type, 203, 206, *206*
  applying, **205–206**, *205*, *206*
  bold type, 200, 203, 205–206, *205*, *206*
  defined, **200**
  fonts and, 205
  italic type, 200, 203, 205–206, *205*, *206*
  keyboard shortcuts, 203
  Old Style numerals, 396
  Roman type style, 200
  small caps, 203, 206, *206*, 394–395, *395*
  strikethrough type, 203, 206, *206*, 397–398, *397*

subscript and superscript type, 203, 206, *206*, 393–394, *393*, *394*
underline type, 203, 206, *206*, 397–398, *397*
Character Set option in Text Import Options dialog box, 118
character styles, **230–241**, **249–257**. *See also* styles
  applying, 249
  assigning keyboard shortcuts to, 236, *236*
  Character Styles palette
    defined, **230**, *230*
    deleting styles, 256–257
    using, 231–232
  creating
    with no text selected, 233, 237–238, *237*
    from selected text or existing styles with changes, 233–236, *233*
    from selected text without changing formatting, 232–233
  defined, **230**, **232**
  deleting
    from documents, 256
    from styles palettes, 256–257
  duplicating, 253, *253*
  editing, **251–252**, *251*
  finding and replacing, 126–128, *127*, *128*
  importing
    from other applications, 115, 232, 254
    from other documents, 115, 232, 253–255, *254*
  New Character Style dialog box, **232–241**
    Advanced Character Formats option, 239, *239*
    assigning keyboard shortcuts to styles, 236, *236*
    Basic Character Formats options, 238–239, *238*
    color settings, 240–241, *240*, *241*
    parent versus child styles, 233–236
    removing or unapplying styles, 255–256
checking for duplicate spot colors, 572–573, *573*

checking spelling, **128–131**, **682**
  customizing dictionaries, 130–131, *130*, 661, *661*, 682
  language setting, 654
  spell checking, 128–130, *129*
child styles, 233–236
circular shapes and frames, 77–78
clearing island spreads, 446
clipping, **700**
clipping paths, **138**, **140**, **520–526**. *See also* paths
  Clipping Path dialog box options, 524–526, *525*, *526*, 685
  creating automatically, 524–526, *525*, *526*
  creating frames from, 138, 140, 520–521
  defined, **520**
  drawing manually, 521–524, *521*, *522*, *524*
  importing images with, 138, 140, 520–521
Close command in File menu, 677
closed paths. *See also* paths
  defined, **478**, *478*
  drawing, 489–490, *489*, *490*
  opening, 507, *508*
closing
  object libraries, 285
  open paths, 506, *507*
CMM (Color Matching Model), 654, **701**
CMYK color
  CMYK color gamut, 292–293, *292*
  CMYK color mode, 294–295
  CMYK color model, **291**, *291*, **293–294**, **587**
collapsing palettes, 44
collation options
  on Macintosh computers, 189
  in Windows, 181
color, **289–326**. *See also* gradients
  applying, **85–88**, **91**, **296–297**, **318–326**
    Apply Color, Apply Gradient, and Apply None Swatch tools, 675
    with Color palette, 87–88, *87*, 297, 320
    color and tints to type, 324
    gradients with Gradient palette, 89–90, *89*, 320–321

COLOR • COLOR

gradients with Gradient tool, 321–324, *321*, *322*, *323*, *324*
gradients to type, 324–326
grayscales or shades, 86
to lines and shape outlines, 91, *91*
overview of, **296**, **318**
to shapes, 85, *85*
from Swatches palette, 297, 320
from Toolbox, 318–319
character style color settings, 240–241, *240*, *241*
Color option
   in Export EPS dialog box, 31
   in Export PDF: PDF Options dialog box, 593
   in Layer Options dialog box, 341
color options for photographs, 139
Color options in Print dialog box, **544–555**
   All to Process option, 551
   color separations and, 544
   Composite options, 548, *548*, *549*
   creating film negatives or positives on Macintosh computers, 552–553, *553*, 555, *555*
   creating film negatives or positives in Windows 98, 552–554, *553*
   creating film negatives or positives in Windows NT, 552–553, *553*, 554–555, *554*
   emulsion settings, 552
   gradients and, 552
   In-RIP option, 549
   selecting composites versus color separations, 544–548, *545*, *546*, *547*
   Separations options, 550–551, *550*
Color palette
   applying colors, 87–88, *87*, 297, 320
   applying grayscales or shades, 86
   creating colors, 297, 309–311
   creating tint swatches, 312–313, *313*
   defined, **692–693**

filling shapes with solid color, 85, *85*
stroking lines and shape outlines, 91, *91*
swatches and, 87
color profile information in exported PDF files, 593
color separations, **544–556**
   versus composites, 544–548, *545*, *546*, *547*
   creating film negatives or positives on Macintosh computers, 552–553, *553*, 555, *555*
   creating film negatives or positives in Windows 98, 552–554, *553*
   creating film negatives or positives in Windows NT, 552–553, *553*, 554–555, *554*
   DCS (Desktop Color Separation) files, **12**, 540, 588
   emulsion settings, 552
   information about electronic prepress and printing, 556
   In-RIP option, 549
   OPI/DCS Image Replacement option in Print dialog box, 540
   overview of, 544
   of PDF files, 592
   printing gradients, 552
   selecting Color Separation options, 550–551, *550*
   Separations option in Application Color Settings dialog box, 709
   setting Composite options, 548, *548*, *549*
   Simulate Separation Printer on Composite Printer option in Application Color Settings dialog box, 710
   Simulate Separation Printer on Monitor option in Application Color Settings dialog box, 709
Color Settings command in File menu, 680
Color Settings options in Image Import Options dialog box, 138–139
color theory, **290–296**
   4-color process printing, 295

additive versus subtractive color, 290–291, *290*, *291*
CMYK color gamut, 292–293, *292*
CMYK color mode, 294–295
CMYK color model, 291, *291*, 293–294, 587
color gamuts, 292–293, *292*
color models, **293–294**
color modes, 294–295
color spaces, 292
L*a*b color model, 294
Lab color gamut, 292, *292*
LAB color mode, 295
process colors, 291, 295
RGB color gamut, 292–293, *292*
RGB color model, 290–291, *290*, 293, 294, 587, 626–627
spot color, 295–296
sRGB color mode, 612–613
Colors and Inks options in Preflight dialog box, 572–573, *573*
commercial color systems, 306–307
DIC Color system, 306–307
Document Color Settings dialog box, 565, *565*
filling shapes, **84–90**
   Fill Color palette, 85–86, *86*
   Fill/Stroke Color Indicator, 674–675
   with gradients, 88–90, *88*, *89*
   with grayscale or color shades, 86
   open shapes, 479, *479*
   overprinting fills, 563–565, *564*
   overview of, 84–85
   selecting colors, 87–88, *87*
   with solid colors, 85–86, *85*, *86*
   text, 84
Focoltone color system, 306–307
grid color options, 659
in HTML files
   color testing documents for print and Web distribution, 615
   converting from print to Web colors, 612–615, *614*, *615*, *616*
   Export HTML dialog box color picker, 624–625, *624*, *625*

Export HTML dialog box
 Override Color option,
  623–624
 sRGB color mode, 612–613
identifying layers with, 353, *353*
Image Color Settings command
 in Object menu, 686
Image Import Options dialog
 box
 Enable Color Management
  option, 138
 File Defined Background Color
  option, 139
 gamma correction options, 140
 Rendering Intent option,
  138–139, 701–702
 White Background option, 139
None or No color options versus
 white, 296, 675
PANTONE color systems,
 306–307
ruler color settings, 64–65, *65*
shape color settings, 84–85
spot color
 checking for duplicate spot
  colors, 572–573, *573*
 defined, **295–296**
Swatches palette, **85**, **86**, **87**,
 240, **297–309**
 adding colors from commercial
  color systems, 306–307
 adding colors from swatches
  libraries, 305–306
 applying color, 297, 320
 Black swatch, 300
 buttons, 299
 Color palette and swatches, 87
 color swatches, 298
 and creating character styles,
  240
 creating gradient swatches,
  298, 316–317, *316*, *317*
 creating swatches, 85, 297,
  300–303, *301*, *302*
 creating tint swatches,
  313–314, *313*
 defined, **297**, *297*
 deleting swatches, 304–305,
  305
 duplicating swatches, 303–304
 editing swatches, 303, *304*
 gradient swatches, 298
 icons, 298

 importing colors from other
  files, 308–309, *308*
 New Color Swatch dialog box,
  300–303, *301*, *302*
 "no color" swatch, 86, 296
 None swatch, 296, 298, 299,
  675
 opening, 297
 out-of-gamut alert icon, 302
 Paper swatch, 299
 Registration swatch, 300
 selecting colors, 297, 320
 selecting swatches, 303
 System color systems, 306–307
 tints, **86**, **312–315**, **318–324**
  applying from Color palette,
   86
  applying from Toolbox,
   318–319
  applying to type, 324
  creating tint swatches with
   Color palette, 312–313, *313*
  creating tint swatches with
   Swatches palette, 313–314,
   313
  defined, **312**
  tint fills for shapes, 86
  tinting objects without saving
   tint swatches, 314
 Toyo Color Finder 1050 color
  system, 306–307
 transparent objects and, 296
 trapping color, **561–565**
  defined, **561–563**, *561*, *562*
  and exporting PDF files, 587
  In-RIP Trapping option, 549,
   561
  overprinting strokes, fills, or
   text, 563–565, *564*
  ScenicSoft Preps software, 557,
   561
  ScenicSoft TrapWise software,
   561
  wet ink trapping, 561–563
 Trumatch color system, 306–307
 Web color system, 306–307
Color Bars option in Print dialog
 box, 558–559
color calibration, **8**, **700**, **715–725**
 Adobe Gamma utility, **716**,
  717–722
  Calibrate the Monitor's
   Gamma option, 720

  Calibrate the Monitor's White
   Point option, 702, 721–722,
   721
  control panel, 719–722, *719*,
   720
  defined, **716**, **717–718**
  opening, 717, *717*, *718*
  preparing for monitor
   calibration, 716–717
  saving monitor profiles, 722,
   722, *723*
  Select the Exact Phosphor Type
   option, 701, 720
  Set Optimum Brightness and
   Contrast Range option, 720
 calibrating and profiling output
  devices, **723–725**
  creating or customizing printer
   profiles, 723–725, *724*
  preparing to calibrate, 723
  Web sites about profiling
   devices, 725
 colorimeters and, 715, *715*
 defined, **700**
 gamma, 140, **701**, 720
 in Illustrator, Photoshop, and
  InDesign, 8
 phosphors, **701**, 720
 white points
  calibrating, 721–722, *721*
  defined, **702**
 workroom environments and,
  715–716
 X-Rite Monitor Optimizer, 715,
  715, 724, 725
color management, **699–725**
 Application Color Settings dialog
  box, **706–714**
  Composite options, 709, *709*
  defined, **707**, *707*
  Download CRDs to Printer
   option, 710
  Engine options, 708
  Illustrator and, 707
  Monitor options, 708, *708*
  Options area, 709–710
  Photoshop and, 707
  selecting color settings,
   706–707
  Separations option, 709
  Simulate Separation Printer on
   Composite Printer option,
   710

Simulate Separation Printer on Monitor option, 709
System Profiles options, 708–709, *708*, *709*
Use Device Independent Color When Printing option, 710
clipping, **700**
CMM (Color Matching Model), 654, **701**
color characterization, **700**
CRDs (Color Rendering Dictionaries), **701**, 710
Document Color Settings dialog box, **565**, **706–707**, **710–714**
   defined, **710–711**, *711*
   overriding embedded profiles, 712
   Preflight dialog box and, 565, *565*
   Rendering Intent options, 701–702, 714, *714*
   selecting color settings, 706–707
   selecting source profiles, 565, *565*, 711–713, *713*
ICC Device Profiles
   adding, 702–705, *703*
   in Application Color Settings dialog box, 708–709, *708*, *709*
   creating or customizing printer profiles, 723–725, *724*
   defined, **701**
   Include ICC Profiles option in Export PDF: PDF Options dialog box, 593
   overriding embedded profiles, 712
   saving monitor profiles, 722, *722*, 723
   selecting source profiles, 565, *565*, 711–713, *713*
   Macintosh ColorSync control panel, 702–705, *703*, 708
   overview of, 699–702
   rendering intents, **701–702**, 714, *714*
   terms defined, **700–702**
   workflows, 705–706
colorimeters, 715, *715*, 724–725
columns of text, **18**, **21**, **60–61**, **104–106**, **158**, **377–382**
   changing number of, 21
   column guides, 18, *19*, 60–61, *61*
   column settings for new documents, 21, 60
   Jump to Next Column option in Text Wrap palette, 158, *158*
   Margins and Columns command in Layout menu, 682
   Margins and Columns dialog box, 60
   in master pages
      changing column settings, 469, *470*
      creating uneven columns, 470, *471*
   versus page columns, 105, *105*
   setting, 377–382, *378*, *381*
   Text Frame Options dialog box
      Columns options, 104–105, *105*
      Fixed Column Width option, 105–106, *106*
commands. *See also* menus
   ellipses (…) in, 39
   in menus, **39**
   that open dialog boxes, 39
comments
   in AppleScript, 749, 751
   OPI (Open Prepress Interface) comments, 25
   in Visual Basic, 733
commercial color systems, **306–307**
compatibility
   of InDesign with Illustrator and Photoshop, 8–9, 699
   of Windows and Macintosh InDesign files, 8
Composer. *See also* hyphenation options
   Composer options in New Paragraph Style dialog box, 244, *245*
   highlighting composition problems, 407, *407*
   hyphenation options and, **398–399**, *400*
   justification settings and, 398, 407
composites
   versus color separations, 544–548, *545*, *546*, *547*
   Composite options in Application Color Settings dialog box, 709, *709*
   Composite options in Print dialog box, 548, *548*, *549*
Composition options in Preferences dialog box, 658, *658*
compound paths, **515–519**. *See also* paths
   Compound Paths command in Object menu, 686
   creating, **516–517**, *517*
   defined, **515–516**, *516*
   editing, 517, *517*
   releasing or breaking up, 519
   reversing, 517–518, *518*, 686
   subpaths and, **516**
compression settings for exported PDF files, **595–600**, *599*
Condensed/Expanded Spacing To option in Microsoft Word Import Options dialog box, 116–117, *116*
connecting
   to Adobe Web site, *636*, 648, 662, *662*
   multiple paths, 508–510, *509*, *510*
Content command in Object menu, 685
context menus, **53–56**, **688**. *See also* menus
   arranging objects, 54, *55*
   changing views, 53, *54*
   defined, **688**
   displaying, 56
   editing graphics, 55, *56*
   editing text, 56, *57*
   entering special characters, 110–111, *110*
continuing open paths, 506
contrast settings in Adobe Gamma utility, 720
Convert Direction Point tool, 502–505, *503*, *504*, *505*
Convert options in Word, WordPerfect, or RTF Import Options dialog box, 116–117, *116*
converting. *See also* exporting; importing
   anchor points, 502–505, *503*, *504*, *505*
   corner points
      to corner points with independent direction lines, 503, *503*, *504*
      to smooth points, 503, *503*, *504*
   HTML files from print to Web colors, 612–615, *614*, *615*, *616*

smooth points
  to corner points with independent direction lines, 504–505, *505*
  to corner points without direction lines, 504, *505*
text files to GIF files in HTML documents, 618
text frames to graphic frames, 76
text outlines to frames, 82–83
text to paths, 519–520, *519*
Copy option in Open a File dialog box, 23
copying. *See also* dragging-and-dropping; moving
  duplicating, **420–423, 431–432**
    creating pages of duplicate objects, 422–423, *422*, *423*
    with Edit menu Duplicate command, 420, *420*, 681
    master pages, 456, *456*
    objects and transforming, 430–432, *431*, *432*, *433*
    spreads, 451–452, *452*
    with Step and Repeat dialog box, 421–423, *422*, *423*, 681
    styles, 253, *253*
    swatches, 303–304
  fonts into package files for service bureaus, 576
  linked graphics into package files for service bureaus, 576
  master pages between documents, 460–461
  objects
    between layers, 344–347, *345*, *346*
    between object libraries, 276–278, *277*, *278*, *279*
    to other layers or pages, 419
    and preserving layers, 349–352, *350*, *351*, *352*
  Save a Copy command, 28, 171–172, *171*, 678
copying and pasting
  Copy command in Edit menu, 681
  graphics, 141
  graphics or text as inline graphics, 159
  objects or text onto layers, 344
  Paste and Paste Into commands in Edit menu, 681
  text, 102, 111

Copying Text and Graphics option in Export PDF: Security dialog box, 604
Corel WordPerfect Import Options dialog boxes, 115, 116–117, *116*
corner effects, 94, 685
corner points. *See also* paths
  Bezier curves and, 484–485, *484*, *485*
  converting smooth points to corner points with independent direction lines, 504–505, *505*
  converting smooth points to corner points without direction lines, 504, *505*
  converting to corner points with independent direction lines, 503, *503*, *504*
  converting to smooth points, 503, *503*, *504*
  defined, **480**, *480*
  drawing curved segments connected by, 494–496
correcting missing fonts problems, 570
crashes, 173
CRDs (Color Rendering Dictionaries), **701**, 710
Create Frame from Clipping Path option in Image Import Options dialog box, 138, 140, 520–521
Create Guides dialog box, 57, 62–63, *63*, 683
Create Outlines command in Type menu, 684
creating. *See also* drawing
  4-page gatefold book inserts, 450–451
  clipping paths
    automatically, 524–526, *525*, *526*
    manually, 521–524, *521*, *522*, *524*
  colors in Color palette, 297, 309–311
  compound paths, 516–517, *517*
  files, **18–21**
    changing initial document settings, 21
    column settings, 21
    Facing Pages option, 19, 441, *442*, 447
    Margin settings, 21

Master Text Frames option, 19–20, 102
Orientation settings, 21
overview of, 18, *19*
Page Size settings, 20–21, *20*
selecting number of pages in document, 18
film negatives or positives
  on Macintosh computers, 552–553, *553*, 555, *555*
  in Windows 98, 552–554, *553*
  in Windows NT, 552–553, *553*, 554–555, *554*
frames from clipping paths, 138, 140, 520–521
gradient swatches
  with Gradient palette, 298, 317–318
  with Swatches palette, 298, 316–317, *316*, *317*
groups from objects on different layers, 436–437
island spreads, 445–446
layers, 339–340
master pages, 455–456, *456*, *457*
object libraries, 266–267, *266*
Object Library palettes, 263, *264*
packaging files for service bureaus
  creating instructions, 575, *576*
  creating packages, 576–578, *577*, *578*
  defined, **575**
  Preflight dialog box and, 575
pages of duplicate objects, 422–423, *422*, *423*
palette groups, 45–46, *45*
printer profiles, 723–725, *724*
shortcut sets, 52–53
styles, **232–248**
  in Character Styles palette, 237–241, *237*
  with no text selected, 233
  in Paragraph Styles palette, 241–248, *242*
  from selected text or existing styles with changes, 233–236, *233*
  from selected text without changing formatting, 232–233
swatches, 85, 297, 300–303, *301*, *302*

text frames
    automatically, 76, 104
    cutting, copying, and pasting
        text and, 111
    drawing with Type tool, 103
    with New Document dialog
        box, 19–20, 102, 104
    placing text and, 76, 104
    tint swatches
        with Color palette, 312–313,
            313
        with Swatches palette,
            313–314, *313*
    uneven columns in master
        pages, 470, *471*
Creation Date option in Subset
    dialog box, 283
cropping
    Crop Image Data to Frames
        option in Export PDF: PDF
        Options dialog box, 594
    Crop Marks option in Print
        dialog box, 535, 558
    Crop To option menu in Place
        PDF dialog box, 144
    graphics, 151
cross mouse pointer, 78
CSS-1 (Cascading Style Sheets) in
    HTML files, 609, 616
cursor keys
    cursor movement shortcuts,
        121–122
    positioning objects with, 420
curves. *See* lines; paths; shapes
customizing. *See also* Preferences
    dialog box
        printer profiles, 723–725, *724*
        spelling dictionaries, 130–131,
            130, 661, *661*, 682
cutting and pasting. *See also* moving
    Cut command in Edit menu, 681
    graphics or text as inline
        graphics, 159
    objects or text onto layers, 344
    Paste and Paste Into commands
        in Edit menu, 681
    text, 102, 111

D

dashed lines and shape outlines,
    95–96

DCS (Desktop Color Separation)
    files
        defined, **12**
        in exported PDF files, 588
        OPI/DCS Image Replacement
            option in Print dialog box, 540
declaring variables in Visual Basic,
    734
default settings in Preferences
    dialog box, 656
Delete Anchor Point tool, 500–501,
    501
deleting
    anchor points, 500–501, *501*,
        502
    clearing island spreads, 446
    guides, 62–63
    inline graphics, 162
    layers, 354–355
    master pages, 460
    object libraries, 285
    objects from object libraries, 266,
        274
    pages, 453
    shortcut sets, 53
    spreads, 453
    styles
        from documents, 256
        removing or unapplying styles,
            255–256
        from styles palettes, 256–257
    swatches, 304–305, *305*
    tab stops, 21
    text with Find/Change dialog
        box, 123
    threaded text frames, 375, *376*,
        377
    words from spelling dictionaries,
        130–131, *131*, 682
descenders, **389**, *390*
Description option in Subset dialog
    box, 284
Deselect All command in Edit
    menu, 681
design in HTML files, 607–608
desktop. *See* menus; palettes;
    Toolbox; work areas
Desktop Color Separation (DCS)
    files
        defined, **12**
        in exported PDF files, 588
        OPI/DCS Image Replacement
            option in Print dialog box, 540

desktop inkjet printers, proofing,
    541
desktop publishing workflow, 9
determining. *See* identifying
device profiles. *See* profiles
dialog boxes. *See also* palettes
    display dialog statements in
        AppleScript, 570
    entering or changing numerical
        values, 46–47, *47*
    Escape key, 172
    Reset buttons, 172
DIC Color system, **306–307**
dictionaries
    CRDs (Color Rendering
        Dictionaries), **701**, 710
    for spelling and hyphenation,
        130–131, *130*, 654, 661, *661*,
        682
digital masters, 586
Dimensions Include Stroke Weight
    option in Transform palette, 415,
    416–417
Direct Selection tool
    anchor points and, 77–78
    defined, **671–672**
    dragging-and-dropping graphics,
        142
    and drawing circular and
        elliptical shapes and frames,
        77–78
    and drawing polygonal shapes
        and frames, 81–82
    and drawing square and
        rectangular shapes and frames,
        79
    and drawing straight lines, 83
    and editing graphics, 55
    graphic frames and, 147
    moving anchor points, 497–498,
        498, 499
    selecting paths and anchor
        points, 496–497, *496*, *497*
    stroking and, 91
    Transform palette and, 412
direction lines
    Bezier curves and, 481–486, *482*,
        486
    converting
        corner points to corner points
            with independent direction
            lines, 503, *503*, *504*

smooth points to corner points with independent direction lines, 504–505, *505*
smooth points to corner points without direction lines, 504, *505*
defined, **481–482**, *482*
direction points
  Bezier curves and, 481–486, *482*, *486*
  changing curved segment shapes by dragging, 510–511, *511*
  Convert Direction Point tool, 502–505, *503*, *504*, *505*
  defined, **481–482**, *482*
disabling automatic hyphenation, 401–402
disaster recovery, **169–173**
  Automatic Recovery feature, 170, 172–173
  Escape key in palettes and dialog boxes, 172
  Reset buttons in palettes and dialog boxes, 172
  Revert command, 172
  Save a Copy command, 28, 171–172, *171*, 678
  Undo command, 169–170
discretionary hyphens, 401, 403
display dialog statements in AppleScript, 570
displaying. *See also* hiding
  context menus, 56
  grids, 60
  guides, 63–64, *64*
  hidden characters, 684
  hidden Toolbox tools, 42
  layers, 338–339, *338*
  messages in Visual Basic, 734
  object libraries, 266, 268–269, *269*
  Object Library palette, 268–270
  palettes, 43
  strokes on screen, 91
  Toolbox, 41
distorting objects, **428–429**, *429*
Distribute Objects options in Align palette, 434–435
Distribute Spacing options in Align palette, 432, 435
distributing objects, **432**, **434–435**
dividing values in palettes, 148, 202
Do Not Allow options in Export PDF: Security dialog box, 603

Document Color Settings dialog box, **565**, **706–707**, **710–714**
  defined, **710–711**, *711*
  overriding embedded profiles, 712
  Preflight dialog box and, 565, *565*
  Rendering Intent options, 701–702, 714, *714*
  selecting color settings, 706–707
  selecting source profiles, 565, *565*, 711–713, *713*
document grids. *See also* grids
  defined, **58**, *59*
  setting up, 58–60, *59*
  Snap to Document Grid option, 58, 60
Document option
  in Check Spelling dialog box, 129
  in Find/Change dialog box, 123
Document Setup command in File menu, 21, 679
document windows
  active document window, 38
  Actual Size command, 669, *669*
  defined, **38**
  Entire Pasteboard command, 669–671, *670*
  Fit Page in Window command, 668, *668*
  Fit Spread in Window command, 668, *669*
documents. *See also* files; pages; Pages palette; printing
  assigning sections to, 466–468, *467*
  copying master pages between, 460–461
  creating, **18–21**
    changing initial document settings, 21
    column settings, 21
    Facing Pages option, 19, 441, *442*, 447
    Margin settings, 21
    Master Text Frames option, 19–20, 102
    Number of Pages option, 18
    Orientation settings, 21
    overview of, 18, *19*
    Page Size settings, 20–21, *20*
  deleting styles from, 256
  flattening, 357

importing styles from other documents, 232, 253–255, *254*
New Document dialog box, **18–21**
  Columns options, 21, 60
  creating text frames, 19–20, 102, 104
  Facing Pages option, 19, 441, *442*, 447
  Margins options, 21, 60
  Master Text Frames option, 19–10, 102
  Number of Pages option, 18
  Orientation options, 21
  overview of, 18, *18*, *19*
  Page Size options, 20–21, *20*
scaling
  to fit paper size, 532–533
  for printing on Macintosh computers, 188
dollar sign ($) in searches, 124–125
dotted lines and shape outlines, 95–96
double-truck printing (two-page spreads)
  on Macintosh computers, 188
  in Windows, 183, *184*
downloading
  Acrobat Reader, 585
  AppleScript software, 747
  CRDs (Color Rendering Dictionaries) to printers, 710
  download times for Web page backgrounds, 626
  fonts to printers, 541–542
Downsample To option in Export PDF: Compression dialog box, 596
dragging-and-dropping. *See also* moving; positioning
  graphics, 141–142
  Illustrator and Photoshop graphics into InDesign, 9, 588
  objects to Object Library palette, 270
  and positioning objects, 419
  and scaling objects, 424–425, *425*
  text files from other applications, 111–112
drawing, **77–85**. *See also* creating; frames; shapes
  arrowheads and other line end shapes, 96–97

circular and elliptical shapes and frames, 77–78, 672–673
clipping paths manually, 521–524, *521*, *522*, *524*
color settings for, 84–85
dashed or dotted lines and shape outlines, 95–96
objects on layers, 344
paths, **486–496**
   closed shapes, 489–490, *489*, *490*
   curved segments, 488–490, *489*, *490*
   curved segments connected by corner points, 494–496
   curved segments followed by straight segments, 492–494
   overview of, 486–487
   straight segments, 487–488
   straight segments followed by curved segments, 490–492
placeholders, 84
polygon shapes and frames, 79–82, 672–673
square and rectangular shapes and frames, 78–79, 672–673
Star Inset and Number of Sides options for polygon shapes and frames, 80–81
straight lines, 83
drop caps
   creating in Paragraph palette, **223–224**
   paragraph styles for, 244, *245*
duplicating. *See also* copying
   Duplicate command in Edit menu, 420, *420*, 681
   master pages, 456, *456*
   objects, **420–423**, **431–432**
      creating pages of duplicates, 422–423, *422*, *423*
      with Edit menu Duplicate command, 420, *420*, 681
      with Step and Repeat dialog box, 421–423, *422*, *423*, 681
      and transforming, 430–432, *431*, *432*, *433*
   spreads, 451–452, *452*
   styles, 253, *253*
   swatches, 303–304
Dynamic HTML, 609

E

Edit menu, **680–682**. *See also* menus
   Check Spelling command, 682
   Copy command, 681
   Cut command, 681
   Deselect All command, 681
   Duplicate command, 420, *420*, 681
   Edit Dictionary command, 682
   Find Next command, 124
   Find/Change command, 122–128, 682
   Macintosh keyboard shortcuts, 778
   Paste command, 681
   Paste Into command, 681
   Redo command, 169–170, 681
   Select All command, 681
   Step and Repeat command, 421–423, *422*, *423*, 681
   Undo command, 169–170, 681
   Windows keyboard shortcuts, 766
Edit Shortcuts command in File menu, 49, 411, 680
editing. *See also* changing
   commercial color system colors, 307
   compound paths, 517, *517*
   exported EPS files, 29
   graphics from context menus, 55, *56*
   imported PDF files, 25
   keyboard shortcuts, 49, *49*, 52, 411, 680
   linked PDF files, 145
   paths, **496–515**
      anchor points and, 496
      changing curved segment shapes by dragging direction points, 510–511, *511*
      closing open paths, 506, *507*
      connecting multiple paths, 508–510, *509*, *510*
      continuing open paths, 506
      opening closed paths, 507, *508*
      selecting paths, 496–497, *496*, *497*
      splitting graphics frames and contents, 515
      splitting paths and frames with Scissors tool, 512–515, *513*, *514*
   shortcut sets, 49, *49*
   spelling dictionaries, 130–131, *131*, 682
   styles, 251–252, *251*
   swatches, 303, *304*
   tab stops, 220–221
   text
      from context menus, 56, *57*
      from Edit menu, 120–121
      with keyboard shortcuts, 121–122
   text shapes, 519–520, *519*
ellipses (…) in menu commands, 39
elliptical shapes and frames, 77–78, 672–673
Em Software plug-ins, 68
Embed Fonts option in Export EPS dialog box, 31
embedding graphics files, **163**, **165**
emulsion settings, 552
enabling
   alerts
      in AppleScript, 762
      in Visual Basic, 747
   automatic hyphenation, 401–402
   Enable Color Management option in Image Import Options dialog box, 138
   Enable Layout Adjustment option in Layout Adjustment dialog box, 471
Encapsulated PostScript files. *See* EPS files
Encoding option in Export EPS dialog box, 31
end caps and shapes for lines, 94–97
end shapes for arrows, 97
end tags in HTML files, 608–609
endpoints in paths, **480**, *480*
Enfocus Software plug-ins, 68
Engine options in Application Color Settings dialog box, 708
entering. *See also* adding
   non-breaking hyphens, 404
   non-breaking spaces, 405
   numerical values in palettes, 46–47, *47*
   special characters, **108–111**
      with context menus, 110–111, *110*

defined, **108**
flush spaces, 406–407
with Insert Character dialog box, 108–109, *109*
with keyboard shortcuts, 109–110
text, 108
values in Paragraph palette, 214
Entire Pasteboard command in View menu, 669–671, *670*
environments for color calibration, 715–716
EPS (Encapsulated PostScript) files
defined, **12**
editing exported EPS files, 29
in exported PDF files, 588
exporting, 26, 29–34, *29*, *30*, *31*
Export EPS dialog box options, 31–34, *33*
to Prepress files, 26, 28, 578–581, *579*, *580*, *581*
importing, 140
Escape key in palettes and dialog boxes, 172
Excel Import Options dialog box, 119, *119*, *120*
Exit command in File menu (Windows), 680
exporting, **28–33**. *See also* importing
EPS files, 26, 29–34, *29*, *30*, *31*
Export EPS dialog box options, 31–34, *33*
to Prepress files, 26, 28, 578–581, *579*, *580*, *581*
Export command in File menu, 679
Export HTML: Document dialog box, **620–622**
Change the Filename and Title option, 621
overview of, 620–623, *620*, *623*
Remove a Page option, 620
View HTML Using option, 621–622, *621*
Export HTML: Formatting dialog box, **623–627**
background options, 625–627, *626*
color picker dialog box, 624–625, *624*, *625*
defined, **623**, *623*
Override Color option, 623–624

Text options, 623–624
Export HTML: Graphics dialog box, **628–631**
converting graphics to GIF or JPEG formats, 628–630, *629*
exporting cropped graphics, 628
GIF file options, 630–631
JPEG file options, 631
Export HTML: Layout dialog box, **627–628**, *628*
Export PDF: Compression dialog box, **595–600**
CCITT option, 598
Compress Text and Line Art option, 598
Downsample To option, 596
JPEG option, 598
No Sample Change option, 597
overview of, 595, *595*
recommended compression settings, 598–600, *599*
resampling options, 596–597
Run Length compression option, 598
setting image compression, 597–598
Subsample To option, 596–597
Zip compression option, 598
Export PDF: Pages and Page Marks dialog box, **600–602**, *601*
Export PDF: PDF Options dialog box, **592–595**
Color option, 593
Crop Image Data to Frames option, 594
Generate Thumbnails option, 594
Images option, 594
Include ICC Profiles option, 593
Omit option, 594
Optimize PDF option, 594–595
overview of, *591*, 592
Subset Fonts Below option, 592
View PDF After Exporting option, 595
Export PDF: Security dialog box, **602–604**
Adding or Changing Notes and Form Fields option, 604

Changing the Document option, 604
Copying Text and Graphics option, 604
Do Not Allow options, 603
overview of, 602, *602*
password options, 603
Printing option, 603
HTML files, 26, 28
overview of, 26, 28, 618–619, *618*, *619*, 631
as Prepress files, 26, 28, 578–581, *579*, *580*, *581*
sample HTML code generated for exported documents, 638–643
selecting export options, 619–621, *619*, *620*, *621*
overview of, 28
PDF files, 26, 29
overview of, 26, 29, 585–586, **589–592**, *590*, *591*, *592*
as Prepress files, 26, 28, 578–581, *579*, *580*, *581*
to Prepress files, 26, 28, 578–581, *579*, *580*, *581*
Extensis plug-ins, 68
Extra Carriage Returns option in Text Import Options dialog box, 118
Extra Spaces option in Text Import Options dialog box, 118

F

Facing Pages option in New Document dialog box, 19, 441, *442*, 447
File Defined Background Color option in Image Import Options dialog box, 139
File menu, **677–680**. *See also* menus
Adobe Online command, 680
Close command, 677
Color Settings command, 680
defined, **677**, *678*
Document Setup command, 21, 679
Edit Shortcuts command, 49, 411, 680
Exit command (Windows), 680
Export command, 679
Links command, 679

Macintosh keyboard shortcuts, 778–779
New command, 18, 677
Open command, 677
Package command, 679
Page Setup command (Macintosh), 679
Place command, 112–114, *113*, 136–140, *137*, 678
Preferences command, 655, 679
Preflight command, 178, 679
Print command, 679
Quit command (Macintosh), 680
Revert command, 172, 678
Save As command, 25–28, *26*, *27*, 678
Save command, 25, 677
Save a Copy command, 28, 171–172, *171*, 678
Windows keyboard shortcuts, 766–768
filename extensions
.APLN, 67
.FLT, 67
.PLN, 67
of plug-ins, 67
.RPLN, 67
files, **11–13**, **18–34**. *See also* documents; exporting; HTML files; importing; PDF files; printing
AI files, **12**
BMP files, **12**
DCS (Desktop Color Separation) files
defined, **12**
in exported PDF files, 588
OPI/DCS Image Replacement option in Print dialog box, 540
EPS (Encapsulated PostScript) files
defined, **12**
editing exported EPS files, 29
Export EPS dialog box options, 31–34, *33*
in exported PDF files, 588
exporting, 26, 29–34, *29*, *30*, *31*
exporting as Prepress files, 26, 28, 578–581, *579*, *580*, *581*
importing, 140
GIF files, **12**
InDr, InDa, and InD3 files, 67

JPEG files
defined, **12**
JPEG option in Export PDF: Compression dialog box, 598
Open a File dialog box, 254, *254*
opening, **21–23**, *22*
password-protected files, 24
supported file formats, **11–13**
packaging for service bureaus, **575–578**, 679
creating instructions, 575, *576*
creating packages, 576–578, *577*, *578*
defined, **575**
Package command in File menu, 679
Preflight dialog box and, 575
PageMaker files, 23
PCX files, **13**
PICT files, **12**
PNG (Portable Network Graphics) files
defined, **13**
importing, 139–140
PostScript files
PostScript Driver installation, 654–655
PostScript option in Export EPS dialog box, 31
printing to on Macintosh computers, 191–193, *193*
printing to non-PostScript printers, 177, 184
printing to in Windows, 191–192
Prepress files, 26, 28, 578–581, *579*, *580*, *581*
PSD files, **12**
QuarkXPress files, 23
ReadMe files, 649, 652
saving, **25–28**
all open files, 25
Prepress files, 26, 28, 578–581, *579*, *580*, *581*
with Save As dialog box, 25–28, *26*, *27*, 678
with Save command, 25, 677
with Save a Copy command, 28, 171–172, *171*, 678
as template or stationery files, 25–26
SCT (Scitex CT) files, **13**

stationery files
defined, **25**
saving files as, 25–26
template files
defined, **25**
saving files as, 25–26
TIFF files, **13**, 588
WMF (Windows Metafiles) files, **13**
filling shapes, **84–90**. *See also* color
Fill Color palette, 85–86, *86*
Fill/Stroke Color Indicator, 674–675
with gradients, 88–90, *88*, *89*
with grayscale or color shades, 86
open shapes, 479, *479*
overprinting fills, 563–565, *564*
overview of, 84–85
selecting colors, 87–88, *87*
with solid colors, 85–86, *85*, *86*
text, 84
film negatives or positives
creating on Macintosh computers, 552–553, *553*, 555, *555*
creating in Windows 98, 552–554, *553*
creating in Windows NT, 552–553, *553*, 554–555, *554*
filters, import filters, 23, 115, 120
Find Next command in Edit menu, 124
Find/Change dialog box, **122–128**, **682**
Case Sensitive option, 124
deleting text, 123
finding and replacing formatting or styles, 126–128, *127*, *128*
finding and replacing special characters, 125–126
finding and replacing text, 123–124
finding text, 123–124
opening, 122–123, *123*, 682
using wildcards, 124–125
Whole Word option, 124
finding
objects in object libraries, 266, 281–285, *282*, *283*
text, 123–124
finding and replacing
fonts, 570

formatting or styles, 126–128,
    127, *128*
special characters, 125–126
text, 123–124
First Baseline option in Text Frame
    Options dialog box, 107
first line indents, 218
First Page command in Layout
    menu, 683
fitting
    contents and frames
        simultaneously, 151
    Fit Content Proportionally
        option, 149–150
    Fit Contents to Frame option,
        150
    Fit Frame to Content option, 149
    Fit Page in Window command in
        View menu, 668, *668*
    Fit Spread in Window command
        in View menu, 668, *669*
    Fitting command in Object
        menu, 685
Fixed Column Width option in Text
    Frame Options dialog box,
    105–106, *106*
flattening documents and layers,
    357
Flip options in Transform palette,
    415
floating graphics in larger frames,
    153–154
.FLT files, 67
flush spaces, **406–407**
Focoltone color system, **306–307**
focus for palette options, 47–48
fonts. *See also* character formatting;
    text
    converting text outlines to
        frames, 82–83
    copying into package files for
        service bureaus, 576
    defined, **204**
    downloading to printers,
        541–542
    Embed Fonts option in Export
        EPS dialog box, 31
    finding and replacing, 570
    Font command in Type menu,
        684
    Font Downloading options in
        Print dialog box, 541–542
    in HTML files, 611–612
    keyboard shortcuts for, 52

missing fonts problems, 570
Open Type fonts, 396
in Preflight dialog box
    correcting missing fonts
        problems, 570
    Fonts options, 568–570, *569*
printer-resident fonts, 541
scaling text, 382–383, *382*, 424
selecting, 204, *204*
selecting font size, 203, 207, 684
Size command in Type menu,
    684
Subset Fonts Below option in
    Export PDF: PDF Options
    dialog box, 592
type
    defined, **102**
    type families, **200**
type styles, **200**, **203**, **205–206**,
    393–398
    all caps type, 203, 206, *206*
    applying, **205–206**, *205*, *206*
    bold type, 200, 203, 205–206,
        205, *206*
    defined, **200**
    fonts and, 205
    italic type, 200, 203, 205–206,
        205, *206*
    keyboard shortcuts, 203
    Old Style numerals, 396
    Roman type style, 200
    small caps, 203, 206, *206*,
        394–395, *395*
    strikethrough type, 203, 206,
        206, 397–398, *397*
    subscript and superscript type,
        203, 206, *206*, 393–394, *393*,
        394
    underline type, 203, 206, *206*,
        397–398, *397*
Type tool
    defined, **672**
    drawing text frames, 103
    editing text, 56, 120
    and filling and stroking type,
        84
    Vertical Type tool, 108
foreign language hyphenation
    options, 396, 654
formatting, **115**, **126–128**,
    199–126. *See also* fonts; styles
    attributes retained and lost in
        exported HTML files, 612,
        616–617

baselines
    ascenders, descenders and,
        389, *390*
    defined, **200**, **389**, *390*
    First Baseline option in Text
        Frame Options dialog box,
        107
    keyboard shortcuts, 203
    raising and lowering text on,
        389–391, *389*, *390*, *391*
changing after applying styles,
    231
character attributes, **200**
Character palette, **201–203**,
    211–213, **690**
    Character palette menu, 201,
        201
    defined, **201–203**, *201*, **690**
    identifying tracking and
        kerning settings, 211–212
    Language option, 396, 654
    manually setting kerning,
        212–213
    manually setting tracking, 212
    No Break option, 403
    Old Style numerals option, 396
    scaling text, 424
    skewing text, 392, *392*, *393*
    small caps option, 394–395,
        395
    strikethrough option, 397–398,
        397
    subscript and superscript
        options, 393–394, *393*, *394*
    switching between metric and
        optical kerning, 211
    underline option, 397–398,
        397
drop caps
    creating in Paragraph palette,
        223–224
    paragraph styles for, 244, *245*
Export HTML: Formatting dialog
    box, **623–627**
    background options, 625–627,
        626
    color picker dialog box,
        624–625, *624*, *625*
    defined, **623**, *623*
    Override Color option,
        623–624
    Text options, 623–624
finding and replacing, 126–128,
    127, *128*

glyph scaling
  defined, **398**
  Glyph Scaling option in Justification dialog box, 405
hyphenation options, **398–405**
  automatic hyphenation options, 402–403, *402*
  Composer and, **398–399**, *400*
  Composer options in New Paragraph Style dialog box, 244, *245*
  discretionary hyphens, 401, 403
  enabling and disabling automatic hyphenation, 401–402
  entering non-breaking hyphens, 404
  highlighting composition problems, 407, *407*
  keyboard shortcuts, 203
  language setting for, 396, 654
  manual hyphenation, 400–401
  in New Paragraph Style dialog box, 246–247, *246*
  preventing hyphenation, 403–404
  in spelling dictionaries, 130–131, *131*, 661, *661*, 682
importing, 115
indents
  defined, **218**
  first line indents, 218
  hanging indents, 222
  indent options in Text Import Options dialog box, 118
  in paragraph styles, 243–244, *244*
  setting, 221–222
Insert/Replace Characters command in Type menu, 684
Keep Options for paragraphs, 247–248, *247*, 387–389, *387*, *388*, *389*
kerning, **200**, **210–213**
  defined, **200**, **210–211**, *211*
  identifying settings, 211–212
  keyboard shortcuts, 203, 213
  metrics kerning, **211**
  optical kerning, **211**
  setting manually, 212–213
keyboard shortcuts
  for aligning paragraphs, 216
  for character formatting, 203
  for kerning, 203, 213
  listed, **772–775**
  on Macintosh computers, **785–787**
  in Windows, **772–775**
leading, **200**, **207–210**
  automatic leading, 208–209
  defined, **200**, **207–208**, *208*
  keyboard shortcuts, 203
  setting manually, 208, 209–210
ligatures, **200**
margin settings
  changing, 21
  gutter margins, 21
  Gutter option in Text Frame Options dialog box, 105, *105*
  InDesign Margins option in Export HTML: Layout dialog box, 627
  margin guides, 18, *19*, 60, *61*
  Margins and Columns command in Layout menu, 682
  Margins and Columns dialog box, 60
  in master pages, 469, *470*
  optical margin alignment or hanging punctuation, 217–218, *217*
  setting margin guides, 18, *19*, 21, 60–61, *61*
paragraph attributes
  applying, 214
  defined, **200**
  Text tool and, 214
Paragraph palette, **201–203**, **213–218**, **691**
  alignment settings, 200, 214–216
  defined, **201–203**, *201*, **213**, *213*, **691**
  drop caps, 223–224
  entering values in, 214
  justification settings, 200, 214–216, 406–407
  optical margin alignment or hanging punctuation, 217–218, *217*
  Paragraph palette menu, 201, *202*
  paragraph rules, 224–226, *225*
  paragraph spacing, 223
  setting hanging indents, 222
  setting indents, 218, 221–222
paragraph rules
  page numbers and, 466
  in Paragraph palette, 224–226, *225*
  in paragraph styles, 248, *248*
paragraph widow and orphan controls, 247–248, *247*, 387–389, *387*, *388*, *389*
scaling text, 382–383, *382*, 424
special characters, **108–111**
  defined, **108**
  entering with context menus, 110–111, *110*
  entering with Insert Character dialog box, 108–109, *109*
  entering with keyboard shortcuts, 109–110
  finding and replacing, 125–126
  flush spaces, 406–407
  metacharacters, 125–126
tab stops, **218–221**, **245–246**, **694**
  defined, **218**
  deleting, 21
  editing, 220–221
  leaders, 221
  in paragraph styles, 245–246, *246*
  setting, 218–220
  tab alignment options, 219
  Tabs palette, 218–221, 694
terms defined, **200**
text frame inset settings, 106, *107*, 226, *226*
tracking, **200**, **210–212**
  defined, **200**, **210**, *210*
  identifying settings, 211–212
  keyboard shortcuts, 203
  setting manually, 212
type
  defined, **102**
  type families, **200**
type styles, **200**, **203**, **205–206**, **393–398**
  all caps type, 203, 206, *206*
  applying, **205–206**, *205*, *206*
  bold type, 200, 203, 205–206, *205*, *206*
  defined, **200**
  fonts and, 205
  italic type, 200, 203, 205–206, *205*, *206*
  keyboard shortcuts, 203
  Old Style numerals, 396

Roman type style, 200
small caps, 203, 206, *206*, 394–395, *395*
strikethrough type, 203, 206, *206*, 397–398, *397*
subscript and superscript type, 203, 206, *206*, 393–394, *393*, *394*
underline type, 203, 206, *206*, 397–398, *397*
4-color process printing, 295, 587
4-page gatefold book inserts, 450–451
frames, **7**, **19–20**, **75–83**. *See also* paths; placeholders; shapes; text frames
   borders for graphic frames, **152–154**
     applying strokes to graphic frames, 152
     floating graphics in larger frames, 153–154
     keylines, **152**
     nesting objects, 153, 154–155, 436
   changing effect of stroking on, 92
   converting
     text frames to graphic frames, 76
     text outlines to frames, 82–83
   creating from clipping paths, 138, 140, 520–521
   Crop Image Data to Frames option in Export PDF: PDF Options dialog box, 594
   defined, **7**, **75–76**
   drawing, **77–82**
     circular and elliptical frames, 77–78, 672–673
     polygon frames, 79–82, 672–673
     square and rectangular frames, 78–79, 672–673
     Star Inset and Number of Sides options of polygon frames, 80–81
   graphic frames, **76**, **145–155**, **515**
     converting text frames to, 76
     cropping or masking with, 151
     Fit Content Proportionally option, 149–150
     Fit Contents to Frame option, 150
     Fit Frame to Content option, 149
     fitting frame and contents simultaneously, 151
     moving contents, 150–151
     moving inline graphic frames, 160–162, *161*
     overview of, 145–146
     resizing, 148
     resizing contents without distorting, 146–147, *146*, 148
     selecting frames and contents, 147–148
     splitting, 515
   identifying, 77
   versus shapes, **76**
   splitting with Scissors tool, 512–515, *513*, *514*
Freehand software, 11
freezes, 173
Full Resolution Images option, 138

G

gamma
   Adobe Gamma utility, **716**, **717–722**, *717*, *718*
     Calibrate the Monitor's Gamma option, 720
     Calibrate the Monitor's White Point option, 702, 721–722, *721*
     control panel, 719–722, *719*, *720*
     defined, **716**, **717–718**
     opening, 717, *717*, *718*
     preparing for monitor calibration, 716–717
     saving monitor profiles, 722, *722*, *723*
     Select the Exact Phosphor Type option, 701, 720
     Set Optimum Brightness and Contrast Range option, 720
   defined, **701**
   gamma correction options in Image Import Options dialog box, 140
gamuts (color)
   defined, **292–293**, *292*
   out-of-gamut alert icon, 302

GATF/PIA (Graphic Arts Technical Foundation/Printing Industries of America), 556
General options in Preferences dialog box, 656, *657*
Generate Thumbnails option in Export PDF: PDF Options dialog box, 594
GIF files, **12**
glyph scaling
   defined, **398**
   Glyph Scaling option in Justification dialog box, 405
Go Back and Go Forward commands in Layout menu, 683
gradients, **88–90**, **298**, **314–326**. *See also* color
   Apply Gradient tool, 675
   applying
     with Gradient palette, 89–90, *89*, 320–321
     with Gradient tool, 321–324, *321*, *322*, *323*, *324*, 673–674
     from Toolbox, 318–319
     to type, 324–326
   creating gradient swatches
     with Gradient palette, 298, 317–318
     with Swatches palette, 298, 316–317, *316*, *317*
   defined, **314–315**, *314*
   filling shapes with, 88–90, *88*, *89*
   Gradient palette
     applying gradients, 89–90, *89*, 320–321
     creating gradient swatches, 298, 317–318
     defined, **693**
     navigating, 315–316, *315*
   gradient swatches, 298
   Gradient tool, 318–319, 321–324, *321*, *322*, *323*, *324*, 673–674
   linear gradients, **88**, *88*, *89*
   printing, 543, 552
   radial gradients, **88**, *88*
Graphic Arts Technical Foundation/Printing Industries of America (GATF/PIA), 556
graphic frames, **76**, **145–155**, **515**. *See also* frames
   borders, **152–154**
     applying strokes to graphic frames, 152

floating graphics in larger frames, 153–154
keylines, **152**
nesting objects, 153, 154–155, 436
converting text frames to, 76
cropping or masking with, 151
Fit Content Proportionally option, 149–150
Fit Contents to Frame option, 150
Fit Frame to Content option, 149
fitting frame and contents simultaneously, 151
moving contents, 150–151
moving inline graphic frames, 160–162, *161*
overview of, 145–146
resizing, 148
resizing contents without distorting, 146–147, *146*, 148
selecting frames and contents, 147–148
splitting, 515
graphics, **135–165**. *See also* bitmap graphics; vector graphics
Allow Graphics and Groups to Resize option in Layout Adjustment dialog box, 471
in AppleScript, 753–756, *754*, *756*
bitmap graphics
BMP files, **12**
defined, **10–11**, *10*
dragging-and-dropping Illustrator and Photoshop bitmaps into InDesign, 9, 588
resizing, 11
resolution and, 11
size of, 11
versus vector graphics, 11
cropping
Crop Image Data to Frames option in Export PDF: PDF Options dialog box, 594
Crop Marks option in Print dialog box, 535, 558
Crop To option menu in Place PDF dialog box, 144
overview of, 151
editing from context menus, 55, 56

embedding graphics files, **163**, **165**
Export HTML: Graphics dialog box, **628–631**
converting graphics to GIF or JPEG formats, 628–630, *629*
exporting cropped graphics, 628
GIF file options, 630–631
JPEG file options, 631
Export PDF dialog box
Compression options, 597–598
PDF Options options, 594
Security options, 604
finding, 125
Full Resolution Images option, 138
Graphics options in Print dialog box, **538–543**
Font Downloading options, 541–542
gradient options, 543
overview of, 538–541, *539*
in HTML files, 612–613
Image Import Options dialog box, **137–140**
Color Settings options, 138–139
EPS options, 140
Image Settings options, 137–138
opening, 137, *137*
PNG Settings options, 139–140
importing
by copying and pasting, 141
by dragging-and-dropping, 141–142
with clipping paths, 138, 140, 520–521
copying and pasting as inline graphics, 159
dragging-and-dropping Illustrator and Photoshop graphics, 9, 588
EPS files, 140
Imported Graphics area in Export EPS dialog box, 32–33
placing graphics, 136–140, *137*
placing graphics files as inline graphics, 159
placing into shapes, 136
placing PDF files as graphics, 142–145, *143*
PNG files, 139–140

inline graphics, **159–162**
defined, **159**
deleting, 162
leading and, 160
moving inline graphic frames, 160–162, *161*
placing graphics files as, 159
resizing, 162
selecting, 160
linking, **145**, **162–165**
copying linked graphics into package files for service bureaus, 576
defined, **162–163**
editing linked PDF files, 145
linking graphics files, 163–165, *165*
Links and Images options in Preflight dialog box, 570–572, *571*, *572*
OPI (Open Prepress Interface) images, 25
in package files for service bureaus, 576
photographs, 139
placing (importing)
graphics files as inline graphics, 159
into shapes, 136
overview of, 136–140, *137*
PDF files as graphics, 142–145, *143*
printing
gradient options, 543, 552
Graphics options in Print dialog box, 538–541, *539*
proxy images, 137–138
resolution of, 137–138
vector graphics
versus bitmap graphics, 11
defined, **11**
dragging-and-dropping Illustrator and Photoshop graphics into InDesign, 9
Illustrator and, 11
Macromedia Freehand and, 11
paths and, 11
resizing, 11
resolution and, 11
size of, 11
in Visual Basic, 738–741, *739*, *741*
wrapping text around graphics, **155–158**, **695**

Bounding Box option, 156, *157*
Invert option, 158, *158*
Jump Object option, 157, *157*
Jump to Next Column option, 158, *158*
No Wrap option, 156, *156*
Object Shape option, 157, *157*
overview of, 155–156, 695
grayscale fills for shapes, 86
grids. *See also* guides; rulers; work areas
    baseline grids, **58–60**, **383–386**
        Align to Baseline Grid option, 58, 386
        defined, **58**, **383**
        locking text to, 58, 386
        setting options, 383–386, *383*, *384*, *385*, *386*
        setting up, 58–60, *59*
    color options, 659
    defined, **57**, **58**
    displaying or hiding, 60
    document grids
        defined, **58**, *59*
        setting up, 58–60, *59*
        Snap to Document Grid option, 58, 60
    Grids Preferences dialog box, 58
    overview of, 57–58
    Preferences: Grids dialog box, 58, 659, *660*
grouping
    objects, **435–437**, **685**
        Allow Graphics and Groups to Resize option in Layout Adjustment dialog box, 471
        creating groups from objects on different layers, 436–437
        HTML files and, 613
        identifying groups, 436
        locked and unlocked objects, 436
        overview of, 435–436, 685
    palettes
        moving palette groups, 45
        reorganizing or creating palette groups, 45–46, *45*
        resizing palette groups, 44
        separating palettes from palette groups, 46

guides. *See also* grids; rulers; work areas
    Create Guides dialog box, 57, 62–63, *63*, 683
    deleting, 62–63
    displaying, hiding, locking, or unlocking, 63–64, *64*, 341
    Layer Options dialog box, 64, *64*
    moving, 57
    overview of, 57–58
    page guides, **62**
    Preferences: Guides dialog box, 660, *660*
    ruler guides
        Allow Ruler Guides to Move option in Layout Adjustment dialog box, 471
        Ignore Ruler Guide Adjustments option in Layout Adjustment dialog box, 472
        Ruler Guides command in Layout menu, 683
        Ruler Guides dialog box, 62
        setting, 57, 62
        Transform palette and, 413
    setting
        evenly spaced guides, 62–63, *63*
        margin and column guides, 18, *19*, 60–61, *61*
        ruler guides, 57, 62
    Show Guides option in Layer Options dialog box, 341
    Snap to Guides option, 58, 60, 64
    spread guides, **62**
Gutter option in Text Frame Options dialog box, 105, *105*

H

Hand tool, 674
hanging indents, 222
hanging punctuation, 217–218, *217*
headlines
    in AppleScript, 758–759, *759*
    in Visual Basic, 743–744, *744*
Height option in Transform palette, 414
Help menu
    defined, **687**, *687*
    Macintosh keyboard shortcuts, 780

    Windows keyboard shortcuts, 767
HexMac Software Systems plug-ins, 69
hidden characters, displaying, 684
hidden Toolbox tools, displaying, 42
hiding. *See also* displaying
    grids, 60
    guides, 63–64, *64*
    layers, 338–339, *338*
    Object Library palette, 268–270
    palettes, 43
highlighting composition problems, 407, *407*
Horizontal Palette option in Transform palette, 416
Horizontal (X) position option in Transform palette, 413, *413*
hotkeys. *See* keyboard shortcuts
HTML files, **607–643**
    books about HTML and other Web topics, 610
    Cascading Style Sheets (CSS-1), 609, 616
    design considerations, 607–608
    Dynamic HTML, 609
    Export HTML: Document dialog box, **620–622**
        Change the Filename and Title option, 621
        overview of, 620–623, *620*, *623*
        Remove a Page option, 620
        View HTML Using option, 621–622, *621*
    Export HTML: Formatting dialog box, **623–627**
        background options, 625–627, *626*
        color picker dialog box, 624–625, *624*, *625*
        defined, **623**, *623*
        Override Color option, 623–624
        Text options, 623–624
    Export HTML: Graphics dialog box, **628–631**
        converting graphics to GIF or JPEG formats, 628–630, *629*
        exporting cropped graphics, 628
        GIF file options, 630–631
        JPEG file options, 631

HYPHENATION OPTIONS • IMPORTING   809

Export HTML: Layout dialog box, **627–628**, *628*
exporting
   overview of, 26, 28, 618–619, *618*, *619*, 631
   as Prepress files, 26, 28, 578–581, *579*, *580*, *581*
   sample HTML code generated for exported documents, 638–643
   selecting export options, 619–621, *619*, *620*, *621*
HTML syntax, 608–609
importing, 117–118, 631
preparing documents for HTML export, **611–618**
   animations, 613
   character and paragraph attributes retained and lost in exported HTML files, 612, 616–617
   color testing documents for print and Web distribution, 615
   converting from print to Web colors, 612–615, *614*, *615*, *616*
   converting text files to GIF files, 618
   fonts, 611–612
   graphics, 612–613
   grouped objects, 613
   naming HTML files, 616
   setting document dimensions and layout, 611
   text, 612
sRGB color mode, 612–613
start tags and end tags, 608–609
testing after exporting, **632–637**, *632*, *637*
viewing, 621–622, *621*, *622*
hyphenation options, **398–405**. *See also* formatting
   automatic hyphenation options, 402–403, *402*
   Composer
      Composer options in New Paragraph Style dialog box, 244, *245*
      highlighting composition problems, 407, *407*
      hyphenation options and, **398–399**, *400*
   discretionary hyphens, 401, 403
   enabling and disabling automatic hyphenation, 401–402
   entering non-breaking hyphens, 404
   keyboard shortcuts, 203
   language setting for, 396, 654
   manual hyphenation, 400–401
   in New Paragraph Style dialog box, 246–247, *246*
   No Break option, 403
   preventing hyphenation, 403–404
   in spelling dictionaries, 130–131, *131*, 661, *661*, 682

I

ICC Device Profiles
   adding, 702–705, *703*
   in Application Color Settings dialog box, 708–709, *708*, *709*
   creating or customizing printer profiles, 723–725, *724*
   defined, **701**
   Include ICC Profiles option in Export PDF: PDF Options dialog box, 593
   overriding embedded profiles, 712
   saving monitor profiles, 722, *722*, *723*
   selecting source profiles, 565, *565*, 711–713, *713*
icons
   Adobe InDesign icon commands on Macintosh computers, 677
   in Windows, 676–677
   icon elements
      in AppleScript, 759, *760*
      in Visual Basic, 744, *745*
   in Swatches palette, 298
identifying
   frames, shapes, and placeholders, 77
   groups, 436
   layers with color, 353, *353*
   Macintosh system configuration, 652, *653*
   plug-in developers, 67
   points of origin, 412, *412*, 417–418, *418*
   tracking and kerning settings, 211–212

Windows 98 system configuration, 650, *650*
Windows NT system configuration, 651, *651*, *652*
Ignore Object and layer Locks option in Layout Adjustment dialog box, 472
Ignore Ruler Guide Adjustments option in Layout Adjustment dialog box, 472
Ignore Text Wrap option in Text Frame Options dialog box, 107
Illustrator
   AI files, **12**
   Application Color Settings dialog box and, 707
   compatibility with InDesign, 8–9, 699
   dragging-and-dropping graphics into InDesign, 9
   vector graphics and, 11
Image Color Settings command in Object menu, 686
Image Import Options dialog box, **137–140**
   Color Settings options, 138–139
   EPS options, 140
   Image Settings options, 137–138
   opening, 137, *137*
   PNG Settings options, 139–140
images. *See* bitmap graphics; graphics; vector graphics
Images option
   in Export EPS dialog box, 33
   in Export PDF: PDF Options dialog box, 594
imagesetters, printing to, 181
importing, **23–25**. *See also* exporting; placing
   colors into Swatches palette from other files, 308–309, *308*
   graphics
      by copying and pasting, 141
      by dragging-and-dropping, 141–142
      with clipping paths, 138, 140, 520–521
      dragging-and-dropping Illustrator and Photoshop graphics, 9, 588
      EPS files, 140
      Imported Graphics area in Export EPS dialog box, 32–33
      placing graphics, 136–140, *137*

placing graphics files as inline graphics, 159
placing into shapes, 136
placing PDF files as graphics, 142–145, *143*
PNG files, 139–140
HTML files, 117–118, 631
Illustrator and Photoshop graphics into InDesign, 9, 588
Image Import Options dialog box, **137–140**
  Color Settings options, 138–139
  EPS options, 140
  Image Settings options, 137–138
  opening, 137, *137*
  PNG Settings options, 139–140
Import Options dialog box, **115–120**
  adding import filters, 23, 115
  Excel Import Options dialog box, 119, *119*, *120*
  opening, 115, 116
  overview of, 115–116
  PageMaker Tagged Text filter, 120
  Text Import Options dialog box, 115, 117–118, *117*
  Word, WordPerfect, and RTF Import Options dialog boxes, 115, 116–117, *116*
import plug-ins, 23, 115
OPI (Open Prepress Interface) images, 25
PageMaker files, 23
PDF files
  overview of, **23–25**
  password-protected files, 24, 144, 603
QuarkXPress files, 23
styles
  from other applications, 115, 232, 254
  from other documents, 232, 253–255, *254*
supported file formats, **11–13**
text files, 111–112
in ports in text frames, 102
Include ICC Profiles option in Export PDF: PDF Options dialog box, 593
Include Inside Edges option in Clipping Path dialog box, 525

indents. *See also* paragraph formatting
  defined, **218**
  first line indents, 218
  hanging indents, 222
  indent options in Text Import Options dialog box, 118
  in paragraph styles, 243–244, *244*
  setting, 221–222
InDesign, **5–6**, **647–662**
  versus Adobe Acrobat, 585–586
  Adobe InDesign icon commands on Macintosh computers, 677
    in Windows, 676–677
  compatibility with Illustrator and Photoshop, 8–9, 699
  defined, **5–6**
  features, **5–6**
  installing, **647–655**
    ATI graphics cards and, 649
    contents of installation package, 647–648
    identifying Macintosh system configuration, 652, *653*
    identifying Windows 98 system configuration, 650, *650*
    identifying Windows NT system configuration, 651, *651*, *652*
    installing Acrobat Reader, 654
    installing InDesign, **652–654**
    installing PostScript Driver, 654–655
    Macintosh system requirements, 649
    ReadMe files, 649, 652
    registering InDesign software, 655
    Windows system requirements, 648, 649
  Preferences dialog box, **655–662**, **679**
    Adobe Online Preferences dialog box, 662, *662*, *663*
    Composition options, 658, *658*
    Dictionary options, 661, *661*
    General options, 656, *657*
    Grids options, 58, 659, *660*
    Guides options, 660, *660*
    navigating, 655–656
    opening, 655, 679
    restoring default settings, 656

Text options, 657, *657*
Units & Increments options, 658–659, *659*
starting, **655**
  with Acrobat Reader, 586
supported file formats, **11–13**
terms defined, **7**, *8*
using QuarkXPress keyboard shortcuts, 6, 49, 52
InDesign Margins option in Export HTML: Layout dialog box, 627
InDr, InDa, and InD3 files, 67
initial caps, **223–224**
inkjet printers, proofing, 541
inline graphics, **159–162**. *See also* graphics
  defined, **159**
  deleting, 162
  leading and, 160
  moving inline graphic frames, 160–162, *161*
  placing graphics files as, 159
  resizing, 162
  selecting, 160
In-RIP option in Print dialog box, 549
In-RIP Trapping option in Print dialog box, 549, 561
Insert Character dialog box, 108–109, *109*
Insert Page Number command in Layout menu, 683
Insert/Replace Characters command in Type menu, 684
inserting. *See* adding; entering; importing
insertion point for text, **102**, **120**
Inset Frame option in Clipping Path dialog box, 525
Inset Spacing options in Text Frame Options dialog box, 106, *107*, 226, *226*
installing
  Acrobat Reader, 585
  InDesign, **647–655**
    ATI graphics cards and, 649
    contents of installation package, 647–648
    identifying Macintosh system configuration, 652, *653*
    identifying Windows 98 system configuration, 650, *650*

identifying Windows NT system configuration, 651, *651*, 652
installing Acrobat Reader, 654
installing InDesign, **652–654**
installing PostScript Driver, 654–655
Macintosh system requirements, 649
ReadMe files, 649, 652
registering InDesign software, 655
Windows system requirements, 648, 649
plug-ins, 67
instruction reports for package files for service bureaus, 577
Invert option
in Clipping Path dialog box, 525
in Text Wrap palette, 158, *158*
island spreads. *See also* Pages palette
adding pages to, 448–449, *449*
clearing, 446
creating, **445–446**
creating 4-page gatefold book inserts, 450–451
defined, **445**
deleting pages from, 453
italic type style, **200**, **203**, **205–206**, *205*, *206*
Item Name option in Subset dialog box, 283

J

Java and JavaScript, 609–610
join effects for corners, 92–93
JPEG files
defined, **12**
JPEG option in Export PDF: Compression dialog box, 598
Jump Object option in Text Wrap palette, 157, *157*
Jump to Next Column option in Text Wrap palette, 158, *158*
justification settings. *See also* alignment
Composer and, 398, 407
defined, **400**
in Justification dialog box, 405–406, *405*
in Paragraph palette, 200, 214–216, 406–407

in paragraph styles, 244–245, *245*

K

Keep Options for paragraphs, 247–248, *247*, 387–389, *387*, *388*, *389*
Keep Tables, Lists, and Indents As Is option in Text Import Options dialog box, 118
kerning, **200**, **210–213**
defined, **200**, **210–211**, *211*
identifying settings, 211–212
keyboard shortcuts, 203, 213
metrics kerning, **211**
optical kerning, **211**
setting manually, 212–213
keyboard shortcuts, **48–53**, **765–789**
for aligning paragraphs, 216
assigning to styles, 236, *236*
for baselines, 203
for character formatting, 203
for cursor movement, 121–122
defined, **48–49**
editing, 49, *49*, 52, 411, 680
for fonts, 52
to Grids or Guides Preferences dialog boxes, 58
for hyphenation, 203
for kerning, 203, 213
for leading, 203
on Macintosh computers, **778–789**
Edit menu, 778
File menu, 778–779
formatting, 785–787
Help menu, 780
Layout menu, 780
Object menu, 780–781
palettes and Toolbox, 783–784
text selection, 782–783
Type menu, 784–785
View menu, 787–788
views, 788
Window menu, 789
for menu commands, 39
for saving all open files, 25
for selecting menu commands, 39
shortcut sets
creating, **52–53**
deleting, 53

editing, 49, *49*
selecting active shortcut set, 50
sharing, 49
viewing or printing, 50, *51*
for special characters, 109–110
for spreads, 445
for text
on Macintosh computers, 782–783
for navigating, editing, and selecting, 121–122
in Windows, 769–771
for tools, 42
for tracking, 203
for type styles, 203
using QuarkXPress shortcuts in InDesign, 6, 49, 52
viewing, 50
views
on Macintosh computers, 788
in Windows, 776–777
in Windows, **766–778**
Edit menu, 766
File menu, 766–768
formatting, 772–775
Help menu, 767
Layout menu, 767–768
Object menu, 768–769
palettes and Toolbox, 771–772
text selection, 769–771
Type menu, 772
View menu, 775–776
views, 776–777
Window menu, 777–778
keylines, **152**. *See also* borders
Kodak
Kodak CMM software and Web site, 654
Kodak SWOP Proofer CMYK—Coated Stock option in Document Color Settings dialog box, 565, *565*

L

L*a*b color model, 294
Lab color gamut, 292, *292*
LAB color mode, 295
landscape orientation
for documents, 21
Macintosh printing options, 187
Windows printing options, 179, *180*, 181

language setting for spelling and
  hyphenation, 396, 654
Last Page command in Layout
  menu, 683
layers, **64**, **275–276**, **329–357**
  adding objects to, 343–344
  changing stacking order of, 354
  copying objects between,
    344–347, *345*, *346*
  creating groups from objects on
    different layers, 436–437
  cutting, copying, and pasting
    objects or text onto, 344
  defined, **329**, **332–334**, *332*, *333*
  deleting, 354–355
  drawing objects on, 344
  flattening documents, 357
  identifying with color, 353, *353*
  Ignore Object and layer Locks
    option in Layout Adjustment
    dialog box, 472
  Layer Options dialog box, 64, *64*,
    340–341, *340*, *341*
  Layers palette, **334–342**, **689**
    creating layers, **339–340**
    defined, **689**
    displaying or hiding layers,
      338–339, *338*
    layer display in, 335
    locking layers, 341, 342
    opening, 334, *334*
    selecting and targeting layers,
      335–337, *336*, *337*, *338*
  in master pages, 455
  merging, 355–357, *356*
  moving or copying objects to
    other layers, 419
  moving objects between, 347,
    348
  naming, 341
  versus object stacks, 330–331,
    437–438
  preserving
    when copying or moving
      objects, 349–352, *350*, *351*,
      352
    when placing library objects,
      275–276
Layout menu
  defined, **682–683**
  Macintosh keyboard shortcuts,
    780
  Windows keyboard shortcuts,
    767–768

layouts
  changing, 470–472, *472*
  Export HTML: Layout dialog
    box, **627–628**, *628*
  Layout Adjustment dialog box,
    470–472, *472*, 683
leaders for tab stops, 221
leading, **200**, **207–210**. *See also*
  formatting
  automatic leading, 208–209
  defined, **200**, **207–208**, *208*
  inline graphics and, 160
  keyboard shortcuts, 203
  setting manually, 208, 209–210
  for text baselines, 107
Letter Spacing option in
  Justification dialog box, 405
libraries. *See also* object libraries
  swatches libraries, 305–306
ligatures, **200**
linear gradients, **88**, *88*, *89*
lines. *See also* paths; shapes
  applying arrowheads and other
    end shapes, 96–97
  changing end caps, 94–95
  changing line or shape outline
    thickness, 90–91, *91*
  Compress Text and Line Art
    option in Export PDF:
    Compression dialog box, 598
  creating dashed or dotted lines
    and shape outlines, 95–96
  drawing straight lines, **83**
  Line tool, 83, 672–673
  paragraph rules
    page numbers and, 466
    in Paragraph palette, 224–226,
      225
    in paragraph styles, 248, *248*
  start point of, 97
  stroking, 91, *91*
linked text frames. *See* threading
  text between linked text frames
linking graphics, **145**, **162–165**
  copying linked graphics into
    package files for service
    bureaus, 576
  defined, **162–163**
  editing linked PDF files, 145
  linking graphics files, 163–165,
    165
  Links and Images options in
    Preflight dialog box, 570–572,
    571, *572*

Links command in File menu, 679
Links palette
  defined, **695**
  imported PDF files and, 25
Lizardtech plug-ins, 69
Loaded Text cursor, 366, 368
locking
  grouping locked and unlocked
    objects, 436
  guides, 63–64, *64*, 341
  layers, 341, 342
  Lock Position and Unlock
    Position commands in Object
    menu, 685
  ruler zero point reference, 66
  text to baseline grid, 58, 386
lowering text on baselines,
  389–391, *389*, *390*, *391*

M

Macintosh computers. *See also*
  AppleScript; Microsoft Windows;
  printing
  Adobe InDesign icon
    commands, 677
  ColorSync control panel,
    702–705, *703*, 708
  compatibility of Windows and
    Macintosh files, 8
  creating film negatives or
    positives, 552–553, *553*, 555,
    555
  identifying system
    configuration, 652, *653*
  InDesign system requirements,
    649
  keyboard shortcuts, **778–789**
    Edit menu, 778
    File menu, 778–779
    formatting, 785–787
    Help menu, 780
    Layout menu, 780
    Object menu, 780–781
    palettes and Toolbox, 783–784
    text selection, 782–783
    Type menu, 784–785
    View menu, 787–788
    views, 788
    Window menu, 789
  memory requirements for
    opening InDesign with Acrobat
    Reader, 586
  Open a File dialog box, 21–23, *22*

PICT files, **12**
Print dialog box
　background printing, 531
　printing thumbnails, 538
printing, **177**, **184–191**, **588**
　background printing, 531
　document dimensions and, 588
　to non-PostScript printers, 177, 184
　opening Print dialog box, 188, 529–530, *530*
　to PostScript files, 191–193, *193*
　printing on both sides of paper, 191
　printing two-page spreads (double-truck printing), 188
　saving print options, 191
　scaling documents for printing, 188
　selecting number of copies and collation options, 189
　selecting number of pages to print, 189–191, *190*
　selecting orientation, 187
　selecting paper size, 185–187, *186*, *187*
　selecting paper source, 191
　selecting printers, 184–185, *185*
　thumbnails, 537, 538
　undocumented features, 529
　Save As dialog box, 27–28, *27*, 678
　System color system, **306–307**
Macromedia Freehand, 11
Managing Editor plug-ins, 69
manually drawing clipping paths, 521–524, *521*, *522*, *524*
manually setting
　hyphenation, 400–401
　kerning, 212–213
　leading, 208, 209–210
　tracking, 212
manually threading text between text frames, 369–375
Mapsoft Computer Services plug-ins, 70
margin settings. *See also* paragraph formatting
　changing, 21
　gutter margins, 21

Gutter option in Text Frame Options dialog box, 105, *105*
InDesign Margins option in Export HTML: Layout dialog box, 627
margin guides, 18, *19*, 60, *61*
Margins and Columns command in Layout menu, 682
Margins and Columns dialog box, 60
in master pages, 469, *470*
optical margin alignment or hanging punctuation, 217–218, *217*
setting margin guides, 18, *19*, 21, 60–61, *61*
masking graphics, 151
master pages, **441**, **454–461**. *See also* Pages palette
　applying to spreads, 457–459, *458*, *459*
　changing margin and column settings, 469, *470*
　copying between documents, 460–461
　creating, **455–456**, *456*, *457*
　creating uneven columns, 470, *471*
　defined, **441**, **454–455**
　deleting, 460
　duplicating, 456, *456*
　layers in, 455
　overriding master objects, 468–469
Master Text Frames option in New Document dialog box, 19–10, 102
measurement units
　for baselines, 391, *391*
　in palettes, 46–47, *47*
　for rulers, 64–65, *65*
　Units & Increments options in Preferences dialog box, 658–659, *659*
memory requirements for opening InDesign with Acrobat Reader, 586
menus, **675–688**. *See also* palettes; Toolbox; work areas
　Adobe InDesign icon commands on Macintosh computers, 677
　in Windows, 676–677
　commands that open dialog boxes, 39
　context menus, **53–56**, **688**
　arranging objects, 54, *55*

changing views, 53, *54*
defined, **688**
displaying, 56
editing graphics, 55, *56*
editing text, 56, *57*
entering special characters, 110–111, *110*
defined, **39**
Edit menu, **680–682**
　Check Spelling command, 682
　Copy command, 681
　Cut command, 681
　Deselect All command, 681
　Duplicate command, 420, *420*, 681
　Edit Dictionary command, 682
　Find Next command, 124
　Find/Change command, 122–128, 682
　Macintosh keyboard shortcuts, 778
　Paste command, 681
　Paste Into command, 681
　Redo command, 169–170, 681
　Select All command, 681
　Step and Repeat command, 421–423, *422*, *423*, 681
　Undo command, 169–170, 681
　Windows keyboard shortcuts, 766
ellipses (…) in, 39
File menu, **677–680**
　Adobe Online command, 680
　Close command, 677
　Color Settings command, 680
　defined, **677**, *678*
　Document Setup command, 21, 679
　Edit Shortcuts command, 49, 411, 680
　Exit command (Windows), 680
　Export command, 679
　Links command, 679
　Macintosh keyboard shortcuts, 778–779
　New command, 18, 677
　Open command, 677
　Package command, 679
　Page Setup command (Macintosh), 679
　Place command, 112–114, *113*, 136–140, *137*, 678
　Preferences command, 655, 679

Preflight command, 178, 679
Print command, 679
Quit command (Macintosh), 680
Revert command, 172, 678
Save As command, 25–28, *26, 27*, 678
Save command, 25, 677
Save a Copy command, 28, 171–172, *171*, 678
Windows keyboard shortcuts, 766–768
Help menu
  defined, **687**, *687*
  Macintosh keyboard shortcuts, 780
  Windows keyboard shortcuts, 767
keyboard shortcuts in menus, 39
Layout menu
  defined, **682–683**
  Macintosh keyboard shortcuts, 780
  Windows keyboard shortcuts, 767–768
Macintosh keyboard shortcuts
  Edit menu, 778
  File menu, 778–779
  Help menu, 780
  Layout menu, 780
  Object menu, 780–781
  Type menu, 784–785
  View menu, 787–788
  Window menu, 789
Object menu
  defined, **684–686**
  Macintosh keyboard shortcuts, 780–781
  Windows keyboard shortcuts, 768–769
overview of, 675–676, *676*
palette menus
  Character palette menu, 201, *201*
  Color palette menu, 87–88, *87*
  defined, **43**
  Paragraph palette menu, 201, *202*
Type menu
  defined, **683–684**
  Macintosh keyboard shortcuts, 784–785
  Windows keyboard shortcuts, 772

View menu, **667–671**, **686**
  Actual Size command, 669, *669*
  Entire Pasteboard command, 669–671, *670*
  Fit Page in Window command, 668, *668*
  Fit Spread in Window command, 668, *669*
  Macintosh keyboard shortcuts, 787–788
  overview of, 668–669, 686
  Windows keyboard shortcuts, 775–776
Window menu
  defined, **687**
  Macintosh keyboard shortcuts, 789
  Windows keyboard shortcuts, 777–778
Windows keyboard shortcuts
  Edit menu, 766
  File menu, 766–768
  Help menu, 767
  Layout menu, 767–768
  Object menu, 768–769
  Type menu, 772
  View menu, 775–776
  Window menu, 777–778
merging layers, 355–357, *356*
metacharacters, **125–126**
metrics kerning, **211**
Microsoft Excel Import Options dialog box, 119, *119, 120*
Microsoft Windows. *See also* Macintosh computers; printing; Visual Basic
  Adobe InDesign icon commands, 676–677
  compatibility of Windows and Macintosh files, 8
  film negatives or positives
    creating in Windows 98, 552–554, *553*
    creating in Windows NT, 552–553, *553*, 554–555, *554*
  identifying system configuration
    in Windows 98, 650, *650*
    in Windows NT, 651, *651*, 652
  InDesign system requirements, 648, 649
  keyboard shortcuts, **766–778**
    Edit menu, 766
    File menu, 766–768

formatting, 772–775
Help menu, 767
Layout menu, 767–768
Object menu, 768–769
palettes and Toolbox, 771–772
text selection, 769–771
Type menu, 772
View menu, 775–776
views, 776–777
Window menu, 777–778
memory requirements for opening InDesign with Acrobat Reader, 586
Open a File dialog box, 21–23, *22*
printing, **177–184**
  to imagesetters, 181
  to non-PostScript printers, 177
  opening Print dialog box, 178, *179*
  to PostScript files, 191–192
  printing two-page spreads (double-truck printing), 183, *184*
  saving print options, 184
  selecting number of copies and collation options, 181
  selecting orientation, 179, *180*, 181
  selecting pages to print, 181–182, *183*
  selecting paper size, 179–181, *180*
  selecting paper source, 179, *180*, 181
  selecting printers, 178
  thumbnails in Windows 98, 536
  thumbnails in Windows NT, 537
Save As dialog box, 26–27, *26*
System color system, **306–307**
WMF (Windows Metafiles) files, **13**
Microsoft Word Import Options dialog boxes, 115, 116–117, *116*
missing fonts problems, 570
miter effects for corners, 92–93
modes, color modes, 294–295
monitors, **8**, **700**, **715–722**
  Adobe Gamma utility, **716**, **717–722**
    Calibrate the Monitor's Gamma option, 720

Calibrate the Monitor's White Point option, 702, 721–722, *721*
control panel, 719–722, *719*, *720*
defined, **716**, **717–718**
opening, 717, *717*, *718*
preparing for monitor calibration, 716–717
saving monitor profiles, 722, *722*, *723*
Select the Exact Phosphor Type option, 701, 720
Set Optimum Brightness and Contrast Range option, 720
calibrating
  colorimeters and, 715, *715*
  defined, **700**
  gamma, 140, **701**, 720
  in Illustrator, Photoshop, and InDesign, 8
  phosphors, **701**, 720
  white points, 702, 721–722, *721*
  workroom environments and, 715–716
  X-Rite Monitor Optimizer, 715, *715*, 724, 725
Monitor options in Application Color Settings dialog box, 708, *708*
moving palettes between, 43
Simulate Separation Printer on Monitor option in Application Color Settings dialog box, 709
mouse
  cross pointer, 78
  dragging-and-dropping graphics, 141–142
    Illustrator and Photoshop graphics into InDesign, 9, 588
    objects to Object Library palette, 270
    and positioning objects, 419
    and scaling objects, 424–425, *425*
    text files from other applications, 111–112
  editing text with, 121
  Loaded Text cursor, 366, 368
  selecting menu commands with, 39
  wheel mouse, 40

moving. *See also* copying; cutting and pasting; dragging-and-dropping; positioning
  anchor points, 497–498, *498*, *499*
  graphic frame contents, 150–151
  guides, 57
  inline graphic frames, 160–162, *161*
  Object Library palette between palette groups, 263, *265*
  objects
    between layers, 347, *348*
    between object libraries, 279
    and preserving layers, 349–352, *350*, *351*, *352*
    objects to other layers or pages, 419
  pages, 446–447, *447*
  palettes
    between monitors, 43
    palettes or palette groups, 45
  points of origin, 412, *412*, 417–418, *418*
  ruler zero point reference, 66, *66*
  spreads, 446–447
  Toolbox, 41
Multi-Line Composer. *See* Composer
multiple linear gradients, **88**, *89*
multiplying values in palettes, 148, 202

N

naming
  HTML files, 616
  layers, 341
  object libraries, 267
  variables in AppleScript, 749
  variables in Visual Basic, 734
navigating
  Gradient palette, 315–316, *315*
  Preferences dialog box, 655–656
  work areas, 40
Navigation Bar option in Export HTML: Layout dialog box, 628
Navigator palette, 420, 690
negatives
  creating on Macintosh computers, 552–553, *553*, 555, *555*
  creating in Windows 98, 552–554, *553*

creating in Windows NT, 552–553, *553*, 554–555, *554*
nesting objects, 153, 154–155, 436
New Character Style dialog box, **232–241**
  Advanced Character Formats option, 239, *239*
  assigning keyboard shortcuts to styles, 236, *236*
  Basic Character Formats options, 238–239, *238*
  color settings, 240–241, *240*, *241*
New Color Swatch dialog box, 300–303, *301*, *302*
New command in File menu, 18, 677
New Document dialog box, **18–21**
  Columns options, 21, 60
  creating text frames, 19–20, 102, 104
  Facing Pages option, 19, 441, *442*, 447
  Margins options, 21, 60
  Master Text Frames option, 19–10, 102
  Number of Pages option, 18
  Orientation options, 21
  overview of, 18, *18*, *19*
  Page Size options, 20–21, *20*
New Library dialog box, 266–268, *266*
New Paragraph Style dialog box, **241–248**
  assigning keyboard shortcuts to styles, 236, *236*
  Drop Caps and Composer options, 244, *245*
  Hyphenation options, 246–247, *246*
  Indents and Spacing options, 243–244, *244*
  Justification options, 244–245, *245*
  Keep Options, 247–248, *247*
  Next Style option, 243
  Paragraph Rules options, 248, *248*
  Tabs options, 245–246, *246*
newspaper columns. *See* columns of text
Next Page command in Layout menu, 683
Next Style option in New Paragraph Style dialog box, 243

No Break option in Character palette, 403
"no color" swatch, 86, 296
No Sample Change option in Export PDF: Compression dialog box, 597
No Wrap option in Text Wrap palette, 156, *156*
non-breaking hyphens, 404
non-breaking spaces, 405
None swatch, 296, 298, 299, 675
non-PostScript printers, printing to, 177, 184
Normal option in Open a File dialog box, 23
Number of Pages option in New Document dialog box, 18
Number of Sides option for polygon shapes and frames, 79–81
numbering pages, **461–468**, **588**
    assigning automatically updated numbers, 463–466, *463*, *465*
    assigning sections to documents, 466–468, *467*
    in exported PDF files, 588
    Insert Page Number command in Layout menu, 683
    inserting section markers, 468
    overview of, 461–462
    setting preferences, 462, *462*
numbers
    entering or changing numerical values in palettes, 46–47, *47*
    Old Style numerals, 396

O

object libraries, **261–285**
    adding objects, **270–274**
        groups of objects, 271–272
        overview of, 270
        pages, 273–274
        ruler guides, 274
        shapes, frames, placeholders, or graphics, 271
        text frames, 272–273
    cataloguing objects, 280–281, *280*, *281*
    closing, 285
    copying objects between, 276–278, *277*, *278*, *279*
    creating, 266–267, *266*
    defined, **261–262**
    deleting, 285
    deleting objects, 266, 274
    displaying, 266, 268–269, *269*
    finding objects, 266, 281–285, *282*, *283*
    moving objects between, 279
    naming, 267
    New Library dialog box, 266–268, *266*
    Object Library palette, **262–266**, **695–696**
        creating, 263, *264*
        defined, **262**, *262*, **695–696**
        deleting objects, 266, 274
        displaying or hiding, 268–270
        displaying object libraries, 266
        dragging objects to, 270
        moving between palette groups, 263, *265*
        opening New Library dialog box from, 268
        selecting object libraries, 262–263
        sorting object libraries, 263
        Swatch Library palette, **696**
    opening, 268, *268*
    placing library objects in documents, 275–276
    Subset dialog box, 282–285, *282*, *283*
Object Shape option in Text Wrap palette, 157, *157*
object stacks, **330–331**, **437–438**
Object Type option in Subset dialog box, 284
objects, **419–438**. *See also* Transform palette
    adding to layers, 343–344
    aligning, **432–435**
    arranging, 54, *55*, 684
    copying
        between layers, 344–347, *345*, *346*
        between object libraries, 276–278, *277*, *278*, *279*
        to other layers or pages, 419
        and preserving layers, 349–352, *350*, *351*, *352*
    cutting, copying, and pasting onto layers, 344
    defined, **7**
    distorting, **428–429**, *429*
    distributing, **432**, **434–435**
    drawing on layers, 344
    duplicating, **420–423**, **431–432**
        creating pages of duplicates, 422–423, *422*, *423*
        with Edit menu Duplicate command, 420, *420*
        with Step and Repeat dialog box, 421–423, *422*, *423*, 681
        and transforming, 430–432, *431*, *432*, *433*
    flipping, 415
    grouping, **435–437**, **685**
        Allow Graphics and Groups to Resize option in Layout Adjustment dialog box, 471
        creating groups from objects on different layers, 436–437
        identifying groups, 436
        locked and unlocked objects, 436
        overview of, 435–436, 685
    Ignore Object and layer Locks option in Layout Adjustment dialog box, 472
    moving
        between layers, 347, *348*
        between object libraries, 279
        and preserving layers, 349–352, *350*, *351*, *352*
    nesting, 153, 154–155, 436
    Object menu
        defined, **684–686**
        Macintosh keyboard shortcuts, 780–781
        Windows keyboard shortcuts, 768–769
    object stacks, **330–331**, **437–438**
    overriding master objects, 468–469
    positioning, **419–420**
        with arrow keys, 420
        with drag-and-drop, 419
        moving or copying to other layers or pages, 419
        Navigator palette and, 420, 690
        with Selection tool, 419
        with Transform palette, 419
    printing an object on top of another, 154
    reflecting, **427–428**, *427*
    rotating, **428–429**, *429*, **673**
    scaling, **423–426**
        with drag-and-drop, 424–425, *425*

overview of, 423–424
  with Scale tool, 424–425, *426*
  with Selection tool, 424, *425*
  text and text frames, 424
  with Transform palette, 425–426
transparent objects, 296
in Visual Basic, **731**
Old Style numerals, 396
Omit option
  in Export EPS dialog box, 33
  in Export PDF: PDF Options dialog box, 594
Open command in File menu, 677
Open a File dialog box, 254, *254*
open paths. *See also* paths
  closing, 506, *507*
  continuing, 506
  defined, **478–479**, *478*, *479*
  filling, 479, *479*
Open Type fonts, 396
opening
  Adobe Gamma utility, 717, *717*, *718*
  Align palette, 432
  closed paths, 507, *508*
  document windows, 38
  files, **21–23**, *22*
    password-protected files, 24
    supported file formats, **11–13**
  Find/Change dialog box, 122–123, *123*
  Image Import Options dialog box, 137, *137*
  Import Options dialog box, 115, *116*
  InDesign, 655
  InDesign with Acrobat Reader, 586
  Layers palette, 334, *334*
  object libraries, 268, *268*
  Pages palette, 442, *443*
  Preferences dialog box, 655, 679
  Print dialog box
    on Macintosh computers, 188
    in Windows, 178, *179*
  Swatches palette, 297
  Text Frame Options dialog box, 104, *104*
  Transform palette, 414
OPI (Open Prepress Interface)
  images
    defined, **32–33**

Export EPS dialog box options, 32–33
importing, 25
OPI/DCS Image Replacement option in Print dialog box, 540
Read Embedded OPI Image Links option in Image Import Options dialog box, 140
optical kerning, **211**
optical margin alignment or hanging punctuation, 217–218, *217*
Optimize PDF option in Export PDF: PDF Options dialog box, 594–595
order of layers, changing, 354
orientation settings
  for documents, 21
  Macintosh printing options, 187
  for palettes, 44
  Windows printing options, 179, *180*, 181
origin points, 412, *412*, 417–418, *418*
Original option in Open a File dialog box, 23
orphan controls, 247–248, *247*, 387–389, *387*, *388*, *389*
out ports in text frames, 102
out-of-gamut alert icon, 302
Overlap option in Print dialog box, 535
overprinting strokes, fills, or text, 563–565, *564*
Override Color option in Export HTML: Formatting dialog box, 623–624
overriding
  embedded profiles, 712
  master objects, 468–469

P

packaging files for service bureaus, **575–578**, 679
  creating instructions, 575, *576*
  creating packages, 576–578, *577*, *578*
  defined, **575**
  Package command in File menu, 679
  Preflight dialog box and, 575
Page Information option in Print dialog box, 558

page marks, **557–560**
  Crop Marks option, 535
  defined, **557**, *557*, *558*
  Export PDF: Pages and Page Marks dialog box, 600–602, *601*
  Page Marks options in Print dialog box, **557**, *557*, *558*
  ScenicSoft Preps trapping software and, 557
  selecting options, 558–559
  selecting page size for page mark specifications, 559–560, *560*
page numbers, **461–468**, 588
  assigning automatically updated numbers, 463–466, *463*, *465*
  assigning sections to documents, 466–468, *467*
  in exported PDF files, 588
  Insert Page Number command in Layout menu, 683
  inserting section markers, 468
  overview of, 461–462
  setting preferences, 462, *462*
Page Setup command in File menu (Macintosh), 679
Page Size options in New Document dialog box, 20–21, *20*
PageMaker
  importing files, 23
  Tagged Text filter, 120
pages. *See also* documents
  adding
    to documents, 447–448
    to island spreads, 448–449, *449*
    when threading text between frames, 368, 371–375, *372*, *373*, *374*
  changing layouts, **470–472**, *472*
  creating pages of duplicate objects, 422–423, *422*, *423*
  defined, **441**
  deleting, 453
  duplicating, 451–452, *452*
  Facing Pages option in New Document dialog box, 19, 441, *442*, 447
  Fit Page in Window command in View menu, 668, *668*
  Layout Adjustment dialog box, **470–472**, *472*, **683**
  moving, 446–447, *447*
  moving or copying objects to other pages, 419

page guides, **62**
page structure elements, 18, *19*
Pages options in Export EPS dialog box, 33–34, *33*
Remove a Page option in Export HTML: Document dialog box, 620
selecting, 444, *444*
User Defined Page Breaks To option in Word, WordPerfect, or RTF Import Options dialog box, 117
Pages palette, **442–470**, **689**
  defined, **689**
  island spreads
    adding pages to, 448–449, *449*
    clearing, 446
    creating, **445–446**
    creating 4-page gatefold book inserts, 450–451
    defined, **445**
    deleting pages from, 453
  master pages, **441**, **454–461**
    applying to other masters, 459, *460*
    applying to spreads, 457–459, *458*, *459*
    changing margin and column settings, 469, *470*
    copying between documents, 460–461
    creating, **455–456**, *456*, *457*
    creating uneven columns, 470, *471*
    defined, **441**, **454–455**
    deleting, 460
    duplicating, 456, *456*
    layers in, 455
    overriding master objects, 468–469
  opening, 442, *443*
  overview of, 442–443
  page numbers, **461–468**, **588**
    assigning automatically updated numbers, 463–466, *463*, *465*
    assigning sections to documents, 466–468, *467*
    in exported PDF files, 588
    Insert Page Number command in Layout menu, 683
    inserting section markers, 468
    overview of, 461–462
    setting preferences, 462, *462*

pages
  adding to documents, 447–448
  adding to island spreads, 448–449, *449*
  deleting, 453
  duplicating, 451–452, *452*
  moving, 446–447, *447*
  selecting, 444, *444*
Pages palette menu, 443
spreads
  applying master pages to, 457–459, *458*, *459*
  defined, **441**
  deleting, 453
  duplicating, 451–452, *452*
  keyboard shortcuts, 445
  moving, 446–447
  reorganizing, 453
  selecting, 444, *444*
  targeting, 444–445
palettes, **42–48**, **688–696**. *See also* menus; object libraries; Pages palette; Toolbox; work areas
  adding, subtracting, multiplying, and dividing values in, 148, 202
  Align palette, **432–435**, **693–694**
    alignment options, 434
    defined, **693–694**
    Distribute Objects options, 434–435
    Distribute Spacing options, 432, 435
    opening, 432
    paragraph alignment and, 433
  Attributes palette, **693**
  Character palette, **201–203**, **211–213**, **690**
    Character palette menu, 201, *201*
    defined, **201–203**, *201*, **690**
    identifying tracking and kerning settings, 211–212
    Language option, 396, 654
    manually setting kerning, 212–213
    manually setting tracking, 212
    No Break option, 403
    Old Style numerals option, 396
    scaling text, 424
    skewing text, 392, *392*, *393*
    small caps option, 394–395, *395*

strikethrough option, 397–398, *397*
subscript and superscript options, 393–394, *393*, *394*
switching between metric and optical kerning, 211
underline option, 397–398, *397*
Character Styles palette
  defined, **230**, *230*, **691**
  deleting styles, 256–257
  using, 231–232
Color palette
  applying colors, 87–88, *87*, 297, 320
  applying grayscales or shades, 86
  creating colors, 297, 309–311
  creating tint swatches, 312–313, *313*
  defined, **692–693**
  filling shapes with solid color, 85, *85*
  stroking lines and shape outlines, 91, *91*
  swatches and, 87
defined, **42**
displaying or hiding, 43
entering or changing numerical values, 46–47, *47*
Escape key, 172
Fill Color palette, 85–86, *86*
Gradient palette
  applying gradients, 89–90, *89*, 320–321
  creating gradient swatches, 298, 317–318
  defined, **693**
  navigating, 315–316, *315*
keyboard shortcuts
  on Macintosh computers, **783–784**
  in Windows, **771–772**
Layers palette, **334–342**, **689**
  creating layers, **339–340**
  defined, **689**
  displaying or hiding layers, 338–339, *338*
  layer display in, 335
  locking layers, 341, 342
  opening, 334, *334*
  selecting and targeting layers, 335–337, *336*, *337*, *338*

Links palette
  defined, **695**
  imported PDF files and, 25
listed, **688**
moving
  between monitors, 43
  palettes or palette groups, 45
Navigator palette, 420, 690
Object Library palette, **262–266**, **695–696**
  creating, 263, *264*
  defined, **262**, *262*, **695–696**
  deleting objects, 266, 274
  displaying or hiding, 268–270
  displaying object libraries, 266
  dragging objects to, 270
  moving between palette groups, 263, *265*
  opening New Library dialog box from, 268
  selecting object libraries, 262–263
  sorting object libraries, 263
  Swatch Library palette, **696**
palette groups
  moving, 45
  reorganizing or creating, 45–46, *45*
  resizing, 44
  separating palettes from, 46
palette menus
  Character palette menu, 201, *201*
  Color palette menu, 87–88, *87*
  defined, **43**
  Paragraph palette menu, 201, *202*
Paragraph palette, **201–203**, **213–218**, **691**
  alignment settings, 200, 214–216
  defined, **201–203**, *201*, **213**, *213*, **691**
  drop caps, 223–224
  entering values in, 214
  justification settings, 200, 214–216, 406–407
  optical margin alignment or hanging punctuation, 217–218, *217*
  Paragraph palette menu, 201, *202*
  paragraph rules, 224–226, *225*
  paragraph spacing, 223

setting hanging indents, 222
setting indents, 218, 221–222
Paragraph Styles palette
  defined, **230–231**, *231*, **691**
  deleting styles, 256–257
  using, 231–232
Reset buttons, 172
resizing, collapsing, or changing orientation of, 44
selecting a focus for options, 47–48
Story palette, **694**
Stroke Color palette, 85, *85*
Stroke palette, **84**, **90–97**, **692**
  applying arrowheads and other line end shapes, 96–97
  applying corner effects, 94, 685
  changing effect of stroking on frames, 92
  changing line end caps, 94–95
  changing line or shape outline thickness, 90–91, *91*
  creating dashed or dotted lines and shape outlines, 95–96
  defined, **84**, **90**, **692**
  Direct Selection tool and, 91
  displaying strokes on screen, 91
  join and miter effects for corners, 92–93
  lines or shape outlines, 91, *91*
  overprinting strokes, 563–565, *564*
  and scaling text, 424
  Stroke Color palette, 85, *85*
  text, 84
Swatch Library palette, **696**
Swatches palette, **85**, **86**, **87**, **240**, **297–309**, **692**
  adding colors from commercial color systems, 306–307
  adding colors from swatches libraries, 305–306
  applying color, 297, 320
  Black swatch, 300
  buttons, 299
  Color palette and swatches, 87
  color swatches, 298
  and creating character styles, 240
  creating gradient swatches, 298, 316–317, *316*, *317*
  creating swatches, 85, 297, 300–303, *301*, *302*

creating tint swatches, 313–314, *313*
  defined, **297**, *297*, **692**
  deleting swatches, 304–305, *305*
  duplicating swatches, 303–304
  editing swatches, 303, *304*
  gradient swatches, 298
  icons, 298
  importing colors from other files, 308–309, *308*
  New Color Swatch dialog box, 300–303, *301*, *302*
  "no color" swatch, 86, 296
  None swatch, 296, 298, 299, 675
  opening, 297
  out-of-gamut alert icon, 302
  Paper swatch, 299
  Registration swatch, 300
  selecting colors, 297, 320
  selecting swatches, 303
Tabs palette, 218–221, 694
Text Wrap palette, **155–158**, **695**
  Bounding Box option, 156, *157*
  Invert option, 158, *158*
  Jump Object option, 157, *157*
  Jump to Next Column option, 158, *158*
  No Wrap option, 156, *156*
  Object Shape option, 157, *157*
  overview of, 155–156, 695
Transform palette, **146–147**, **148**, **150**, **411–418**, **690**
  defined, **412**, **690**
  Dimensions Include Stroke Weight option, 415, 416–417
  Direct Selection tool and, 412
  duplicating and transforming objects, 430–432, *431*, *432*, *433*
  Flip Horizontal, Flip Vertical, and Flip Both options, 415
  Horizontal/Vertical Palette options, 416
  moving points of origin, 412, *412*, 417–418, *418*
  opening, 414
  positioning objects, 419
  Proxy for Origin option, 412, *412*, 417–418, *418*
  reflecting objects, 427–428

resizing graphics
proportionally, 146–147, 148, 150
Rotate 180, Rotate 90 CW, and Rotate 90 CCW tools, 415, 673
Rotate tool and, 414, 428–429, *429*
Rotation Angle option, 414, *414*
ruler guides and, 413
Scale Content option, 415, 426
Scale tool and, 414
Scale X Percentage option, 414
Scale Y Percentage option, 415
scaling objects, 425–426
Selection tool and, 411
Shear Angle option, 414
Shear tool and, 414
Text tool and, 411
Transformations Are Totals option, 414, 415–416
Width and Height options, 414
X (Horizontal) and Y (Vertical) position options, 413, *413*
units of measure in, 46–47, *47*
PANTONE color systems, **306–307**
Pantone plug-ins, 70
paper size settings
on Macintosh computers, 185–187, *186*, *187*
in Windows, 179–181, *180*
paper source settings
on Macintosh computers, 191
in Windows, 179, *180*, 181
Paper swatch, 299
paragraph formatting, **200–203, 213–226**. *See also* formatting; styles
drop caps
creating in Paragraph palette, **223–224**
paragraph styles for, 244, *245*
in exported HTML files, 612, 616–617
finding and replacing, 126–128, *127*, *128*
importing, 115
indents
defined, **218**
first line indents, 218
hanging indents, 222
indent options in Text Import Options dialog box, 118

in paragraph styles, 243–244, *244*
setting, 221–222
Keep Options, 247–248, *247*, 387–389, *387*, *388*, *389*
margin settings
changing, 21
gutter margins, 21
Gutter option in Text Frame Options dialog box, 105, *105*
InDesign Margins option in Export HTML: Layout dialog box, 627
margin guides, 18, *19*, 60, *61*
Margins and Columns command in Layout menu, 682
Margins and Columns dialog box, 60
in master pages, 469, *470*
optical margin alignment or hanging punctuation, 217–218, *217*
setting margin guides, 18, *19*, 21, 60–61, *61*
paragraph attributes
applying, 214
defined, **200**
Text tool and, 214
Paragraph palette, **201–203, 213–218**, 691
alignment settings, 200, 214–216
defined, **201–203**, *201*, 213, *213*, **691**
drop caps, 223–224
entering values in, 214
justification settings, 200, 214–216, 406–407
optical margin alignment or hanging punctuation, 217–218, *217*
Paragraph palette menu, 201, *202*
paragraph rules, 224–226, *225*
paragraph spacing, 223
setting hanging indents, 222
setting indents, 218, 221–222
paragraph rules
page numbers and, 466
in Paragraph palette, 224–226, *225*
in paragraph styles, 248, *248*

tab stops, **218–221, 245–246, 694**
defined, **218**
deleting, 21
editing, 220–221
leaders, 221
in paragraph styles, 245–246, *246*
setting, 218–220
tab alignment options, 219
Tabs palette, 218–221, 694
terms defined, **200**
text frame inset settings, 106, *107*, 226, *226*
widow and orphan controls, 247–248, *247*, 387–389, *387*, *388*, *389*
paragraph styles, **230–236, 241–257**. *See also* styles
applying, 249–251
assigning keyboard shortcuts to, 236, *236*
creating
with no text selected, 233, 241–243, *242*, *243*
from selected text or existing styles with changes, 233–236, *233*
from selected text without changing formatting, 232–233
defined, **230**, **232**
deleting
from documents, 256
from styles palettes, 256–257
duplicating, 253, *253*
editing, **251–252**, *251*
finding and replacing, 126–128, *127*, *128*
importing
from other applications, 115, 232, 254
from other documents, 232, 253–255, *254*
New Paragraph Style dialog box, **241–248**
assigning keyboard shortcuts to styles, 236, *236*
Drop Caps and Composer options, 244, *245*
Hyphenation options, 246–247, *246*
Indents and Spacing options, 243–244, *244*

Justification options, 244–245, *245*
Keep Options, 247–248, *247*
Next Style option, 243
Paragraph Rules options, 248, *248*
Tabs options, 245–246, *246*
Paragraph Styles palette
  defined, **230–231**, *231*
  deleting styles, 256–257
  using, 231–232
  parent versus child styles, 233–236
  removing or unapplying styles, 255–256
parent styles, 233–236
passwords
  importing password-protected PDF files, 24, 144, 603
  password options in Export PDF: Security dialog box, 603
Paste and Paste Into commands in Edit menu, 681
pasteboard
  defined, **38**
  Entire Pasteboard command in View menu, 669–671, *670*
paths, **7**, **75**, **138**, **140**, **477–526**. *See also* lines; shapes
  anchor points, **7**, **77–78**, **479–482**
    adding, 499–500, *500*
    Bezier curves and, 481–486
    converting, 502–505, *503*, *504*, *505*
    corner points and, **480**, *480*
    defined, **7**, **479–480**, *480*
    deleting, 500–501, *501*, *502*
    Direct Selection tool and, 77–78
    direction lines, direction points and, 481–486, *482*, *486*
    and editing paths, 496
    endpoints and, **480**, *480*
    moving, 497–498, *498*, *499*
    selecting, 496–497, *496*, *497*
    smooth points and, **481**, *481*
    Bezier curves theory and, 481–486, *481*, *486*
  clipping paths, **138**, **140**, **520–526**

Clipping Path dialog box options, 524–526, *525*, *526*, 685
  creating automatically, 524–526, *525*, *526*
  creating frames from, 138, 140, 520–521
  defined, **520**
  drawing manually, 521–524, *521*, *522*, *524*
  importing images with, 138, 140, 520–521
closed paths
  defined, **478**, *478*
  drawing, 489–490, *489*, *490*
  opening, 507, *508*
compound paths, **515–519**
  Compound Paths command in Object menu, 686
  creating, **516–517**, *517*
  defined, **515–516**, *516*
  editing, 517, *517*
  releasing or breaking up, 519
  reversing, 517–518, *518*, 686
  subpaths and, **516**
converting text to paths, **519–520**, *519*
corner points
  Bezier curves and, 484–485, *484*, *485*
  converting smooth points to corner points with independent direction lines, 504–505, *505*
  converting smooth points to corner points without direction lines, 504, *505*
  converting to corner points with independent direction lines, 503, *503*, *504*
  converting to smooth points, 503, *503*, *504*
  defined, **480**, *480*
  drawing curved segments connected by, 494–496
  defined, **7**, **75**, **477–481**, *478*, *479*, *480*, *481*
direction lines
  Bezier curves and, 481–486, *482*, *486*
  converting corner points to corner points with independent direction lines, 503, *503*, *504*

converting smooth points to corner points with independent direction lines, 504–505, *505*
  converting smooth points to corner points without direction lines, 504, *505*
  defined, **481–482**, *482*
direction points
  Bezier curves and, 481–486, *482*, *486*
  changing curved segment shapes by dragging, 510–511, *511*
  Convert Direction Point tool, 502–505, *503*, *504*, *505*
  defined, **481–482**, *482*
drawing, **486–496**
  closed shapes, 489–490, *489*, *490*
  curved segments, 488–490, *489*, *490*
  curved segments connected by corner points, 494–496
  curved segments followed by straight segments, 492–494
  overview of, 486–487
  straight segments, 487–488
  straight segments followed by curved segments, 490–492
editing, **496–515**
  anchor points and, 496
  changing curved segment shapes by dragging direction points, 510–511, *511*
  closing open paths, 506, *507*
  connecting multiple paths, 508–510, *509*, *510*
  continuing open paths, 506
  opening closed paths, 507, *508*
  selecting paths, 496–497, *496*, *497*
  splitting graphics frames and contents, 515
  splitting paths and frames with Scissors tool, 512–515, *513*, *514*
editing text shapes, **519–520**, *519*
endpoints, **480**, *480*
open paths
  closing, 506, *507*
  continuing, 506

defined, **478–479**, *478*, *479*
filling, 479, *479*
Reverse Path command in Object menu, 686
segments
  changing curved segment shapes by dragging direction points, 510–511, *511*
  defined, **479**, *480*
  drawing curved segments, 488–490, *489*, *490*
  drawing curved segments connected by corner points, 494–496
  drawing curved segments followed by straight segments, 492–494
  drawing straight segments, 487–488
  drawing straight segments followed by curved segments, 490–492
selecting, 496–497, *496*, *497*
smooth points
  Bezier curves and, 483–484, *483*
  converting corner points to, 503, *503*, *504*
  converting to corner points with independent direction lines, 504–505, *505*
  converting to corner points without direction lines, 504, *505*
  defined, **481**, *481*
subpaths, **516**
vector graphics and, 11
PCX files, **13**
PDF files, **13**, **585–604**
  defined, **13**
  digital masters and, 586
  Export PDF: Compression dialog box, **595–600**
    CCITT option, 598
    Compress Text and Line Art option, 598
    Downsample To option, 596
    JPEG option, 598
    No Sample Change option, 597
    overview of, 595, *595*
    recommended compression settings, 598–600, *599*
    resampling options, 596–597
    Run Length compression option, 598
    setting image compression, 597–598
    Subsample To option, 596–597
    Zip compression option, 598
  Export PDF: Pages and Page Marks dialog box, **600–602**, *601*
  Export PDF: PDF Options dialog box, **592–595**
    Color option, 593
    Crop Image Data to Frames option, 594
    Generate Thumbnails option, 594
    Images option, 594
    Include ICC Profiles option, 593
    Omit option, 594
    Optimize PDF option, 594–595
    overview of, *591*, 592
    Subset Fonts Below option, 592
    View PDF After Exporting option, 595
  Export PDF: Security dialog box, **602–604**
    Adding or Changing Notes and Form Fields option, 604
    Changing the Document option, 604
    Copying Text and Graphics option, 604
    Do Not Allow options, 603
    overview of, 602, *602*
    password options, 603
    Printing option, 603
  exporting
    overview of, 26, 29, 585–586, **589–592**, *590*, *591*, *592*
    as Prepress files, 26, 28, 578–581, *579*, *580*, *581*
  importing, **23–25**
    editing imported PDF files, 25
    editing linked PDF files, 145
    password-protected files, 24, 144
  InDesign versus Adobe Acrobat, 585–586
  InDesign and, 9
  placing as graphics, 142–145, *143*
  preparing for export, **586–589**
    for high-resolution composite PDF files, 586–588
    for Web or CD-ROM applications, 588–589
  printing color separations of PDF files, 592
Pen tool, **486–496**, **672**. *See also* paths
  adding anchor points, 499–500, *500*
  closing open paths, 506, *507*
  connecting multiple paths, 508–510, *509*, *510*
  continuing open paths, 506
  defined, **672**
  deleting anchor points, 500–501, *501*
  drawing clipping paths manually, 521–524, *521*, *522*, *524*
  drawing closed shapes, 489–490, *489*, *490*
  drawing curved segments, 488–490, *489*, *490*
  drawing curved segments connected by corner points, 494–496
  drawing curved segments followed by straight segments, 492–494
  drawing straight segments, 487–488
  drawing straight segments followed by curved segments, 490–492
  editing compound paths, 517, *517*
  overview of, 486–487
Perceptual (Images) option in Image Import Options dialog box, 138
Perform OPI Replacement option in Export EPS dialog box, 33
phosphors, **701**, 720
photographs, 139
Photoshop
  Application Color Settings dialog box and, 707
  compatibility with InDesign, 8–9, 699
  dragging-and-dropping graphics into InDesign, 9
  Macintosh ColorSync plug-in, 704

Photoshop graphics in exported
  PDF files, 588
PSD files, **12**
PICT files, **12**
pictures. *See* bitmap graphics;
  graphics; vector graphics
placeholders. *See also* frames; shapes
  defined, **7**, **76**
  drawing, 84
  identifying, 77
placing. *See also* importing
  graphics
    graphics files as inline
      graphics, 159
    into shapes, 136
    overview of, 136–140, *137*
    PDF files as graphics, 142–145,
      143
    library objects into documents,
      275–276
    Place command in File menu,
      112–114, *113*, 136–140, *137*,
      678
    text, **102**, **112–114**, *113*
      and creating text frames, 76,
        104
      HTML files, 117–118
      importing character and
        paragraph styles, 115
      importing formatting, 115
Platform option in Text Import
  Options dialog box, 118
.PLN files, 67
plug-ins, **7**, **23**, **66–71**, 586
  A Lowly Apprentice Production
    (ALAP) plug-ins, 67–68
  Adobe Acrobat plug-ins, 586
  defined, **7**, **66–67**
  Em Software plug-ins, 68
  Enfocus Software plug-ins, 68
  Extensis plug-ins, 68
  filename extensions of, 67
  HexMac Software Systems plug-
    ins, 69
  identifying plug-in developers,
    67
  import plug-ins, 23, 115
  installing, 67
  Lizardtech plug-ins, 69
  Macintosh ColorSync plug-in,
    704
  Managing Editor plug-ins, 69
  Mapsoft Computer Services plug-
    ins, 70

Pantone plug-ins, 70
PowrTools Software plug-ins, 70
ShadeTree Marketing plug-ins,
  70–71
Ultimate Technographics plug-
  ins, 71
updates on Adobe Web page, 67
Virginia Systems Software
  Services plug-ins, 71
PNG (Portable Network Graphics)
  files
  defined, **13**
  importing, 139–140
points of origin, 412, *412*, 417–418,
  418
polygon shapes and frames, 79–82,
  672–673
Portable Document Format. *See* PDF
  files
portrait orientation
  for documents, 21
  Macintosh printing options, 187
  Windows printing options, 179,
    180, 181
positioning objects, **419–420**. *See
  also* dragging-and-dropping;
  moving
  with arrow keys, 420
  with drag-and-drop, 419
  moving or copying to other
    layers or pages, 419
  Navigator palette and, 420, 690
  Positioning option in Export
    HTML: Layout dialog box, 627
  with Selection tool, 419
  with Transform palette, 419
PostScript files. *See also* EPS
  (Encapsulated PostScript) files
  PostScript Driver installation,
    654–655
  PostScript option in Export EPS
    dialog box, 31
  printing to, **191–193**
    on Macintosh computers,
      191–193, *193*
    in Windows, 191–192
  printing to non-PostScript
    printers, 177, 184
PowrTools Software plug-ins, 70
Preferences dialog box, **655–662**,
  679
  Adobe Online Preferences dialog
    box, 662, *662*, *663*
  Composition options, 658, *658*

Dictionary options, 661, *661*
General options, 656, *657*
Grids options, 58, 659, *660*
Guides options, 660, *660*
navigating, 655–656
opening, 655, 679
restoring default settings, 656
Text options, 657, *657*
Units & Increments options,
  658–659, *659*
Preflight dialog box, **178**, **565–575**
  checking for duplicate spot
    colors, 572–573, *573*
  Colors and Inks options,
    572–573, *573*
  correcting missing fonts
    problems, 570
  Document Color Settings dialog
    box and, 565, *565*
  and exporting PDF files, 587
  Fonts options, 568–570, *569*
  Links and Images options,
    570–572, *571*, *572*
  and packaging files for service
    bureaus, 575
  Print Settings options, 573, *573*
  printing Preflight reports,
    573–574, *574*
  Specifications for Web Offset
    Publications (SWOP) and,
    565–566
  Summary options, 566–567, *567*,
    568
preparing
  documents for HTML export,
    611–618
    animations, 613
    character and paragraph
      attributes retained and lost in
      exported HTML files, 612,
      616–617
    color testing documents for
      print and Web distribution,
      615
    converting from print to Web
      colors, 612–615, *614*, *615*,
      616
    converting text files to GIF
      files, 618
    fonts, 611–612
    graphics, 612–613
    grouped objects, 613
    naming HTML files, 616

824 PREPRESS FILES • PRINTING

setting document dimensions and layout, 611
text, 612
for monitor calibration, 716–717
PDF files for export, **586–589**
  for high-resolution composite PDF files, 586–588
  for Web or CD-ROM applications, 588–589
Prepress files, exporting to, 26, 28, 578–581, *579, 580, 581*
preserving layers
  when copying or moving objects, 349–352, *350, 351, 352*
  when placing library objects, 275–276
preventing
  hyphenation, 403–404
  printing of exported PDF files, 603
Previous Page command in Layout menu, 683
Print dialog box, **532–565**
  Color options, **544–555**
    All to Process option, 551
    color separations and, 544
    Composite options, 548, *548, 549*
    creating film negatives or positives on Macintosh computers, 552–553, *553, 555, 555*
    creating film negatives or positives in Windows 98, 552–554, *553*
    creating film negatives or positives in Windows NT, 552–553, *553,* 554–555, *554*
    emulsion settings, 552
    gradients and, 552
    In-RIP option, 549
    selecting composites versus color separations, 544–548, *545, 546, 547*
    Separations options, 550–551, *550*
  Graphics options, **538–543**
    Font Downloading options, 541–542
    gradient options, 543
    overview of, 538–541, *539*
    on Macintosh computers background printing, 531
    printing thumbnails, 538

overview of, 177, 529–530, *530*
Page Marks options, **557–560**
  Crop Marks option, 535
  defined, **557**, *557, 558*
  Page Marks options in Print dialog box, **557**, *557, 558*
  ScenicSoft Preps trapping software and, 557
  selecting options, 558–559
  selecting page size for page mark specifications, 559–560, *560*
Scale and Fit options, **532–535**
  Overlap option, 535
  scaling documents to fit paper sizes, 532–533
  tiling options, 533–535, *534, 535*
thumbnails, **535–538**
  Generate Thumbnails option in Export PDF: PDF Options dialog box, 594
  on Macintosh computers, 537, 538
  overview of, 535–536
  in Windows 98, 536
  in Windows NT, 537
Trapping options, **561–565**
  defined, **561–563**, *561, 562*
  In-RIP Trapping option, 549, 561
  overprinting strokes, fills, or text, 563–565, *564*
  ScenicSoft Preps software, 557, 561
  ScenicSoft TrapWise software, 561
  wet ink trapping, 561–563
printers
  calibrating and profiling, **723–725**
    creating or customizing printer profiles, 723–725, *724*
    preparing to calibrate, 723
    Web sites about profiling devices, 725
  downloading CRDs (Color Rendering Dictionaries) to, 710
  downloading fonts to, 541–542
  printer-resident fonts, 541
  proofing desktop inkjet printers, 541
  RIPs (Raster Image Processors), 541–542, 549, 561

selecting on Macintosh computers, 184–185, *185*
selecting in Windows, 178
virtual printer feature, **191–193**
  on Macintosh computers, 191–193, *193*
  in Windows, 191–192
printer's marks. *See* page marks
printing, **50**, **154**, **177–193**, **529–581**
  4-color process printing, 295
  color separations, **544–556**
    versus composites, 544–548, *545, 546, 547*
    creating film negatives or positives on Macintosh computers, 552–553, *553, 555, 555*
    creating film negatives or positives in Windows 98, 552–554, *553*
    creating film negatives or positives in Windows NT, 552–553, *553,* 554–555, *554*
    DCS (Desktop Color Separation) files, **12**, 540, 588
    emulsion settings, 552
    information about electronic prepress and printing, 556
    In-RIP option, 549
    OPI/DCS Image Replacement option in Print dialog box, 540
    overview of, 544
    of PDF files, 592
    printing gradients, 552
    selecting Color Separation options, 550–551, *550*
    Separations option in Application Color Settings dialog box, 709
    setting Composite options, 548, *548, 549*
    Simulate Separation Printer on Composite Printer option in Application Color Settings dialog box, 710
    Simulate Separation Printer on Monitor option in Application Color Settings dialog box, 709
  exporting to Prepress files, **26**, **28**, **578–581**, *579, 580, 581*

Font Download options, 541–543
graphics
    gradient options, 543, 552
    Graphics options in Print dialog box, 538–541, *539*
from Macintosh computers, 177, **184–193**
    background printing, 531
    document dimensions and, 588
    to non-PostScript printers, 177, 184
    opening Print dialog box, 188, 529–530, *530*
    to PostScript files, 191–193, *193*
    printing on both sides of paper, 191
    printing two-page spreads (double-truck printing), 188
    saving print options, 191
    scaling documents for printing, 188
    selecting number of copies and collation options, 189
    selecting number of pages to print, 189–191, *190*
    selecting orientation, 187
    selecting paper size, 185–187, *186*, *187*
    selecting paper source, 191
    selecting printers, 184–185, *185*
    thumbnails, 537, 538
    undocumented features, 529
an object on top of another, 154
packaging files for service bureaus, **575–578**, **679**
    creating instructions, 575, *576*
    creating packages, 576–578, *577*, *578*
    defined, **575**
    Package command in File menu, 679
    Preflight dialog box and, 575
page marks, **557–560**
    Crop Marks option, 535
    defined, **557**, *557*, *558*
    Export PDF: Pages and Page Marks dialog box, 600–602, *601*
    Page Marks options in Print dialog box, **557**, *557*, *558*

ScenicSoft Preps trapping software and, 557
    selecting options, 558–559
    selecting page size for page mark specifications, 559–560, *560*
to PostScript files, **191–193**
    on Macintosh computers, 191–193, *193*
    in Windows, 191–192
Preflight dialog box, **178**, **565–575**
    checking for duplicate spot colors, 572–573, *573*
    Colors and Inks options, 572–573, *573*
    correcting missing fonts problems, 570
    Document Color Settings dialog box and, 565, *565*
    and exporting PDF files, 587
    Fonts options, 568–570, *569*
    Links and Images options, 570–572, *571*, *572*
    and packaging files for service bureaus, 575
    Print Settings options, 573, *573*
    printing Preflight reports, 573–574, *574*
    Specifications for Web Offset Publications (SWOP) and, 565–566
    Summary options, 566–567, *567*, *568*
preventing printing of exported PDF files, 603
scaling documents to fit paper size, 532–533
shortcut sets, 50, *51*
thumbnails, **535–538**
    Generate Thumbnails option in Export PDF: PDF Options dialog box, 594
    on Macintosh computers, 537, 538
    overview of, 535–536
    in Windows 98, 536
    in Windows NT, 537
tiling options, 533–535, *534*, *535*
trapping color, **561–565**
    defined, **561–563**, *561*, *562*
    and exporting PDF files, 587
    In-RIP Trapping option, 549, 561

overprinting strokes, fills, or text, 563–565, *564*
ScenicSoft Preps software, 557, 561
ScenicSoft TrapWise software, 561
wet ink trapping, 561–563
from Windows, **177–184**, **191–192**
    to imagesetters, 181
    to non-PostScript printers, 177
    opening Print dialog box, 178, *179*, 529–530, *530*
    to PostScript files, 191–192
    printing on both sides of paper, 181–182, *183*
    printing two-page spreads (double-truck printing), 183, *184*
    saving print options, 184
    selecting number of copies and collation options, 181
    selecting orientation, 179, *180*, 181
    selecting pages to print, 181–182, *183*
    selecting paper size, 179–181, *180*
    selecting paper source, 179, *180*, 181
    selecting printers, 178
    thumbnails in Windows 98, 536
    thumbnails in Windows NT, 537
process colors, **291**, **295**
profiles
    creating or customizing printer profiles, 723–725, *724*
    ICC Device Profiles
        adding, 702–705, *703*
        in Application Color Settings dialog box, 708–709, *708*, *709*
        defined, **701**
        Include ICC Profiles option in Export PDF: PDF Options dialog box, 593
        overriding embedded profiles, 712
        saving monitor profiles, 722, *722*, *723*
        selecting source profiles, 565, *565*, 711–713, *713*

Profile option in Image Import Options dialog box, 138
projecting cap for lines, 94
proofing
    Proof Print option in Print dialog box, 540–541
    proofing desktop inkjet printers, 541
properties in Visual Basic, **731**
Proxy Image Resolution option in Image Import Options dialog box, 137–138
Proxy for Origin option in Transform palette, 412, *412*, 417–418, *418*
proxy points, **412**
PSD files, **12**

Q

QuarkXPress
    importing QuarkXPress files, 23
    keyboard shortcuts in InDesign, 6, 49, 52
question mark (?) in searches, 124–125
Quit command in File menu (Macintosh), 680

R

radial gradients, **88**, *88*
raising text on baselines, 389–391, *389*, *390*, *391*
Ranges option in Export EPS dialog box, 34
Raster Image Processors (RIPs), 541–542, 549, 561
raster images. *See* bitmap graphics
Read Embedded OPI Image Links option in Image Import Options dialog box, 140
ReadMe files, 649, 652
recommended compression settings for exported PDF files, 598–600, *599*
recovery, **169–173**
    Automatic Recovery feature, 170, 172–173
    Escape key in palettes and dialog boxes, 172
    Reset buttons in palettes and dialog boxes, 172
    Revert command, 172

Save a Copy command, 28, 171–172, *171*, 678
Undo command, 169–170
rectangular shapes and frames, 78–79, 672–673
Redo command, 169–170, 681
reflecting objects, **427–428**, *427*
registering InDesign software, 655
Registration Marks option in Print dialog box, 558
Registration swatch, 300
Relative Colorimetric option in Image Import Options dialog box, 139
releasing compound paths, 519
Remove a Page option in Export HTML: Document dialog box, 620
removing. *See* deleting
Rendering Intent options
    defined, **701–702**
    in Document Color Settings dialog box, 701–702, 714, *714*
    in Image Import Options dialog box, 138–139
reorganizing
    palette groups, 45–46, *45*
    spreads, 453–454
replacing. *See* finding and replacing
reports
    instruction reports for package files for service bureaus, 577
    Preflight reports, 573–574, *574*
resampling options in Export PDF: Compression dialog box, 596–597
Reset buttons in palettes and dialog boxes, 172
resizing
    bitmap graphics, 11
    frame and contents simultaneously, 151
    graphic frame contents without distorting, 146–147, *146*, 148
    graphic frames, 148
    inline graphics, 162
    palette groups, 44
    palettes, 44
    vector graphics, 11
resolution
    bitmap graphics and, 11
    Full Resolution Images option, 138
    of graphics, 137–138

Proxy Image Resolution option in Image Import Options dialog box, 137–138
Use High Resolution Image option in Clipping Path dialog box, 525
vector graphics and, 11
restoring default settings in Preferences dialog box, 656
reversing compound paths, 517–518, *518*, 686
Revert command in File menu, 172, 678
RGB color
    RGB color gamut, **292–293**, *292*
    RGB color model, **290–291**, *290*, **293**, **294**, **587**, **626–627**
    sRGB color mode, 612–613
right-click menus. *See* context menus
RIPs (Raster Image Processors), 541–542, 549, 561
Rochester Institute of Technology (RIT) T&E Center, 556
Roman type style, 200
Rotate tool
    defined, **673**
    duplicating and transforming objects, 430–432, *431*, *432*, *433*
    points of origin and, 417
    rotating and distorting objects, **428–429**, *429*
    Transform palette and, 414, 428–429, *429*
Rotate tools in Transform palette, 415, 673
Rotation Angle option in Transform palette, 414, *414*
round cap for lines, 94
rounded join effect for corners, 93
.RPLN files, 67
RTF Import Options dialog boxes, 115, 116–117, *116*
ruler guides. *See also* guides
    Allow Ruler Guides to Move option in Layout Adjustment dialog box, 471
    Ignore Ruler Guide Adjustments option in Layout Adjustment dialog box, 472
    Ruler Guides command in Layout menu, 683
    Ruler Guides dialog box, 62
    setting, 57, 62

Transform palette and, 413
rulers, **57–58**, **64–66**. *See also* grids; guides; work areas
  overview of, 57–58
  setting units of measure, color, and threshold preferences, 64–65, *65*
  zero point reference
    defined, **65**, *65*
    locking or unlocking, 66
    moving, 66, *66*
rules in paragraphs
  page numbers and, 466
  in Paragraph palette, 224–226, *225*
  in paragraph styles, 248, *248*
Run Length compression option in Export PDF: Compression dialog box, 598

S

Saturation (Graphics) option in Image Import Options dialog box, 139
saving
  files, **25–28**
    all open files, 25
    Prepress files, 26, 28, 578–581, *579*, *580*, *581*
    with Save As dialog box, 25–28, *26*, *27*, 678
    with Save command, 25, 677
    with Save a Copy command, 28, 171–172, *171*, 678
    as template or stationery files, 25–26
  monitor profiles, 722, *722*, *723*
  print options
    on Macintosh computers, 191
    in Windows, 184
Scale Content option in Transform palette, 415, 426
Scale and Fit options in Print dialog box, **532–535**
  Overlap option, 535
  scaling documents to fit paper sizes, 532–533
  tiling options, 533–535, *534*, *535*
Scale tool
  defined, **673**
  duplicating and transforming objects, 430
  points of origin and, 417

scaling objects, 424–425, *426*
Transform palette and, 414
Scale X Percentage option in Transform palette, 414
Scale Y Percentage option in Transform palette, 415
scaling
  documents
    to fit paper size, 532–533
    for printing on Macintosh computers, 188
  glyph scaling
    defined, **398**
    Glyph Scaling option in Justification dialog box, 405
  objects, **423–426**
    with drag-and-drop, 424–425, *425*
    overview of, 423–424
    with Scale tool, 424–425, *426*
    with Selection tool, 424, *425*
    text and text frames, 424
    with Transform palette, 425–426
  type, 382–383, *382*
ScenicSoft Preps software, 557, 561
ScenicSoft TrapWise software, 561
Scissors tool
  defined, **673–674**
  opening closed paths, 507, *508*
  splitting paths and frames, 512–515, *513*, *514*
scripts. *See also* AppleScript; Visual Basic
  Java and JavaScript, 609–610
scroll bars, 40
SCT (Scitex CT) files, **13**
sections in documents, 466–468, *467*
security
  Export PDF: Security dialog box, **602–604**
    Adding or Changing Notes and Form Fields option, 604
    Changing the Document option, 604
    Copying Text and Graphics option, 604
    Do Not Allow options, 603
    overview of, 602, *602*
    password options, 603
    Printing option, 603
  importing password-protected PDF files, 24, 144

segments. *See also* paths
  changing curved segment shapes by dragging direction points, 510–511, *511*
  defined, **479**, *480*
  drawing curved segments, 488–490, *489*, *490*
  drawing curved segments connected by corner points, 494–496
  drawing curved segments followed by straight segments, 492–494
  drawing straight segments, 487–488
  drawing straight segments followed by curved segments, 490–492
selecting. *See also* Direct Selection tool; Selection tool
  active shortcut set, 50
  anchor points, 496–497, *496*, *497*
  Application Color Settings dialog box options, 706–707
  Color Separation options, 550–551, *550*
  colors for filling shapes, 87–88, *87*
  colors in Swatches palette, 297
  Document Color Settings dialog box options, 706–707
  export options, 619–621, *619*, *620*, *621*
  a focus for palette options, 47–48
  font size, 203, 207, 684
  fonts, 204, *204*
  graphic frames and contents, 147–148
  inline graphics, 160
  layers, 335–337, *336*, *337*, *338*
  Macintosh printing options
    number of copies and collation options, 189
    number of pages to print, 189–191, *190*
    orientation, 187
    paper size, 185–187, *186*, *187*
    paper source, 191
    printers, 184–185, *185*
  object libraries, 262–263
  page marks options, 558–559
  page size for page mark specifications, 559–560, *560*

pages, 444, *444*
paths, 496–497, *496*, *497*
phosphor types, 701, 720
Select All command in Edit
 menu, 681
source profiles, 565, *565*,
 711–713, *713*
spreads, 444, *444*
swatches, 303
text, 120, 121–122
 Macintosh keyboard shortcuts,
 782–783
 Windows keyboard shortcuts,
 769–771
tools, 41
Windows printing options
 number of copies and collation
 options, 181
 orientation, 179, *180*, 181
 pages to print, 181–182, *183*
 paper size, 179–181, *180*
 paper source, 179, *180*, 181
 printers, 178
Selection option
 in Check Spelling dialog box,
 129
 in Find/Change dialog box, 124
Selection tool
 defined, **671–672**
 dragging-and-dropping graphics,
 142
 and drawing circular and
 elliptical shapes and frames,
 77–78
 and drawing polygonal shapes
 and frames, 81–82
 and drawing square and
 rectangular shapes and frames,
 79
 and drawing straight lines, 83
 duplicating and transforming
 objects, 430
 graphic frames and, 147
 positioning objects, 419
 reflecting objects, 427, *427*
 scaling objects, 424, *425*
 Transform palette and, 411
Send Image Data option in Print
 dialog box, 540
separating palettes from palette
 groups, 46
separations, **544–556**
 versus composites, 544–548, *545*,
 546, *547*

creating film negatives or
 positives on Macintosh
 computers, 552–553, *553*, 555,
 555
creating film negatives or
 positives in Windows 98,
 552–554, *553*
creating film negatives or
 positives in Windows NT,
 552–553, *553*, 554–555, *554*
DCS (Desktop Color Separation)
 files, **12**, 540, 588
emulsion settings, 552
information about electronic
 prepress and printing, 556
In-RIP option, 549
OPI/DCS Image Replacement
 option in Print dialog box, 540
overview of, 544
of PDF files, 592
printing gradients, 552
selecting Color Separation
 options, 550–551, *550*
Separations option in
 Application Color Settings
 dialog box, 709
setting Composite options, 548,
 548, *549*
Simulate Separation Printer on
 Composite Printer option in
 Application Color Settings
 dialog box, 710
Simulate Separation Printer on
 Monitor option in Application
 Color Settings dialog box, 709
service bureaus. *See* packaging files
 for service bureaus
Set Dictionary To option in Text
 Import Options dialog box, 118
setting
 baseline grid options, 383–386,
 383, *384*, *385*, *386*
 columns of text, 377–382, *378*,
 381
 Composite options, 548, *548*,
 549
 guides
 evenly spaced guides, 62–63,
 63
 margin and column guides, 18,
 19, 60–61, *61*
 ruler guides, 57, 62

image compression in Export
 PDF: Compression dialog box,
 597–598
indents, 221–222
 hanging indents, 222
kerning manually, 212–213
leading manually, 208, 209–210
margins in new documents, 21
page number preferences, 462,
 462
page size for new documents,
 20–21, *20*
ruler units of measure, color, and
 threshold preferences, 64–65,
 65
tab stops, 218–220
setting up baseline or document
 grids, 58–60, *59*
Seybold Seminars, 725
shades. *See* tints
ShadeTree Marketing plug-ins,
 70–71
shapes, **7**, **75–97**. *See also* frames;
 paths
 closed shapes, **478**, *478*
 defined, **7**, **76**
 drawing, **77–85**
 arrowheads and other line end
 shapes, 96–97
 circles and ellipses, 77–78,
 672–673
 color settings for, 84–85
 dashed or dotted lines and
 shape outlines, 95–96
 placeholders, 84
 polygons, 79–82, 672–673
 squares and rectangles, 78–79,
 672–673
 Star Inset and Number of Sides
 options for polygons, 79–81
 straight lines, 83
 filling, **84–90**
 Fill Color palette, 85–86, *86*
 Fill/Stroke Color Indicator,
 674–675
 with gradients, 88–90, *88*, *89*
 with grayscale or color shades,
 86
 open shapes, 479, *479*
 overprinting fills, 563–565, *564*
 overview of, 84–85
 selecting colors, 87–88, *87*
 with solid colors, 85–86, *85*, *86*
 text, 84

versus frames, **76**
identifying, 77
lines
  applying arrowheads and other end shapes, 96–97
  changing end caps, 94–95
  changing line or shape outline thickness, 90–91, *91*
  Compress Text and Line Art option in Export PDF: Compression dialog box, 598
  creating dashed or dotted lines and shape outlines, 95–96
  drawing straight lines, **83**
  Line tool, 83, 672–673
  start point of, 97
  stroking, 91, *91*
paragraph rules
  page numbers and, 466
  in Paragraph palette, 224–226, *225*
  in paragraph styles, 248, *248*
placeholders
  defined, **7**, **76**
  drawing, 84
  identifying, 77
points and origin and, 417–418, *418*
stroking, **84**, **90–97**
  applying arrowheads and other line end shapes, 96–97
  applying corner effects, 94, 685
  changing effect of stroking on frames, 92
  changing line end caps, 94–95
  changing thickness of lines or shape outlines, 90–91, *91*
  creating dashed or dotted lines and shape outlines, 95–96
  defined, **84**, **90**
  Dimensions Include Stroke Weight option in Transform palette, 415, 416–417
  Direct Selection tool and, 91
  displaying strokes on screen, 91
  join and miter effects for corners, 92–93
  lines or shape outlines, 91, *91*
  overprinting strokes, 563–565, *564*
  Stroke Color palette, 85, *85*

Stroke palette and scaling text, 424
  text, 84
sharing shortcut sets, 49
Shear Angle option in Transform palette, 414
Shear tool
  defined, **673**
  duplicating and transforming objects, 430
  points of origin and, 417
  rotating and distorting objects, **428–429**, *429*
  Transform palette and, 414
Shift key
  drawing circles with, 78
  drawing lines with, 83
shortcut keys. *See* keyboard shortcuts
shortcut menus. *See* context menus
Show Guides option in Layer Options dialog box, 341
Show Hidden Characters command in Type menu, 684
Show Layer option in Layer Options dialog box, 341
Simulate Separation Printer on Composite Printer option in Application Color Settings dialog box, 710
Simulate Separation Printer on Monitor option in Application Color Settings dialog box, 709
Single-Line Composer. *See* Composer
size
  of bitmap graphics, 11
  of imported OPI (Open Prepress Interface) images, 25
  of vector graphics, 11
Size command in Type menu, 684
sizing
  bitmap graphics, 11
  frame and contents simultaneously, 151
  graphic frame contents without distorting, 146–147, *146*, 148
  graphic frames, 148
  inline graphics, 162
  palette groups, 44
  palettes, 44
  vector graphics, 11
skewing text, 392, *392*, 393

small caps type style, 203, 206, *206*, 394–395, *395*
smooth points. *See also* paths
  Bezier curves and, 483–484, *483*
  converting corner points to, 503, *503*, *504*
  converting to corner points with independent direction lines, 504–505, *505*
  converting to corner points without direction lines, 504, *505*
  defined, **481**, *481*
snapping
  Snap to Guides option, 58, 60, 64
  Snap Zone option in Layout Adjustment dialog box, 471
  text to baseline grid, 58, 386
solid color fills for shapes, 85–86, *85*, *86*
sorting object libraries, 263
source profiles, 565, *565*, 711–713, *713*
spaces
  flush spaces, 406–407
  in imported text, 118
  non-breaking spaces, 405
spacing
  Distribute Spacing options in Align palette, 432, 435
  finding white space, 125
  Inset Spacing options in Text Frame Options dialog box, 106, *107*, 226, *226*
  paragraph spacing, 223
  paragraph spacing in paragraph styles, 243–244, *244*
special characters, **108–111**. *See also* character formatting; text
  defined, **108**
  entering with context menus, 110–111, *110*
  entering with Insert Character dialog box, 108–109, *109*
  entering with keyboard shortcuts, 109–110
  finding and replacing, 125–126
  flush spaces, 406–407
  metacharacters, 125–126
Specifications for Web Offset Publications (SWOP), 565–566

spell checking, **128–131**, **682**
    checking spelling, 128–130, *129*
    customizing dictionaries, 130–131, *130*, 661, *661*, 682
    language setting, 654
splitting paths and frames with Scissors tool, 512–515, *513*, *514*
spot color
    checking for duplicate spot colors, 572–573, *573*
    defined, **295–296**
spread guides, **62**
spreads. *See also* Pages palette
    applying master pages to, 457–459, *458*, *459*
    defined, **441**
    deleting, 453
    duplicating, 451–452, *452*
    Fit Spread in Window command in View menu, 668, *669*
    island spreads
        adding pages to, 448–449, *449*
        clearing, 446
        creating, **445–446**
        creating 4-page gatefold book inserts, 450–451
        defined, **445**
        deleting pages from, 453
        keyboard shortcuts, 445
        moving, 446–447
        reorganizing, 453
        selecting, 444, *444*
        targeting, 444–445
square shapes and frames, 78–79
sRGB color mode, 612–613
stacking order of layers, changing, 354
Star Inset option for polygon shapes and frames, 79–81
start point of lines, 97
start tags in HTML files, 608–609
starting InDesign, **655**
    with Acrobat Reader, 586
stationery files
    defined, **25**
    saving files as, 25–26
Step and Repeat dialog box, 421–423, *422*, *423*, 681
Story option
    in Check Spelling dialog box, 129
    in Find/Change dialog box, 124
Story palette, **694**

strikethrough type style, 203, 206, *206*, 397–398, *397*
string variables in AppleScript, 749
stroking, **84**, **90–97**
    applying arrowheads and other line end shapes, 96–97
    applying corner effects, 94, 685
    changing effect of stroking on frames, 92
    changing line end caps, 94–95
    changing thickness of lines or shape outlines, 90–91, *91*
    creating dashed or dotted lines and shape outlines, 95–96
    defined, **84**, **90**
    Dimensions Include Stroke Weight option in Transform palette, 415, 416–417
    Direct Selection tool and, 91
    displaying strokes on screen, 91
    Fill/Stroke Color Indicator, 674–675
    graphic frames, 152
    join and miter effects for corners, 92–93
    lines or shape outlines, 91, *91*
    overprinting strokes, 563–565, *564*
    Stroke Color palette, 85, *85*
    Stroke palette and scaling text, 424
    text, 84
styles, **115**, **126–128**, **229–257**. *See also* formatting
    applying, **249–251**
        changing formatting after applying styles, 231
        character styles, 249
        paragraph formatting without character formatting, 251
        paragraph styles, 249–251
        removing or unapplying styles, 255–256
    assigning keyboard shortcuts to, 236, *236*
    Cascading Style Sheets (CSS-1) in HTML files, 609, 616
    character styles
        applying, 249
        assigning keyboard shortcuts to, 236, *236*
        defined, **230**, **232**
        deleting from documents, 256

        deleting from styles palette, 256–257
        duplicating, 253, *253*
        editing, **251–252**, *251*
        finding and replacing, 126–128, *127*, *128*
        importing from other applications, 115, 232, 254
        importing from other documents, 115, 232, 253–255, *254*
        parent versus child styles, 233–236
        removing or unapplying, 255–256
    Character Styles palette
        defined, **230**, *230*, **691**
        deleting styles, 256–257
        using, 231–232
    creating, **232–248**
        with Character Styles palette, 237–241, *237*
        with no text selected, 233
        with Paragraph Styles palette, 241–248, *242*
        from selected text or existing styles with changes, 233–236, *233*
        from selected text without changing formatting, 232–233
    defined, **229–230**
    deleting
        from documents, 256
        removing or unapplying styles, 255–256
        from styles palettes, 256–257
    duplicating, 253, *253*
    editing, **251–252**, *251*
    finding and replacing, 126–128, *127*, *128*
    importing
        from other applications, 115, 232, 254
        from other documents, 232, 253–255, *254*
    New Character Style dialog box, **232–241**
        Advanced Character Formats option, 239, *239*
        assigning keyboard shortcuts to styles, 236, *236*
        Basic Character Formats options, 238–239, *238*

color settings, 240–241, *240*, *241*
New Paragraph Style dialog box, **241–248**
   assigning keyboard shortcuts to styles, 236, *236*
   Drop Caps and Composer options, 244, *245*
   Hyphenation options, 246–247, *246*
   Indents and Spacing options, 243–244, *244*
   Justification options, 244–245, *245*
   Keep Options, 247–248, *247*
   Next Style option, 243
   Paragraph Rules options, 248, *248*
   Tabs options, 245–246, *246*
paragraph styles
   applying, 249–251
   assigning keyboard shortcuts to, 236, *236*
   defined, **230**, 232
   deleting from documents, 256
   deleting from styles palette, 256–257
   duplicating, 253, *253*
   editing, **251–252**, *251*
   finding and replacing, 126–128, *127*, *128*
   importing from other applications, 115, 232, 254
   importing from other documents, 232, 253–255, *254*
   removing or unapplying, 255–256
   Paragraph Styles palette
      defined, **230–231**, *231*, **691**
      deleting styles, 256–257
      using, 231–232
sub-headlines
   in AppleScript, 760
   in Visual Basic, 745
subpaths, **516**
Subsample To option in Export PDF: Compression dialog box, 596–597
subscript and superscript type styles, 203, 206, *206*, 393–394, *393*, *394*
Subset dialog box, 282–285, *282*, *283*

Subset Fonts Below option in Export PDF: PDF Options dialog box, 592
subtracting values in palettes, 148, 202
subtractive color, **290–291**, *291*
Summary options in Preflight dialog box, 566–567, *567*, *568*
supported file formats, 11–13
Swatch Library palette, **696**
Swatches palette, **85**, **86**, **87**, **240**, **297–309**, **692**. *See also* color
   adding colors from commercial color systems, 306–307
   adding colors from swatches libraries, 305–306
   applying color, 297, 320
   Black swatch, 300
   buttons, 299
   Color palette and swatches, 87
   color swatches, 298
   and creating character styles, 240
   creating gradient swatches, 298, 316–317, *316*, *317*
   creating swatches, 85, 297, 300–303, *301*, *302*
   creating tint swatches, 313–314, *313*
   defined, **297**, *297*, **692**
   deleting swatches, 304–305, *305*
   duplicating swatches, 303–304
   editing swatches, 303, *304*
   gradient swatches, 298
   icons, 298
   importing colors from other files, 308–309, *308*
   New Color Swatch dialog box, 300–303, *301*, *302*
   "no color" swatch, 86, 296
   None swatch, 296, 298, 299, 675
   opening, 297
   out-of-gamut alert icon, 302
   Paper swatch, 299
   Registration swatch, 300
   selecting colors, 297, 320
   selecting swatches, 303
switching between metric and optical kerning, 211
SWOP (Specifications for Web Offset Publications), 565–566
System color systems, **306–307**
system crashes, 173
System Profiles options in Application Color Settings dialog box, 708–709, *708*, *709*

T

T&E Center of Rochester Institute of Technology (RIT), 556
tab stops, **218–221**, **245–246**, **694**. *See also* formatting
   defined, **218**
   deleting, 21
   editing, 220–221
   leaders, 221
   in paragraph styles, 245–246, *246*
   setting, 218–220
   tab alignment options, 219
   Tabs palette, 218–221, 694
Tagged Text filter for PageMaker, 120
tails for arrows, 97
targeting
   layers, 335–337, *336*, *337*, *338*
   spreads, 444–445
template files
   defined, **25**
   saving files as, 25–26
testing
   AppleScript scripts, 762
   color in documents for print and Web distribution, 615
   HTML files after exporting, 632–637, *632*, *637*
   Visual Basic scripts, 734–735
text, **101–131**. *See also* columns of text; fonts; formatting
   in AppleScript, 756–757, *758*
   applying
      color and tints to type, 324
      gradients to type, 324–326
   Compress Text and Line Art option in Export PDF: Compression dialog box, 598
   converting text outlines to frames, 82–83
   converting to paths, 519–520, *519*
   Copying Text and Graphics option in Export PDF: Security dialog box, 604
   cutting, copying, and pasting, **102**, **111**
      as inline graphics, 159
      onto layers, 344
   defined, **102**

dragging-and-dropping text files
  from other applications,
    111–112
editing
  from context menus, 56, *57*
  from Edit menu, 120–121
  with keyboard shortcuts,
    121–122
  text shapes, 519–520, *519*
entering, 108
filling, 84
Find/Change dialog box,
  122–128, **682**
  Case Sensitive option, 124
  deleting text, 123
  finding and replacing
    formatting or styles,
    126–128, *127*, *128*
  finding and replacing special
    characters, 125–126
  finding text, 123–124
  opening, 122–123, *123*, 682
  replacing text, 123–124
  using wildcards, 124–125
  Whole Word option, 124
glyph scaling
  defined, **398**
  Glyph Scaling option in
    Justification dialog box, 405
in HTML files
  converting text files to GIF files
    in HTML documents, 618
  Export HTML: Formatting
    dialog box Text options,
    623–624
  overview of, 612
Ignore Text Wrap option in Text
  Frame Options dialog box, 107
Import Options dialog box,
  115–120
  adding import filters, 23, 115
  Excel Import Options dialog
    box, 119, *119*, *120*
  opening, 115, 116
  overview of, 115–116
  PageMaker Tagged Text filter,
    120
  Text Import Options dialog
    box, 115, 117–118, *117*
  Word, WordPerfect, and RTF
    Import Options dialog boxes,
    115, 116–117, *116*

keyboard shortcuts
  on Macintosh computers,
    782–783
  for navigating, editing, and
    selecting text, 121–122
  in Windows, 769–771
Old Style numerals, 396
overprinting, 563–565, *564*
overview of, 101–102
placing (importing), **102**,
  112–114, *113*
  and creating text frames, 76,
    104
  HTML files, 117–118
  importing character and
    paragraph styles, 115
  importing formatting, 115
Preferences: Text dialog box, 657,
  657
raising and lowering on
  baselines, 389–391, *389*, *390*,
  391
scaling, 382–383, *382*, 424
selecting, 120, 121–122
  Macintosh keyboard shortcuts,
    782–783
  Windows keyboard shortcuts,
    769–771
skewing, 392, *392*, *393*
special characters, **108–111**,
  125–126
  defined, **108**
  entering with context menus,
    110–111, *110*
  entering with Insert Character
    dialog box, 108–109, *109*
  entering with keyboard
    shortcuts, 109–110
  finding and replacing, 125–126
  flush spaces, 406–407
  metacharacters, 125–126
spell checking, **128–131**, **682**
  checking spelling, 128–130,
    129
  customizing dictionaries,
    130–131, *130*, 661, *661*, 682
  language setting, 654
stroking, 84
text insertion point, **102**, **120**
Text Wrap command in Object
  menu, 685
threading between linked text
  frames, **7**, **363–375**

and adding text frames and
  pages, 368, 371–375, *372*,
  373, *374*
automatically threading text,
  366–368
defined, **7**, **363–366**
deleting threaded text frames,
  375, *376*, *377*
Loaded Text cursor, 366
and loading cursor with
  overflow text, 368
manually threading overflow
  text, **369–375**
one frame at a time, 366–367,
  367, 369–371, *370*, *371*
unthreading text frames, 375
type
  defined, **102**
  type families, **200**
Type menu
  defined, **683–684**
  Macintosh keyboard shortcuts,
    784–785
  Windows keyboard shortcuts,
    772
Type option in Print dialog box,
  558
type styles, **200**, **203**, **205–206**,
  393–398
  all caps type, 203, 206, *206*
  applying, **205–206**, *205*, *206*
  bold type, 200, 203, 205–206,
    205, *206*
  defined, **200**
  fonts and, 205
  italic type, 200, 203, 205–206,
    205, *206*
  keyboard shortcuts, 203
  Old Style numerals, 396
  Roman type style, 200
  small caps, 203, 206, *206*,
    394–395, *395*
  strikethrough type, 203, 206,
    206, 397–398, *397*
  subscript and superscript type,
    203, 206, *206*, 393–394, *393*,
    394
  underline type, 203, 206, *206*,
    397–398, *397*
Type tool
  defined, **672**
  drawing text frames, 103
  editing text, 56, 120

TEXT FRAMES • TOOLBOX   833

and filling and stroking type, 84
Vertical Type tool, 108
in Visual Basic, 742, *743*
wrapping around graphics, **155–158**, *695*
    Bounding Box option, 156, *157*
    Invert option, 158, *158*
    Jump Object option, 157, *157*
    Jump to Next Column option, 158, *158*
    No Wrap option, 156, *156*
    Object Shape option, 157, *157*
    overview of, 155–156, 695
    Text Wrap command in Object menu, 685
text frames, **19–20**, *76*, **102–108**. *See also* frames
    converting to graphic frames, 76
    creating
        automatically, 76, 104
        cutting, copying, and pasting text and, 111
        drawing with Type tool, 103
        with New Document dialog box, 19–20, 102, 104
        placing text and, 76, 104
    inset settings, 106, *107*, 226, *226*
    Master Text Frames option in New Document dialog box, 19–20, 102
    in ports and out ports, 102
    scaling, 424
    setting columns of text, 377–382, *378*, *381*
    Text Frame Options dialog box, **104–107**
        Columns options, 104–105, *105*
        First Baseline option, 107
        Fixed Column Width option, 105–106, *106*
        Gutter option, 105, *105*
        Ignore Text Wrap option, 107
        Inset Spacing options, 106, *107*, 226, *226*
        opening, 104, *104*
    threading text between linked frames, *7*, **363–375**
        and adding text frames and pages, 368, 371–375, *372*, *373*, *374*

automatically threading text, **366–368**
defined, **7**, **363–366**
deleting threaded text frames, 375, *376*, *377*
Loaded Text cursor, 366
and loading cursor with overflow text, 368
manually threading overflow text, **369–375**
one frame at a time, 366–367, *367*, 369–371, *370*, *371*
unthreading text frames, 375
in Web pages, 612
Text tool
    and applying paragraph attributes, 214
    converting text to paths, 519–520, *519*
    Transform palette and, 411
Text Wrap palette, **155–158**, *695*. *See also* graphics
    Bounding Box option, 156, *157*
    Invert option, 158, *158*
    Jump Object option, 157, *157*
    Jump to Next Column option, 158, *158*
    No Wrap option, 156, *156*
    Object Shape option, 157, *157*
    overview of, 155–156, 695
thickness settings for lines and shape outlines, 90–91, *91*
threading text between linked text frames, **7**, **363–375**
    and adding text frames and pages, 368, 371–375, *372*, *373*, *374*
    automatically threading text, **366–368**
    defined, **7**, **363–366**
    deleting threaded text frames, 375, *376*, *377*
    Loaded Text cursor, 366
    and loading cursor with overflow text, 368
    manually threading overflow text, **369–375**
    one frame at a time, 366–367, *367*, 369–371, *370*, *371*
    unthreading text frames, 375
Threshold option in Clipping Path dialog box, 525
threshold preferences for rulers, 64–65, *65*

thumbnails, **535–538**. *See also* printing
    Generate Thumbnails option in Export PDF: PDF Options dialog box, 594
    on Macintosh computers, 537, 538
    overview of, 535–536
    in Windows 98, 536
    in Windows NT, 537
TIFF files, **13**, 588
tiling options for printing documents, 533–535, *534*, *535*
tints, **86**, **312–315**, **318–324**. *See also* color
    applying
        from Color palette, 86
        from Toolbox, 318–319
        to type, 324
    creating tint swatches
        with Color palette, 312–313, *313*
        with Swatches palette, 313–314, *313*
    defined, **312**
    tint fills for shapes, 86
    tinting objects without saving tint swatches, 314
title headlines
    in AppleScript, 758–759, *759*
    in Visual Basic, 743–744, *744*
To End of Story option
    in Check Spelling dialog box, 129
    in Find/Change dialog box, 124
Tolerance option in Clipping Path dialog box, 525
Toolbox, **40–42**, **671–675**. *See also* menus; palettes; work areas
    Add Anchor Point tool, 499
    Adobe Online tool, 671
    Apply Color, Apply Gradient, and Apply None Swatch tools, 675
    applying color or tints from, 318–319
    color controls, 84–85
    Convert Direction Point tool, 502–505, *503*, *504*, *505*
    defined, **40**, *41*, **671**, *671*
    Delete Anchor Point tool, 500–501, *501*
    Direct Selection tool
        anchor points and, 77–78

defined, **671–672**
dragging-and-dropping graphics and, 142
drawing circular and elliptical shapes and frames, 77–78
drawing polygonal shapes and frames, 81–82
and drawing square and rectangular shapes and frames, 79
and drawing straight lines, 83
and editing graphics, 55
graphic frames and, 147
moving anchor points, 497–498, *498*, *499*
selecting paths and anchor points, 496–497, *496*, *497*
stroking and, 91
Transform palette and, 412
displaying, 41
displaying hidden tools, 42
Ellipse tool, 77–78, 672–673
Fill/Stroke Color Indicator, 674–675
Gradient tool, 318–319, 321–324, *321*, *322*, *323*, *324*, 673–674
Hand tool, 674
keyboard shortcuts
on Macintosh computers, **783–784**
for tools, 42
in Windows, **771–772**
Line tool, 83, 672–673
moving, 41
Pen tool, **486–496**, 672
adding anchor points, 499–500, *500*
closing open paths, 506, *507*
connecting multiple paths, 508–510, *509*, *510*
continuing open paths, 506
defined, **672**
deleting anchor points, 500–501, *501*
drawing clipping paths manually, 521–524, *521*, *522*, *524*
drawing closed shapes, 489–490, *489*, *490*
drawing curved segments, 488–490, *489*, *490*

drawing curved segments connected by corner points, 494–496
drawing curved segments followed by straight segments, 492–494
drawing straight segments, 487–488
drawing straight segments followed by curved segments, 490–492
editing compound paths, 517, *517*
overview of, 486–487
Polygon tool, 79–82, 672–673
Rectangle tool, 78–79, 672–673
Rotate tool
defined, **673**
duplicating and transforming objects, 430–432, *431*, *432*, *433*
points of origin and, 417
rotating and distorting objects, **428–429**, *429*
Transform palette and, 414, 428–429, *429*
Scale tool
defined, **673**
duplicating and transforming objects, 430
points of origin and, 417
scaling objects, 424–425, *426*
Transform palette and, 414
Scissors tool
defined, **673–674**
opening closed paths, 507, *508*
splitting paths and frames, 512–515, *513*, *514*
selecting tools, 41
Selection tool
defined, **671–672**
dragging-and-dropping graphics, 142
and drawing circular and elliptical shapes and frames, 77–78
and drawing polygonal shapes and frames, 81–82
and drawing square and rectangular shapes and frames, 79
and drawing straight lines, 83
duplicating and transforming objects, 430

graphic frames and, 147
positioning objects, 419
reflecting objects, 427, *427*
scaling objects, 424, *425*
Transform palette and, 411
Shear tool
defined, **673**
duplicating and transforming objects, 430
points of origin and, 417
rotating and distorting objects, **428–429**, *429*
Transform palette and, 414
Text tool
and applying paragraph attributes, 214
converting text to paths, 519–520, *519*
Transform palette and, 411
Type tool
defined, **672**
drawing text frames, 103
editing text, 56, 120
and filling and stroking type, 84
Vertical Type tool, 108
Zoom tool, 40, 674
Toyo Color Finder 1050 color system, **306–307**
tracking, **200**, 210–212. *See also* formatting
defined, **200**, **210**, *210*
identifying settings, 211–212
keyboard shortcuts, 203
setting manually, 212
Transform palette, **146–147**, **148**, **150**, **411–418**, **690**. *See also* objects
defined, **412**, **690**
Dimensions Include Stroke Weight option, 415, 416–417
Direct Selection tool and, 412
duplicating and transforming objects, 430–432, *431*, *432*, *433*
Flip Horizontal, Flip Vertical, and Flip Both options, 415
Horizontal/Vertical Palette options, 416
moving points of origin, 412, *412*, 417–418, *418*
opening, 414
positioning objects, 419
Proxy for Origin option, 412, *412*, 417–418, *418*

reflecting objects, 427–428
resizing graphics proportionally, 146–147, 148, 150
Rotate 180, Rotate 90 CW, and Rotate 90 CCW tools, 415, 673
Rotate tool and, 414, 428–429, *429*
Rotation Angle option, 414, *414*
ruler guides and, 413
Scale Content option, 415, 426
Scale tool and, 414
Scale X Percentage option, 414
Scale Y Percentage option, 415
scaling objects, 425–426
Selection tool and, 411
Shear Angle option, 414
Shear tool and, 414
Text tool and, 411
Transformations Are Totals option, 414, 415–416
Width and Height options, 414
X (Horizontal) and Y (Vertical) position options, 413, *413*
transparent objects, 296
trapping color, **561–565**. *See also* color; printing
 defined, **561–563**, *561*, *562*
 and exporting PDF files, 587
 In-RIP Trapping option, 549, 561
 overprinting strokes, fills, or text, 563–565, *564*
 ScenicSoft Preps software, 557, 561
 ScenicSoft TrapWise software, 561
 wet ink trapping, 561–563
Trumatch color system, **306–307**
turning off automatic hyphenation, 401–402
turning on
 alerts
  in AppleScript, 762
  in Visual Basic, 747
 automatic hyphenation, 401–402
 Enable Color Management option in Image Import Options dialog box, 138
 Enable Layout Adjustment option in Layout Adjustment dialog box, 471
two-page spreads (double-truck printing)
 on Macintosh computers, 188

in Windows, 183, *184*
type. *See also* fonts; text
 defined, **102**
 type families, **200**
Type menu
 defined, **683–684**
 Macintosh keyboard shortcuts, 784–785
 Windows keyboard shortcuts, 772
Type option in Print dialog box, 558
type styles, **200**, **203**, **205–206**, **393–398**
 all caps type, 203, 206, *206*
 applying, **205–206**, *205*, *206*
 bold type, 200, 203, 205–206, *205*, *206*
 defined, **200**
 fonts and, 205
 italic type, 200, 203, 205–206, *205*, *206*
 keyboard shortcuts, 203
 Old Style numerals, 396
 Roman type style, 200
 small caps, 203, 206, *206*, 394–395, *395*
 strikethrough type, 203, 206, *206*, 397–398, *397*
 subscript and superscript type, 203, 206, *206*, 393–394, *393*, *394*
 underline type, 203, 206, *206*, 397–398, *397*
Type tool
 defined, **672**
 drawing text frames, 103
 editing text, 56, 120
 and filling and stroking type, 84
 Vertical Type tool, 108

U

Ultimate Technographics plug-ins, 71
unapplying styles, 255–256
underline type style, 203, 206, *206*, 397–398, *397*
Undo command, 169–170, 681
undocumented printing features on Macintosh computers, 529
Ungroup command in Object menu, 685
units of measure
 for baselines, 391, *391*

in palettes, 46–47, *47*
for rulers, 64–65, *65*
Units & Increments options in Preferences dialog box, 658–659, *659*
Unlock Position command in Object menu, 685
unlocking
 guides, 63–64, *64*
 ruler zero point reference, 66
unthreading text frames, 375
updating
 graphic links in package files for service bureaus, 576
 InDesign plug-in information from Adobe Web site, 67
 Kodak CMM software, 654
Use Device Independent Color When Printing option in Application Color Settings dialog box, 710
Use High Resolution Image option in Clipping Path dialog box, 525
Use Transparency Information option in Image Import Options dialog box, 139
User Defined Page Breaks To option in Word, WordPerfect, or RTF Import Options dialog box, 117
utilities. *See* Adobe Gamma utility; plug-ins

V

variables
 in AppleScript, 749
 in Visual Basic, 733–734
vector graphics. *See also* bitmap graphics; graphics
 versus bitmap graphics, 11
 defined, **11**
 dragging-and-dropping Illustrator and Photoshop graphics into InDesign, 9
 Illustrator and, 11
 Macromedia Freehand and, 11
 paths and, 11
 resizing, 11
 resolution and, 11
 size of, 11
Vertical Palette option in Transform palette, 416
Vertical (Y) position option in Transform palette, 413, *413*

video cards, ATI graphics cards, 649
View menu, **667–671**, **686**
   Actual Size command, 669, *669*
   Entire Pasteboard command, 669–671, *670*
   Fit Page in Window command, 668, *668*
   Fit Spread in Window command, 668, *669*
   Macintosh keyboard shortcuts, 787–788
   overview of, 668–669, 686
   Windows keyboard shortcuts, 775–776
viewing
   HTML files, 621–622, *621*, *622*
   instruction reports for package files for service bureaus, 577
   keyboard shortcuts, 50
   PDF files after exporting, 595
   Print Settings in Preflight dialog box, 573, *573*
   shortcut sets, 50, *51*
views
   changing, 53, *54*
   keyboard shortcuts
      on Macintosh computers, 788
      in Windows, 776–777
   view controls, 40
Virginia Systems Software Services plug-ins, 71
virtual printer feature, **191–193**
   on Macintosh computers, 191–193, *193*
   in Windows, 191–192
Visual Basic, **729–762**
   assigning and displaying messages, 734
   comments, 733
   InDesign scripts, **735–747**
      adding body text, 746, *746*
      adding icon elements, 744, *745*
      communicating with InDesign, 737–738
      composing sub-headlines, 745
      composing text, 742, *743*
      composing title headlines, 743–744, *744*
      enabling alerts, 747
      overview of, 735–737
      placing and fitting large images, 738–739, *739*
      placing and fitting small images, 740–741, *741*

   objects, **731**
   properties, **731**
   scripts
      creating a button script, 732–734
      overview of, 729–730
      testing, 734–735
      variables, 733–734

W

W3C (World Wide Web Consortium), 610
wet ink trapping, 561–563
wheel mouse, 40
White Background option in Image Import Options dialog box, 139
white versus None or No color options, 296
white points
   calibrating, 721–722, *721*
   defined, **702**
white space, finding, 125
Whole Word option in Find/Change dialog box, 124
widow controls, 247–248, *247*, 387–389, *387*, *388*, *389*
Width option in Transform palette, 414
width settings for lines and shape outlines, 90–91, *91*
wildcard characters in Find/Change dialog box, 124–125
Window menu
   defined, **687**
   Macintosh keyboard shortcuts, 789
   Windows keyboard shortcuts, 777–778
windows. *See* document windows
Windows. *See* Microsoft Windows
WMF (Windows Metafiles) files, **13**
Word Import Options dialog boxes, 115, 116–117, *116*
Word Spacing option in Justification dialog box, 405
WordPerfect Import Options dialog boxes, 115, 116–117, *116*
Words Longer Than option in Hyphenation dialog box, 403
work areas, **8**, **37–66**. *See also* grids; guides; menus; palettes; Toolbox
   defined, **37–38**, *38*
   document windows

active document window, 38
Actual Size command, 669, *669*
defined, **38**
Entire Pasteboard command, 669–671, *670*
Fit Page in Window command, 668, *668*
Fit Spread in Window command, 668, *669*
in Illustrator, Photoshop, and InDesign, 8
navigating, 40
pasteboard
   defined, **38**
   Entire Pasteboard command in View menu, 669–671, *670*
ruler zero point reference
   defined, **65**, *65*
   locking or unlocking, 66
   moving, 66, *66*
rulers, **57–58**, **64–66**
   overview of, 57–58
   Ruler Guides dialog box, 62
   setting ruler guides, 57, 62
   setting units of measure, color, and threshold preferences, 64–65, *65*
scroll bars, 40
view controls, 40
zoom tools, 40, 674
workflows
   color workflows, 705–706
   desktop publishing workflows, 9
workroom environments for color calibration, 715–716
World Wide Web. *See also* HTML files
   Adobe Web site
      Adobe Online tool, 671
      connecting to, *636*, 648, 662, *662*
      downloading Acrobat Reader, 585
      plug-ins updates, 67
   Java and JavaScript, 609–610
   Web color system, **306–307**
   Web sites
      anti-aliased text in Web pages, 612, 618
      Apple Computer, 747
      Birmy Graphics Corporation, 541
      Kodak, 654

about profiling devices, 725
Seybold Seminars, 725
World Wide Web Consortium (W3C), 610
wrapping text
    around graphics, **155–158**, **695**
        Bounding Box option, 156, *157*
        Invert option, 158, *158*
        Jump Object option, 157, *157*
        Jump to Next Column option, 158, *158*
        No Wrap option, 156, *156*
        Object Shape option, 157, *157*
        overview of, 155–156, 695
    Ignore Text Wrap option in Text Frame Options dialog box, 107
    Text Wrap command in Object menu, 685

X

X (Horizontal) position option in Transform palette, 413, *413*
X-Rite Monitor Optimizer, 715, *715*, 724, 725

Y

Y (Vertical) position option in Transform palette, 413, *413*

Z

zero point reference in rulers
    defined, **65**, *65*
    locking or unlocking, 66
    moving, 66, *66*
Zip compression option in Export PDF: Compression dialog box, 598
zoom tools, 40, 674

SYBEX BOOKS ON THE WEB

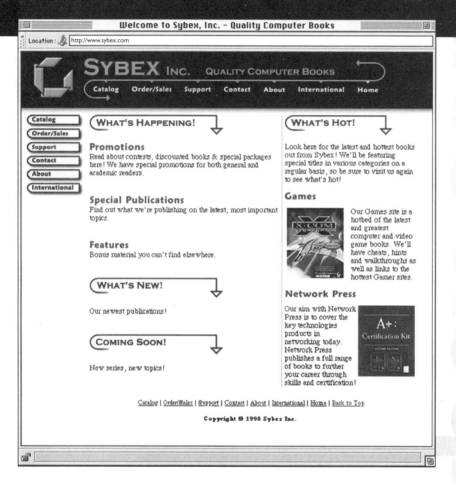

At the dynamic and informative Sybex Web site, you can:

- view our complete online catalog
- preview a book you're interested in
- access special book content
- order books online at special discount prices
- learn about Sybex

www.sybex.com

SYBEX Inc. • 1151 Marina Village Parkway, Alameda, CA 94501 • 510-523-8233